The Organization of Information

Recent Titles in
Library and Information Science Text Series

Library and Information Center Management, Ninth Edition
Barbara B. Moran and Claudia J. Morner

Collection Management Basics, Seventh Edition
Margaret Zarnosky Saponaro and G. Edward Evans

Young Adult Literature in Action: A Librarian's Guide, Third Edition
Rose Brock

Children's Literature in Action: A Librarian's Guide, Third Edition
Sylvia M. Vardell

Library Information Systems, Second Edition
Joseph R. Matthews and Carson Block

Data Science for Librarians
Yunfei Du and Hammad Rauf Khan

Research Methods in Library and Information Science, Seventh Edition
Lynn Silipigni Connaway and Marie L. Radford

The Collection Program in Schools: Concepts and Practices, Seventh Edition
Marcia A. Mardis

Library Programs and Services: The Fundamentals, Ninth Edition
Stacey Greenwell with G. Edward Evans

The School Library Manager: Leading through Change, Seventh Edition
Blanche Woolls, Joyce Kasman Valenza, and April M. Dawkins

Reference and Information Services: An Introduction, Seventh Edition
Melissa A. Wong and Laura Saunders, Editors

The Organization of Information

Daniel N. Joudrey

Fifth Edition

With the assistance of Emily Baldoni

Library and Information Science Text Series

BLOOMSBURY LIBRARIES UNLIMITED
NEW YORK • LONDON • OXFORD • NEW DELHI • SYDNEY

Online resources to accompany this book are available at https://bloomsbury.pub/org-of-info-5e. If you experience any problems, please contact Bloomsbury at: onlineresources@bloomsbury.com

BLOOMSBURY LIBRARIES UNLIMITED
Bloomsbury Publishing Inc, 1359 Broadway, New York, NY 10018, USA
Bloomsbury Publishing Plc, 50 Bedford Square, London, WC1B 3DP, UK
Bloomsbury Publishing Ireland, 29 Earlsfort Terrace, Dublin 2, D02 AY28, Ireland

BLOOMSBURY, BLOOMSBURY LIBRARIES UNLIMITED and the Diana logo are trademarks of Bloomsbury Publishing Plc

First published in the United States of America 2025

Copyright © Daniel N. Joudrey, 2025

Daniel N. Joudrey has asserted his right under the Copyright Designs and Patents Act, 1988, to be identified as Author of this work.

It is important for readers to understand that the definitions, information, and lesson ideas presented in this text are only applicable to United States copyright law. Readers must conduct their own due diligence to be sure that the lessons within this book and the resources on the accompanying website are applicable to their locale.

Cover image: Pawel Czerwinski/Unsplash

All rights reserved. No part of this publication may be: i) reproduced or transmitted in any form, electronic or mechanical, including photocopying, recording or by means of any information storage or retrieval system without prior permission in writing from the publishers; or ii) used or reproduced in any way for the training, development or operation of artificial intelligence (AI) technologies, including generative AI technologies. The rights holders expressly reserve this publication from the text and data mining exception as per Article 4(3) of the Digital Single Market Directive (EU) 2019/790.

Bloomsbury Publishing Inc does not have any control over, or responsibility for, any third-party websites referred to or in this book. All internet addresses given in this book were correct at the time of going to press. The author and publisher regret any inconvenience caused if addresses have changed or sites have ceased to exist, but can accept no responsibility for any such changes.

Library of Congress Cataloging-in-Publication Data
Names: Joudrey, Daniel N., author.
Title: The organization of information / Daniel N. Joudrey.
Description: Fifth edition. | New York : Bloomsbury Libraries Unlimited, 2025. | Series: Library and Information Science Text Series | Includes bibliographical references and index.
Identifiers: LCCN 2024051074 (print) | LCCN 2024051075 (ebook) | ISBN 9781440878619 (PB) | ISBN 9781440878596 (HC) | ISBN 9798216184331 (eBook) | ISBN 9781440878602 (ePDF)
Subjects: LCSH: Information organization. | Metadata.
Classification: LCC Z666.5 .T39 2025 (print) | LCC Z666.5 (ebook) | DDC 025–dc23/eng/20241028
LC record available at https://lccn.loc.gov/2024051074
LC ebook record available at https://lccn.loc.gov/2024051075

ISBN:	PB:	978-1-4408-7861-9
	HB:	978-1-4408-7859-6
	ePDF:	978-1-4408-7860-2
	eBook:	979-8-2161-8433-1

Series: Library and Information Science Text Series

Typeset by Integra Software Services Pvt. Ltd.

For product safety related questions contact productsafety@bloomsbury.com.

To find out more about our authors and books visit www.bloomsbury.com and sign up for our newsletters.

For Arlene

This book is dedicated to Dr. Arlene G. Taylor. She has been one of the most influential people in my life. Without her, I would not be the person that I am today. She has been my teacher, my mentor, my friend, and my writing partner. She has been generous, supportive, encouraging, challenging, and thought provoking since the moment I met her in the fall of 1998. She has been an inspiration in my career as a teacher, a scholar, a faculty member, and a conscientious writer. It has been an honor and a pleasure to work with her over the years. I hope she likes the fifth edition. It would not exist without her vision for a new way to introduce LIS students to the longstanding processes of organizing information. She will forever have my love and respect. Thank you, Arlene, for everything.

Contents

	Preface	xx
	Acknowledgments	xxiii
	List of Acronyms and Initialisms	xxiv
1	**Organization of Recorded Information**	1
	1.1 The Need to Organize	2
	1.2 The Nature of Information	5
	1.2.1 The Nature of Information Organization	7
	1.3 Organization of Information in Different Contexts	11
	1.3.1 Libraries	11
	1.3.1.1 Collections and Acquisitions	12
	1.3.1.2 Cataloging	13
	1.3.1.3 Physical Processing	15
	1.3.1.4 The Catalog	15
	1.3.2 Archives	16
	1.3.3 Museums	18
	1.3.4 Online Settings and Contexts	22
	1.3.4.1 The Internet and the Semantic Web	23
	1.3.4.2 Digital Collections	27
	1.3.4.3 Information Architecture	29
	1.3.5 Indexing and Abstracting	31
	1.3.5.1 Indexing	31
	1.3.5.1.1 Back-of-the-Book Indexing	31
	1.3.5.1.2 Database Indexing	32
	1.3.5.1.3 Periodical Indexing	32
	1.3.5.1.4 Web Indexing	33
	1.3.5.2 Abstracting	34
	1.3.6 Records Management	35
	1.3.7 Personal Information Management	37
	1.3.8 Knowledge Management	37

	1.4 Conclusion	39
	1.5 Discussion Questions and Exercises	41
	1.6 Suggested Readings	42
	1.7 Notes	45
2	**Development of the Organization of Recorded Information in Western Civilization**	**49**
	2.1 Inventories, Bibliographies, and Catalogs	49
	2.1.1 Antiquity	49
	2.1.2 Middle Ages and the Renaissance	55
	2.1.3 From Inventories to Finding Lists to Collocating Devices	57
	2.2 The Modern Era	62
	2.2.1 Nineteenth Century: A Period of Codification	62
	2.2.2 Twentieth Century: Description and Access	68
	2.2.3 Subject Access in the Modern Era	78
	2.2.3.1 Controlled Vocabularies	78
	2.2.3.2 Classification	79
	2.2.4 Special Materials	81
	2.2.4.1 Archives and Museums	81
	2.2.4.2 Subject Access to Special Materials	83
	2.2.5 Mechanization of the Information Professions	83
	2.2.5.1 The Documentation Movement	83
	2.2.5.2 Library Automation	86
	2.2.5.3 Integrated Library Systems	87
	2.3 Conclusion	89
	2.4 Discussion Questions and Exercises	92
	2.5 Suggested Readings	92
	2.6 Notes	93
3	**Retrieval Tools**	**99**
	3.1 The Need for Retrieval Tools	99
	3.2 Types of Retrieval Tools	100
	3.2.1 Bibliographies	100
	3.2.2 Catalogs	102
	3.2.2.1 Functions of Catalogs	103

		3.2.2.2	Forms of Catalogs	105
			3.2.2.2.1 Book Catalogs	105
			3.2.2.2.2 Card Catalogs	106
			3.2.2.2.3 Microform Catalogs	108
			3.2.2.2.4 Online Catalogs	108
		3.2.2.3	Arrangement and Displays within Catalogs	109
			3.2.2.3.1 Classified Arrangements	110
			3.2.2.3.2 Alphabetical Arrangements	111
			3.2.2.3.3 Other Arrangements	114
	3.2.3	Finding Aids		115
	3.2.4	Registers and Museum Databases		116
	3.2.5	Search Engines		121
	3.2.6	Internet Directories		124
	3.2.7	Indexing and Abstracting Databases		125
3.3	The Need for Retrieval Tools Revisited			127
3.4	Conclusion			128
3.5	Discussion Questions and Exercises			130
3.6	Suggested Readings			130
3.7	Notes			130

4	**Information Systems, Retrieval, and Other Technology Concerns**			**133**
	4.1	Systems and System Design		134
		4.1.1	What Is a System?	134
		4.1.2	System Design	134
		4.1.3	Databases and Query Languages	136
		4.1.4	Retrieval Models	138
		4.1.5	Searching Information Systems	138
			4.1.5.1 Querying	139
			4.1.5.2 Browsing	140
			4.1.5.3 Federated Searching	141
	4.2	Standardization Issues		143
		4.2.1	Display	144
			4.2.1.1 Display of Retrieved Results	144
			4.2.1.2 Display of Records	146
		4.2.2	Basic Search Queries	147

		4.2.3 Initial Articles	149
		4.2.4 Truncation, Boolean Operators, and Proximity	149
		4.2.5 Punctuation	150
		4.2.6 Authority Control Integration	151
		4.2.7 The Z39.50 Communication Protocol	154
	4.3	Systems Used in the LIS Professions	155
		4.3.1 Bibliographic Networks	155
		4.3.2 Resource Management Systems	155
		4.3.2.1 Integrated Library Systems or Library Services Platforms?	156
		4.3.2.2 Developments in Resource Management Systems	157
		4.3.3 Systems in Archives and Museums	159
	4.4	Conclusion	160
	4.5	Discussion Questions and Exercises	162
	4.6	Suggested Readings	162
	4.7	Notes	163
5	**Encoding Standards**		167
	5.1	Introduction to Encoding	167
	5.2	Encoding Records	169
	5.3	MARC (Machine-Readable Cataloging)	170
		5.3.1 MARC 21	170
		5.3.1.1 Components of MARC Records	171
		5.3.1.2 Components of MARC Fields	173
		5.3.2 UNIMARC	180
		5.3.3 The Future of MARC	180
	5.4	Markup Languages	181
		5.4.1 SGML (Standard Generalized Markup Language)	181
		5.4.2 HTML (Hypertext Markup Language)	183
		5.4.3 XML (Extensible Markup Language)	186
		5.4.3.1 TEI (Text Encoding Initiative)	188
		5.4.3.2 EAD (Encoded Archival Description)	191
		5.4.3.3 MARCXML	192
	5.5	BIBFRAME: A Future Standard?	194
	5.6	Conclusion	197
	5.7	Discussion Questions and Exercises	199
	5.8	Suggested Readings	199
	5.9	Notes	199

6	**Introduction to Metadata**		203
	6.1 Metadata? What's That?		203
	6.2 The Basics of Metadata		205
	6.3 Metadata Schemas		208
	6.4 Metadata Characteristics		209
	6.5 Categories of Metadata		210
		6.5.1 Descriptive Metadata	211
		6.5.2 Administrative Metadata	211
		6.5.2.1 Technical Metadata	213
		6.5.2.2 Preservation Metadata	214
		6.5.2.3 Rights and Access Metadata	214
		6.5.2.4 Meta-Metadata	215
		6.5.3 Structural Metadata	216
		6.5.3.1 METS (Metadata Encoding & Transmission Standard)	217
	6.6 Metadata Management Tools		218
		6.6.1 Application Profiles	218
		6.6.2 Metadata Registries	219
		6.6.3 Crosswalks	220
		6.6.4 Other Tools	221
	6.7 Conclusion		221
	6.8 Discussion Questions and Exercises		223
	6.9 Suggested Readings		223
	6.10 Notes		223
7	**Conceptual Models**		225
	7.1 What is a Model?		225
	7.2 Entity-Relationship Models		226
	7.3 Specific Conceptual Models		227
		7.3.1 Libraries: IFLA's *Library Reference Model* (LRM)	227
		7.3.1.1 History of LRM	227
		7.3.1.2 User Tasks	228
		7.3.1.3 Entities	230
		7.3.1.3.1 Resource Entities (WEMI)	232
		7.3.1.3.2 Agent Entities	233
		7.3.1.3.3 Other Entities	234
		7.3.1.4 Attributes and Relationships	236
		7.3.1.4.1 Attributes	236
		7.3.1.4.2 Relationships	238

	7.3.2 Archives: *Records in Contexts* (RiC)	241
	7.3.2.1 Entities	243
	7.3.2.2 Attributes	244
	7.3.2.3 Relationships	246
	7.3.3 Museums: CIDOC Conceptual Reference Model (CRM)	248
	7.3.4 The Semantic Web and Linked Data	250
	7.3.4.1 Resource Description Framework (RDF)	253
	7.3.4.2 Microdata	259
	7.3.4.3 The Future of the Semantic Web	260
	7.3.5 DCMI Abstract Model (DCAM)	261
7.4	Conclusion	262
7.5	Discussion Questions and Exercises	264
7.6	Suggested Readings	264
7.7	Notes	265

8 Description and Access — 269

8.1	Creation of Metadata Descriptions	270
8.2	Principles of Description and Access	271
	8.2.1 IFLA's *Statement of International Cataloguing Principles* (ICP)	271
	8.2.2 *General International Standard Archival Description* (ISAD(G))	273
	8.2.3 *Describing Archives: A Content Standard* (DACS)	273
	8.2.4 *Cataloging Cultural Objects* (CCO)	275
	8.2.5 Cataloguing Code of Ethics	276
8.3	Some Preliminary Considerations	277
	8.3.1 Resource Types	277
	8.3.2 Resource Entities from LRM	278
	8.3.3 Mode of Issuance	279
	8.3.4 Level of Description	282
	8.3.5 Sources	283
	8.3.6 Relationships	285
8.4	Access	285
	8.4.1 Types of Access Points	287
	8.4.2 Relationships between Agents and Resources	288
	8.4.3 Relationships between Resources	288
	8.4.4 Describing Relationships	290

				8.5	Common Attributes across Resource Types	293

- 8.5 Common Attributes across Resource Types — 293
  - 8.5.1 Title, or, What Is It Called? — 293
  - 8.5.2 Edition, or, Which Version Is It? — 294
  - 8.5.3 Dissemination Information, or, Where Did It Come from and When? — 295
  - 8.5.4 Physical Description, or, What Does It Look Like? — 297
  - 8.5.5 Creator, or, Who Is Responsible for It? — 297
  - 8.5.6 Other Common Characteristics — 299
- 8.6 Conclusion — 299
- 8.7 Discussion Questions and Exercises — 302
- 8.8 Suggested Readings — 302
- 8.9 Notes — 303

9 Standards for Description and Access — 305
- 9.1 Bibliographic and General Metadata Standards — 305
  - 9.1.1 *RDA: Resource Description & Access* (2020) — 306
    - 9.1.1.1 Entities — 308
    - 9.1.1.2 Elements — 309
    - 9.1.1.3 Data Recording Methods — 311
    - 9.1.1.4 Conditions and Options — 313
    - 9.1.1.5 Levels of Description — 315
    - 9.1.1.6 Supplementary Materials and Implementation Considerations — 315
  - 9.1.2 *RDA: Resource Description & Access* (2010) — 321
  - 9.1.3 *International Standard Bibliographic Description* (ISBD) — 329
  - 9.1.4 *Anglo-American Cataloguing Rules, Second Edition* (AACR2) — 333
  - 9.1.5 The Dublin Core (DC) — 336
  - 9.1.6 Metadata Object Description Schema (MODS) — 339
- 9.2 Archives Metadata Standards — 342
  - 9.2.1 *General International Standard Archival Description* (ISAD(G)) — 342
  - 9.2.2 *Describing Archives: A Content Standard* (DACS) — 345
- 9.3 Other Domain-Specific Metadata Schemas — 347
  - 9.3.1 *Cataloging Cultural Objects* (CCO) — 347
  - 9.3.2 VRA Core — 348
  - 9.3.3 *Categories for the Description of Works of Art* (CDWA) — 350

		9.3.4 ONIX (Online Information Exchange)	351
		9.3.5 Index and Bibliography Records	356
	9.4	Conclusion	357
	9.5	Discussion Questions and Exercises	359
	9.6	Suggested Readings	360
	9.7	Notes	360

10 Authority Control — 365

- 10.1 Authority Control — 365
  - 10.1.1 Authority Control of Names — 366
  - 10.1.2 Authority Control of Works and Expressions — 369
  - 10.1.3 Authority Work — 370
  - 10.1.4 Authority Files — 373
  - 10.1.5 International Authority Control Efforts — 377
- 10.2 Bibliographic Standards For Authority Control — 377
  - 10.2.1 IFLA's *Library Reference Model* (LRM) and Its Precursors — 378
    - 10.2.1.1 *Functional Requirements for Bibliographic Records* (FRBR) — 378
    - 10.2.1.2 *Functional Requirements for Authority Data* (FRAD) — 379
    - 10.2.1.3 IFLA's *Library Reference Model* (LRM) — 380
  - 10.2.2 IFLA's *Statement of International Cataloguing Principles* (ICP) — 382
  - 10.2.3 *RDA: Resource Description & Access* (2020) — 383
    - 10.2.3.1 Nomens and Appellations — 384
    - 10.2.3.2 Describing Agents — 386
      - 10.2.3.2.1 Persons: Appellation Elements — 387
      - 10.2.3.2.2 Persons: Relationship Elements — 388
      - 10.2.3.2.3 Persons: Attribute Elements — 390
    - 10.2.3.3 Describing Works and Expressions — 390
      - 10.2.3.3.1 Works and Expressions: Appellation Elements — 391
      - 10.2.3.3.2 Works and Expressions: Relationship Elements — 392
      - 10.2.3.3.3 Works and Expressions: Attribute Elements — 393
  - 10.2.4 *RDA: Resource Description & Access* (2010) — 394
    - 10.2.4.1 Describing and Establishing Access Points for Agents — 395
      - 10.2.4.1.1 Describing Persons: Names — 395
      - 10.2.4.1.2 Creating Access Points for Persons — 396

	10.2.4.1.3 Other Attributes for Describing Persons	398
	10.2.4.2 Describing and Creating Access Points for Works and Expressions	399
	10.2.4.3 Describing Relationships	402
10.2.5	*Anglo-American Cataloguing Rules, Second Edition* (AACR2)	405
10.2.6	Metadata Authority Description Schema (MADS)	407
10.3	Standards for Archives	408
10.3.1	*International Standard Archival Authority Record for Corporate Bodies, Persons, and Families* (ISAAR(CPF))	409
10.3.2	*Describing Archives: A Content Standard* (DACS)	410
10.3.3	Encoded Archival Context for Corporate Bodies, Persons, and Families (EAC-CPF)	410
10.4	Standards for Art and Museums	411
10.4.1	*Cataloging Cultural Objects* (CCO)	412
10.4.2	*Categories for the Description of Works of Art* (CDWA)	415
10.4.3	VRA Core	416
10.5	Standards and Projects in Online Settings	417
10.6	Conclusion	418
10.7	Discussion Questions and Exercises	420
10.8	Suggested Readings	421
10.9	Notes	422

11 Subject Analysis — 425

11.1	Subject Analysis and Aboutness	425
11.2	What is Subject Analysis?	427
11.3	Challenges in Subject Analysis	431
	11.3.1 Cultural Differences	432
	11.3.2 Consistency	433
	11.3.3 Non-textual Information	434
	11.3.4 Exhaustivity	435
	11.3.5 Objectivity	437
11.4	Some Methods Used to Determine Aboutness	438
	11.4.1 Langridge's Approach	439
	11.4.2 Wilson's Approaches	440
	11.4.3 Use-Based Approaches	440

    11.5 Conceptual Analysis Process 441
        11.5.1 Resource Examination 441
            11.5.1.1 Cover, Jacket, or Container 442
            11.5.1.2 Title and Subtitle 442
            11.5.1.3 Tables of Contents 442
            11.5.1.4 Introductions or Prefaces 442
            11.5.1.5 Illustrations and Other Visual Features 443
            11.5.1.6 Other Bibliographic Features 443
            11.5.1.7 The Text 443
            11.5.1.8 Non-textual Information 443
        11.5.2 Content Examination 444
            11.5.2.1 Identification of Concepts 444
                11.5.2.1.1 Topics 444
                11.5.2.1.2 Names 444
                11.5.2.1.3 Chronological Elements 445
            11.5.2.2 Content Characteristics 445
                11.5.2.2.1 Research Methods 446
                11.5.2.2.2 Point of View 446
                11.5.2.2.3 Language, Tone, Audience, and Intellectual Level 446
                11.5.2.2.4 Genre and Form 447
            11.5.2.3 Content Examination Strategies 448
        11.5.3 Stages in Aboutness Determination 449
    11.6 Next Steps in Subject Analysis 449
    11.7 Future of Subject Analysis 450
    11.8 Conclusion 451
    11.9 Discussion Questions and Exercises 452
    11.10 Suggested Readings 452
    11.11 Notes 453

12 Systems for Vocabulary Control 455
    12.1 What are Controlled Vocabularies? 456
    12.2 Types of Controlled Vocabularies 458
        12.2.1 Simple Term Lists 458
        12.2.2 Synonym Rings 458
        12.2.3 Taxonomies 459
        12.2.4 Thesauri and Subject Heading Lists 460

12.3	Relationships in Controlled Vocabularies	461
	12.3.1 Equivalence Relationships	462
	12.3.2 Hierarchical Relationships	464
	12.3.3 Associative Relationships	465
	12.3.4 Displaying Relationships	465
	12.3.5 Lexical Relationships	466
12.4	Controlled Vocabulary Challenges	467
	12.4.1 Specific versus General Terms	467
	12.4.2 Synonymous Concepts	468
	12.4.3 Inclusive Terms	468
	12.4.4 Word Form for One-Word Terms	469
	12.4.5 Sequence and Form for Multi-word Terms and Phrases	470
	12.4.6 Compound Headings	470
	12.4.7 Homographs and Homophones	471
	12.4.8 Qualification of Terms	471
	12.4.9 Abbreviations, Acronyms, and Initialisms	472
	12.4.10 Popular versus Technical Terms	472
	12.4.11 Pre-Coordination versus Post-Coordination (Subdivision of Terms)	473
12.5	Principles for Creating Controlled Vocabularies	475
	12.5.1 Specificity	475
	12.5.2 Literary Warrant	476
	12.5.3 Direct Entry	477
12.6	Principles for Applying Vocabulary Terms	477
	12.6.1 Specific Entry and Coextensive Entry	478
	12.6.2 Number of Terms Assigned	478
	12.6.3 Concepts Not in the Controlled Vocabulary	479
12.7	Controlled Vocabulary Standards	479
	12.7.1 *Library of Congress Subject Headings* (LCSH)	479
	12.7.2 *Sears List of Subject Headings* (*Sears*)	482
	12.7.3 *Medical Subject Headings* (MeSH)	483
	12.7.4 *Library of Congress Genre/Form Terms for Library and Archival Materials* (LCGFT)	484
	12.7.5 *Library of Congress Demographic Group Terms* (LCDGT)	487
	12.7.6 *Art & Architecture Thesaurus* (AAT)	488
	12.7.7 *Thesaurus of ERIC Descriptors*	491

		12.7.8 Faceted Application of Subject Terminology (FAST)	492
		12.7.9 Homosaurus	493
	12.8	Ontologies	494
	12.9	Natural Language Approaches to Subjects	498
		12.9.1 Keywords	498
		12.9.2 Natural Language Processing	499
		12.9.3 Tagging and Folksonomies	501
	12.10	Conclusion	505
	12.11	Discussion Questions and Exercises	507
	12.12	Suggested Readings	507
	12.13	Notes	508
13	**Systems for Categorization**		**513**
	13.1	What are Categories, Classifications, and Taxonomies?	513
	13.2	Theory of Categorization	516
		13.2.1 The Rise and Fall of the Classical Theory of Categories	516
		13.2.2 Cracks in the Classical Theory of Categories	516
		13.2.3 Prototype Theory	518
	13.3	Bibliographic Classification	518
		13.3.1 Components of Classification Schemes	520
		13.3.2 Hierarchical and Enumerative Classification	522
		13.3.3 Faceted Classification	527
	13.4	Classification Concepts	529
		13.4.1 Broad versus Close Classification	529
		13.4.2 Classification of Knowledge versus Classification of a Particular Collection	530
		13.4.3 Integrity of Numbers versus Keeping Pace with Knowledge	530
		13.4.4 Closed versus Open Stacks	532
		13.4.5 Fixed versus Relative Location	533
		13.4.6 Location Device versus Collocation Device	533
	13.5	The Use of Categories and Taxonomies Online	533
	13.6	Conclusion	535
	13.7	Discussion Questions and Exercises	536
	13.8	Suggested Readings	537
	13.9	Notes	537

Appendix A: Arrangement of Metadata Displays 539
Appendix B: Arrangement of Physical Information
             Resources in Libraries 545
Appendix C: EAD3 Encoded Finding Aid 549
Appendix D: BIBFRAME Record 555
Appendix E: An Approach to Subject Analysis 571
Glossary 576
Selected Bibliography 612
Index 624
About the Author 654

Preface

The preface to the first edition of this book began with a statement from the original author, Arlene G. Taylor:

> As I began work on the ninth edition of *Introduction to Cataloging and Classification* I became more and more aware that another work was needed that would precede the cataloging text. Core courses in many schools of library and information science now include a course in organizing information. These courses typically cover much more than cataloging and classification. They discuss the concept of organization and its role in human endeavors; many kinds of retrieval tools, such as bibliographies, indexes, finding aids, catalogs, and other kinds of databases; encoding standards, such as MARC, SGML, various SGML DTDs, and XML; creation of metadata; all kinds of controlled vocabularies, including thesauri and ontologies, as well as subject heading lists; classification theory and methodology; arrangement and display of metadata records and physical information–bearing packages; and system design. *The Organization of Information* addresses this need, leaving *Introduction to Cataloging and Classification* as a textbook for courses devoted to the specifics of cataloging and classification.[1]

This statement is as true now as it was when it was written more than a quarter century ago. Changes have come in degree, however. Information organization has replaced cataloging as a core course in most schools of library and information science.[2] Encoding standards, metadata standards, and systems continue to evolve, new ones have been developed, and old ones have disappeared. New concepts have become useful additions to the discussion of organization of information—concepts such as linked data, tagging, and microdata.

The goal of the fifth edition of *The Organization of Information* is to be a key resource for anyone who is seeking accurate, clear, and up-to-date guidance on organizing information. It seeks to enable students, practicing librarians and other information professionals, and others to understand the theories, principles, standards, and tools behind information organization in all types of environments. To this end, more figures and tables have been added to better illustrate the concepts used in organizing information. Textboxes for acronyms and important vocabulary terms are found at the end of each chapter. The glossary has been significantly expanded, and a chapter/section numbering system has been introduced to ensure that readers can easily understand the placement of subtopics within each chapter. Additionally, explanatory footnotes have been separated from the bibliographic reference endnotes, keywords are highlighted (using both bold and italics) throughout the text, and discussion questions and activities end each chapter.

To accomplish the book's goals effectively, it was necessary to make some changes to the structure of the work. The beginning chapters continue to cover the same concepts as in the previous edition but with extensive updating and some reordering. Chapter 1, "Organization of Recorded Information," looks at our basic human need to organize and how it is approached in various contexts. Some of the detailed content found in the fourth edition of the work has been moved to later chapters so that this first chapter is more of an overview. Some sections, however, have been expanded, including the sections on museums, nature of information, and indexing. Two new work process figures have been added: one for archives and one for museums. Chapter 2 addresses the history of organization principles and milestones that have developed over the centuries in the Western world. In this edition, there are amplifications of a few historical occurrences that were treated more briefly in earlier editions (e.g., the development of libraries in the Mediterranean region, the development of online catalogs in the late twentieth century). A multi-figure visual timeline of events has been spread throughout the chapter to provide some chronological context, and additional images have been added. Chapter 3 is concerned with the formats and functions of basic retrieval tools. The individual sections on catalogs, indexes, finding aids, museum registers, and search engines have been updated and new examples have been provided in some cases. Chapter 4, "Information Systems, Retrieval, and Other Technology Concerns," follows directly after the retrieval tools chapter as the two chapters are related; they can be read together to get a better sense of the technology and system issues that underlie the profession's various retrieval tools. Chapter 4 has been updated and completely restructured to enhance the flow of the content; it now includes more information about library services platforms and briefly discusses information systems in museums and archives. Chapter 5, "Encoding Standards," has been updated. Two standards, TEI and EAD, which were previously addressed across multiple chapters, are now addressed solely in Chapter 5. ONIX and MODS—two other hybrids standards that were addressed in both the encoding and description chapters in the previous edition—are now covered in a new descriptive standards chapter (Chapter 9).

After these initial chapters that provide background and context for the activities of information organization, the following chapters begin to discuss the processes associated with organizing information. Chapter 6 discusses the broad concept of *metadata*, its attributes, its various types, and metadata management tools. It has been restructured and updated. The section on metadata models, previously found in this chapter, has been revised and expanded into its own chapter: Chapter 7, "Conceptual Models." The new chapter expands the discussion of entity-relationship models and the *Records-in-Contexts* model designed for archives; the section on library conceptual models now focuses on the *IFLA Library Reference Model* (LRM), replacing *Functional Requirements for Bibliographic Records* (FRBR). Chapter 7 also includes a revised and restructured section on linked data and the Semantic Web.

The next three chapters reflect another change in structure. In previous editions, there were two chapters: one on Resource Description and the other on Access and Authority Control. In this fifth edition, these two chapters have been reorganized into three chapters. Chapter 8, "Description and Access," contains information about creating descriptive metadata, principles of description (including the recently updated "Cataloguing Code of Ethics"), resource types, LRM entities, mode of issuance, levels of description, relationships, types of access points, and common attributes across all resource types. The extensive coverage of various content and metadata structure standards has been moved to a new chapter titled, "Standards for Description and Access." Chapter 9 contains information about various standards, including a new section on Official RDA. Because not everyone will likely switch to Official RDA quickly, there is still significant content about Original RDA and AACR2, as well as Dublin Core, MODS, DACS, CCO, VRA Core, CDWA, ONIX, and so on. Chapter 10, "Authority Control," contains an overview of the process, the MARC standard for authority records, and standards related to authority control (including a new section on Official RDA).

Subject approaches to organizing information are covered in Chapter 11, "Subject Analysis," Chapter 12, "Systems for Vocabulary Control," and Chapter 13, "Systems for Categorization." These are updated and rewritten for the fifth edition. Highlights include a brief section on artificial intelligence (AI), new examples, a brief section on the Homosaurus vocabulary, and an expanded discussion of faceted classification.

One concept newly introduced in this edition—and one that will likely assume greater prominence over time—is the use of AI in organizing information. As of this writing in 2025, its full potential and limitations remain uncertain; the technology is still in a relatively early stage. I have no doubt that AI will play an increasingly important role in the years ahead. However, I remain cautious about making strong predictions. There are legitimate concerns about the implications of shifting a task traditionally entrusted to trained information professionals to automated systems—including questions of accuracy, accountability, and broader ethical considerations.

Notes

1. Arlene G. Taylor, *The Organization of Information* (Englewood, CO: Libraries Unlimited, 1999), xvii.
2. Daniel N. Joudrey and Ryan McGinnis, "Graduate Education for Information Organization, Cataloging, and Metadata," *Cataloging & Classification Quarterly* 52, no. 5. (2014): 525–6.

Acknowledgments

I want to acknowledge the assistance and support of the people who made my job easier in this long overdue update to the book. I am grateful for the input of Ralph Holley (MS-LIS) for his suggestions on the systems chapter; Dr. Kyong Eun Oh for her review of the section on personal information management; and Dr. Ann Graf for her early attempts to keep me in line. I would especially like to thank Emily Baldoni (MS-LIS) for assisting me during the last nine months of revising the manuscript for publication. Preparing the text was a bumpy, multi-year process for a variety of reasons. Emily's assistance was invaluable. She read through the entire manuscript, caught most of my typos, made valuable suggestions, added content of her own (especially the sections on Official RDA), and was a thoughtful sounding board. I trust her knowledge, judgment, and instincts. I am also immensely grateful to Emma Bailey, my editor at Bloomsbury Libraries Unlimited, for her professionalism, kindness, encouragement, patience, and dedication to this project. She is the best.

On a more personal note, I would like to say the writing of this book has not been easy. As I was just getting started, COVID-19 hit. As everyone knows, it was *a lot*. Thank heavens for Maggie, my beautiful cockapoo, who has been my constant companion since the beginning of the pandemic. By the time things started to get back to "normal," my father died unexpectedly. This also turned my world upside down. Most of my energy was focused on my loved ones after that, and that delayed this book. This amounted to a three-year delay in getting a foothold on the revisions. At times, I did not think I would be able to complete the task, but with the support of my partner, my dog, my family, and my friends, I was able to get back to the work.

I would especially like to thank my partner, my friend, my one true love, Jesús Alonso Regalado, Subject Librarian for Romance Languages and Literatures, and Latin American, Caribbean, and U.S. Latino Studies at the University at Albany, State University of New York. During these challenging times, he often put my needs above his own so that I could focus on my family, my work, and this book. I thank him for inspiring me with his expertise, his dedication, and his love of librarianship. He is *still* the best librarian that I have ever known. And it is not just me! Others have recognized his brilliance and dedication as well. In 2020, he received the ALA I Love My Librarian award! Finally, I thank the universe for Orientation Day at the School of Information Sciences at the University of Pittsburgh in August 1999. That day started my career and introduced me to Jesús. It was the best day of my life.

List of Acronyms and Initialisms

AACR:	*Anglo-American Cataloging Rules*
AACR2:	*Anglo-American Cataloguing Rules, Second Edition*
AAP:	Authorized Access Point
AAT:	*Art & Architecture Thesaurus*
AI:	Artificial Intelligence
ALA:	American Library Association
ANSI:	American National Standards Institute
APPM:	*Archives, Personal Papers, and Manuscripts*
ASCII:	American Standard Code for Information Interchange
ASIS&T:	Association for Information Science and Technology
BC2:	*Bibliographic Classification*, 2nd ed.
BIBFRAME:	Bibliographic Framework Initiative
BT:	Broader Term
CC:	*Colon Classification*
CCO:	*Cataloging Cultural Objects*
CDWA:	*Categories for the Description of Works of Art*
CIDOC:	International Committee on Documentation
COM:	Computer Output Microform
CONA:	*Cultural Objects Name Authority*
CQL:	Contextual Query Language
CRG:	Classification Research Group
CRM:	Conceptual Reference Model
CV:	Controlled Vocabulary
DACS:	*Describing Archives: A Content Standard*
DC:	Dublin Core
DCAM:	DCMI Abstract Model
DCMES:	Dublin Core Metadata Element Set
DCMI:	Dublin Core Metadata Initiative
DDC:	*Dewey Decimal Classification*
DDI:	Data Documentation Initiative
DOI:	Digital Object Identifier
DPLA:	Digital Public Library of America
DTD:	Document Type Definition
EAC-CPF:	Encoded Archival Context-Corporate Bodies, Persons, and Families

EAD:	Encoded Archival Description
EBCDIC:	Extended Binary Coded Decimal Interchange Code
EGAD:	Expert Group on Archival Description
ERIC:	Education Resources Information Center
Exif:	Exchangeable Image File Format
FAST:	Faceted Application of Subject Terminology
FRAD:	*Functional Requirements for Authority Data*
FRBR:	*Functional Requirement for Bibliographic Records*
FRSAD	*Functional Requirements for Subject Authority Data*
GARR:	*Guidelines for Authority Records and References*
GUI:	Graphical User Interface
HTML:	Hypertext Markup Language
IA:	Information Architecture
IBM:	International Business Machines
ICA:	International Council on Archives
ICOM:	International Council of Museums
ICP:	*Statement of International Cataloguing Principles*
IFLA:	International Federation of Library Associations and Institutions
ILS:	Integrated Library System
IR:	Information Retrieval
IRI:	Internationalized Resource Identifier
ISAAR(CPF):	*International Standard Archival Authority Record for Corporate Bodies, Persons, and Families*
ISAD(G):	*General International Standard Archival Description*
ISBD:	*International Standard Bibliographic Description*
ISBN:	International Standard Book Number
ISNI:	International Standard Name Identifier
ISO:	International Organization for Standardization
ISSN:	International Standard Serial Number
JSON:	JavaScript Object Notation
JSON-LD:	JavaScript Object Notation for Linked Data
KOS:	Knowledge Organization System
KWAC:	Keyword and Context *or* Keyword Augmented in Context
KWIC:	Keyword in Context
KWOC:	Keyword Out of Context
LC:	Library of Congress
LC-MARC:	Library of Congress MARC
LC-PCC:	Library of Congress-Program for Cooperative Cataloging
LC-PCC PS:	Library of Congress-Program for Cooperative Cataloging Policy Statements
LCC:	*Library of Congress Classification*
LCCN:	Library of Congress Control Number
LCDGT:	*Library of Congress Demographic Group Terms*

LCGFT:	*Library of Congress Genre/Form Terms for Library and Archival Materials*
LCNAF:	Library of Congress/NACO Authority File
LCRI:	*Library of Congress Rule Interpretations*
LCSH:	*Library of Congress Subject Headings*
LIS:	Library and Information Science
LRM:	*IFLA Library Reference Model*
LSP:	Library Services Platform
MADS:	Metadata Authority Description Schema
MARC:	Machine-Readable Cataloging
MARC-AMC:	MARC Format for Archival and Manuscripts Control
MARCXML:	MARC 21 XML Schema
MDR:	Metadata Registry
MeSH:	*Medical Subject Headings*
METS:	Metadata Encoding & Transmission Standard
MGD:	Metadata Guidance Documentation
MIX:	NISO Metadata for Images in XML Schema
MLA:	Music Library Association
MODS:	Metadata Object Description Schema
NACO:	Name Authority Cooperative Program
NISO:	National Information Standards Organization
NLM:	National Library of Medicine
NLP:	Natural Language Processing
NoSQL:	Not Only Structured Query Language
NT:	Narrower Term
OAI:	Open Archives Initiative
OAI-PMH:	Open Archives Initiative Protocol for Metadata Harvesting
OCLC:	Online Computer Library Center
ODRL:	Open Digital Rights Language
ONIX:	Online Information Exchange
OPAC:	Online Public Access Catalog
ORCID:	Open Researcher and Contributor ID
OWL:	Web Ontology Language
PCC:	Program for Cooperative Cataloging
PDF:	Portable Document Format
PREMIS:	Preservation Metadata: Implementation Strategies
RAD:	*Rules for Archival Description*
RDA:	*Resource Description & Access*
RDF:	Resource Description Framework
RDFa:	Resource Description Framework in Attributes
RiC:	*Records in Contexts*
RiC-AG:	*Records in Contexts: Application Guidelines*
RiC-CM:	*Records in Contexts: Conceptual Model*

RiC-FAD:	*Records in Contexts: Foundations of Archival Description*
RiC-O:	*Records in Contexts: Ontology*
RNG:	Relax (Regular Language for XML) Next Generation
RT:	Related Term
SA:	See Also
SAA:	Society of American Archivists
SAC:	Subject Analysis Committee
SEO:	Search Engine Optimization
SGML:	Standard Generalized Markup Language
SHM:	*Subject Headings Manual*
SNAC:	Social Networks and Archival Context
SQL:	Structured Query Language
SRU:	Search/Retrieval via URL
TEI:	Text Encoding Initiative
TGN:	*Getty Thesaurus of Geographic Names*
UBC:	Universal Bibliographic Control
UCS:	Universal Coded Character Set
UDC:	*Universal Decimal Classification*
UF:	Used For
ULAN:	*Union List of Artist Names*
UNIMARC:	Universal MARC
URI:	Uniform Resource Identifier
URL:	Uniform Resource Locator
USMARC:	United States MARC
VAP:	Variant Access Point
VIAF:	Virtual International Authority File
VRA:	Visual Resources Association
W3C:	World Wide Web Consortium
WEMI:	Work-Expression-Manifestation-Item
XHTML:	Extensible Hypertext Markup Language
XML:	Extensible Markup Language

Chapter 1

Organization of Recorded Information

Organization is everywhere! It is a part of our lives, employed in formal information environments such as libraries and archives, but also in our everyday mundane interactions with the world around us. Kitchens are organized so that cooking equipment is easily accessible, and foodstuffs and spices can be used as needed. Grocery stores are organized to bring like items together (and, more so, to maximize profits). Items in a newspaper, either digital or on newsprint, are organized into specific sections so that similar stories are presented together, which results in a separation of unlike items. Accordingly, *Garfield* and *Peanuts* are not collocated with obituaries or local politics. Personal music collections are organized so that we can find just the right song when we want it. Workplaces are organized so tasks can be accomplished efficiently and effectively. Auto body shops are organized so that mechanics can find just the right part to prevent the wheels from falling off a car while it is being driven down the highway. Organization is a very important part of everyday life; it is key for efficiency, progress, and even survival!

What does it mean to organize? Merriam-Webster's dictionary gives several senses in its definition of the word **organize**. The ones that we are interested in are

- to arrange or order things so that they can be found or used easily and quickly,
- to put in a certain order, and
- to arrange elements into a whole of interdependent parts.[1]

This book, then, is dedicated to explaining the processes of arranging or ordering elements. It, however, has a narrower focus than what is described above. We are interested in organizing information for the purpose of retrieval. This book examines the activities carried out and the tools used by people who work in places that accumulate information resources (e.g., books, maps, documents, datasets, images) for the use of humankind, both immediately and for posterity. This text discusses the processes that are in place to make resources findable, whether someone is performing a known-item search or browsing through hundreds of search results hoping to discover something useful. Information organization supports a myriad of information-seeking scenarios.

This chapter provides an overview of information organization. It also introduces different environments within the library and information science (LIS) discipline in which we organize resources. New terms and acronyms (so, so many acronyms) are introduced throughout this chapter and the chapters that follow. A list of acronyms and a list of important terms are provided at the end of each chapter, in addition to the acronym list provided in the front matter of this book. Terms, which may be unfamiliar to readers who are new to the LIS field or information organization, are explained in more detail in later chapters. In the meantime, readers will find definitions of most unfamiliar terms in the book's extensive glossary. Over the years, many readers have commented that they find the glossary to be a particularly helpful feature of this textbook; please consult it as needed.

1.1 The Need to Organize

There appears to be a basic human drive to organize. Psychologists tell us that babies' brains organize images into categories such as *faces* or *foods*. Small children do a lot of organizing and matching during play. For example, children may divide their toys by shape, color, or type before playing or as a form of play in its own right. Many toys for toddlers are sorting and stacking toys that are designed to help young minds develop the ability to categorize. **Categorization** is the cognitive function that involves grouping together like entities, concepts, objects, resources, and so on. As we grow, humans develop more sophisticated cognitive abilities to categorize, to recognize patterns, to sort, to relate, and to create groups of things and ideas. Learning occurs through analysis and organization of data and information that are added to our stores of knowledge. Cognitive scientist Steven Harnad has succinctly summed up categorization's centrality and significance in the statement: "Cognition is categorization."[2]

With some individuals the need to organize appears to be much stronger than with others. Those who follow the maxim "A place for everything and everything in its place" may not be able to begin to work until their desk is cleared and stray objects have been put away. That is, such persons may have to be organized before beginning a new project. But even those whose workspaces appear to be cluttered or chaotic may have a sense of organization in their heads. Such persons usually have some idea, or perhaps certain knowledge, of what is in the various piles or collections of stuff. In terms of personal information management, both popular culture and some scholarly research categorize people as *filers* or *pilers*, depending on how they organize their own materials.[3] (The two categories are rather self-explanatory.) Regardless of one's personal style, however, human learning is based upon the ability to

- analyze, organize, and retrieve data,* information, and knowledge;
- recognize patterns;
- compare experiences, concepts, and ideas; and
- process the relationships among all of these.

---

*In this text, the terms *data* and *metadata* are treated as mass nouns and take singular verbs. I believe that treating the term *data* as plural, although correct (and still popular in the hard sciences), is unnecessarily formal and feels a bit stodgy; the same goes for *metadata*. And, on another note, I am also a supporter of the singular *they* and you may see it from time to time in this text. If a reader is upset by this usage, too bad for *them*; *they* will have to get over it!

Why do we organize? In addition to the sheer pleasure of having everything in its place (whether that is in a folder, on a shelf, or in a particular pile), we organize for more significant reasons. We organize to

- **Understand**. Organization helps us to make sense of many things in daily life. For example, one can live in the Fenway, a neighborhood in Boston, a city in Suffolk County, which is a political division in the Commonwealth of Massachusetts, which is a state located in New England, the northeastern-most part of the United States, located near N 42° 20' 18.311", W 71° 05' 58.921". There are both formal and informal organization systems of geography that help us to understand where we are and to communicate geographic locations to others.
- **Save time**. We organize to be efficient. We want to access information, things, and services in a timely manner. If, for example, the documents in an archival storage box are not grouped according to series, we may have to sort through hundreds of pieces of paper to find what is needed. That would take too much time.
- **Collocate**. We organize to bring similar things or ideas together into groups. For example, if we have many articles on the same subject or sound recordings in the same musical genre, it is helpful to label them consistently so that they can be searched and presented together. When we find a useful article or a piece of music that is appealing, we can discover similar resources.
- **Document**. The organization of information allows us to save copies and keep records of all kinds of resources that have resulted from human endeavors (e.g., books, artworks, music). Through the organization of information, humans keep a record of these resources for posterity.
- **Retrieve**. Most of all, we organize because we need to retrieve. The world is filled with objects and ideas. We need to find them (and perhaps re-find them at another time), whatever and wherever they are. Organizing makes this possible.

Efficient and effective retrieval of information is dependent upon its having been organized.[†] Information is needed in all aspects of life—for example, for health reasons, for entertainment, to understand each other, to learn about one's relationships, to fix things that are broken, or simply to expand our knowledge. Some of this information has already been assimilated and is in one's knowledge reserves, while other information must be sought. If this information is not organized, it can be difficult, and at times impossible, to find. (Can you imagine the inconvenience of using a printed dictionary that is not arranged alphabetically?) So, we have many structured tools to aid in the process of finding information: directories, dictionaries, encyclopedias, bibliographies, indexes, catalogs, databases, inventories, and the like.

The reasons we organize information can be summarized by using language found in the International Federation of Library Associations and Institutions' (IFLA) *Library Reference Model* (LRM).[4] LRM is a conceptual model that identifies key components of the universe of recorded

---

[†]There is an important caveat to mention: the process of organizing information does not always lead users directly to the information that they seek. Often, they point users to documents that contain the information sought. It is then up to the reader to locate what they need within those sources.

information.‡ It states that we organize our resource collections and information so that users can accomplish the following tasks:[5]

Task	Explanation	Example
Find	to search for entities that match specific criteria	to find *La Biblioteca de Babel* by Jorge Luis Borges in the catalog through a specific search or through browsing
Identify	to confirm that an entity corresponds to the one sought; to tell similar entities apart	to identify that the author found is the Argentine Jorge Borges who wrote *La Biblioteca de Babel* and not Jorge Borges, a Brazilian biologist who writes about sustainability
Select	to choose a resource that is appropriate to the user's needs	to select a version of *La Biblioteca de Babel* that is in a language understood by the reader, such as the English translation: *The Library of Babel*
Obtain	to gain access to the resource described	to obtain *La Biblioteca de Babel* from the library stacks or to request it from another institution
Explore	to discover resources and entities and to gain greater understanding of resources	to explore other works created by Borges, which leads to the discovery of *El Hacedor* and *El Aleph*

According to Jennifer Rowley, there are three longstanding principles we must keep in mind regarding information organization.

- Information is organized for communities, which means we must understand our communities.
- In designing tools to support information organization, we must understand our community's linguistic, semantic, and cognitive frameworks.
- Standards and standardization enhance interoperability between systems; this benefits both the organizers and communities they serve.[6]

Libraries, archives, museums, and other cultural institutions have been organizing resources for their surrounding communities for many years, both physically and digitally. We examine their processes throughout the rest of this book. Although some examples may come from the corporate world, this book is not particularly concerned with the organization of information, resources, or materials in commercial enterprises and other profit-driven ventures that may have put together collections of items for the purpose of sale, rather than collecting items to benefit humanity and our collective knowledge reserves.

---

‡LRM is the successor to IFLA's *Functional Requirements for Bibliographic Records* (FRBR). First published in 1998, FRBR is a well-known conceptual model in the library community. LRM replaced it in 2018, but FRBR is still mentioned in LIS literature.

1.2 The Nature of Information

Consider the following terms: *understanding, data, knowledge, wisdom,* and *information.* If you were asked to place these terms in order, how would you do it? Would you rank them from the lowest level of thinking to the highest? In alphabetical order? By the length of each word? In some other way? Clifford Stoll, in his book *Silicon Snake Oil: Second Thoughts on the Information Highway,* discussed these words that we use to indicate different levels of comprehension of symbols.[7] His order, indicating symbols from the least meaningful to the most meaningful, is Data→Information→Knowledge→Understanding→Wisdom. (His order just happens to be in alphabetical order, too!)

Others have addressed these same concepts—or a subset of them—both before and after Stoll. In 1989, Russell L. Ackoff, in a presidential address to the International Society for General Systems Research, presented some ideas about the nature of and the hierarchical relationships among the concepts represented in Figure 1.1.[8]

Rowley states,

> The hierarchy referred to variously as the "Knowledge Hierarchy," the "Information Hierarchy" and the "Knowledge Pyramid" is one of the fundamental, widely recognized and "taken-for-granted" models in the information and knowledge literatures. It is often quoted, or used implicitly, in definitions of data, information and knowledge in the information management, information systems and knowledge management literature.[9]

Over the years, many, including Ackoff and Rowley, have defined the terms in various ways. Many of these definitions have been combined to come up with the following descriptions:[10]

- ***Data***: unprocessed and unorganized information; discrete objective facts, statistics, or properties; products of observation; akin to evidence and/or facts; has little to no meaning or value because it is without context and interpretation.

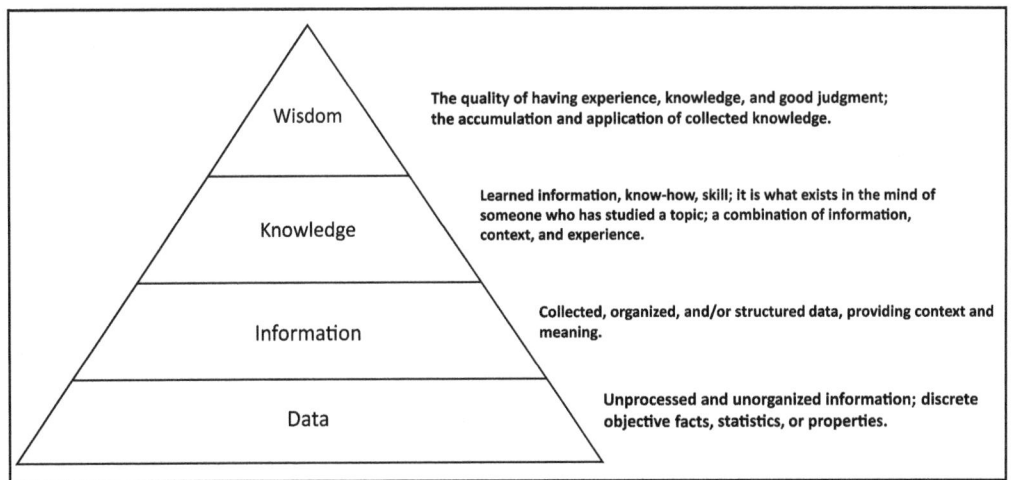

Figure 1.1 The DIKW Pyramid.

- ***Information***: collected, organized, and/or structured data, providing context and meaning; meaning given by humans to collected data with a presumption of truth; answers questions that begin with who, what, where, when, and how many.
- ***Knowledge***: what exists in the mind of someone who has studied a topic; know-how; learned information transmitted through education or experience.
- ***Wisdom***: the quality of having extensive experience, knowledge, and good judgment; the accumulation and application of collected knowledge to generate an understanding of others and society.

Which of these concepts are we organizing in libraries, museums, archives, and other such institutions? At various times, there have been spirited discussions over what it is that we are organizing. Some believe we are organizing information, and others believe we are organizing knowledge. As stated in earlier editions of *The Organization of Information*,

> The authors' bias is evident from the title of this book. It seems to us that we can use our knowledge to write a book, but until you read that book, understand it, and integrate it into your own knowledge, it is just information. That is why we believe we organize information—so that others can find it, read or otherwise absorb it, and use it to add to their own reserves of knowledge.[11]

Notice that the authors said that you read, understand, and then integrate the information into your own knowledge. So, there is some question about Stoll's putting understanding *after* knowledge. Perhaps the two concepts are intertwined. You need to have some understanding to incorporate something into your knowledge, but you must have a certain amount of knowledge to understand new things.

Some dictionaries define *information* as the communication or reception of knowledge. Such communication occurs in great part through the recording of knowledge in some fashion. People write, speak, compose, paint, sculpt, and attempt to communicate their knowledge to others in many other ways. This book, for example, is a representation of my knowledge (and that of the original author, Arlene G. Taylor), but it is not a complete representation of our knowledge of the subject. And it is, no doubt, an imperfect representation, in the sense that some concepts may not be explained as thoroughly as we truly understand them. However, it is not a representation of the reader's knowledge until the reader has read it, processed it, and understood it. That is, it is information that can be placed into a scheme of organization from which it can be retrieved for study by those interested in increasing their knowledge of the subject. Thus, I choose to use the term *information* rather than *knowledge* as my expression of what I believe we organize when organizing for the benefit of others.

This, however, is not a rejection of the phrases *organization of knowledge* and *knowledge organization*. The knowledge existing in the brains of people is being harnessed in many situations. Authors work on organizing their own knowledge every time they write. The knowledge of reference librarians is used in an organized way when they assist patrons in answering questions. The phrase *knowledge management* has come into use in the administration of organizations. And, in more recent years, some information professionals have begun to refer to classification schemes, thesauri, and other controlled vocabularies as *knowledge organization systems* (KOS). Ultimately, I think it does not matter whether we say that we are organizing information or knowledge, as long as we keep our collections of resources organized and retrievable for users!

1.2.1 The Nature of Information Organization

As mentioned earlier, this book addresses the organization of recorded information, as other means are necessary to organize information that has only been spoken, heard, or thought about. Recorded information, however, includes much more than just text. Video and audio recordings, images, notated music, and cartographic representations are all examples of recorded information that are not text. Therefore, instead of using words such as *book, short story, issue,* or *article* to refer to describable units of information, the terms *resource* and *information resource* are used in this book (interchangeably, it should be noted). A resource, thus, is an instance of recorded information; it is a generic term encompassing all materials collected by information institutions. Resources, therefore, include books, maps, artworks, personal papers, videos, datasets, sound recordings, correspondence, websites, blog posts, and so on. It can be anything from a 300-character post on Bluesky to an organized collection of 300 rock and mineral samples.

Despite the various forms in which information may be recorded, all resources have some basic *attributes* (i.e., characteristics or properties) in common, such as *title* (what we call a resource), *creator* (the agent responsible for originating and developing a resource), and *subject* (what a resource is about). These and other attributes are recorded to help organize information; collectively, attributes can be referred to as *metadata*. Metadata, in its most informal but most prevalent definition, is "data about data." This means that the attributes used to describe an information resource are metadata about that resource. Metadata is discussed throughout this book, particularly in Chapter 6, and specific aspects of metadata are addressed in Chapters 7–13.

Ronald Hagler, in his book *The Bibliographic Record and Information Technology*, identified five functions of bibliographic control.[12] *Bibliographic control* (more often referred to as *information organization* today) is the process of describing information resources and providing name, title, and subject access to the descriptions, resulting in metadata records that serve as surrogates for the actual items of recorded information. Metadata records are usually placed into information retrieval tools, where they act as pointers to the resources being described. The descriptions provide users with enough information to determine the potential value of the resources without having to view the items directly. Metadata may be stored in a variety of *retrieval tools* (a collective term used to describe bibliographies, catalogs, indexes, finding aids, museum registers, bibliographic databases, search engines, and other tools that help users find resources).

Hagler's list reflects the purpose of his book—that is, the emphasis is upon the work of *catalogers* (i.e., librarians responsible for creating and managing metadata for the library catalog). However, the list, presented and enlarged below, with wording altered to be inclusive of all types of recorded information, reflects the major activities involved not just in cataloging, but in organizing recorded information more generally.

1. *Identifying the existence of all types of information resources as they are made available.*

In short, we organize to make things known. Books may be published and streaming music may be released, but if no one apart from their creators knows of their existence, those resources will be of no use to anyone. Existence and identity can be made known in a variety of ways: publishers' announcements (through social media platforms, mailers, or email), reviews (both formal and informal), and subject-related listings, to name a few. Most publishers create sales catalogs listing their products with accompanying marketing blurbs. Some academic journals send announcements to inform readers when a new issue is available and indicate the nature of its contents. Some organizations, publications, and individual content creators allow people to sign up to receive notifications (through email, RSS feeds, etc.) about new resources, information available at their websites, and so on. (How many times have you heard, "Click below to subscribe!" on YouTube?) Reference tools such as *Books in Print* are also products of this first function of bibliographic control. And, of course, listing these resources in bibliographies, catalogs, and other retrieval tools is a way to make resources known when they are added to a collection.

2. *Identifying the works contained within those resources.*

This function indicates that we need to know what it is that we are organizing and describing: physical items, intellectual works, or both. In many cases, one information resource is equal to one intellectual, literary, or artistic work (e.g., a DVD that contains one feature film). That is fairly simple to address. We provide details in the description about the physical resource and the artistic work that it contains. In some cases, however, a single resource may contain numerous individual works. For example, a DVD may be a compilation of a half-dozen short films by different directors on a specific theme. The compilation DVD is an aggregate with individual short films that are works in their own right. For this resource, we might create metadata for the compilation primarily, but include contents notes listing the individual films on the DVD. If we decided, however, that each individual film is of greater importance, we could instead choose to describe each short film separately, but also include metadata about the larger resource containing them. Or we might choose another approach entirely. The level at which resources are described depends upon how much **granularity** (i.e., level of detail) is desired, standard institutional practices, and predicted user needs.

3. *Producing lists of these information resources prepared according to standard rules for citation.*

Organizers tend to be list makers. That is something we do; we create lists of resources that are in our collections. The lists may be of varying levels of sophistication, but they are, in the end, still lists. The types of lists created in the process of describing information resources include, among others,

- bibliographies,
- library catalogs,
- archival finding aids,
- museum registers, and
- various kinds of indexes.

Creating lists accompanies the process of developing collections of information resources. Traditionally, the activity of creating collections has been thought of as the province of institutions such as libraries, archives, and museums. Collections, however, have been created in many other situations. For example, personal collections are created because of an interest in a particular subject or creator, collections of internal documents and information are needed to carry out the work of an office, university departments may collect materials needed for teaching in a particular discipline, and so on. Whereas in the past these collections might have remained hidden from view, it is now easy to make these collections known publicly through various electronic means.

Although a list often reflects what an institution owns, collections of resources today also include digital materials that are not held or owned locally. Many institutions procure the right to allow their users to access resources online. Some such resources are accessible only electronically, while others are also available in print. Unless a collection is well organized (e.g., through the creation of lists), it can be difficult to determine what is already contained within the collection and which new resources will enrich the collection further. Developers of collections rely on metadata to avoid adding something that is already owned.

Lists (e.g., catalogs, finding aids) are important for the retrieval of individual information resources. If one is looking for a known resource—especially a tangible one that has a physical location—it is necessary to find it listed somewhere in order to access it. Such lists may still be in print form, but over the past few decades the preference has moved gradually toward providing online access to them, often exclusively. These lists have varying levels of complexity. Some, such as bibliographies, may be quite simple and easy to use; others, such as library catalogs, may contain more complete and more complex information that requires greater sophistication in methods of access.

To ensure consistency and accuracy in our lists, many institutions use the instructions in a **content standard** (i.e., a set of guidelines or rules for metadata creation) to create resource descriptions. Different types of institutions follow different content standards (some of which will be addressed in later chapters of this book). Most content standards, at a minimum, provide an overview of the description process, an indication of what data elements may be recorded, and guidelines for how to record the metadata. Not all metadata creators, however, adhere to a formal content standard when producing descriptions.

   4.   *Providing name, title, subject, and other useful access to these information resources.*

The successful retrieval of resources through lists depends on the inclusion of sufficient metadata. The provision of authority-controlled access points increases the value, usefulness, and retrieval potential of the metadata. An **access point** is a term (typically a name or a prescribed string) in a surrogate record that is used to retrieve that record. Access points are often singled out from other descriptive data to identify entities associated with the resource (e.g., creators, titles of works, and subjects), and are often under authority control. **Authority control** is the process of ensuring the use of unique character strings and/or identifiers to represent each entity associated with a resource to achieve consistency within a retrieval tool. It also involves creating explicit relationships between related names, works, and subjects.

Keyword access, by contrast, can be provided more or less automatically—that is, any information in digital form can be found by searching for any word that appears in the resource. However, keyword searching is not always efficient or precise, and not everything on that topic may be retrieved due to a lack of semantic controls. With larger collections, keyword searches become less and less satisfactory because of the overwhelming number of returned results, many of which may not be relevant to the searcher's information needs. More satisfactory retrieval comes from being able to search for specific names, titles, and subjects that have been chosen and constructed under authority control to bring together variant forms and related terms and to disambiguate homographs. Authority-controlled access is of little use, however, unless systems are designed to take advantage of it. The retrieval systems designed for searching and displaying organized information are not always sophisticated, intuitive, or easy to navigate. Without the support of thoughtful user-oriented system design, the benefits of information organization can be diminished or lost entirely.

5. *Providing the means of locating a resource.*

Location of information resources has been, for more than a century, a value added by institutions with collections. The printed catalogs or other lists created in these institutions gave information on the physical location of the resource. Most library catalogs, some museum information, and many archival finding aids are now available online. In many online catalogs, circulation information is available so that if a resource has been taken out of the library, that information is made available to the patron. This does not apply to archives and museums because they generally do not circulate their collections to the public. (Sorry, but you cannot take Dali's *Persistence of Memory* home for the weekend from the Museum of Modern Art!) Bibliographic networks, such as OCLC Online Computer Library Center, are also helpful because they indicate which member institutions own specific resources. One can discover which libraries own the resource sought, and then learn from individual library sites if the resource is available or has been borrowed by a patron.

Traditionally, bibliographies and journal indexes have not given location information. Bibliographies list information resources that exist somewhere, but seldom tell where you may find copies of them. Indexes give the larger resource in which a smaller work being listed can be found (e.g., the journal volume, issue, and page numbers for an article), but they do not give the physical location of the larger resource (that is, which libraries subscribe to the journal). All of this is still true for tangible resources, but for online resources it is now common to give the direct location in the form of a **Uniform Resource Locator** (URL)—a web address for an online resource. For example, in a catalog, you might see the following:

Title: The Internet Movie Database
Links: http://www.imdb.com
http://bibpurl.oclc.org/web/273

To accomplish Hagler's functions of bibliographic control, sufficient well-formed metadata is needed. Without metadata, information resources could not be made known to the world, contained works could not be identified, consistent lists could not be produced for collections, access could not be granted, and locating the resources would be impossible. Metadata is necessary to meet these and other functions as well. Metadata, however, will not look the same in all cases. There are differences in how metadata is created for different types of materials, in different environments, among different communities, and in different contexts.

1.3 Organization of Information in Different Contexts

There are many contexts in which there is a desire to organize information so that it will be retrievable for various purposes and so that at least some of it will be preserved for posterity. The ones to be discussed here are

- Libraries
- Archives
- Museums
- Online settings and contexts, such as
  - The Internet and the Semantic Web
  - Digital collections
  - Information architecture
- Indexing and abstracting
- Records management
- Personal information management
- Knowledge management

1.3.1 Libraries

Libraries are places in which collections of information resources are kept for people to use or borrow (rather than purchase). We consider libraries first in this text because they have the longest traditions of organizing information for the purpose of retrieval and for posterity. For centuries, **librarians**[§] have overseen the daily operations of libraries, organized and managed collections of resources, provided access to those collections, and assisted patrons in myriad ways. In most modern libraries, information organization activities are centered in the technical services department. The term ***technical services*** (often shortened to *tech services* in casual conversation) refers to the "behind-the-scenes" activities that address developing, acquiring, organizing, and preparing a library's collection of resources.[13] Additionally, there may be other units within the department focused on serials, digital resources, preservation and conservation, archives, or technology. There is no universal agreement on which activities belong in technical services departments; each library may have a different configuration of units placed under the technical services banner. For example, in some libraries, collection development may be more closely associated with ***public services*** (a library's front-of-house operations including reference services, instruction, and circulation) or it may be its own department. Figure 1.2 provides a basic overview of selected technical services activities, many of which are described further in the text.

[§]In this context, I am referring simply to persons who work in libraries. This is not the venue for a discussion of who is and who is not a librarian, what qualifications are or are not required, the status and responsibilities of various staff positions in libraries, the need for a master's degree, and so on.

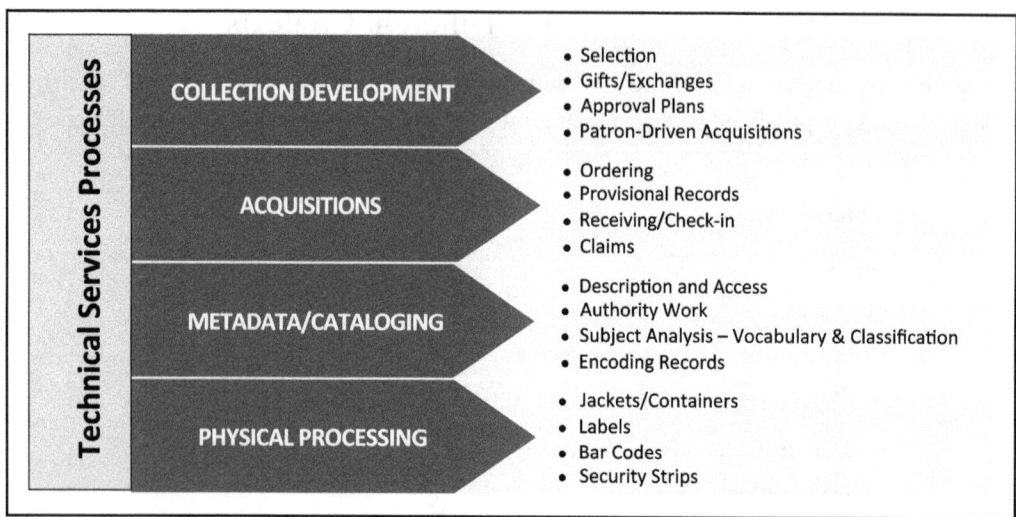

Figure 1.2 Some Library Technical Services Processes.

1.3.1.1 Collections and Acquisitions

As mentioned earlier, the process of organizing recorded information begins with collections. Collections in libraries are created through the *collection development* process, that is, the activities performed to build a collection of resources that meets the information needs of the population that the library serves. These activities may include any of the following methods.

- *Approval Plans*: a method in which a library contracts with one or more vendors to receive new resources according to pre-selected profiles outlining the collection's needs.
- *Selection*: the process in which collection development librarians (who may also be known as *subject librarians* or *bibliographers*) learn about the existence of works through vendors' product catalogs, reviews, publishers' announcements and websites, requests from users of the library, and the like, and then choose the most appropriate materials for the collection.
- *Gifts and Exchanges*: *gifts* are information resources that are donated to a library; *exchanges* are made when a library has a mutually beneficial trade agreement with one or more other libraries to swap its duplicate or unwanted resources for resources that they want or need.
- *Patron-Driven Acquisitions*: also known as *demand-driven acquisitions*; the process by which a library obtains certain resources (usually electronic) only after the need for them has been definitively established. For example, a library may provide access to a large number of e-book records in the catalog, but the library only purchases an individual e-book after it has been accessed by a patron.

Less frequently, but still practiced in some academic and research libraries, collection development librarians may take resource-buying trips to purchase special materials, including particularly difficult-to-find foreign language materials.

Acquisitions, another function related to the development and organization of collections, is responsible for managing orders and budgets (e.g., ordering materials, paying bills, overseeing standing orders, monitoring budgets). Additionally, they may be responsible for receiving the resources, checking them in, claiming missing items, and managing returns. The acquisitions staff may also be responsible for obtaining or creating temporary catalog records at the time of ordering materials.[14] After the materials have been checked in, these provisional records are expanded upon in the next process: cataloging.

1.3.1.2 Cataloging

Once resources arrive at the library, they must be organized and integrated into the collection and its catalog. A *catalog* is a retrieval tool that contains an organized compilation of bibliographic metadata that represents the holdings of a particular collection, an institution, or a group of institutions. The process of organizing and describing resources in libraries is called *cataloging*, and its goal is to create a multifaceted list of resources to which the library can provide access. The activities described in this section are addressed in more detail in Chapters 8–13.

Cataloging comprises two major activities. The first is *descriptive cataloging*, which entails documenting the most significant attributes of resources to allow users to find, identify, select, obtain, and explore them. The description, often, is a straightforward representation of the "facts" of the resource addressing *who*, *what*, *where*, and *when*. A minimal description for a published resource typically includes elements such as:

- title proper
- statement of responsibility
- version or edition
- resource type
- publication location
- publisher's name
- publication date
- extent
- dimensions
- series information
- standard number

Descriptive cataloging also entails choosing access points for the agents and titles associated with the resource. Access points are useful for finding the resource in a catalog. Another component of descriptive cataloging is authority control, which ensures consistency of access points. The preferred name of an agent and the most common version of a widely known title are selected as the bases of *authorized access points*—the standardized, consistently used character strings chosen to represent agents and some titles. This means, for example, catalogers use the authorized access point **Onassis, Jacqueline Kennedy, 1929-1994** in the metadata for resources that are by or about the former First Lady of the United States, no matter what form of name appears in the resource (Jackie Kennedy, Jackie O, Jacqueline Bouvier Kennedy).

Subject cataloging, the second major cataloging component, entails analyzing the subject matter of a resource in order to describe it using controlled terminology and classification notation. It comprises two key activities: *conceptual analysis* and *translation*. **Conceptual analysis** is the process of determining what a resource is about and what the resource is. Using professional jargon, we might say the conceptual analysis is performed to determine the resource's "*aboutness*" (i.e., its subject matter and its genre/form properties). A resource cannot be accurately described if it has not been thoughtfully examined and understood. The other subject cataloging activity, *translation*, is the process of transforming the cataloger's understanding of the aboutness into one or more controlled subject access systems. Translation involves choosing appropriate controlled vocabulary terms and the most relevant classification notation(s) to describe the resource.

When materials are organized into collections, physical entities must be arranged in some fashion. They may be placed on shelves in the order in which they arrive, or they may be placed in some more meaningful order. They could be arranged in alphabetical order, the way that fiction and biography sections are often arranged in many public and school libraries. Most resources, however, are arranged by classification. For tangible resources, classification notations are used to create a location device referred to as a **call number**. A call number is used to identify the physical resource and to provide a unique shelf address; it is usually established by adding a cutter number to the classification notation assigned to the resource. A **cutter number** is a sequence of alphanumeric characters that usually represents the primary creator's name, or lacking such a name, the title. There are different approaches to establishing call numbers depending on the classification scheme used.

Most records created through the cataloging process are encoded with the Machine-Readable Cataloging (MARC) format.[15] MARC is a set of numeric tags and alphanumeric subfields that are used to identify the various types of metadata being recorded about a library resource. MARC allows the metadata to be ingested into the catalog, searched, and then presented to library users in response to their queries. A single line from a MARC record might look something like this:

> 245 10 $a Bridges and crowns : $b an introduction / $c by D.N. Allan.

This states that the resource has a title proper (245 $a), a subtitle (245 $b), and a statement of who is responsible for creating the resource (245 $c). The online catalog, however, will display this metadata in a more user-friendly manner. Perhaps something like this:

> **Title:** Bridges and crowns : an introduction / by D.N. Allan.

The online catalog, or *online public access catalog* (OPAC), is just one part of a library's larger automation tool known as an **integrated library system** (ILS) or a **library services platform** (LSP). Both are library management systems that include various modules to perform different functions (e.g., cataloging, circulation, reserves) while sharing access to the same database.

The process of cataloging just described, where a cataloger does all this work "from scratch," is referred to as **original cataloging**. Fortunately, it is not necessary for every information resource in every library to be cataloged originally in that library. Because libraries frequently acquire copies of the same resources, their catalogers can share metadata by adapting a copy of the original cataloging record created by another library for their own catalogs, a process commonly called **copy cataloging**. This is related to the idea of **cooperative cataloging**—the working together by independent institutions to create cataloging that can be shared with others. There are various ways to obtain copies of existing cataloging records, such as through membership in a consortium or a bibliographic network (e.g., downloading records from OCLC), from vendors (e.g., paying for catalog records to be sent along with purchased resources), or from libraries that make their metadata freely available (e.g., downloading records from the catalog of the Library of Congress).

1.3.1.3 Physical Processing

Once resources have been chosen, received, and added into the catalog, the physical items are sent to the physical processing unit so that they can be prepared to be added to the collection. This involves removing or adding book jackets, placing security strips in or on materials, placing call number labels and barcodes on the resources, sending a resource to the conservation/preservation department if it is not in good shape, and so forth. Once resources are processed, they may be shelved in the stacks to be accessed by users and circulated, if appropriate.

1.3.1.4 The Catalog

The two major outcomes of cataloging are (1) the arrangement of collections and (2) the creation and maintenance of the catalog that provides the primary means of access to the collections. The catalog can show what exists in the collection by certain creators, having certain titles, or on certain subjects. It also collocates all the works of a creator, all the editions of a work, and all works on a subject, even though they might not be brought together in the physical collection. Finally, the catalog provides some kind of location device to indicate where an item will be found, assuming it is not circulating to a user.

Until recently the online catalog primarily contained records only for resources physically held by the library system. As libraries have entered into cooperative relationships, the longstanding principle of the catalog showing "what the library has"[16] has eroded. In *union catalogs*—catalogs that contain records from more than one library (e.g., the libraries in a consortium)—the concept was expanded to show what at least one of the cooperating libraries had. The addition of online resources has meant that catalogs now contain records for what the library provides access to (in addition to what the library owns).

Online catalogs can act as gateways to outside resources. Over time, catalogs evolved to provide direct access to remote internet resources, marking a major advance in their functionality. Now, a URL in a catalog record can provide immediate access to:

- additional metadata (e.g., tables of contents),
- additional or complementary content (e.g., a supplement, an image of a book cover), or
- the entire full-text resource represented in the description, if available (e.g., a link to a PDF version of a resource).

Catalogs may also connect to the catalogs of other institutions or to bibliographic networks (e.g., OCLC's WorldCat database) that can show where a resource may be found if it is not available locally. The resource can then be requested through *interlibrary loan* (ILL) or some other form of document delivery.

In addition to searching the inventory of tangible library resources found in the catalog, bibliographic and full-text databases may be accessed through a catalog's discovery layer (also referred to as a *discovery interface*, *discovery tool*, or *discovery service*). A **discovery layer** is a technological add-on to the ILS or LSP that allows users to have a greater variety of interactions with a library's information stores. For example, through the discovery layer, patrons may be able to search for books, journal articles, and digital objects all in one search, or they may be able to browse keyword search results that have been sorted into *facets* (i.e., fundamental aspects, features, or characteristics of resources) such as genre, resource type, creator, subject, publication date, location, and so on. The technologies used to present metadata to the public continue to evolve.

1.3.2 Archives

Archives are organizations that preserve records of enduring value that document organizational or personal activities accumulated in the course of daily life and work. Archives may contain any type of material, but some of the more common types found in collections of organizational records include things such as annual reports, correspondence, and personnel records. Personal records might consist of items such as correspondence, manuscripts, and personal papers, or perhaps a collection of memorabilia or a scrapbook. Even though materials in archives often are thought to be old, this is not necessarily so. Further, archival materials can be in many different formats: texts, objects, images, moving image recordings, and so forth. These can exist in both physical and digital forms.

Over the twentieth century, libraries became more and more standardized, with many information resources in a library being duplicates of resources held in others; this led to sharing metadata for such resources. This, however, is not the situation in archives. An archives[17]** usually contains unique items. Therefore, it was once thought that standardization was not applicable or necessary. Archives could not take advantage of previously created metadata because they were not describing materials that were also owned elsewhere. However, in the past several decades, archives have seen significant standardization in their descriptive practices. Although their collections may be unique, the attributes that make those collections findable and identifiable are not. The information we want to know about archival collections is often the same, no matter which specific collection we are addressing.

Archival materials have been arranged and described for centuries, despite the lack of universal descriptive standards for most of that time. Unlike library materials, archival materials are typically arranged and described in groups. Until the last few decades, each archives chose its own way to organize its collections, particularly regarding the level of control and the depth of description. There have been several schools of thought as to the best approach for organizing the materials in archival collections and creating appropriate representations for those materials.

Two fundamental principles serve as a foundation for current archival standards: *provenance* and *original order*. **Provenance** refers to the individual, family, organization, or institution that is responsible for the creation, maintenance, or use of the materials. It is related to the French concept, **respect des fonds**, a principle that dictates that records of different origins should be kept separate to preserve their context.[18]

**In North American professional jargon, the institution is generally referred to as *an archives*, though some may refer to it in the singular.

Respect des fonds declared simply that the overall corpus of records resulting from a single high-level administrative entity—for example, the records of the Foreign Office—should be maintained as an indivisible whole and that no materials from other discrete governmental entities should be added into them. That was the extent of it, its proponents not much concerned with how the many records comprising the *fonds* should themselves be arranged.[19]

Original order directs archivists to maintain the organization or sequence of materials established by the creator of those materials. This may or may not be evident in the collection. If the original order has been lost or the collection was never truly organized by the creator or collector, then an archivist may need to construct a logical order for the collection. In establishing a logical order, whether original or devised by the archivist, ***series*** (subgroupings) among the materials may be identified. The description of the collection should reflect the arrangement of those groupings. Most archives keep the contents of individual collections within the archives as a whole, in original order, and the collections are maintained according to provenance. An overview of processing archival collections is provided in Figure 1.3.

Standardization and cooperation came to the archival world beginning in the 1980s because of increased interest in research involving documents and archival collections housed all over the globe. In the 1990s and 2000s, interest also grew in making descriptions of archival collections accessible online and in including summary descriptions of archival collections in the same databases with library catalog records.

Descriptions of archival materials can take different forms and perform different types of functions. An ***accession record*** summarizes information about the source of the collection, gives the circumstances of its acquisition (which are more fully treated in the donor file), and briefly describes physical details and contents for a collection. A ***finding aid*** provides detailed notes on the historical and organizational context of the collection and continues by describing its content,

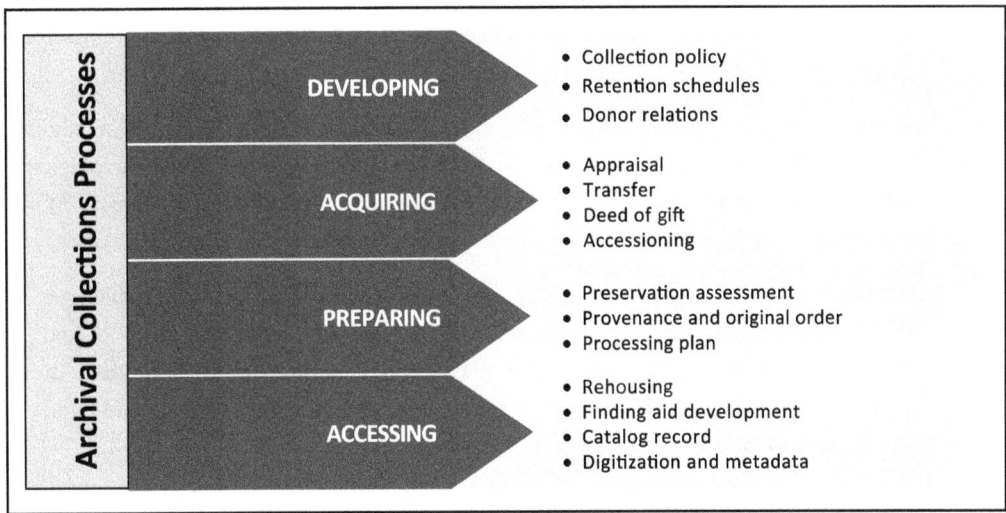

Figure 1.3 Processing Archival Collections. (Courtesy of Sarah Martin, Archivist.)

providing an inventory outlining what is in each box. It may also contain subject headings, authority-controlled access points, and physical details such as the presence of brittle or fragile materials. Finding aids can also be referred to as *registers, inventories,* or *container lists.* A separate record, which describes the collection (or a part or parts of the collection), also may be created for inclusion in a library catalog. MARC can be used to code archival catalog records. In the late 1990s, the Encoded Archival Description (EAD)[20] standard was released and has been implemented internationally to encode finding aids so that they can be manipulated and displayed online.

To meet the responsibilities of taking care of records of enduring value while at the same time providing access to those materials, archival materials are generally housed in boxes kept in **closed stacks**, where the shelves of materials are accessible only to staff. There is no public browsing of archival repositories, so the arrangement of the individual archival collections in the stacks does not need to be classified, unlike in a library with **open stacks** where anyone can browse the resources. In addition, the varied nature of archival collections would require such a broad classification as to diminish the utility of that assignment.

The organization of archival materials is a fundamental activity in the management and provision of access to collections. Archival description serves many purposes. It provides guidance to researchers on the utility of the material for their information needs. It also assists archivists in the management and preservation of their collections. When collections are well organized and documented, archival materials can fulfill a wide variety of uses and user needs.

1.3.3 Museums

What is a **museum**? Although we all think that we know, the definition of a museum has become a point of contention in the late 2010s and early 2020s. For many years, the standard definition was something akin to that provided by the International Council of Museums (ICOM):

> A museum is a non-profit, permanent institution in the service of society and its development, open to the public, which acquires, conserves, researches, communicates and exhibits the tangible and intangible heritage of humanity and its environment for the purposes of education, study and enjoyment.[21]

That definition, however, is not satisfactory to all and there have been ongoing attempts to redefine the term within ICOM. One critic pointed out that the definition, "does not speak the language of the 21st century," and that it does not reply to current demands of "cultural democracy."[22] One proposed definition from 2019 received a good deal of attention, but not all of it was positive.

> Museums are democratising, inclusive and polyphonic spaces for critical dialogue about the pasts and the futures. Acknowledging and addressing the conflicts and challenges of the present, they hold artefacts and specimens in trust for society, safeguard diverse memories for future generations and guarantee equal rights and equal access to heritage for all people.
>
> Museums are not for profit. They are participatory and transparent, and work in active partnership with and for diverse communities to collect, preserve, research, interpret,

exhibit, and enhance understandings of the world, aiming to contribute to human dignity and social justice, global equality and planetary wellbeing.[23]

ICOM's proposed definition was controversial. Some members of the committee appointed to revise the definition even resigned in protest. *The New York Times* stated, "For some, these disagreements reflect a wider split in the museum world about whether such institutions should be places that exhibit and research artifacts, or ones that actively engage with political and social issues."[24] One critic of the proposed definition stated, "This is not a definition but a statement of fashionable values."[25] In 2022, ICOM announced their approval of yet another version of the definition:

> A museum is a not-for-profit, permanent institution in the service of society that researches, collects, conserves, interprets and exhibits tangible and intangible heritage. Open to the public, accessible and inclusive, museums foster diversity and sustainability. They operate and communicate ethically, professionally and with the participation of communities, offering varied experiences for education, enjoyment, reflection and knowledge sharing.[26]

From these various definitions, however, it is clear that museums contain specimens valuable for understanding the world around us. Although libraries and archives may contain some visual materials (notably photographs, but also slides, art prints, and the like), the collections of museums, galleries, and other institutions that collect artifacts and objects of material culture consist primarily of visual material in two- or three-dimensional form. Both the organization of these materials and their documentation traditionally have been for internal use only. Research needs, institutional mandates, and public interest, however, have led such institutions to begin organizing their collections in ways that libraries and archives have for many years. Metadata schemas, controlled vocabularies, classification systems, and content standards have emerged in the last few decades as a response to museums' needs to disseminate more information about their collections.

For internal use, museums must establish a ***registration*** process, which is "simply a system of record keeping to help track and care for the items in a museum collection."[27] (See Figure 1.4.) The records created by a registrar in a museum, historical society, or special collections department establish organizational control over the artworks and artifacts. The system contains "policies, procedures, practices, and documents that provide a link between the objects and their history."[28] Registration may comprise processes such as acquisitions, accessioning, documentation, and cataloging.

The first stage of registration is usually the acquisition process through various methods including donations, purchases, exchanges or transfers, bequests, or collection through fieldwork. Some major concerns in the acquisitions process relate to the rights to the object, in particular acquiring title and possession of it. Bills of sale, donation documentation, and acknowledgments, among other paperwork, must be collected for the accession file. In museums, the provenance of an object or a collection of objects is essential information in determining the name and other elements describing that particular object. *Provenance* means slightly different things in museums and archives. *Provenance* in archives drives the principles of organization; collections are organized

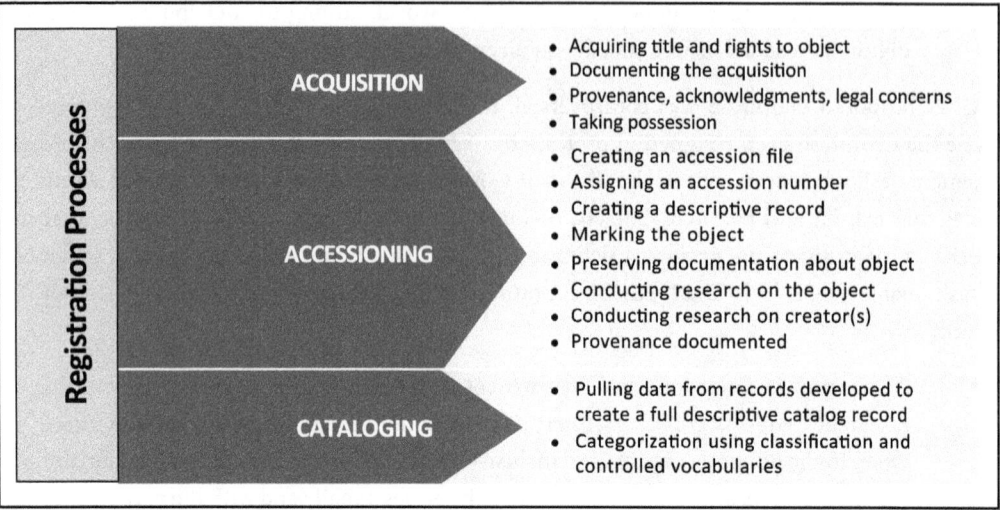

Figure 1.4 A Sample Museum Registration Process.

around their creators. In art history, the ***provenance*** of a work is connected to the ownership, history, and authenticity of the work.

Items are accessioned after being acquired. "The ***accessioning*** process consists of making a place for the object in the museum registration system and creating a permanent record of it. The accessioning process consists of the following steps: acquiring right and title to the object; assigning an accession number; making a record of the object; and marking the object."[29] An accession record is created using the documents developed during the acquisitions process (e.g., rights and title of the object). Practice in natural history museums, where artifacts are acquired largely from fieldwork, can differ somewhat as a preliminary field record is created first. If it is decided to keep the objects in the collection, then accession records are made. In some cases, groups of similar objects (e.g., gemstones) are described as a single lot that is given a single accession number. The curation of individual objects, which may not happen for some time, results in departmental-level catalog records with their own numerical sequences. A crucial aspect of accessioning is assigning an ***accession number***: a unique identifier assigned to each object to track that object as part of the collection. It is used consistently throughout all documentation. The numbering system can be tailored to the needs of the museum with as much or as little complexity as required. Other accession information needed may include the following:[30]

- name of the object
- source, donor, or vendor
- restrictions
- value/worth
- size
- description
- date of acquisition
- location
- images

During the accessioning process, further documentation is gathered, and a description of the object is built. Documentation includes information that accompanies the object or is discovered while conducting research about the object. Information may also be recorded about those who created or previously held custody over the object. Both provenance and physical condition of the object must appear with all other information about the object in the accession file. One aspect of creating records for museum objects and art that differs significantly from creating records for bibliographic resources is that the objects are often imperfectly known at the time of acquisition or registration. There may be an accumulation of information over time, some of which may be conflicting or contradictory, which becomes part of the object's documentation.

Cataloging, in the context of museums, has a similar purpose to that of library cataloging: creating a full description about the specimen, artifact, or art object, but there are some differences. According to Reibel,

> There are actually several different processes that are called cataloging. They mainly fall into two classes: (1) The creation of the catalog by extracting data from your records and presenting it in some useful format. (2) The updating of the information in the collection records. Every generation of professionals that works with the collection expands the museum's knowledge about the collection. If this new understanding of the collection is written into the permanent records, it will destroy primary data. Therefore, the new information is written into the catalog. Often a completely new catalog record is created and then becomes the record of choice. When people talk about cataloging, they are usually talking about this updating process.[31]

As part of the cataloging process, categorization is employed. Registrars and curators assign to objects one or more categories from organized controlled vocabularies or classification systems. It collocates objects with similar subjects, genres, forms, purposes, origins, time periods, and so on. Examples of standards for categorizing museum objects include *Art & Architecture Thesaurus*[32] and *Nomenclature for Museum Cataloging*.[33]

Description of visual material can be more difficult than describing textual material. There is more reliance on the perceptions of the person doing the describing. Often there are no words associated with items at all; it is necessary for the registrars and curators of such items to use their own words. A single object record may have many more fields than does the usual library catalog record. Some fields that are typically needed for art objects that are not used in libraries are materials, technique(s), provenance, exhibition history, installation considerations, and appraised value. Even with additional fields, it is not possible to anticipate all the uses a researcher might find in works of art or artifacts. A street scene from a century ago may be useful to historians, architects, urban planners, cultural historians, medical researchers, sociologists, students of photography, or others. Systems have been developed that start with queries that use the text of the description; then query results allow the searcher to browse surrogate images.

Subject analysis presents challenges for visual materials—an image does not state in words what it is about, nor does the title of a visual work always clearly convey what the work is about. Additionally, the line between description and subject analysis is harder to draw. One might describe a work of art as being a painting of a woman in a blue dress holding and looking at a baby—this is a description. But if one gives the subject of the work as "Mary and Jesus," one has crossed the line into interpretation (unless, perhaps, this is the title of the work given by the artist). And if one uses a description like "maternal love," one is definitely interpreting.

A perceived barrier to shared metadata about museum objects has been the fact that museums often hold unique objects. This is perhaps less true of natural history collections than other museum and art collections; although each specimen of an insect or a bird is unique, each represents a class of organisms that can be identified to the genus–species level and is kept not for its unique characteristics but for its representational qualities. In the case of these natural history specimens, there may be copy-specific notes, but this does not preclude the idea of reusing metadata for cooperative access. However, as was true of libraries when cooperative cataloging was first introduced, museum curators in other types of museums fear a loss of individual control and a diminished level of detail. Until the advent of initiatives like Artstor[34] and OCLC's WorldCat,[35] museums had been reluctant to give up their local terminology and idiosyncratic ways of organizing their information to participate in union catalogs or federated retrieval tools. This has been changing in recent years.

Besides their major collections, museums can also have archives, records management programs, and libraries. A museum library may contain published materials that document or relate to the museum collections. Museum archives document the institutional records of the museum as it accumulates, displays, and creates programming based on its collections. And because museums are institutions with responsibilities for proving their tax status (often nonprofit), among other things, they also have records management programs to ensure that appropriate and adequate documentation is kept over time.

As with archival materials, museum collections are accessible only to staff. Unlike the open stacks in the library, patrons of a museum are usually not allowed to touch or hold the specimens or the art (unless, perhaps, it is tactile art). Much of the collection is stored behind the scenes while only a portion of it is on display at any one time. Behind the scenes, the items are numbered in such a way that they can be retrieved as needed. Persons responsible for the exhibits make heavy use of the system of organizational control. These collections are increasingly also being used for research by persons with diverse research needs, but mediated access has not required a change in strategy for organizational control.

1.3.4 Online Settings and Contexts

In the twenty-first century, the internet has become omnipresent in our personal and professional lives. The internet—particularly the World Wide Web (or the web)—is a tool that we use for nearly everything. We use it to conduct business transactions, to manage our calendars and bank accounts, to find answers to quick questions, and to investigate almost anything that we are curious about. The internet, however, is not a panacea for all of life's information problems. The internet is unpredictable and inconstant; it can be unkind and untrue; it is full of opinions that may masquerade as facts, and it is very messy. The internet has been likened to a library where all the books have been dumped on the floor and there is no catalog.[36] For many years, efforts have been made to find ways to gain some intellectual control over it. One cannot say, however, that the internet is organized, and this is unlikely to change anytime soon. Portions of it—certain types of online spaces and many individual sites—may be organized in some fashion, but they are not representative of the entire internet. The next three subsections discuss some of these online settings and contexts: the internet, digital collections, and information architecture.

1.3.4.1 The Internet and the Semantic Web

In the rapidly advancing, technology-centered environment of the third millennium, much of our lives is facilitated by the internet. A high volume of the world's information has been transferred to the web, as has much of its metadata. Many of our modern work processes and methods of communication are dependent on its technologies (e.g., Zoom). The internet is indispensable. It has gone from a luxury to a basic necessity in our twenty-first century lives, but as we have already discussed, it is flawed. Machines are amazing in so many ways, but they are not smart; they lack intelligence, sentience, and intuition. They are not good at inferring connections or understanding context without being fed massive amounts of additional data and using massive amounts of resources. Consequently, we are sometimes frustrated with the current state of our technology, yearning for the promised technologies of tomorrow. Although we would all like to experience the interactive technology of *Star Trek*, we are just not there yet despite the advances made in the early 2020s with generative artificial intelligence (AI). Although AI has made tremendous leaps forward in a very short time, information professionals are only beginning to investigate the role of this technology in the organization of information. Early experiments have proved somewhat frustrating with AI hallucinations being used to fill in metadata blanks. AI as an organizing tool is not yet ready for prime time, but the potential is there, and exploration is ongoing.[37]

In the mid-1990s, shortly after the birth of the web, some librarians and LIS researchers enthusiastically and somewhat naively attempted to design projects to help organize the internet—the *whole* internet.[38] These efforts began in earnest only after the web became the face of the internet. These information professionals, however, were quick to realize that there was so much rapid change on the internet that many efforts were out of date in a short time. Early on, libraries attempted to use traditional means of organization, but it soon became clear that full-scale library cataloging was not well suited for describing what often turned out to be ephemeral web resources.

Instead of creating individual records for each website, some librarians began to compile bibliographies of sites, some of which eventually became more formal directories or subject gateways to the internet. An ***internet directory*** is an organized collection of links to websites on particular topics. A small number of internet directories were organized according to traditional library classifications, such as the *Dewey Decimal Classification*, but most directories had organization schemes consisting of 12–16 top-level home-grown categories (e.g., Arts, Business, Computers, Finance, Games) from which users could drill down further to find varying levels of subtopics:

   📁 Arts
    📁 Performing Arts
     📁 Theater
      📁 Stagecraft
       📁 Lighting and Electrics
        📁 Designers

Although a small number of them still exist, hierarchical directories are mostly relics of the internet's past. As information architects Louis Rosenfeld, Peter Morville, and Jorge Arango state, "The findability techniques that were effective in the late 1990s (e.g., Yahoo!'s curated hierarchical directory) are ineffective today."[39] An example of an enduring subject gateway, at least at the time of this writing, is *SciCentral*, which provides up-to-date links to science-related news stories, journals, job resources, conferences, and so on.[40]

Another attempt to control the information on the internet resulted in the development of one of the world's most recognized metadata schemas. In 1995, 52 librarians, archivists, humanities scholars, and geographers, as well as standards makers working with the internet and associated technologies, met at an invitational metadata workshop sponsored by OCLC Online Computer Library Center and the National Center for Supercomputing Applications. The goals were to

- identify the scope of the problem (i.e., the exponential growth of internet resources and the growing difficulty in retrieving them),
- achieve consensus on a list of metadata elements that would yield simple descriptions, and
- lay the groundwork for achieving further progress in the definition of metadata elements that describe electronic information.[41]

This team of people developed a metadata standard for describing online resources known as the **Dublin Core**.[42] It was designed as a relatively small set of basic metadata elements, because most websites and other document-like objects on the internet at that time did not require as much detail as was typically found in the library catalog. The schema, which contains 15 basic elements applicable to most resources (e.g., title, identifier, subject, type), was created to enhance resource discovery. In the late 1990s, OCLC established a way for libraries to catalog online resources cooperatively and to have ready access to a database of metadata describing important web resources. This system was eventually incorporated into OCLC's WorldCat database.

Much work on organizing and searching the internet has been done by persons other than librarians. For example, computer scientists and programmers have primarily developed **search engines**—the principal tool used to access web resources. Information professionals and the general public value search engines highly, even though they may be somewhat frustrated that these tools are not more selective and precise. Most programs or agents (e.g., crawlers, bots, spiders) sent out to find websites to add to the search engine are better able to interpret and index text than other formats; videos, sound files, and images can be recognized as such, but their contents may not be indexed adequately unless they also have accompanying text or labels. In addition, these programs cannot analyze a site's purpose, history, policies, and so forth. To improve this situation, work to advance our technologies continues, but so does work focused on improving our metadata standards and our approaches to digital information.

Appropriate information *could* be gleaned by bots from metadata that has been added to a site by its creator or by someone trained in describing and analyzing resources; in the past two decades, however, misuse of metadata has kept many search engines from making extensive use of it. This misuse (e.g., the addition of keywords that are popular words but may have nothing to do with the content of the site) can be seen as unethical, homegrown attempts at *search engine optimization* (SEO)—an activity aimed at raising the visibility of websites (i.e., getting sites to be ranked higher in search engine results). Legitimate SEO activities focus on sets of best practices in digital marketing, web design, information architecture, and content organization to achieve their goals, rather than on deception. SEO tends to be focused on commercial activities; consequently, there is little exploration of SEO in this text.[43]

In recent years, the attitude toward including metadata in web resources has begun to change. Some of the world's most popular search engines (i.e., Google, Bing, Yahoo!, and Yandex) are starting to embrace certain semantic technologies that embed small amounts of metadata (known as *microdata*) into Hypertext Markup Language (HTML) code to make the data found within websites more meaningful to search engines and web crawlers. Properly used, metadata and microdata can include, among other things, information about creators, titles, subjects, and other traditional descriptive attributes; non-textual parts of a site; textual portions of the site; entities, roles, and relationships; and the site's purpose and history.

That initial desire among librarians and others to describe everything on the internet quickly dissipated. It was naive to think that every web resource could be cataloged like a book or a DVD in a library. Instead, the profession and the general public have embraced search engines to retrieve materials sought on the internet. Although their results are sometimes overwhelming (e.g., millions of results) and sometimes erroneous (e.g., often full of *false drops*[††]), search engines are excellent for satisfying most general internet searching needs. Information professionals, researchers, and other conscientious information seekers, however, do not perform all of their in-depth, scholarly research using only search engines, though they may start their preliminary exploration of a topic that way. Search engines, like other more narrowly focused retrieval tools, have an important role to play in information retrieval, and we anticipate that their scope, power, and effectiveness will continue to grow in the future as more meaningful metadata is added to web content and is taken into consideration by AI-powered search algorithms.

Although some believe that organizing the internet is impossible, not everyone has given up on this dream. Some computer scientists, programmers, and library and information professionals believe that the parts of the internet that are important for retrieval and for posterity are likely to be brought under some form of control. It is human nature to want to organize, and the principles learned over centuries of organizing print information can be an inspiration, and in some cases can be used alongside newer tools to help organize online information. The current effort to create the Semantic Web is a case in point, wherein online data will be more meaningfully defined and linked to other pertinent data for the purpose of improved discovery of information.

So, why do we need improvements? Search engines today rely on keywords. As previously mentioned, keyword-based searching tends to lack semantic controls. Synonyms and homographs make searching our current keyword-matching systems an obstacle course of false drops. For example, when we search Google for information about spiders on the web (i.e., programs or bots

---

[††]*False drops* are search results that meet your search criteria but have nothing to do with the information you were trying to find.

that crawl the internet looking for new websites), we are inundated with pages about and pictures of the cobwebby things created by arachnids to catch their dinner. And, for the most part, users are accustomed to it; they accept it as a part of the search process. Not everyone, however, feels that this is okay. Some believe we can do better; hence the efforts to develop the Semantic Web.

The **Semantic Web** is intended as an extension of the current web. It is based on the notion of **linked data**. On the web today, pages provide a limited number of hand-selected links to other resources. Creators point to other documents that they consider to be relevant to the information they are presenting—generally at the level of the whole resource. In other words, we click the link and go to another document. A goal of the Semantic Web is to increase technology's abilities to connect to an even wider variety of related resources through automatic means (rather than relying on a content creator's few selected links). The Semantic Web will provide links in a format semantically meaningful to and actionable by computers to automatically gather additional, relevant information. If we can clearly identify entities on the web and their relationships to other entities (e.g., persons, concepts, other resources), we can link the resources that have properties in common (e.g., all information about Cameroon, all resources by Celeste Ng). Linked data is meant to "smarten" our machines; to help them "understand" meaning, rather than just matching alphanumeric character strings.

This means that the web must shift from identifying and retrieving documents for human consumption *only* to identifying and retrieving the data in those documents for humans *and* for better machine understanding, manipulation, and processing. In many ways, it is an attempt to turn the web into something like a giant global database rather than an enormous document warehouse. So, if we go back to that analogy of the internet being a library where all the books are dumped on the floor,[44] then the Semantic Web is a library where the books have been ripped apart into individual pages, paragraphs, or even sentences, so that discrete chunks of data can be clearly identified and relationships between the chunks can be explicitly indicated in order for machines to connect them on a more granular level. Instead of being pointed to a website, we may be pointed right to the data we are seeking (within a website). The Semantic Web is not to be based on the document as a unit; it is more concerned with what information is contained within those documents.

Among some, there is great excitement about the potential of the Semantic Web and the changes that could occur as the result of its maturation. There will be far-reaching effects on information organization and cataloging, but exactly *how* things will change is not completely evident at this time. Although some have expressed hope about this journey, there are still plenty of naysayers who do not expect the promises of the Semantic Web to come to fruition.[45,‡‡] Some believe that Semantic Web technologies may not be necessary due to the rapid development of generative AI tools. Although it is too early to begin prognosticating about the future of internet search, it seems likely that Semantic Web technologies combined with generative AI developments could be exponentially better than either of those developments on their own.

---

‡‡More information about the Semantic Web can be found in Chapter 7.

1.3.4.2 Digital Collections

The development of the internet has changed many things. We now have much faster means of communication, instantaneous shopping, news and entertainment on demand, endless pictures of pets, new ways to meet the love of your life, and plenty of other distractions. It has also redefined the notion of space. We now live much of our lives in online spaces—venues to visit for a range of reasons (e.g., to catch up with friends, to attend classes, to watch TikToks). One of the more ambitious and beneficent uses of them has been the development of **digital collections**. These spaces, generally, contain collections of digitized or born-digital resources that have been selected for inclusion for the purposes of access and preservation for posterity. A specific digital collection may be referred to as a *digital library*, a *digital archives*, or an *institutional repository*. These terms are not always precisely defined; what is a *repository* in one institution may be very similar to the *digital archives* of another. What an individual digital collection is called may depend on the nature of the content and the nature of the institution establishing the collection. For example, one would expect to find mostly digitized primary sources (i.e., original documents) in digital archives.

What might be found in a digital collection? Almost anything if it can be presented in digital form. One can certainly find large amounts of text among most digital collections, but much more excitement often centers around the inclusion of multimedia resources and complex digital objects. Some digital collections are very narrowly focused, with limited resource types; for example, in the Franklin D. Roosevelt Presidential Library and Museum's digital collection FRANKLIN, one primarily encounters digitized texts—speeches, correspondence, diaries, press conference transcripts, executive orders, and so on.[46] But other collections are more sweeping in scope, and one will find a great variety of digital resource types. For example, in the digital collections of the Library of Congress or the Digital Public Library of America (DPLA), one may find sound files of historic speeches, interviews, lectures, entire long-playing record albums from yesteryear, and so on. Short films, video clips, television programs, political ads, news footage, public service announcements, and the like are not unusual, nor are digitized photographs, drawings, advertisements, and advanced geospatial data renderings. This diversity is now practically *de rigueur* for digital collections.

Digital collections are more sophisticated and more accessible than ever before, but they came from humble beginnings. In the 1990s the definition of *digital library* was a matter of debate. There were many types of experiments and projects labeled as digital libraries that would not be considered to be so today. For example, at the simplest level were collections of links to resources related to a particular subject; sometimes, such collections (really internet directories) were coordinated among individual librarians at cooperating institutions. To some, the term referred to sites like Project Gutenberg, which in its earliest form was a large collection of "e-texts" to be read online as simply formatted web pages. Candy Schwartz states, "It is an understatement to say that the phrase 'digital library' . . . means different things to different people." As part of a class project, her students found 64 formal and informal definitions of *digital library*.[47] Over time the phrase *digital collection* has come to refer to collections in which a site provides digitized information resources with a defined architecture and a service for the retrieval of such resources. Summarizing the definitions that had become predominant by the turn of the century, it can be said that a digital collection

- must contain an organized collection of digital resources (it is not a set of hyperlinks to other material);
- is created for a particular audience, group of users, or community;
- takes advantage of technology and human resources (e.g., librarians);
- provides fast and efficient access to digital resources, often without cost (although membership in a community might be required); and
- owns, controls, or has rights to the digital resources distributed by it.

Christine Borgman emphasizes that digital libraries are for communities of users and that they are really extensions of the physical places (e.g., libraries, museums, archives) where resources are selected, collected, organized, preserved, and accessed.[48] One example of a digital collection usually found in academic settings is the *institutional repository*—an online system that collects, manages, disseminates, and preserves digital resources related to the intellectual activity of an academic community (i.e., a university, a college, a department).

Organizing digital collections is often accomplished using many of the same methods used in physical libraries, archives, and museums, but these approaches are supplemented with the use of additional standards. Approaches to organization can vary from institution to institution and among software packages. As with tangible resources, the most important attributes of digital resources are described, access points are chosen, and the resources are analyzed so that subject matter and genre/form can be described. In addition to the metadata generated from those activities, further metadata may be needed to address the resource's digital lifecycle. For example, although users need to know that the resource is text-based and 120 pages in length, they also need to know in which formats the resource is available (e.g., as HTML or PDF). If the resource is downloadable or if it requires software to interact with it, the size and the system requirements are necessary metadata. If there are restrictions on access or use, these should be stated clearly. The description, in addition to identifying those parties responsible for the creation of the content, might also include those who digitized the resource and when that occurred, as well as who created the metadata, when it was created, and when it was last updated. Some structural metadata might also be needed to help the pieces of complex digital objects fit together to operate smoothly (e.g., so the video can be viewed or the pages of an e-book can be turned).

To contain the necessary metadata for each resource, some digital collections use established schemas such as the Metadata Encoding and Transmission Standard (METS), Metadata Object Description Schema (MODS), the Dublin Core, or even traditional library cataloging standards. Other institutions, however, develop their own approaches, often partly or fully based on one or more previously existing metadata schemas. For example, the DPLA's Metadata Application Profile[49] identifies several existing metadata schemas as sources for their set of metadata elements. Rather than reinventing the wheel, they reused elements from Dublin Core, the Europeana Data Model,[50] and other schemas. Like many other digital collections, DPLA employs strategies that are compliant with the protocols used by the Open Archives Initiative (OAI) to ensure easy sharing of digital resources and metadata. Projects such as these may also use one or more lists of controlled terminology to describe subjects, names, places, titles, forms, genres, resource types, and so on. In short, the organization of digital collections is being accomplished by using many of the same approaches used in libraries, archives, museums, and other cultural heritage institutions, with tools such as content standards, metadata schemas, encoding standards, controlled vocabularies, taxonomies, and so forth. These components are described more fully in later chapters of this book.

1.3.4.3 Information Architecture

Digital libraries, general websites, online news sources, online banks and bookstores, mobile applications, Facebook, and the like are all examples of online spaces. Just as architects determine the needs of the people who will use a physical space and then design buildings that will serve those needs, so must information architects anticipate how information might be used and create pathways to finding needed information in online spaces.

Information architecture, then, is more than just an aesthetic exercise in website design, although its development as a discipline is closely tied to web design; it is connected to areas of study within LIS, such as usability and the organization of information, as well as to other disciplines.[51] Andrew Dillon defines **information architecture** (IA) as "the process of designing, implementing and evaluating information spaces that are humanly and socially acceptable to their intended stakeholders."[52] He says he purposely leaves the definition "open so that we cover the organizational, blueprinting, and experience aspects, and allow for IA roles to cover these aspects."[53] Rosenfeld, Morville, and Arango define *information architecture* as follows:

- The structural design of shared information environments.
- The synthesis of organization, labeling, search, and navigation systems within digital, physical, and cross-channel ecosystems.
- The art and science of shaping information products and experiences to support usability, findability, and understanding.
- An emerging discipline and community of practice focused on bringing principles of design and architecture to the digital landscape.[54]

Then, they jokingly ask, "Were you expecting a single definition? Something short and sweet? A few words that succinctly capture the essence and expanse of the field of information architecture? Keep dreaming!"[55]

There is still disagreement about what is included in information architecture. Andrew Dillon and Don Turnbull describe some differences in points of view:

> In the absence of formal definition, a line of division has been drawn between two competing views of the field, known generally as the Big IA vs. Little IA perspectives. Big IA is … the process of designing and building information resources that are useful, usable, and acceptable. From this perspective IA must cover user experience and even organizational acceptance of the resource. On the other hand, Little IA refers to … a far more constrained activity that deals with information organization and maintenance, but does not involve itself in analyzing the user response or the graphical design of the information space. Big IA tends to be seen as top-down, conceiving the full product and its human or organizational impact; Little IA is viewed as more bottom-up, addressing the metadata and controlled vocabulary aspects of information organization, without

dealing directly with, and certainly never evaluating formally, the user experience of the resulting space.[56]

Some information architects reject the notion that information architecture is a new approach to the longstanding organizing practices used in libraries, archives, and museums. But the parallels are striking. Librarians have long understood the necessity of organizing information resources in ways that will aid users in gaining access to them as needed. There does appear to be some agreement, however, on the desire to design complete and helpful "information ecologies." To do this, the information architect must

- create online spaces with users' needs, behaviors, and limitations in mind;
- understand the specific context of the site (e.g., the mission, goals, strategies, etc., that are unique to the institution creating the space); and
- organize the online information (e.g., the stuff that users are looking for) logically and clearly to provide easy access to that information.[57]

The process includes designing usable interfaces and navigation systems (e.g., sitemaps, taxonomies, menus) in addition to creating a pleasing overall graphic design. Rosenfeld, Morville, and Arango identify the following as stages in the information architecture process:[58]

- *Research* includes a review of background materials, goals, context, content, the existing information architecture, and intended audiences. In this stage, an understanding of the content must be developed, including existing metadata.
- *Strategy* arises from contextual understanding developed in the first phase and defines the top levels of the site's organization and navigation structures, while also considering document types and the metadata schema. For example, one must develop ideas about how users will access the site's information (e.g., via alphabetic, chronological, topical, or task-oriented means).
- *Design* involves creating detailed blueprints, metadata schemas, and the like. In this stage, content categories, browsing menus, controlled vocabularies, search functions, and label systems are created.
- *Implementation* is where designs are used in the building, testing, and launching of the site; organizing and tagging documents, troubleshooting, and developing documentation occur in this phase.
- *Administration* involves the continuous evaluation and improvement of the site's information architecture.

The strategy and design stages, in particular, are the ones that require a thorough understanding of the theoretical underpinnings of information organization and the system design that will allow display of results in a logical and usable fashion.

1.3.5 Indexing and Abstracting

Indexing and abstracting are two approaches to distilling information content into an abbreviated, but comprehensive, representation of an information resource. Indexing has a long and shifting tradition in terms of what it is, who has done it, why it is done, and how it is done. The history of abstracting is less volatile and has evolved in the twentieth and twenty-first centuries into specific formats with targeted audiences.

1.3.5.1 Indexing

Indexing and *index* are difficult terms to understand because they are used in a variety of ways in the LIS professions. *Indexing* can refer to a process performed by humans or a process performed by machines. It produces a product, an *index* (i.e., a list), that may be used by humans or primarily by machines. The content in the list might be rich in descriptive detail or it might contain little more than a reference to the location of some information (e.g., a page number, a link to a record, or a URL). So, if you are confused about what these terms mean, you are not alone. Thus, we start with some definitions.

An ***index*** is a list of entries "designed to enable users to locate information in a document or specific documents in a collection."[59] It is usually in alphabetical order, and points to where each item in the list can be found, whether that is in a book, a web page, a journal issue full of articles, or a set of records in a database. So, indexes are a form of locator device that assists users to find information resources based on their search terms (e.g., subject, author, title).

Accordingly, ***indexing*** is the process of creating an index. It is the process by which the content of an information resource is analyzed, the aboutness of that item is determined and expressed in a concise manner, and the resource is described in such a way that users are aware of the basic attributes of a document, such as author, title, length, and the location of the content. Indexing often concerns textual items, although image and media indexing are also important areas of practice. Four types of indexing are addressed in this section: back-of-the-book indexing, database indexing, periodical indexing, and web indexing. Be forewarned, these are not the only uses of the term; it will appear in other chapters in other contexts.

1.3.5.1.1 Back-of-the-Book Indexing

In ***back-of-the-book indexing***, the index is a list of terms or phrases arranged alphabetically with locator references that make it possible for the user to retrieve the desired content from a print or electronic book. The index terms are typically derived from the language used in the text; this type of indexing is known as ***derived indexing***. A good book index will also include second-level entries or subheadings, *see* references for synonyms and variant forms of names, and *see also* cross-references for related concepts or names. Book indexing is primarily done by freelance specialists who contract with publishers (although some publishers may maintain an in-house indexing staff), or it may be performed by the authors themselves. Entries in a back-of-the-book index may look similar to this:

EAC-CPF. *See* Encoded Archival Context

EAD. *See* Encoded Archival Description

EBSCO, 82, 150, 504

Editions, 304–305; statement, 304

Element mapping, 202

Encoded Archival Context (EAC-CPF), 407–415, 532. *See also* Authority Control.

1.3.5.1.2 Database Indexing

In **database indexing** (or *journal indexing*), the focus is not just a single resource like a book. Instead, the scope and coverage are considerably larger. The goal is to provide access to the large body of periodical literature published for a specific subject area or discipline. For example, *Library & Information Science Source* is a journal index that includes content from more than 3,200 different LIS scholarly journals, magazines, trade publications, reports, and monographic collections.

Each item added to the database (e.g., a scholarly article in a journal or a technical report) is represented by a brief description of the most important attributes of that item along with a set of descriptor terms and, in some instances, a classification code. A database index may include the following elements, more or less, in a standard description:

- Article title
- Authors
- Contact information
- Author affiliation
- Source
- Subjects/Keywords
- Abstract
- Language
- Volume, issue, and date
- ISSN
- Page numbers
- Document type
- Digital Object Identifier (DOI)

Controlled vocabulary terms are frequently used to describe the subjects addressed in articles. These may be enhanced by the addition of author-supplied keywords. The scope and number of descriptor terms assigned to an item is determined by the editorial policies of the given database, and in-house or specially trained indexers usually perform the indexing. An example of a database index entry can be found in Figure 3.10 (page 126).

1.3.5.1.3 Periodical Indexing

Periodical indexing is similar to journal indexing, except that instead of describing the literature of an entire knowledge domain, the index focuses on the contents of a single periodical, such as a magazine or a newspaper. Because the contents of periodicals expand considerably on a daily, weekly, monthly, or annual basis, new entries must be systematically added to the index for names, keywords, and subjects appearing in every major item in the publication. The format of entries can range from a simple reference (issue number or date, along with page numbers) to more complete entries (including a brief abstract or summary). For much of the twentieth century, these indexes appeared in the form of print volumes, which could be purchased for inclusion in a library's reference collection, with entries collected and issued in monthly, quarterly, or annual installments. In more recent years, web interfaces are prevalent, and periodical indexes may be updated continuously. Rarely do we see these resources in print.

Perhaps the most prominent print periodical index was that of *The New York Times*, but even that esteemed index ceased publication in 2016, after more than a century in print. Many print indexes have been replaced by a publication's "archives" or "vault," where content from the distant past is often isolated from more current articles. In some cases, a publication's periodical index (or a portion of it) has been incorporated into a general database/journal index. For example, in the Academic One-File Select database, one can perform a search of the contents of *The New York Times*, although for a much narrower range of dates than is available in the *Times*' archives.

Some publications share their periodical indexes as web documents. An example of this approach comes from the journal *Rochester History*, published by the Rochester Public Library; its index entries provide topics, subtopics, and locator references made up of the volume number, the issue number in parentheses, page numbers, and dates. Conveniently, the locator references are hyperlinked to digitized issues of the journal.[60]

>**Rochester Academy of Art**
>   demise, 17(2):8 (Apr 1955)
>   exhibits
>   Sibley collection, 7(3):15 (Jul 1945)
>   termination, of second, 17(2):7 (Apr 1955)
>   founding-1870s, 17(2):6 (Apr 1955)
>   incorporation, 7(3):10 (Jul 1945)
>   reorganization-1870s, 18(4):8 (Oct 1956)
>
>**Rochester Academy of Medicine**
>   cerebral palsy group and, 55(2):20 (Spr 1993)
>   location, 12(2&3):12 map (Apr 1950); 18(1):18 (Jan 1956); 28(2&3):40 (Apr & Jul 1966)

1.3.5.1.4 Web Indexing

Web indexing (or *internet indexing*) is a type of indexing still in development, in terms of both its jargon and its actual practice. Currently, web indexing falls into two basic categories:

- *Search engine indexing*—automatic indexing of websites, and
- *A–Z indexing*—back-of-the-book indexing using hyperlinks within a website rather than page references.

In search engine indexing, websites are searched based on user query terms, an index of the words found and where they were found is maintained, and future searching on these same queries uses the saved indexes. Because search engine indexing is automated, the question of who performs web indexing applies primarily to the A–Z style. Freelance contractors, often book indexers who have expanded their repertoire of services, create A–Z web indexes. An example from an A–Z web index for the United States Census Bureau looks something like this:[61]

> **J**
> Jeffersonville National Processing Center
> Jobs - Census Careers
> Journey to Work, Commuting and Place of Work
> > Back to top
>
> **K**
> Kids' Site (Student State Facts)

The entries under the letters are links to the relevant pages for those topics.

Several software tools have been created to generate indexes. They use a variety of techniques, the efficacy of which depends upon variables such as cost, time constraints, type and size of files to be indexed, and individual preferences. The American Society for Indexing lists several types of tools used for indexing.[62]

1.3.5.2 Abstracting

Abstracting is the process of analyzing the content of an information resource and then writing a succinct summary or synopsis of the resource (i.e., an ***abstract***). Typically, abstracting is done for academic publications or professional journals. The length, style, and amount of detail in an abstract may vary depending on its intended audience. Generally, an abstract is not a review of the work nor does it evaluate or interpret the work that is being abstracted, though *critical* abstracts do include some evaluative text. Although it contains keywords and concepts found in the larger document, the abstract is an original text rather than an excerpted passage. There are several types of abstracts:

- **Indicative**: descriptive of the content, but without providing results or outcomes (also can be referred to as a *descriptive abstract*);
- **Informative**: summative with the results or outcomes emphasized;
- **Critical**: condensed critical review;
- **Structured**: non-narrative in format, it includes labeled sections (e.g., objectives, methods, results, discussion);
- **Modular**: includes five discrete sections—citation, annotation, indicative abstract, informative abstract, and critical abstract.

Technically, an abstract is the summary text; in practice, a formal abstract consists of the title, the citation of the abstracted work, and the summary itself. An example of an abstract is included in Figure 3.10 (page 126).

Abstracting is done by both authors and specially trained information professionals. Scholarly journals often require that an abstract accompany the articles that authors submit for publication. The rubrics provided by journal publishers can be inconsistent or vague, and the quality of published abstracts can suffer as a consequence. Abstracts are also written by professionals who are either in-house or are contracted by the publishers. Editorial policies are employed to guide abstractors in this instance; the policies are not all the same but are designed in response to specific audience needs.

Abstracts have several uses in information organization and retrieval. Users needing to stay abreast of a field or a given topic can do so by reviewing abstracts published in that area. Many researchers find that reviewing abstracts instead of full texts saves time. Abstracts aid in the decision of which articles need to be read in full versus which can be skimmed or skipped altogether. In a related fashion, because it is sometimes the practice to publish English-language abstracts for non-English-language articles, the user can decide from reading the abstract if it is cost- and time-effective to have the full article translated. Librarians and other information professionals find that the use of abstracts improves the speed and utility of patron literature searches. Database indexers, who typically index only using the title and abstract of a text, require that the abstract be well written and accurate.

1.3.6 Records Management

Records management is the terminology applied to the control and disposition of records created in offices and other administrative settings. It has its roots in the office filing systems that developed throughout the twentieth century. These systems have been significantly influenced by developments in technology—typewriters, photocopiers, and computers (starting with sorters and collators). The use of computers in this context has sometimes been referred to as *data administration*. Records management systems have a strong relationship with archives, as that is where an organization's records may be deposited when their active operating life has passed, and they have become inactive records.

As was true in other parts of our society, records management originally involved the keeping, filing, and maintaining of paper records. It was a simpler time but also a frustrating time, because usually only one copy of a record was filed in only one place. One records manager's file labels were not necessarily logical to the next. As information began being entered and stored in electronic files, access points (the file labels) became invisible. This was not an immediate problem if the people who developed the electronic files documented what was contained in them. The situation became more complicated when powerful personal computers began to allow persons to store and file their own information on their desktops. A problem of continuity developed when these personal files were abandoned.

For many years various operations were automated, each with its own system. For example, payroll, general ledger, accounts payable, inventories, and other such systems were automated separately. During the 1990s integration of these systems took place with the result that the systems had many redundant data fields with little documentation of their content. It appeared that many of the fields were meant to contain the same information, but what was actually there was often different (e.g., name given in full in the payroll file, but middle name shortened to an initial in the faculty file).

The International Organization for Standardization (ISO) updated its standard for records management in 2016 (reviewed and reaffirmed in 2021). It defines records management as the "field of management responsible for the efficient and systematic control of the creation, receipt, maintenance, use and disposition of records, including processes for capturing and maintaining evidence of and information about business activities and transactions in the form of records."[63] Further, in describing records system characteristics, the standard states:

> Records systems should:
>
> a) routinely capture records within the scope of the business activity they support;
> b) routinely function as the primary source of authoritative information about actions documented in the records;
> c) enable the participation of any authorized agents;
> d) present records in useable form;
> e) support timely access to records;
> f) protect records from unauthorized use, alteration, concealment or destruction;
> g) store records for as long as they are needed;
> h) provide mechanisms, where necessary, for importing (or otherwise incorporating) records and metadata for records into the system or exporting them from one system to another; and
> i) allow for disposition actions to be carried out on records.[64]

A number of commercially available records management systems have now been developed that track and store records, provide security and auditing functions, have content management and user identity modules, and more. Records management systems are a growing industry as corporate settings (as well as college and university, governmental, and other more traditional institutional settings) engage in records management activities and seek technological solutions to long-standing data management problems.

Records managers have dealt with the information explosion by using principles of information organization. The units that need to be organized in the administrative environment are such things as directories, files, programs, and, at another level, such things as field values. Organization can be by system (e.g., payroll, budget) or by type of record (e.g., registration records). Records managers must keep track of information that crosses system boundaries (e.g., personal names cross boundaries when the same names are entered into several different files). There must be methods for handling identically named concepts with different purposes (e.g., *part-time* can have different meanings in a university depending upon whether one is talking about payroll, faculty, graduate students, or undergraduate students).

1.3.7 Personal Information Management[§§]

Personal information management is defined as "the practice and the study of the activities a person performs in order to acquire or create, store, organize, maintain, retrieve, use, and distribute the information needed to complete tasks and fulfill various roles and responsibilities."[65] Because personal information management is directly connected to an individual's everyday life, there has been growing interest in the development of tools and devices that facilitate personal information management, as well as more investigation of how people manage their personal information.

People organize their personal information in various formats: books, paper-based documents, music albums, recipes, photos, emails, apps, and different types of digital files. These are stored in their personal spaces such as offices and homes, as well as on personal devices or tools including computers, tablets, smartphones, and cloud storage. When organizing personal information, people have different habits and processes. For instance, some people have neatly organized offices while others' offices are messy with piles of paper documents.[66] In the case of organizing digital files, there have been ongoing debates on the necessity of organizing them into folders, particularly since people can now simply search for them in personal devices. However, many people report that they still organize digital files into folders; the act of organizing files has more functions than just finding specific items. These functions include reminding people of tasks and helping them further understand the relationships among information items. In addition, a search function can be less useful when there are a number of files with similar names or the exact keywords cannot be recalled.

There are many factors that influence organization decisions, such as where and how to organize items. Primary factors include use/purpose of the information item, format of the information item, and topic of the information item.[67] Organizing personal information can be challenging because it involves various decisions that need to be made based on the future use of, need for, interest in, and value of the information, all of which can be hard to predict (and can change easily). Today, two issues also make personal information organization even more challenging. These are ***information overload***, which is when a person receives more information than can be processed, and ***information fragmentation***, which is having information items scattered across multiple personal devices and tools in different formats.[68] However, regardless of the format, effectively organizing personal information items facilitates finding and using information efficiently, which can increase an individual's productivity.

1.3.8 Knowledge Management

Everyone has heard the phrase "knowledge is power." Originally, the phrase applied to individuals and implied that persons who increased their knowledge would be able to increase their power in society. During the 1980s, it came to be understood that the same thing applied to organizations. At that time, there was much downsizing of organizations to reduce overhead and increase profits.

[§§]This section was written by Dr. Kyong Eun Oh, School of Library and Information Science, Simmons University, Boston, MA.

In the process, it became obvious that organizations lost important knowledge as employees left and took their accumulated years of experience with them. In the same period there was much technological development that was seen at first as a way to save costs by replacing human workers. Again, though, all the knowledge held and applied by humans could not be replaced by machines. For an organization to survive, knowledge is brought to bear in the challenges the organization faces. Management of that knowledge increases its power.

The idea of passing on knowledge gained in a work setting has existed for centuries. Apprentices learned various trades by working alongside experts. Children often followed parents into family businesses. More recently, there are people who take on mentoring responsibilities to help newcomers in a profession. Also, sometimes, a person leaving a job may be asked to train their replacement before leaving.

Knowledge management is the process of capturing, developing, sharing, and using organizational information to make good, well-informed decisions. This concept came into being as an attempt to capture employees' knowledge with advanced technology so that knowledge could be stored and shared easily. As people became overwhelmed with the increased availability of information through rapid technological developments, knowledge management took on the additional role of coping with the explosion of information. In the knowledge management context, the process comprises three major components: people, processes, and technology.

Managing knowledge requires a definition of *knowledge*, a concept that has been discussed by philosophers for years without complete resolution. It has been characterized in several ways—for example, as residing in people's minds rather than in any stored form; as being a combination of information, context, and experience; as being that which represents shared experience among groups and communities; or as a high value form of information that is applied to decisions and actions. R. D. Stacy makes the following observation:

> Knowledge is not a "thing," or a system, but an ephemeral, active process of relating. If one takes this view then no one, let alone a corporation, can own knowledge. Knowledge itself cannot be stored, nor can intellectual capital be measured, and certainly neither of them can be managed.[69]

However, Rosenfeld, Morville, and Arango posit, "Knowledge managers develop tools, processes, and incentives to encourage people to share" what they know.[70]

Dave Snowden notes that knowledge management started in 1995 with the popularization of ideas about *tacit knowledge* versus *explicit knowledge* put forward by Ikujiro Nonaka and Hirotaka Takeuchi.[71] Nonaka and Takeuchi postulated that tacit knowledge is hidden, residing in the human mind, and cannot be easily represented via technology, but it can be made explicit to the degree necessary to accomplish a specific innovation.[72] They described a spiral process of sharing tacit knowledge with others through socializing, followed by listeners internalizing the knowledge, and then new knowledge being created, in turn, to be shared. Snowden says that it does not follow that all knowledge in people's minds could or should be made explicit. Often, the knowledge that can be made explicit is just the tip of the iceberg. Over time, software programs were created to store and share this knowledge. Some of the software tools useful in knowledge management include document and/or content management systems, intranets, wikis, and data warehouses.

Core issues of concern to people in the information organization business are those of describing, classifying, and retrieving what has been stored. In the context of knowledge management, this means that the organization's knowledge must be sorted out, labeled (i.e., described), and categorized using a list of different subjects or groups (i.e., a taxonomy) if it is to be retrieved when needed. Nick Milton and Patrick Lambe emphasize "the need to have a systematic and evidence-based methodology for organizing explicit knowledge and supporting documents" and identify the three crucial components of organizing knowledge: a taxonomy, metadata, and information architecture.[73] In their study of knowledge management in consulting firms, Ling-Ling Lai and Arlene G. Taylor found that the firms required creation of a knowledge piece at the end of each project. Further, each organization had a template with attributes and facets appropriate to describing both tacit and explicit knowledge gained during a consultation. The researchers observed that the actions of capturing tacit knowledge and then describing it are much like the process of organizing information in libraries: "Essentially, descriptive cataloging and subject cataloging (in LIS terminology) are achieved when consultants work on describing a knowledge piece by completing a standardized template with a number of attributes, and further when they use facets to categorize the knowledge piece. Whether it is called facet analysis, tagging, or providing metadata, the core meaning of cataloging and classification exists in consulting firms as well as in libraries."[74]

1.4 Conclusion

This chapter discusses the basic human need to organize, defines information organization, and presents an overview of different kinds of organizing contexts and environments. Although there are differences among these environments, there are also many points of convergence. All the contexts and environments entail describing resources for retrieval purposes, providing access to resources, helping users to select what is most appropriate for their needs, helping users to understand and explore the information they encounter, analyzing content and describing it consistently, using categories in beneficial ways, and so on.

The following chapters discuss in more detail the processes that have been developed for information organization, those currently under development, and the issues that affect their implementation. But first, the next chapter provides a historical look at the development of organizing processes over several centuries, giving us perspective on where we have been, where we are now, and how far we might go.

Some Important Terms in This Chapter
(Definitions Provided in the Glossary)

Aboutness
Abstract
Abstracting
Access point
Accession number
Accession record
Accessioning
Acquisitions
Approval plan
Archives
Attribute
Authority control
Authorized access point
A–Z Indexing
Back-of-the-book indexing
Bibliographic control
Call number
Catalog
Cataloger
Cataloging
Categorization
Closed stacks
Collection development
Conceptual analysis
Content standard
Cooperative cataloging
Copy cataloging
Creator
Cutter number
Data
Database indexing
Derived indexing
Descriptive cataloging
Digital collection

Discovery layer
Dublin Core
Explore
Facet
False drop
Find
Finding aid
Gifts and exchanges
Granularity
Identify
Index
Indexing
Information
Information architecture
Information fragmentation
Information organization
Information overload
Information resource
Institutional repository
Integrated library system
Interlibrary loan
Internet directory
Keyword
Knowledge
Knowledge management
Knowledge organization
Librarian
Library
Library services platform
Linked data
Metadata
Microdata
Museum
Obtain

Open stacks
Organize
Original cataloging
Original order
Patron-driven acquisitions
Periodical indexing
Personal information management
Provenance
Public services
Records management
Registration
Resource
Respect des fonds
Retrieval tool
Search engine
Search engine optimization
Search engine indexing
Select
Selection (Collection development)
Semantic web
Series (Archives)
Subject
Subject cataloging
Technical services
Title
Translation (Subject cataloging)
Union catalog
Uniform Resource Locator
Web indexing
Wisdom

Some Important Acronyms in This Chapter

AI:	Artificial Intelligence
DOI:	Digital Object Identifier
DPLA:	Digital Public Library of America
EAD:	Encoded Archival Description
FRBR:	*Functional Requirements for Bibliographic Records*
HTML:	Hypertext Markup Language
IA:	Information Architecture
IFLA:	International Federation of Library Associations and Institutions
ICOM:	International Council of Museums
ILL:	Interlibrary Loan
ILS:	Integrated Library System
ISO:	International Organization for Standardization
KOS:	Knowledge Organization System
LIS:	Library and Information Science
LRM:	*IFLA Library Reference Model*
LSP:	Library Services Platform
MARC:	Machine-Readable Cataloging
METS:	Metadata Encoding & Transmission Standard
MODS:	Metadata Object Description Schema
OAI:	Open Archives Initiative
OCLC:	Online Computer Library Center
OPAC:	Online Public Access Catalog
SEO:	Search Engine Optimization
URL:	Uniform Resource Locator

1.5 Discussion Questions and Exercises

- Is there a basic need to organize?
- Why do we organize?
- What is information organization?
- How is organizing information in a library different from organizing information in
    - an archives?
    - a museum?
    - an online setting?
    - your own office, bookshelves, desk?

- What are your personal organizational strengths? Alternatively, where are some areas where you struggle to stay organized?
- Take a little time to organize your spice cabinet or spice rack. After completing the task, try to articulate how you sorted the products there and the choices you made. Are there alternative arrangements you could have chosen? What are the benefits and weakness of these approaches?

1.6 Suggested Readings

General Information Organization and Metadata

Glushko, Robert J., ed. *The Discipline of Organizing*. 4th Professional ed. Berkeley, CA: University of California, 2020.

Hider, Philip. *Information Resource Description: Creating and Managing Metadata*. 2nd ed. Chicago: ALA Neal-Schuman, 2018.

Rowley, Jennifer, and Richard Hartley. *Organizing Knowledge: An Introduction to Managing Access to Information*. 4th ed. Aldershot, UK: Ashgate, 2008.

Weinberger, David. *Everything Is Miscellaneous: The Power of the New Digital Disorder*. New York: Times Books, 2007.

Zeng, Marcia Lei, and Jian Qin. *Metadata*. 3rd ed. Chicago: ALA Neal-Schuman, 2022.

Organization of Information in Libraries

Baldoni, Emily, and Daniel N. Joudrey. "Cataloging." In *Encyclopedia of Libraries, Librarianship, and Information Science*, edited by David Baker and Lucy Ellis. Cambridge, MA: Elsevier, 2025.

Hoffman, Gretchen. *Organizing Library Collections: Theory and Practice*. Lanham, MD: Rowman & Littlefield, 2019.

Hoffman, Gretchen, and Karen Snow, eds. *Cataloging and Classification: Back to Basics*. New York: Routledge, 2022.

Joudrey, Daniel N. "Cataloging." In *Encyclopedia of Library and Information Sciences*. 4th ed., edited by John D. McDonald and Michael Levine-Clark. Boca Raton, FL: Taylor & Francis, 2017.

Joudrey, Daniel N., Arlene G. Taylor, and David P. Miller. *Introduction to Cataloging and Classification*. 11th ed. Santa Barbara, CA: Libraries Unlimited, 2015.

Salaba, Athena, and Lois Mai Chan. *Cataloging and Classification: An Introduction*. 5th ed. Lanham, MD: Rowman & Littlefield, 2023.

Weihs, Jean, and Sheila Intner. *Beginning Cataloging*. 2nd ed. Santa Barbara, CA: Libraries Unlimited, 2017.

Organization of Information in Archives

Bastian, Jeannette, Megan Sniffin-Marinoff, and Donna Webber. *Archives in Libraries: What Librarians and Archivists Need to Know to Work Together*. Chicago: Society of American Archivists, 2015.

Carmichael, David W. *Organizing Archival Records*. 4th ed. Lanham, MD: Rowman & Littlefield, 2019.

Gilliland, Anne J. *Conceptualizing 21st-century Archives*. Chicago: Society of American Archivists, 2014.

Hamill, Lois. *Archival Arrangement and Description: Analog to Digital*. Lanham, MD: Rowman & Littlefield, 2017.

Meissner, Dennis. *Arranging and Describing Archives and Manuscripts*. Chicago: Society of American Archivists, 2019.

Millar, Laura A. *Archives: Principles and Practices*. 2nd ed. New York: Neal-Schuman, 2017.

Roe, Kathleen D. *Arranging & Describing Archives & Manuscripts*. Chicago: Society of American Archivists, 2005.

Organization of Information in Museums

Bierbaum, Esther Green. "Records and Access: Museum Registration and Library Cataloging." *Cataloging & Classification Quarterly* 9, no. 1 (1988): 97–111.

Bourcier, Paul, Heather Dunn, and Nomenclature Task Force, eds. *Nomenclature 4.0 for Museum Cataloging*. 4th ed. Lanham, MD: Rowman & Littlefield, 2015.

Neilson, Dixie. "Museum Registration and Documentation." In *Encyclopedia of Library and Information Sciences*. 4th ed., edited by John D. McDonald and Michael Levine-Clark, 3199–213. Boca Raton, FL: CRC Press, 2017.

Reibel, Daniel B., and Deborah Rose Van Horn. *Registration Methods for the Small Museum*. 5th ed. Lanham, MD: Rowman & Littlefield, 2018.

Simmons, John E., and Toni M. Kiser, eds. *MRM6: Museum Registration Methods*. 6th ed. Lanham, MD: Rowman & Littlefield, 2020.

Vanderwarf, Sandra, and Bethany Romanowski. *Inventorying Cultural Heritage Collections: A Guide for Museums and Historical Societies*. Lanham, MD: Rowman & Littlefield, 2022.

Organization of Information on the Semantic Web and the Internet

Berners-Lee, Tim, James Hendler, and Ora Lassila. "The Semantic Web." *Scientific American* 284, no. 5 (May 2001): 34–8, 40–3.

Carlson, Scott, Cory Lampert, Darnelle Melvin, and Anne Washington. *Linked Data for the Perplexed Librarian*. Chicago: ALA Editions, 2020.

DeWeese, Keith P., and Dan Segal. *Libraries and the Semantic Web*. San Rafael, CA: Morgan & Claypool, 2015.

Organization of Information in Digital Collections

Banerjee, Kyle. *Building Digital Libraries: A How-to-Do-It Manual for Librarians*. 2nd ed. Chicago: ALA Neal-Schuman, 2019.

Gartner, Richard. *Metadata in the Digital Library*. London: Facet, 2021.

Information Resources Management Association, ed. *Digital Libraries and Institutional Repositories: Breakthroughs in Research and Practice*. Hershey, PA: IGI Global, 2020.

Landis, William E., and Robin L. Chandler, eds. *Archives and the Digital Library*. Binghamton, NY: Haworth Information, 2006.

Miller, Steven J. *Metadata for Digital Collections: A How-to-Do-It Manual*. Chicago: ALA Neal-Schuman, 2022.

Weiss, Andrew. *Using Massive Digital Libraries: A LITA Guide*. Chicago: American Library Association, 2014.

Information Architecture

Covert, Abby. *How to Make Sense of Any Mess: Information Architecture for Everybody*. North Charleston, SC: CreateSpace, 2014.

Dillon, Andrew, and Don Turnbull. "Information Architecture." In *Encyclopedia of Library and Information Sciences*. 3rd ed., edited by Marcia J. Bates and Mary Niles Maack, 2361–8. New York: Taylor & Francis, 2009.

Martin, Lisa Marie. *Everyday Information Architecture*. New York: A Book Apart, 2019.

Rosenfeld, Louis, Peter Morville, and Jorge Arango. *Information Architecture: For the Web and Beyond*. 4th ed. Sebastopol, CA: O'Reilly, 2015.

Indexing and Abstracting

Badgett, Nan. *The Accidental Indexer*. Medford, NJ: Information Today, 2015.

Cleveland, Donald B., and Ana D. Cleveland. *Introduction to Indexing and Abstracting*. 4th ed. Santa Barbara, CA: Libraries Unlimited, 2013.

Hedden, Heather. *The Accidental Taxonomist*. 3rd ed. Medford, NJ: Information Today, 2022.

Keyser, Pierre de. *Indexing: From Thesauri to the Semantic Web*. Oxford: Chandos, 2012.

Lancaster, F. W. *Indexing and Abstracting in Theory and Practice*. 3rd ed. London: Facet, 2003.

Mulvany, Nancy C. *Indexing Books*. 2nd ed. Chicago: University of Chicago Press, 2005.

Neal, Diane Rasmussen, ed. *Indexing and Retrieval of Non-text Information*. Berlin: De Gruyter Saur, 2012.

O'Connor, Brian C., Jodi Kearns, and Richard L. Anderson. *Doing Things with Information: Beyond Indexing and Abstracting*. Westport, CT: Libraries Unlimited, 2008.

Records Management

ARMA International Education Development Committee, eds. *Records and Information Management Core Competencies*. 2nd ed. Overland Park, KS: ARMA International, 2017.

Franks, Patricia C. *Records and Information Management*. Chicago: ALA Neal-Schuman, 2018.

Saffady, William. *Records and Information Management: Fundamentals of Professional Practice*. 4th ed. Lanham, MD: Rowman & Littlefield, 2021.

Yeo, Geoffrey. *Record-making and Record-keeping in Early Societies*. New York: Routledge, 2021.

Personal Information Management

Jones, William, and Jaime Teevan, eds. *Personal Information Management*. Seattle: University of Washington Press, 2007.

Marshall, Brianna H., ed. *The Complete Guide to Personal Digital Archiving*. Chicago: ALA Editions, 2018.

Reyes, Vanessa. *Saving Your Digital Past, Present, and Future: A Step-By-Step Guide*. Lanham, MD: Rowman & Littlefield, 2020.

Whittaker, Steve. "Personal Information Management: From Information Consumption to Curation." *Annual Review of Information Science and Technology*. Volume 41. Medford, NJ: Information Today, 2007.

Knowledge Management

Collison, Chris J., Paul J. Corney, and Patricia Lee Eng. *The KM Cookbook: Stories and Strategies for Organisations Exploring Knowledge Management Standard ISO30401*. London: Facet, 2019.

Dalkir, Kimiz. *Knowledge Management in Theory and Practice*. 4th ed. Cambridge, MA: MIT Press, 2023.

Desouza, Kevin C., and Scott Paquette. *Knowledge Management: An Introduction*. New York: Neal-Schuman, 2011.

Husain, Shabahat. *Knowledge Management Systems: Concepts, Technologies and Practices*. Bingley, UK: Emerald Publishing, 2021.

Schopflin, Katharine, and Matt Walsh. *Practical Knowledge and Information Management*. London: Facet, 2019.

1.7 Notes

All URLs accessed April 2025.

1. "Organize," Merriam-Webster.com, https://www.merriam-webster.com/dictionary/organize.
2. Steven Harnad, "To Cognize is to Categorize: Cognition is Categorization," in *Handbook of Categorization in Cognitive Science*, ed. Henri Cohen and Claire Lefebvre (Amsterdam: Elsevier, 2005), 20–45.
3. Mark Lansdale, "The Psychology of Personal Information Management," *Applied Ergonomics* 19, no. 1 (1988): 55–66; Thomas W. Malone, "How Do People Organize Their Desks? Implications for the Design of Office Information Systems," *ACM Trans Office Info Systems* 1, no. 1 (1983): 99–112; Lisa Frederick, "Are You a Filer or a Piler?" HGTV, https://www.hgtv.com/design/remodel/interior-remodel/are-you-a-piler-or-a-filer.
4. Pat Riva, Patrick Le Boeuf, and Maja Žumer, *IFLA Library Reference Model: A Conceptual Model for Bibliographic Information* (The Hague: IFLA, 2017), https://www.ifla.org/resources/?oPubId=11412 [henceforth cited as LRM].
5. LRM, 15–16.
6. Jennifer Rowley and Richard Hartley, *Organizing Knowledge: An Introduction to Managing Access to Information* (Aldershot, UK: Ashgate, 2008): 12.
7. Clifford Stoll, *Silicon Snake Oil: Second Thoughts on the Information Highway* (New York: Doubleday, 1995), 193.
8. Russel L. Ackoff, "From Data to Wisdom," *Journal of Applied Systems Analysis* 16 (1989): 3–9.
9. Jennifer Rowley, "The Wisdom Hierarchy: Representations of the DIKW Hierarchy." *Journal of Information Science* 33, no. 2 (2007): 163–80.
10. Ackoff, 3–4, 9; Rowley, 170–4; Martin Frické, "The Knowledge Pyramid," *Knowledge Organization* 46, no. 1 (2019): 35–8; Heather J. Van Meter, "Revising the DIKW Pyramid and the Real Relationship Between Data, Information, Knowledge, and Wisdom," *Law, Technology, and Humanities* 2, no. 2 (2020): 71–6.
11. Daniel N. Joudrey and Arlene G. Taylor, *The Organization of Information*, 4th ed. (Santa Barbara, CA: Libraries Unlimited, 2018), 5.
12. Ronald Hagler, *The Bibliographic Record and Information Technology*, 3rd ed. (Chicago: American Library Association, 1997), 13.
13. For a more robust exploration of all aspects of technical services in libraries, please see G. Edward Evans, Sheila S. Intner, and Jean Weihs, *Introduction to Technical Services*, 8th ed. (Santa Barbara, CA: Libraries Unlimited, 2011); Stacey Marien, *Library Technical Services: Adapting to a Changing Environment* (West Lafayette, IN: Purdue University Press, 2020); and Kimberly A. Edwards and Tricia Mackenzie, eds. *Telling the Technical Services Story: Communicating Value* (Chicago: American Library Association, 2021).
14. To learn more in-depth information about collection development and acquisitions, please consult the following: Wayne Disher, *Crash Course in Collection Development*, 3rd ed. (New York: Bloomsbury Libraries Unlimited, 2024); Vicky L. Gregory, *Collection Development and Management for 21st Century Library Collections: An Introduction*, 2nd ed. (Chicago: American Library Association, 2019); Peggy Johnson, *Fundamentals of Collection Development and Management*, 4th ed. (Chicago: American Library Association, 2018); Margaret Zarnosky Saponaro and G. Edward Evans, *Collection Management Basics*, 7th ed. (Santa Barbara, CA: Libraries Unlimited, 2019); and Frances C. Wilkinson, Linda K. Lewis, and Rebecca L. Lubas, *The Complete Guide to Acquisitions Management*, 2nd ed. (Santa Barbara, CA: Libraries Unlimited, 2015).
15. "MARC Standards," Library of Congress, Network Development and MARC Standards Office, http://www.loc.gov/marc/.

16. Charles A. Cutter, *Rules for a Dictionary Catalog*, 4th ed. (Washington, DC: Government Printing Office, 1904; reprint, London: The Library Association, 1962), 10.
17. "Archive," *SAA Dictionary of Archives Terminology*, https://dictionary.archivists.org/entry/archive.html.
18. "Provenance," *SAA Dictionary of Archives Terminology*, https://dictionary.archivists.org/entry/provenance.html.
19. Dennis Meissner, *Arranging and Describing Archives and Manuscripts* (Chicago: SAA, 2019), 18.
20. "EAD: Encoded Archival Description," Library of Congress, http://www.loc.gov/ead/.
21. "Museum Definition," International Council on Museums, https://icom.museum/en/resources/standards-guidelines/museum-definition/.
22. Jette Sandahl, as quoted by Vincent Noce, "What Exactly Is a Museum? ICOM Comes to Blows over New Definition," *The Art Newspaper*, August 19, 2019, https://www.theartnewspaper.com/news/what-exactly-is-a-museum-icom-comes-to-blows-over-new-definition.
23. "ICOM Announces the Alternative Museum Definition that Will Be Subject to a Vote," International Council on Museums, July 25, 2019, https://icom.museum/en/news/icom-announces-the-alternative-museum-definition-that-will-be-subject-to-a-vote/.
24. Alex Marshall, "What Is a Museum? A Dispute Erupts Over a New Definition," *The New York Times*, August 6, 2020, https://www.nytimes.com/2020/08/06/arts/what-is-a-museum.html.
25. François Mairesse, as quoted by Vincent Noce, "What Exactly Is a Museum? ICOM Comes to Blows over New Definition," *The Art Newspaper*, August 19, 2019, https://www.theartnewspaper.com/news/what-exactly-is-a-museum-icom-comes-to-blows-over-new-definition.
26. "ICOM Approves a New Museum Definition," International Council on Museums, August 24, 2022, https://icom.museum/en/news/icom-approves-a-new-museum-definition/.
27. Daniel B. Reibel, *Registration Methods for the Small Museum*, 5th ed., revised by Deborah Rose Van Horn (Lanham, MD: Rowman & Littlefield, 2018), 1.
28. Reibel, 11.
29. Reibel, 43.
30. Reibel, 48.
31. Reibel, 64–5.
32. "Art & Architecture Thesaurus Online," The Getty Research Institute, https://www.getty.edu/research/tools/vocabularies/aat/.
33. "Nomenclature for Museum Cataloging," Nomenclature, https://page.nomenclature.info/apropos-about.app?lang=en.
34. Artstor, https://www.jstor.org/images.
35. "WorldCat," OCLC, https://www.worldcat.org/.
36. Joshua Quittner quoting Ed Krol, "Getting Up to Speed on the Computer Highway," *Newsday*, November 3, 1992, 51; cited in Arlene G. Taylor, "The Information Universe: Will We Have Chaos or Control?" *American Libraries* 25, no. 7 (1994): 629.
37. Richard Urban, "Getting Ready for AI," Hanging Together: The OCLC Research Blog, June 24, 2024, https://hangingtogether.org/getting-ready-for-ai/.
38. Norman Oder, "Cataloging the Net: Can We Do It?" *Library Journal* 123, no. 16 (1998): 47–51.
39. Louis Rosenfeld, Peter Morville, and Jorge Arango, *Information Architecture: For the Web and Beyond*, 4th ed. (Sebastopol, CA: O'Reilly, 2015), 12.
40. SciCentral, http://www.scicentral.com/index.html.
41. Stuart Weibel, "Metadata: The Foundations of Resource Description," *D-Lib Magazine* 1, no. 1 (July 1995), https://www.dlib.org/dlib/July95/07weibel.html.
42. "DCMI: Home," Dublin Core Metadata Initiative, http://dublincore.org/.

43. For more information, a simple Google search for "search engine optimization" or "SEO" will retrieve information about this topic if you are interested in exploring it further. Recent books on the topic include Richard Conway, *How to Get to the Top of Google Search: A Practical SEO Guide* (Auckland, NZ: Random House NZ, 2019) and Subhankar Das, *Search Engine Optimization and Marketing* (Boca Raton, FL: CRC Press, 2021).
44. Quittner, 51.
45. Seth Grimes, "Semantic Web Business: Going Nowhere Slowly," *InformationWeek*, January 7, 2014, http://www.informationweek.com/software/information-management/semantic-web-business-going-nowhere-slowly/d/d-id/1113323.
46. "FRANKLIN: Access to the FDR Library's Digital Collections," Franklin D. Roosevelt Presidential Library and Museum, http://www.fdrlibrary.marist.edu/archives/collections/franklin/.
47. Candy Schwartz, "Digital Libraries: An Overview," *Journal of Academic Librarianship* 26, no. 6 (2000): 385.
48. Christine L. Borgman, *From Gutenberg to the Global Information Infrastructure: Access to Information in the Networked World* (Cambridge, MA: MIT Press, 2000), 42.
49. "Metadata Application Profile," DPLA Digital Public Library of America, https://pro.dp.la/hubs/metadata-application-profile.
50. "Metadata," Europeana pro, https://pro.europeana.eu/share-your-data/metadata.
51. Andrew Dillon and Don Turnbull, "Information Architecture," in *Encyclopedia of Library and Information Sciences*, 3rd ed., ed. Marcia J. Bates and Mary Niles Maack (New York: Taylor & Francis, 2009), 2362.
52. Andrew Dillon, "Information Architecture in JASIST: Just Where Did We Come From?" *Journal of the American Society for Information Science and Technology* 53, no. 10 (2002): 821.
53. Dillon, 821.
54. Rosenfeld, Morville, and Arango, 24.
55. Rosenfeld, Morville, and Arango, 24.
56. Dillon and Turnbull, 2362.
57. Rosenfeld, Morville, and Arango, 31–4.
58. Rosenfeld, Morville, and Arango, 311–15.
59. International Organization for Standardization, *Information and Documentation: Guidelines for the Content, Organization and Presentation of Indexes*, ISO 999:1996 (Geneva: ISO 1996), Section 3.5.
60. "Rochester History," Rochester Public Library, https://roccitylibrary.org/digital-collections/rochester-history/.
61. "Index A–Z," United States Census Bureau, https://www.census.gov/about/index.html.
62. "Software," American Society for Indexing, http://www.asindexing.org/reference-shelf/software/.
63. International Organization for Standardization, *Information and Documentation: Records Management*, ISO 15489-1, Pt. 1. Concepts and Principles (Geneva: ISO, 2016), Section 3.15.
64. ISO 15489: 2016, Pt. 1, 6–7.
65. William Jones, "Personal Information Management," in *Annual Review of Information Science and Technology*, Volume 41 (Medford, NJ: Information Today, 2007), 453.
66. Malone, "How Do People Organize Their Desks?," 104.
67. Deborah K. Barreau, "Context as a Factor in Personal Information Management Systems," *Journal of the American Society for Information Science* 46, no. 5 (1995): 333; Deborah K. Barreau, "The Persistence of Behavior and Form in the Organization of Personal Information," *Journal of the American Society for Information Science and Technology* 59, no. 2 (2008): 315–16; Barbara Kwasnik, "The Influence of Context on Classificatory Behavior" (PhD diss., Rutgers, 1989), 85–6; and Kyong Eun Oh, "The Process of Organizing Personal Information" (PhD diss., Rutgers, 2013), 222–4.
68. William Jones, *Keeping Found Things Found: The Study and Practice of Personal Information Management* (San Francisco, CA: Morgan Kaufmann, 2008), 391–2.

69. R. D. Stacy, *Complex Responsive Processes in Organizations: Learning and Knowledge Creation* (New York: Routledge, 2001), as quoted in Dave Snowden, "Complex Acts of Knowing: Paradox and Descriptive Self-Awareness," *Bulletin of the American Society for Information Science and Technology* 29, no. 4 (April–May 2003): 24.
70. Rosenfeld, Morville, and Arango, 25.
71. Snowden, 23.
72. Ikujiro Nonaka and Hirotaka Takeuchi, *The Knowledge-Creating Company* (Oxford: Oxford University Press, 1995).
73. Nick Milton and Patrick Lambe, *The Knowledge Manager's Handbook: A Step-by-Step Guide to Embedding Effective Knowledge Management in Your Organization* (London: Kogan Page, 2016), 151–5.
74. Ling-Ling Lai and Arlene G. Taylor, "Knowledge Organization in Knowledge Management Systems of Global Consulting Firms," *Cataloging & Classification Quarterly* 49, no. 5 (2011): 387–407.

Chapter 2

Development of the Organization of Recorded Information in Western Civilization*

It is often said that you cannot tell where you are going until you know where you have been. This chapter looks back at where we have been. Practices and principles of organizing that we now take for granted were once thought of for the first time by intelligent and serious scholars, just as we are coming up with innovative ideas for today's organization that will likely be taken for granted in the next decades.

The history outlined in this chapter is primarily a story of the Western development of information organization. This is not intended to diminish the activities and histories of other parts of the world. The focus of this chapter is to contextualize the systems of organization currently used in the information environments of the Western world, which were predominantly influenced by traditions developed in Europe and in the Middle East. Other parts of the world have their own rich histories in librarianship and information organization,[1] but because they have not led to our current Anglo-American systems, they are not systematically woven into this historical overview.

The period covered in this chapter is vast. The story spans approximately 4,000 years from 2000 BCE to 2000 CE. Developments in the late twentieth and early twenty-first centuries are primarily covered in other chapters in the book, as many of them are still in use.

2.1 Inventories, Bibliographies, and Catalogs

2.1.1 Antiquity

Organization usually begins with a list. One of the oldest lists of books that we know of appears on a Sumerian tablet found at Nippur from about 2000 BCE. The tablet records 62 titles, 24 of which are currently known literary works. Although we don't know the exact purpose the list served, the Sumerians were tireless writers, making it easy to believe that it may have resembled what we would recognize as a *catalog*.[†2] They seem to have kept everything: history books, medical prescriptions, love poems, business invoices, school children's homework assignments, and the

---

*Much of the material in the first half of this chapter is based on Ruth French Strout, "The Development of the Catalog and Cataloging Codes," *Library Quarterly* 26, no. 4 (1956): 254–75. Rather than making citation after citation, line after line, I want to acknowledge this huge intellectual debt at the beginning of the chapter.
†A catalog is a type of retrieval tool that contains an organized compilation of bibliographic metadata that represents the holdings of a particular collection, an institution, or a group of institutions.

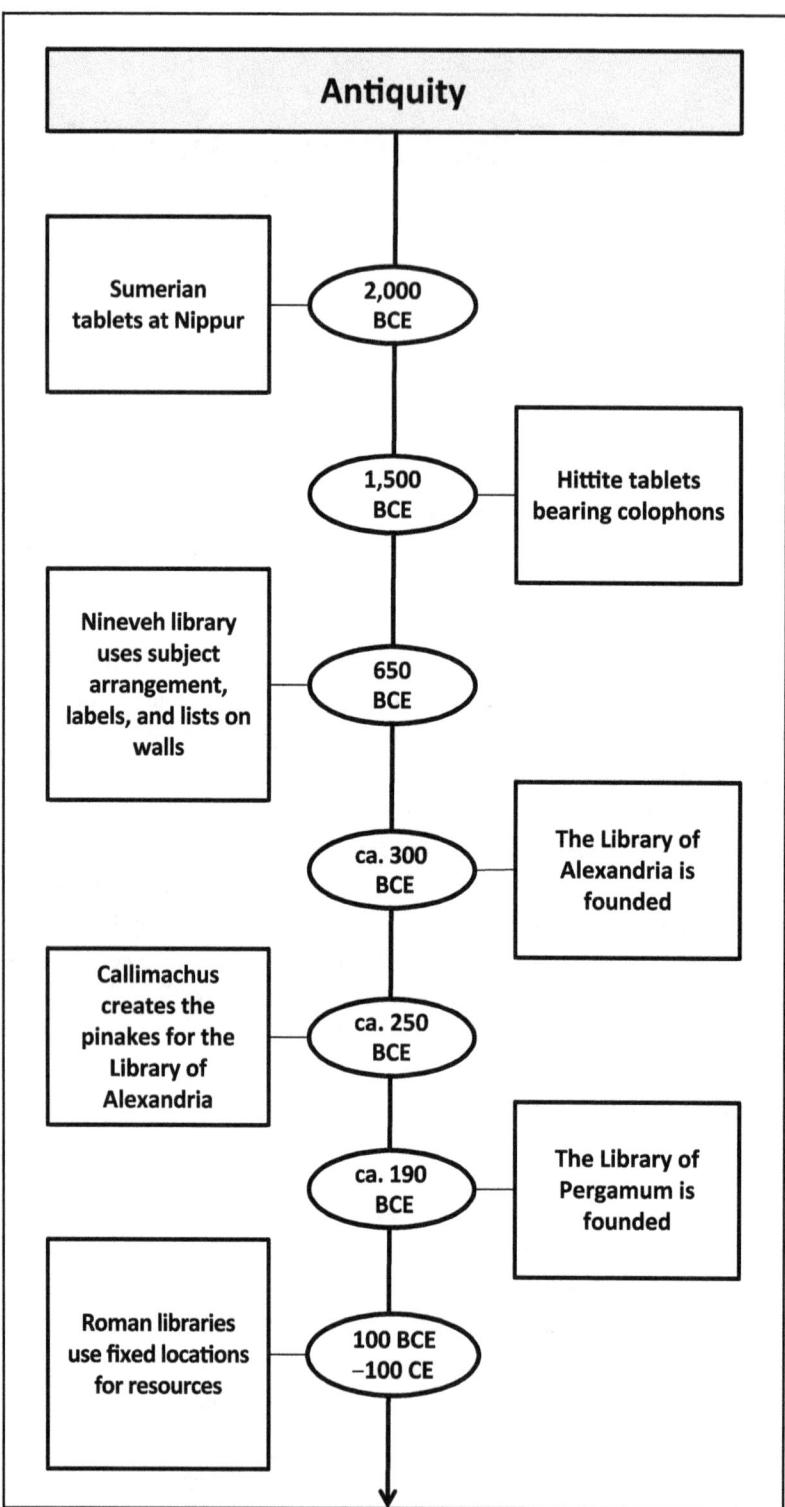

Figure 2.1 Timeline 1: Antiquity.

first-known letter home from a student who threatens to drop out of school unless his parents fork over more money for a suitable wardrobe.

Through the archaeological discoveries and excavations of ancient civilizations, we know that tablets and other resources were used to inscribe titles of books, but we do not know for what purpose. They might have been ownership tags (e.g., the ones that had the names of the king and queen and a title on each small plaque), or they might have been relics of something like a bibliography or a catalog. There are more remnants of early records from Babylonia than from Egypt, probably because Babylonians wrote on clay tablets, while Egyptians wrote on less-enduring papyrus.

Around 1500 BCE, the Hittites evidently saw the need to convey bibliographic information as part of a written work. Their tablets bore colophons that identified the number of the tablet in a series, its title, and often the name of the scribe. A *colophon* is an inscription, often at the end of a book, with facts about its publication and production.

Around 650 BCE, Ashurbanipal, a king of the Neo-Assyrian empire, developed a library in the city of Nineveh. This library comprised nearly 30,000 clay tablets and was arranged by subject in a series of rooms. Identification tags were affixed to jars that contained the tablets. Additionally, lists on walls could be found in each room to detail what works were found in that room. This early example of a library is often discussed because of the great care taken to preserve order and authenticity as well as its early catalog-like activities, despite not having anything beyond these informal management tools.[3]

Two of the great libraries of antiquity were in Alexandria and Pergamum—two active centers of Greek civilization. The **Library of Alexandria** in Egypt was founded around 300 BCE. It was a research hub of great prestige, and it was open to the public—that is, to anyone in the public with "scholarly or literary qualifications."[4] The Library of Alexandria was the largest and most famous library of antiquity. Libraries throughout the ancient world competed "in rivalries that proved as dangerous and unscrupulous as actual wars. Perhaps the most vicious rivalry of all was between the libraries of Alexandria and Pergamum in … present-day Bergama, Turkey. In this conflict, the ego-driven kings of both cities enforced various sneaky maneuvers to stunt the growth of the opposing collections."[5]

The collection of the Library of Alexandria contained books (i.e., scrolls or rolls) that were purchased from all over the Mediterranean. "What they couldn't buy the Ptolemies commandeered: for example, they confiscated any books found on ships unloading at Alexandria; the owners were given copies (one advantage the Ptolemies did have was plenty of papyrus paper for copying), and the originals went to the library. Ptolemy III … was willing not only to lay out an enormous amount of money but to resort to swindling in the bargain."[6]

Each acquisition obtained by the library had a tab attached to it to contain basic metadata—authors and their places of origin, ownership information, sometimes titles (but sometimes not), and so on. There were more than 500,000 scrolls in the library, but it is unclear how many books or authors were contained within those scrolls.[7] A single work might be transcribed on several scrolls and a single scroll might contain several shorter works; additionally, some important works had more than one copy in the library. As is the case today, there was no one-to-one correlation between physical items and intellectual works.

The first director of the Library of Alexandria was Zenodotus, an educator, critic, and Homeric scholar. He was appointed as director in 284 BCE and purportedly was a great innovator as an organizer of information. He is presumed to have set up the shelving system in the library, based on the nature of the contents of the scrolls and the information on their tabs. Scrolls about the same subject matter were kept in the same room or in the same part of a room. Within those subject sections, the scrolls were organized alphabetically by author.

> This brings us to one of the great contributions that we owe to the scholars at the library of Alexandria—alphabetical order as a mode of organization. So far as we know, Zenodotus was the first to have employed it, in a glossary of rare words that he compiled. ... Zenodotus, having found the system useful for his glossary, applied it to the collection. The alphabetization went only as far as the first letter. ... Not until the second century A.D. does fuller alphabetization make an appearance.[8]

When its collection was relatively small there was little need at the library for additional information about its holdings, but as the collection grew the staff and scholars using the library could no longer rely on memory to know just what was in the collection. A system had to be developed; that system was called the **pinakes**.[‡] It is not quite clear, however, whether the pinakes was a catalog of the library's holdings or if it was a bibliography of contemporary intellectual and literary works. The full title of the pinakes is translated as *Tables of Persons Eminent in Every Branch of Learning Together with a List of Their Writings*.[9]

The pinakes of Alexandria was created by Callimachus, who is credited as the first cataloger or bibliographer of whom we have knowledge. The pinakes has not survived the ages, but later scholarly writings have referred to them; our understanding of this tool comes from secondary sources. "This gigantic work [the pinakes], said to have comprised 120 books, has not been preserved, but it is possible to reconstruct it in outline from quotations by later Greek scholars. It listed Greek authors by classes according to literary forms or by scholarly disciplines."[10] There are a few generalizations about the bibliographic practices of the time that can be drawn from quotations of scholars who referenced Callimachus's work. For example, a few broad categories were considered sufficient for subject access.

- Epic poetry
- Non-dramatic poetry
- Drama
- Law
- Philosophy
- History

- Oratory
- Medicine
- Mathematical science
- Natural science
- Miscellanea

---

‡*Pinakes* is the plural of *pinax*, a word that means *tray* or *dish*. It is thought that such trays had slightly raised edges and that wax could be poured in the middle; when hardened, the wax could be written in with a stylus. If this was indeed the medium, it is no wonder that no remnants have survived.

A scholar would go to a general subject category and then look for the author of interest. In the pinakes, Callimachus "listed not only authors of important works in the arts and sciences (poetry, oratory, etc.) but also all persons who had written a work held by the library, even if these dealt with the baking of cakes or the relations with courtesans."[11] An *entry* (i.e., an item in a list) in the pinakes contained the author's name, a biographical sketch, and a list of the author's works typically arranged in alphabetical order by initial letter. There are no examples of arrangement by any letter past the first one. The lack of comprehensive alphabetization probably indicates that their lists were not nearly as long as ours.

Greek civilization seems to have given us the basis for our Western idea of the primacy of the author. This creates the idea that the main entry, or the thing that dictates where an item falls in the list, ought to be the author. This kind of entry has not appeared in any work that has survived from early Eastern civilizations. Even today in Asian countries the traditional entry for a book is its title. Librarian and library science professor Ruth French Strout stated that a Japanese librarian of her acquaintance once observed that the principle of author entry goes along with democracy, since it rests upon belief in the importance of the individual.[12]

Little information is available about Roman libraries, other than the fact that they tended to be private collections among the wealthiest families. From sources that mention them, there is evidence that there was some way of finding a designated book when it was requested. This was probably through shelf arrangement based on *fixed location* (i.e., a set, physical space assigned to each item). One story goes that if a nobleman got into an intellectual argument, he would send an enslaved servant to the library to retrieve a certain book that would prove his point.

Ambitions to provide more widespread access to information were not unheard of at this time though.

> Julius Caesar, in the days when he "bestrode the world like a colossus," had plans to enhance Rome's cultural status by giving it a public library; his assassination cut the project short. It was revived by one of his supporters, Asinius Pollio. … In 39 B.C., Pollio commanded a successful military expedition and returned to Rome laden with spoils. This gave him the funds to bring into being what Caesar had brought only as far as the drawing board—Rome's first public library.[13]

Pollio's library was divided into two collections—works in Greek and works in Latin. This division was used in later Roman libraries as well. Little else is known about his library other than it was located near the Forum.

Caesar Augustus in 28 BCE created Rome's second public library—the Palatine Library. Because it followed the division of Greek and Roman resources, the library was designed as two identical chambers set side by side, each housing one of the language collections. The library contained 18 niches to contain the bookshelves and the books. "The bookcases would have been numbered and the appropriate number entered in the catalogue alongside each title to indicate the location. The rolls of the library's collection would have been laid horizontally on the shelves with the ends bearing the tag of identification facing outward."[14]

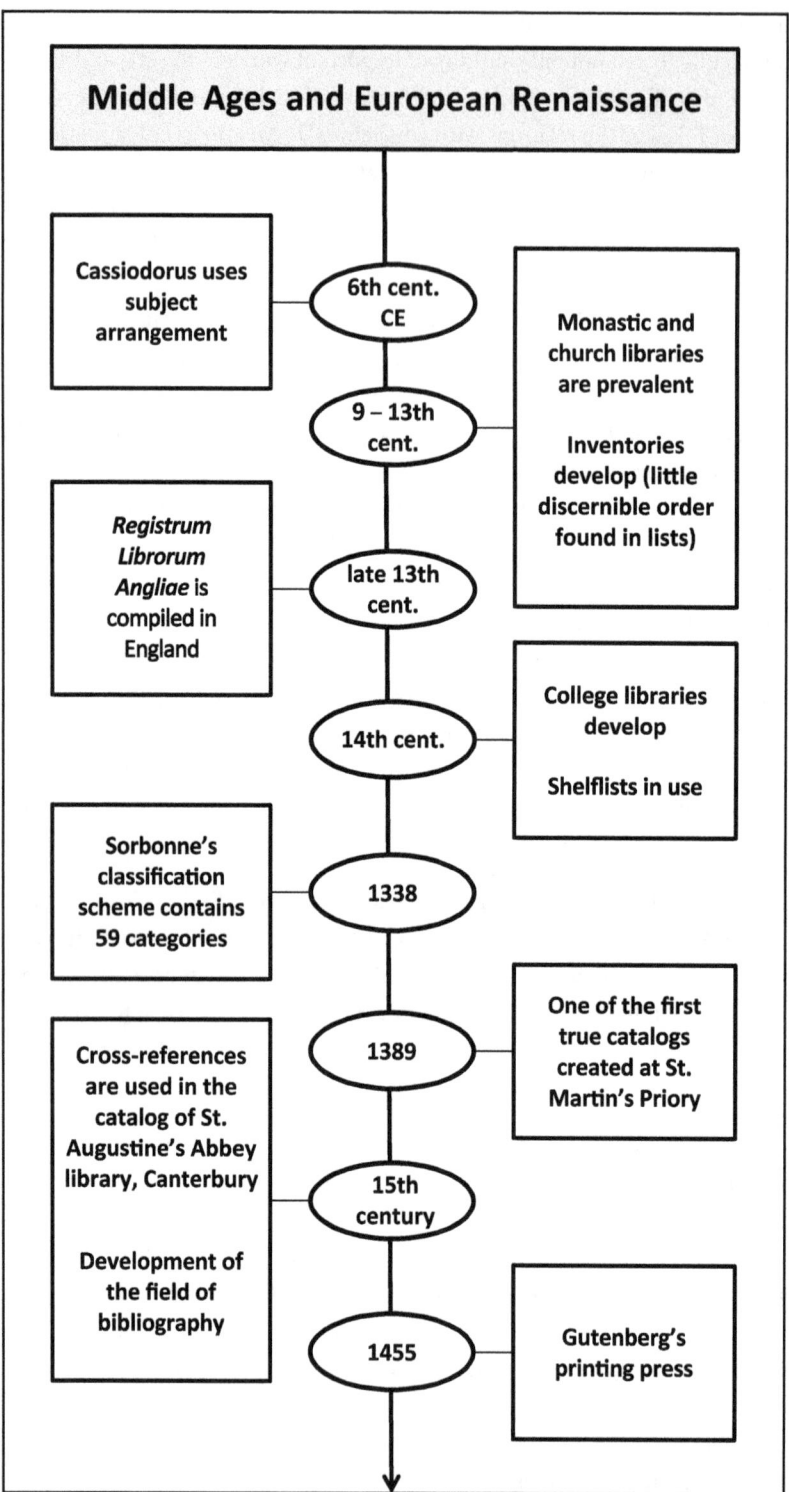

Figure 2.2 Timeline 2: Middle Ages to the Renaissance.

2.1.2 Middle Ages and the Renaissance

We know that during the Middle Ages (circa the fifth to the fourteenth centuries CE) there were church and monastery libraries in Europe and in the Byzantine empire. Outside of those enclaves and the imperial library of Constantinople, there was little to no demand for books, and knowledge was not sought in any way that would require the use of catalogs. Through monks in scriptoriums acting as scribes and illuminators, a system was set up by which monasteries became the sole keepers, manufacturers, and finally, list makers of books through many centuries.

One of the earliest listings of the holdings of a medieval library was dated in the eighth century. It was written on the final *flyleaf* of a book (i.e., the blank pages at the end of a book) and consisted of a list of brief titles with authors added to some of them. It probably served as an **inventory** (i.e., a complete list of resources owned by an institution or a person) and may have represented the shelf arrangement, although there were no location symbols accompanying the titles. This list was typical of most of the so-called "catalogs" of the following centuries—the briefest sort of inventories recorded in the most casual places.

From the ninth through the thirteenth centuries, libraries continued to produce lists that seemed to be no more than inventories. One list, which specified that its purpose was for inventory, stated that the library contained 246 volumes. It would be quite unrealistic to expect libraries of this size to feel any need for a more sophisticated retrieval tool, such as a catalog. Even after libraries grew to the size of 600 or 700 volumes, lists were still just inventories. Occasionally such a list would use author entries, but in no discernible order. A few lists gave works contained in each volume, and the number of volumes to a work. Books into which works were copied were often bound blank pages. Works were copied into them in the order in which the scribe picked them up. Several works could be copied into one bound blank volume, but it might take several bound volumes to copy a very long work.

The library established in the sixth century by Cassiodorus at Vivarium—a monastery, library, and biblical studies center in Squillace, Italy—is another early example of a subject arrangement, with the collection arranged into at least ten different subject areas (although it is not clear exactly what those areas were).[15] Subjects during the medieval period were broadly defined, with some libraries using only two categories: *biblical* and *humanistic*. By the mid-fourteenth century, however, more sophisticated classification systems began to emerge. One such system is the 1338 catalog for the Sorbonne, which included 59 different classes, including topics such as the Bible, history, medicine, law, and so on.[16] At least one list from the thirteenth century, that of Glastonbury Abbey, added some unusual descriptions in designating books variously as *useless*, *legible*, *old*, and *good*, but we do not know whether they were used as an aid in identification for inventory or to help the reader by pointing out which books could be more or less easily read.

In the late thirteenth century, a project that might be considered a milestone in the history of catalogs began. This was the compilation of the *Registrum Librorum Angliae*, "a union list of holdings of English monastery libraries in which, in a quite modern way, each library was assigned a number for coding purposes. The *Registrum* was never finished."[17] There is evidence of later attempts to compile continuations of it, although no completed version has survived.

The fourteenth century in Europe brought some improvements to information organization, and a few lists of this period might be called *shelflists* (i.e., lists of resources ordered as they are arranged on the bookshelves). The most notable contribution of the fourteenth century, compiled by John Whytefield, is the list describing the collection at St. Martin's Priory at Dover, England dated 1389. It may be the first of the lists that could be accurately described as a catalog. It is a list of the holdings of a particular library, divided into three parts. The first is a listing by a number that represents the fixed location of individual volumes. The second section of the catalog is also arranged by these numbers but gives the contents of each volume as well, including pagination and the opening words for each work. The third section, however, is an innovation in the development of cataloging: a list of analytical entries and an alphabetical listing. An *analytical entry* is an entry made for each work in a volume, as opposed to making only one entry for the entire volume. The entries are a mishmash of types: some under an author's name, some under the title, some under words describing the resource such as *book*, *part*, or *codex*. There is no obvious importance attached to the entry word.

As monasticism declined, educational institutions began to flourish. At the outset, the best library collections were property of individual faculty members, and students would access necessary resources from their tutors.[18] Centralized college libraries began to be available in the fourteenth century but did not bring any innovations to the development of information organization. The earliest lists from college libraries retained the prevalent, less sophisticated inventory style of the preceding centuries. As with the monastic libraries before them, college library collections were small and, therefore, required fewer mechanisms for the organization of information resources. In fact, it was not unusual for a college library at that time to have only 100 books.

A new practice introduced in the fifteenth century was the use of *cross-references* (or, simply, *references*). A cross-reference is a pointer from one part of the catalog where someone may logically search to another place where the information is actually found. For example, in a modern catalog, you might see a cross-reference pointing you from an unused term to an authorized *heading*.[§]

> Death penalty
> *See*: **Capital punishment**

In one catalog, the references were not separate entries but were appended to a sort of contents note pointing out in what other place in the library a certain item might be found (e.g., "which seek in the 96th volume of theology"[19]). In the catalog of St. Augustine's Abbey, Canterbury, England, though, references reached the status of separate entries.[20] A typical example of the kind of reference employed is

> The Meditations of Bernard, not here because it is above in the Bible [which was given by] W. Wylmynton.[21]

[§]A *heading* is the exact string of characters of the authorized form of an access point or subject heading as it appears in an authority record or in a controlled vocabulary.

In the middle of the fifteenth century came an event that challenged everything about information organization—the invention of movable type printing by Johannes Gutenberg. This is the conventional wisdom on the subject, but it is not quite correct. Gutenberg did not, in fact, invent movable type printing. "The first overtures towards printing … began around roughly 800 AD, in China, where early printing techniques [involved] chiseling an entire page of text into a wood block backwards, applying ink, and printing pages by pressing them against the block. … Later efforts would create early movable type—including the successful but inefficient use of ideograms chiseled in wood and a brief, abortive effort to create ceramic characters."[22] The thousands of ideograms needed made the widespread use of the technique somewhat impractical for mass production.[23]

Knowledge of these efforts was imported to Korea, where the process was improved. "The innovation that Johannes Gutenberg is said to have created was small metal pieces with raised backwards letters, arranged in a frame, coated with ink, and pressed to a piece of paper, which allowed books to be printed more quickly. But Choe Yun-ui did that—and he did it 150 years before Gutenberg was even born."[24] The ideas and innovations apparently spread further westward via the Silk Road into the Uyghur homeland and the western-most parts of the Mongol empire. Whether or not this knowledge made its way into Europe via the Mongols is still a matter of debate, but the widespread perception that Gutenberg invented movable type completely ignores the contributions of China, Korea, and other parts of Asia.

Gutenberg and others in fifteenth-century Europe did innovate through the development and perfection of the mechanics of the printing press and the development and commercialization of a printing industry. Gutenberg's innovation was adapting a wine press with woodblocks and metal movable type to create a printing press.[25] This industrial form of printing allowed resources to be produced quickly, accurately, and inexpensively. Resources could be mass produced and information (and misinformation) could be spread far and wide. Suddenly, instead of relatively few, unique manuscript copies of works, now identical printed duplicates of works were more readily available for sale. The popularization of the printing press was a watershed moment in Western history that reverberated in cultural, economic, and political spheres. It should be no surprise that it had a significant impact on the bibliographic universe.

The spread of the printing press ushered in the need for greater bibliographic control, previously unnecessary due to small collection sizes. This need created a new area of expertise, **bibliography**: the study of books as physical and cultural objects, which often results in creating extensive lists. Toward the close of the fifteenth century, German abbot and bibliographer Johannes Trithemius (also known as Johann Tritheim) is noted for an innovation in the history of bibliographic control. He compiled a bibliography in chronological order, which was innovative enough for his time, but he also appended to this an index of author names in alphabetical order. Strout notes that it is difficult to understand why such a simple and useful device had not always been used, yet it took centuries of compiling book lists to reach this degree of accomplishment.[26]

2.1.3 From Inventories to Finding Lists to Collocating Devices

In the sixteenth century, improvements to information organization continued, often through the efforts of bibliographers. One of these, Conrad Gessner (also known as Konrad Gesner),

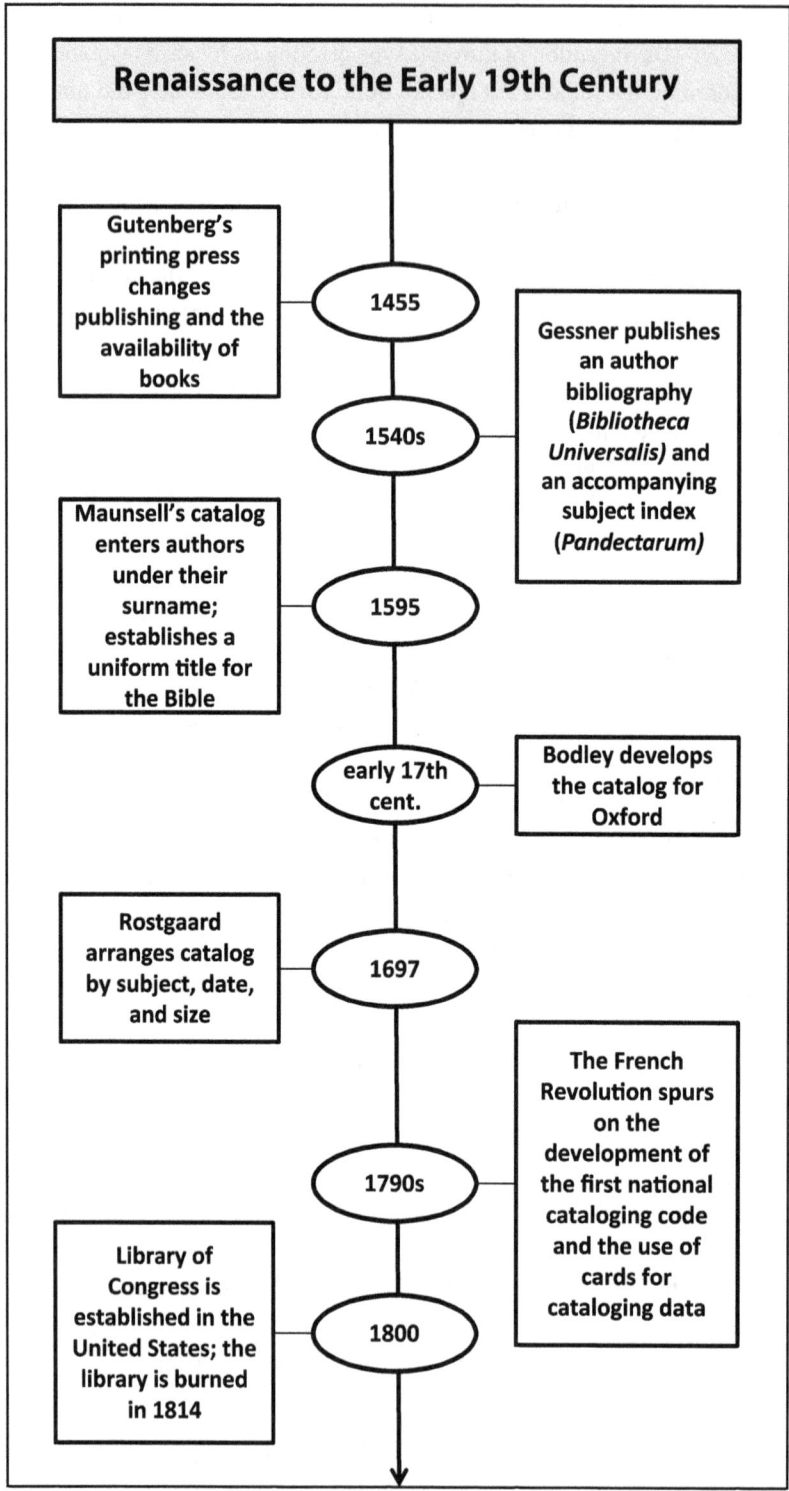

Figure 2.3 Timeline 3: Renaissance to the Early Nineteenth Century.

published an author bibliography, *Bibliotheca Universalis*, in 1545 and a subject index (known as the *Pandectarum*) in 1548, and in the process set a new standard of excellence. He continued to use forenames (i.e., first names or given names) of authors for entry words, according to the tradition of the time, but he recognized the possible inconvenience of this practice and so he prefixed to his bibliography an alphabetical list of authors in which the names were inverted. In addition, his main listing included references from variant spellings of names to the accepted form (e.g., "Thobias, see Tobias"). Gessner suggested that libraries use copies of his bibliographies as their catalogs by inserting call numbers next to the entries for resources that were in their collections, thus providing themselves with both an author and a subject catalog.

The end of the sixteenth century saw even greater advances in bibliography, and some of the conventions that we now take for granted were introduced. For example, "in 1595 Andrew Maunsell, an English bookseller, compiled his *Catalogue of English Printed Books* and in the Preface stated his rules for entry. He advocated the entry of personal names under surnames rather than Christian names, noting that this was contrary to the usage set up by Gesner."[27] He set up the principle of uniform entry for the Bible, copies of which, prior to Maunsell's collocating them, had been entered under whatever the title page said (*Holy Bible*, *The Word of God*, *Bible*, *Wycliffe's Bible*). He insisted that one should be able to find a book under three types of entries—the author's surname, the subject, and the translator. Strout notes that these were radical and sudden advances in the development of bibliographic control.[28]

By the beginning of the seventeenth century, catalogs were beginning to be looked upon as finding lists rather than inventories. Early in the century, Sir Thomas Bodley offered to build up the University of Oxford library, which had been dissolved some fifty years before when in 1550 the dean of Christ Church, "hoping to purge the English church of all traces of Catholicism including 'superstitious books and images,' removed all the library's books—some to be burnt."[29] Bodley took a great interest in the catalog because he expected that it would be useful in his acquisitions program; he wanted the catalog to tell him if the library already owned a work. He insisted upon a classified catalog with an alphabetical author index arranged by surname, and he also wanted analytical entries.

In 1697 Frederik Rostgaard published a discourse on cataloging in which he called for subject arrangement subdivided at once chronologically and by volume size. For the preceding century, size of volume had been a way of dividing catalogs. Rostgaard proposed a printed catalog, with the spread of two facing pages divided into four parallel columns, each column to contain books of a certain size (folios, quartos, octavos, and duodecimos), arranged so that books of various sizes that had been published on a certain subject within the same year would come directly opposite each other in parallel columns. He recommended an alphabetical index of subjects and authors to be placed at the end of the catalog, with authors entered by surname. The word order of titles as found on the title page was to be preserved. His final suggestion was that his rules should not be followed when it seemed best to arrange things differently!

As the eighteenth century began, information organization seemed to have hit a plateau that did not change for most of the century. Catalogs were sometimes classified and sometimes alphabetical and usually divided according to the size of books; indexes were considered useful, though by no means necessary; authors were now almost always entered under surname; the wording

Duodecimos	Octavos	Quartos	Folios
Art 1608 Title 1 Title 2	Art 1608 Title 3	Art 1608 Title 4	Art 1608 Title 5
1609 Title 1	1609	1609 Title 2	1609
1610 Title 1	1610 Title 2	1610 Title 3	1610 Title 4
Biology 1610 Title 1	Biology 1610 Title 2	Biology 1610 Title 3	Biology 1610

Figure 2.4 Illustration of Rostgaard's Catalog.

of the title page had become sacrosanct and was now being transcribed precisely without being paraphrased; *imprints* (i.e., publication information) were included; bound-with notes were used; cross-references were common; and some analytical entries were used.

The French Revolution provided the impetus for the creation of a new kind of catalog. In 1791 the new French government sent out instructions for cataloging the collections of the libraries that had been confiscated throughout the country. These collections were to be sold to help cover the government's expenses or to be kept in order to form a national library, open to the public, to engender the diffusion of knowledge believed to be necessary in a democratic government. To fulfill this program, they created the first instance of a national *cataloging code* (i.e., a set of guidelines or rules on how to catalog). The need for the code was twofold: first, the inexperience of the catalogers required that instructions be provided; and second, and more importantly, uniformity would allow identification of duplicate items, facilitating decisions about the disposition of specific copies.[30] The instructions identified playing cards as the medium on which to record cataloging data:

> That there might be enough blank space for writing, it was recommended, in case of very long titles, that the playing cards chosen should be those with the smallest

Development of the Organization of Recorded Information 61

Figure 2.5 and Figure 2.6 Front and Back Views of a Catalog Card from the French Revolution. (Images courtesy of Larry T. Nix. http://libraryhistorybuff.blogspot.com/.)

number of pips, as the ace, deuce, etc., and with as plain backs as possible, so that, if the space for the title was insufficient on the face of the card, the back might be used to complete it.[31]

This is possibly the first appearance in history of a card catalog. A ***card catalog*** is a list of resources in which the descriptions are recorded on cards that are arranged in a particular order. In France it was introduced, not because someone thought it would be a convenient form, but because, with wartime shortages, it was a practical way of using available materials. Confiscated playing cards were to be used for the purpose. Playing cards of the time were blank on the back, rather than having pictures.[32] They were also larger than today's cards. See Figures 2.5 and 2.6.

It is notable that even though the card catalog of the French Revolution is thought to be the first card catalog recorded in history,[33]** and it provided the first national instructions on how to create card entries, the catalog itself is unremarkable. The purpose of the code was not to provide a catalog of a library for access purposes but to serve an administrative function for the creation of

---

**The Austrian National Library claims that the first card catalog was created by Gottfried van Swieten in 1780.

a union catalog that would assist in the appropriate confiscation of unique resources. As stated in the instructions (translated by Joseph Smalley[††]),

> It is necessary to set up catalogs having no other object than of procuring an exact knowledge of all the books, printed as well as manuscripts, that exist in those libraries of each department that make up part of the "biens nationaux."[34][‡‡]

That this catalog was not meant for public consumption surely affected the construction of the catalog itself. The rules themselves contain instructions on the physical process of cataloging as well as on the intellectual content needed. There was no theory or philosophizing in this code. The title page was to be transcribed on the card and the author's surname underlined for the filing word. If there was no author, a keyword in the title was to be underlined. A **collation**, a detailed description of the physical attributes of a book, was added that was to include number of volumes, size, a statement of illustration, the material of which the book was made, the kind of type, any missing pages, and a description of the binding if it was outstanding in any way. This elaborate collation was partly for the purpose of identifying valuable books that the government might offer for sale to increase government revenue. After the cards were filled in and put in order by the underlined filing word, they were to be strung together by running a needle and thread through the lower left corners to keep them in order.[35]

Despite the lack of intention, the French Revolution card catalog established some procedures that have continued to the present. The resulting cataloging code was the first systematic national effort to standardize cataloging, and it is notable for its use of cards in the production of a catalog. Although it would be another 100 years before card catalogs became the standard for libraries in the Anglo-American world, this code, coming at the end of the eighteenth century, provides a stepping stone to the extensive cataloging developments of the nineteenth century.

2.2 The Modern Era

2.2.1 Nineteenth Century: A Period of Codification

The nineteenth century brought a period of much debate over the relative virtues of different types of catalogs, not only among librarians, but also among readers and scholars in general and even in reports to the House of Commons of Great Britain. Feelings ran very high on the subject, and rather emotional arguments were made, "from the statement that classified catalogs and indexes were not needed because living librarians were better than subject catalogs, to the opinion that any intelligent man who was sufficiently interested in a subject to want to consult material on it could just as well use author entries as subject, for he would, of course, know the names of all the authors who had written in his field."[36]

[††]Smalley provides a complete translation of the catalog code as distributed to the libraries, which were confiscated property of the crown in France and therefore under the decree of the National Constituent Assembly.

[‡‡]*Biens nationaux* refers to goods confiscated from the church, the monarchy, and other elites during the French Revolution.

What was needed was a person who could persuade others of the value of cataloging and subject analysis. That person turned out to be Antonio Genesio Maria Panizzi (better known as Anthony Panizzi), a lawyer and Italian political refugee who was appointed assistant librarian at the British Museum in 1831. When he was appointed Keeper of the Printed Books in 1837, there was much objection. One historian, Dorothy May Norris, states that it was because "firstly, Panizzi was an Italian by birth, and it was felt that only an Englishman should be in charge of one of our national institutions; secondly, it was said that Panizzi had been seen in the streets of London selling white mice."[37] No further explanation is given! Louis Fagan, in his biography of Panizzi, gives this account: "Meetings were held against the 'Foreigner;' and one of the speakers made an open statement that Panizzi had been seen in the streets of London selling white mice: had it been a few years later, possibly the distinctive title of organ-grinder would have been added."[38]

In 1836 a committee of the House of Commons was charged with inquiry into the management and activities of the British Museum. One of the concerns was the state of the institution's catalogs and cataloging. During hearings on the topic, witnesses came to testify for and against the existing catalogs of that time. Many of the witnesses became quite vehement about various details, large and small; Strout states, "Surely such great interest in the minutiae of cataloging has never been displayed at any other time by scholar, reader, and government."[39] Panizzi was able again and again to persuade the committee members to accept his ideas. Panizzi wrote his views into a cataloging code titled, "Rules for the Compilation of a Catalogue" (more commonly known as the "91 Rules"). It appeared in the first and only volume of *The Catalogue of Printed Books in the British Museum*.[40] This code gained official approval in 1839, although Panizzi had to give up his concept of corporate authorship to get approval due to opposition by those who believed that only individual persons are capable of authorship.

It is generally accepted that the catalog code of the British Museum, published in 1841, begins the current period of cataloging. The legacy of the "91 Rules," however, is not as simple as merely being the first formal English-language catalog code. Although Panizzi managed to print only the first volume of his planned catalog due to political infighting, the rules themselves provided a foundation upon which later codes were built. Panizzi's code shows that we had, at last, arrived at modern cataloging, because he tried to deal with many of the same problems we are still faced with today.

In the United States, cataloging experienced the same growing pains as in Europe. Prior to the nineteenth century, American cataloging had been generally a century behind European cataloging. For example, the earliest catalogs printed at Harvard were divided by size and then alphabetized according to author, title, or keyword, with shelf locations and very brief records, but no subject access.[41] Preceding the introduction of mechanized card production in 1901 by the Library of Congress (LC), much of the cataloging performed in the United States resulted in book catalogs, both print and manuscript.[42] Cataloging was one area under scrutiny by the leadership of the nascent profession of librarianship. Charles Coffin Jewett is one of the leaders who placed this activity at the center of his work.

Jewett was a librarian during a period when printed catalogs were considered premier. He trained in cataloging at the beginning of his career, and, throughout his professional life, he was

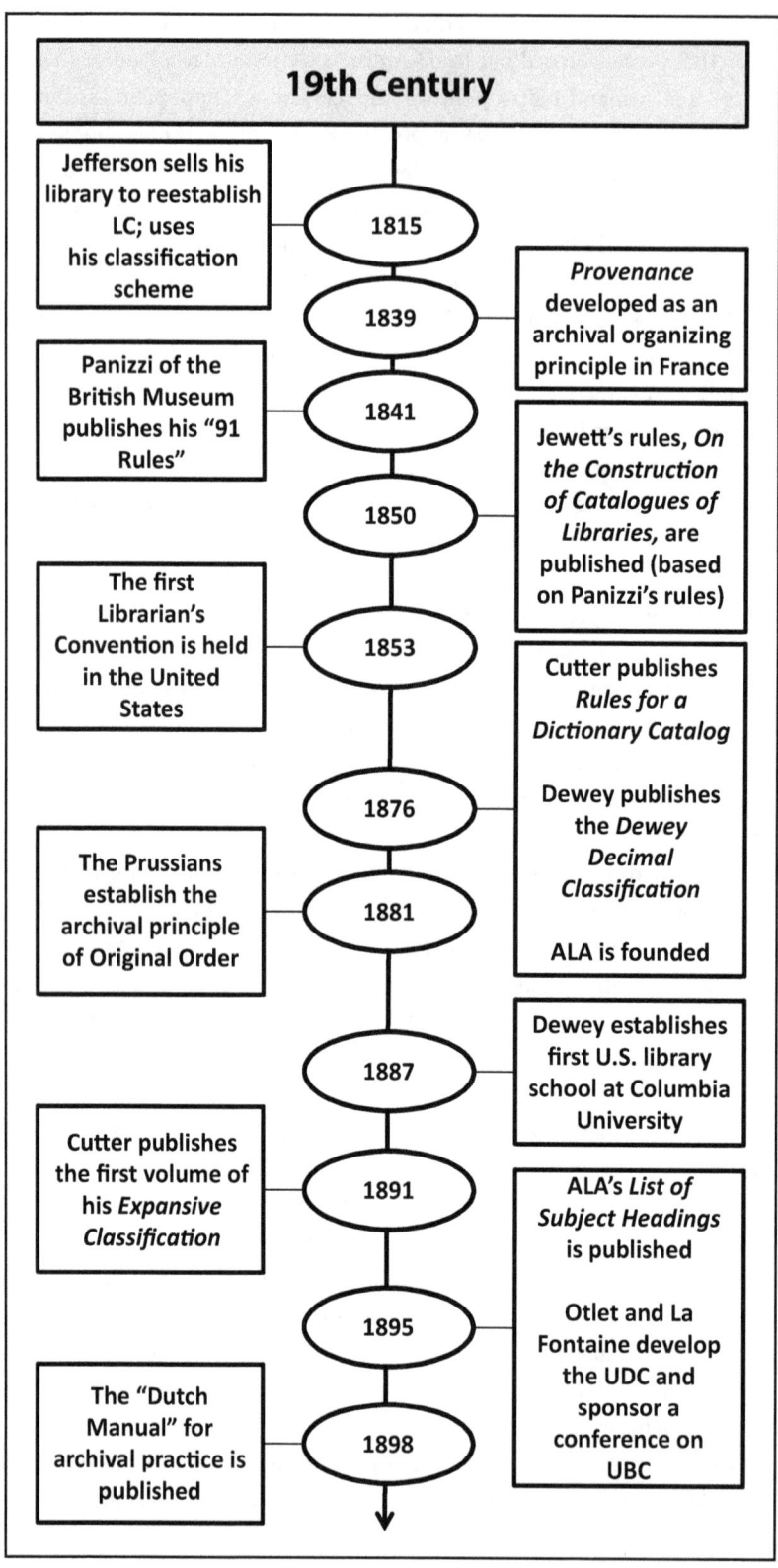

Figure 2.7 Timeline 4: Nineteenth Century.

Figure 2.8 Photograph of Anthony Panizzi. (Photograph in the Public Domain.)

considered an expert in the practice of constructing and evaluating library catalogs. He enjoyed success at the Brown University library, and then was appointed librarian for the newly established Smithsonian Institution. Later in his career he had a significant impact on the Boston Public Library as superintendent.

In 1850 Jewett published a code for the catalog of the Smithsonian Institution. With this code the United States began to have influence in cataloging. Jewett acknowledged his debt to Panizzi and in only a few instances varied from the instructions in the "91 Rules." Jewett is given credit for extending the principle of corporate authorship further than Panizzi had. Research now shows that Jewett copied his rule from Panizzi's original draft, which had a rule for corporate bodies as authors, but which did not appear in the published "91 Rules" because Panizzi was forced by the British Museum trustees to drop his rules for entry under corporate author.[43] So what Jewett did was to bring Panizzi's concept of corporate authorship to public attention.

Jewett's philosophy of the purpose of a code was this: "*Uniformity* is, then, imperative; but, among many laborers, can only be secured by the adherence of all to rules embracing, as far as possible, the minutest details of the work."[44] In light of this philosophy, it is interesting to observe that the second edition of Jewett's rulebook contains only 39 rules on pages 29–64 with pages 67–90 devoted to examples. The title of Jewett's book, *On the Construction of Catalogues of Libraries, and Their Publication by Means of Separate, Stereotyped Titles*, makes it clear that Jewett was addressing more than just rules for cataloging. The first part of the volume is devoted to his plan to create a stereotyped plate of each title cataloged, to store the plates, and to use them over and over for production of printed catalogs. **Stereotyping** was a method of printing using a metal copy of a typeset image. Jewett planned to have the plates numbered in the order in which they were printed and to keep them in alphabetical order in shallow drawers. The numbers could be used by libraries to indicate which titles were owned by each, and then a catalog could be produced for a library by pulling out the plates for titles owned by that library. Also, a union catalog could be produced from the plates. Jewett's plan, however, was never implemented. Apparently, he was technologically a bit ahead of his time.[45] To say that Jewett influenced American librarianship—from his contributions to cataloging, his vision of a national library (which he hoped would be the Smithsonian), and his leadership in the burgeoning library profession, particularly at the 1853 Librarian's Convention (often credited as a precursor to the American Library Association)—would be an understatement. Even his contemporaries, without the benefit of hindsight, recognized Jewett as a visionary in cataloging and a leader in librarianship. Although Jewett made significant contributions to American librarianship and cataloging specifically, his contributions are overshadowed by those of Charles Ammi Cutter and Melvil Dewey (discussed below).

Cutter, as librarian of the Boston Athenaeum, created his masterwork, *Rules for a Dictionary Catalog*,[46] which ran to four editions and can be credited as the foundation of American

Figure 2.9 Portrait of Charles Coffin Jewett. (Photograph in the Public Domain. This image is available from the United States Library of Congress's Prints and Photographs division under the digital ID cph.3c28407.)

Development of the Organization of Recorded Information 67

Figure 2.10 Photograph of Charles Ammi Cutter. (Photograph in the Public Domain.)

cataloging. His set of cataloging rules, influenced by the work of Panizzi and Jewett, still informs our cataloging standards today. Cutter, along with Dewey and others, was instrumental in the establishment of the American Library Association just over two decades after the 1853 Librarian's Convention. Like Jewett before him, Cutter was considered a leader in the profession. He also created the *Expansive Classification* and was the originator of book numbers, still in use today and known as *cutter numbers*. His legacy, though, rests squarely in his articulation of the objectives of the catalog,[§§] in addition to his innumerable contributions to cataloging, the profession, and the larger library mission.

When Cutter published his rules in 1876, he strengthened the concept that catalogs should not only point the way to an individual publication but also assemble and organize literary units.[47] That is, catalogs should be collocating devices. This was not an entirely new idea: Maunsell had used the heading **Bible** to bring together all versions of that work no matter the title presented on the title page; Panizzi had strengthened it by introducing corporate and government entries; and Jewett had given further support by using real names rather than pseudonyms. Cutter, though, was the first to state it as a formal principle.

[§§]Cutter's "objects" of the catalog are discussed in Chapter 3.

Cutter was also the first to make rules for subject headings to provide subject access to materials through the catalog. And he was the last to incorporate instructions for the description of resources, guidelines for subject headings, and rules for filing entries into a single set of rules. At the end of the nineteenth century each of these areas (i.e., description and access, subject headings, and filing) took on lives of their own and followed separate paths of development. We will now follow the first two paths separately. Filing is discussed in Appendix A: Arrangement of Metadata Displays.

2.2.2 Twentieth Century: Description and Access

In the area of description, the twentieth century was an era of codes. The British and the Americans collaborated on a code published in 1908, titled *Catalog Rules: Author and Title Entries*. It was compiled by committees of the American Library Association (ALA) and Great Britain's Library Association. Members of the committees included famous librarians of the day such as Charles Cutter, James Hanson (one of the developers of the *Library of Congress Classification*), James Duff Brown (creator of the *Subject Classification* scheme), and E. Wyndham Hulme (who developed the idea of **literary warrant*****). Reflective of the times, the committee primarily consisted of men; of the 24 committee members listed, only three were women, all of whom were on the American committee.[48] The 1908 code's importance lies in being the first international cataloging code, and in the extent of its rapid and widespread adoption and use by all types and sizes of libraries in the two countries. But it was not, by any means, a perfect code.

> Lacking a guiding hand and a single set of unified principles, this, the first of the committee codes that have lumbered through the 20th century, was an assemblage of the best practices of Anglophone libraries. It was inevitable that such a code would be based on cases and ever more minute distinctions between cases. The latter reached its reductio ad absurdum in the full page devoted to the rule on Exploring expeditions, with its two subrules, the second of which has 6 sub-subrules.[49]

In the 1920s four prominent American librarians helped write the Vatican code, which was published in Italian in 1931. It was quickly accepted by catalogers in many countries as the best and most complete code in existence, but because it was in Italian, most Americans could not use it. A second edition of the Vatican code was published in 1939. Due to delays associated with the Second World War, an English translation did not appear until 1948, long after other codes had taken root in the United States. "Had it not been for the Second World War, it is quite possible that work on the Vatican code would have taken the place of the work that led to the abortive 1941 draft rules and the unmitigated disaster of the 1949 ("Red Book") rules."[50]

In the 1930s, British and American catalogers began cooperative work toward a second edition of *Catalog Rules: Author and Title Entries* (the 1908 code), but the outbreak of the Second World War ended this cooperation. ALA proceeded independently in producing a preliminary second edition in 1941. This code was published in two parts: one for entry and heading and one for

---

***Literary warrant is the principle that new notations are created for a classification scheme and new terms are added to a controlled vocabulary only after information resources exist about those concepts.

description of books.[51] It was widely attacked for its complexity and the proliferation of rules for every circumstance. The most famous critique was by Andrew Osborn in his article, "The Crisis in Cataloging,"[52] in which he identified four principal theories of cataloging.

- **Legalistic**: cataloging with a rule for everything, and an authority to settle any question at issue
- **Perfectionistic**: cataloging performed so well the first time that it is done once and for all
- **Bibliographic**: cataloging made into a branch of descriptive bibliography with extremely detailed physical descriptions and notes
- **Pragmatic**: cataloging according to the needs of particular types of libraries and/or users

He called for both the cataloging process and the rules governing it to become pragmatic, with simple rules supplemented by cataloger judgment. Osborn's article is one of the classic statements in cataloging theory and certainly one of the historical turning points in code development.

In response to the criticism, the ALA Division of Cataloging and Classification undertook a revision of the first part (entry and heading) of the 1941 code. In 1949, the revision was published as the *A.L.A. Cataloging Rules for Author and Title Entries* (known as the "Red Book" for its color). The *Rules for Descriptive Cataloging* published by LC was substituted for the second part (description of books) of the 1941 rules. The ALA portion of the 1949 rules again was criticized as being a continuation of Osborn's "legalistic" characterization. In 1951, ALA commissioned Seymour Lubetzky to do a critical study of cataloging rules. The objective of the study was to point out weaknesses in the current cataloging code and to indicate how they could be improved. It was to clear the ground and lay the foundation for a revision. Lubetzky concluded the current set of rules was deficient in principles and structure. A revision of the rules was not needed; a complete reconstruction of objectives and principles was! He believed that cataloging should be performed according to principles, and he drafted a code based on them.[53] Progressives welcomed it, but conservatives began worrying about probable costs of changes.

An International Conference on Cataloguing Principles was held in Paris in 1961, the first major initiative for the International Federation of Library Associations and Institutions (IFLA), at which a draft statement of principles, based on Lubetzky's code, was submitted. The goal of this conference was to agree on principles that would inform cataloging standards internationally. The participants agreed to adopt these principles and to work in their various countries for revised rules that would be in agreement with the accepted principles. These principles, referred to as the ***Paris Principles***, are important because for the first time there was multinational agreement upon which to base future international developments.

Participants, including Lubetzky, Osborn, and Eva Verona, debated many ideas at the conference. Verona was a Croatian librarian and professor who worked at the National and University Library in Zagreb, a library system that had fewer economic advantages than libraries familiar to Osborn and Lubetzky. Consequently, she had a different perspective on many issues raised at the conference, such as the purpose of main entry in the catalog.

According to the Paris Principles, one of the headings chosen to represent a resource in the catalog is to be selected as the primary one, which is called the ***main entry***. A main entry is usually

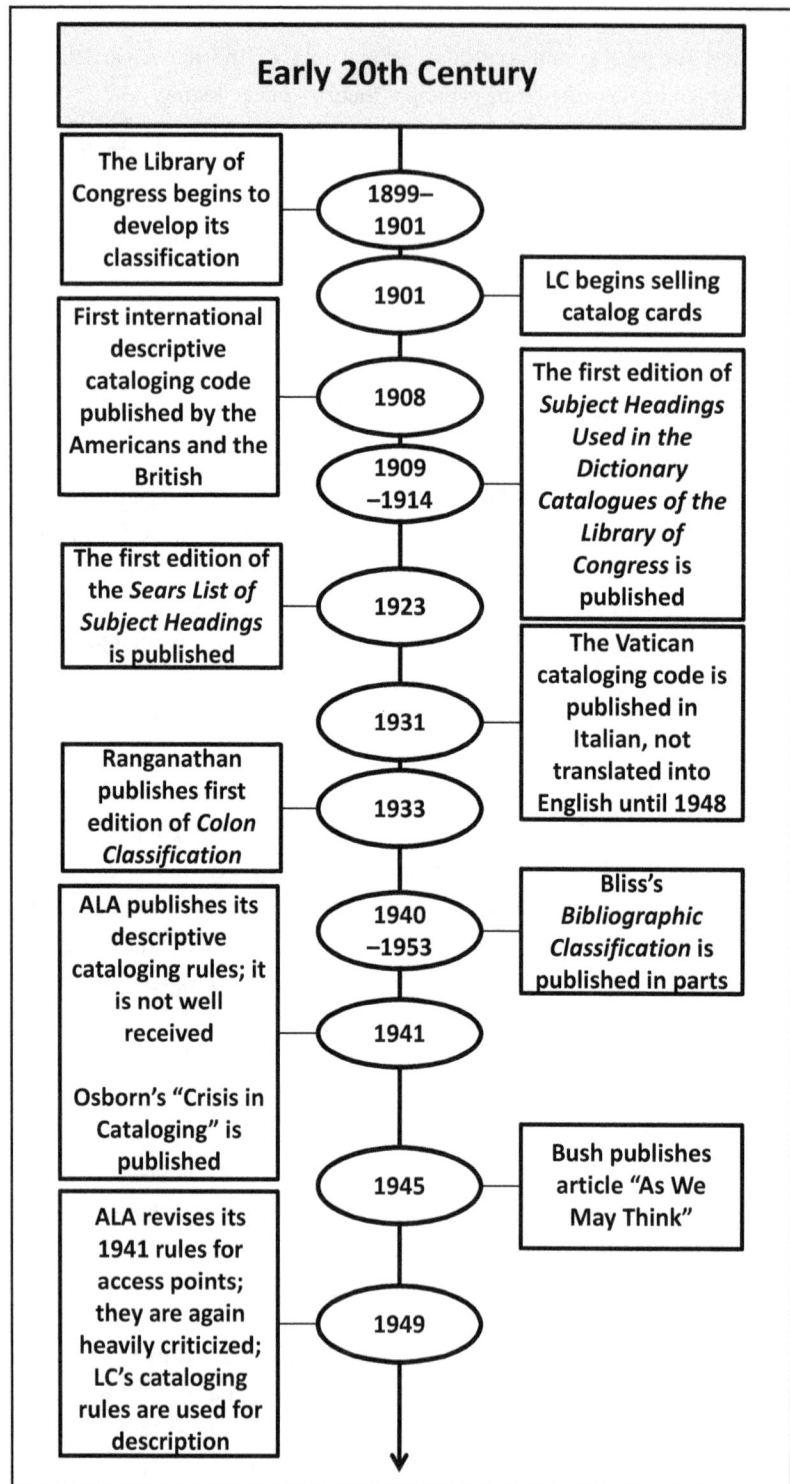

Figure 2.11 Timeline 5: Twentieth Century.

Development of the Organization of Recorded Information 71

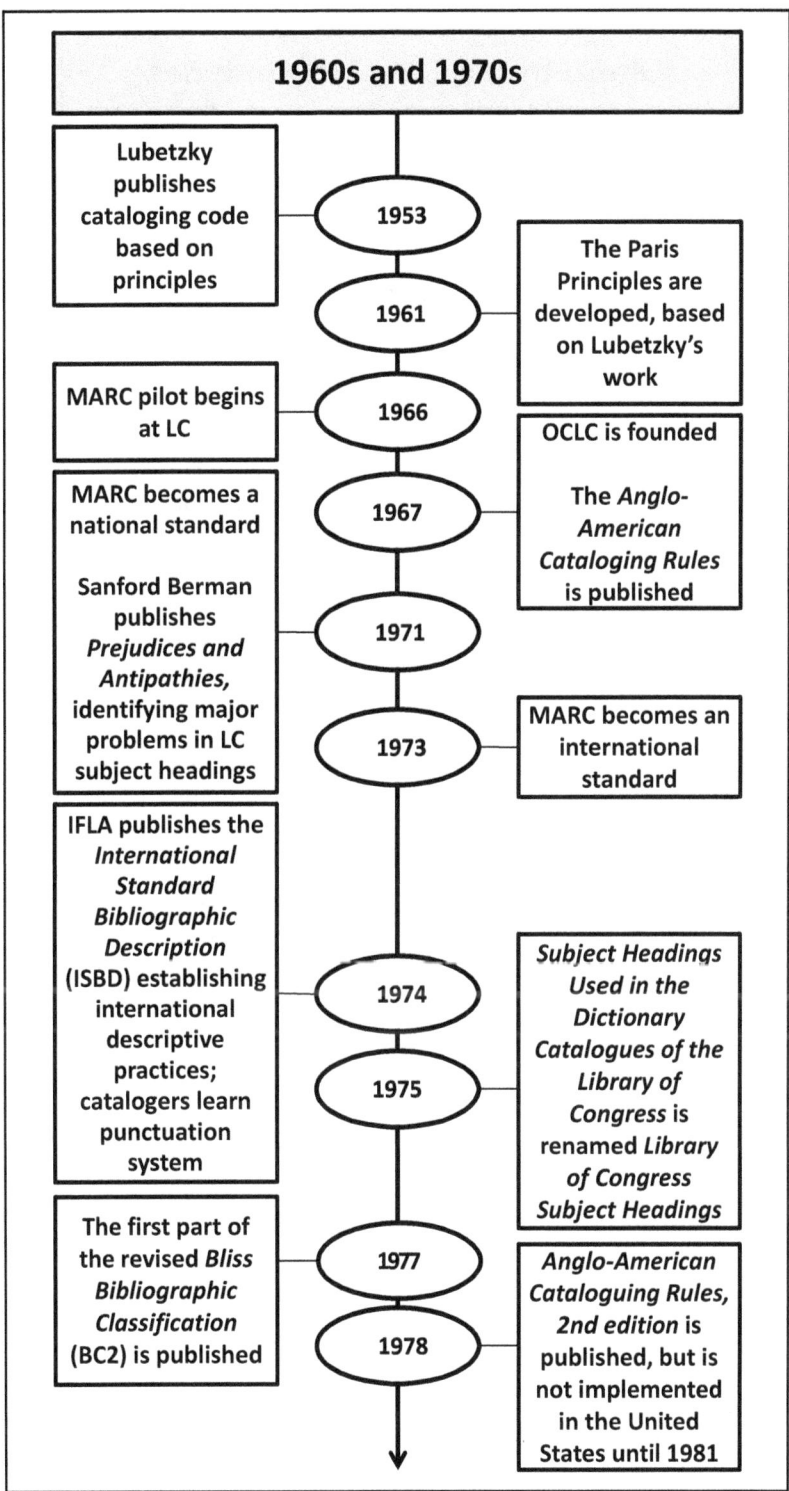

Figure 2.11 *(Continued)*

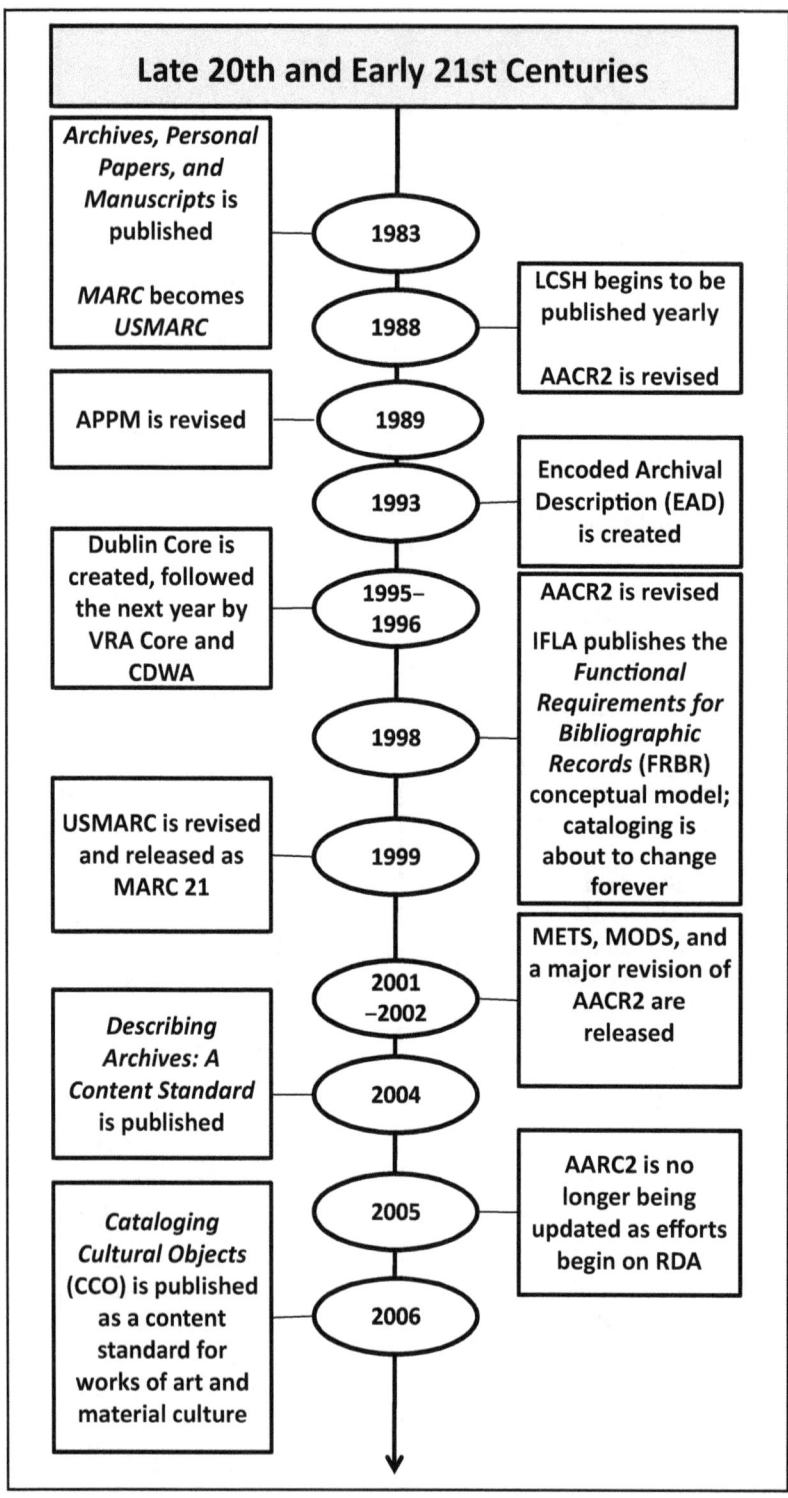

Figure 2.11 *(Continued)*

Development of the Organization of Recorded Information

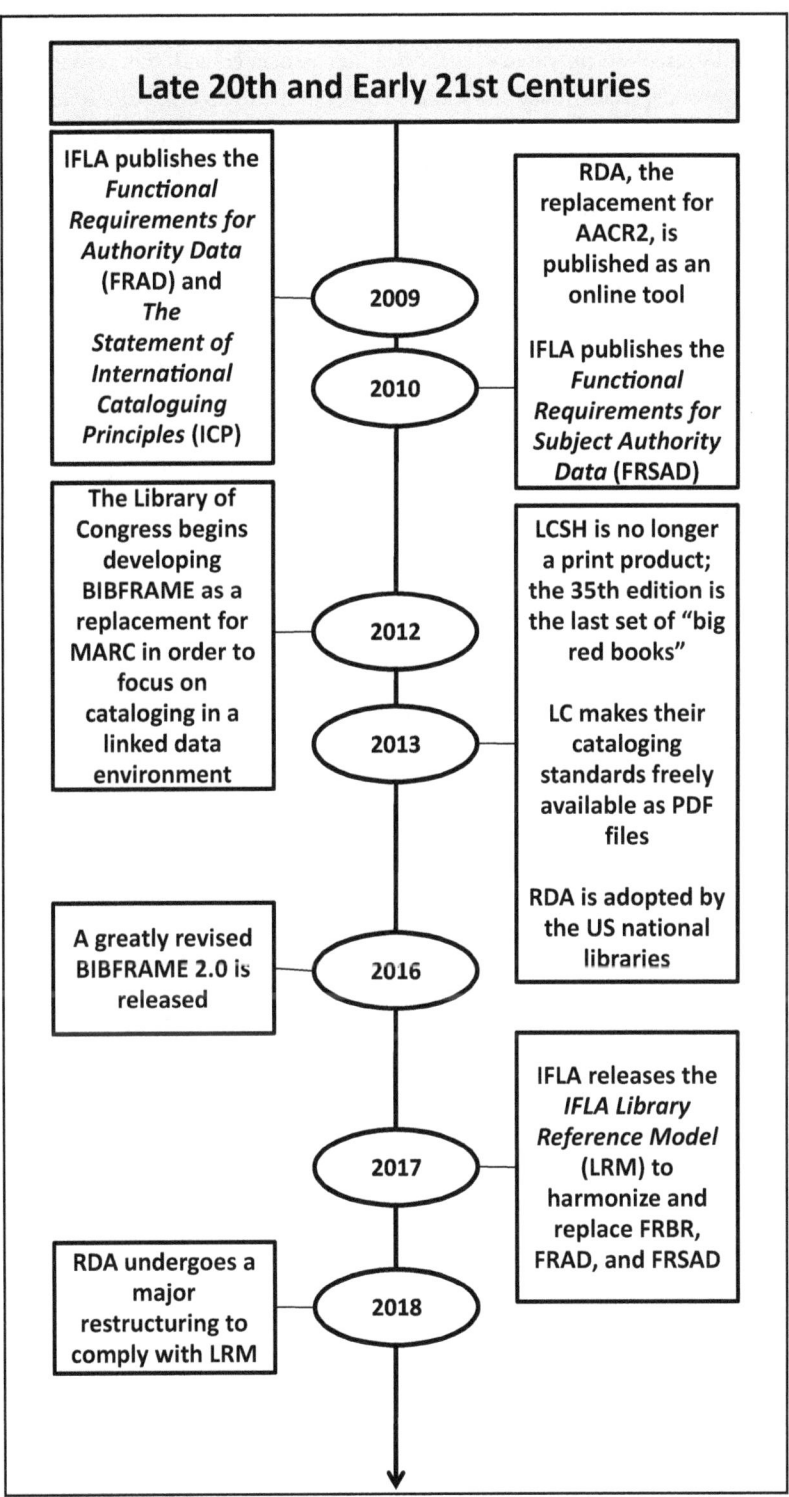

Figure 2.11 *(Continued)*

(but not always) the first-named creator of a resource.[†††] In catalogs of that day, a bibliographic description for a resource was provided at every heading associated with that resource (e.g., author, co-authors, title, subjects, series, illustrators, and so on), but the main entry alone was used to create a ***standard citation*** for the resource (i.e., a consistent way to refer to the resource). The standard citation usually entailed combining the main entry's authorized heading with the standardized title of the work to create a name/title heading (e.g., **Shakespeare, William, 1564–1616. Twelfth night**).

Lubetzky believed that main entry was needed to support the gathering function of the catalog (i.e., to collocate the same work by the same creator, no matter the title used or the form of the creator's name). This is sensible in a relatively wealthier environment where in a single collection many versions of the same work might be found (in different languages, translations, editions, etc.). Verona felt the finding function of the catalog (i.e., to support direct retrieval of a resource) was the more important objective; a sensible approach especially where a library collection would typically have only one version of a work due to limited resources. There is a basic conflict in the use of main entry regarding the two functions: main entry can be used to accomplish one or the other, but not necessarily both. Both are important, and this issue had to be resolved. The solution they found addressed both concerns, as seen in Section 5 of the Paris Principles:

> The two functions of the catalogue … are most effectively discharged by
> 5.1 an entry for each book under a heading derived from the author's name or from the title as printed in the book, *and*
> 5.2 when variant forms of the author's name or of the title occur, an entry for each book under a *uniform heading*, consisting of one particular form of the author's name or one particular title, or, for books not identified by author or title, a uniform heading consisting of a suitable substitute for the title, *and*
> 5.3 appropriate added entries and/or references.[54]

This means that transcribed data directly from the source as well as authority-controlled headings (for names and some titles) are included in a bibliographic description of a resource.

The Paris Principles also state that the description found at a resource's main entry must be a ***full entry*** (i.e., a complete description of a resource containing all its details). Although this is not relevant in today's information environment, this made sense in the days of card and book catalogs where it was necessary to place as many descriptions of the same resource into a catalog as there were headings. Though a separate entry was made for each heading, it was necessary to save time and space by having only one full entry for each resource, with the rest of the descriptions under the other headings found in abbreviated form (e.g., omitting certain details and notes). The Paris Principles state that the place where the fullest entry should be filed is under the resource's main entry. Soon it was common to conflate the two terms: *full entry* and *main entry*, which caused confusion throughout the last several decades of the twentieth century. By the time online catalogs

---

[†††]In certain circumstance, main entry may be the title of a resource. This often occurs with works by unknown creators, motion pictures and television programs, sacred scriptures, and collections of separate works by different creators.

were being used, catalogers no longer had a need for a full entry; a complete MARC record was used to represent a resource. The concept of *full entry* is not applicable in online catalogs, yet the basic concept of *main entry* is still used to establish a standard citation for a resource.

Several years later, the Americans and the British again cooperated on a new set of cataloging rules, and in 1967 published the *Anglo-American Cataloging Rules*, though it had to be published in separate North American and British editions because of the inability to come to agreement on some points. These rules, known as AACR, were based on the Paris Principles, although they deviated in some respects. The first edition of AACR was used for almost fifteen years before a revised edition, the *Anglo-American Cataloguing Rules, Second Edition* (AACR2), was published.[55]

In 1974, IFLA issued the *International Standard Bibliographic Description* (ISBD), produced as a means for the international communication of bibliographic information. ISBD's original objectives were to make records from different sources interchangeable, to facilitate their interpretation against language barriers, and to facilitate the conversion of such records to machine-readable form. To meet these objectives, ISBD provided a standard set of bibliographic elements with which to describe resources, a standard order for those elements, and a system of punctuation symbols to be used to identify individual elements (allowing for the identification of individual elements when the language of the cataloging data is unfamiliar). Because ISBD is still being used in many libraries around the world, it is addressed further in Chapter 9.

Published in 1978, but not adopted until 1981, AACR2 was the primary descriptive cataloging standard in the United States and other Anglo-American countries for more than three decades. This edition of the Anglo-American rules sought

- to incorporate ISBD into the rules for description,
- to bring non-book materials into the mainstream,
- to take into account machine processing of bibliographic records,
- to reconcile the British and American texts of AACR, and
- to conform more closely to the Paris Principles.

Four national libraries (Australia, Canada, Great Britain, and the United States) agreed on the content of the rules and to implement the standard; other countries later adopted it for their own use. Revised editions of AACR2 were published in 1988 and 1998. These were mainly cumulations of changes incurred in the process of continuous revision. A significant revision of AACR2 was published in 2002, with updates distributed annually until 2005. Updates ceased in 2005, as efforts were focused on the creation of a new descriptive cataloging content standard—originally referred to as AACR3, but later given a new title: *RDA: Resource Description & Access*.

There have always been contentious discussions during the development of cataloging codes. In the course of developing AACR2 in the mid-to-late 1970s, there were several issues of concern. One centered on the use of main entry in cataloging records. (Yes, more debate over main entry!) In 1978, Seymour Lubetzky and Michael Gorman, two notable figures in cataloging, disagreed quite publicly at a conference on the emergence of AACR2.[56] AACR2's introduction included the observation that main entry might have outlived its time. However, there had not been enough time to research the idea, and so the concept was included in AACR2. The introduction stated that if they wished, a library could choose access points without designating one creator as the primary one. Lubetzky argued that this was a step backward instead of forward. It would undermine the identification of different works that shared the same title. Gorman believed that identifying a main entry (or primary creator for a work) was only necessary when a cataloger needed to cite a related work in the record for the work being described, a situation that he guessed would happen "less than 1 percent" of the time.[57] Research, however, has shown this estimate to be quite low. Richard Smiraglia found that approximately 50 percent of a sample of works had **derivative relationships**.[58] Derivative relationships exist when one work is descended from another (e.g., later editions, translations, adaptations, performances). A bibliographic description for a resource containing a derivative work should cite or refer to the work from which it has been derived. Because of these circumstances, main entry continued to be used throughout the life of AACR2 and beyond. In fact, the practice of identifying a primary creator is still around today; we simply do not refer to it as *main entry*. In today's parlance, we add an authorized access point for an agent to the preferred title for a work to create a standard citation for the work.

Another controversy from this time was related to what exactly was being described in our bibliographic metadata: an intellectual work or a physical item. This was another source of debate between Lubetzky and Gorman. Lubetzky, whose Paris Principles influenced the original AACR, believed that the intellectual work had primacy, whereas Gorman advocated centering the description on the item in hand. Because Gorman was the editor of AACR2, his approach was implemented in the new version of the standard. Ultimately, despite the debates, catalogers knew that both the work and the item must be addressed in the process of resource description.

In the mid-to-late 1990s, concerns about works, items, and other entities continued to be discussed. These topics were placed at the front and center of a conceptual framework for information organization developed by IFLA. This conceptual framework, still in place today, has gone through several iterations; it has greatly influenced the development of the modern approach to descriptive cataloging. This framework began with *Functional Requirements for Bibliographic Records* (FRBR), a conceptual model which enumerated the entities found in the bibliographic universe (i.e., resource entities, agent entities, and subject entities) and gathered them into groups. FRBR identified attributes associated with each entity, as well as a variety of important relationships. FRBR was also the source of the **user tasks** that were described in Chapter 1—tasks that users perform while using information retrieval tools and interacting with bibliographic data (find, identify, etc.). The model pointed out the connections between what is recorded about a resource and how different attributes support one or more user tasks. FRBR's influence was far reaching in the library community, although it was not deemed especially useful for archives, museums, and other information institutions. Two companion models, *Functional Requirements for Authority Data* (FRAD) and *Functional Requirements for Subject Authority Data* (FRSAD) followed in 2009 and 2010, respectively. These three models, which comprised IFLA's conceptual framework for resource description, had different foci and conflicted on some topics. This led to efforts to harmonize the three. This work resulted in the *IFLA Library Reference Model* (LRM), which supplanted the three FR conceptual models when it was adopted in 2017.

For decades, implementation of AACR2 in the United States was dominated by the policies of the Library of Congress. Anyone using AACR2 was expected to also consult the *Library of*

Congress Rule Interpretations (LCRI),[59] which recorded how LC catalogers interpreted and applied certain AACR2 instructions. LC stopped updating the LCRIs in 2010 when it became clear that they would soon be adopting the new content standard *RDA: Resource Description & Access*. The primary instructions in RDA incorporated a large majority of the rule interpretation outlined in the LCRIs, thus making them unnecessary. RDA, though, would require its own set of interpretations. Institutions using RDA now consult *policy statements* to help them interpret RDA instructions. For example, in the United States, the Library of Congress-Program for Cooperative Cataloging Policy Statements (LC-PCC PSs) are consulted to explicate various instructions.

RDA: Resource Description & Access, the replacement for AACR2, was published in 2010. As was the case with AACR2, implementation of the new standard was delayed by several years. In the United States, RDA was not adopted by the national libraries (LC, the National Agricultural Library, and the National Library of Medicine) until 2013. Although many of the instructions in RDA were like those in AACR2, there were some changes. Much of the impetus for creating RDA stemmed from dissatisfaction with AACR2, especially its inadequate rules for more complex resource types (e.g., streaming video, online maps, websites). More significantly, the overall structure of the rules was revised to reflect the original conceptual models developed by IFLA: primarily FRBR and FRAD. Other differences exist, especially in terms of access points, but the major changes found in RDA included:

- replacing *general material designations* with three new metadata elements: *content type*, *media type*, and *carrier type*;
- reducing the use of English abbreviations (e.g., ill., ed., col.) and eliminating all Latin abbreviations (e.g., et al.);
- eliminating restrictions on the number of creators and contributors included in the description and as access points;
- eliminating the correction of typos found on a resource (in other words, mistakes are recorded as found);
- allowing families to be identified as creators and contributors;
- introducing additional descriptive attributes (such as place of birth, occupation, and affiliation) to describe agents (i.e., persons, corporate bodies, and families acting as creators and contributors); and
- changing cataloging vocabulary (e.g., *headings* became *authorized access points*; *authors* became *creators*).

In 2018, another major restructuring of the cataloging rules began. RDA was reorganized to reflect a structure like that of a data dictionary, and it was rewritten to incorporate changes introduced in LRM. FRBR was one of the underlying foundations of the original version of RDA, so when LRM replaced FRBR, revisions to RDA appeared necessary (although this has been debated). This coincided with a major upgrade in the functionality of the RDA Toolkit, the subscription-based online service that contains the content standard. In December 2020, the RDA overhaul was complete, but, reminiscent of AACR2 and RDA in 2010, the revised standard was not immediately implemented. Those responsible for the 2020 version of RDA do not consider it a second edition of the same work, though some librarians have referred to it as "RDA 2.0." Both versions of RDA are now accessible; to differentiate between the two they are being referred to as "Original RDA" and "Official RDA."

2.2.3 Subject Access in the Modern Era

2.2.3.1 Controlled Vocabularies

For centuries philosophers worked on classifying knowledge; Callimachus, Plato, Aristotle, and Bacon are among the most famous. Librarians tried to adapt these classifications for use with books by assigning letters and/or numbers to the concepts classified by the philosophers. Other than this, there was only intermittent interest in subject access in libraries before Charles Cutter. As already mentioned, Cutter included a section of guidelines for subject headings in his *Rules for a Dictionary Catalog*.[60]

ALA's *List of Subject Headings for Use in Dictionary Catalogs* was first published in 1895, and the preface stated that it was to be considered an appendix to Cutter's rules. It was based on headings found in five major catalogs of the time, including the catalog of the Boston Athenaeum and the Harvard subject index. A second revised edition, "with an appendix containing hints on subject cataloging and schemes for subheads under countries and other subjects," was published in 1898 with the statement that "further changes are not to be expected for many years."[61] However, new terminology became necessary rapidly, and interleaved and annotated editions became unwieldy. Many librarians asked for the list of subject headings that were appearing on LC catalog cards, and so from 1909 to 1914 the first edition of *Subject Headings Used in the Dictionary Catalogues of the Library of Congress* was published in parts. This list rapidly replaced the ALA list as the distribution of LC catalog cards spread. The title of LC's list was changed to *Library of Congress Subject Headings* (LCSH) in 1975. LCSH has appeared in multiple editions in its printed version, and from 1988 to 2013 a new edition was published every year (or nearly so). The 35th edition was the last print edition of "the big red books" (as they were sometimes called). Although the print editions are no longer available, the system of subject headings is available electronically in different forms. Many institutions access LCSH through a searchable, interactive, web-based subscription service, *Classification Web Plus*.[62] This service, however, may be cost prohibitive for smaller libraries. Others access LCSH through the LC subject authority file that is freely available at LC's website or through a subscription to a bibliographic network, such as OCLC Online Computer Library Center. Starting in 2014, LC began providing free access to LCSH through print-ready, downloadable PDF files. Each year, a new edition is published on the LC website.[63] LC has adopted a process of continuous revision for its subject heading list; new and revised headings are approved regularly.

The *Sears List of Subject Headings* was first published in 1923 as the *List of Subject Headings for Small Libraries: Compiled from Lists Used in Nine Representative Small Libraries*. It was prepared by Minnie Earl Sears in response to demands for a list of subject headings that was more suitable to the needs of smaller libraries. Recognizing the need for uniformity, Sears followed the form of the LC subject headings, although she eliminated the more detailed headings and simplified some terminology. *Sears* continues to be published in print. The online version, available by subscription, is updated annually.[64]

2.2.3.2 Classification

In the early nineteenth century, classification had developed at LC from arrangement by size in the early 1800s to arrangement by 18 broad categories inspired by the scheme of human knowledge originally developed by Francis Bacon.[65] A more structured approach to classification was needed because the collection had grown significantly between its inauguration in 1802 (with 740 books) and 1812, when the new scheme was implemented and the collection had grown to more than 3,000 resources. That growth, however, was stunted in 1814 when LC was burned by the British during the War of 1812. To reestablish the library's collection, Thomas Jefferson sold Congress his library of 6,487 volumes, which was classified using 44 main subjects.

> He organized his library according to a classification scheme based on Francis Bacon's *Advancement of Learning* (1674) and very likely also on an expanded scheme by Jean [le Rond] d'Alembert in the monumental *Encyclopédie* (1751). Jefferson divided human knowledge into three major categories: history, philosophy, and fine arts, which corresponded to Bacon's "faculties of the soul," namely, memory, reason, and imagination.[66]

By the end of the century, though, it was clear that the rapidly growing collection (nearly 1.5 million volumes) needed even more detail in its classification.

In 1876 Melvil Dewey anonymously issued the first edition of his classification. He divided all knowledge into 10 main classes, with each of those divided again into 10 divisions, and each of those divided into 10 sections—giving 1,000 categories into which books could be classified. Like its predecessors, it was enumerative in that it listed specific categories one by one. In later editions he added decimals so that the 1,000 categories could be divided into 10,000, then 100,000, and so on. He also introduced the first hints of **number building** when he included tables for geographic areas and for forms of material. Notations from these tables—with their own defined meanings (today referred to as **subdivisions**)—could be appended to a base number to show a certain subject as being relevant to a particular geographic area or being presented in a particular form.

> **641.05:** Periodicals about public health
> **641:** Public health (*topic*) + **05**: Periodical (*form*)

By the end of the nineteenth century, LC had decided it had outgrown Jefferson's classification. The *Dewey Decimal Classification* (DDC) was popular and already in its fifth edition. Cutter had also developed his own scheme, called the *Expansive Classification*, which used notation that began with letters of the alphabet, expanded with second letters, and then expanded further with numbers for different aspects of a topic. LC representatives talked with Dewey to convince him to allow them to adapt his scheme but ran afoul of his intransigence. They turned to Cutter but found his scheme a bit too complicated for their liking. They did not adopt Cutter's classification directly but instead created their own scheme based upon his main class structure. This was the origin of the *Library of Congress Classification* (LCC).

The *Universal Decimal Classification* (UDC), meanwhile, was developed in 1895 by two Belgian lawyers and peace activists, Paul Otlet and Henri La Fontaine. UDC was based on the DDC (then in its fifth edition) but was, with Dewey's permission, expanded by the addition of detailed subdivisions and the use of symbols to indicate complex subjects. Why Otlet and La Fontaine were able to get Dewey's permission when LC was not is unclear, but it may have been because UDC was not at the outset intended as a library classification but rather as a means to organize documents (see section 2.2.5.1 below). UDC expanded Dewey's subdivisions to about a dozen generally applicable auxiliaries, which could be joined together as needed—an approach that we now call *faceting*. **Faceting** is an approach to categorizing in which discrete concepts or terms with similar functions or shared characteristics will be clustered together in the classification or vocabulary (e.g., keeping together all geographic locations or languages or time periods). This allows the organizer to choose a term or a concept with its own notation from an applicable facet to represent a specific aspect of the resource's subject matter. Numerous individual facets can then be combined to describe complex topics.

The use of facets is the cornerstone of a type of classification scheme developed and popularized during the twentieth century. **Faceted classification** entails the use of these small notations, which stand for subparts (i.e., facets) of a whole topic, that are strung together to create a complete multi-topic representation of a resource's subject matter. Faceted classification is appealing because it allows the classifier to express multiple aspects of an interdisciplinary subject in the same classification notation. This type of classification is also referred to as *analytico-synthetic classification*.

Figure 2.12 Photograph of Melvil Dewey. (Photograph in the Public Domain.)

The term *facet* (i.e., a component, piece, side, or aspect of a subject) was first used with this meaning by S. R. Ranganathan in the early 1930s in his *Colon Classification*, named for its use of the colon punctuation mark as a major facet indicator. As mentioned earlier, Dewey had already provided for some number building, but Ranganathan introduced a fully faceted approach by means of classification notations constructed entirely from individual facets in a prescribed sequence from the most specific to the most general. The work of Ranganathan inspired many librarians and information scientists in the second half of the twentieth century, most notably a cohort of classificationists in Great Britain collectively known as the Classification Research Group (CRG). The CRG's work led to the revision of the *Bliss Bibliographic Classification*, the creation of the *Preserved-Context Indexing System* (also known as PRECIS), and the development of several faceted classifications used in various disciplines and industries. Classification is discussed further in Chapter 13.

Since the late 1800s, classification notation has been the foundation for the call numbers used to organize books and other resources on library shelves. The arrangement of physical resources, using cutter numbers and work marks, is discussed in Appendix B.

2.2.4 Special Materials

2.2.4.1 Archives and Museums

In the United States, developments in the organization of special materials (e.g., archival collections, museum objects) have nearly all taken place since the turn of the twentieth century. European archival practice stemmed from working with public archives (e.g., land grants, laws). Archival materials were kept because of legal and other administrative value. The concept of **provenance**—the origins or ownership trail of an archival document or collection—emerged in France in about 1840, and the concept of **original order**—maintaining the sequence of records as established by the creator of those records—came from the Prussians shortly thereafter.[67]

The first articulation of principles for archives was published in 1898 by Dutch archivist Samuel Muller, Dutch lawyer and historian Johan Feith, and Dutch historian Robert Fruin, and is typically regarded as the foundation of archival theory.[68] The "Dutch manual" articulates 100 rules that would assist with "uniformity in the handling of inventories both in essentials and in details."[69] The concepts articulated in the manual include the definition of archives, the importance of arrangement (including the principle of **respect des fonds**[‡‡‡]), the organic nature of archival collections, the role of description and its relationship to arrangement, and terminological definitions. All these concepts appear in later codified international descriptive standards. The manual was quickly adapted by other European countries, first being translated into German, then Italian and French. Bulgarian, Russian, and Estonian editions appeared in the second decade of the twentieth century. It was finally published in English in 1940.[70] As Marjorie Rabe Barritt articulates in her account

---

[‡‡‡]The principle that states that archival materials created together or collected together should be kept together without mixing in records or materials from other creators or collections.

of its introduction to the United States, "the spread of ideas and theories can be subtle; they often do not wait for translation to begin to effect change."[71] The principles and concepts published in the "Dutch manual" gained traction in the United States through the endorsement of individuals willing to argue for their relevance. American archival practice, before the distribution of the English-language edition of the manual, was influenced more by historians and librarians than it was grounded in archival theory. The establishment of the Society of American Archivists in 1936, and the subsequent publication of the manual in English in 1940, would initiate a half-century search for standards and codification.[72]

As in libraries, the first archival catalogs were lists and then inventories. In early archival practice in the United States, material was collected for its artifactual value. It was often cataloged at the item level without any concern for provenance or original order. Collections were sometimes formed based on similar topics. Thus, the context in which the archival record was originally created was lost. This practice lasted in the United States through the 1930s, when the European ideas articulated in the "Dutch manual" began to influence U.S. practice. Early cataloging codes in the United States (e.g., Cutter, AACR) dealt with cataloging manuscripts, but at the item level. In the early 1980s, Steve Hensen, while working for LC, was asked to construct a cataloging code for archival materials. His work resulted in the publication of *Archives, Personal Papers, and Manuscripts* (later known as APPM), which brought library and archival traditions closer together.[73] APPM was based on ISBD and AACR2 but also included archival principles. A second edition of APPM was published in 1989 and served as the content standard for archival description for the next fifteen years.[74] APPM provided guidelines for the content of Machine-Readable Cataloging (MARC) records for the description of archival materials. A special MARC format was developed (called MARC-AMC for "archival and manuscript control"). It has since been incorporated with the other special MARC formats into the current MARC bibliographic format used for all types of materials. APPM, though, only provided guidance for MARC records and did not adequately address the needs of finding aids, the primary descriptive tool created by archivists. To that end, *Describing Archives: A Content Standard* (DACS), the descriptive standard used in the creation of finding aids and MARC records for archival collections in the United States, was first published in 2004, superseding APPM. A second edition of DACS was released in 2013. The latest editions of DACS are now found primarily online and can be accessed freely through the website of the Society of American Archivists.[75]

As in libraries and archives, museums began first with lists and later expanded to include inventories. Museum **registration** is terminology that has often been applied to the cataloging of art and artifacts. It is a system that provides an indispensable record of information associated with these objects. Museums are now joining the library and archives communities in codification of descriptive practice. The internet has spurred this action because of the demand from researchers for access to images and textual descriptions of artifacts and art. The visual resource community has developed standard means for creating surrogate records (e.g., *Cataloging Cultural Objects*). Libraries with these kinds of collections may use RDA, which can be used to describe any type of information object, or they may still use AACR2's chapters for cataloging realia and graphics, and then enter these descriptions into a MARC record.

2.2.4.2 Subject Access to Special Materials

Subject access to special materials follows the needs of the user communities. For controlled vocabularies, archivists use LCSH and the *Art & Architecture Thesaurus* (AAT), among other resources. The museum community has developed specialized lists and thesauri (often called *lexicons*). One example is Robert G. Chenhall's *Nomenclature*, originally published in 1978 and currently in its fourth edition. It is a system for classifying human-made objects, which has been adopted by thousands of museums and historical societies in the United States and Canada.[76] Museums may also use AAT.

The collective nature of archival description does not lend itself to the use of classification. Some collections of art and artifacts are classified, however. Some natural history museums classify specimens of organisms that can be identified to the genus–species level. Two other examples include natural history museums, which may still use Romer's classification of vertebrates,[77] and art collections with Christian iconographic themes that use *Iconclass*,[78] a classification scheme developed in the Netherlands.

2.2.5 Mechanization of the Information Professions

Technology first became entrenched in the activities of information organization in the 1870s when the typewriter was introduced into libraries. You may not think of typewriters as a form of technology, but this was an important step in the profession's use of machines. Typewriters were highly controversial at first because they were so noisy. Many libraries were one-room operations with the cataloger sitting at a table in the back. Patrons, who had been used to the quiet of the cataloger creating handwritten cards, found the clacking of the typewriter annoying. Some librarians also objected, finding typed cards less aesthetically pleasing than those written in **library hand**, a method of writing in which the letters were carefully formed to be completely readable (see Figure 2.13).

2.2.5.1 The Documentation Movement

The trend to mechanize bibliography began with the Documentation Movement in Europe in the 1890s. The nineteenth century brought the development of professional organizations and

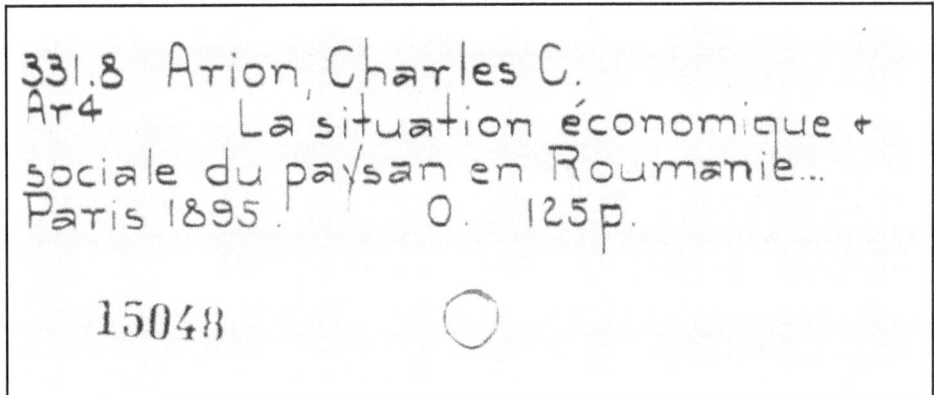

Figure 2.13 A Catalog Card Written in Library Hand.

the growth of scientific research, both of which created a dramatic increase in the number of published journals. Otlet and La Fontaine (introduced earlier in this chapter in relation to UDC) spearheaded a movement to expand bibliographic control in libraries beyond books, providing access to parts of books, journal articles, research documents, brochures, catalogs, patents, government records, archives, photographs, and newspapers. The goal of the Documentation Movement was to capture, record, and provide access to all information in all formats for the improvement of science.

A conference organized by Otlet and La Fontaine was held in Brussels in 1895, with a focus on **Universal Bibliographic Control** (UBC).[79] They wanted to create a central file that would include surrogate records for all information resources, particularly for scientific articles in all the scientific journals of the world. As UBC evolved throughout the twentieth century, it came to mean that each country of the world would be responsible for creating descriptions for its information resources and would share those records with all other countries. The magnitude of the undertaking necessitated an entirely new body of techniques, different from conventional library practice, for organization, subject analysis, bibliographic description, authority control, and annotation. This quest for new techniques of bibliographic control naturally led to a search for new technology.

The concept of documentation was transported to the United States in the 1930s, and in 1937 the American Documentation Institute was formed. In 1938, the International Federation for Documentation was established and was devoted almost exclusively to the promotion of *Universal Decimal Classification* (UDC). From its inception, UDC was not intended as a library classification but rather as a means to organize and analyze ***documents***, a term then defined to include such things as journal articles, scientific papers, patents, and the like, but not books or journals.

An important technological advance for the documentation field was the development of microphotography by Eastman Kodak in 1928. This was seen as a means of collecting, storing, and accessing vast quantities of information, and it was predicted that microfilm would supplant the conventional book. This, of course, did not happen,[§§§] but the use of microfilm for certain types of materials in libraries (e.g., dissertations, old newspapers) has long been established.

The Second World War had an impact on the mechanization of bibliographic control in two ways. First, it created an immediate scientific information explosion, as the U.S. government's imperative was to "get the bomb first." Scientific research was conducted rapidly and in secrecy, with a critical need for immediate dissemination of research results from lab to lab. This heightened the government's awareness of the need for bibliographic control and brought with it government funding to develop a mechanized process. Second, as the outcome of the war shifted in favor of the Allies, huge quantities of German scientific literature were confiscated. This material needed immediate document control in order to be useful. Microfilms were made and distributed through a committee attached to the Office of Strategic Service, a wartime intelligence agency that is the predecessor of the Central Intelligence Agency. The distribution was

---

[§§§]Speculation and rumors about the demise of the book have existed for a century, but the book is not dead yet!

under the direction of Frederick Kilgour, who later oversaw the development and expansion of OCLC. At the same time, the Central Information Division of the Office of Strategic Service was working on the subject analysis of documents using IBM punched card equipment. The war itself was the impetus for many technological advances; some of these advances could now be applied to organizing and accessing the hoards of scientific and technical literature that also were an outgrowth of the war.

In 1945, Vannevar Bush opened the way for a new era in documentation and information science with his article "As We May Think." Bush developed the idea of the *memex*, a hypothetical "device in which an individual stores all … books, records and communications, and which is mechanized so that it may be consulted with exceeding speed and flexibility."[80] Bush's memex is, in some ways, similar to Otlet's vision for what he called the "televised book" in a "radiated library." Today, their foresighted concepts are seen as precursors to or inspirations for the internet.[81] Using the medium of microfilm (in 1945, remember), Bush described in detail what has become the web-based access to information we have today. His memex concept was based on the human thought process, where items are linked together based on a variety of associations and any item can immediately lead to the access of other related information. Bush even predicted new forms of encyclopedias where information could be coded and connected to pertinent articles. A man of vision, Bush believed that science should implement the ways in which we produce, store, and consult the record of the human race.

The 1950s and 1960s saw many and varied attempts at mechanization using the technology of that time. In 1950, Calvin Mooers coined the term **information retrieval** to describe the use technology to find resources in document collections. He and other information scientists of the day, such as Ralph Shaw and Mortimer Taube, worked on developments such as the Rapid Selector, designed to provide subject access to microfilm by a method that used holes punched in the sides of the film. Another technique used a knitting-type needle to access subjects on punched cards. Taube was especially concerned with the linguistic problems of documentary analysis and retrieval.

In the 1950s people began working on automatic indexing, relying on the power of computers to perform repetitive tasks at high speed. The first such method, introduced by Hans Peter Luhn in 1958, became known as KWIC (*Key Word in Context*) indexing. In a KWIC index, titles are arranged so that each of the words in a title appears once in alphabetical order in the center of a page, with all other words to the left or right of the center word printed in the order in which they appear in the title (so that the alphabetized word is in context).

KWIC

Introduction to	**Cataloging** and Classification.
Introduction to Cataloging and	**Classification**.
	Introduction to Cataloging and Classification.

An adaptation of the KWIC method is known as KWOC (*Key Word Out of Context*), which prints the significant words in the left-hand margin instead of in the middle of the page, and the title is printed to the right or beneath the keyword.

KWOC
Cataloging   Introduction to Cataloging and Classification.
Classification   Introduction to Cataloging and Classification.
Introduction   Introduction to Cataloging and Classification.

Two additional types, both identified as *KWAC*, were used somewhat less frequently. The first, *Key Word and Context* is a combination of KWIC and KWOC, in which the significant word appears in the heading position, followed by the remainder of the title.

KWAC: Key Word and Context

Cataloging and Classification. Introduction to
Classification. Introduction to Cataloging and
Introduction to Cataloging and Classification.

The second, *Key Word Augmented in Context*, allows the indexer to augment the title with additional words to provide more meaning and to enhance access to the resource.

KWAC: Key Word Augmented in Context

Cataloging and Classification [in Libraries]. Introduction to
Classification [in Libraries]. Introduction to Cataloging and
Introduction to Cataloging and Classification [in Libraries].
Libraries. Introduction to Cataloging and Classification

In 1957, Sputnik, the first artificial satellite launched into space from Earth, pushed information needs to the forefront of the scientific community once again. There was increased interest in improving access to recorded knowledge in both the government (the National Science Foundation, the National Library of Medicine, the Library of Congress, etc.) and the private sector (IBM, General Electric, Kodak, etc.). The field of documentation evolved into the field of information science with a great deal of money made available for research and development. The 1960s saw a period of tremendous technological advances in communication and information processing. The computer became established as the means of storing massive amounts of data and providing high-speed access. In 1968, the American Documentation Institute changed its name to the American Society for Information Science (ASIS) and then changed its name again in 2000 to the American Society for Information Science & Technology (ASIS&T). In 2013, it changed its name yet again to Association for Information Science and Technology (also ASIS&T) to reflect its growing international membership. By the late 1960s, the use of machines for the retrieval of information was solidly entrenched in the information science community—a community that had developed quite separately from libraries until this point.

2.2.5.2 Library Automation

In the late 1960s, two developments changed the face of information organization forever. At LC, Henriette Avram engineered the creation of the MARC format, enabling the machine readability of bibliographic records. Building on early experiments to create machine-readable entries, a pilot project was embarked on in 1965 under the Office of Information Systems Specialists. Avram, a systems analyst who had recently joined LC, collaborated with Kay Guiles, a descriptive cataloger, and Ruth Freitag, a reference librarian, to construct an "input format that is reasonable to produce, function codes to explicitly define those elements that cannot be recognized by machine today, and programming rules to define those elements implicitly defined."[82] The work on the development of MARC in the 1960s and early 1970s resulted not only in machine-readable bibliographic data but also in records that facilitated data exchange and opened the door to what has now been more than half a century of expansion through automation and data sharing.

Around the same time, the Ohio College Association, seeking to promote library cooperation to maximize resource availability and minimize costs, brought in Ralph Parker of the University of Missouri and Frederick Kilgour of Yale University as consultants. Parker and Kilgour envisioned a new approach: a cataloging system and union catalog that leveraged emerging technologies. Kilgour went on to become the first executive director of the Ohio College Library Center (OCLC) and to oversee a startling period of growth, starting with six staff members after its first two years and expanding to over 200 staff members after its first decade. With the development of the MARC format, OCLC was able to provide cataloging information via cable and terminal to all its member libraries, which in turn were able to put their original cataloging online for the use of all other members. In 1977, another major network came into being particularly to serve research libraries—the Research Libraries Information Network, which in 2006 was absorbed into OCLC. Other bibliographic networks are operational today (e.g., SkyRiver, Auto-Graphics), but they would not be possible without the pioneering work of Avram, Kilgour, LC, and OCLC. Kilgour continued to serve as director of OCLC until 1980. Over that period, the online system of shared cataloging became fully operational and extended its membership to libraries outside of Ohio. In 1981, OCLC changed its name to OCLC Online Computer Library Center, Inc. The following three decades saw numerous projects and partnerships that underscored the basic mission of the organization, including the incorporation of technological advances when they occurred.[83] OCLC continues to expand its offerings to the larger library community. It currently offers management services, metadata services, discovery services, and resource sharing services and maintains the most substantial bibliographic network, WorldCat.[84] OCLC was also instrumental in the development of the Dublin Core metadata scheme (discussed in Chapter 9).

2.2.5.3 Integrated Library Systems

An ***integrated library system*** is a fully integrated resource management system in which primary library functions are addressed by a set of software programs organized into modules that share common databases. Its purpose is to incorporate the functionality of what would have been five or six separate databases into one integrated system. Before the first ILSs appeared on the scene in the 1970s, computers were already being used to organize information. Computers were used in the 1960s and 1970s to produce card, book, and microform catalogs. At that time, computers were not the desktop machines we think of today but were instead large mainframe systems that were run in batch mode. A quick search in the computer was not possible; jobs were sent in batches and often the results were not available until the next day. It was not until the late 1970s that minicomputers, which could provide some online access to information, began appearing in libraries.[85] In order to have online catalogs, there had to be a convergence of computing power, mass storage, low costs, software that could handle large files, and the files themselves in an electronic format (e.g., MARC).[86]

The first automated library systems were created in the 1970s. Many of these products were ***turnkey systems*** (computer systems customized to include all the hardware and software necessary for a particular function or application). Often these products were developed to manage only one specific type of function, such as circulation. Then as more vendors got into the library automation business (increasing competition), additional modules were created to expand functionality. Numerous systems failed, but by the 1980s a second generation of online catalogs began to appear with increased search capabilities.[87] In recent years, some smaller and midsized vendors have survived by focusing on specific types of libraries or by catering to specific niches.[88] A number of early systems were created as in-house products, but by the end of the twentieth century, most of those systems had been replaced by commercially developed packages. LC was one of the last holdouts before it announced in 1999 that it would replace its thirty-year-old in-house computer systems with the commercially produced Voyager system. A major reason that LC replaced its homegrown approach (which consisted of seven separate record systems) was that data in an ILS can be shared among the different modules.

In the last fifty years, there have been tremendous improvements in library automation. Although many of these developments have centered around the OPAC, others have affected the entire system. Major developments included the creation of web-accessible catalogs, the move to graphical user interfaces (GUIs), widespread implementation of client-server architecture (later to be replaced by web-based platforms), the use of industry-standard relational databases, support for Unicode to enable the use of multiple scripts and multiple languages, implementation of self-service features, personalized interfaces, and the creation of authentication mechanisms for remote users.[89]

To patrons, the OPAC is the most familiar module in a library system. Three decades ago, Charles Hildreth stated, "The online public access catalog is the first major development that brings the benefits of automation directly to the user as a means of expanded access to library collections and as a means of organizing and presenting bibliographic information for effective self-services."[90] The evolution of the OPAC is often described in terms of *generations*. The first generation of OPACs appeared in the early 1980s as crude finding lists, often based on circulation system records[91] or simple MARC records, perhaps with a circulation, serials, or acquisitions module added on.[92] The systems were designed based on what we knew: card catalogs and early online retrieval systems; thus, their searching capabilities were generally limited to authors and titles, using only left-anchored searching. The interface of first-generation OPACs was menu-based; today, they would be considered quite primitive. These early systems had little or no subject access or reference structures. They were little more than poor imitations of print catalogs. Some systems were programmed to respond to commands in which a code (e.g., *a:* for author, *t:* for title) was to be followed by an exact string of characters that would be matched against the system's internal indexes. In others, derived key searching was supported. This entailed taking parts of names and/or titles to create a search string. For example, *int,to,ca,a* could be used to search for the title *Introduction to Cataloging and Classification.***** These first-generation systems were highly intolerant of user mistakes. There was little or no browsing or keyword searching. First-generation OPACs were primarily book finding lists and worked best for known-item searching.[93]

With designers learning from the problems of the first generation, the second generation of OPACs in the late 1980s showed major improvements. This generation was marked by significantly improved user interfaces. Keyword searching and use of Boolean operators were introduced, thus increasing accessibility to other parts of catalog records. This meant that searches were no longer required to be exact left-anchored word or phrase searches; words could now be matched, even if they were in the middle of a text string. Also greatly enhancing the searching process were truncation support, browsing capabilities, use of full MARC records, interactive search refinement, and greater subject access to resources. Second-generation OPACs also provided greater manipulation of search results and provided better help systems with more informative error messages (although there is still a lot of work to be done in this area).[94]

Through the first and second generations of OPACs, the characteristics distinguishing each generation were somewhat clear. There have been, however, differences in how the profession refers to more recent developments in OPACs. Some consider older systems that are currently in use—web accessible, GUI-based OPACs—to be third-generation OPACs. Many others, thankfully, have just simply stopped referring to "generations" altogether. Catalogs are discussed further in Chapter 3; ILSs and their replacement, *library services platforms* (LSP), are discussed in Chapter 4.

2.3 Conclusion

We see here the coming together of the information science track and the library science track, which had previously developed separately. Some see a wide gulf between information science and library science, but both are interested in and working on the organization of information, as we see in the chapters that follow. And the distinctions are becoming less and less obvious as our technology and information infrastructures grow relentlessly intertwined.

****This example is from a derived search approach used in OCLC and is based on the prescribed formula for title searching of 3,2,2,1. That means the first three letters of the first non-stopword in the title, followed by the first two letters of the next word (whether stopword or not), and so on. An author/title derived search for the same book uses a 4,4 formula: joud,intr (i.e., the first four letters of the first author's entry word [Joudrey] and the first four letters of the first non-stopword of the title [*Introduction*]). Derived searching is kind of fun and efficient but seems to be going the way of the dinosaurs!

Some Important Terms in This Chapter
(Definitions Provided in the Glossary)

Analytical entry	Fixed location	Paris principles
Bibliography	Flyleaf	Pinakes
Card catalog	Full entry	Provenance
Catalog	Heading	Registration
Cataloging code	Imprint	*Respect des fonds*
Collation	Information retrieval	Shelflist
Colophon	Integrated library system	Standard citation
Cross-reference	Inventory	Stereotyping
Derivative relationship	Library hand	Subdivision
Document	Library of Alexandria	Turnkey system
Entry	Literary warrant	Universal bibliographic control
Facet	Main entry	
Faceted classification	Number building	User tasks
Faceting	Original order	

Some Important Historical Figures and Other Entities in This Chapter

Ashurbanipal	Gorman, Michael	Muller, Samuel
Avram, Henriette	Guiles, Kay	Otlet, Paul
Bodley, Thomas, Sir	Gutenberg, Johannes	Osborn, Andrew
Brown, James Duff	Hanson, James	Panizzi, Anthony
Bush, Vannevar	Hensen, Steve	Parker, Ralph
Callimachus	Hulme, Edward Wyndham	Ranganathan, S. R.
Cassiodorus	Jefferson, Thomas	Rostgaard, Frederik
Classification Research Group	Jewett, Charles Coffin	Sears, Minnie Earl
	Kilgour, Frederick	Shaw, Ralph
Cutter, Charles Ammi	La Fontaine, Henri	Taube, Mortimer
Dewey, Melvil	Lubetzky, Seymour	Trithemius, Johannes
Feith, Johan	Luhn, Hans Peter	Verona, Eva
Freitag, Ruth	Maunsell, Andrew	Whytefield, John
Fruin, Robert	Mooers, Calvin	Zenodotus
Gessner, Conrad		

Some Important Acronyms in This Chapter

AACR:	*Anglo-American Cataloging Rules*
AACR2:	*Anglo-American Cataloguing Rules, Second Edition*
AAT:	*Art & Architecture Thesaurus*
ALA:	American Library Association
APPM:	*Archives, Personal Papers, and Manuscripts*
ASIS&T:	Association for Information Science and Technology
CRG:	Classification Research Group
DACS:	*Describing Archives: A Content Standard*
DDC:	*Dewey Decimal Classification*
EAD:	Encoded Archival Description
FRAD:	*Functional Requirements for Authority Data*
FRBR:	*Functional Requirement for Bibliographic Records*
FRSAD:	*Functional Requirements for Subject Authority Data*
HTML:	Hypertext Markup Language
IFLA:	International Federation of Library Associations and Institutions
ISAD(G):	*General International Standard Archival Description*
ISBD:	*International Standard Bibliographic Description*
KWAC:	Keyword and Context *or* Keyword Augmented in Context
KWIC:	Keyword in Context
KWOC:	Keyword Out of Context
LC:	Library of Congress
LC-PCC PS:	Library of Congress-Program for Cooperative Cataloging Policy Statements
LCC:	*Library of Congress Classification*
LCSH:	*Library of Congress Subject Headings*
LCRI:	*Library of Congress Rule Interpretations*
LRM:	*IFLA Library Reference Model*
MARC:	Machine-Readable Cataloging
MARC-AMC:	MARC Format for Archival and Manuscripts Control
OCLC:	Online Computer Library Center
OPAC:	Online Public Access Catalog
RDA:	*Resource Description & Access*
UBC:	Universal Bibliographic Control
UDC:	*Universal Decimal Classification*

2.4 Discussion Questions and Exercises

- How have technological innovations impacted the development of information organization over time?
- Many features of modern information retrieval tools that we now take for granted were radical innovations when they were first introduced. Select one major development from antiquity, the Middle Ages, or the Renaissance and discuss:
    - How did it diverge from previous practice?
    - What new options did it offer for information retrieval?
    - Are there analogous features in modern information retrieval tools?
- What arguments have shaped modern cataloging codes?

2.5 Suggested Readings

Baker, Nicholson. "Discards." *New Yorker* 70, no. 7 (April 4, 1994): 64–86.

Berner, Richard C. "Historical Development of Archival Theory and Practices in the United States." *Midwestern Archivist* 7, no. 2 (1982): 103–17.

Burke, Frank G. "Archives: Organization and Description." In *World Encyclopedia of Library and Information Services*. 3rd ed., edited by Robert Wedgeworth, 63–8. Chicago: American Library Association, 1993.

Bush, Vannevar. "As We May Think." *Atlantic Monthly* 176 (July 1945): 101–8. Also available at: https://www.theatlantic.com/magazine/archive/1945/07/as-we-may-think/303881/.

Carpenter, Michael. "The Original 73 Rules of the British Museum: A Preliminary Analysis." *Cataloging & Classification Quarterly* 35, no. 1/2 (2002): 23–36.

Denton, William. "FRBR and the History of Cataloging." In *Understanding FRBR: What It Is and How It Will Affect Our Retrieval Tools*, edited by Arlene G. Taylor, 35–57. Westport, CT: Libraries Unlimited, 2007.

Dunkin, Paul S. *Cataloging U.S.A.* Chicago: American Library Association, 1969.

Fishbein, Meyer H. "Archives: Records Management and Records Appraisal." In *World Encyclopedia of Library and Information Services*. 3rd ed., edited by Robert Wedgeworth, 60–3. Chicago: American Library Association, 1993.

Harris, Michael H. *History of Libraries in the Western World*. 4th ed. Lanham, MD: Scarecrow, 1999.

Hopkins, Judith. "The 1791 French Cataloging Code and the Origins of the Card Catalog." *Libraries & Culture* 27, no. 4 (Fall 1992): 378–404.

Humbert, de Romans. *Regulations for the Operation of a Medieval Library*. St. Paul: Associates of the James Ford Bell Library, University of Minnesota, 1980.

Jackson, Sidney L. *Libraries and Librarianship in the West: A Brief History*. New York: McGraw-Hill, 1974.

Joudrey, Daniel N., Arlene G. Taylor, and David P. Miller. *Introduction to Cataloging and Classification*. 11th ed. Santa Barbara, CA: Libraries Unlimited, 2015.

Lancaster, F. W. "Whither Libraries? or Wither Libraries." *College & Research Libraries* 39, no. 5 (September 1978): 345–57.

Osborn, Andrew D. "The Crisis in Cataloging." *Library Quarterly* 11, no. 4 (October 1941): 393–411.

Reynolds, Dennis. *Library Automation: Issues and Applications*. New York: Bowker, 1985.

Russell, Beth M. "Hidden Wisdom and Unseen Treasure: Revisiting Cataloging in Medieval Libraries." *Cataloging & Classification Quarterly* 26, no. 3 (1998): 21–30.

Smalley, Joseph. "The French Cataloging Code of 1791: A Translation." *Library Quarterly* 61, no. 1 (January 1991): 1–14.

Stauffer, Suzanne M., ed. *Libraries, Archives, and Museums: An Introduction to Cultural Heritage Institutions Through the Ages*. Lanham, MD: Rowman & Littlefield, 2021.

Stoll, Clifford. *Silicon Snake Oil: Second Thoughts on the Information Highway*. New York: Doubleday, 1995.

Strout, Ruth French. "The Development of the Catalog and Cataloging Codes." *Library Quarterly* 26 (October 1956): 254–75.

Taylor, Arlene G. "Cataloguing." In *World Encyclopedia of Library and Information Services*. 3rd ed., edited by Robert Wedgeworth, 177–81. Chicago: American Library Association, 1993.

Witty, Francis J. "The Beginnings of Indexing and Abstracting: Some Notes Towards a History of Indexing and Abstracting in Antiquity and the Middle Ages." *The Indexer* 8 (1973): 193–8.

2.6 Notes

All URLs accessed April 2025.

1. For example, see the special 2002, four-issue series on historical aspects of cataloging and classification in *Cataloging & Classification Quarterly*, featuring overviews of cataloging in Africa, Argentina, Central America, Chile, China, Germany, Iran, Japan, and Mexico. For a deeper dive, search for monographs about regions of interest. For example, for a history of Chinese bibliography or Chinese cataloging, you might consult Hur-Li Lee's *Intellectual Activism in Knowledge Organization: A Hermeneutic Study of the Seven Epitomes* (Taipei: Taiwan National University, 2016) or Hong Gao's *A History of Cataloging Perspectives* (Beijing: Beijing Library Press, 2008).
2. Lionel Casson, *Libraries in the Ancient World* (New Haven, CT: Yale University Press, 2001), 4.
3. Michael H. Harris, *History of Libraries in the Western World*, 4th ed. (Lanham, MD: Scarecrow, 1999), 19–20.
4. Casson, 31.
5. Lauren Young, "The Fierce, Forgotten Library Wars of the Ancient World," *Atlas Obscura*, August 26, 2016, https://www.atlasobscura.com/articles/the-fierce-forgotten-library-wars-of-the-ancient-world.
6. Casson, 35.
7. Casson, 36.
8. Casson, 37.
9. Casson, 39.
10. Rudolf Blum, *Kallimachos: The Alexandrian Library and the Origins of Bibliography* (Madison: University of Wisconsin Press, 1991), 2.
11. Blum, 151.
12. Ruth French Strout, "The Development of the Catalog and Cataloging Codes," *Library Quarterly* 26, no. 4 (1956): 257.
13. Casson, 80.
14. Casson, 81–2.
15. Martin Davies, "Medieval Libraries," in *International Dictionary of Library Histories*, ed. David Stam (Chicago: Fitzroy Dearborn Publishers, 2001), 104–5.

16. Alain Besson, *Medieval Classification and Cataloguing: Classification Practices and Cataloging Methods in France from the 12th to 15th Centuries* (Biggleswade, UK: Clover Publications, 1980), 38.
17. Strout, 260.
18. Hugo Kunoff, *The Foundations of the German Academic Library* (Chicago: American Library Association, 1982), 10.
19. Strout, 262.
20. Montague Rhodes James, *The Ancient Libraries of Canterbury and Dover* (Cambridge: Cambridge University Press, 1903), lx.
21. Strout, 262.
22. M. Sophia Newman, "So, Gutenberg Didn't Actually Invent Printing as We Know It," *Literary Hub*, July 19, 2019, https://lithub.com/so-gutenberg-didnt-actually-invent-the-printing-press/.
23. Paul Gray, "Johann Gutenberg," *Time* 154, no. 27 (1999): 108.
24. Newman.
25. Gray, 108.
26. Strout, 262.
27. Strout, 263–4.
28. Strout, 264.
29. "History of the Bodleian," Bodleian Libraries, University of Oxford, https://visit.bodleian.ox.ac.uk/plan-your-visit/history-bodleian.
30. Judith Hopkins, "The 1791 French Cataloging Code and the Origins of the Card Catalog," *Libraries and Culture* 27, no. 4 (Fall 1992): 379–83.
31. George Watson Cole, "An Early French 'General Catalog,'" *Library Journal* 25, no. 7 (July 1900): 330.
32. Mary Ellen Quinn, "Catalog Card," in *Historical Dictionary of Librarianship* (Lanham, MD: Rowman & Littlefield, 2014), 76.
33. Österreichische Nationalbibliothek, "1780: The Oldest Card Catalogue," https://www.onb.ac.at/en/more/about-us/timeline/1780-the-oldest-card-catalogue.
34. Joseph Smalley, "The French Cataloging Code of 1791: A Translation," *Library Quarterly* 61, no. 1 (January 1991): 5.
35. Smalley, 1–14.
36. Strout, 268.
37. Dorothy May Norris, *A History of Cataloguing and Cataloguing Methods, 1100–1850* (London: Grafton, 1939), 206.
38. Louis Fagan, *The Life of Sir Anthony Panizzi*, 2nd ed., reprint (New York: Burt Franklin, 1970), 134. (Originally published 1880.)
39. Strout, 268.
40. British Museum, Department of Printed Books, "Rules for the Compilation of the Catalogue," in *Catalogue of Printed Books in the British Museum*, ed. Anthony Panizzi, vol. 1 (London: British Museum, 1841), [v]–ix.
41. Harvard College Library, *Catalogus Librorum Bibliothecae Collegij Harvardini: quod est Cantabrigiae in Nova Anglia* (Boston, MA: B. Green), 1723–36, https://iiif.lib.harvard.edu/manifests/view/drs:42282481$5i.
42. Jim Ranz, *The Printed Book Catalogue in American Libraries, 1723–1900* (Chicago: American Library Association, 1964).
43. Personal communication between former author Arlene G. Taylor and Michael Carpenter. For further information about the drafts of Panizzi's rules, see Michael Carpenter, "The Original 73 Rules of the British Museum: A Preliminary Analysis," *Cataloging & Classification Quarterly* 35, no. 1/2 (2002): 23–36.

44. Charles Coffin Jewett, *On the Construction of Catalogues of Libraries, and Their Publication by Means of Separate, Stereotyped Titles*, 2nd ed. (Washington, DC: Smithsonian Institution, 1853), 18.
45. Elaine Svenonius, *The Intellectual Foundation of Information Organization* (Cambridge, MA: MIT Press, 2000), 79.
46. Charles A. Cutter, *Rules for a Printed Dictionary Catalogue* (Washington, DC: Government Printing Office, 1876). [The title changed to the more commonly known title, *Rules for a Dictionary Catalogue* after the first edition.]
47. Charles A. Cutter, *Rules for a Dictionary Catalog*, 4th ed. (Washington, DC: Government Printing Office, 1904; reprint, London: Library Association, 1962), 12. [Note that there is another change in the title: the spelling of *catalog*.]
48. *Catalog Rules: Author and Title Entries*, compiled by committees of the American Library Association and the (British) Library Association, American ed. (Chicago: ALA, 1908), verso of title page.
49. Michael Gorman, "From Card Catalogues to WebPACs: Celebrating Cataloguing in the 20th Century," *Proceedings of the Bicentennial Conference on Bibliographic Control for the New Millennium: Confronting the Challenges of Networked Resources and the Web, Washington, D.C., November 15–17, 2000*, sponsored by the Library of Congress Cataloging Directorate; edited by Ann M. Sandberg-Fox (Washington, DC: Library of Congress, Cataloging Distribution Service, 2001), https://www.loc.gov/catdir/bibcontrol/gorman_paper.html.
50. Gorman, https://www.loc.gov/catdir/bibcontrol/gorman_paper.html.
51. *A.L.A. Catalog Rules: Author and Title Entries*, prepared by the Catalog Code Revision Committee of the American Library Association with the collaboration of a Committee of the (British) Library Association, Preliminary American 2nd ed. (Chicago: ALA, 1941).
52. Andrew Osborn, "The Crisis in Cataloging," *Library Quarterly* 11, no. 4 (October 1941): 393–411.
53. Seymour Lubetzky, *Cataloging Rules and Principles: A Critique of the A.L.A. Rules for Entry and a Proposed Design for their Revision* (Washington, DC: Library of Congress, 1953).
54. International Conference on Cataloguing Principles, Paris, 9th–18th October, 1961, *Report* (London: International Federation of Library Associations, 1963), 91–96.
55. *Anglo-American Cataloguing Rules, Second Edition, 2002 Revision* (AACR2R), prepared under the direction of the Joint Steering Committee for Revision of AACR (Ottawa: Canadian Library Association; Chicago: American Library Association, 2002, loose-leaf, with updates), D-2.
56. Doris Hargrett Clack, ed., *The Making of a Code: The Issues Underlying AACR2* (Chicago: American Library Association), 1980.
57. Michael Gorman, "AACR2: Main Themes," in *The Making of a Code: The Issues Underlying AACR2*, ed. Doris Hargrett Clack (Chicago: American Library Association, 1980), 46.
58. Richard P. Smiraglia, "Authority Control and the Extent of Derivative Bibliographic Relationships" (PhD diss., University of Chicago, 1992).
59. *Library of Congress Rule Interpretations*, 2nd ed. (Washington, DC: Cataloging Distribution Service, Library of Congress, 1990–2010).
60. Cutter, *Rules for a Dictionary Catalog*, 66–79.
61. American Library Association, *List of Subject Headings for Use in Dictionary Catalogs*, 2nd ed., rev. (Boston: Library Bureau, 1898), vi.
62. *Classification Web Plus* (Washington, DC: Library of Congress, Cataloging Distribution Service), https://classweb.org/. [requires ID and password]
63. "Library of Congress Subject Headings PDF Files," Library of Congress, https://www.loc.gov/aba/publications/FreeLCSH/freelcsh.html.

64. "Sears List of Subject Headings," Grey House Publishing, https://searslistofsubjectheadings.com/.
65. Francis Bacon, *The Advancement of Learning* (Oxford: Clarendon, Press, 2000).
66. Endrina Tay, "Jefferson, Thomas and Books," *Encyclopedia Virginia*, December 07, 2020, https://encyclopediavirginia.org/entries/jefferson-thomas-and-books/.
67. Ernst Posner, "Some Aspects of Archival Development since the French Revolution," *American Archivist* 3, no. 2 (April 1940): 159–72.
68. Samuel Muller, Johan A. Feith, and Robert Fruin, *Handleiding voor het Ordenen en Beschrijven van Archieven* (Groningen: Erven B. van der Kamp, 1898).
69. Samuel Muller, Johan A. Feith, and Robert Fruin, *Manual for the Arrangement and Description of Archives*, translation of the second edition by Arthur H. Leavitt; with new introductions by Peter Horsman [and others] (Chicago: Society of American Archivists, 2003), 9.
70. Samuel Muller, Johan A. Feith, and Robert Fruin, *Manual for the Arrangement and Description of Archives*, drawn up by the Netherlands Association of Archivists (New York: H. W. Wilson, 1940).
71. Marjorie Rabe Barritt, "Coming to America: Dutch *Archivistiek* and American Archival Practice," *Archival Issues* 18, no. 1 (1993). Reprinted in Muller, Feith, and Fruin, *Manual* (2003), xxxvi.
72. Barritt, l.
73. Steven L. Hensen, *Archives, Personal Papers, and Manuscripts: A Cataloging Manual for Archival Repositories, Historical Societies, and Manuscript Libraries* (Washington, DC: Cataloging Distribution Service, 1983).
74. Steven L. Hensen, *Archives, Personal Papers, and Manuscripts: A Cataloging Manual for Archival Repositories, Historical Societies, and Manuscript Libraries*, 2nd ed. (Chicago: Society of American Archivists, 1989).
75. *Describing Archives: A Content Standard*, Society for American Archivists, https://www2.archivists.org/groups/technical-subcommittee-on-describing-archives-a-content-standard-dacs/describing-archives-a-content-standard-dacs-second-.
76. Paul Bourcier, Heather Dunn, and the Nomenclature Task Force, *Nomenclature 4.0 for Museum Cataloging: Robert G. Chenhall's System for Classifying Cultural Objects* (Lanham, MD: Rowman & Littlefield/AASLH, 2015), https://page.nomenclature.info/apropos-about.app?lang=en.
77. Alfred Sherwood Romer, *Vertebrate Paleontology*, 3rd ed. (Chicago: University of Chicago Press, 1966).
78. Netherlands Institute for Art History, *Iconclass* (The Hague, RKD, 2012), https://iconclass.org/.
79. W. Boyd Rayward, "The Origins of Information Science and the International Institute of Bibliography/International Federation for Information and Documentation (FID)," *Journal of the American Society for Information Science* 48, no. 4 (1997): 289–300.
80. Vannevar Bush, "As We May Think," *Atlantic Monthly* 176 (July 1945): 101–8. Also available at: https://www.theatlantic.com/magazine/archive/1945/07/as-we-may-think/303881/.
81. For a quick and fun overview of Otlet's idea, originally discussed in his *Traité de Documentation: Le Livre Sur le Livre, Théorie et Pratique* (Brussels: Editiones Mundaneum, 1934), see the video clip, "Paul Otlet, Visioning a Web in 1934," on YouTube, https://www.youtube.com/watch?v=hSyfZkVgasI. The clip is from the documentary by Françoise Levie and produced by Sofidoc Productions, *The Man Who Wanted to Classify the World* (New York: Filmakers Library, 2004).
82. Henriette Avram, "Defining the Fields of Data for the LC Machine-Readable Bibliographic Records," as quoted in Karen M. Spicher, "The Development of the MARC Format," *Cataloging & Classification Quarterly* 21, no. 3/4 (1996): 81.
83. Donna Rosenheck, "OCLC: From an Historical Perspective," *The Katharine Sharp Review*, no. 4 (1997), https://www.ideals.illinois.edu/handle/2142/78252.
84. "WorldCat," OCLC, http://www.oclc.org/en/worldcat.html.
85. Lucy A. Tedd, "OPACs through the Ages," *Library Review* 43, no. 4 (1994): 27–37.

86. Larry Milsap, "A History of the Online Catalog in North America," in *Technical Services Management, 1965-1990: A Quarter Century of Change, A Look to the Future: A Festschrift for Kathryn Luther Henderson*, eds. Linda C. Smith and Ruth C. Carter (Binghamton, NY: Haworth, 1996), 79.
87. Milsap, 85–6.
88. Marshall Breeding, "Power Plays: Library Systems Report 2016," *American Libraries* 47, no. 5 (May 2016): 36.
89. John Akeroyd and Andrew Cox, "Integrated Library Management Systems: Overview," *Vine*, no. 115 (2000): 3–10.
90. Charles R. Hildreth, "Online Catalog Design Models: Are We Moving in the Right Direction? A Report Submitted to the Council on Library Resources August, 1995," https://web.archive.org/web/20150923010236/http://myweb.cwpost.liu.edu/childret/clr-opac.html.
91. Akeroyd and Cox, 3.
92. Mary K. Bolin, "Catalog Design, Catalog Maintenance, Catalog Governance," *Library Collections, Acquisitions, & Technical Services* 24 (2000): 53–63.
93. Tedd, 28.
94. Hildreth, "Online Catalog Design Models."

Chapter 3

Retrieval Tools

3.1 The Need for Retrieval Tools

Retrieval tools are systems created for discovering information. They are designed to help users find, identify, select, obtain, and explore information resources of all types. They assist users by retrieving information directly (e.g., through a web search) or through relevant documents that are part of organized collections (e.g., a catalog search). At the time of this writing, retrieval tools typically contain records that act as surrogates for resources. That is, each ***surrogate record*** (also called a *description* or *metadata*) provides enough information so that it can serve as a short representation for a resource. The surrogates facilitate access to individual resources in a collection by providing metadata such as creator, title, subject, location information, etc. Currently, the surrogate record remains the primary unit of description in most libraries, archives, and other cultural heritage institutions, and, thus, is a focus of this chapter.* Surrogate records are arranged and retrieved in retrieval tools through the use of ***access points.*** An access point can be a name, title, or subject chosen by an indexer, archivist, or cataloger. In online systems, keyword searching of every word (that is not a stopword) is another way of retrieving surrogate records.

Retrieval tools are building blocks in the efforts to organize as much of the world's recorded information as possible. A dream of being able to provide access to all recorded information has existed since the 1890s when Paul Otlet and Henri La Fontaine organized a conference to create Universal Bibliographic Control (UBC). In the twentieth century, the efforts of the International Federation of Library Associations and Institutions (IFLA), combined with the ideals of UBC, led to the development of numerous initiatives aimed at the sharing of bibliographic data on an international level. The many retrieval tools that have been developed because of Otlet and La Fontaine's dream have brought us closer to UBC.

The following retrieval tools are discussed in this chapter:

- bibliographies
- catalogs
- finding aids
- registers
- search engines
- directories
- indexes

---

*Surrogate records, however, are not the only way to retrieve information. As Semantic Web technologies advance, the emphasis on the surrogate record as a unit of description may wane. In some instances, creating individual metadata statements—separately linked to a resource as a form of identification and description—may suffice.

Databases and bibliographic networks have distinct roles in housing retrieval tools. They are discussed in the next chapter.

3.2 Types of Retrieval Tools

3.2.1 Bibliographies

Fundamentally, **bibliographies** are lists of resources. They are essential to scholars and to those involved professionally with books and other sources of information (e.g., collectors, dealers, librarians), and they are also useful resources for serious readers. Bibliographies bring together lists of sources based on subject matter, creator, time period, and other facets (see the more detailed list below). Some bibliographies include **annotations**, that is, brief reviews indicating the subject matter and/or commenting on the usefulness of the information resource; these are called **annotated bibliographies**.

Bibliographies can be attached to a scholarly work and consist of the information resources that were consulted by the author of the work, or they can be separate entities—works in their own right. Each resource represented in the list has a short description referred to as a **citation** or *bibliographic entry* (not to be confused with an *annotation*). A citation typically includes the following components.

For a book or another whole entity:	For a part of a work (e.g., a journal article):
Creator	Creator
Title	Title
Edition/Version	Title of the larger containing work
Publication information	Volume/Issue (if applicable)
Publication date	Publication date
Page numbers or other part designation	Page numbers or other part designation

Some citations also include physical characteristics, series, dates accessed, duration, revision information, and a Uniform Resource Locator (URL) or a Digital Object Identifier (DOI) for quick and easy access.

In a bibliography, each citation usually appears in only one place, most often under the last name of the creator of the work (or under the last name of the first creator listed if there is more than one). This is an example of a retrieval tool that generally provides only one access point. In a bibliography that is arranged only by creators' names, other attributes such as titles, the names of other contributors, and subjects are not access points. For example, if a user only knows the fourth-named author of a book, the resource may not be easily found in a printed bibliography.

Citations may be constructed according to various styles, one of which is chosen by the creator of the bibliography or by a publisher (for bibliographies attached to published scholarly works). Examples of some style manuals and a citation from each are provided below:

- **APA (American Psychological Association)**[1]

  Mitchell, T. R., & Larson, J. R., Jr. (1987). *People in organizations: An introduction to organizational behavior* (3rd ed.). McGraw-Hill.

- **Chicago Manual of Style**[2]

  Mitchell, Terence R., and James R. Larson, Jr. *People in Organizations: An Introduction to Organizational Behavior.* 3rd ed. New York: McGraw-Hill, 1987.

- **MLA (Modern Language Association)**[3]

  Mitchell, Terence R., and James R. Larson, Jr. *People in Organizations: An Introduction to Organizational Behavior.* 3rd ed., McGraw-Hill, 1987.

- **Scientific Style and Format (*The CSE Manual*)**[4]

  Mitchell TR, Larson JR Jr. People in organizations: an introduction to organizational behavior. 3rd ed. McGraw-Hill; 1987.

- **Turabian**[5]

  Mitchell, Terence R., and James R. Larson, Jr. *People in Organizations: An Introduction to Organizational Behavior.* 3rd ed. New York: McGraw-Hill, 1987.

- **Vancouver Style (*Citing Medicine*)**[6]

  Mitchell, TR, Larson, JR Jr. People in organizations: an introduction to organizational behavior. 3rd ed. New York (NY): McGraw-Hill; 1987. 602 p.

These examples are for a book, but each style manual provides guidelines for citing all types of resources, including journal articles, theses and dissertations, and web resources, to name a few. Some publishers use their own in-house style manuals; authors submitting works to those publishers may be required to reformat their citations to meet the house style.

Each bibliography has a specific focus or arrangement. The most common include the following:

Focus	Purpose	Example
Subject	Gathers resources about a particular topic.	*A Bibliography of Female Economic Thought Up to 1940*
Creator	Gathers some or all works of a creator (sometimes including sources about the creator).	*A Bibliography of Jane Austen*
Language	Gathers resources in one or more languages.	*An Extensive Bibliography of Studies in English, German, and French on Turkish Foreign Policy, 1923–1997*
Period	Gathers resources published in a specific era.	*Russian and Soviet Education 1731–1989*

Focus	Purpose	Example
Locale	Gathers resources created in a specific location or by a particular institution.	*Area Bibliography of China*
Publisher	Gathers the products of a publisher.	*The Stinehour Press: Work of the First Fifty Years*
Form	Gathers resources in a certain form (e.g., videocassettes, electronic resources, poetry, biographies).	*An Annotated Bibliography of the 16th century Italian Plays in Suzzallo Library, the University of Washington, Seattle*

Two or more of these foci may be combined in bibliographies. The example above used to illustrate *language* is a combination of language, subject, and period.

There is a special kind of bibliography found in libraries that is truly meant to be a retrieval tool. They were for many years called *pathfinders*, but now they are usually referred to as **research guides** (sometimes as *library guides*, *libguides*, or *subject guides*). These tools are subject bibliographies with a special function in the library world. Although most bibliographies do not indicate whether an individual institution owns a specific resource, research guides focus on the resources in a defined subject area available in a particular setting. In addition to the list of relevant resources, the guide may also include a list of locally accessible databases to search, specific instructions on how to search the local catalog, and a list of specific reference sources related to the subject area. For example, the guide may provide a list of relevant subject headings that may be used in the local catalog. Subject librarians have created these tools for decades. Originally pathfinders were printed documents available only in the library, but now these guides are primarily found on a library's website.[†] In recent years, software products have been developed for the creation and management of library research guides, ranging from proprietary software products to open source software. Another option is to adapt other web tools, such as wikis or blogs, to meet the purpose as they are relatively inexpensive and easy to implement.

3.2.2 Catalogs

A *catalog* is a retrieval tool that contains an organized compilation of bibliographic metadata that represents the holdings of a particular collection, an institution, or a group of institutions. Although catalogs are most frequently associated with libraries, museums and archives might also have catalogs. Catalogs provide access to information about individual items in a collection. Each resource is represented by a description that is somewhat longer than an entry in a bibliography. The descriptions are assigned one or more access points. As mentioned earlier, an access point can be almost any word in a record when keyword searching is used; however, the term *access point* is usually applied to the names, titles, and subjects that are listed on the record separately from the description. An access point is constructed in a certain order (e.g., surname followed by forename

---

[†]For an example of a research guide, please look at https://libguides.library.albany.edu/latinx.

and middle initial), and is usually under authority control. **Authority control** is the process of bringing together all the forms of name that apply to a single entity; gathering all the variant titles that apply to a single work; and relating synonyms, broader terms, and narrower terms to a particular subject heading. The descriptions and access points in a catalog are constructed according to a content standard designed by a particular community (e.g., *RDA: Resource Description & Access* for libraries). Several different standards for description and access are discussed in more detail in Chapter 9.

3.2.2.1 Functions of Catalogs

Catalogs have traditionally served two main user groups: the patrons and the staff of a library. The employees of a library (or another information institution) interact with resources on a daily basis and retrieve information about those resources (i.e., metadata) in order to work with the collection. For example, the catalog is used by collection development librarians to see what the library does and does not own before selecting new materials; another such use is by an employee of a museum who is looking for objects to place in a new exhibit. The most well-known use of the catalog, though, is by the patrons of the institution who wish to borrow materials or make use of them on-site. If such users have a known resource in mind, they may search for it in the catalog by creator or title (this is called ***known-item searching***). Users might also try searching by keyword if they only remember certain words of the title or part of a name. If users do not know of a particular resource but are searching for something on a particular topic, they may use a subject heading search, a subject keyword search, or a general keyword search (which is quite often the default search in the catalog's interface). In online catalogs, keyword searches are often appropriate for helping a person find a record that looks like it might be on the user's topic. Once a potentially useful record is found, the user may identify authority-controlled subject headings or a classification notation for their topics of interest. Then the user may conduct a search in the catalog, usually by clicking on hyperlinks in the record, for the subject headings or the classification notation. Alternatively, one may go to the location of the classification notation in the stacks to browse for other pertinent works shelved nearby.

A number of attempts have been made through the years to identify the purposes of catalogs. In 1876, as part of his cataloging rules, Charles A. Cutter published his "objects" (i.e., objectives) of a catalog, which are presented in Figure 3.1.[7] The first object, the finding function, says that a catalog should help a user to retrieve a resource if one of its key access points is known (if the resource is part of the collection). The second object, the gathering function, states that a catalog should be able to display *all* resources in the collection by a creator, on a specific subject, or in a particular genre or literary form. The third object, the selecting function, is to help users to choose the resource that they need based on bibliographic attributes (e.g., version, language, format, date) or the nature of the content (e.g., genre, subject matter). Cutter was speaking only of library catalogs, but if these objectives were broadened to archives, museums, and other collecting institutions, they would still represent what catalogs and other retrieval tools are supposed to do today.

> **Objects**
> 1. To enable a person to find a book of which either
>   - (A) the author
>   - (B) the title   } is known.
>   - (C) the subject
> 2. To show what the library has
>   - (D) by a given author
>   - (E) on a given subject
>   - (F) in a given kind of literature.
> 3. To assist in the choice of a book
>   - (G) as to its edition (bibliographically)
>   - (H) as to its character (literary or topical).

Figure 3.1 Cutter's Objects of the Catalog.

Seymour Lubetzky worked in the mid-twentieth century to simplify cataloging rules, positing that the cataloging code should be reconstructed "in accordance with deliberately adopted objectives ... and well considered principles."[8] He then stated that:

> The first objective is to enable the user of the catalog to determine readily whether or not the library has the book he wants. ... The second objective is to reveal to the user of the catalog, under one form of the author's name, what works the library has by a given author and what editions or translations of a given work.[9]

Lubetzky's work was the basis for the Paris Principles adopted in 1961 at the International Conference on Cataloguing Principles in Paris. The second principle, "Functions of the Catalogue," stated that the catalog should be an efficient instrument for ascertaining

> 2.1 whether the library contains a particular book specified by
>   (a) its author and title, *or*
>   (b) if the author is not named in the book, its title alone, *or*
>   (c) if author and title are inappropriate or insufficient for identification, a suitable substitute for the title; and
>
> 2.2 (a) which works by a particular author *and*
>   (b) which editions of a particular work are in the library.[10]

In 1998, the International Federation of Library Associations and Institutions (IFLA) published *Functional Requirements for Bibliographic Records* (FRBR), which identified four generic user tasks that the bibliographic record is intended to support. These four tasks were built on the work of Cutter, Lubetzky, and the Paris Principles, and essentially represent four main functions of a catalog:

- to *find* entities that correspond to a user's search criteria
- to *identify* entities (e.g., persons, works, subjects)

- to *select* resources appropriate to the user's needs
- to *obtain* access to the resources described[11]

The fourth user task in FRBR is an addition to the functions identified by Cutter, but it was recognized by several writers in the late twentieth century that a catalog differs from certain other retrieval tools in that it facilitates physically locating the information resources that are listed in the catalog.[12] In 2017 a fifth user task was added to the *IFLA Library Reference Model* (LRM)—a document that harmonizes FRBR and two other functional-requirements models established by IFLA. The fifth task is to *explore* resources based on the relationships identified in the catalog.[13]

Another important function of catalogs has traditionally been to act as an inventory of the collection—that is, to provide a record of what is owned. Often a *shelflist* has been used to accomplish this purpose. A shelflist includes one copy of every record in a catalog arranged in the order in which the information resources, objects, and so forth, are arranged on the shelves. So, for example, one could use the shelflist in the process known as *shelf reading* to determine whether resources from the collection were misshelved. Originally, shelflists were literally in the order of items on the shelf, starting a new sequence with each change in format, collection location, or size. Later, shelflists often were arranged by classification notation regardless of format or other categorization. This is the way the concept works in online catalogs. The purpose of serving as an inventory is still there, but the mental image of a shelflist arranged as it is on the shelf is lost.

A *union catalog* is a variation of the concept that a catalog represents just the holdings of one institution. A union catalog represents the holdings of more than one institution or collection. For example, a union catalog can show the resources held by any member of a large regional consortium of libraries, with location information showing which resources are housed in which of the cooperating institutions. The ultimate union catalog is the one maintained by the largest bibliographic network, OCLC Online Computer Library Center, where each information resource is represented by a bibliographic record and associated with that record is a code for each OCLC member library that has cataloged the resource through the network or has asked that its code be added to the record because it holds that resource.

3.2.2.2 Forms of Catalogs

Catalogs can appear in different forms and can have different arrangements. The following formats are discussed in this section:

- book catalogs
- card catalogs
- microform catalogs
- online catalogs

3.2.2.2.1 Book Catalogs

Book catalogs were originally just handwritten lists. After the widespread adoption of printing with movable type, book catalogs were printed, but not always in a discernible order. Eventually, entries were printed in alphabetical or classified order, but book catalogs were very expensive to produce and were, therefore, not updated often. By the early 1900s, book catalogs were almost completely replaced with card catalogs that could be updated as soon as the cards could be filed and were relatively inexpensive to create and maintain. Book catalogs had a brief renaissance in the 1960s and 1970s when (1) computers made them easier and less expensive to produce, (2) large card catalogs became unwieldy, and (3) rapid growth of new libraries and new branches made it desirable to have multiple copies of catalogs. But to update a book catalog, supplements were usually produced, resulting in multiple searches across several documents for a single inquiry. In addition, it was usually three to six months before supplements were produced, meaning that new materials were not represented in the catalog in the interim.

Online catalogs have replaced both book and card catalogs in most technologically advanced and economically advantaged countries, but book catalogs are still used in some cases for rare materials, catalogs of exhibits, artists' works, and so forth. Book catalogs provide a way to make the contents of special collections known to users in many locations. For example, book catalogs of historical societies are popular acquisitions by collectors of genealogical materials. This use, though, may be replaced by the availability of such catalogs online. Book catalogs also still exist in some libraries and archives as the only retrieval tool available to access older materials, because some institutions have chosen not to convert their metadata for rarely used resources into machine-readable form for the online catalog.

An advantage of book catalogs over online catalogs once was that book catalogs are compact and portable; they can be consulted anywhere they can be carried. However, with smartphones and laptop computers, online catalogs are now accessible from almost anywhere. One advantage of book catalogs, though, is that glancing over a page of book catalog entries is relatively fast, and some people prefer this to paging through screen after screen of online responses. Figure 3.2 is an illustration of a book catalog.

3.2.2.2.2 Card Catalogs

In a *card catalog*, each bibliographic description is prepared on a standard 7.5 × 12.5 cm card (roughly 3 × 5 in.) and interfiled into drawers full of cards in specially designed cabinets. The dimensions of the cards were not always standard; in the early days of card catalogs, different sizes were in use (3 × 5 in., 1 1/2 × 5 in., 4 × 6 in., etc.). Card catalogs were popularized in the United States by Library of Congress (LC) cards, first made available for sale in 1901, and by H. W. Wilson cards, which began production in 1938 in response to the needs of small libraries. (Both have now ceased card production.)

Technological advances encouraged further use of the card catalog. The descriptions on cards were at first hand-written, using a standardized type of handwriting developed by Melvil Dewey in the 1870s (see an example of *library hand* in Figure 2.13 on page 83). Later, typewriters, one of the great technological innovations in libraries at the turn of the century, made handwritten cards unnecessary. Later, offset printing was used by LC for its cards. Then photocopying allowed the local creation of whole card sets from one master card. Finally, the advent of computer printing made it possible to have customized cards made either locally or at a distant facility. When created at a distance, the cards were often shipped pre-alphabetized and ready to file. Figure 3.3 contains an example of a catalog card.

Due to the influence of LC cards, card catalogs and the order of the information on cards were standardized in libraries for many decades. Patrons could go from library to library with confidence that they would be able to use an unfamiliar catalog with as much ease as they did their local one. But that is no longer the case as card catalogs have mostly disappeared in many economically advantaged countries, where online catalogs are now more common.

Puppyville Free Library
Dictionary Catalog

HV9644 .H8 1887	**Jottings from jail** : notes and papers on prison matters / by the Rev. J.W. Horsley. – London : T.F. Unwin, 1887. – viii, 259 pages ; 19 cm
PQ2311 .J73 A22 1983	**Joubert, Joseph, 1754-1824.** The notebooks of Joseph Joubert : a selection / edited and translated by Paul Auster ; with an afterword by Maurice Blanchot. – San Francisco : North Point Press, 1983. – x, 181 pages ; 23 cm. – Translation of: Les carnets de Joseph Joubert.
Z693 .W94 2015	**Joudrey, Daniel N.** Introduction to cataloging and classification / Daniel N. Joudrey, Arlene G. Taylor, and David P. Miller. – Eleventh edition. – Santa Barbara, California : Libraries Unlimited, 2015. – xxv, 1048 pages : illustrations ; 26 cm. – Library and information science text series. – Includes bibliographical references (pages 1001-1022) and index.
Z666.5 .T39 2009	The organization of information / Arlene G. Taylor and Daniel N. Joudrey. – Third edition. – Westport, Conn. : Libraries Unlimited, 2009. – xxvi, 512 pages : illustrations ; 26 cm. – Library and information science text series. – Includes bibliographical references (pages 479-498) and index.
Z666.5 .T39 2018	The organization of information / Daniel N. Joudrey and Arlene G. Taylor ; with the assistance of Katherine M. Wisser. – Fourth edition. – Santa Barbara, California : Libraries Unlimited, 2018. – xxi, 722 pages : illustrations ; 27 cm. – Library and information science text series. – Includes bibliographical references and index.
PQ2635 .A25 J6 1925	**Les joues en feu** : poèmes anciens et poèmes inédits 1917-1921 / Raymond Radiguet. – Paris : B. Grasset, 1925. – 104 pages : 1 portrait ; 19 cm
E237 .J6 H34 1973	**Jouett, Jack, 1754-1822—Juvenile fiction.** Jack Jouett's ride / written and illustrated by Gail E. Haley. – 1st edition. – New York : Viking Press, ©1973. – 31 unnumbered pages : color illustrations ; 23 x 29 cm
LB2332 .J68 1967	**Joughin, Louis.** Academic freedom and tenure : a handbook of the American Association of University Professors / edited by Louis Joughin. – Madison : University of Wisconsin Press, 1967. – xiv, 343 pages : illustrations ; 22 cm
PN1997 .J68 C35 1970	**Le jour se lève** / a film by Marcel Carné and Jacques Prévert. English translation and description of action by Dinah Brooke and Nicola Hayden. – New York : Simon and Schuster, 1970. – 128 pages : illustrations ; 21 cm
	Jouve, Nicole Ward *See* Ward Jouve, Nicole

Figure 3.2 A Page from a Dictionary-style Alphabetical Catalog in Book Form.

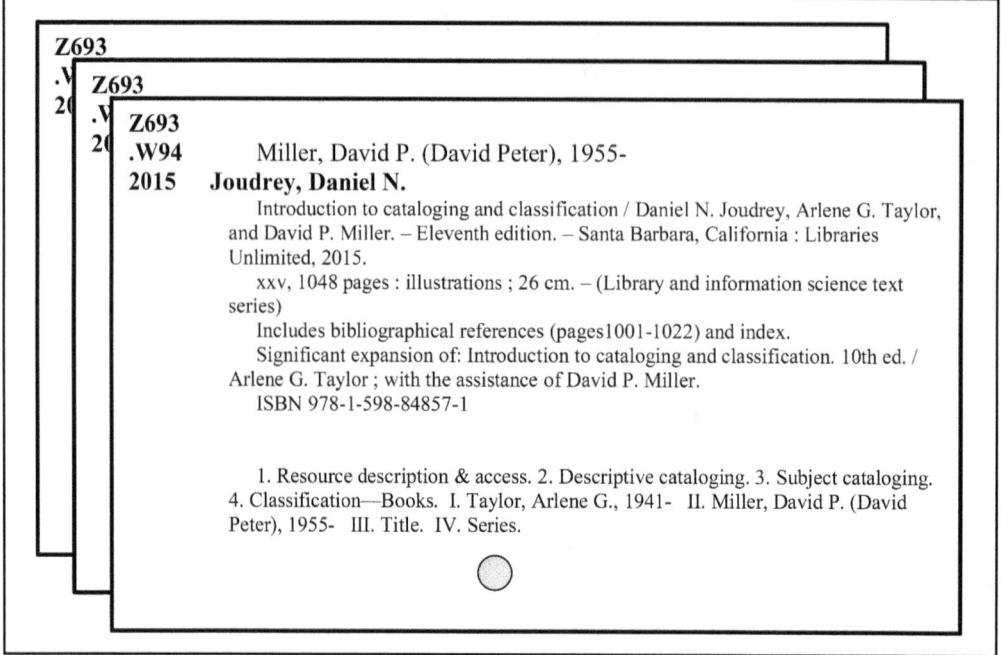

Figure 3.3 A Set of Catalog Cards.

Although many card catalogs have been replaced, that is not true of every information institution. Some libraries, archives, and museums still have card catalogs, especially smaller institutions without funds for automation projects. And it is important to remember that in some countries, the card catalog is still the predominant form of catalog. Not everyone in the world has equal access to resources (money, equipment, electricity, and so on) to be able to enjoy the luxury of automated information retrieval.

3.2.2.2.3 Microform Catalogs

The creation of **computer output microform catalogs** (or COM catalogs) became possible in the 1960s. They are produced on either microfiche or microfilm and require a microform reader to be able to use them. They are produced like book catalogs, but because they do not have to be printed on paper and bound, they can be completely reproduced with new additions every three months or so without having to go through the supplement stage. Due to unpopularity, microform catalogs were replaced rather quickly by online catalogs. It has been found that users will use microfilm if that is the only way to get the information they need, but most people find the readers hard to use and microform images difficult to read.

3.2.2.2.4 Online Catalogs

Online catalogs, sometimes referred to as *online public access catalogs* or OPACs, are the predominant form of catalog in the United States and in many other countries today. In these catalogs, records are stored on a local or remote server. The records are displayed only as needed. There is much flexibility in the look of the displays. Figure 3.4 shows the basic search screen of the OPAC used at Simmons University Library. Figure 3.5 shows the view of a single record in that library's catalog.

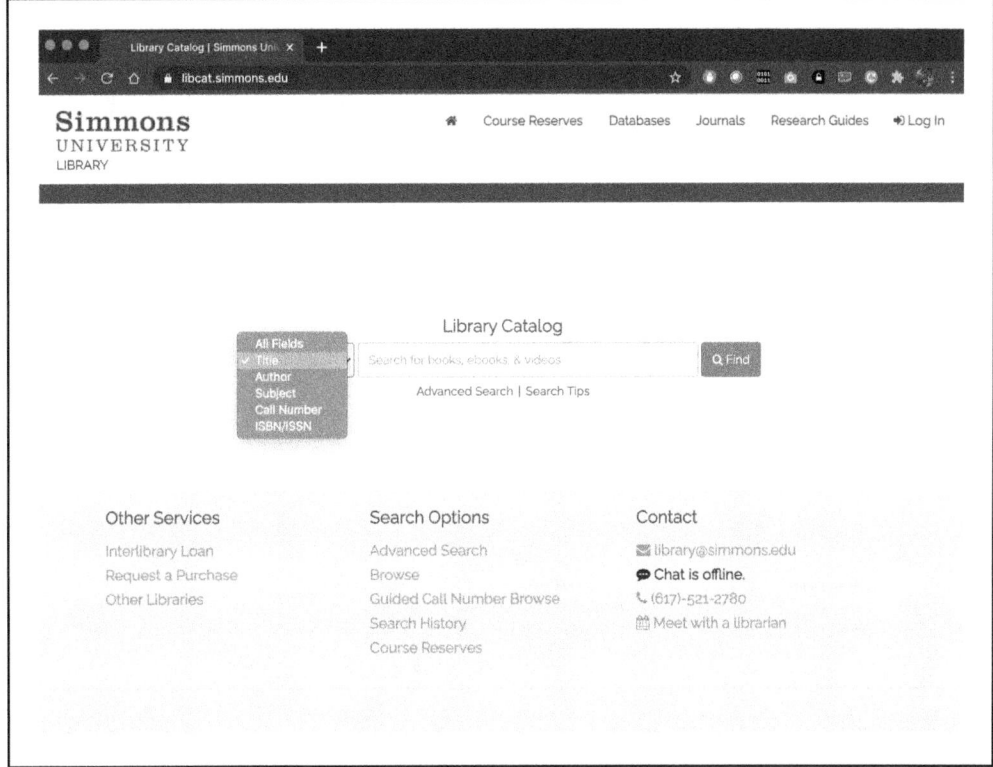

Figure 3.4 Basic Search Screen in an Online Catalog. (Source: Simmons University Library, Boston, Mass.)

Online catalogs have not been standardized, although in two or more institutions that have purchased the same system, the displays may look somewhat similar. Librarians have long called for standardization, so that patrons can move from catalog to catalog and find records displayed in the same manner, but this has yet to happen.[14] In recent years, dissatisfaction with online catalogs has been expressed by many in the library and information professions. This frustration—that the online catalog is still difficult to use—is intensified by comparisons to internet search engines that are relatively easy to use. At times, this discontent has led some to question the long-term prospects for the online catalog. If catalog vendors respond by improving arrangements of displayed responses (e.g., by emphasizing relationships among resources), online catalogs may again be seen as providing something not available in search engines and then may survive. Some believe that when the Semantic Web is realized and all types of resources (bibliographic and otherwise) are connected using linked data techniques, then perhaps general search engines will replace the OPACs that we use today to find information in libraries. This, however, may be a long time coming.

3.2.2.3 Arrangement and Displays within Catalogs

The records within catalogs must be arranged in some fashion or they are unusable. In card catalogs, records are arranged by being filed in a certain order. In book and microform catalogs, records are arranged by being printed one after another in a particular order. Records in OPACs,

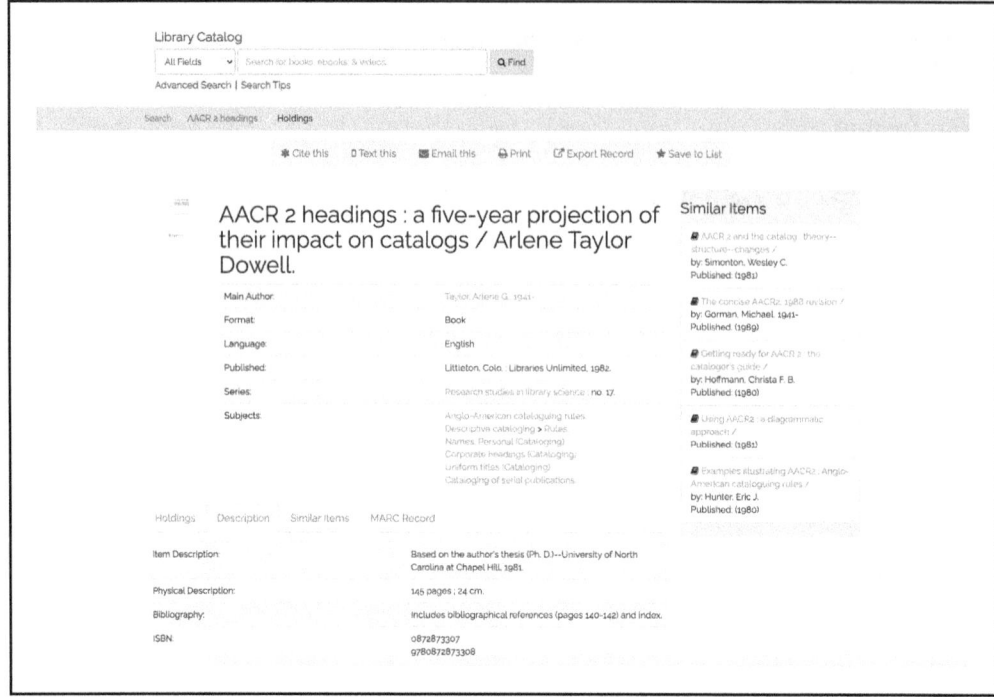

Figure 3.5 A Bibliographic Record in an Online Catalog. (Source: Simmons University Library, Boston, Mass., https://libcat.simmons.edu/Record/b1055231.)

however, are not set in one place. Records are arranged within the database either in sequential order of entry into the system or in random order; no matter which arrangement is used, the records can be rearranged for display in a variety of ways. This allows for the customization of the display of search results in online catalogs. So, the arrangement discussed here applies to the arrangement of the displayed responses to search queries in the case of online catalogs and not to the internal order within the database. (For more information about arrangement of metadata displays, see Appendix A.)

In general, there were two basic arrangements that made sense in ***printed catalogs*** (i.e., all the formats of catalogs occurring before the online version). Catalog records were either in classified order or in alphabetical order. These arrangements are possible in the online catalog, although they are no longer the *only* choices for display. In today's OPACs, many options for displaying search results are offered; users may choose the display option that works best for any given search. In the next sections, the two traditional approaches to the arrangement of printed catalogs are discussed; a brief section then follows on the choices for display in the online catalog.

3.2.2.3.1 Classified Arrangements

Classified catalogs usually have more than one section. In what is considered the "main" section of the catalog, the arrangement or display is in the order of the classification scheme used by that institution. That is, this section is arranged in subject order, where the subject is represented by classification notation rather than by subject terminology. For example, a book of slow cooker recipes is represented and arranged by the *Dewey Decimal Classification* (DDC) notation **641.5884** rather than by its analogous subject heading, **Electric cooking, Slow**. There can be as many classification notations assigned to a single record as there are subject concepts in the information resource.

Classified catalogs have the advantage that users can look at records for broader and narrower concepts at the same place they are looking for records on a specific concept. In a way, it is like browsing in the stacks with a classification notation, except that in the case of the classified catalog, each information resource is represented by several notations signifying all its subject concepts, rather than just one. An example from a printed classified catalog is found in Figure 3.6; in it one can see the entries arranged by the call number associated with each resource.

As it is nearly impossible for anyone to know all the classification notations relating to a subject, there should be a section of the catalog that lists verbal representations of all topics and gives the notation for each topic.

Slow cooking	641.588
Slow cooking, Electric	641.5884
Slow food movement	641.013
Slow learners	371.926
Slugs	594.38

In some situations, this need could be met by placing a copy of the classification scheme at the catalog, because most classification schemes include an index of topics in alphabetical order. And, of course, there are users who want to search for authors or titles, so there must be other sections of the catalog for those entities as well. In printed catalogs, the subject term, author, and title sections are arranged in alphabetical order. In OPACs, they are word-searchable, and the order of displays varies.

The United States never really embraced classified catalogs, but they have been used in other parts of the world, particularly in countries where several languages are spoken and represented in the collection. Among the reasons the concept is still relevant today is that there is now global access to online catalogs, and a classified catalog can hold and display records in any language with classification notations that are universal. If indexes to a classified catalog are made in many languages, access can be gained through any one of the many languages. In addition, it makes broadening and narrowing of searches, as well as browsing, easier.

3.2.2.3.2 Alphabetical Arrangements

Early American catalogs were arranged by broad subject categories in alphabetical order. With a collection consisting of a few books, there was little need for elaborate classification or arrangement. As catalogs expanded along with collections, the broad categories used for subject access needed to be subdivided, so somewhat narrower categories were created and placed alphabetically within each broad category. For example, if the broad category were **Domestic animals**, the sub-categories under it might be **Cats, Cows, Dogs, Horses, Mules**, and so forth. Catalogs using this approach were called ***alphabetico-classed catalogs***. As subject categories multiplied, it became more difficult to predict the subject category and where it would be found. It began to make sense to place all categories and sub-categories in alphabetical order. Cutter was instrumental in the

Puppyville Free Library
Classified Catalog

641.3
R523w
	Richardson, Joan.
	    Wild edible plants of New England : a field guide : including poisonous plants often encountered / by Joan Richardson. – Yarmouth, Maine : DeLorme Publishing, 1981. – x, 217 pages, 32 pages of plates : illustrations (some color) ; 23 cm.
	    Includes bibliographical references (pages 189-190) and index.
	    ISBN 0-993301-09-6

641.303
T373n
	Thayer, Samuel.
	    Nature's garden : a guide to identifying, harvesting, and preparing edible wild plants / by Samuel Thayer – Birchwood, Wisconsin : Forager's Harvest Press, 2010. – 512 pages : color illustrations ; 23 cm.
	    Subtitle from cover.
	    Includes bibliographical references (pages 481-492) and index.
	    ISBN 978-0-9766-2661-9

641.58
D417b
	Denzer, Kiko.
	    Build your own earth oven : a low-cost, wood-fired mud oven, simple sourdough bread, perfect loaves / Kiko Denzer, with Hannah Field. – 3rd edition. – Blodgett, Oregon : Hand Print Press, 2007. – 129 pages : illustrations (some color) ; 26 cm.
	    "Revised, expanded, updated" – Cover.
	    Includes bibliographical references (pages 122-124) and index.
	    ISBN 978-0-96798-467-4

641.58
G618o
	Goldenson, Suzanne, 1944-
	    The open-hearth cookbook : recapturing the flavor of early America / by Suzanne Goldenson with Doris Simpson.- Revised edition. – Chambersburg, PA : Alan C. Hood & Co., 2006. – ix, 164 pages : illustrations ; 23 cm.
	    ISBN 978-0-911469-26-4

641.58
Y28g
	Yarnell, Elizabeth.
	    Glorious one-pot meals : a revolutionary new quick and healthy approach to Dutch-oven cooking / Elizabeth Yarnell. – New York : Broadway Books, 2009. – xii, 223 pages ; 21 cm.
	    Previously published: Denver, Colorado : Pomegranate Consulting, 2005.
	    Includes index.
	    ISBN 978-0-76793-010-9

641.5884
P558s
	Phillips, Diane.
	    Slow cooker : the best cookbook ever with more than 400 easy-to-make recipes / Diane Phillips ; photographs by James Baigrie. – San Francisco : Chronicle Books, 2009. – 543 pages : illustrations (some color) ; 24 cm.
	    "Glorious meals at the flip of a switch. The slow cooker is your new best friend for delicious breakfasts, lunches, dinners, and desserts"-- Page 4 of cover.
	    ISBN 978-0-81186-657-6

Figure 3.6 A Page from a Classified Book Catalog.

development of what he called the ***dictionary catalog***. He recommended alphabetical arrangement with authors, titles, and subjects all interfiled in the same catalog. An example of a printed dictionary catalog is found in Figure 3.2 on page 107. It contains the following mix of entries:

1. a title entry for *Jottings from Jail*
2. an author entry for Joseph Joubert's notebooks
3. an author entry for Daniel N. Joudrey for a book on cataloging
4. an author entry for Joudrey for an earlier edition of this book, *The Organization of Information*
5. another author entry for another edition of this book
6. a title entry for a book of French poems, *Les Joues en Feu*
7. a subject entry for a biographical children's book about Jack Jouett
8. an entry for a handbook edited by Louis Joughin
9. a title entry for a book about the film *Le Jour se Lève*
10. a personal name cross-reference (from Jouve to Ward Jouve)

The interfiling of the various types of entries is what defines this type of arrangement as a dictionary catalog.

The dictionary card catalog was the standard for the first half of the twentieth century. Later, it became quite complicated to file new cards into large catalogs because of the complexity of filing rules that seemed to grow as the catalogs grew. Early filing rules had reflected the influence of the classified catalog and presorted catalog entries into categories. Cutter recommended alphabetical filing, but names and titles beginning with a word that could also be a topical subject (e.g., Glass) were supposed to be filed in the order: personal name, geographic entity, corporate body, subject heading, title. This is seen in the following example:

Glass, Richard	[personal name]
Glass Mountains (Tex.)	[geographic entity]
Glass Art Society	[corporate body]
Glass	[subject heading]
Glass art	[subject heading]
Glass menagerie	[title]

These entries are not in simple alphabetical order, and it is easy to see how complicated such an arrangement was in large catalogs.

Attempts to break up the large files resulted in ***divided catalogs***. Divided catalogs were alphabetical catalogs that were partitioned into two or three sections. If there were two, they were often divided so that authors and titles were in one part and subject headings were in the other. In a catalog with three sections, the division was usually authors, titles, and subjects. In this tripartite arrangement, records for resources about a person were usually filed in the subject section, and records for works created by that person were filed in the author section. However, some considered it useful to keep records for works by and about a person together, so sometimes all names were placed in one part of the catalog whether it was for the name as a creator or for the name as a subject. In a divided card catalog, there might be separate cabinets (or sets of cabinets) used for the different sections of the catalog (see Figure 3.7). The divided catalog was easier and less expensive for the keepers of the catalog, but it was assumed that users knew the differences among author, title, and subject entries, which was not always the case.

With the development of OPACs in the 1980s, the divided catalog was moved online. One usually had to search either by author, by title, or by subject (although, later, more options for searching became available). In this case, though, it was seldom possible to retrieve works both by and about a person in the same search; this was not possible until general keyword searching became available in the online catalog, and even then, it was not terribly precise because the name might appear in parts of the record other than a creator or subject field. General keyword searches are similar to the dictionary catalog approach to arranging a catalog, because one does not have to choose the type of search one wishes to conduct; search terms are retrieved no matter where they appear in the catalog record. The classified arrangement is also available in today's OPAC; it is usually achieved by performing a call number browse, if that is available. In some ways, the sophistication that had been built into the design of card catalogs through elaborate intellectual filing rules was abandoned in exchange for the convenience of automated searching.

3.2.2.3.3 Other Arrangements

In modern OPACs, the displays of search results are usually not in alphabetical or classified order. A specific OPAC's programming determines which types of arrangements are possible and when each arrangement is used as the default display. In some catalogs, searches for creators or titles may

Figure 3.7 A Divided Alphabetical Card Catalog.

bring up an alphabetical display of authority-controlled access points for creators or a list of titles in alphabetical order, but other systems may have a default setting that is used for almost every type of search: ***relevance ranking***. Arrangement by relevance can be mysterious to users and information professionals alike. The idea is that the resources that are most closely connected to the search terms are ranked higher in the search results. Relevancy is determined algorithmically, and it is defined differently by each system. It is based on a combination of factors (e.g., placement, field weighting, term frequency) that may be adjusted somewhat according to an institution's preferences.

The choice of display arrangements and the choice of searches available vary from catalog to catalog. Some, for example, do not provide users with the ability to conduct a classification search or call number browse, but they may allow title or creator search results to be sorted in call number order. Some OPACs do not allow browsing of authority-controlled lists of names, instead focusing primarily on keyword searching. Most online catalogs now allow users a choice of the order in which search results are to be displayed. In addition to relevance ranking, catalogs may allow sorting based on the following attributes:

- creator's name (alphabetical by last name)
- title (alphabetical by first non-article word)
- call number
- ascending chronological order (i.e., publication date from earliest to latest)
- descending chronological order (i.e., from latest to earliest)
- most popular resources first
- format or material type

The choices offered by catalogs may vary from just two or three of these sorting options to, perhaps, many or most of the types listed. In some systems, these arrangements can include options for a variety of sub-arrangements under the primary sort key (e.g., sorting first by creator but then choosing sub-arrangement by title or publication date).

3.2.3 Finding Aids

Finding aids are descriptions of archival collections, and they tend to be longer than typical catalog records. Archives usually maintain control over entire collections of archival materials from personal, corporate, or institutional sources. Thus, a finding aid describes a collection, not a single letter or record within that collection. Although some finding aids are not publicly accessible, this is becoming increasingly rare as archives add more finding aids to the web. The finding aid, itself a retrieval tool, is often linked to a summary description of the collection in a catalog record. Summary records provide name, title, and subject access points for archival collections in the catalog and provide a means to point users to more detailed finding aids. *Describing Archives: A Content Standard* (DACS) is used in the United States to create both finding aids and MARC-based catalog records. The equivalent standard in Canada is *Rules for Archival Description* (RAD), whereas in the United Kingdom, *General International Standard Archival Description* (ISAD(G)) is used.

A finding aid may be a brief or quite lengthy description, depending upon the size of the archival collection, the complexity of its organization, and the level of granularity desired in the description. Because the materials in archives are different from the types of information resources found in other institutions, the types of metadata recorded in a finding aid are different from those found in catalogs or indexes. The following types of information are found in a typical finding aid.

- **Provenance information**: including creator, title, dates, and biographical or administrative history
- **Physical extent and condition**: including the collection's physical size (quantity, volume, and measurements in linear/cubic feet) and a statement of the collection's condition
- **Scope and content notes**: including a narrative description of the nature of the collection, what is included, the depth of the collection, gaps, types of materials, and access points for names and subjects
- **Order and structure**: including how the collection is arranged and organized, and detailed container lists
- **Administrative information:** including location, conditions of use, restrictions, processing, citation, acquisition and accession, repository, and conservation information

Finding aids for many years were in paper form, but now it is much more common to access them through digital means. Some finding aids are encoded using Encoded Archival Description (EAD), but others may simply be marked up using HTML (Hypertext Markup Language) or provided as a Portable Document Format (PDF) file. Although many institutions post their individual finding aids on their institution's website, some institutions are attempting to make their finding aids more accessible by aggregating them in searchable databases, either at the local level (e.g., Archives at Yale) or through participation in a multi-institution aggregator (e.g., Archives Grid from OCLC). Users interested in certain topics or in the documents related to a particular entity can find relevant archival collections through such search systems. An example of a brief finding aid is presented in Figure 3.8.

3.2.4 Registers and Museum Databases

A *register* (also known as an *accession log* or an *accession system*) constitutes the primary collections control tool for museums. It functions somewhat like a catalog, but it is more involved than that. The registration system covers a wide range of documentation of the object beyond the basic description. For example, museums must have documentation showing that they have rights to possess and exhibit the object, information about the origins of the object and its ownership history (provenance), valuation and insurance documentation, and so on.

The process of registration in a museum is similar to the process of cataloging in a library; it includes metadata about the resource (e.g., title, creator, physical description), but there are also metadata elements that are far different from those used for most library resources (e.g., culture, methods, materials). During the registration process, the registrar identifies the object, the donor, provenance, any information needed for insurance purposes, and so forth. An accession number

Guide to the Industrial School for Girls (Dorchester, Boston, Mass.) records, 1873-1934

Archivist's View

Descriptive Summary

Creator	Industrial School for Girls (Dorchester, Boston, Mass.)
Title	Industrial School for Girls (Dorchester, Boston, Mass.) records
Dates	1873-1934
Identification	CC 30
Quantity	0.5 linear feet (1 manuscript box)
Collection Abstract	The Industrial School for Girls collection contains the annual reports of the Board of Managers, arranged chronologically with a concentration of reports from 1873 to 1934. Also, there is a paper read at the 50th anniversary of the Dorchester Industrial School on June 7, 1904, as well as a bound copy of *Suggestions to Visitors of Dependent Children*, 1874.
Historical Abstract	The Industrial School for Girls was established in 1853 and incorporated 1855 in the names of Lucretia O. Everett and Maria Greenwood. It moved from Winchester, Massachusetts, to Dorchester, Massachusetts, in 1858, located at 232 Centre Street. It provided a home and training school for various branches of housework to develop the habits and principles to become upright, self-supported women. By the mid-1940s the Industrial School for Girls had evolved into the Everett House located at the same place, and in the 1950s the New England Home for Little Wanderers acquired it.
Language	Material in English.
Location	Collection may be stored offsite. Please contact Archives staff for more information.

Information for Users

Access Restrictions
Collection is open.

Copyright Notice
Copyright for materials resides with the creators of the items in question, unless otherwise designated.

Publishing Permission
Please contact the College Archivist with requests to publish any material from the collection.

Preferred Citation
[Identification of item: description and date], Industrial School for Girls (Dorchester, Boston, Mass.) records, CC 30, Simmons College Archives, Boston, MA, USA.

Acquisitions Information
Transferred from the Simmons College School of Social Work Library, 1991
Accession number: 2002.178

Processing Information
Processed by Molly Tierney, December 2002; Supervised by Jason Wood. This collection guide was encoded as part of the LEADS project by Katie Sallade, November 2012

Figure 3.8 An Example of a Finding Aid. (Source: Simmons University Library Collection: CC30, Simmons University Archives, Boston, Mass.)

Organizational History

The Industrial School for Girls was established in 1853 and incorporated 1855 in the names of Lucretia O. Everett and Maria Greenwood. It moved from Winchester, Massachusetts, to Dorchester, Massachusetts, in 1858, located at 232 Centre Street. It provided a home and training school for various branches of housework to develop the habits and principles to become upright, self-supported women. They accepted on average 25 students through an application process, … girls between 10 to 14 years of age, whose family or friends are unable or unfit to care for them. The original age of acceptance was between the ages of 6 to 10, which gradually rose with modern social standards. Reductions of boarding charges were made when relatives could not pay. The girls attend public schools (this started in 1881) and Congregational church. They would go out to earn their living as soon as able under the immediate care of the head of household, usually in country families, and each one, unless returned to relatives, would be supervised under the care of one of the managers. By the mid-1940s the Industrial School for Girls had evolved into the Everett House located at the same place. And in the 1950s the New England Home for Little Wanderers acquired it.

Information taken from *Directory of Charitable and Beneficent Organizations*, Boston, 1907 and 1940 or the *Report of the Board of Managers*, 1926 and the finding aid for CC 6, "Guide to the New England Home for Little Wanderers records."

Collection Overview

The Industrial School for Girls records consist of the annual reports of the Board of Managers, arranged chronologically with a concentration of reports from 1873 to 1934. Also, there is a paper read at the 50th anniversary of the Dorchester Industrial School June 7, 1904, which has a summation of the first 50 years of the School and a bound copy of Suggestions to Visitors of Dependent Children, 1874, which provides guidance for guardians of the girls.

There has been an annual report printed every year except in 1858 when they were moving from Winchester to Dorchester. The reports cover officers' positions, brief history of the School, student population, admission application statistics, requests for student help placement, expense reports, list of subscribers for previous year, donations made and by-laws of the organization. Missing are the years: 1919, 1923, 1925, 1928, 1930, and 1932.

Online Catalog Headings

These and related materials may be found under the following headings in online catalogs.
    Charities-- Massachusetts-- Boston
    Dorchester (Boston, Mass.)
    Industrial School for Girls (Dorchester, Boston, Mass.)
    New England Home for Little Wanderers-- History
    Winchester (Mass.)

Figure 3.8 (*Continued*)

Collection Arrangement

Collection is arranged into 3 series:

Series I: <u>Annual Reports</u>
Series II: <u>Manual</u>
Series III: <u>50th Anniversary Paper</u>

Related Material

Part of the <u>School of Social Work Library Charities Collection</u>.

Detailed Description of the Collection

Series I: Annual Reports, 1873-1934 (3 folders)

This series contains the Industrial School for Girls' annual reports printed each year except in 1858. The reports cover officers' positions, brief history of the School, student population, admission application statistics, requests for student help placement, expense reports, list of subscribers for previous years, donations made, and by-laws of the organization. Missing years include: 1919, 1923, 1925, 1928, 1930, and 1932.

Box 1
- Folder 1: **Bound 1873-1885, 1886-1900**
- Folder 2: **1874-1920**
- Folder 3: **1921-1934**

Series II: Manual, 1879 (1 folder)

This series contains a bound copy of *Suggestions to Visitors of Dependent Children*, 1874, which provides guidance for guardians of the girls.
- Folder 4: 1879

Series III: 50th Anniversary Paper, 1904 (1 folder)

This series contains a paper read at the 50th anniversary of the first 50 years of the Dorchester Industrial School on June 7, 1904, which has a summation of the first 50 years of the School.
- Folder 5: 1904

Figure 3.8 (*Continued*)

is assigned as a permanent identifier, which must be used in all records kept about the resource. This process of documentation is internal and seldom made available to the public. The accession record is the basis for one or more files that help provide organization and control of the museum's content.

Additionally, museums sometimes provide online databases for public access. For example, the Pitt Rivers Museum in Oxford, England allows their collections to be searched online. Anyone can search the databases by filling in various fields in the advanced search form (based on the fields included in the record structure). For example, the databases have search boxes for: accession number, description, geographical reference, cultural groups, names and roles, date, date of acquisition, and more.¹⁵ This approach is very factual, with a good deal of information provided by the databases, but it contains a more visually oriented, polished presentation than what is found in most library catalogs.

An example of a more comprehensive and sophisticated interface is found at the National Gallery of Art (NGA) in Washington, DC. The entire collection (drawings, paintings, photographs, prints, and sculptures) is searchable in at least three distinct methods through their website. The first interface is labeled "Search the Collection." It allows the public to search the collection's object records by artist name, keywords in the title or in the object description, donors and owners, accession number, exhibition history, and a few other fields.¹⁶ After an initial search is complete, users may filter their search results by nationality, time span, style, and so on. A digital image for many, but not all, works is provided.

In addition, some artworks have extensive descriptions. For example, the search results for Luis Meléndez's eighteenth-century painting *Still Life with Figs and Bread* begin with some brief information:

Location:	West Building, Main Floor–Gallery 34
Medium:	oil on canvas
Dimensions:	
Overall:	47.6 × 34 cm (18 3/4 x 13 3/8 in.)
Framed:	65.6 × 49.2 × 4.4 cm (25 13/16 x 19 3/8 x 1 3/4 in.)
Credit Line:	Patrons' Permanent Fund
Accession number:	2000.6.1
Artists/Makers:	Luis Meléndez (painter) Spanish, 1715-1780
Image Use:	This image is in the public domain.

Following this, there is an image description, a concise overview essay, a bibliography, a description of the work's provenance, and its exhibition history.¹⁷ Some artworks in the collection have more detailed entries than this.

The second interface is a simple "Artists Search" page, where users can search for the name of an artist (assisted by autofill) to find an overview of that artist. In addition, users will find that artist's works of art, a bibliography, and a section labeled "Related Content." The related content may contain audio-visual materials, educational resources, and exhibition information, among other things.¹⁸ A third interface is available through the the NGA's free image and open access repository.¹⁹ This separate browsing tool allows users to narrow down a collection of 50,000 downloadable images using various filters, such as nationality, classification (the type of art: painting, sculpture, media art), style, subjects, and dates. The results provide downloadable digital images and a link to the object record (mentioned above). This is one specific museum's approach to providing information about its collections to the public. Other cultural heritage institutions approach it in different ways. As time goes along, we may or may not see more consistency among presentations of retrieval tools on museum websites.

Figure 3.9 *Still Life with Figs and Bread* by Luis Meléndez. (This image is in the Public Domain. Provided by the National Gallery of Art, Washington, D.C.)

3.2.5 Search Engines

For most information seekers, ***search engines*** are probably the most familiar of all the retrieval tools discussed in this chapter. Search engines are tools developed for computer systems, particularly the internet, to find instances of requested words or phrases that can be found in the documents covered by the scope of the tool. They were developed for the purpose of searching full text documents (or indexes of those documents) for particular words or phrases. Some search engines are used to search only a single resource, such as the website for an organization like OCLC. Other search engines are for searching the entire internet (although only a small percentage of the internet is actually covered by each search engine). Using a program called a ***web crawler*** (also known as a *spider*, a *crawler*, or a *bot*), each search engine automatically collects information from web resources and places it into a database of records or in a full-text index that is similar to a concordance. The web crawler is typically programmed to go onto the web to retrieve and download copies of web pages and everything linked to them, everything linked to the links, and so on. Massive collective indexes—created from the web crawler's database—are stored in data centers around the world. These indexes (some comprising over 100 million gigabytes of data) are what are searched when users enter terms into the search box.

Obviously, not every web resource has been indexed. Some resources may be indexed by only a few search engines—thus, a variety of responses can be had when searching different engines for the same concept. In addition, not every search engine indexes every type of material available online. It has only been in more recent years that images, PDF files, videos, and PowerPoint slides have become searchable online. In some cases, resources may be password protected, and as a result, they may not be indexed in a search engine because they are not accessible to the crawler. In other cases, some resources may be indexed and returned as search results, despite being restricted—a fact that the searcher may discover only after trying to access the information. In general, only the surface web is included in search engine indexes; the so-called ***deep web*** (or hidden web) includes many things the public would not want to see indexed in search engines (e.g., email correspondence, financial transactions, dating profiles, nefarious dealings).

Unlike catalogs and finding aids, search engines have become a ubiquitous part of users' routine interactions with the world (at least for those privileged enough to have consistent and reliable internet access). Due to a general familiarity with search engines and their relative ease of use (just throw some keywords into the search box!), other retrieval tools often look antiquated and too complex in comparison. Although search engines may or may not provide results that are as intellectually satisfactory as the results from other retrieval tools, users often report satisfaction because they quickly find *something* related to their information need. But most users do not know if what they found is necessarily authentic, authoritative, or the best resource that is available on their topic. Searches for known items or for specific names are sometimes less satisfactory than searches for topical information. Some users do not always realize that search engines may push advertisements and sponsored links to the top of the results page, or that more in-depth information may be found much further down in the list of results.

There is no doubt that search engines have become more advanced in recent years. Google is one of the most sophisticated both in giving searching assistance (e.g., asking, "Did you really mean to search for … ?" in response to a misspelled word) and in the display of results, but there are still drawbacks. At the time of this writing, there is still no real distinction among homographs. For example, on the first page of search results for the term *bridge*, Google brings back various definitions, a panel labeled an artificial intelligence (AI) overview, and a mixture of resources about card games, structures spanning geographic spaces or gaps, specific named highway structures, and some local and international organizations with the word *bridge* in their names. The handling of synonyms and related terms is somewhat mysterious. In Google, searching *funny pets* brings back videos about funny pets, but some of the search results are for *funny dogs* (where the word *pets* is nowhere to be found on the page). Although humans understand that dogs are a type of pet, machines do not *know* this; they must be programmed to connect these strings of characters and to treat them as related concepts. Although Google acknowledges that it has a "synonyms system" of which they are very proud and that it involves analyzing "petabytes of web documents and historical search data to build an intricate understanding of what words can mean in different contexts,"[20] Google is not particularly detailed in describing how synonym control works, but they do state that they address the problem through an expansion of the original query using the Boolean operator *OR*.[21] They essentially extend the search, through a synonym ring,‡ for each word in the query, by adding supplemental related terms connected by OR. Using one of their simple examples, a search for *cycling tours in Italy* might end up being processed as

**(cycling OR cycle OR bicycle OR bike OR biking)
AND (tours OR tour OR holidays OR vacation)
AND (Italy OR Italian).**

Disappointingly, the synonyms system is not something that users can explore directly. The need for synonyms systems to expand natural language queries has increased exponentially with the now wide-spread availability of generative AI tools.

With most search engines, displays of search results are usually arranged according to **relevance**, which can be calculated in various ways. A search engine may calculate relevance by giving different weights to factors such as how many search terms are found in each web page, how often each term is found in a page, whether the terms are in proximity or dispersed, whether the terms are in the header or buried further down in its body, and how common (or rare) a particular search term is. Search engines continue to strive for more sophisticated methods of calculating relevance and for displaying results. For example, Google uses a formula that examines over 200 different factors in determining relevance. Google uses common factors, such as word placement and word frequency, in its formula, but also less-expected criteria such as site quality, geographic region, search history, recency, and site popularity (i.e., frequency that a page is linked to from other web pages) as elements in the ranking of search results.[22] Google, Bing, and other search engines are continuously updating, refining, and testing their algorithms and formulas in their quests to improve the internet searching experience.

When metadata was first being developed to describe web documents, most search engines did not take user-supplied metadata into consideration in their relevance ranking due to metadata mischief and malfeasance (e.g., including popular terms that have no relationship to the site being described). With the development of linked data, however, the major search engines are now embracing the inclusion of more structured data as part of the underlying textual markup of web resources. Encoding approaches such as JSON-LD (Java Script Object Notation

---

‡See Chapter 12 for more information about synonym rings.

for Linked Data), microdata, and RDFa (Resource Description Framework in Attributes)—in combination with specialized vocabularies (such as the categories established in Schema.org) to identify necessary semantics—may be used to add more contextual metadata directly into web resources. For example, when searching recipes on a culinary website, it would be helpful if the search engine could distinguish between dietary restrictions (e.g., gluten-free) and the actual ingredients of the recipe. Support for linked data and the processing of contextual metadata embedded within web documents enables search engines to make such distinctions—and these capabilities are expected to improve significantly in the coming decades.

3.2.6 Internet Directories

In the 1990s and early 2000s, alternatives to search engines for finding web resources still existed—most notably, *internet directories*. As mentioned in Chapter 1, internet directories were organized collections of links to websites. In many directories, human indexers curated the links at first, but as technology developed, some began to collect links through automatic means. INFOMINE, established in 1994, is an example of an internet directory created by cooperating librarians from several academic institutions. It contained pages dedicated to various topics (e.g., cultural diversity resources, government information, maps and geographic data), each of which contained lists of links to recommended websites. The links could be browsed in alphabetical lists or searched using title words, creator names, subjects, or keywords. Its organization was similar to, but simpler than, that of the Yahoo! directory, which also debuted in 1994.

The directory created by Yahoo! was one of the largest and the best known. In its heyday, Yahoo! employed human indexers to create and maintain its directory. Humans added subject terms and categorized the records into a hierarchical subject tree index. Yahoo! favored a more hierarchical, drill-down method of browsing, where one started with one of the 14 top-level categories that were divided into myriad subtopics or facets. In any given category, one could easily find five or six levels of subtopics and, in some cases, many more. Hierarchically structured directories of websites, however, eventually lost favor to general search engines, such as Alta Vista and Google, after many improvements increased the efficacy of search engines. After two decades of operation, both Yahoo! and INFOMINE closed their directories in December 2014 after experiencing significant declines in usage in later years.[23]

Directories, once the first place to look for websites, have waned considerably in popularity due to the ascendancy of the search engine and the tremendous efforts and resources needed to maintain extensive lists of ever-changing web resources. Most of the long-standing internet directories have ceased operations. Although a small number still exists, hierarchical directories are mostly relics of the internet's past. "The findability techniques that were effective in the late 1990s … are ineffective today."[24] To get a sense of how these directories were organized, and what searching for information on the web was like in the previous millennium, please visit one of the last large-scale internet directories: *The Best of the Web* directory.[25]

3.2.7 Indexing and Abstracting Databases

Indexes (or indexing databases) are retrieval tools that provide access to the analyzed contents of information resources (e.g., articles in journals, short stories in collections, papers in conference proceedings). Although **back-of-the-book indexes** provide access to the analyzed contents of one resource, they are not retrieval tools in the sense defined in this chapter; they are prepared at the time of publication of the resource, not at a later time in an effort to provide bibliographic control. They do, however, aid with retrieval of the information found in the item in hand. Some websites also have indexes that function very much like back-of-the-book indexes, but instead of page locator references, each entry links directly to an HTML anchor within the site being indexed. Online these may be called **A–Z indexes** (to distinguish them from search trees, directories, and search engines). Like back-of-the-book indexes, an A–Z web index should contain properly identified major topics along with second-level entries (i.e., subheadings), variant entries, and cross-references.

The indexes that are retrieval tools (in the sense discussed in this chapter) are resources in their own right that are created separately from the resources being analyzed. **Database indexes** (also called *journal indexes* or *periodical indexes*) are the longest-lived examples of indexes as retrieval tools. Database indexes contain descriptions of the contents found in either (1) an array of related journals in a discipline (e.g., *Library and Information Science Source*) or (2) a single publication (e.g., the now-defunct index for *The New York Times*).

The sample index entry in Figure 3.10 illustrates the types of information included in an index for scholarly journal articles. It begins with the title of the article and then lists various characteristics of the article, including who wrote it, contact information, and affiliations. There is also information about the journal, including its title, type, and an identifier, usually the International Standard Serial Number (ISSN). Other information includes the publisher's name, the volume and issue in which the article is found, the page numbers, and the article's length. There is also an abstract and associated subjects.

Indexes may not have authority control of names. A name such as Lois Mai Chan, for example, can be entered into the same index at different times as Chan, L.; Chan, LM; Chan, L. M.; Chan, Lois M; Chan, Lois Mai; and even Mai Chan, Lois. Indexes do, however, usually maintain authority control over subjects. Indexers tend to use hierarchical controlled vocabularies (called **thesauri**) for the topical terms they wish to bring out in the index. A thesaurus contains systematized language that subsumes narrower terms under broader terms and provides a structure of relationships between related terms.[5]

Unlike catalogs, indexes are not limited to what is available in a local setting or a particular collection, and they do not usually give location information as such. They do provide, as part of the description, the larger resource in which the smaller work can be found. It may then be necessary for a user of the index to search for a copy of the larger work. In online indexes, there exists the capacity to link to online catalogs to allow users to see quickly if their library owns the

---

[5]See Chapter 12 for more information on thesauri and other controlled vocabularies.

> *Describing Entities and Identities: The Development and Structure of Encoded Archival Context—Corporate Bodies, Persons, and Families.*
>
> | | |
> |---|---|
> | **Author:** | **Wisser, Katherine M.** |
> | **Email Address:** | wisser@simmons.edu |
> | **Author Affiliations:** | School of Library and Information Science, Simmons College, USA |
> | **Source:** | **Journal of Library Metadata** |
> | **Source Type:** | Scholarly journal |
> | **ISSN:** | 1938-6389 |
> | **Volume:** | 11 |
> | **Issue:** | 3-4 |
> | **Date:** | Jul-Dec 2011 |
> | **Pages:** | 166-175 |
> | **Length:** | 10 pages |
> | **Publisher:** | Taylor & Francis, Philadelphia, PA |
> | **Document Type:** | Journal Article |
> | **Subjects:** | Archives |
> | | Encoded Archival Context-Corporate Bodies, Persons, and Families |
> | | International Standard Archival Authority Record for Corporate Bodies, Persons & Families |
> | **Abstract:** | |
> | | In January 2011, the Society of American Archivists fully endorsed the standard Encoded Archival Context-Corporate Bodies, Persons, and Families (EAC-CPF). This article details the development of the standard, from its conceptual beginnings in 1998 to its dissemination and adoption in 2011. It provides an overview of the general structure of EAC-CPF and discusses variables that were considered important in the design of the standard. It concludes with a reflection on the strength of international participation in the development and review of the standard in order to ensure that EAC-CPF would be applicable across many different boundaries. [ABSTRACT FROM AUTHOR] |
> | **DOI:** | 10.1080/19386389.2011.629960 |
> | **Accession Number:** | 12349876 |
> | ... | |

Figure 3.10 An Index Entry for a Scholarly Journal Article.

larger work. If the larger work is not found in the local catalog, the user may have to search a union catalog, such as WorldCat, to request the resource through interlibrary loan (ILL). Increasingly, online indexes have links to full-text versions of many articles, but that is entirely dependent upon the library's electronic resources budget.

Indexing can be carried out by people or by machines or by a combination of both. Database indexing is still mostly completed by specially trained indexers, although they may have machine assistance. For many decades, indexes were available in print form, but today they are primarily online tools. Some print versions were arranged in alphabetical dictionary fashion, with entries for authors, titles, and subjects interfiled. Others reflected a divided arrangement, having an author/title part separate from the subject index. Online indexes have interfaces that dictate how they are searched and how results are displayed.

As with OPACs, there is little standardization from index to index. OPACs, at least, have the standardization that comes from using RDA (or another set of descriptive rules), whereas, until recently, there was no such standard commonly used by indexing services. In 1996, the National Information Standards Organization (NISO) tried to update *Basic Criteria for Indexes* (ANSI Z39.4-1984),[26] but committees could not come to agreement with the American Society for Indexing, and proposed changes to Z39.4 were withdrawn. A standard from the International Organization for Standardization (ISO), which the British and others have adopted, was published in 1996; it was reviewed and re-confirmed in 2020[27] but it had not been universally adopted in the United States. After many long years, Z39.4 was finally updated and renamed. *Criteria for Indexes* (ANSI/NISO Z39.4-2021) is now available to provide U.S. indexing agencies with "guidelines for the content, organization, and presentation of indexes used for retrieval of documents and parts of documents."[28]

Another difference between catalogs and indexes is that indexes tend to be created by for-profit organizations, such as H. W. Wilson, or by professional societies, such as the American Chemical Society. Often there is a charge for access to the online versions. Libraries pay for the right to allow their patrons to use the indexes online without cost. Some libraries have both print and online access, although there seems to be a trend to continue only with the online versions. In any case, the index often is cataloged so that the whole index can be found through the catalog.

Most of the indexing already discussed is performed by humans. However, as early as the 1950s people began working on automatic indexing that would rely on the power of computers to perform repetitive tasks at high speed. The current application of automatic indexing is in search engine indexing. A search engine is sometimes referred to as an *index* but, more accurately, a search engine creates lists of terms that are referred to as *indexes*. Search engines are discussed more fully in sections 1.3.4.1 and 3.2.5 of this text.

3.3 The Need for Retrieval Tools Revisited

In today's heavily web-focused information environment, it is often tempting to think that nothing more than a search engine is ever needed. Some feel that if a resource cannot be found through Google's web, scholar, or book search, then that resource may not be worth finding. This, however, could not be further from the truth. It can be easy to forget that much of the world's information is still not online at this time and that much of that information probably never will be. In addition, a great deal of what is available in electronic form is not necessarily freely available to all. Information is a commodity. Most e-books are not free; they are sold. A needed article may be behind a paywall. There can be costs associated with online information access.

Although this may change in the future, individual retrieval tools (beyond search engines) still have vital roles to play in information gathering. Catalogs, indexes, and other retrieval tools, however, are often compared negatively to search engines. Students and scholars alike have asked, "Why is the catalog still hard to use?"[29] and "Why can't the catalog be more like Google or Amazon?" The desire for straightforward and user-friendly tools is understandable and pervasive, and there are information professionals who are working to rectify the situation. However, we must be careful to remember that this is not a contest. Not everything is as simple as putting keywords into a single Google search box. There are times when users and information professionals need more advanced types of searching that are currently not available in the search engine approach (e.g., an author search rather than a general keyword search).

Different types of retrieval tools have been designed to describe different kinds of materials for various communities. Information professionals must understand where and how to access the best information for each situation. For example, one must access a finding aid if one wants detailed information about an archival collection—relying on the brief catalog record for the collection usually will not suffice. Using Google to get to the Wikipedia page for Eleanor Roosevelt might be a fine starting point for a school report, but it will not provide comprehensive information about her life and accomplishments; published print materials, such as biographies and histories, will provide a greater depth of information and analysis—and a catalog will easily retrieve those materials (if they are in that collection). As psychologist Abraham Maslow said, "I suppose it is tempting, if the only tool you have is a hammer, to treat everything as if it were a nail."[30] We must be very cautious about overreliance on a single type of retrieval tool. We must not let the web search engine become our hammer. The trick is to make sure that all the tools in the toolbox are understood, and that they are used when necessary and appropriate.

3.4 Conclusion

A century ago, Charles Cutter stated that catalogs should enable people to find books for which titles, authors, or subjects were known; should show what was available in a library by a particular author, on a particular subject, or in a kind of literature; and should assist in the choice of a book by its edition or character (content). A century later, Cutter's "objects" are still appropriate, except that they should be expanded to all kinds of information resources beyond just books in libraries and to different kinds of retrieval tools beyond just the catalog.

This chapter has discussed the major retrieval tools used in the organization and retrieval of recorded information. The surrogate records that make up a retrieval tool must be created and encoded, either by humans or automatically by software programs created by humans. The individual retrieval tools discussed in this chapter are types of information systems. In the next chapter, we provide an overview of some of the issues and problems in organizing information as they relate to technology. Chapters on encoding and metadata follow, before settling into a multi-chapter discussion of the descriptive metadata found in retrieval tools.

Some Important Terms in This Chapter
(Definitions Provided in the Glossary)

A–Z index	Database index	Register
Access point	Deep web	Relevance
Alphabetico-classed catalog	Dictionary catalog	Relevance ranking
Annotated bibliography	Divided catalog	Research guide
Annotation	Explore	Retrieval tool
Authority control	Find	Search engine
Back-of-the-book index	Finding aid	Select
Bibliography	Identify	Shelflist
Book catalog	Index	Shelf reading
Card catalog	Internet directory	Surrogate record
Catalog	Known-item searching	Thesaurus
Citation	Obtain	Union catalog
Classified catalog	Online catalog	Web crawler
Computer output microform catalog	Printed catalog	

Some Important Acronyms in This Chapter

AI:	Artificial Intelligence
COM:	Computer Output Microform
DACS:	*Describing Archives: A Content Standard*
DOI:	Digital Object Identifier
FRBR:	*Functional Requirements for Bibliographic Records*
IFLA:	International Federation of Library Associations and Institutions
ISO:	International Organization for Standardization
JSON-LD:	Java Script Object Notation for Linked Data
LC:	Library of Congress
LRM:	*IFLA Library Reference Model*
NISO:	National Information Standards Organization
OCLC:	Online Computer Library Center
OPAC:	Online Public Access Catalog
PDF:	Portable Document Format
RAD:	*Rules for Archival Description*
RDA:	*Resource Description & Access*
RDF:	Resource Description Framework
RDFa:	RDF in Attributes
UBC:	Universal Bibliographic Control
URL:	Uniform Resource Locator

3.5 Discussion Questions and Exercises

- What is a retrieval tool?
- Select two of the retrieval tools discussed in this chapter and discuss:
  - What characteristics do they share?
  - How do they differ?
  - How do they reflect the information environments (libraries, archives, museums, etc.) they were created for?
- Can search engines do it all? What role is there for other types of retrieval tools in information seeking?

3.6 Suggested Readings

Bettington, Jackie, ed. *Keeping Archives*. 3rd ed. Canberra: Australia Society of Archivists, 2008.

Breeding, Marshall. *Next-Gen Library Catalogs*. New York: Neal-Schuman, 2010.

Buckland, Michael K. "What Is a 'Document'?" *Journal of the American Society for Information Science* 48, no. 9 (September 1997): 804–9. http://people.ischool.berkeley.edu/~buckland/whatdoc.html.

Chambers, Sally, ed. *Catalogue 2.0: The Future of the Library Catalogue*. U.S. ed. Chicago: Neal-Schuman, 2013.

Cleveland, Donald, and Ana Cleveland. *Introduction to Indexing and Abstracting*. 4th ed. Santa Barbara, CA: Libraries Unlimited, 2013.

Joudrey, Daniel N., Arlene G. Taylor, and David P. Miller. *Introduction to Cataloging and Classification*. 11th ed. Santa Barbara, CA: Libraries Unlimited, 2015.

Kumar, Shiv. "From Clay Tablets to Web: Journey of Library Catalogue." *DESIDOC Journal of Library & Information Technology* 33, no. 1 (January 2013): 45–54.

Markey, Karen. "The Online Library Catalog: Paradise Lost and Paradise Regained?" *D-Lib Magazine* 13, no. 1/2 (2007). http://www.dlib.org/dlib/january07/markey/01markey.html.

Meissner, Dennis. *Arranging and Describing Archives and Manuscripts*. Chicago: Society of American Archivists, 2019.

Millar, Laura A. *Archives: Principles and Practices*. 2nd ed. Chicago: Neal-Schuman, 2017.

OCLC. *Online Catalogs: What Users and Librarians Want: An OCLC Report*. Dublin, OH: OCLC, 2009. https://www.oclc.org/content/dam/oclc/reports/onlinecatalogs/fullreport.pdf.

Reibel, Daniel B., and Deborah Rose Van Horn. *Registration Methods for the Small Museum*. 5th ed. Lanham, MD: Rowman & Littlefield, 2018.

Rowley, Jennifer, and Richard Hartley. *Organizing Knowledge: An Introduction to Managing Access to Information*. 4th ed. Burlington, VT: Ashgate, 2008.

3.7 Notes

All URLs accessed April 2025.

1. *Publication Manual of the American Psychological Association*, 7th ed. (Washington, DC: American Psychological Association, 2020).

2. *Chicago Manual of Style*, 18th ed. (Chicago: University of Chicago Press, 2024).
3. *MLA Handbook*, 9th ed. (New York: Modern Language Association of America, 2021).
4. Council of Science Editors, *The CSE Manual: Scientific Style and Format for Authors, Editors, and Publishers*, 9th ed. (Chicago: Council of Science Editors in cooperation with the University of Chicago Press, 2024).
5. Kate L. Turabian, *A Manual for Writers of Research Papers, Theses, and Dissertations*, 9th ed., revised by Wayne C. Booth, Gregory G. Colomb, Joseph M. Williams, Joseph Bizup, William T. FitzGerald, and the University of Chicago Press editorial staff (Chicago: University of Chicago Press, 2018).
6. Karen Patrias, *Citing Medicine: The NLM Style Guide for Authors, Editors, and Publishers*, 2nd ed. (Bethesda, MD: National Library of Medicine, 2007), https://www.ncbi.nlm.nih.gov/books/NBK7256/.
7. Charles A. Cutter, *Rules for a Printed Dictionary Catalogue* (Washington, DC: Government Printing Office, 1876), 10.
8. Seymour Lubetzky, *Cataloging Rules and Principles: A Critique of the A.L.A. Rules for Entry and a Proposed Design for Their Revision* (Washington, DC: Processing Dept., Library of Congress, 1953), 36.
9. Lubetzky, 36.
10. International Conference on Cataloguing Principles, Paris, 9th–18th October 1961, *Report* (London: International Federation of Library Associations, 1963), 91–6. Also available in: *Library Resources & Technical Services* 6 (1962): 162–7; *Statement of Principles Adopted at the International Conference on Cataloguing Principles, Paris, October, 1961*, annotated ed., with commentary and examples by Eva Verona (London: IFLA Committee on Cataloguing, 1971); and A. H. Chaplin and Dorothy Anderson, eds., *Report/International Conference on Cataloguing Principles, Paris, 9th–18th October 1961* (London: IFLA International Office for UBC, 1981).
11. International Federation of Library Associations and Institutions, IFLA Study Group, *Functional Requirements for Bibliographic Records* [FRBR]: *Final Report* (Munich: Saur, 1998), 82, https://www.ifla.org/resources/?oPubId=591. [Henceforth cited as FRBR.]
12. Arlene G. Taylor, "Cataloging in Context," in Bohdan S. Wynar and Arlene G. Taylor, *Introduction to Cataloging and Classification*, 8th ed. (Englewood, CO: Libraries Unlimited, 1992), 8.
13. Pat Riva, Patrick Le Boeuf, and Maja Žumer, *IFLA Library Reference Model: A Conceptual Model for Bibliographic Information* (The Hague: IFLA, 2017), 15–16, https://www.ifla.org/resources/?oPubId=11412.
14. Martha M. Yee and Sara Shatford Layne, *Improving Online Public Access Catalogs* (Chicago: ALA, 1998).
15. "Collections Online," Pitt Rivers Museum, https://www.prm.ox.ac.uk/databases.
16. "Search the Collection," National Gallery of Art, https://www.nga.gov/collection/collection-search.html.
17. Luis Meléndez, "Still Life with Figs and Bread, c. 1770," National Gallery of Art, https://www.nga.gov/collection/art-object-page.111627.html.
18. "Artists Search," National Gallery of Art, https://www.nga.gov/collection/artists-search.html.
19. "Free Images and Open Access," National Gallery of Art, https://www.nga.gov/open-access-images.html.
20. Steven Baker, "Helping Computers Understand Language," *Official Google Blog*, January 19, 2010, https://googleblog.blogspot.com/2010/01/helping-computers-understand-language.html.
21. Paul Haahr, "Improving Search Over the Years," November 4, 2019, in Web Master Conference, Mountain View, video, 19:42, https://www.youtube.com/watch?v=DeW-9fhvkLM&t=101s&ab_channel=GoogleSearchCentral.
22. "How Search Works," Google, https://www.google.com/search/howsearchworks/how-search-works/.
23. "INFOMINE: Scholarly Internet Resource Collections," University of California, Riverside, https://web.archive.org/web/20160311214940/http://library.ucr.edu/view/infomine; Danny Sullivan, "The Yahoo Directory—Once the Internet's Most Important Search Engine—Is To Close," Search Engine Land, http://searchengineland.com/yahoo-directory-close-204370.
24. Louis Rosenfeld, Peter Morville, and Jorge Arango, *Information Architecture: For the Web and Beyond*, 4th ed. (Sebastopol, CA: O'Reilly, 2015), 12.

25. Best of the Web Directory, https://botw.org/.
26. American National Standards Institute, *American National Standard for Library and Information Sciences and Related Publishing Practices—Basic Criteria for Indexes*, ANSI Z39.4-1984 (New York: American National Standards Institute, 1984).
27. International Organization for Standardization, *Information and Documentation: Guidelines for the Content, Organization and Presentation of Indexes*, ISO 999:1996 (Geneva: ISO, 1996).
28. American National Standards Institute and National Information Standards Organization, *Criteria for Indexes*, ANSI/NISO Z39.4-2021 (Baltimore, MD: National Information Standards Organization, 2021).
29. Christine L. Borgman, "Why Are Online Catalogs *Still* Hard to Use?" *Journal of the American Society for Information Science* 47, no. 7 (1996): 493–503.
30. Abraham H. Maslow, *The Psychology of Science: A Reconnaissance* (New York: Harper & Row, 1966), 15.

Chapter 4

Information Systems, Retrieval, and Other Technology Concerns

Among the information and cultural heritage institutions discussed in this book, libraries were the first to automate. Though the question "Why automate?" is rarely asked these days, Larry Milsap reminds us that libraries automated in order to

- provide access to the complete catalog from multiple locations,
- increase and improve access points,
- increase and improve search capabilities,
- eliminate or reduce inconsistencies and inaccuracies of card catalogs,
- reduce the increasing problems and costs of maintaining card catalogs, and
- deal with pressures and influences for change.[1]

With automation came major changes in the ways that libraries performed daily tasks and fulfilled their obligations to patrons. Archives, museums, and other institutions also embraced the use of information technology in making their resources accessible. Today, the automation revolution is a thing of the past (at least in affluent nations); the importance and prevalence of information technology in organizing processes and in institutions are now just taken for granted. From yesterday's quills and typewriters to today's mobile apps, artificial intelligence-powered tools, and linked data principles, technology has been and will continue to be a vital part of information organization. This does not mean, however, that all problems related to systems and organizing information have been resolved. Information professionals still have much work to do, and it is unlikely that all the problems will be completely resolved before new ones come along.

This chapter provides an overview of some of the issues and problems in technology as they relate to organizing information. The retrieval tools described in the previous chapter require a solid and reliable technological infrastructure and adequate design to allow users to find the information they seek. These retrieval tools are useful for illustrating the problems of technology and system design in a familiar and practical way. This chapter looks at some technological components and issues that affect information organization and retrieval, but this is not meant to be a comprehensive discussion of technology's role in the library and information science (LIS) discipline. Some technology issues, many highly technical in nature, are not addressed because they go beyond the scope of this book.[2]

4.1 Systems and System Design

4.1.1 What Is a System?

The term *system* is defined in *A Dictionary of Computing* as "anything we choose to regard (a) as a whole and (b) as comprising a set of related components. ... In computing the word is freely used to refer to all kinds of combinations of hardware, software, data and other information, procedures, and human activities."[3] Therefore, the management of systems may involve a single source of data handled through a single type of software or a more complex mixture of various data sources, pieces of hardware, and software components.

In information organization, the term *system* generally refers to what we call an *information system* or an *information retrieval system*. An **information system** is a type of technology that performs three basic functions:

- **Storage**: Data is stored in a system using a specific format that is suitable for containing the type of information being amassed. Data is normalized to reduce redundancies and improve data integrity, and then it is partitioned into logical groupings (e.g., in tables or indexes) based on the nature or function of the data. The groupings are based on how the individual pieces of data are encoded or tagged. For example, all creator metadata in a system is stored together in one index, and this metadata is identified by specific codes such as 100 or 700 (in Machine-Readable Cataloging (MARC)) or natural language tags such as <creator>, <agent>, <author>, <artist>, and so on.

- **Retrieval**: To retrieve the information, a user or another system formulates a search string, which is converted into the query language used to access the data stored in the system. Quick retrieval is achieved through a thorough and meticulous indexing process. It allows the query to look at only the appropriate indexes or tables rather than trying to match the query to individual pieces of data in individual records, one record at a time.

- **Display**: Once the sought-after data is retrieved, the proper presentation renders the raw data usable and understandable in user-friendly ways (e.g., in a prescribed order, with labels).

Each one of these functions is necessary and vital to the system, and the operation of each depends on the other two. System design decisions take into consideration all three of these functions (see Figure 4.1).

4.1.2 System Design

System design refers to the process of creating an architecture for the different components, interfaces, and modules of an information system.[4] To ensure resource discovery, systems must be designed to store, retrieve, and display data in useful and logical ways. At times, it is unclear where the process of organizing information ends and where system design begins. In a display of metadata records from an information retrieval tool, both aspects come together to present information to the user. This set of results combines features of the organizing process (standard

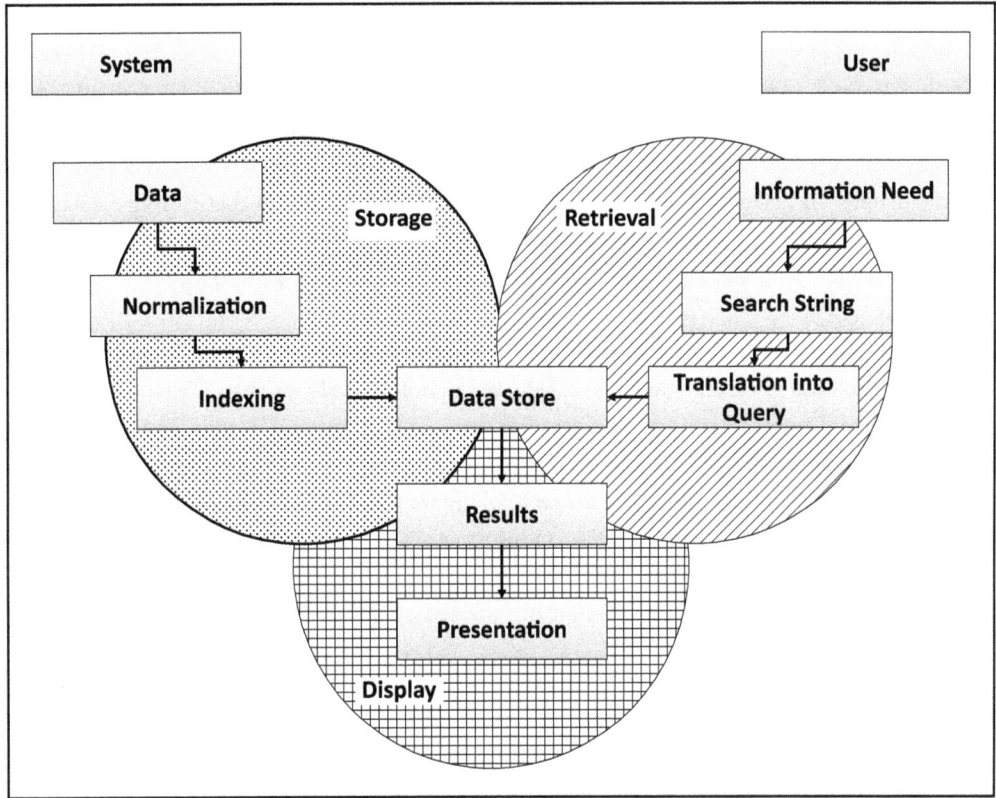

Figure 4.1 Basic Functions of and Activities in an Information System.

punctuation, forms of access points, etc.) and features of system design (labels, screen layout, etc.) in the presentation of the data. When the metadata is clear, understandable, easily retrieved, and well presented, the user usually does not notice system design or organizing elements. It is only when there are problems or confusion that these elements are discussed.

In the print world, system design was not separate from the process of creating surrogate records. Panizzi's "91 Rules" included principles for what information to include in surrogate records and also standards for placing those records into a cohesive catalog.[5] Cutter's rules included record-creation rules that emphasized collocation (i.e., placing those records in logical juxtaposition with one another) and also included a section of filing rules (i.e., Cutter's design for the card catalog).[6] Each subsequent set of cataloging rules published by the American Library Association assumed the system design of a card catalog, at least until 2010 with the publication of *RDA: Resource Description & Access*. Standards for the creation of bibliographies and indexes often assumed a print format, generally in book form, but this has changed in the twenty-first century. Published indexes and bibliographies are now rarely anything but web-based products (e.g., in database form) or as PDF documents.

Of course, the term *system design* was not used for the process of deciding how print tools would be arranged and laid out. The same people who created surrogate records also controlled the display of those records. They did not think of themselves as system designers. Yet some print tools were and still are quite sophisticated finding and collocation systems. They could be sophisticated because the designers knew the contents of the surrogate records intimately. As tools became automated, the task of design was taken on by people who understood technology, but often had little or no knowledge of the contents of the records that would make up the retrieval system.

System design is a necessity for the retrieval of organized information, whether it is done by the same people who create surrogate records or not. It can be a design that simply displays, in no order, every record that contains a certain keyword. Or it can be a design that displays records in a sophisticated way to show relationships among resources, as well as responding to requested search words.

System design research can be divided into two categories: (1) technology-focused research and (2) user-centered research. These two categories are not mutually exclusive. There are overlapping concerns and interconnections between the two (e.g., the system's search functionality and the user's information-seeking behavior have important connections). Users' needs and search behavior should influence the design of the technology we use (whether they do or not is another issue). Although this book is not a treatise on information-seeking behavior, it is helpful to start with a basic underlying assumption that users generally approach retrieval tools with an information need. How they meet that need is greatly affected by the characteristics of the system they encounter.

4.1.3 Databases and Query Languages

One of the most basic technologies used to organize information is the ***database***. A database provides the underlying structure for our information retrieval systems. Records are the fundamental components of a database. Typically, a database comprises a set of records all constructed in the same way, with common attributes (fields) and connected by relationships, where each record represents a specific entity (a product, an employee, a library book, etc.). Records may contain text, numeric information, graphic representations, or a combination of these. A record comprises data fields (such as name, stock number, date of birth, title) chosen to describe entities of interest. A database *can* be represented in a paper format (e.g., a phone book), but today it is nearly always thought of as containing machine-readable data. Databases become necessary when there is too much information for humans to process and analyze by themselves. Simply put, databases are highly organized collections of data.

An everyday example to help clarify the basic components of a database is a checkbook or an online banking activity log. Each transaction has a record (e.g., a row in the checkbook). Transactions have attributes, such as date, check number, payee, transaction description, amount, and adjusted balance. In each column, there is a field for holding the value of each attribute. The attribute values identify, describe, and explain the transactions.[7]

Of course, most databases are more complex than this, but the checkbook example does contain elements of a basic database structure. A variety of organizational methods may be used to manage the data stored inside a database, and these methods vary among systems. A key feature of bibliographic databases is the use of indexes created to hold distinct types of information. For example,

Date	Check #	Payee	Description	Amount	Balance
1/15/25			ATM withdrawal	$ -100.00	$ 1,536.34
1/17/25	132	American Library Association	Student Membership Fee	$ -46.00	$ 1,490.34
2/01/25			Salary	$ 2,000.00	$ 3,490.34
2/01/25	133	Mr. Fishoeder	Rent	$ -1,200.00	$ 2,290.34

separate indexes may be created to track creator data, title data, subject data, and the like; the number and types of indexes that are created differ from system to system.

Today, most database applications are relational databases. These are databases designed using an entity-relationship model. In the relational database model, the collection of metadata typically found in a surrogate record is divided into parts (entities), which are held in various tables. These parts are linked to each other to form individual metadata displays that show how the various entities are related. Each individual piece of information is stored in only one place, reducing data redundancy, but it may be used in multiple displays. For example, an author's name may be stored only once in a table of names, but the display for each work written by that author includes the author's name. To interact with the information held in a database, a query language is used. Structured Query Language (SQL) is a common programming language used to manage and retrieve information contained within most relational databases.

In the past, some systems were based on hierarchical databases, which used a traditional tree structure as the model for holding information. They consisted of one file composed of many records, which in turn were made up of numerous data fields. These databases tended to be rather inflexible and used more space as data was often repeated. Hierarchical structures are rarely used in today's information systems, and the ones that exist are being replaced primarily by relational models. The early 2010s saw the development of several alternative database structures lumped under the heading *non-relational databases*, sometimes called NoSQL* databases. Non-relational databases have a few sub-types including graph databases, document databases, object-oriented databases, and more.[8] The more technical aspects of database structures are beyond the scope of this book,[9] but what is important to understand is that more than just a single type of database is found in the larger computing environment.

Databases serve various functions. They may hold administrative data, a collection of images, or raw numerical data. They may contain surrogate records or hold the actual information resources of interest. They may be repositories of full-text articles, or they might keep track of inventory and sales. The functions of databases can be divided into two categories:

1. **Reference databases** that contain links or pointers to information sources held outside of the database, for example, a journal index containing information about the location and contents of articles that are stored elsewhere.

2. **Source databases** that contain the actual information sought, for example, a human resources database containing employee information.

---

*NoSQL stands for *not only SQL*.

Databases created as information retrieval tools generally contain surrogate records. The retrieval tools described in the previous chapter can all be held in computer databases, although bibliographies and finding aids are more likely to be displayed as online documents. Databases underlie many tools that we use to organize information. Indexing and abstracting services, book sellers, museums, and libraries, to name a few, all rely on databases to hold the records of their inventories.

4.1.4 Retrieval Models

Despite the presence of browsing in some retrieval tools, our current information systems are frequently oriented toward **Boolean retrieval**, which uses exact-match queries, wherein the exact specifications of the query must be satisfied to create a match. This may include the use of familiar **Boolean operators**: **AND**, **OR**, and **NOT**. For this type of system to work reasonably well, users must know what they are looking for and be able to construct a query that translates their interests into a logical search strategy. A simple query using Boolean logic might seek more than one term where either

- both terms must appear together in the record to create a match (**AND**), or
- only one of the terms must be present in the record to create a match (**OR**).

Also, terms may be added to the query to invalidate any records that contain those terms (**NOT**), that is, the presence of the terms make a record undesirable and therefore not retrieved as part of the results set. If the query contains multiple elements, parentheses may be used to nest the operations, although this is often more useful to the searcher to ensure clarity than it is for the system itself.

((Cats **OR** Dogs) **AND** Pets) **NOT** (Feral **OR** Wild)

Exact match, Boolean searching tends to be an all-or-nothing approach. It is precise, rigid, purely mechanistic, and the burden is placed on users, not on the system. If there is no exact match, then nothing may be retrieved.

Other retrieval models do exist such as statistical models like the vector space and probabilistic approaches. **Probabilistic retrieval**, for example, is based on term weighting and frequency, and attempts to estimate the probable relevance of information to a query; it returns results that match the query to some degree and are displayed in the order of decreasing similarity. Such models have been the subject of research for many years. They represent attempts to find ways around the limitations of exact-match, Boolean-based retrieval. These retrieval models are not without criticism though. For example, they may not consider information-seeking behaviors such as browsing or exploratory searching, which are not query-based. In the best of all possible systems, a variety of search options and retrieval techniques would be available.

4.1.5 Searching Information Systems

According to Charles Hildreth, there are two basic approaches to searching: (1) querying and (2) browsing. Each can be subdivided into more specific methods.[10] Figure 4.2 provides an illustration of the breakdown.

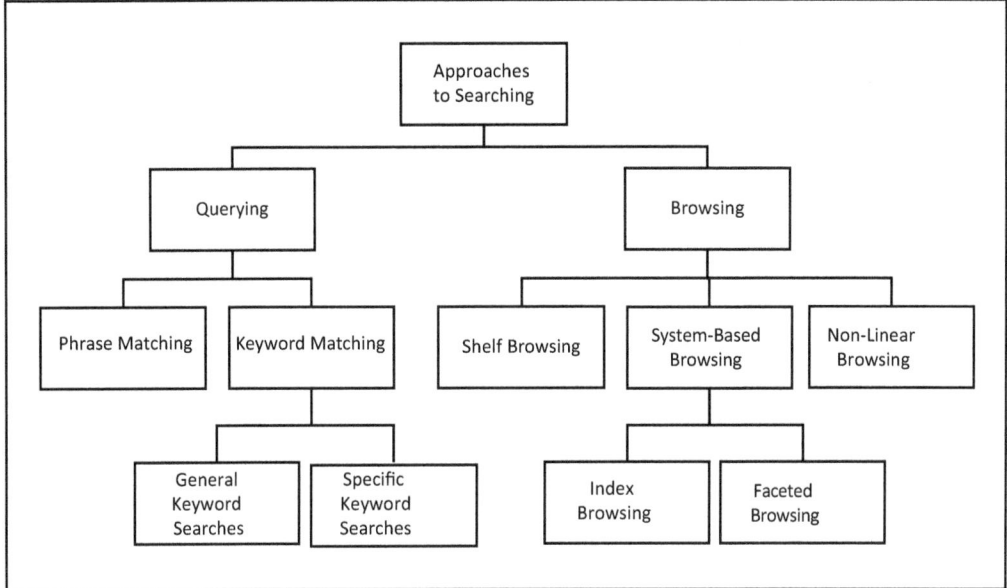

Figure 4.2 Basic Approaches to Searching.

4.1.5.1 Querying

The first approach is ***querying***, which is asking questions or requesting information from a retrieval tool (i.e., conducting a search). This can be subdivided into two types of retrieval approaches: *phrase matching* and *keyword matching*. ***Phrase matching*** is comparing and matching a search string to the exact text located in records found in the system (or more precisely, matching the search string to specific indexes created by the system from those records). This type of query demands that the words of the string be found together in the exact order as given in the search query.[†] This is processed as ***left-anchored searching*** because character matching starts with the first letter of the first word of the phrase working from left to right. It matches character by character until there is a mismatch. If, for example, a user was searching for books by Lev Grossman in a system that supports left-anchored searching, the user would simply enter the following string into the search box:

Creator/Author: Grossman, Lev

The system would then search the creator index (only) and search the string letter-by-letter from left to right.

G-R-O-S-S-M-A-N L-E-V

As the system begins to compile the results, it includes all the Grossmans, up to the point where it begins to match the letters of the first names. Then the presence of the letter "L" in the query would eliminate Allen Grossman and Evelyne Grossman, leaving only authors named Grossman whose first names begin with "L." Then it goes to the next letter, "E," and removes L.P. Grossman

---

[†]This process is similar to using quotation marks around a phrase in an internet search engine.

and Lloyd Grossman, leaving only Lev and Leah. The next letter, "V," ends the query completely because Leah is eliminated, leaving only authors with the last name Grossman and the first name Lev (or perhaps Levi, Levon, Leva, etc., depending on whether automatic truncation is activated in the search system). It is also important to note that there could be more than one person named Lev Grossman found in the search results—names are not unique!

Phrase matching does not allow the terms in search strings to be retrieved from more than one field (or index). Phrase matching requires the terms to come from the same data source. For example, when performing the earlier phrase matching query for Lev Grossman, you will not retrieve results where *Grossman* is from the creator index but *lev* (the Hebrew word for *mind, heart, consciousness*) is found only in a summary, table of contents, or elsewhere. Allowing sought terms to be separated across fields (indexes) is a characteristic of the second type of query: **keyword matching**.

Keyword searching involves matching discrete words to the system's indexes, often using Boolean operators or proximity formulations (e.g., near, within) to combine them. Keywords may be matched against terms that occur in more than one field or index. Keyword matching may involve querying a general keyword index (a compilation of all keywords found in the records), or it may be more specific, where users can limit the search to one type of keyword (e.g., a title keyword search or a subject keyword search). For example, a general keyword search for *twelfth night* will bring back records for Shakespeare's play, but it will also bring back, among many other things, a novel titled *Trial by Treason* published by *Night* Shade Books with a summary indicating that the story is set in *twelfth*-century England. A search, however, could also specify that the keywords *twelfth* and *night* must appear only in the title index; this will again retrieve the play, but also *Doctor Who: Twelfth Night, Carol on Twelfth Night*, and *Montmartre 1924–1939*, which contains songs with the titles "Twelfth Year" and "Night and Day." The terms *twelfth* and *night* do not have to appear together as a phrase or be the first words of the title to match the keyword search.

4.1.5.2 Browsing

Browsing—surveying or perusing information—can also be divided into sub-categories. Upon hearing the word, what most likely comes to mind is ***shelf browsing***. This, of course, refers to inspecting the area of the stacks where a user has already found an item of interest to see if other relevant items are in proximity. This does not relate specifically to searching a system, but it is the most familiar form of browsing to users. When it comes to browsing in an information system, one approach is pre-sequenced, linear, ***system-based browsing***. This entails users scanning lists of topics, creators, or titles to find items of interest. System-based browsing can be divided further into index browsing and faceted browsing. ***Index browsing*** is a very structured approach, using the system's internal data organization to guide browsing activities. In other words, it relies on the system's indexes to provide browsable lists of names, subjects, titles, and so on. For example, in a system that allows users to browse authority-controlled headings, a user could enter the creator list at whatever point they choose, such as authors with the last name of *Grossman* and the first initial *L*. The system would then return a list like this:

Grossman, Leonard
Grossman, Leonid Petrovich, 1888-1965
 See: **Grossman, L. P. (Leonid Petrovich), 1888-1965**

Grossman, Leonid Zinovèvich
Grossman, Leroy Whitney
Grossman, Leslie, 1947-
Grossman, Lev
Grossman, Lewis A., 1964-
Grossman, Libah Jane

From that point, the user may scan names either before or after the entry point into the list.

Many institutions augment their information systems with a *discovery layer*—a front-end interface designed to facilitate more flexible interaction with the system's information stores. A feature of many discovery layers is the provision of *faceted browsing*, another form of system-based browsing that exploits facets (i.e., individual aspects) of the data gathered from the original records ingested into the system. Faceted browsing provides new and interesting ways of grouping keyword search results into clusters based on a wide variety of characteristics. Instead of simply putting a keyword into a search box and retrieving a large randomly returned set of results, discovery layers separate the results into smaller chunks based on certain facets they believe will be helpful, such as subjects, format, genre, language, classification number, region, date range, and so on. An example of a faceted browsing interface can be seen in Figure 4.3.

The final type of browsing is *non-linear browsing*. This is browsing that is more serendipitous and multi-directional. It is unstructured and uses hypertext links to navigate between assorted items; it is more exploratory in nature and can appear to be more random.

Although querying is useful when users know what they want, browsing in some cases may be a more efficient alternative to retrieving thousands of records in response to a keyword query. In cases where the user is unsure of what is wanted, or when the user does not know the exact string used in the system to describe what is sought, browsing may provide a more manageable approach to meeting the user's information need. In recent years, many systems seem to have moved away from allowing users to browse system-generated indexes or perform left-anchored searches. Instead, the focus has shifted to keyword searching, with or without faceted browsing. The reasons for this change are not entirely clear.

4.1.5.3 Federated Searching

Federated searching, also known as *meta-searching*, is the ability to search and retrieve results from multiple sources of information while using only a single, common interface. It features an all-inclusive overlay (one-search box) to multiple systems, which may include catalogs, indexes, databases, and other electronic resources. This, too, is a popular feature of discovery layers. William Frost states:

> Metasearching (a.k.a. federated searching or broadcast searching) is considered by some to be the next evolutionary step of database searching. Proponents believe that novice users, such as undergraduates, are baffled by the number of databases they have to choose from and need one common interface to meet all their research needs. A common interface, they claim, could wean novice searchers from using the Internet as their primary source for research.[11]

Narrow Your Search	**Search**
	Subject: Subject cataloging
	Sort by: Date Descending

Year of Publication:
 From   To
 [2010]   [2023]
 	
 Resource Type ▲
 ☐ Articles (1,355)
 ☐ Books (122)
 ☐ eBooks (71)
 ☐ Serials (2)
      Show more....
 	
 Library of Congress Call Number ▲
 Z – Library Science (121)
 L – Education (1)
 	
 Subject ▼
 	
 Place ▼
 	
 Form/Genre ▼
 	
 Author/Creator ▼
 	
 Language ▼
 	
 Location/Branch ▼
 	
 Journal Title ▼
 	
 Series ▼
 	
 Audience ▼
	Search Results (1–10 of 47 results)
	
	 1. **Cos'è l'indicizzazione**
	      Guarasci, Roberto [author] / Milano : Editrice Bibliografica / (Biblioteconomia e scienza dell'informazione ; 40) / 2022.
	
	 2. **Cruising the library : perversities in the organization of knowledge**
	      Adler, Melissa [author] / First edition / New York, NY : Fordham University Press 2017.
	
	 3. **Introduction to cataloging and classification**
	      Joudrey, Daniel N. [author] / Eleventh edition / Daniel N. Joudrey, Arlene G. Taylor, and David P. Miller / Santa Barbara, California : Libraries Unlimited / (Library and information science text series) / 2015.
	
	 4. **Cataloguing and classification : an introduction to AACR2, RDA, DDC, LCC, LCSH and MARC 21 standards**
	      Lazarinis, Fotis [author] / Waltham, Massachusetts ; Oxford, England : Chandos Publishing, 2015.
	
	 5. **Essential classification**
	      Broughton, Vanda [author] / Chicago : ALA Neal-Schuman, an imprint of the American Library Association, 2015.
	
	 6. **Guidelines for subject access in national bibliographies.**
	      International Federation of Library Associations and Institutions. Working Group on Guidelines for Subject Access by National Bibliographic Agencies [author] ; edited by Yvonne Jahns. / Berlin : De Gruyter Saur, 2012 / (IFLA series on bibliographic control, 1868-8434 ; v. 45.
	
	 7. **FAST: Faceted Application of Subject Terminology : principles and applications**
	      Chan, Lois Mai [author] / Santa Barbara, CA : Libraries Unlimited, 2010.

Figure 4.3 An Example of a Faceted Browsing Interface.

Others believe its popularity is simply due to the *principle of least effort*,[12] where users will choose convenience and ease over a raft of other benefits including specificity, precision, and exhaustivity. Although it appears that users may desire this type of searching for one reason or another, there are downsides, the biggest being that federated searching functionality is limited to the level of the lowest common denominator among all the systems that the interface searches (e.g., catalog, various databases, digital collections). Frost also states that reliance on meta-searching prevents students and other users from developing a better understanding of the multiple, diverse, specialized resources available to them and how to take advantage of the different systems.[13]

4.2 Standardization Issues

Standardization was a key feature of the card catalog. Users who were familiar with one catalog could apply the same knowledge and skills to other catalogs they encountered with a minimum of difficulty. Standardization, however, does not happen overnight. It takes time to develop. The lack of standardization today is reminiscent of a time more than a century ago, when catalogs contained cards of varying sizes (e.g., 2 × 5 inches, 2 × 10 inches, 3 × 5 inches) and the information placed on cards lacked a standard order. Standardization came when Melvil Dewey's 7.5 × 12.5-centimeter catalog cabinets won out over other sizes.‡ In the library cataloging community, throughout the latter part of the twentieth century, there were calls for standard interfaces for online public access catalogs (OPACs). As Martha Yee stated, "The lack of standardization across OPACs can make it difficult for catalogue users to apply their knowledge of one OPAC to searching another OPAC in a different library."[14] David Thomas notes that a user's need for standardized description has not been acknowledged in online systems, and this leads to a loss of familiarity for the user.[15]

Today, there are still no real standards, just broad guidelines and suggestions. Due to the competitive nature of vendors in the information technology marketplace, a standard interface is unlikely to occur anytime soon. Vendors develop new features, and each vendor places different levels of importance on various aspects of its system design. Some have diverse internal organization schemes; some have limited search capabilities. Vendors try to develop the most appealing interface, search features, and modules in order to gain a greater market share. This competition contributes to the lack of standardization in system design, but it can also contribute to long-term system innovations and progress. This is a question of finding the right balance between standardization and market forces. Online indexes, too, have a great deal of variety and little standardization. This is a continuation of a long history of lack of standardization in print indexes. The following are some areas in which standardization has been recommended over the years.

- Display
- Basic search queries
- Initial articles

---

‡This was reinforced by the Library of Congress (LC) selling its cataloging on 3 × 5 in. cards. The size of the LC cards was and continued to be 7.5 × 12.5 cm, but the United States did not change to the metric system as Dewey believed was imminent. The size was just under 3 × 5 in., and the cards came to be called "3 × 5 cards."

- Truncation, Boolean operators, and proximity
- Punctuation

They are discussed further below.

4.2.1 Display

One of the key areas in which the lack of standardization is most apparent is in system displays. Displays can be divided into two categories: (1) the display of sets of retrieved results and (2) the display of metadata found in surrogate records. Both are concerned with issues of screen layout and design. Concerns over displays led some in the LIS profession to work toward standardization guidelines. In 1997, a task force of the International Federation of Library Associations and Institutions (IFLA) was established to develop guidelines for the display of authority and bibliographic information.[16] In 2005, the guidelines were finalized and published. "The intent of these guidelines is to provide a set of recommendations that meet the core requirements for displays that catalogues should present, regardless of any other options that may be offered to the users," including users who want to begin searching right away without much instruction.[17] The efforts of the IFLA task force and additional LIS researchers have focused on users' needs for powerful but easy-to-use search tools. Despite the development of these recommendations by an international body, system vendors are under no obligation to comply with them. Neither the decades of external user experience research nor the 2005 IFLA guidelines appears to have made much impact on commercial information systems.

4.2.1.1 Display of Retrieved Results

Regarding display, our first concern is what is being presented to the user as initial search results. Do the results appear as individual records or as a list of names or terms? The former is a list of individual resources to sort through and the latter is a list of formal access points and cross references. Examples may help to clarify the difference.

In response to a search for a creator with the surname *Benson,* some systems return lists of resources related to all creators named Benson without first identifying how many there are and who those Bensons are. For example, a user might see the following results:

1. African beginnings / James Haskins & Kathleen Benson.
2. Agriculture / O.H. Benson.
3. All kids are our kids / Peter L. Benson
4. Beading for the first time / Ann Benson.
5. Beside still waters / Arthur Christopher Benson.
6. Counter cultures / Susan Porter Benson.
7. The desert islander / Stella Benson.
8. Emily / Sally Benson.
9. Endangered species / Sonia Benson.
10. Forty-eight hours in Miami / Sara Benson.

Users are required to page through the list of titles—which may or may not be in a self-evident order (e.g., alphabetical by title)—instead of being able to browse a list of creator names first. Other systems, in response to the same search, display all creators in the system named Benson, alphabetized by forename. Users then must browse through this list and find the appropriate access point for the desired Benson before clicking on its link to retrieve a list of resources to sift through.

74 **Benson, Sally, 1897-1972**
75 **Benson, Sara**
76 **Benson, Sonia**
77 **Benson, Stella, 1892-1933**
78 **Benson, Susan Porter, 1943-2005**
79 **Benson, Thomas W.**
80 **Benson, Warren, 1924-2005**
81 Benson, Warren E. (Warren Edgar), 1931-
   See: **Benson, Warren Edgar, 1931-**
82 **Benson, Warren Edgar, 1931-**
83 Benson, Warren Frank, 1924-2005
   See: **Benson, Warren, 1924-2005**
84 **Benson, Wayne**

This display is used when the creator search is run against the controlled headings found in a system's authority file (if the system has one) or when the retrieval tool supports system-based browsing, allowing users to scan through a list of all creators (usually, but not always, from the authority file).

Another concern in displaying results is the order in which results are shown. First-generation information systems often worked on the "last in, first out" principle. Although this was not entirely random, the order lacked meaning for users. As systems matured, designers took users' needs into account to provide a more logical order of search results. In many catalogs and indexes, results were then presented in alphabetical order by the last name of the primary (or first-named) creator.

In time, as programming became more sophisticated, additional options for sorting were developed. Search results could then be displayed in different ways for different types of searches. For example, the results from a subject search could be sorted alphabetically by the primary creator, while a title search in the same system could be displayed in alphabetical order by the first significant word of the title. This development began to allow local institutions to make their own choices as to what would best serve their users.

As systems have advanced further, control of search results displays has been given to the user. In most systems, users can specify, from a brief list of options, how they wish search results to be sorted. Such sorting, however, may still present problems. For example, if one chooses to have results sorted by creator, then the access point for the primary or first-named author is displayed in the sorted list, but that access point may not be the author that the user knows about or is interested in (e.g., the Benson being sought could be a second or later author of a resource, as seen in the *African beginnings* example above).

Of the sorting options now provided to users, one is usually **relevance**. Relevance means many things in the LIS landscape. In terms of retrieval systems, Rebecca Green defines *relevance* as "the property of a text's being potentially useful to a user in the resolution of a need."[18] Howard White states:

> When [information retrieval] systems are formally evaluated, judges decide the goodness of fit between documents and the sense of the query that elicited them. In everyday life we constantly do the same thing less formally when we search the Web. Relevance is thus a variable; in judgments of documents it can take at least two values, "Relevant" and "Not Relevant," and many IR system evaluators have used scales that allow values in between.[19]

Relevance ranking, in theory, allows the most pertinent search results to be displayed first and results determined to be less relevant to the query to be displayed later.

There are various methods for determining the relevance of a result. One method employed by some systems is to break up the elements of a query. Consider this search string:

music **AND** notation **AND** (software **OR** package)

The results of this query, ranked by relevance, would start with results that include three or more of the above terms: *music*, *notation*, *software*, and *package*. Less relevant results would follow (e.g., results that include just two terms), with the least relevant results listed at the end (e.g., those that match just a single term).[20] Some companies with proprietary search tools, such as EBSCO Information Services, have released basic details about how their tools rank relevance. For example, their EBSCO Discovery Service assigns different weights to metadata fields when calculating relevance, giving higher priority to information from subject fields than to information from free-text fields.[21] In discovery layers that allow for faceted browsing, users can narrow sets of search results to only the most pertinent results by choosing facets that reflect their immediate information needs, avoiding the requirement to scroll through page after page of results ranked by system-defined relevance.

In addition, users now have different choices for sorting lists of retrieved results. If the list is in chronological order, it may be in ascending or in descending order. If the list is arranged alphabetically, there are numerous ways a computer can be programmed for alphabetical order, affected by punctuation, spacing, and other such factors. Numerical order is likewise unpredictable, not to mention the problem of whether numbers come before or after letters. These and other issues are discussed in Appendix A: Arrangement of Metadata Displays.

4.2.1.2 Display of Records

Display of retrieved records also varies from system to system. In the case of library catalogs containing MARC records, there is often far more data in the record than is displayed to the public. Much of the record goes unseen because it contains information that is not useful to the general user. At the local level, the library staff may determine which fields are displayed and which are not. Thus, in one library the record display may be longer or shorter than that found in another nearby library.

Some LIS professionals have expressed concerns about display inconsistencies across systems.[22] Some of the variations include the suppression of notes and the treatment of subjects. Notes are designed to give information that clarifies data given in other areas of the description. Without some or all notes, users may be misled by the information that is given. In some systems, subjects may not be presented on the preliminary display (sometimes they appear on a separate tab in the display or in a subsequent fuller display screen). These display disparities could cause users to overlook potentially relevant or useful resources based on what is initially shown.

So, what *should* be displayed? The 2005 IFLA recommendations state, "a single record display should contain the data necessary to fulfill the functions of the catalogue,"[23] that is, the IFLA user tasks (find, identify, select, obtain, and explore). Thomas, however, recognized that users find only a small number of fields useful.[24] Additional guidelines may be needed for selecting the most essential metadata fields to display to improve consistency.

Similarly, information contained in index records is quite variable. Commercial indexes use their own encoding schemes and may have their own standards for inclusion of information in records. Differences may include length of citation, abbreviations, inclusion of abstracts, and the presence or absence of controlled vocabulary terms. They also display records in a variety of ways, often allowing the user some control over the types and amount of information they see.

The labeling of metadata in records also varies among systems, and there are differences in the terminology used for labeling. In addition, the need for labeling metadata at all has been questioned. Labels can be confusing and do not necessarily cover everything in a field. For example, in the MARC format, the 245 field may contain, among other things, a title proper, subtitles, a parallel title and parallel subtitles, a part title, part numbering, and statements of responsibility; this complex collection of data elements may simply be labeled as *Title*. Thomas points out that although many assert the need for labels, there is no empirical evidence that labeled displays are more effective.[25] One might assume, then, that using unlabeled displays would cause relatively few problems for users. To serve the most inexperienced users, however, the persistence of labels is probably for the best.

4.2.2 Basic Search Queries

When approaching an unfamiliar information system, users who wish to search with precision must determine the ways in which they can search. Keyword, creator, title, and subject searches are found in most retrieval tools. Although these searching options are generally available, some systems may present only an empty keyword-focused Google-style search box as the initial interface. Some, but not all, OPACs also allow call number searching. In a few systems, the user may be offered searches that are less common, such as combined name/title, standard number, or journal title searches. Although some search types may be typical across various systems, the ways in which those systems are indexed are not consistent. To illustrate, consider some of the following questions that might arise when a user encounters a new search system:

- What types of searches can be conducted (left-anchored, keyword, browsing)?
- Which fields are indexed for the various types of searches?

- Can specific fields be searched in some way (e.g., genre/form, publisher, publication location)?

Due to the lack of standardization among systems, the answers will vary.

Users may or may not be able to choose whether a creator search is interpreted by the system as an exact match, browse, or keyword search. If a search for *Smith, William* is entered:

- Will the system search for that word string exactly, no more and no less (i.e., a left-anchored phrase-matching search with no truncation)?
- Will it search for any entry beginning with that exact word string (i.e., a browse search with automatic truncation)?
- Will it search any creator-related field that contains both *William* and *Smith*, returning results for **Barney, William Smith** and **William, Jonathan Smith** (i.e., a creator keyword search)?

In these examples, if a user wishes to find a particular *William Smith* whose middle names and/or dates are not known or remembered, then a phrase match or a keyword match may not be satisfactory. Browsing may be the only efficient solution. Unfortunately, users may not understand the differences in these types of interactions, and the system may not make these choices discernible or available.

The results of keyword searching are determined by the fields that are searched in the system. Some systems have generic keyword searches that search almost every field of a record—or more precisely, they search a general keyword index that includes all fields except for **stopwords**, which are extremely common words (such as *the, it, an, to*) that are typically ignored during searching because they add little value to retrieval. In other systems, there may be separate pull-down menus so that users can choose the type of keyword search they want to perform (e.g., subject keyword, title keyword, creator keyword). The fields included in these distinct types of keyword indexes vary from system to system. For example, some subject keyword indexes contain terms from subject heading fields, summary notes, contents notes, genre/form headings, and title fields, while others include only subject heading fields. Although general notes fields may contain subject-laden terminology, system designers often exclude them as fields to be searched for subject keywords.

Not all systems allow direct searching of certain types of data. For example, very few systems offer the public a *publisher* search or a dedicated *series* search. To search this type of data, users may have to rely on general keyword searches or searches that include multiple data types (e.g., relying on the title search for series title searching). Although separate genre/form searching has been implemented in some systems, it is far from universal. If users are interested in autobiographies or in specialized dictionaries, it would be helpful for them to be able to include genre/form terms in the search. For certain materials, like art and other visual resources, genre/form concepts are essential for a successful query, but this type of search is still relatively rare in library catalogs. Genre/form browsing, though, is available through some discovery layers (such as EBSCO Discovery Service or VuFind).

Other searching considerations include choosing the collection or the library branch to search. Users should be aware of search limits available in a system (e.g., language, date, format). As is true of most of the choices discussed here, all these options are managed differently across systems.

4.2.3 Initial Articles

Another example of the lack of standardization is the handling of initial articles (*a, an, the,* and their equivalents in other languages). In many systems, there are instructions to omit initial articles when entering a search string. Users tend to follow this advice if the instruction can be seen from the search box. If a search still includes the initial article, the system may

- return a message that the user received no hits, with no explanation given;
- provide the user with a message to remove the article and try again;
- treat an initial article differently depending on whether it is a keyword, browse, or exact word search; or
- eliminate the article without notifying the user and perform the search.

The last possibility in the above list may be good for most searches, but there are times when the article (or what appears to be an article) is needed for the search to be successful (e.g., a book titled *A is for Apple*).

4.2.4 Truncation, Boolean Operators, and Proximity

Other examples of lack of consistency are found in the way systems manage truncation, Boolean operators, and proximity. Users should know if there is automatic right-hand truncation and, if not, what they must do to apply it. In a system with automatic right-hand truncation, when a user inputs a search word, the system returns everything that contains that word, but also anything else that begins with that word. For example, a search for *catalog* retrieves not only records for *catalog* but also records that contain the terms:

- cataloged
- cataloger
- catalogers
- catalogic
- cataloging
- catalogise
- catalogize
- Catalogne

- catalogs
- catalogue
- catalogued
- cataloguer
- cataloguers
- catalogues
- cataloguing
- cataloguise (and more!)

If right-hand truncation is not automatic, then a symbol must be used to indicate that truncation is desired in a search. The symbol may be an asterisk (*), a question mark (?), a pound sign (#), a dollar sign ($), or another symbol, depending on the system. For example, the search mentioned above may need to be formulated as *catalog#* in a system without automatic truncation to bring about the same results. The use of truncation might also change depending on the type of search conducted. For example, in a single system, title searches and creator searches may always use automatic truncation, but in keyword searches the user may need to input a specific truncation symbol. In many systems, information about how truncation works is presented in the help screens, but if not, experimentation may be necessary to better understand the mechanics of the search process.

Use of Boolean logic is not always consistent among systems. Most allow more than one word per search, but the ways in which multiple terms are treated can vary. The default Boolean operator is often **AND**, but it could be **OR**. Most online catalogs, for example, treat a keyword search with multiple terms as if the operator **AND** has been inserted between them. That is, all terms in the search must be present in a record for that record to be retrieved. Many internet search engines, though, treat such a search as if **OR** has been inserted between terms. That is, each record retrieved contains at least one of the terms, but not necessarily all the terms. When Boolean operators are expressly inserted, a user must know the order in which operations are conducted. For example, in a search for "catalog **OR** index **AND** libraries," most systems execute the operators from left to right (i.e., records with either *catalog* or *index* combined with the word *libraries*). Some online retrieval systems, however, may search for records with the term *catalog* or records containing both *index* and *libraries*. In other words, the query might be interpreted as either of the following:

> (catalog **OR** index) **AND** libraries
> catalog **OR** (index **AND** libraries)

The best solution would be to use nesting to ensure that the execution will be conducted as desired—although this may be beyond the knowledge of many users.

Advanced users may also want to know if ***proximity operators*** are supported and, if so, how specific the formulations are. Proximity formulations are often used in indexes and some search engines, but less frequently in library catalogs. They allow the user to specify the maximum distance between two or more words in a search query. The degree of sophistication in formulation may range from a simple **NEAR** or **ADJ** (adjacent) to an indication of the distance allowed to appear between terms (e.g., **w2** or **w/2**—meaning within two words). Unfortunately, there is little consistency in the use of these helpful search tools across the various types of information systems.

4.2.5 Punctuation

Punctuation can be a source of great confusion for users and information professionals alike. When approaching a new system, several questions arise, such as:

- Are quotation marks used to indicate exact phrases? For example, will a search for "organization of information" retrieve only that phrase as it appears, or will it also retrieve "information organization" and other variations?
- Are diacritical marks used and understood? For example, are the accent marks in *résumé* necessary? If so, how are they to be entered?
- Should all punctuation be stripped from the query? If not, which symbols can be used, and which ones should be deleted? For example, should one search, "**Shakespeare, William, 1564-1616**" or should the search be "**Shakespeare William 1564 1616**" or some other variation?

- Are there filing rules or conventions based on punctuation that will thwart a user's ability to find desired search results? For example, are *meta-data* and *metadata* filed next to each other in a list of results, or are they separated in the list because of the hyphen?

Removing punctuation from a string of text to provide better potential for matches is called ***normalization***. Data normalization often occurs when the system indexes metadata records as they are entered into the database.

String	**Benson, Susan Porter, 1943-2005.**
Normalized string	**Benson Susan Porter 1943 2005**

Normalization allows better matching because users are not always precise in the placement of diacritics, commas, and other punctuation marks. However, depending upon the algorithm used for normalization, results may be different from system to system.

A telling example of how the lack of standardization can affect users comes from an article by J. H. Bowman, who looked at how the ampersand (&) and the hyphen (-) are treated in various online catalogs.[26] Bowman found that in separate systems the symbols behaved quite differently. The hyphen affected searching and indexing in at least six ways. Sometimes the hyphen was treated as

- a space
- a null character (i.e., nothing there, not even a space, thereby bringing the two pieces of the hyphenated word together into one word)
- both a null character and as a space (which meant the terms were indexed at least twice)
- as a hyphen (the punctuation mark)
- as a Boolean **NOT** (i.e., the hyphen as a minus sign)
- as an invalidating character (e.g., completely disrupting the search)

In addition, Bowman found that the hyphen was sometimes processed differently in keyword searches than it was in phrase-matching queries. The ampersand, too, had a variety of treatments. It was seen as an ampersand, as a Boolean **AND**, as a search string terminator, and as a null character. Besides the obvious effects that these different treatments have on the results and the arrangement of results lists (and on the frustration levels of users scrolling through long lists of results), they can also have an impact on federated searching. Although the impact of this issue has lessened over time in online catalogs, the various uses of ampersands and hyphens still affect other types of retrieval tools, particularly internet search engines.

4.2.6 Authority Control Integration

Another issue of standardization is whether authority control is supported in the system. ***Authority control*** is a mechanism for creating consistency in online systems and for allowing greater precision and better recall in searching (it is addressed in detail in Chapter 10). ***Precision*** is a measurement of how many of the documents retrieved are relevant, and **recall** is a measurement of how many of the relevant documents stored in a system are *actually* retrieved. LIS professionals believe that users (including themselves) would like both high precision and high recall in their search results.[§] In other words, we would like our systems to allow users to find all the resources that are related to their searches with very few non-relevant items in the mix. Precision is enhanced using standardized forms of names and subjects, while recall is improved by a system of cross-references; both are features of authority control. In some information systems, primarily those in libraries, authority control is an integral part of the retrieval process. It is built into the system to enhance precision and recall. Not all information systems, however, include authority control integration, even in libraries. Some systems rely on data gathered solely from bibliographic records, rather than a mix of authority and bibliographic data.

For authority control to be successful, authority work must be consistent and thorough. In an information system where authority control is integrated, authority records are linked to bibliographic records to ensure collocation of records that all relate to the same name, standardized title, or subject heading. These linkages may be

- one-to-one (e.g., a creator who is associated with only one resource),
- one-to-many (e.g., a single creator who has created two or more works), or
- many-to-one (e.g., linking more than one creator to a single information resource).

For subject headings, it is less common to find one-to-one relationships, as there is usually more than one work on a topic. For a graphic representation of the relationship between bibliographic and authority records, see Figure 4.4. The figure shows the many-to-one and one-to-many relationships between authority records and bibliographic records.

In simple terms, each authorized access point for a name (and for subjects and *some* titles) in a bibliographic record has an authority record. Each authority record may be linked to as many bibliographic records as are appropriate (e.g., the authority record for Dolly Parton is connected to the bibliographic record describing *9 to 5*, to the one for *Rainbowland*, and to every other bibliographic record acting as a surrogate for her works), and each bibliographic record may be linked to as many authority records as are appropriate (e.g., the record describing *Rainbowland* is connected to two performers' authority records and one genre/form authority record). In Figure 4.4, there are arrows from the authority records in the name authority file to the associated names in the records in the bibliographic file. This illustration is much simpler than what one would find in most catalogs, where a single bibliographic record may be linked to 10 or more different authority records for persons, corporate bodies, subject headings, genre/form headings, series titles, and so on.

In a retrieval system with authority control integration, there are links (or pointers) from each authority record to each bibliographic record that uses the name, title, or subject in that authority

---

[§]This, however, might not be universally true. Many users are satisfied by retrieving *some* relevant results. Whether they retrieve all relevant results and only relevant result may be immaterial in any given situation.

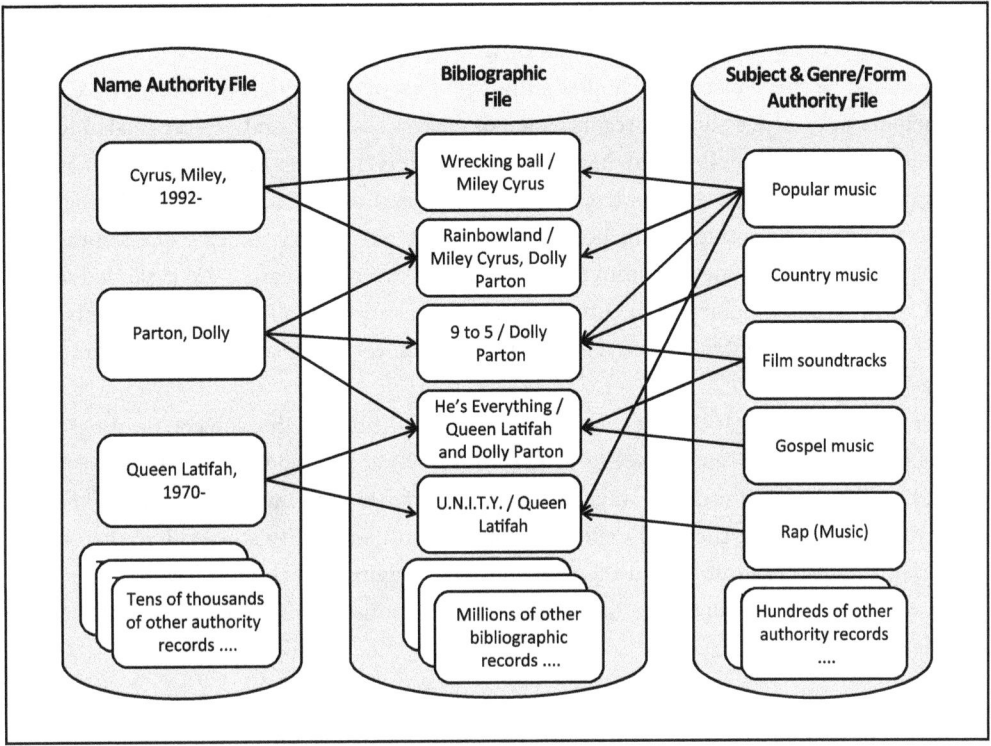

Figure 4.4 Linkages between Authority Records and Bibliographic Records.

record. There would also be links in each bibliographic record back to the multiple authority records that represent all the names, titles, and subjects for that record. The result is that if a user searches for an unused subject term, the authority record presents a reference to the authorized subject term used. Then when the user requests records for the authorized term (usually by clicking on a hyperlink), all the bibliographic records using that term are displayed. Going in the other direction, if a user has found a bibliographic record that looks promising and wants more on that subject, the link from the subject heading back to the authority record allows the system to display all the bibliographic records that contain that subject heading.

Because authority work on names and controlled vocabularies is expensive, time-consuming, human-based work, keyword searching is often touted as being a sufficient method for retrieving information resources. However, research has shown that keyword searching may result in *false drops* (i.e., irrelevant retrievals) because the word retrieved has a different meaning from the intended meaning and may result in loss of recall because synonyms or near-synonyms were not retrieved with the word sought. In addition, Tina Gross, Arlene G. Taylor, and Daniel N. Joudrey found that over one-quarter of keyword searches could fail if the authorized subject terminology is not included in the bibliographic records in the catalog, because the only place some keywords are found in some records is in the subject heading fields.[27] If the system lacks authority-controlled names, titles, and subjects, users will have to think of all synonyms, related terms, and different forms of a name on their own.

Users should be made aware of whether authority-controlled subject relationships are available to help them browse a subject area, broaden or narrow searches, and explore related topics. In the area of subject searching there have been suggestions that keyword searches be matched against both free text terms and controlled vocabulary, and that system additions be made to assist users in taking advantage of the power of controlled vocabulary. An example comes from database indexes, which sometimes provide the ability to "explode a search." An ***exploded search*** is one in which the vocabulary term chosen is searched along with all its narrower terms. This allows a user to take advantage of the relationships among terms that are built into a controlled vocabulary.

Another improvement to subject access might be to enhance the subject headings with user-supplied tags. At this time, it seems rather unlikely that user tagging will enhance subject retrieval in a consistent and useful way, because the "problems of homographs, synonyms and polysemy, are common in them. Therefore, skepticism and ambiguity still exist in the professional cataloguing community about the value of social tagging."[28] It is, however, an area where research will likely continue as more user-centered applications are incorporated into traditional system designs.

4.2.7 The Z39.50 Communication Protocol

The Z39.50 communication protocol is a national standard developed by the National Information Standards Organization (NISO). It began as an attempt to get diverse information systems to communicate and share data. The protocol establishes how one computer (the client) can query another computer (the server) and transfer search results from one to the other. It was developed and is maintained by the Library of Congress. In simple terms, when using the Z39.50 protocol, one system translates a set of local commands into a set of universal commands that are then sent to another computer. The second system translates the universal commands into equivalent commands for the second system. The results are then returned to the first computer in the same fashion. If two institutions both have Z39.50 clients installed, users can search the information system in other institutions using their locally available tools. Z39.50, however, limits the searching of various systems to the lowest common denominator. The sophisticated programming of one system cannot be passed through Z39.50 to the other system.[29]

Although Z39.50 has been a useful protocol for communicating among information systems, developers have explored other ways to perform the same tasks through updated, web-based processes. LC oversees a standard called *Search/Retrieval via URL* (SRU 2.0).[30] SRU is a standard XML search protocol for internet search queries that uses the Contextual Query Language (CQL), a standard syntax for representing queries. It incorporates many of the ideas found in Z39.50. It attempts to preserve many of the intellectual contributions that Z39.50 has accumulated over the decades. SRU can be viewed as an update or modernization of that protocol for the web environment.

4.3 Systems Used in the LIS Professions

4.3.1 Bibliographic Networks

Bibliographic networks have as their main resource a huge database of catalog-type records. Access to the database is available for a fee, and members of the network can contribute new records and download existing ones. Bibliographic networks acquire many MARC records from the Library of Congress (LC) and other subscription sources. The databases also include cataloging records contributed by participating libraries. The records contain two kinds of information: (1) cataloging data (such as title, subject, creator, dates), and (2) holdings information for libraries that have added specific items to their collections.

Bibliographic networks were organized in the 1970s to support library technical services operations through cooperative cataloging and computer-assisted card production. They have steadily expanded their activities, but their continued emphasis on cooperative cataloging most clearly distinguishes them from other online information firms that provide access to surrogate records. For example, LC MARC records are available online through other sources, but these services do not offer online entry of original cataloging data, record editing, interlibrary loan, or other services that specifically support cataloging activities. To facilitate cataloging decisions and promote consistency, bibliographic networks provide online access to the LC name and subject authority files.

As mentioned, bibliographic networks offer vast databases of existing bibliographic records and record editing interfaces that can be used to edit individual records to meet local requirements. When an institution downloads an existing record for local use, it is called ***copy cataloging***. If no cataloging copy is available, a cataloger must create a new record from "scratch" (i.e., ***original cataloging***).

Two major bibliographic networks are OCLC and SkyRiver. Bibliographic networks differ in their administrative structures and customer bases. OCLC Online Computer Library Center, the largest and most comprehensive bibliographic network, operates as an international, nonprofit membership organization.[31] The public interface for OCLC's database is known as WorldCat; librarians interact with cataloging data through OCLC's Connexion client or WorldShare Record Manager. SkyRiver, which operates for profit, offers similar resources, but at a smaller scale. Both are general-purpose bibliographic networks that are available to libraries of all types and sizes.

4.3.2 Resource Management Systems

Resource management system is a generic term that refers to various kinds of technology applications used to manage work processes in libraries and other information institutions. Any number of tools can be included under this umbrella term, but the primary topic of this section is the long-established ***integrated library system*** (ILS). The ILS has also been known as an *integrated library management system*, *library management support system*, or *library housekeeping system*. In the 2010s, a new generation of resource management systems was developed, and additional terms began to augment the professional lexicon. These include *webscale management solution*, *uniform management system*, and most commonly, ***library services platform*** (LSP).

4.3.2.1 Integrated Library Systems or Library Services Platforms?

So, what are ILSs and LSPs? According to library technology expert Marshall Breeding, who coined the term *library services platform* in 2013,[32]

> Both are types of resource management systems and can serve as the primary business process automation environment for a library. Library services platforms might reasonably be considered just the next round of integrated library systems with expanded functionality and newer technology [but] I see more fundamental differences and consider these to be distinct genres.[33]

Integrated library systems and library services platforms share similar purposes and some characteristics. Both are tools to manage a library's collections but the recognizable difference between the two is that ILSs were designed for managing print collections, whereas LSPs are designed for managing physical, digital, and electronic materials. Library services platforms "aimed to address the fundamental disconnect in academic libraries between the dominance of electronic resources in collections and the integrated library systems' inherent focus on print materials."[34] Although an ILS can be used to manage electronic resources, LSPs were specifically designed to take advantage of newer processes used to manage them. Their development was not an adaptation of the traditional architecture of the ILS, but instead a redevelopment of the underlying processes. Thus, LSPs are a change in approach rather than just another iteration of the previous technology.

An ILS is a fully integrated resource management system in which primary library functions are addressed by a set of software programs organized into modules that share common databases. Its purpose is to incorporate the functionality of what would have been five or six separate databases into one integrated system. The greatest benefit comes from sharing information among the various modules, reducing duplication of data and effort. An ILS may have modules to support the following work functions:

- acquisitions
- authority control
- cataloging
- circulation
- course reserves
- digital collections management
- interlibrary loan
- public access (the OPAC)
- serials management
- system administration

Though many ILSs are still in use today in all library sectors, fewer academic libraries are interested in installing new ILS systems, opting instead for the newer, more sophisticated LSPs.[35] Breeding states,

> The technology and functional scope of an integrated library system should not be considered obsolete. The products are generally reliable, stable, and can scale to support large organizations. ... The integrated library system will likely continue its evolutionary development trajectory for decades to come. The integrated library system continues as a viable and appropriate automation model for many libraries. ... especially in the public library sector, in which lending of physical materials continues as its primary

service, supplemented by increasing proportions of audiobooks, ebooks, and streaming audio and video. Integrated library systems and their associated catalogs and discovery interfaces have evolved and adapted to accommodate these digital services.[36]

Library services platforms go beyond the capabilities of the print-focused ILS. Breeding and others have identified what makes an LSP different from an ILS. An LSP

- seamlessly integrates the management of many kinds of resources, which often entail quite different processes;[37]
- supports multiple procurement models, including those for ownership, paid licenses and subscriptions, demand-driven acquisitions, and open-access materials;
- supports multiple metadata schemas;
- enables managing electronic resources at the product or portfolio level rather than as individual journal titles;
- is usually hosted by a vendor rather than locally;
- is accessed through a discovery layer rather than directly through an OPAC module;
- provides all staff and patron functionality through browser-based interfaces; and
- provides knowledge bases that represent the body of content extending beyond the library's specific collection.[38]

An LSP also incorporates more current web technologies and architectures, such as cloud computing, which are often unavailable in the traditional ILS.[39] In 2018, LC announced that they would begin searching for a new LSP to replace their twenty-year-old ILS system, Voyager. In 2022, a press release stated that the Library of Congress had awarded a contract to EBSCO Information Services to further develop FOLIO, their open source library service platform, to meet the scale and complexity of LC's work processes.[40]

4.3.2.2 Developments in Resource Management Systems

Over the years, librarians have debated and speculated about the role of technology in cataloging, something that continues today with the advent of artificial intelligence (AI). In the first decades of the twenty-first century, boisterous discussions prevailed about how inadequate OPACs were and how changes were needed (the language used was a bit more colorful than that).[41] The question on everyone's mind was how to improve library automation. These discussions, which were taking place at conference sessions and on various blogs, forums, and discussion lists, were mostly focused on determining just what the future ILS should be and what it should do in this increasingly web-based, Google-influenced information environment. Some improvements argued for —and have since been implemented—include the following:

- **Simpler interfaces**: Many of today's ILSs, LSPs, and discovery layers begin with a single search box (like Amazon or Google). In fact, in some tools it can be difficult to locate browsing or advanced search functions.

- **Expanded searching**: Through an LSP or a discovery layer, many libraries now provide their users the ability to search all parts of the collection at the same time (i.e., federated searching). No longer do searchers have to search the catalog for print materials and search separate databases for electronic full-text articles; both may be searched with a single, integrated search box, for good and for bad.
- **Increased direct access**: In both discovery interfaces and catalogs, access to more than just surrogate records is provided. Direct links to full-text documents and digital objects may be provided. In discovery layers, full-text articles may be easily accessed through a single interface, if the searcher is an authenticated user and a link resolver is in place.
- **Faceted browsing**: Discovery layers allow users to browse keyword search results in new ways. Browsing can be done using facets such as subject, genre, format, call number, library branch, language, geographic area, period, and so on.
- **Increased interaction**: In recent years, resource management systems and discovery layers have allowed more user input, like Web 2.0 applications where users may review, rank, recommend, or tag information resources.

In recent years, vendors have developed innovative approaches to digital collections management, license and rights management, collection management that integrates print and electronic resources, and search and discovery. Of these, the developments in discovery layers have received the most attention. Breeding states

> Reacting to the need for libraries to compete with other web destinations, much ... energy focused on development and marketing of new web-based interfaces. The battle is on to deliver interfaces that showcase faceted browsing, relevance-ranked results, end user rating or tagging, and visual navigation—all standard fare in commercial web interfaces.[42]

Some of these resource discovery tools were created by companies outside of the ILS vendor marketplace, while others were created by the vendors themselves. Most of these products profess to work with all major ILS/LSP systems and to combine information from multiple sources in multiple formats into one seamless interface.

Interest in open source software has led to the development of a few viable open source systems for libraries, such as EBSCO's FOLIO LSP,[43] Koha's ILS,[44] Evergreen's ILS,[45] and the VuFind discovery interface.[46] Compared to the commercial products in the library technology marketplace, the number of open source systems is still relatively small, but open source software systems are gaining a greater market share.[47] In 2023, Breeding stated

> Although proprietary products continue to dominate, open-source alternatives are becoming increasingly competitive. Interest in open systems has been growing within the library world for at least 15 years, and recent procurements reflect important breakthroughs. The selection of the open-source library services platform FOLIO by Library of Congress, the MOBIUS consortium, the National Library of Australia, and others has solidified FOLIO's position as a major competitor in the market.[48]

Both Koha and Evergreen "are well established among specific library sectors."[49]

These advances represent an exciting area where information organization and information technology intersect. Although these changes have happened, we are still in a period of transition, and it is expected that lively discussions of where we are heading will continue. For example, the promise of linked data is always at the forefront for many LIS professionals. Linked data principles are becoming more influential in the plans being developed for the future management and dissemination of our metadata, and linked data functionalities are being tested in some information systems. In addition, libraries are facilitating access to information that has been structured through linked data platforms, such as the United States government data.gov site.[50] Another example is the movement toward increasing the involvement of users in our processes. Wikipedia has been noted as having an infrastructure that could be emulated in library catalogs to great benefit.[51] The introduction of such capabilities in catalogs could offer many benefits to users, patrons, and librarians alike. Furthermore, such capabilities would bring user experiences with catalogs closer to what is expected when using online information tools. Finally—perhaps most importantly—information workers of all levels are anxiously awaiting some clarity and insight as to how AI will play a role in the LIS professions, our retrieval tools, and search. Stay tuned for further developments.**

4.3.3 Systems in Archives and Museums††

Although this section of the chapter has focused primarily on library systems, there are information systems in other environments that should be mentioned. ArchivesSpace is an open source web-based archives management system. Its organizational home is with Lyrasis, a non-profit organization that supports open source projects for libraries, archives, and museums. It is the result of a project to merge two other software packages: Archon and the Archivists' Toolkit. Development of ArchivesSpace began in 2012. The platform was released in 2013 and has received regular updates since. The software supports functionality such as accessioning, collection management, description and arrangement, and management of authority data. Like the previously mentioned LSPs, it also supports a wide variety of metadata formats, including EAD, Dublin Core, and METS.[52] ArchivesSpace supports both physical and digital materials, however, it is not a document repository. Other software, such as the commercial product Preservica can be used for digital preservation and digital access needs while also linking metadata from ArchivesSpace.[53]

ArchivesGrid, another system, is a product of OCLC that was developed in 2006 as a subscription-based discovery service for archival materials. In 2012, OCLC made it accessible free of charge. Its goal is to connect researchers to primary sources of information through a search engine that contains information about specific collections of archival materials. It is a "collection of over

---

**For more information about current trends in library systems, see Breeding's annual "Library Systems Report" in *American Libraries*.

††Much of this section was written by Ralph M. Holley, M.S., Adjunct Professor, School of Library and Information Science, Simmons University.

seven million archival material descriptions, including MARC records from WorldCat and finding aids harvested from the web [in a variety of formats including HTML, PDF, and EAD-encoded‡‡ finding aids]."⁵⁴ The interface allows users to browse archives in their geographic areas, as well as search for collections related to specific persons, organizations, topics, places, events, and archives. From 2020–2023, OCLC has also been a research partner in a National Finding Aid Networking building project along with the California Digital Library (the project lead), the University of Virginia Library, Shift Collective, and Chain Bridge Group. With the research complete, the data "will inform the next steps for the NAFAN project and offers a wealth of information on archival user behavior and needs and the current state of archival description workflows and data."⁵⁵ This is something to watch for in the near future.

An example of an information system used in museums is PastPerfect. Its features include collection management functions, image hosting within records, contact management, authority control, and web functionality.⁵⁶ First released in 1998, it is now offered as both a cloud-based web application and as a desktop application. At the time of this writing, the software has been obtained by "over 11,000 museums, historical societies, archives, libraries, and other collecting institutions. ... [the] PastPerfect Version 5.0 desktop software contains tools for cataloging and tracking diverse collections along with tools for managing members, donors, and volunteers including their payments and gifts. The program's robust research and report functions provide staff and researchers multiple methods for searching and sharing information. ... PastPerfect Online, enables PastPerfect 5.0 users to select and share collections information as a fully searchable online database."⁵⁷

4.4 Conclusion

This chapter discusses a hodgepodge of search, systems, system design, and standardization issues as they relate to information organization. Though libraries, archives, and museums each face unique challenges when it comes to organizing information, the above sections illustrate commonalities in the activities that they need to perform. Each type of institution must have a system in place to allow for the retrieval and display of surrogate records, authority control, and collection management. Increasingly, all three environments have demonstrated a need for internet connectivity, the ability to work with multiple metadata formats, and more sophisticated search capabilities. Despite their differences, libraries, archives, and museums require the same functionality from their information systems.

Over the years, many researchers and practitioners have made suggestions for improving online retrieval systems, but the creators of this technology have not always paid attention. Evidence of this comes from two articles by Christine Borgman. Back in 1986, she wrote an article titled, "Why Are Online Catalogs Hard to Use?"⁵⁸ A decade later she authored "Why Are Online Catalogs *Still* Hard to Use?"⁵⁹ Thirty years later, her questions remain pertinent. In these articles, Borgman stated that retrieval systems were hard to use because their design did not reflect an understanding

---

‡‡EAD stands for Encoded Archival Description, an encoding format.

of user searching behavior. She suggested that a long-term goal of system designers should be to design intuitive systems that require a minimum of instruction.[§§60]

Borgman, other researchers, and practitioners have long aimed at resolving problems that users encounter in retrieval systems. There are large bodies of research on information-seeking behavior, user needs, usability, the importance of subject access, and various retrieval methods. After a half century of using automated information systems to organize information, it is unfortunate that we must continue to ask the question, "Why are systems still hard to use?" There are ways to institute standard features in all systems that will not detract from the ability of vendors to create innovative and competitive products for the marketplace but will allow users to develop a lasting familiarity with retrieval tools.

For users to get the most benefit from the information systems available, organizers and system designers must work closely together. This seems to be happening in the development and use of discovery interfaces. These tools are allowing users to discover, browse, and explore resources in our collections, making some resources accessible that may have been hidden in traditional displays of retrieval results. Although there has been progress in system design and in communication between organizers and designers, there is still a long way to go. Perhaps a goal today might be for organizers and system designers to become much more conversant in each other's languages so that meaningful conversations about what is needed can be had. Sophisticated design is wasted if the metadata that the system presents is inadequate, and sophisticated metadata is wasted if the system design is lacking.

Some Important Terms in This Chapter
(Definitions Provided in the Glossary)

Authority control	Index browsing	Querying
Bibliographic network	Information system	Recall
Boolean operator	Integrated library system	Reference database
Boolean retrieval	Keyword matching	Relevance
Browsing	Left-anchored searching	Resource management system
Copy cataloging	Library services platform	
Database	Non-linear browsing	Shelf browsing
Discovery layer	Normalization	Source database
Exploded search	Original cataloging	Stopword
Facet	Phrase matching	System
Faceted browsing	Precision	System-based browsing
False drop	Probabilistic retrieval	System design
Federated searching	Proximity operators	Turnkey system

[§§]Instruction has often been touted as the way around inadequate system design, but in this age of remote access, where instruction may not be available, one must agree with Borgman: good training is not a substitute for good system design.

Some Important Acronyms in This Chapter

CQL:	Contextual Query Language
GUI:	Graphical User Interface
IFLA:	International Federation of Library Associations and Institutions
ILS:	Integrated Library System
LC:	Library of Congress
LIS:	Library and Information Science
LSP:	Library Services Platform
MARC:	Machine-Readable Cataloging
NISO:	National Information Standards Organization
NoSQL:	Not Only Structured Query Language
OCLC:	Online Computer Library Center
OPAC:	Online Public Access Catalog
SQL:	Structured Query Language
SRU:	Search/Retrieval via URL
XML:	Extensible Markup Language

4.5 Discussion Questions and Exercises

- Select a local library catalog and explore the search and display options that it offers. Try to determine:
    - What kinds of searching does it support (e.g., keyword, left-anchored, phrase-matching)?
    - Does it support browsing? What kinds of indexes can be browsed?
    - How does it handle truncation, wildcards, and Boolean operators?
    - What options does it provide for sorting, filtering, and displaying results?
    - What kind of help screens/documentation are available? How easy is it to determine how/why search results are being retrieved?
- Should library catalogs be more like Google and Amazon? Compare and contrast these platforms and discuss potential advantages and disadvantages for different types of information retrieval needs.

4.6 Suggested Readings

Badke, William. *Research Strategies: Finding Your Way Through the Information Fog*. 7th ed. Bloomington, IN: iUniverse, 2021.

Bates, Marcia J. "The Design of Browsing and Berrypicking Techniques for the Online Search Interface." *Online Review* 13, no. 5 (October 1989): 407–24.

Bilal, Dania. *Library Automation: Core Concepts and Practical Systems Analysis*. 3rd ed. Santa Barbara, CA: Libraries Unlimited, 2014.

Breeding, Marshall. "Library Systems Report." *American Libraries*. May 1st issue each year.

Breeding, Marshall. *Library Technology Buying Strategies*. Chicago: ALA Editions, 2016.

Breeding, Marshall. *Library Technology Guides*. http://www.librarytechnology.org/.

Breeding, Marshall. *Next-Gen Library Catalogs*. New York: Neal-Schuman, 2010.

Brown, Christopher C. *Librarian's Guide to Online Searching: Cultivating Database Skills for Research and Instruction*. 6th ed. Santa Barbara, CA: Libraries Unlimited, 2021.

Chambers, Sally, ed. *Catalogue 2.0: The Future of the Library Catalogue*. Chicago: Neal-Schuman, 2013.

Foster, Elvis, with Shripad V. Godbole. *Database Systems: A Pragmatic Approach*. 3rd ed. Boca Raton: CRC Press, 2023.

Gates, Lynn E., and Joel D. Tonyan. *Making the Most of Your ILS: A User's Guide to Evaluating and Optimizing Library Systems*. Santa Barbara, CA: Libraries Unlimited, 2023.

Gross, Tina, Arlene G. Taylor, and Daniel N. Joudrey. "Still a Lot to Lose: The Role of Controlled Vocabulary in Keyword Searching." *Cataloging & Classification Quarterly* 53, no. 1 (2015): 1–39.

Hernandez, Michael J. *Database Design for Mere Mortals, 25th Anniversary Edition: A Hands-on Guide to Relational Database Design*. 4th ed. Hoboken, NJ: Pearson Education, 2020.

Hildreth, Charles R. "The Use and Understanding of Keyword Searching in a University Online Catalog." *Information Technology and Libraries* 16, no. 2 (June 1997): 52–62.

Joudrey, Daniel N., Arlene G. Taylor, and David P. Miller. *Introduction to Cataloging and Classification*. 11th ed. Santa Barbara, CA: Libraries Unlimited, 2015.

OCLC. *Online Catalogs: What Users and Librarians Want: An OCLC Report*. Dublin, OH: OCLC, 2009.

Pace, Andrew. "21st Century Library Systems." *Journal of Library Administration* 49, no. 6 (2009): 641–50.

Webber, Desiree, and Andrew Peters. *Integrated Library Systems: Planning, Selecting, and Implementing*. Santa Barbara, CA: Libraries Unlimited, 2010.

4.7 Notes

All URLs accessed April 2025.

1. Larry Milsap, "A History of the Online Catalog in North America," in *Technical Services Management, 1965–1990: A Quarter Century of Change, A Look to the Future: A Festschrift for Kathryn Luther Henderson*, eds. Linda C. Smith and Ruth C. Carter (Binghamton, NY: Haworth, 1996), 79–91.
2. For more in-depth information on technology, system design, or technology management, please see Carson Block, *Managing Library Technology: A LITA Guide* (Lanham, MD: Rowman & Littlefield, 2017); Richard Fox, *Information Technology: An Introduction for Today's Digital World*, 2nd ed. (Boca Raton, FL: CRC Press, 2021); Brice G. Hobrock, ed., *Library Management in the Information Technology Environment: Issues, Policies, and Practice for Administrators* (London: Routledge, 2019); and Kenneth E. Kendall and Julie E. Kendall, *Systems Analysis and Design*, 11th ed. (New York: Pearson, 2023).
3. *A Dictionary of Computing*, 4th ed. (Oxford: Oxford University Press, 1996), 489–90.
4. "What is System Design?" *Geeks for Geeks*, https://www.geeksforgeeks.org/what-is-system-design-learn-system-design/.
5. British Museum, Department of Printed Books, "Rules for the Compilation of the Catalogue," in *Catalogue of Printed Books in the British Museum*, ed. Anthony Panizzi, vol. 1 (London: British Museum, 1841), [v]–ix.
6. Charles A. Cutter, *Rules for a Dictionary Catalog*, 4th ed. (Washington, DC: Government Printing Office, 1904), 84–130.

7. M. Jay Norton, "Knowledge Discovery in Databases," *Library Trends* 48, no. 1 (Summer 1999): 9–21.
8. Neal Leavitt, "Will NoSQL Databases Live Up to Their Promise?" *Computer* 43, no. 2 (2010): 12–14.
9. For more technical introductions to databases, please see resources such as Carlos Coronel and Steven Morris, *Database Systems: Design, Implementation, & Management*, 14th ed. (Boston, MA: Cengage, 2023); Sufyan bin Uzayr, ed., *Mastering SQL: A Beginner's Guide* (Boca Raton, FL: CRC Press, 2024).
10. Charles R. Hildreth, "Online Catalog Design Models: Are We Moving in the Right Direction? A Report Submitted to the Council on Library Resources August, 1995," https://web.archive.org/web/20150923010236/http://myweb.cwpost.liu.edu/childret/clr-opac.html.
11. William F. Frost, "Back Talk: Do We Want or Need Metasearching?" *Library Journal* 129, no. 6 (April 1, 2006): 68.
12. Thomas Mann, *The Oxford Guide to Research*, 4th ed. (Oxford: Oxford University Press, 2015), xxvi, 244; George Kingsley Zipf, *Human Behavior and the Principle of Least Effort* (Cambridge, MA: Addison-Wesley Press, 1949) 1, 5–8.
13. Frost, 68.
14. Martha M. Yee, "Guidelines for OPAC Displays: 1999," in *From Catalog to Gateway: Charting a Course for Future Access: Briefings from the ALCTS Catalog Form and Function Committee*, eds. Bill Sleeman and Pamela Bluh (Chicago: Association for Collections & Technical Services, American Library Association, 2005), 83.
15. David Thomas, "The Effect of Interface Design on Item Selection in an Online Catalog," *Library Resources & Technical Services* 45, no. 1 (January 2001): 20–45.
16. IFLA Task Force on Guidelines for OPAC Displays, *Guidelines for Online Public Access Catalogue (OPAC) Displays, Final Report May 2005* (München: K.G. Saur, 2005), 9.
17. IFLA Task Force, 10.
18. Rebecca Green, "Topical Relevance Relationships. I. Why Topic Matching Fails." *Journal of the American Society for Information Science* 46, no. 9 (1995): 647.
19. Howard D. White, "Relevance in Theory," *Encyclopedia of Library and Information Science*, 4th ed., ed. by John D. McDonald and Michael Levine-Clark (Boca Raton, FL: CRC Press, 2018), 3926.
20. Jennifer Rowley and Richard Hartley, *Organizing Knowledge: An Introduction to Managing Access to Information*, 4th ed. (Burlington, VT: Ashgate Publishing Limited, 2008), 157.
21. "How is Relevance Ranking Determined in EBSCO Discovery Service (EDS)?" EBSCO, https://connect.ebsco.com/s/article/How-is-relevance-ranking-determined-in-EBSCO-Discovery-Service-EDS?language=en_US.
22. Yee, 83.
23. IFLA Task Force, 21.
24. Thomas, 42–4.
25. Thomas, 32.
26. J. H. Bowman, "The Catalog as Barrier to Retrieval—Part 1: Hyphens and Ampersands in Titles," *Cataloging & Classification Quarterly* 29, no. 4 (2000): 39–60.
27. Tina Gross, Arlene G. Taylor, and Daniel N. Joudrey, "Still a Lot to Lose: The Role of Controlled Vocabulary in Keyword Searching," *Cataloging & Classification Quarterly* 53, no. 1 (2015): 1–39.
28. Praveenkumar Vaidya and N. S. Harinarayana, "The Comparative and Analytical Study of LibraryThing Tags with Library of Congress Subject Headings," *Knowledge Organization* 43, no. 1 (2016): 41.
29. Paul Miller, "Z39.50 for All," *Ariadne* 21 (September 20, 1999), http://www.ariadne.ac.uk/issue/21/z3950/.
30. "SRU: Search/Retrieval via URL," Library of Congress, http://www.loc.gov/standards/sru/.
31. "OCLC," OCLC Online Computer Library Center, http://www.oclc.org/.
32. Marshall Breeding, "Serials Solutions to Launch Summon 2.0," *Smart Libraries* Newsletter 33, no. 5 (May 2013): 2–5, https://journals.ala.org/index.php/sln/issue/view/281.

33. Marshall Breeding, "Smart Libraries Q&A: Differences between ILS and LSP," *Smart Libraries Newsletter* 40, no. 10 (2020): 3–4.
34. Breeding, "Smart Libraries Q&A," 3–4.
35. Marshall Breeding, "2021 Library Systems Report: Advancing Library Technologies in Challenging Times," *American Libraries* 52, no. 5 (May 2021): 25.
36. Breeding, "Smart Libraries Q&A," 3–4.
37. Carl Grant, "The Future of Library Systems: Library Services Platforms," *Information Standards Quarterly* 24, no. 4 (2012): 5.
38. Marshall Breeding, "Library Services Platforms: A Maturing Genre of Products," *Library Technology Reports* 51, no. 4 (2015): 8; Breeding, "Smart Libraries Q&A," 3–4.
39. Grant, 5.
40. "Library of Congress Launches Effort to Transform Collections Management and Access," Library of Congress Newsroom, September 21, 2022, https://newsroom.loc.gov/news/library-of-congress-launches-effort-to-transform-collections-management-and-access/s/c432d3c2-780b-4bfe-9123-bbb6c25631bc.
41. For example: Karen G. Schneider, "How OPACs Suck, Part 2: The Checklist of Shame," in "ALA TechSource," https://web.archive.org/web/20231210165335/http://www.ala.org/tools/article/ala-techsource/how-opacs-suck-part-2-checklist-shame.
42. Marshall Breeding, "Automation System Marketplace 2007: An Industry Redefined," *Library Journal* 132, no. 6 (April 1, 2007): 36.
43. "FOLIO: Open Source Library Services Platform," Folio, https://www.folio.org/.
44. "Koha Library Software," Koha, https://koha-community.org/.
45. "Evergreen: Open Source Library Software," Evergreen, http://evergreen-ils.org/.
46. "VuFind: Search. Discover. Share," Villanova University Falvey Memorial Library, https://vufind.org/vufind/.
47. Matt Enis, "Open for Growth," *Library Journal* 147, no. 10 (October 2022): 41–4.
48. Marshall Breeding, "2023 Library Systems Report: The Advance of Open Systems," *American Libraries* 54, no. 5 (May 1, 2023): 21
49. Breeding, "Power Plays," 37.
50. Robin Hastings, "Linked Data in Libraries: Status and Future Directions," *Computers in Libraries* 35, no. 9 (2015): 15, https://www.infotoday.com/cilmag/nov15/Hastings--Linked-Data-in-Libraries.shtml.
51. Kris Joseph, "Wikipedia Knows the Value of What the Library Catalog Forgets," *Cataloging & Classification Quarterly* 57, no. 2–3 (February 2019): 170–2.
52. "Mission and Guiding Principles," ArchivesSpace, https://archivesspace.org/about/mission.
53. "Integrate your ArchivesSpace Catalog with Preservica," Preservica, https://preservica.com/resources/knowledge-centre/archivesspace-connector-overview.
54. "ArchivesGrid," OCLC, https://www.oclc.org/research/areas/research-collections/archivegrid.html.
55. "Research Findings from the Building a National Finding Aid Network Project," OCLC, May 2023, https://www.oclc.org/research/publications/2023/nafan/nafan-summary-research.html.
56. "PastPerfect Museum Software," PastPerfect Software, Inc., https://museumsoftware.com/.
57. "About Us," PastPerfect Software, Inc., https://museumsoftware.com/about.html.
58. Christine L. Borgman, "Why Are Online Catalogs Hard to Use? Lessons Learned from Information Retrieval Studies," *Journal of the American Society for Information Science* 37, no. 6 (June 1986): 387–400.
59. Christine L. Borgman, "Why Are Online Catalogs *Still* Hard to Use?" *Journal of the American Society for Information Science* 47, no. 7 (July 1996): 493–503.
60. Borgman, Why Are Online Catalogs *Still* Hard to Use?" 501.

Chapter 5

Encoding Standards

In the digital information environment of the twenty-first century, encoding is necessary for libraries, museums, archives, and other cultural heritage institutions to communicate, use, process, and share their **metadata** (i.e., information about the resources in their collections). **Encoding** is the process of converting data into electronic form. If surrogate records and metadata statements are not encoded, they cannot be stored in and retrieved from online retrieval tools or the web. This chapter addresses several ways to encode documents, metadata, and surrogate records. It also provides an overview of an approach to encoding for the linked data landscape of the Semantic Web.

5.1 Introduction to Encoding

In the information professions, there are different contexts in which encoding standards are used. *Encoding* may refer to the process of creating a metadata record using a standardized coding scheme that allows the record to be accessed by computer systems and shared among institutions. This is the most common use for the Machine-Readable Cataloging (MARC) encoding format in libraries. *Encoding* may also refer to the process of making any document machine-readable or machine-processable. This is seen in the use of myriad XML schemas to structure documents in an electronic environment. These documents may or may not contain metadata. The term is also used to refer to the character encoding within a document, such as the use of Unicode.

The MARC format is the encoding standard used to create bibliographic records that are stored in most library catalogs. It is a mature standard that was designed in the mid-1960s, became an international standard in 1973, and has been in worldwide use for over half a century.[1] Although some call it a *mature* standard, others might refer to it as an *aging* standard. In the first decades of the twenty-first century, MARC began to show its limitations, and many in the LIS professions support replacing it with something less proprietary and more compatible with the web technologies of today (and tomorrow).

Another standard, SGML (Standard Generalized Markup Language), also had its origins in the mid-1960s. It is a markup language used to identify the structural components of documents. SGML became an international standard in 1986.[2] In addition to its standard function of marking up a wide variety of electronic documents, SGML and its derivatives have been adapted for encoding metadata or surrogate records (our primary concern in this chapter). Various applications of SGML have been created over the years, including HTML (Hypertext Markup Language) and XML (Extensible Markup Language). Specific XML schemas and DTDs (document type definitions) have been designed to encode data for individual communities or for specific document types. All these standards may be used to store, share, and retrieve metadata in retrieval tools or to manage and structure documents on the web or in other electronic environments. Although XML-based schemas are now widespread, XML is not without its detractors, with some saying it is far too verbose and difficult to understand.[3]

Some information professionals view metadata content and its encoding as inseparable concepts, but they are actually distinct. The descriptive content of metadata can be determined independently of how it will be stored or formatted. Rather than simply filling in template fields during creation, metadata content can first be decided upon and then encoded afterward. Think of encoding or syntax as a container—like a box or a bucket that holds the metadata content. The various encoding standards discussed in this chapter are different types of containers. The same metadata content can be placed in different containers (for example, the same information could appear in either a MARC record or an XML-encoded document header). Before working with metadata, it is helpful to understand the characteristics of these different container formats, so we will review several encoding standards.

The metadata content held in the containers may conform to a separate **content standard** (i.e., a set of rules or guidelines for metadata creation), or in a few rare cases, it may be guided by the encoding standard itself.* Some metadata standards include both encoding and content specifications, but in this book encoding standards are discussed separately before covering the creation of metadata content. This further illustrates that creating content and encoding metadata are not the same processes. Metadata creation is covered in later chapters.

Before addressing the encoding of records and documents, it may be useful to say a few words about how computers encode the characters that appear in a record. Each character (each letter, numeral, and symbol) is represented by a numeric code, because, fundamentally, computers process numbers. ISO/IEC 10646 *Universal Coded Character Set* (UCS) is a standard from the International Organization for Standardization (ISO) and is the first standardized character set with the purpose of including all characters in all written languages of the world (including mathematical and all other symbols). **Unicode** is an American industry counterpart that is kept compatible with ISO/IEC 10646. Unicode is overseen by the Unicode Consortium and was named for its aim to embrace three characteristics: *universality*, covering all modern written languages; *uniqueness*, with no duplication of characters even if they appear in more than one language; and *uniformity*, with each character being the same length in bits. UCS/Unicode provides a unique code for every character in every modern language, as well as thousands of emojis. For example,

---

*For example, the metadata entered into a MARC record is usually controlled by outside descriptive cataloging rules (e.g., *RDA: Resource Description & Access*), by the conventions of a subject thesaurus (e.g., *Library of Congress Subject Headings*), and by the rules of a classification scheme (e.g., *Dewey Decimal Classification*). There are, however, some MARC 21 fields for which the rules for content appear only in the MARC 21 standard itself (e.g., the 007 field gives specific codes for aspects of certain materials, such as microforms or motion pictures).

😜 = U+1F61C.

Before UCS/ Unicode, there were a multitude of different encoding systems for the display of characters, such as ASCII (American Standard Code for Information Interchange) and EBCDIC (Extended Binary Coded Decimal Interchange Code). For information about the latest version of Unicode (e.g., the newest scripts, emojis, and ideographs), please see its website.[4]

5.2 Encoding Records

For metadata to be accessible, it must be conveyed to users through an information system. Now that retrieval tools are primarily online (at least in economically advantaged nations), metadata is usually created in electronic form. Although some print retrieval tools may still be used, even those are typically created through electronic means.

Metadata records and statements are encoded by assigning *tags* (or *codes*) made up of numbers, letters, punctuation marks, and so forth, that designate the kind of field in an encoding standard. Tags are assigned to discrete pieces of information in a description. For example, a primary creator's personal name is coded with a "100" tag in MARC, but in an XML schema, such as the Text Encoding Initiative (TEI), the name is preceded by <author> and is followed by </author>. Such encoding is often referred to as the *syntax*.

> **MARC:** 100 1# $a Kobabe, Maia
> **TEI:** <author>Kobabe, Maia</author>

Surrogate records are encoded to provide users with access to the contents of those records. Encoding allows for individual parts of the metadata to be distinguished and marked for specific purposes. This enables the creation of software programs that allow for the indexing and searching of only certain metadata fields at one time. For example, if a user wishes to narrow their search to creators only, the retrieval system can search only the subset of metadata that has been coded for creators. In a library catalog, this means the system will retrieve only names that have been encoded with a MARC creator tag (e.g., 100, 700, 110). As noted above, the same result is achieved in some XML schemas by placing a name between opening and closing <author>, <creator>, or <contributor> tags.

Encoding is also used to support metadata display. With tags that identify the function or purpose of each chunk of metadata, programs and style sheets can be written so that each metadata element can be displayed and labeled in a specified position on the screen. When a TEI <author> tag or a MARC 100 or 700 field is used, creator information can be presented consistently in the system display. For example, the tags used to identify the creator can tell the system to display the name at the top of the screen or just after the title; to present the name in 18-point boldface type or in italics; and to precede the name with a specific label or not.

Another use for encoding is to allow many languages and scripts to be displayed and searched in the same file. It has always been possible to interfile languages that use the Roman alphabet, although filing them alphabetically was sometimes a problem (see discussion of filing issues in Appendix A: Arrangement of Metadata Displays). Languages in other scripts had to be romanized to be interfiled in the paper world. Online, however, if the display of non-Latin scripts is provided for, record encoding allows for identification of the fields of the surrogate record regardless of the language or script.

Quick and easy transmission is yet another important reason to encode data. Institutions that collect information resources tend to have their own online systems into which they place encoded metadata for their resources. When these information resources are duplicates of those found in other institutions' online systems, cooperative arrangements are made to exchange the metadata. This means that each institution does not have to create a metadata description for every resource "from scratch." Shared, standardized encoding allows such exchanges of metadata to occur among institutions around the world.

The following encoding standards are discussed in this chapter:

- MARC (Machine-Readable Cataloging)
    - MARC 21
    - UNIMARC (Universal MARC)
- SGML (Standard Generalized Markup Language)
    - HTML (Hypertext Markup Language)
    - XML (Extensible Markup Language) and its DTDs and Schemas
        - TEI (Text Encoding Initiative) Schema
        - EAD (Encoded Archival Description) DTD and Schema
        - MARCXML Schema

5.3 MARC (Machine-Readable Cataloging)

In the 1960s, the Library of Congress (LC) created the ***MARC (Machine-Readable Cataloging)*** format to share bibliographic data. The MARC format is used for encoding bibliographic metadata and transmitting it from one system to another. MARC is primarily used in libraries, although it has been used by some museums and archives. MARC was developed from 1965 to 1968 at LC under the leadership of Henriette Avram. The encoding format was identified simply as "MARC" until other versions were developed in the 1970s, when the first version was referred to as "LC-MARC." Later, the name USMARC came to distinguish the version used in the United States from more than 20 other national versions that were developed (e.g., UKMARC, RUSMARC, IBERMARC). In 2000, MARC 21 was released. It is the version currently used in the United States, Canada, Great Britain, Germany, and other places around the world.

5.3.1 MARC 21

MARC 21 (named for the twenty-first century) is based on ANSI/NISO standard Z39.2-1994 (R2016), *Information Interchange Format*.[‡5] The international version is ISO 2709:2008, *Information*

[‡]The original standard was the *American National Standard for Bibliographic Information Interchange on Magnetic Tape* published in 1971, revised in 1979, and again in 1984.

and Documentation—Format for Information Exchange.[6] MARC 21 records may be encoded with either an 8-bit encoding called MARC-8 or with the Unicode UTF-8 encoding rules.[7]

MARC 21 was released in the year 2000 after an agreement was made between the United States and Canada to merge their national MARC formats (USMARC and CAN/MARC), compromising on the differences between them. In 2004 the British Library adopted MARC 21 as its cataloging format, and that same year, the Deutsche Nationalbibliothek announced it also would be moving to MARC 21.

MARC 21 has five formats for encoding distinct types of metadata.

- **Bibliographic format**: for data describing information resources in surrogate records
- **Authority format**: for authority data describing persons, corporate bodies, subjects, etc., in authority records
- **Community information format**: for information about events, programs, organizations, and services that can be integrated into catalogs
- **Holdings format**: for data elements that show the holdings and location information for resources
- **Classification data format**: for data elements related to classification numbers, the captions associated with them, their hierarchies, and associated subject headings

For a more complete description of the MARC 21 standard, please see the extensive MARC documentation available on the web.[8]

5.3.1.1 Components of MARC Records

The MARC 21 format comprises several components: a leader, a directory, and two types of variable fields (control fields and data fields). The *leader* identifies the beginning of a new record and contains 24 alphanumeric characters that, among other things, identify record length, record status, character-coding scheme (e.g., UCS/Unicode), encoding level, and the kind of information resource being described. The leader can be seen in Figure 5.1 (the top line in boldface type).

The *directory* contains a series of fixed-length segments (each containing 12 characters) that identify the field tag, length, and starting position of each data field in the record. The directory is visible in Figure 5.1, but it is the focus of Figure 5.2. In Figure 5.2, one segment is highlighted; it conveys that the 700 field is 39 characters long and begins at the 3,258th character position in the record. The MARC directory was a major contribution to information science. Instead of containing only fixed-length fields, which was common in databases in the 1960s, the directory structure allowed for variable-length fields, which are now prevalent.

The MARC format identifies two types of variable fields: control fields and data fields. *Control fields* are of a predictable length and are perfect for carrying alphanumeric codies; they are used for processing machine-readable bibliographic records. In MARC 21 these field tags begin with two zeros (i.e., 00X fields). Control fields are used, among other things, for fixed-length descriptive data, LC control numbers, and codes for date and time of latest transaction. Control fields are all fixed-length fields, but one of them (the 008 field) is often called *the fixed field* and is displayed differently from other fields in some online systems.

```
04277cam 2200781 i 4500
001001300000000300060001300500170001900800410003601000170007704001000009401900360019402000470023
002000440027702000420032102000390036302000260040203500750042804200080050305000200051108200140053108400340054
508400320057908400180061104900090062910000330063824501110067125000220078226400060020080430000300086633600260080
963370028009223380027009504900040089775000152010255040069011775050944012465200381021906500020829571650000240
599650002702623630003502650650010402685650006102789630000610285065000530291165000540029646500050030186300061
0303865000400312965000450316965000044032147000039032587000053032977000096033508300049034446
ocn911180115OCoLC20170607111220.0150616s2015    cau    b    001 0 eng    a 2015012911 aDLCbengerdacDLC
dYDXdMBBdYDXCPdBDXdBTCTAdOCLCFdNTEdCDXdNDSdlBIdCHVBKdGBVCPdOCLCO a881400756a881446762a935877570
a9781598848571 (hardback : acid-free paper) a1598848577 (hardback : acid-free paper) a9781598848564 (pbk : acid-free paper)
a1598848569 (pbk : acid-free paper) z9781440837456 (ebook) 1 a(OCoLC)911180115z(OCoLC)881400756z(OCoLC)881446762
z(OCoLC)935877570 apcc00aZ693b.W94 201500a025.3223 aLAN025030aLAN0200002bisacsh a06.709Katalogisierung2bcl aAN
740002rvk aDD0A1 aJoudrey, Daniel N.,eauthor.10aIntroduction to cataloging and classification /cDaniel N. Joudrey, Arlene G. Taylor,
and David P. Miller.  aEleventh edition. 1aSanta Barbara, California :bLibraries Unlimited,c[2015]  axxv, 1048 pages ;c27 cm.
atextbtxt2rdacontent aunmediatedbn2rdamedia avolumebnc2rdacarrier1 aLibrary and information science text series aSignificant
expansion of: Introduction to cataloging and classification. Tenth edition / Arlene G. Taylor ; with the assistance of David P. Miller.
aIncludes bibliographical references (pages 1001-1022) and index.0 aCataloging in context -- Development of catalogs and cataloging
codes -- Underlying principles and conceptual models -- Resource Description and Access (RDA) basics -- Manifestations and items --
Works and expressions -- Persons, families, places, and corporate bodies -- Relationships and the use of access points -- RDA metadata
in the MARC format -- Authority control -- Subject access -- Verbal subject access -- Library of Congress subject headings (LCSH) -- Sears
list of subject headings (Sears) -- Other verbal access systems -- Classification -- Decimal classification -- Library of Congress classification
(LCC) -- Creation of complete call numbers -- Other classification systems -- MAchine-Readable Cataloging (MARC) encoding --
Alternative containers for metadata -- International standard bibliographic description (ISBD) -- Cataloging management and support --
Appendix A: RDA outline -- Appendix B: ICC11 RDA book template.  aThis new edition reintroduces the topic of library cataloging from a
modern perspective. This textbook delineates the new cataloging landscape; shares a principles-based perspective; provides
introductory text for beginners and intermediate students; emphasizes descriptive and subject cataloging, as well as format-neutral
cataloging, and covers new cataloging rules and RDA. 0aDescriptive cataloging. 0aSubject cataloging.
0aClassificationxBooks.00aResource description & access. 7aLANGUAGE ARTS & DISCIPLINES / Library & Information Science /
Cataloging & Classification.2bisacsh 7aLANGUAGE ARTS & DISCIPLINES / Study & Teaching.2bisacsh07aResource description &
access.2fast0(OCoLC)fst01791077 7aClassificationxBooks.2fast0(OCoLC)fst00863572 7aDescriptive
cataloging.2fast0(OCoLC)fst00891123 7aSubject cataloging.2fast0(OCoLC)fst0113645007aResource description and access.0(DE-
588)7710221-62gnd 7aBibliothek.0(DE-588)4006439-62gnd 7aKatalogisierung.0(DE-588)4163418-42gnd 7aKlassifikation.0(DE-
588)4030958-72gnd1 aTaylor, Arlene G.,d1941-eauthor.1 aMiller, David P.q(David Peter),d1955-eauthor.1 iBased on (work):aTaylor,
Arlene G.,d1941-tIntroduction to cataloging and classification. 0aLibrary and information science text series.
```

Figure 5.1 A MARC Bibliographic Record Displayed in the Communication Format. (Source: OCLC Connexion, WorldCat—Record Number 911180115.)

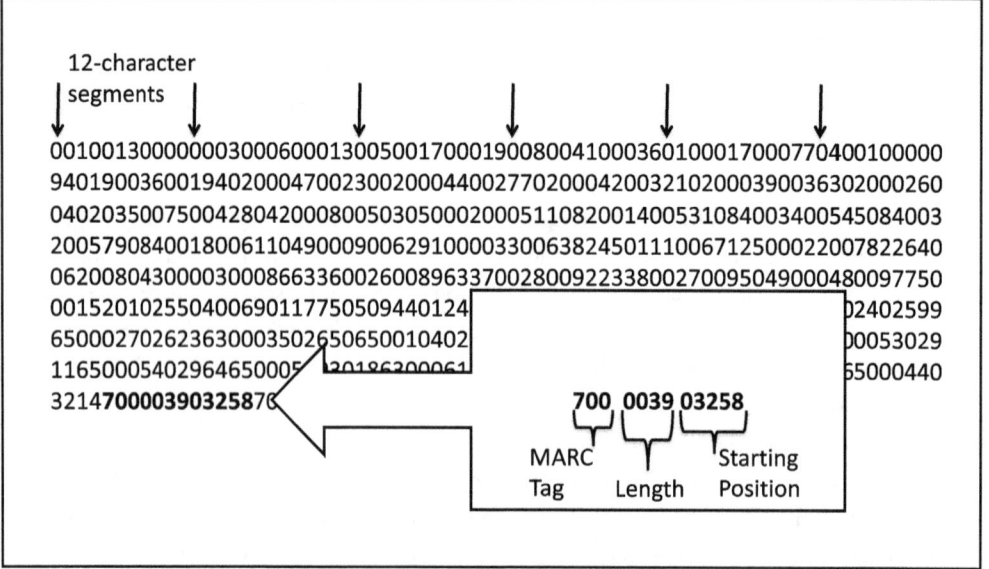

Figure 5.2 The Directory in a MARC Bibliographic Record. (Source: OCLC Connexion, WorldCat—Record Number 911180115.)

Variable data fields carry alphanumeric data of variable length. Because they are of varying length, the record must identify the beginning and the end of each varying data field; thus, the need for the directory. These fields contain traditional cataloging data but also may carry information such as playing time, URLs, and linking entries. Variable data fields are often divided into ***subfields*** to achieve greater granularity in encoding. Some variable fields are repeatable in a single record (e.g., 650 fields containing subject headings), and others are not repeatable (e.g., a 100 field containing the primary creator)—it depends on the purpose of the field.

5.3.1.2 Components of MARC Fields

Variable data fields are made up of tags, indicators, and subfield codes. ***MARC tags*** are the three-digit numbers (from 001 to 999) that designate the kind of content in the field. Although there is a potential to have as many as 999 MARC tags, far fewer (nearer to 275) are defined, and even fewer are frequently used. In 2010 an OCLC report showed that only 11 MARC tags were found in 20 percent or more of their 145 million bibliographic records, and that 22 tags occurred in 10 percent or more of those records.[9] Of the available MARC tags, clearly most are used only rarely. William Moen and Penelope Benardino presented similar research findings in 2003.[10] A list of frequently used MARC tags is provided in Table 5.1.

Table 5.1 Frequently Used MARC 21 Tags in Bibliographic Records

Tag	Description	Example	
001	Control Number	001	18660797
007	Physical Description Fixed Field	007	sd fungnnmmneu
008	*The* Fixed Field	008	150616s2015 cau b 001 0 eng
010	Library of Congress Control Number	010	$a 2015012911
020	International Standard Book Number	020	$a 9781598848564
040	Cataloging Source	040	$a DLC $b eng $e rda $c DLC $d YDX
043	Geographic Area Code	043	$a n-us-ma
050	Library of Congress Call Number	050 00	$a Z693 $b.W94 2015
082	Dewey Decimal Classification Number	082 00	$a 025.3 $2 23
100	Main Entry – Personal Name	100 1#	$a Joudrey, Daniel N., $e author.
245	Title Statement	245 10	$a Introduction to cataloging and classification / $c Daniel N. Joudrey, Arlene G. Taylor, and David P. Miller.
250	Edition Statement	250	$a Eleventh edition.
264	Production, Publication, Distribution, Manufacture, and Copyright Notice	264 #1	$a Santa Barbara, California : $b Libraries Unlimited, $c [2015]
300	Physical Description	300	$a xxv, 1048 pages : $b illustrations ; $c 27 cm
336	Content Type	336	$a text $b txt $2 rdacontent

Tag	Description	Example	
337	Media Type	337	$a unmediated $b n $2 rdamedia
338	Carrier Type	338	$a volume $b nc $2 rdacarrier
490	Series Statement	490 1#	$a Library and information science text series
500	General Note	500	$a Significant expansion of: Introduction to cataloging and classification. Tenth edition / Arlene G. Taylor ; with the assistance of David P. Miller.
504	Bibliography, etc. note	504	$a Includes bibliographical references (pages 1001-1022) and index.
505	Contents notes	505 0#	$a Cataloging in context – Development of catalogs and cataloging codes – Underlying principles and conceptual models – Resource Description and Access (RDA) basics – ….
520	Summary, etc.	520	$a This new edition reintroduces the topic of library cataloging from a modern perspective.
650	Subject Added Entry – Topical Term	650 #0	$a Subject cataloging.
650	Subject Added Entry – Topical Term	650 #0	$a Descriptive cataloging.
655	Index Term – Genre/Form	655 #7	$a Textbooks $2 lcgft
700	Added Entry – Personal Name	700 1#	$a Taylor, Arlene G., $d 1941- $e author.
700	Added Entry – Related work	700 1#	$i Based on (work): $a Taylor, Arlene G., $d 1941- $t Introduction to cataloging and classification.
830	Series Added Entry – Uniform Title	830 #0	$a Library and information science text series.

When records are received in the MARC communications format, each system displays them according to its own programming. OCLC Online Computer Library Center, for example, puts the fixed field at the top of the record and uses mnemonic labels to interpret the various codes that make up the 008 field. OCLC also hides the $a subfield code for the first metadata element in each field. The Library of Congress's catalog, however, displays $a, and the fixed field is presented as a single string of alphanumeric characters in the 008 field as seen in Table 5.1. Local systems have staff interfaces that differ significantly from public-facing displays. The public interface to the catalog generally does not display any subfield codes or the fixed field (except in implementations that allow for a MARC view). System displays also vary in such things as spacing, placement of certain subfields, and so on (see Figures 5.3 and 5.4).

OCLC 911180115				No holdings in DD0 - 305 other holdings					
Books		Rec Stat	c	Entered 20150616			Replaced 20240202		
	Type	a	ELvl		Srce	Audn	Ctrl		Lang eng
	BLvl	m	Form		Conf 0	Biog	MRec		Ctry cau
			Cont	b	GPub	LitF 0	Indx	1	
	Desc	i	Ills	a	Fest 0	DtSt t	Dates	2015,2015	

010	2015012911
040	DLC ‡b eng ‡e rda ‡c DLC ‡d YDX ‡d MBB ‡d YDXCP ...
020	9781598848571 ‡q (hardback : ‡q acid-free paper)
020	9781598848564 ‡q (pbk : ‡q acid-free paper)
050 00	Z693 ‡b .W94 2015
082 00	025.3 ‡2 23
100 1#	Joudrey, Daniel N., ‡e author.
245 10	Introduction to cataloging and classification / ‡c Daniel N. Joudrey, Arlene G. Taylor, and David P. Miller.
250	Eleventh edition.
264 #1	Santa Barbara, California : ‡b Libraries Unlimited, ‡c [2015]
264 #4	‡c ©2015
300	xxv, 1048 pages : ‡b illustrations ; ‡c 27 cm.
336	text ‡b txt ‡2 rdacontent
337	unmediated ‡b n ‡2 rdamedia
338	volume ‡b nc ‡2 rdacarrier
490 1#	Library and information science text series
500	Significant expansion of: Introduction to cataloging and classification. Tenth edition / Arlene G. Taylor ; with the assistance of David P. Miller.
504	Includes bibliographical references (pages 1001-1022) and index.
505 0#	Cataloging in context – Development of catalogs and cataloging codes – Underlying principles and conceptual models – Resource Description and Access (RDA) basics – Manifestations and items – [*Table of contents continues*] – Appendix B: ICC11 RDA book template.
520	This new edition reintroduces the topic of library cataloging from a modern perspective. This textbook delineates the new cataloging landscape; shares a principles-based perspective; provides introductory text for beginners and intermediate students; emphasizes descriptive and subject cataloging, as well as format-neutral cataloging, and covers new cataloging rules and RDA.
650 #0	Descriptive cataloging.
650 #0	Subject cataloging.
650 #0	Classification ‡x Books.
630 00	Resource description & access.
700 1#	Taylor, Arlene G., ‡d 1941- ‡e author.
700 1#	Miller, David P. ‡q (David Peter), ‡d 1955- ‡e author.
700 1#	‡i Based on (work): ‡a Taylor, Arlene G., ‡d 1941- ‡t Introduction to cataloging and classification.
758	‡i has work: ‡a Introduction to cataloging and classification (Text) ‡1 https://id.oclc.org/worldcat/entity/E39PCGqjgm9CTXftWhtwXYjkCP ‡4 https://id.oclc.org/worldcat/ontology/hasWork
830 #0	Library and information science text series.

Figure 5.3 A Partial MARC 21 Record as Displayed in the OCLC Connexion Client. (Source: OCLC Connexion, WorldCat—Record Number 911180115.)

000		02436cam a2200469 i 4500
001		18660797
005		20170607111220.0
008		150616s2015 cau b 001 0 eng
010	__	|a 2015012911
020	__	|a 9781598848571 (hardback : acid-free paper)
020	__	|a 9781598848564 (pbk : acid-free paper)
040	__	|a DLC |b eng |c DLC |e rda |d DLC
050	00	|a Z693 |b .W94 2015
082	00	|a 025.3 |2 23
100	1_	|a Joudrey, Daniel N., |e author.
245	10	|a Introduction to cataloging and classification / |c Daniel N. Joudrey, Arlene G. Taylor, and David P. Miller.
250	__	|a Eleventh edition.
264	_1	|a Santa Barbara, California : |b Libraries Unlimited, |c [2015]
264	_4	|c ©2015
300	__	|a xxv, 1048 pages : |b illustrations ; |c 27 cm.
336	__	|a text |b txt |2 rdacontent
337	__	|a unmediated |b n |2 rdamedia
338	__	|a volume |b nc |2 rdacarrier
490	0_	|a Library and information science text series
500	__	|a Significant expansion of: Introduction to cataloging and classification. Tenth edition / Arlene G. Taylor ; with the assistance of David P. Miller.
504	__	|a Includes bibliographical references (pages 1001-1022) and index.
650	_0	|a Descriptive cataloging.
650	_0	|a Subject cataloging.
650	_0	|a Classification |x Books.
630	00	|a Resource description & access.
650	_7	|a LANGUAGE ARTS & DISCIPLINES / Library & Information Science / Cataloging & Classification. |2 bisacsh
650	_7	|a LANGUAGE ARTS & DISCIPLINES / Study & Teaching. |2 bisacsh
700	1_	|a Taylor, Arlene G., |d 1941- |e author.
700	1_	|a Miller, David P. |q (David Peter), |d 1955- |e author.
700	1_	|a Taylor, Arlene G., |d 1941- |t Introduction to cataloging and classification. |i Based on (work):

Figure 5.4 A Partial MARC 21 Record as Displayed by the Library of Congress Catalog. (Source: LC Online Catalog—Record Number 18660797.)

Fields in MARC records are grouped together based on their first digit to create logical categories of related fields.

Group	Purpose
0XX	Control, number, and code fields
1XX	Main entry (primary creator) fields
2XX	Title, edition, and publication fields
3XX	Physical description fields

Group	Purpose
4XX	Series field (490 only)
5XX	Notes fields
6XX	Subject fields
7XX	Added entries (additional creators and contributors) and linking fields
8XX	Series added entry and holdings data fields
9XX	Local data fields

These groupings mean, for example, that all 1XX fields are related to the primary creator of a resource and all 6XX fields are related to subject access (e.g., 600 is for personal names used as subjects, 650 is for topical terms, 651 is for geographic names).

Indicators consist of two character-positions following a MARC tag. These positions contain coded information interpreting or supplementing the data in the field. The number and meaning of indicators depend on the individual MARC tag. For some fields, no indicators are used, so the indicator positions are empty. In other fields, one or both indicators may be defined and used. Each indicator position is independent of the other. Here is an example with two indicators appearing immediately after the MARC 245 tag.

> 245 14 $a The organization of knowledge in libraries : $b and the subject-approach to books / $c by Henry Evelyn Bliss.

The first indicator ("1") tells whether a title added entry is needed in the catalog.[†] The second indicator is the number of non-filing characters; it tells how many characters should be ignored (counting blank spaces as characters) to get to the first non-article word in the title. In this example, the second indicator contains the value "4" because the title begins with an initial article (*The*), and should be skipped so the resource can be filed with other titles that begin with the letter *O* (*Organization of Knowledge in Libraries*), not with the *T* titles.

A *subfield code* marks the beginning of a subfield and consists of a delimiter and a letter or number. The purpose of subfields is to introduce a greater level of granularity into MARC encoding. They identify elements in a field that might require separate treatment; they break down the larger field into smaller, more manageable chunks. Some subfields may be repeatable to accommodate multiple values for a particular element (e.g., two publication locations or two geographic subdivisions); repeatability depends on the specific MARC field and the purpose of the individual subfield. For example, the MARC subject heading field below requires $z to be repeated in order to achieve the appropriate level of geographic specificity.

[†]This is a holdover from the card catalog: an additional card for the title proper was not made when the title was already the main entry (i.e., the primary access point because no creator was identified or when more than three creators were involved). In most cases now, it functions as an indicator of whether a title is the primary access point for the record (0 = yes; 1= no).

650 #0 $a Judges $z New Hampshire $z Jaffrey $v Biography.

Delimiters are unique characters (e.g., $ or ‡ or |) that indicate the beginning of a particular subfield code. The symbol used as a delimiter may vary depending on the system. Whether it is the dollar sign, double dagger, or pipe does not matter because the characters used as delimiters are equivalent (**$a = ‡a = |a**); the difference is in style, not substance. The lowercase letter or number that follows the delimiter is a ***data element identifier***. It specifies the content found in the subfield. In the two examples above, the following subfields were used.

Tag	Subfield	Purpose
245	$a	Title proper
	$b	Remainder of title (e.g., subtitles, parallel titles)
	$c	Statement of responsibility
650	$a	Topical term used as a subject
	$z	Geographic subdivision
	$v	Form subdivision

The meaning of $a differs in each field. It is important to remember that while subfield letters and numbers can be defined consistently across a handful of fields, more often their meanings vary. Take $b as an example. Its meaning depends on the context of the MARC tag being used.

Tag	Subfield	Purpose
245	$b	Remainder of title
246	$b	Remainder of title
264	$b	Name of publisher, distributor, manufacturer
300	$b	Other physical details
338	$b	Carrier type code
520	$b	Expansion of summary note
600	$b	Numeration
710	$b	Subordinate unit of a corporate body

In the 245 and 246 fields, $b has the same meaning—remainder of title. Its meaning in other fields, however, is significantly different. Tags, indicators, and subfields can be confusing when first learning about this encoding format. To help clarify these components, Figure 5.5 labels and identifies them. For greater assistance, see the extensive MARC 21 documentation provided by the Library of Congress and OCLC.[11]

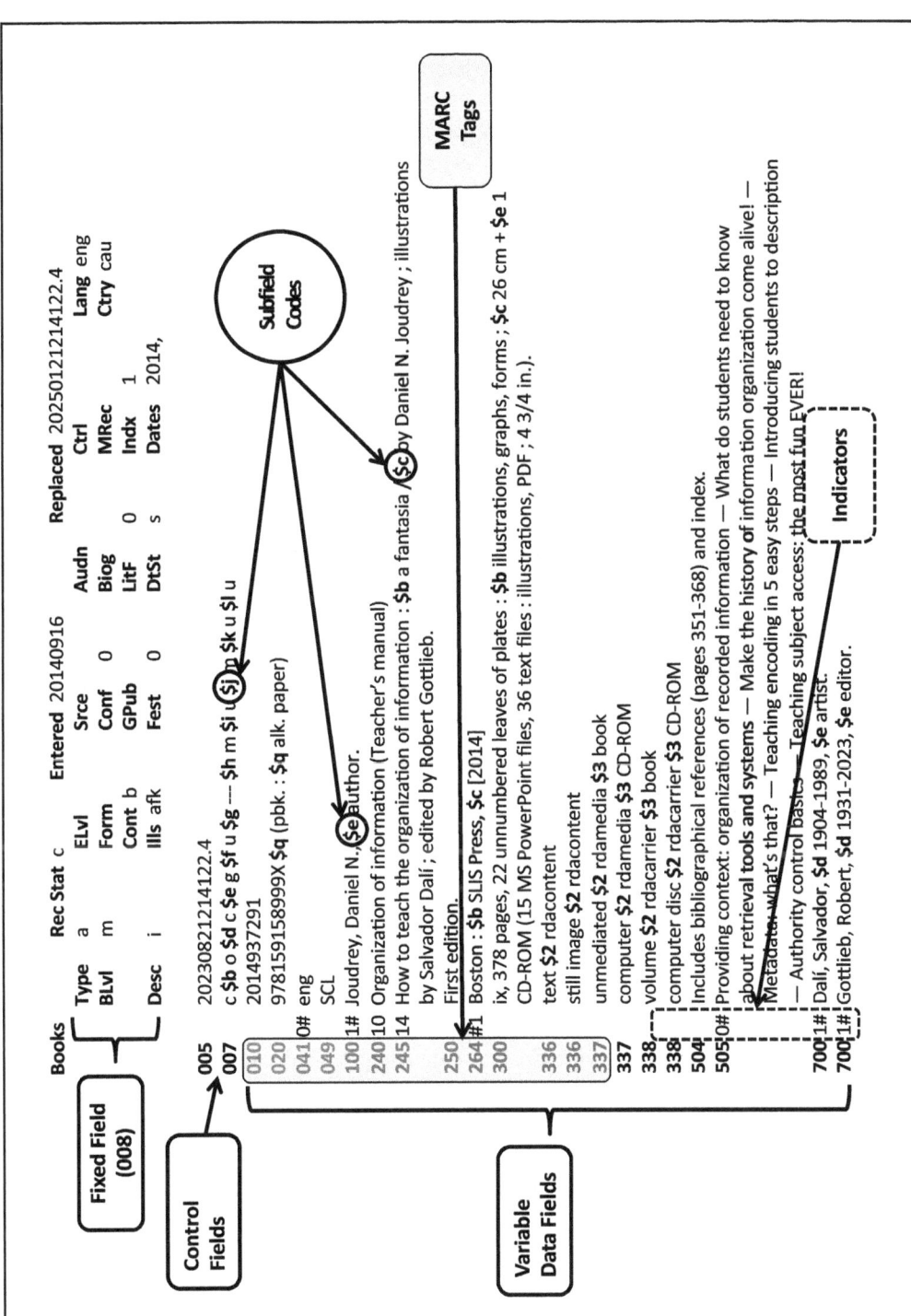

Figure 5.5 A MARC 21 Record with the Components Highlighted. (Based on the OCLC format.)

5.3.2 UNIMARC

UNIMARC (Universal MARC)[12] was developed in 1977 as a vehicle for the exchange of MARC records between national bibliographic agencies. It is a standard maintained by the Permanent UNIMARC Committee of the International Federation of Library Associations and Institutions (IFLA). It conforms to ISO 2709, as does MARC 21. UNIMARC calls for use of ISO character-set standards but also allows parties to agree on the character set to be used when exchanging records.

The proliferation of national MARC formats necessitated the development of UNIMARC. At first it was thought that UNIMARC would primarily be a conversion format. In this capacity, it is necessary for each national bibliographic agency to create a translator to change records from UNIMARC to their national MARC format and vice versa. When a translator is in place, records can be converted to UNIMARC to be sent to other countries, and records received from other countries can be translated from UNIMARC to a specific national format. In addition to this translation function, a few national agencies, which did not already have a MARC format, have adopted UNIMARC as the MARC standard in their countries.

Differences between UNIMARC and MARC 21 are immediately apparent upon looking at the list of code blocks beginning with 0, 1, 2, and so on. For example, the 1XX fields are coded information rather than main entry fields, and the 2XX block is a descriptive information block in which a title field is designated 200, rather than 245 as found in MARC 21. Also, the second indicator of the 200 field is blank and therefore does not tell how many characters to skip for an initial article. It de-emphasizes main entry in the 7XX block, where 700 is for Personal Name–Primary Intellectual Responsibility, but if the concept of main entry does not exist or is not distinguished in a source format, then 701 is used for all personal names.

5.3.3 The Future of MARC

In recent decades, some information professionals have expressed dissatisfaction with the limitations of the MARC format. They have suggested that librarians should be developing another encoding format for their bibliographic metadata to remain current and relevant in today's web-based information environment. Others have defended the MARC standard, stating that it has more than met its purpose over the years and continues to be relevant. As with most standards, there are both strengths and weaknesses associated with MARC. Strengths include MARC's maturity and its widespread use for roughly six decades. It is well understood and well tested. It has been widely adopted by libraries around the world. Over half a billion records have been created in the last sixty years and are available to libraries through bibliographic networks.

Weaknesses include MARC's limited recognition outside the library community, which hinders its interoperability with other information systems and limits the reuse of bibliographic data created by libraries. Some believe this marginalizes librarians and library metadata in the wider web-based information environment. Others find MARC's size limitations and its inability to convey hierarchical or complex relationships among entities to be problematic. Some dislike

MARC's inability to embed related objects in the record (e.g., book covers), and see this as symptomatic of MARC's antiquated data structure.

For many years, some suggested that an XML schema should replace MARC. Others declared that instead of arguing over MARC versus XML, we should be discussing MARC *and* XML to take advantage of the interoperability of XML without giving up the established content designation structure of MARC. In more recent years, many LIS professionals believe libraries need to provide bibliographic metadata in a linked data format for use outside the silo of resource management systems. Since 2011, LC has actively been pursuing this direction in its Bibliographic Framework Initiative (BIBFRAME).[§] At the time of this writing, however, BIBFRAME is still being evaluated, and widespread implementation has yet to occur. The future of MARC seems assured for at least the next decade, but as technology continues to advance, MARC's age and limitations become more apparent.

5.4 Markup Languages

Markup languages are used to describe the structure, formatting, contents, or the relationships of parts within documents through rules and a standard set of symbols. To develop markup languages, principles and guidelines are needed to provide consistency. There are several types of markup languages: punctuational, presentational, procedural, referential, descriptive, and meta-markup.[13] Of these, this chapter focuses on ***descriptive markup***, which entails identifying logical structures within a document rather than focusing on its appearance. Descriptive markup is designed to be easy for both people and computers to read and understand. Several descriptive markup languages owe their existence to a single progenitor: SGML.

5.4.1 SGML (Standard Generalized Markup Language)

The Standard Generalized Markup Language (SGML) was developed as a ***meta-language*** for encoding electronic texts. In other words, it is a markup language for creating markup languages; it provides a set of rules by which other more specific markup languages may be created. Its origins can be traced back to work done at IBM. In 1969, Charles Goldfarb, Ed Mosher, and Ray Lorie developed what was at first named the *Text-Description Language* but was eventually called *Generalized Markup Language*.[14] In the 1980s, it continued to evolve until it was published as an international standard: ISO 8879:1986, *Information Processing—Text and Office Systems—Standard Generalized Markup Language* (SGML).[15]

Unlike MARC, SGML does not provide standardized content designation—that is, it does not contain a predefined set of tags. Nor is it a standard template for producing specific types of

---

[§]BIBFRAME is discussed further toward the end of this chapter.

documents. Instead, it is a set of guidelines for designing hardware-independent markup languages to describe the structures of documents so that documents may be interchanged across computer platforms. Both text and markup are encoded in the same character set (e.g., Unicode or ASCII text), but SGML allows documents to be represented in such a way that the document structure may be identified independently from the content. **Document structure** refers to various components of the text that are marked up (encoded) to indicate their function within the document. For example, it might indicate

- this piece of text is the title,
- this content is the first chapter,
- this string of characters is a section heading,
- these lines constitute a paragraph,
- this is a quoted statement, and so on.

Or, for surrogate records, the markup may identify a piece of text as a title element, a creator element, a date element, and so on. It is said that SGML is flexible enough to define an infinite number of markup languages.

SGML defines data in terms of entities, elements, and attributes. An *entity* is a thing to be encoded (e.g., a document, a part of a document, a surrogate record). An *element* is a particular component in the entity, such as a title, a chapter title, a section heading, a paragraph, a publisher name, a classification number, and so forth. An *attribute* provides information about an element (e.g., the type of place, the language used in the element). The relationships between entities, elements, and attributes are described using SGML.

```
<teiHeader>
    <fileDesc>
        <titleStmt>
            <title>Introduction to Cataloging and Classification</title>
            <author>Daniel N. Joudrey</author>
            <author>Arlene G. Taylor</author>
            <author>David P. Miller</author>
            <respStmt>
                <resp>Encoded by</resp>
                <name>Ralph M. Holley</name>
            </respStmt>
        </titleStmt>
        ...
    </fileDesc>
</teiHeader>
```

Figure 5.6 An Example of Nesting Tags in a TEI Header. (TEI coding shown in bold.)

SGML prescribes markup that consists of delimiters and tags. Delimiters are defined symbols such as <, >, and </, which are used to construct tags (e.g., <author>). Tags usually appear before and after an element. For example, if an element (such as an author's name) is to be coded, then that name is placed between two tags identifying the type of element.

<**author**>Edward Gaynor</**author**>

Attribute values are delimited by quotation marks (" … " or ' … ').

<**quote lang='spa'**>¿Que pasa?</**quote**>

Tags may be nested hierarchically. An example of a nested set of tags from TEI (described below) is found in Figure 5.6.

Because SGML does not contain a prescribed set of tags, it requires some form of structure to be provided through a particular application or through a document type definition (DTD). An internal DTD may appear at the beginning of a document, or an external, pre-established DTD may be declared as the one being followed. Before discussing DTDs further, two specific applications or derivations of SGML are addressed. Although SGML was widely used for decades in many contexts (particularly web-based communications and data exchange), it has essentially been replaced by HTML and XML, two markup languages that were originally derived from SGML.

5.4.2 HTML (Hypertext Markup Language)

Hypertext Markup Language (HTML), originally a derivation of SGML, is a basic markup language developed for the creation of web pages. It allows almost anyone to be a web author. It defines the content, the layout, and the formatting and display of web documents. It provides for the creation of a simple structure, enables display of multimedia, and provides for establishment of links between documents. Users of an HTML-encoded document can navigate through the text itself if internal links have been made or can move from one website to another with external links. In HTML there are specific provisions for elements that can be used to describe properties of a document (e.g., title, date, keywords), making it possible to encode rudimentary metadata. For decades, the World Wide Web Consortium (W3C)[16] maintained the HTML standard across several versions, but in 2004 concerns were raised about the future direction of HTML, particularly about the W3C's interest in moving HTML closer to another standard, XML. By 2008, multiple versions of HTML had been created (HTML5, HTML4, XHTML 2.0). In addition, competing oversight bodies—W3C and the Web Hypertext Application Technology Working Group (WHATWG),[17] a consortium of the major web browser vendors (Apple, Google, Mozilla, and Microsoft)—sought control over the standard. The two organizations competed, but also, at times, collaborated on the standard. "Most of the work relating to web standards was always done first at WHATWG before it was proposed as an official standard at the W3C."[18] In 2019, the two organizations came to an agreement that WHATWG would be solely responsible for the standard. The latest version of HTML is now referred to as the *HTML Living Standard*.[19]

Until recently, it was somewhat rare to find metadata encoded in HTML. In the early years of the web, the creation and insertion of meta tags in the headers of HTML documents was encouraged by the W3C. Although specific metadata elements were not defined in the HTML standard, page creators could use any metadata element set in the generic meta tags if a Uniform Resource Identifier (URI) could be provided for that set of elements. The Dublin Core Metadata Initiative also encouraged web designers to insert Dublin Core metadata into their document headers as part of the creation process. Much to the disappointment of many information professionals, however, the make-your-own-metadata approach never really caught on with most creators of web content; or when it did, it often involved metadata mischief or malfeasance (e.g., attempts to fool search engines into directing users to an irrelevant page through misrepresentations of the content). By 2002, no existing search engine gave any credence to the keyword meta tags found in web documents.[20]

More recently, major search engines have started to trust metadata annotations being embedded within the HTML coding of web documents. Annotations may come in a variety of forms. For example, some may use microdata to annotate the content of a resource,[21] but others may prefer to use microformats,[22] RDFa (Resource Description Framework in Attributes),[23] or another form. The simplest format, **microdata**, is an HTML specification that can be used to nest metadata, in the form of name-value pairs, within the content of web resources. Annotations must be made using a controlled vocabulary to provide semantic structure. Some annotation systems, such as microdata, depend on external vocabularies to provide the semantics (e.g., it can use the Schema.org vocabulary), but others, such as microformats, have developed their own semantic structures for specific information types commonly found on the web. For example, to describe a recipe using microdata, you can use the nine properties provided by Schema.org for that type of information.

- cookTime
- cookingMethod
- nutrition
- recipeCategory
- recipeCuisine
- recipeIngredient
- recipeInstructions
- recipeYield
- suitableForDiet

Schema.org also acknowledges that many of the properties associated with describing creative works and other categories of resources may also be needed (e.g., *name* for the title of the recipe). No matter which annotation format is used, the goal is still the same: to embed additional structure, context, and metadata into the HTML coding of web documents to enhance the efficiency of search engines. An example of simple HTML, with microdata added, is presented in Figure 5.7.

Over the years, as the web has grown and become more sophisticated in the kinds of activities and information that is stored there, HTML has been criticized as being too simple because it is not particularly good at representing complex document structures and because it focused (at least initially) on display aspects, such as text size, bullet points, background colors, and so on. To remedy this, some believed that full support of SGML on the web was the answer. SGML, however, is complex and has features that make programming complicated and lengthy. XML, a subset of SGML, was developed to address some of these concerns and is somewhat simpler than SGML.

```html
<html>
<head>
<title>LIS 417 Syllabus</title>
</head>
<body itemscope itemtype="http://schema.org/WebPage">
...
<h1 align="center" itemprop="name" >LIS 417:  Subject Cataloging and Classification</h1>
<h2 align="center" itemprop="description">Syllabus</h2>
<div itemscope itemtype="http://schema.org/Person">
<ul>
<li><b>Instructor:</b><span itemprop="name">Daniel N. Joudrey</span>
<li><b>Title:</b><span itemprop="jobTitle">Professor</span>
<li><b>Email:</b><span itemprop="email">joudrey@simmons.edu</span>
<li><b>Affiliation:</b><span itemprop="affiliation">School of Library and Information Science, Simmons University</span></div><br><br>
<img src="me.jpg" itemprop="image" alt="Photo of DNJ"/>
</ul>
<br>
<br>
<div itemprop="address" itemscope itemtype="http://schema.org/PostalAddress">
        <span itemprop="streetAddress">300 The Fenway C-330K</span><br>
        <span itemprop="addressLocality">Boston</span>,
        <span itemprop="addressRegion">MA</span>
        <span itemprop="postalCode">02115</span><br>
        <span itemprop="telephone">(617) 555-5555</span>
</div>
<br>
<br>
<div itemscope itemtype="http://schema.org/CreativeWork">
<h2>Course Description:</h2>
<p itemprop="description"> This course addresses the theories, principles, and practices of subject cataloging and classification. It covers the application of national standards to the creation of bibliographic records and to the construction of catalogs in libraries and other information environments.
<br>
<br>
...
                    <!-- SYLLABUS goes on and on and on-- >

</body>
</html>
```

Figure 5.7 Simple HTML with Microdata Added. (HTML coding shown in bold; microdata elements shown in italics.)

5.4.3 XML (Extensible Markup Language)

Extensible Markup Language (XML) is a markup language, used for electronic documents, which can be read by both humans and machines. It is used to structure data and is touted by its developers as being just as easy to use as HTML but at the same time being as powerful as SGML.[24] Unlike basic HTML, XML focuses on structural markup to facilitate searching and data exchange; it leaves issues of display to style sheets. It also allows developers to create their own sets of tags, as needed—thus the word *extensible* as part of its name. XML tags "effectively act as a standard set of database field[s]," so that data can be exchanged once a tag set has been agreed upon.[25] In addition, because XML was developed some years after SGML, it incorporates techniques needed for multimedia files, such as the ability to identify the format used to encode an illustration. It is a simplified, web-compatible version of SGML. Its components are the same: entities, elements, and attributes. XML, however, allows for—but does not require—a DTD.

A ***document type definition*** (DTD) is an XML or SGML application that defines, with its own notation, the structure of a particular type of document. It gives advance notice of what elements can be used in a particular document type, so that all documents that belong to a particular type will be alike. It could be thought of as a template. Typically, the following are defined in a DTD:

- the elements that might be part of that specific document type
- element names and whether they are repeatable
- whether an element contains child elements or text
- whether an element is required or optional
- tag attributes and default values
- names of permissible entities

For example, the DTD providing the underlying structure for this (erroneous) memo

> **To:** All Veridian Dynamic Employees
> **From:** Human Resources
> **Subject:** Offensive language
> **Reference:** M-314
>
> Employees must *now* use offensive or insulting language in the workplace.[26]

might have the following lines:

```
<!DOCTYPE memo [
<!ELEMENT memo (to, from, subject?, reference, para+) >
<!ELEMENT to (#PCDATA) >
<!ELEMENT from (#PCDATA) >
<!ELEMENT subject (#PCDATA) >
<!ELEMENT reference (#PCDATA) >
<!ELEMENT para (#PCDATA) >
] >
```

This DTD states that the document type is a *memo*, and that a memo includes a *to* element, a *from* element, and a *reference* element; it includes one or more paragraphs, as indicated by the plus sign; and it may or may not include a *subject* element, as per the question mark. It also states that the *to*, *from*, and the other elements are made up of alphanumeric character strings (#PCDATA).

In the XML environment, there is an alternative to DTDs known as **XML schemas**. XML schemas have evolved as richer forms of DTDs, which define not only the structure of documents, but also their content and semantics. Unlike DTDs, XML schemas are expressed in the XML syntax and follow XML rules. Therefore, a developer does not have to learn another notation, and the software does not require a different parser. An XML schema can also define shared vocabularies with links to the namespaces in which those vocabularies reside—something not supported in DTDs. In large part, schemas have replaced DTDs because of these and other enhancements. In short, an XML schema defines:

- elements and attributes that can appear in a document
- parent–child relationships among elements
- the order and number of child elements
- whether an element is empty or can include text
- data types for elements and attributes
- default and fixed values for elements and attributes[27]

An XML schema for a memo would be written in XML and look like XML tagging:

```
<xs:element name="memo">
    <xs:complexType>
        <xs:sequence>
            <xs:element name="from" type="xs:string"/>
            <xs:element name="to" type="xs:string"/>
            <xs:element name="date" type="xs:string"/>
            <xs:element name="subject" minOccurs="0" maxOccurs="1"
                type="xs:string"/>
            <xs:element name="para" minOccurs="1"
                maxOccurs="unbounded" type="xs:string"/>
        </xs:sequence>
    </xs:complexType>
</xs:element>
```

This XML schema states that the document is a memo composed of multiple elements in a specific sequence, including elements such as *from*, *to*, and *date*, each consisting of alphanumeric character strings.

An XML schema (or DTD) may be created for only one document, in which case it may be contained at the beginning of the text, but creating a schema is time consuming. It makes more sense to create schemas that can be used for many documents. These exist separately from the texts that refer to them. Many XML schemas have been created and are in widespread use. A few of these are discussed below as examples:

- **Text Encoding Initiative (TEI):** for encoding literary texts
- **Encoded Archival Description (EAD):** for encoding archival finding aids
- **MARCXML:** for encoding MARC 21 records in XML

5.4.3.1 TEI (Text Encoding Initiative)

The schema developed by the Text Encoding Initiative provides a way to encode literary or scholarly texts so that electronic versions can be exchanged easily. It is "widely used by libraries, museums, publishers, and individual scholars to present texts for online research, teaching, and preservation."[28] Thus, it plays a significant role in the digital humanities field. When it was created in the late 1980s, TEI was designed as an SGML DTD, but over the years it has evolved first into an XML DTD, and then into an XML schema in TEI P5 (the latest version of the standard).

TEI was created to overcome difficulties caused by the use of multiple encoding schemes to encode literary or scholarly texts. Once encoded, the documents could not be exchanged easily. TEI makes the semantic features of a text explicit in a format that allows the processing of that text by different programs running on different machines. The text can be represented exactly as it appears in its original form (in the case of encoding text from books or manuscripts). Texts can be exchanged for research purposes (e.g., textual analysis). TEI can also be used for newly created documents, especially in cases where authors have a particular vision of how the text should be presented. TEI is no longer limited to texts in the arts and humanities; the guidelines provide a framework that can be used to describe many additional kinds of texts.

> The impact of the TEI on digital scholarship has been enormous. Today, the TEI is internationally recognized as a critically important tool, both for the long-term preservation of electronic data, and as a means of supporting effective usage of such data in many subject areas. It is the encoding scheme of choice for the production of critical and scholarly editions of literary texts, for scholarly reference works and large linguistic corpora, and for the management and production of detailed metadata associated with electronic text and cultural heritage collections of many types.[29]

TEI represents a constellation of encoding protocols for various literary forms that are used to mark up a wide variety of materials for numerous user communities. By necessity, the set of tags included in the schema is large (and considered unwieldy to some). It is suggested in the guidelines that one needs to customize TEI to get the best from it. To facilitate the ease of use of TEI, the consortium has designed specific customizations (i.e., more manageable subsets of the schema). These include tag sets specially designed for speech representations, dramas, manuscripts, journal articles, and the like. A popular customization that is used by a core constituency is *TEI Lite*. It contains a core set of tags from TEI to "meet '90% of the needs of 90% of the TEI user community.' Due to its simplicity and the fact that it can be learned with relative ease, [TEI Lite] has been widely adopted, particularly by beginners and by big institutional projects. ..."[30]

A notable part of TEI is the TEI Header, created to provide metadata about the electronic version of the resource encoded in the TEI schema. A strong motivation for the creation of a standard for the TEI Header was to provide a source of information for cataloging. TEI creators collaborated with library catalogers for the file description element of the header. They wanted the mapping from TEI to a catalog record as simple as possible in both directions. The standard TEI Header requires many of the same elements and therefore the content resembles that in a catalog record.

The TEI Header has five sections, only one of which is required. The five components are listed below:

- **File Description <fileDesc>**: The file description is required and contains a bibliographic description of the electronic version of the text. It includes the title statement, with author information; edition statement; extent; publication statement; series statement; notes statement; and the source description, which is a description of the original source from which the electronic text was derived.

- **Encoding Description <encodingDesc>**: This section explains the relationship between an electronic text and its source, and what rules were used or editorial decisions were made in transcribing the text (e.g., information about how quotations and spelling variations were treated, information about the tags used in the document). This area includes elements that cover project description, tagging, text sampling, references, geographic coordinates, and so on.

- **Text Profile <profileDesc>**: The text profile has information characterizing various non-bibliographic descriptive aspects of a text. It contains language information, subject terminology, and classification notation(s) as well as contextual information to help understand the situation in which the resource was produced. This section may include abstracts, creation information, language usage, classifications, correspondence descriptions, and a description of the calendar system used for dates in the resource.

- **Container Element <xenoData>**: This section contains any non-TEI metadata that the project wishes to include.

- **Revision History <revisionDesc>**: The revision history contains a record of every change that has been made to the electronic version of the text, including when each change was made and by whom.

```xml
<TEI version="5.0" xmlns="http://www.tei-c.org/ns/1.0">
<teiHeader>
    <fileDesc>
        <titleStmt>
                <title>Introduction to Cataloging and Classification</title>
                <author>Daniel N. Joudrey</author>
                <author>Arlene G. Taylor</author>
                <author>David P. Miller</author>
                <respStmt>
                        <resp>Digitized and encoded in TEI P5 by</resp>
                        <name>Ralph M. Holley</name>
                </respStmt>
        </titleStmt>
        <editionStmt>
                <edition n="1">First digital edition</edition>
                <respStmt>
                        <resp>Proofread and edited by</resp>
                        <name>Emily Baldoni</name>
                        <name>Monica Shin</name>
                </respStmt>
        </editionStmt>
        <extent>
                <measure unit="Mb" quantity="132.5">132.5 megabytes</measure>
                <measure unit="pages" quantity="1048">1048 pages</measure>
        </extent>
        <publicationStmt>
                <pubPlace>Santa Barbara, CA</pubPlace>
                <publisher>ABC-CLIO eBooks</publisher>
                <date>2015</date>
                <idno type="ISBN">978-1-44083-745-6</idno>
                <availability status="restricted">
                        <p>Available under license from the publishers</p>
                </availability>
        </publicationStmt >
        <seriesStmt>
                <title>Library and Information Science Text series</title>
        </seriesStmt>
        <notesStmt>
                <note>Significant expansion of: Introduction to cataloging and classification. Tenth edition / Arlene G. Taylor ; with the assistance of David P. Miller</note>
        </notesStmt>
        <sourceDesc>
                <p>This first digital edition is based on the 11th edition of <title>Introduction to Cataloging and Classification</title> published in <date>2015</date> by Libraries Unlimited, an imprint of ABC-Clio</p>
        </sourceDesc>
    </fileDesc>
    ...
</teiHeader>
                <!--A full TEI-encoded document follows the TEI Header-->
```

Figure 5.8 The File Description from a TEI Header. (TEI coding shown in bold.)

The form of the content that is entered into the fields is not dictated in the guidelines for TEI Headers. Examples may be found on the TEI website and through the TEI By Example project.[31]

5.4.3.2 EAD (Encoded Archival Description)

Encoded Archival Description (EAD) is used to encode finding aids in archives, museums, and libraries.[32] It facilitates the exchange of finding aids among institutions and allows users to discover collections in distant places. Its design principles state: "EAD is ... not a data content standard. It does not prescribe how one formulates the data that appears in any given data element—that is the role of external national or international data content standards."[33] Content standards for finding aids exist (e.g., *Describing Archives: A Content Standard*), so EAD does not need to contain prescriptions for content. Instead, EAD defines the encoding designations.

EAD Version 2002[34] is available as an XML schema as well as a DTD that conforms to all SGML/XML specifications. The minimum set of EAD tags required for an online finding aid includes the following elements:

```
<ead>
    <eadheader>
        <eadid> ... </eadid>
        <filedesc>
            <titlestmt>
                <titleproper> ... </titleproper>
            </titlestmt>
        </filedesc>
    </eadheader>
    <archdesc level="collection">
        <did>
            <unittitle> ... </unittitle>
        </did>
    </archdesc>
</ead>**
```

EAD 2002 has a header section that contains metadata about the creation and maintenance of the EAD document itself. This header has been replaced in EAD3 with a <control> element for recording bibliographic and administrative information about an EAD-encoded document.

The latest official version of EAD at the time of this writing is EAD3, which was released in 2015. It too is available as an XML schema and a DTD. It was introduced to update and simplify the encoding standard. A decade after the release of EAD3, many archives are still using EAD 2002. LC notes:

> EAD 2002 is deprecated and no longer supported by the Technical Subcommittee on Encoded Archival Standards. ... As of 2021, this version of the standard is still used in the archival community and will hence remain available at this location and on GitHub.[35]

**In the above example, "collection" is one of the valid values for the *level* attribute. Also, the Descriptive Identification element requires a sub-element, of which Title of the Unit is one option.

EAD3 contains 165 elements and more than 80 attributes. Each element in the tag library is presented with at least some of the following information:

- Tag name
- Element name
- Summary
- May contain
- May occur within
- Attributes
- Description and Usage
- Availability
- References
- Examples

Changes in EAD3 are outlined in the preface to the EAD3 Tag Library and were driven by four principles:

- Achieving greater conceptual and semantic consistency in the use of EAD.
- Exploring mechanisms whereby EAD-encoded information might more seamlessly and effectively connect with, exchange, or incorporate data maintained according to other protocols.
- Improving the functionality of EAD for representing descriptive information created in international and particularly in multilingual environments.
- Being mindful that a new version will affect current users.[36]

As stated, EAD3 was not immediately adopted. In some instances, archives chose to continue using EAD Version 2002, while others catalog their archival collections using MARC (this may be in lieu of or in addition to creating finding aids). It should be remembered that some institutions have not adopted any version of EAD whatsoever, instead using PDF documents or HTML-encoded web pages to share their archival metadata. Some organizations simply may not have the staff, funding, expertise, or technological infrastructure to support the creation of EAD-encoded metadata.

In late 2023, SAA announced that the development of EAD 4.0 had begun.[37] For a complete listing of elements used in EAD3 or EAD 2002, please consult the tag libraries at the EAD Official Site.[38] For an example of an EAD3-encoded finding aid, see Appendix C in this text.

5.4.3.3 MARCXML

In the mid-1990s LC developed two SGML DTDs to provide access to MARC data in an SGML format without a loss of data.[39] As technology evolved, these two SGML DTDs were converted to XML DTDs. The two MARC XML DTDs defined all the elements that appear in a MARC record and specified how they were tagged and represented with XML coding. But as DTDs have gone somewhat out of fashion in favor of XML schemas, the MARC DTDs have been deprecated.

An XML schema based on MARC has been developed by LC.[††] The MARCXML schema supports XML markup of full MARC 21 records, featuring lossless conversion to and from MARC 21 records, a conversion toolkit, and style sheets. It duplicates the MARC content designation structure in a native XML encoding format. For an example of a MARCXML-encoded record, see Figure 5.9.

[††]In truth, two XML schemas have been developed. The other one, Metadata Object Description Schema (MODS) is addressed in Chapter 9 Description and Access Standards. Unlike MARCXML, which does not have a unique approach to content designation, MODS is a metadata structure standard, with its own set of unique elements that is encoded using XML.

```xml
<record xmlns="http://www.loc.gov/MARC21/slim"
xmlns:cinclude="http://apache.org/cocoon/include/1.0" xmlns:zs="http://www.loc.gov/zing/srw/">
    <leader>02384cam a2200457 i 4500</leader>
    <controlfield tag="001">18660797</controlfield>
    <controlfield tag="005">20160818094544.0</controlfield>
    <controlfield tag="008">150616s2015 cau b 001 0 eng</controlfield>
    <datafield tag="010" ind1=" " ind2=" ">
        <subfield code="a">2015012911</subfield></datafield>
    <datafield tag="020" ind1=" " ind2=" ">
        <subfield code="a">9781598848571 (hardback : acid-free paper)</subfield>
    </datafield>
    <datafield tag="050" ind1="0" ind2="0">
        <subfield code="a">Z693</subfield>
        <subfield code="b">.W94 2015</subfield></datafield>
    <datafield tag="082" ind1="0" ind2="0">
        <subfield code="a">025.3</subfield>
        <subfield code="2">23</subfield></datafield>
    <datafield tag="100" ind1="1" ind2=" ">
        <subfield code="a">Joudrey, Daniel N.,</subfield>
        <subfield code="e">author.</subfield></datafield>
    <datafield tag="245" ind1="1" ind2="0">
        <subfield code="a">Introduction to cataloging and classification /</subfield>
        <subfield code="c">Daniel N. Joudrey, Arlene G. Taylor, and David P. Miller.
        </subfield></datafield>
    <datafield tag="250" ind1=" " ind2=" ">
        <subfield code="a">Eleventh edition.</subfield></datafield>
    <datafield tag="264" ind1=" " ind2="1">
        <subfield code="a">Santa Barbara, California :</subfield>
        <subfield code="b">Libraries Unlimited,</subfield>
        <subfield code="c">[2015]</subfield></datafield>
    <datafield tag="300" ind1=" " ind2=" ">
        <subfield code="a">xxv, 1048 pages :</subfield>
        <subfield code="b">illustrations ;</subfield>
        <subfield code="c">27 cm.</subfield></datafield>
    <datafield tag="700" ind1="1" ind2=" ">
        <subfield code="a">Taylor, Arlene G.,</subfield>
        <subfield code="d">1941-</subfield>
        <subfield code="e">author.</subfield>
    </datafield>
    <datafield tag="700" ind1="1" ind2=" ">
        <subfield code="a">Miller, David P.</subfield>
        <subfield code="q">(David Peter),</subfield>
        <subfield code="d">1955-</subfield>
        <subfield code="e">author.</subfield>
    </datafield>
    <datafield tag="700" ind1="1" ind2=" ">
        <subfield code="a">Taylor, Arlene G.,</subfield>
        <subfield code="d">1941-</subfield>
        <subfield code="t">Introduction to cataloging and classification.</subfield>
        <subfield code="i">Based on (work):</subfield>
    </datafield>
</record>
```

Figure 5.9 An Excerpt from a MARCXML Record. (MARCXML coding shown in bold.)

5.5 BIBFRAME: A Future Standard?

In the early twenty-first century, there were increasingly urgent calls to replace MARC as the primary encoding standard in libraries. Although MARC was a groundbreaking achievement and has adapted to libraries' needs over time, critics have declared that MARC has reached the end of its useful life. One of the more prominent critics is Roy Tennant, whose provocative and influential article, "MARC Must Die," captured the profession's attention.[40] As new conceptual models for bibliographic metadata were developed, with their emphasis on identifying multiple and diverse relationships, the MARC format's limitations and its inflexibility became clearer.

Since 2011, a different approach to encoding—one that embraces the potential of and the technologies supporting the Semantic Web—has been under development at LC.‡‡ The LC MARC-replacement project is called the Bibliographic Framework Initiative but is more commonly known as BIBFRAME. BIBFRAME comprises a set of linked data tools for creating bibliographic metadata that is compatible with the wider networked computing environment. It is designed to make bibliographic data more accessible, yet still serve the specific needs of libraries.

BIBFRAME is intended to move library metadata from the record-bound MARC structure to metadata statements that are not confined to a catalog record.

> Instead of bundling everything neatly as a "record" and potentially duplicating bibliographic information across multiple records, the BIBFRAME Model relies heavily on relationships between resources. ... In short, the BIBFRAME Model is the library community's formal entry point for becoming part of a much larger web of data, where the links between things are paramount.[41]

Although the initiative is an ambitious attempt to replace MARC, at the same time LC intends to retain the huge investment made by libraries in the creation of authoritative and reliable metadata. As the LC report, *Bibliographic Framework as a Web of Data*, states:

> Libraries generate, maintain and curate an enormous amount of high-quality data ... that is valuable well beyond traditional library boundaries. ... In modeling the MARC 21 format as a Web of Data it is important to deconstruct and then reconstruct the informational assets that comprise MARC.[42]

Beyond retaining the metadata content of MARC records, BIBFRAME is also designed to continue the basic MARC functions of "representation and communication of bibliographic and related information in machine-readable form."[43] Unlike previous calls for the "death" of a standard, BIBFRAME will not consign the billions of existing MARC records to a sealed-off zone of legacy records but instead will move their value forward into the Semantic Web by converting them into a linked data-compatible format.

Although BIBFRAME has been in the works for over a decade, it still has not been widely implemented. LC continues to promote its development, but some libraries may not be capable of converting to another format due to financial constraints. And, as BIBFRAME tools become more sophisticated, conversion programs between MARC and BIBFRAME have improved to a point where perhaps either format can be used. Whether a record is created in BIBFRAME or MARC,

---

‡‡The Semantic Web, linked data, and the Resource Description Framework (RDF) are discussed in more detail in Chapter 7.

the data can be used by all. So, MARC may not need to "die" after all—at least not in the immediate future. At professional conferences and in personal conversations, many catalogers expect to continue to work in the MARC format for the foreseeable future.

BIBFRAME comprises two major components: the BIBFRAME Vocabulary and the BIBFRAME Model. The **BIBFRAME Vocabulary** is "the key to the description of resources."[44] Similar to the defined set of tags and subfields for the purpose of content designation found in the MARC bibliographic format, the BIBFRAME Vocabulary has a defined set of *classes* (groups of things or entities) and *properties* (relationships or attributes) to describe bibliographic resources. The BIBFRAME Vocabulary, at this writing, contains over 200 classes, some of which contain one or more subclasses, a sample of which is provided below.

Classes	Associated Subclasses
AdminMetadata	
Agent	Family
	Jurisdiction
	Meeting
	Organization
	Person
Carrier	
Classification	ClassificationDdc
	ClassificationLcc
	ClassificationNlm
	ClassificationUdc

There are also nearly 150 properties identified, some of which are seen below.

Properties	Associated Class
dimensions	Instance
dissertation	Work or Instance
duration	Work or Instance
edition	Classification

The **BIBFRAME Model** describes the structure of bibliographic resources and their potential relationships to other entities; it comprises three high-level core classes: *work*, *instance*, and *item*. This structure may be familiar to those conversant in the conceptual models of the cataloging and metadata world; these core classes are like the resource entities found in the *IFLA Library Reference Model* (LRM): *work, expression, manifestation,* and *item*.[§§]

Work in the BIBFRAME Model is the "conceptual essence of the cataloged resource"; it entails the distinct ideas and the artistic or intellectual vision of a creator. In BIBFRAME, however, the work incorporates not only the intellectual or artistic content but also the way in which that content is communicated (e.g., language, translations, form of work). Thus, it is a fusion of the

---

[§§]LRM has been mentioned in passing in previous chapters. It is discussed in more detail in Chapter 7.

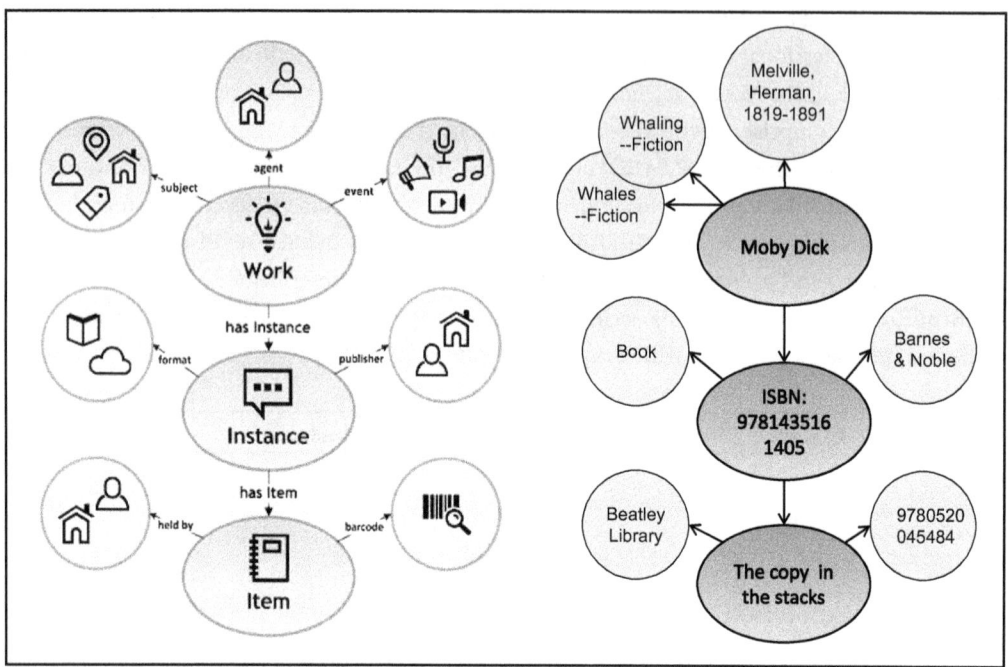

Figure 5.10 The Basic Conceptual Model for BIBFRAME 2.0 with an Example. (Source of Model: Library of Congress, BIBFRAME 2.0 Model, https://www.loc.gov/bibframe/docs/bibframe2-model.html.)

work and expression entities found in the LRM model. *Instance*—one or more material embodiments of a work—is equivalent to LRM's manifestation. The definition of *item*, too, is similar to that in the LRM model. BIBFRAME's item is "an actual copy (physical or electronic) of an Instance." In addition to these three high-level core classes, the BIBFRAME Model identifies three related key concepts: *agents*, *subjects*, and *events*. **Agents** are persons, corporate bodies, families, or governments associated with a work or an instance. Agents play roles in the creation of a work or an instance, such as author, publisher, illustrator, translator, and the like. **Subjects** reflect what the resource is about, and *events* are occurrences related to the content of a work (e.g., the Battle of Gettysburg).[45]

Additional classes may also be used to identify relationships and attributes of the resources being described. The basic BIBFRAME conceptual model is illustrated in Figure 5.10; an example is provided next to the model to illustrate relationships. An encoded BIBFRAME description for the item in Figure 5.4 is presented in Appendix D.*** At the time of this writing, a BIBFRAME editor, MARVA,††† can be used to create BIBFRAME records.[46]

***The figure is too large to include in this chapter.
†††MARVA was chosen to honor Henriette Avram (the mother of MARC); MARVA is Avram spelled backward.

5.6 Conclusion

This chapter has discussed some ways of encoding metadata. We have reviewed the MARC format that has long been used in library catalogs. Although it has largely fulfilled its role for more than half of a century, there are difficulties associated with this aging standard. In the late 1990s and early 2000s, many suggested that an XML-based approach to encoding metadata was the answer. As technology developed further, the creation of XML records with natural language tags began to seem somewhat out of date. Progress continued and another approach was offered: using RDF-structured linked data statements to record and share descriptive metadata. Although not quite ready for widespread adoption, many information professionals are actively working to advance this model.

An understanding of encoding has been important ever since MARC became a routine part of organizing information in libraries. Catalogers, archivists, and other information professionals have been responsible not only for the descriptive metadata content but also for the encoding which allows institutions to share that metadata easily and efficiently. As technology continues to develop, though, there may be less need to be actively involved in the direct encoding of metadata. We may come to rely more on automated template tools or editors that will take descriptive content in, convert that information to RDF triples behind the scenes, and then present metadata that is ready to be shared in the linked data environment. In short, while catalogers once needed to understand MARC in detail to do their work, such depth of interaction may no longer be required with the adoption of BIBFRAME.

Some Important Terms in This Chapter
(Definitions Provided in the Glossary)

Agent	Document type definition	Meta-language
Attribute	Encoding	Microdata
BIBFRAME model	Entity	ONIX message
BIBFRAME vocabulary	Event	Property
Class	Fixed field	Subfield
Code	Indicator	Subfield code
Content standard	Instance	Subject
Control field	Item	Tag
Data element identifier	Leader	TEI header
Delimiter	MARC tag	Variable data field
Descriptive markup	Markup language	Work
Directory	Metadata	XML schema
Document structure		

Some Important Acronyms in This Chapter

ANSI:	American National Standards Institute
ASCII:	American Standard Code for Information Interchange
BIBFRAME:	Bibliographic Framework Initiative
DTD:	Document Type Definition
EAD:	Encoded Archival Description
EBCDIC:	Extended Binary Coded Decimal Interchange Code
HTML:	Hypertext Markup Language
IBM:	International Business Machines
IFLA:	International Federation of Library Associations and Institutions
ISO:	International Organization for Standardization
LC-MARC:	Library of Congress MARC
LRM:	*IFLA Library Reference Model*
MARC:	Machine-Readable Cataloging
MARCXML:	MARC 21 XML Schema
MODS:	Metadata Object Description Schema
NISO:	National Information Standards Organization
OCLC:	Online Computer Library Center
ONIX:	Online Information Exchange
RDF:	Resource Description Framework
RDFa:	RDF in Attributes
RNG:	Relax (Regular Language for XML) Next Generation
SGML:	Standard Generalized Markup Language
TEI:	Text Encoding Initiative
UCS:	Universal Coded Character Set
UNIMARC:	Universal MARC
URI:	Uniform Resource Identifier
USMARC:	United States MARC
W3C:	World Wide Web Consortium
XHTML:	Extensible Hypertext Markup Language
XML:	Extensible Markup Language

5.7 Discussion Questions and Exercises

- Some say MARC is outdated and needs to be replaced; others argue MARC is doing the job it was designed to do and there is no need to rush away from it. What are the arguments for replacing MARC? What potential challenges might there be to moving away from the standard?
- Select an XML encoding standard discussed in section 5.4:
    - What is the origin of the standard? What problems was it created to solve?
    - What are the advantages and disadvantages of this schema?
    - How does it compare to the older MARC standard?

5.8 Suggested Readings

"EAD: Encoded Archival Description." Library of Congress. http://www.loc.gov/ead/.

Furrie, Betty. *Understanding MARC Bibliographic: Machine-Readable Cataloging*. 8th ed. Washington, DC: Library of Congress, Cataloging Distribution Service, 2009. http://www.loc.gov/marc/umb.

Joudrey, Daniel N., Arlene G. Taylor, and David P. Miller. *Introduction to Cataloging and Classification*. 11th ed. Santa Barbara, CA: Libraries Unlimited, 2015.

Library of Congress, Network Development and MARC Standards Office. "BIBFRAME: Bibliographic Framework Initiative." http://www.loc.gov/bibframe/.

Library of Congress, Network Development and MARC Standards Office. "MARC Standards." http://www.loc.gov/marc/.

Library of Congress, Network Development and MARC Standards Office. "MARCXML: MARC 21 XML Schema." http://www.loc.gov/standards/marcxml/.

Text Encoding Initiative. "TEI: P5 Guidelines." Version 3.1.0. http://www.tei-c.org/release/doc/tei-p5-doc/en/html/index.html.

W3C. "Extensible Markup Language." https://www.w3.org/XML/.

Web Hypertext Application Technology Working Group (WHATWG). "HTML Living Standard." https://html.spec.whatwg.org/.

5.9 Notes

All URLs accessed April 2025.

1. Henriette Avram, "Machine Readable Cataloging (MARC): 1961–1974 [Classic from 1975]," in *Encyclopedia of Library and Information Sciences*, 4th ed., eds. John D. McDonald and Michael Levine-Clark (Boca Raton, FL: Taylor & Francis, 2017), 2963.
2. Kevin S. Clarke, "Extensible Markup Language (XML)," in *Encyclopedia of Library and Information Sciences*, 4th ed., eds. John D. McDonald and Michael Levine-Clark (Boca Raton, FL: Taylor & Francis, 2017), 1808.
3. Clarke, 1809.
4. "About the Unicode Standard," Unicode Consortium, https://www.unicode.org/standard/standard.html.

5. National Information Standards Organization, *ANSI/NISO Standard Z39.2-1994 (R2016): Information Interchange Format* (Baltimore, MD: NISO, 2016).
6. International Organization for Standardization, *Information and Documentation—Format for Information Exchange*, ISO 2709:2008, 4th ed. (Geneva: ISO, 2008). [Reviewed and confirmed in 2022.]
7. "MARC 21 Specifications for Record Structure, Character Sets, and Exchange Media: Character Sets and Encoding Options," Library of Congress, Network Development and MARC Standards Office, http://www.loc.gov/marc/specifications/speccharintro.html.
8. "MARC Standards," Library of Congress, Network Development and MARC Standards Office, http://www.loc.gov/marc; "Bibliographic Formats and Standards," OCLC, https://www.oclc.org/bibformats/en.html.
9. Karen Smith-Yoshimura, Catherine Argus, Timothy J. Dickey, Chew Chiat Naun, Lisa Rowlinson de Ortiz, and Hugh Taylor, *Implications of MARC Tag Usage on Library Metadata Practices* (Dublin, OH: OCLC, 2010), 19–20, http://www.oclc.org/research/publications/library/2010/2010-06.pdf.
10. William E. Moen and Penelope Benardino, "Assessing Metadata Utilization: An Analysis of MARC Content Designation Use," *International Conference on Dublin Core and Metadata Applications* (S.l.: DCMI, 2003), 171–80, http://dcpapers.dublincore.org/pubs/article/view/745.
11. "MARC Standards," http://www.loc.gov/marc; "Bibliographic Formats and Standards, https://www.oclc.org/bibformats/en.html.
12. IFLA, *UNIMARC Manual: Bibliographic Format*, 3rd ed., ed. Alan Hopkinson (Munich: K.G. Saur, 2008).
13. James Coombs, Allen H. Renear, and Steven J. DeRose, "Markup Systems and the Future of Scholarly Text Processing," *Communications of the ACM* 30 (Nov. 1987): 933–47, http://xml.coverpages.org/coombs.html.
14. Airi Salminen, "Markup Languages," in *Encyclopedia of Library and Information Sciences*, 4th ed., eds. John D. McDonald and Michael Levine-Clark (Boca Raton, FL: Taylor & Francis, 2017), 3074.
15. International Organization for Standardization, *Information Processing: Text and Office Systems: Standard Generalized Markup Language (SGML)*, ISO 8879:1986 (Geneva: ISO, 1986). [Reviewed and confirmed in 2020.]
16. "Making the Web Work," W3C, https://www.w3.org/.
17. "Welcome to the WHATWG Community," WHATWG, https://whatwg.org/.
18. Catalin Cimpanu, "Browser Vendors Win War with W3C over HTML and DOM Standards," *ZDNET*, https://www.zdnet.com/article/browser-vendors-win-war-with-w3c-over-html-and-dom-standards/.
19. "HTML Living Standard," WHATWG, https://html.spec.whatwg.org/.
20. Kristine Schachinger, "How to Use HTML Meta Tags," *Search Engine Watch*, 2001, https://www.searchenginewatch.com/2012/05/01/how-to-use-html-meta-tags/.
21. "Microdata," WHATWG, https://html.spec.whatwg.org/multipage/microdata.html.
22. Microformats: Meaningful Metadata, https://microformats.io/; Microformats, http://microformats.org/.
23. "RDFa 1.1 Primer: Rich Structured Data Markup for Web Documents," 3rd ed., W3C, 2015, https://www.w3.org/TR/rdfa-primer/.
24. "Extensible Markup Language (XML)," W3C, https://www.w3.org/XML/; "XML in 10 Points," W3C, https://www.w3.org/XML/1999/XML-in-10-points-19990327.
25. Jennifer Rowley and Richard Hartley, *Organizing Knowledge*, 4th ed. (Aldershot, UK: Ashgate, 2008), 41.
26. *Better Off Ted*, Season 2, episode 8, "The Impertence of Communicationizing," directed by Michael Fresco, written by Victor Fresco, Michael Teverbaugh, and Ingrid Escajeda, featuring Jay Harrington, Portia de Rossi, and Andrea Anders, aired January 12, 2010, on ABC, https://www.amazon.com/gp/video/detail/0LCOF6ZZL5G0RZ8Z3DL599IYK1.
27. "XML Schema," W3Schools.com, http://www.w3schools.com/xml/xml_schema.asp.

28. "TEI Guidelines," Text Encoding Initiative, http://www.tei-c.org/Guidelines/.
29. "TEI: History," Text Encoding Initiative, https://www.tei-c.org/about/history/.
30. "TEI Lite," Text Encoding Initiative, https://tei-c.org/release/doc/tei-p5-exemplars/html/tei_lite.doc.html.
31. "TEI: Text Encoding Initiative," Text Encoding Initiative, https://www.tei-c.org/index.en.html; "Welcome to the TEI by Example Project," TEI By Example, https://teibyexample.org/exist/examples/.
32. "EAD: Encoded Archival Description," Library of Congress, http://www.loc.gov/ead/. [Henceforth cited as EAD.]
33. "Design Principles for Enhancement to EAD (December 2002)," Library of Congress, http://www.loc.gov/ead/eaddesgn.html.
34. EAD.
35. EAD.
36. Society of American Archivists (SAA), *Encoded Archival Description Tag Library, Version EAD3 1.1.2*, Edition 2023, Library of Congress, https://www.loc.gov/ead/EAD3taglib/EAD3-TL-eng.html.
37. SAA, "Major revision of EAD – Call to action," https://www2.archivists.org/groups/technical-subcommittee-on-encoded-archival-standards-ts-eas/major-revision-of-ead-call-to-act.
38. EAD.
39. "MARCXML: MARC 21 XML Schema," Library of Congress, http://www.loc.gov/standards/marcxml/.
40. Roy Tennant, "MARC Must Die," *Library Journal* 127, no. 17 (2002): 26–7.
41. "Marva BIBFRAME User Manual: What is BIBFRAME?" Library of Congress, https://guides.loc.gov/c.php?g=1170551&p=8987094&preview=003264c97f504caf990125066b248e24.
42. *Bibliographic Framework as a Web of Data: Linked Data Model and Supporting Services* (Washington, DC: Library of Congress, 2012), http://www.loc.gov/bibframe/pdf/marcld-report-11-21-2012.pdf.
43. Kevin M. Ford, "LC's Bibliographic Framework Initiative and the Attractiveness of Linked Data," *Information Standards Quarterly* 24, no. 2/3 (2012): 47.
44. "BIBFRAME Frequently Asked Questions," Library of Congress, http://www.loc.gov/bibframe/faqs/.
45. "Overview of the BIBFRAME 2.0 Model," Library of Congress, http://www.loc.gov/bibframe/docs/bibframe2-model.html.
46. "Marva," Library of Congress, https://bibframe.org/marva/editor/.

Chapter 6

Introduction to Metadata

In the preceding chapters, we have referred to the concept of *metadata* in numerous contexts. This chapter explores metadata in greater detail—its types, forms, characteristics, and uses. It also examines definitions of the concept, common metadata management tools, and the role metadata plays in supporting the goals of information retrieval tools.

6.1 Metadata? What's That?

Metadata is commonly described as "data about data"—a definition that assumes information resources (e.g., books, maps, streaming video) are themselves data. The information used to describe a resource's contents and attributes is, in turn, also data—hence the phrase "data about data." This definition represents the very broadest level of the concept. Across professional literature, numerous definitions of *metadata* exist ranging from simple phrases like "data about data" to more complex definitions. What they all have in common is the notion that metadata is structured information that describes the important attributes and relationships of resources for the purposes of identification, discovery, selection, use, access, and management. *FOLDOC: Free On-Line Dictionary of Computing* defines metadata as "definitional data that provides information about or documentation of other data managed within an application or environment. ... Metadata may include descriptive information about the context, quality and condition, or characteristics of the data."[1] This definition implies that metadata includes not only descriptive information, such as that found in traditional retrieval tools for the purpose of resource discovery, but also information necessary for the management, use, and preservation of the information resource (e.g., data about where the resource is located, how it is displayed online, its ownership, its condition).

Even among information professionals, metadata concepts can be confusing. This is due in part to the multifaceted nature of the topic and in part to the overly simplistic, pervasive "data about data" definition. With that as a primary description, it is no wonder that many refer to any number of interrelated concepts as *metadata*. Discussions of metadata may be about any of the conceptual components listed in Table 6.1.

Although in theory we may discuss any or all of these as distinct conceptual components, in practice the divisions among them are not quite so clear. At times, the concepts are so intertwined that efforts to separate them only result in more confusion. This complexity is evident in the Machine-Readable Cataloging (MARC) format. While many consider MARC to be an encoding format,

Table 6.1 Components That May Be Described as Metadata

Component	Explanation	Examples
Attributes of Information Resources	The identifying characteristics of resources (i.e., the data used to describe them)	• *Jaws*—the title of a film • 2015—the manufacture date of a specimen collection • Fondue—the subject of a resource
Elements	Individual units of data that contain specific attributes used to describe resources	• \<title> • \<date> • \<subject>
Data Structure Standards (or Metadata Schemas)	Sets of metadata elements created by particular communities or for particular types of resources	• Dublin Core Metadata Element Set (DCMES) • VRA Core
Data Content Standards	Sets of rules, guidelines, or best practices used to create resource descriptions	• *RDA: Resource Description & Access* • *Describing Archives: A Content Standard* (DACS) • *Cataloging Cultural Objects* (CCO)
Data Value Standards (or Controlled Vocabularies)	Lists of controlled values used to populate specific metadata elements	• *Library of Congress Subject Headings* (LCSH) • Getty's *Union List of Artist Names* (ULAN) • Dublin Core Metadata Initiative (DCMI) Type Vocabulary
Data Format Standards (or Encoding Standards)	Syntaxes used to convert resource descriptions into machine-readable form	• Machine-Readable Cataloging (MARC) bibliographic format • Encoded Archival Description (EAD)
Models	Holistic representations of the principles, entities, attributes, and relationships used to describe information resources	• *Library Reference Model* (LRM) • *Records in Contexts* (RiC) • Dublin Core Abstract Model (DCAM)
Records	Documented descriptions of (or surrogates for) information resources	• A catalog record • A finding aid • A metadata statement

others refer to it as a metadata schema (or structure standard). The confusion stems from MARC's exhibiting properties of both. On closer examination, MARC even acts as a data value standard by dictating the values of certain data elements in the record (particularly for the MARC control fields). So, it is not surprising that there are misunderstandings about what metadata is. The components outlined in Table 6.1 are addressed throughout later chapters of this book.*

It is important to remember that the term *metadata* may signify different things to different communities. The information resources found in libraries are quite different from those found in museums, historical societies, scientific data repositories, or on the open web. Differences in the nature, characteristics, and uses of the resources may require diverse approaches to description and to the metadata created. Distinct types of information professionals (and non-professionals of all types) will therefore have different perceptions of what metadata entails. For example, when librarians, who are mostly familiar with bibliographic data, speak of metadata, they often have a different understanding of metadata than, say, a database designer or someone working with complex geospatial information encoded in an Extensible Markup Language (XML) schema.

6.2 The Basics of Metadata

Metadata is often divided into three broad categories:

- Administrative metadata
- Descriptive metadata
- Structural metadata

These categories of metadata are described in more detail later in this chapter. Keep in mind that these categories are somewhat fluid; the boundaries among them are not fixed and their definitions are not standardized or precise. Individual metadata elements may fit into more than one category (e.g., a unique identifier may be considered useful as descriptive, administrative, and structural metadata). In addition, these three categories are not the only ways to classify metadata. Some authors have identified five types of metadata:[2]

- Administrative
- Descriptive
- Preservation
- Technical
- Use

Others, though, have identified as many as 11 metadata types:[3]

- Administrative
- Behavior
- Descriptive
- Image quality assessment

---

*Information resources and metadata records are addressed throughout this text, but identifying attributes are primarily addressed in Chapters 8 and 9, along with metadata elements, structure standards, and content standards. Value standards that are not subject-based are addressed in Chapter 10, and subject-related value standards are addressed in Chapters 12 and 13. Encoding is addressed in Chapter 5 and data models are addressed in Chapter 7.

- Meta-metadata
- Preservation
- Recordkeeping
- Rights
- Structural
- Technical
- Tracking

Some authors have offered additional types of metadata to consider, such as contextual metadata[4] and analytical metadata.[5] Others, however, view these as part of the descriptive metadata category. We must remember that because there is no formal taxonomy of metadata types with precise definitions, what one author might refer to as *use metadata* another might call *administrative metadata*. The three broad categories employed in this text (descriptive, administrative, and structural) reflect the most prevalent categorization used today. The other types are subsumed under these three main categories. For a broad overview of these metadata types, see Table 6.2.

Another way of looking at metadata is to consider its level of complexity. The simplest metadata may be little more than data extracted from the resource itself, as reflected by the search engine approach to organizing the web through automated indexing techniques. Another level of structure and complexity can be added by using general-use element sets to create a basic template for metadata creation that does not require professional-level description (for example, as in the use of Hypertext Markup Language (HTML) meta tags to describe web resources). A still more complex approach is prevalent in most libraries, archives, and museums, where information professionals create rich, meticulously detailed descriptions. They are more comprehensive and combine metadata elements with encoding and content standards. Examples of rich metadata are found in bibliographic records that are created using *RDA: Resource Description & Access*, *International Standard Bibliographic Description* (ISBD), and MARC, and in online finding aids created using *Describing Archives: A Content Standard* (DACS) and Encoded Archival Description (EAD).

At times, the need for comprehensive, rich description has been questioned by those interested in developing more cost-effective approaches to metadata creation, often advocating for greater use of automatically generated metadata whenever possible.† Others, however, are convinced that this will result in a reduction of the quality of the metadata produced and are opposed to making radical changes in metadata-creation processes. As the popular saying goes (popular among catalogers and archivists, that is), "Metadata is a love letter to the future." In other words, many information professionals strongly believe it is better to create rich, full, well-formed metadata now, than to regret the lack of it later—we should be kind to future generations.

Metadata can be used to describe information resources at various levels of **granularity** (i.e., detail or depth). It can be created for individual information resources, for discrete components of those resources, or for established collections comprising multiple resources. In other words, metadata could be used to describe

---

†As noted in several places in this text, the library and information science professions are starting to investigate the potential role of artificial intelligence (AI) in information organization processes. Although the developments show promise for streamlining organizing processes, the current state of AI is not yet good enough to replace current workflows. When the various bugs are worked out, it is likely that AI will be adopted by many in the information professions.

Table 6.2 Metadata Types

Type	Definition	Sub-types	Typical Elements	Examples
Administrative Metadata	Supports management, decision making, preservation, rights management, technical support, metadata management, usage tracking, assessment, and recordkeeping	<ul><li>Image-quality assessment</li><li>Meta-metadata</li><li>Preservation</li><li>Recordkeeping</li><li>Rights</li><li>Technical</li><li>Tracking</li><li>Use</li></ul>	<ul><li>Acquisition</li><li>Condition</li><li>Digitization information</li><li>File size</li><li>Metadata creation data</li><li>Preservation actions</li><li>Responsibility</li><li>Software requirements</li><li>Storage requirements</li><li>Usage information</li><li>User tracking</li></ul>	<ul><li>Metadata for Images in XML Standard (MIX)</li><li>Open Digital Rights Language (ODRL)</li><li>Preservation Metadata: Implementation Strategies (PREMIS)</li></ul>
Structural Metadata	Technical information that is needed to ensure that a digital resource functions properly, displays onscreen, and can be navigated by users	<ul><li>Behavior</li></ul>	<ul><li>Behavior</li><li>File sequencing</li><li>Next page</li><li>Previous page</li><li>Resource map</li></ul>	<ul><li>Material eXchange Format (MXF)</li><li>Metadata Encoding & Transmission Standard (METS)</li><li>Open Archives Initiative Object Reuse and Exchange (OAI-ORE)</li><li>Page-turner models</li></ul>
Descriptive Metadata	Describes the identifying characteristics and intellectual contents of information resources for the purposes of discovery, identification, selection, acquisition, context, and understanding	<ul><li>Analytical</li><li>Contextual</li></ul>	<ul><li>Contributors</li><li>Creator or Author</li><li>Dates</li><li>Edition or Version</li><li>Notes</li><li>Provenance</li><li>Series</li><li>Standard numbers</li><li>Style</li><li>Subject</li><li>Table of contents</li><li>Title</li></ul>	<ul><li>*Categories for the Description of Works of Art* (CDWA)</li><li>Dublin Core Metadata Element Set (DCMES)</li><li>Friend of a Friend (FOAF)</li><li>RDA elements</li><li>Schema.org</li><li>VRA Core Categories</li></ul>

- a single web page, which may contain text, images, multimedia files, or any combination of these;
- an individual streaming video clip embedded on that page or one of the other components; or
- the entire website that contains the page with the video clip, as well as any number of other pages that are part of the site.

Different communities may choose to describe their resources at different levels of granularity. Some might describe resources using one or more of these levels, depending on the type of resource, the community's approach to organizing information, and the needs of their users. For example, libraries typically describe printed books on the individual resource level (e.g., one book equals one metadata record). Archival materials, however, are traditionally described with less granularity, usually at the collection level. Digital libraries may combine or alternate between collection-level and item-level descriptions, based on the nature of a particular collection, the size of the collection, and the users of the collection. In other words, a digital library might describe individual objects (e.g., a digitized map), individual collections (e.g., a collection of 2,000 digitized documents), or both.

Metadata may be found in various places and in different forms. For example, the metadata for an online resource may be part of the document itself (entered in the header as meta tags) or it may be found as embedded annotations within the HTML code (using microdata to mark up web documents). Metadata found in these forms may be viewed by looking at the encoding for the document, and it may or may not be indexed by an internet search engine. Metadata may also be found "wrapped" into a digital object's complex packaging. The descriptive metadata may be one small section of a multi-file digital object (such as a digitized music album comprising 10 tracks, cover photos, liner notes, searchable lyrics, etc.), and may only be searched and viewed within the content management system used to house the digital repository. Metadata may also be viewed as a surrogate record that is separate from the information resource it describes. These records may be held in various retrieval tools to allow users to browse or search for the records, instead of trying to navigate through each individual resource in the collection. For online materials, there may or may not be direct links to the individual resources from their surrogate records, depending on the nature of the resource, the institution, and the sophistication of the retrieval tool. Because metadata is usually created in the electronic environment (e.g., in an online catalog, in an XML database, or on the web), the term is rarely applied to records found in paper tools.

6.3 Metadata Schemas

For it to be used to its full potential, metadata cannot consist of unstructured descriptions of resources; it must be standardized and controlled. Without formal structure or rules, metadata description is no better than keyword access. Two basic units of metadata are the element and the schema. Metadata **elements** are individual fields that hold discrete pieces of a resource description. Typical metadata elements include *title, creator, identifier, creation date, subject,* and the like. Metadata **schemas** are sets of elements designed to meet the needs of individual communities. Although some schemas are general in nature, most are created for specific types of information resources or for specific purposes. Individual schemas have been designed to manage government, geospatial, visual, educational, and other types of resources. Consequently, it is not surprising that these schemas vary greatly. They differ in the number of data elements, in the use of mandatory and repeatable elements, in encoding requirements, and in the use of value standards, among other things. Much to the chagrin of students and information professionals alike, it is simply not possible to create a perfect, one-size-fits-all metadata schema that will satisfy the needs of different communities. Diversity in metadata is both desirable and unavoidable. The goal is to find ways for these communities to share their own metadata in useful and meaningful ways.

According to Sherry Vellucci, there are three characteristics found in all metadata schemas. They are semantics, syntax, and structure.[6] *Semantics* refers to meaning, specifically the meaning of the various metadata elements. Semantics help metadata creators understand, for example, what the element *title* means in each schema that contains it. *Syntax* refers to the encoding of the metadata. Encoding standards, as discussed in Chapter 5, include the MARC bibliographic format and a variety of specific XML schemas. Stuart Weibel writes that syntax allows us to "take a set of metadata assertions and pack them so that one machine can send them to another, where they can be unpacked and parsed. ... Syntax is arranging the bits reliably so they travel comfortably between computers."[7] *Structure* refers to the data model used to shape the way that metadata statements are expressed.[‡] Weibel states, "structure is the specification of the details necessary to layout [sic] and declare metadata assertions so they can be embedded unambiguously in a syntax. A data model is the specification of this structure."[8] For example, do metadata statements conform to the Resource Description Framework (RDF)?[§]

The semantics of a metadata schema do not dictate the content placed into the elements. This is the province of content standards and controlled vocabularies. *Content standards* specify how content should be recorded. For example, a content standard might state that all dates are to be recorded using the YYYY-MM-DD format or require personal names to be entered with family name first, followed by a comma, and then by the remainder of the name. Controlled vocabularies (or data value standards) also may be used to standardize the contents of elements such as *subject* or *resource type*. *Controlled vocabularies* are lists of words in which certain terms are chosen as preferred, and their synonyms function as pointers to the preferred terms, thereby limiting the range of values that can be entered into a particular metadata element. If tools such as content standards and data value standards did not exist, information retrieval would be less consistent and less effective.

6.4 Metadata Characteristics

For metadata to be as useful as possible in meeting the diverse needs of information users, some specific metadata characteristics require attention: interoperability, flexibility, and extensibility.[9] *Interoperability* refers to the ability of various systems to interact with each other no matter the hardware or software being used. Achieving interoperability helps to minimize the loss of information due to technological differences. Interoperability can be divided into semantic, syntactic, and structural interoperability.

[‡]Metadata structure should not be confused with structural metadata. *Structural metadata* refers to the internal digital file organization of a resource, while *metadata structure* refers to the composition and expression of metadata statements.

[§]RDF is discussed further as a data model in Chapter 7.

- **Semantic interoperability**: This refers to ways in which diverse metadata schemas express meaning in their elements. In other words, does the element *author* in one schema mean exactly or nearly the same thing as *creator* in another? Does *title* refer to the name of a resource or to a position held by a person?
- **Syntactic interoperability**: This refers to the ability to exchange and use metadata from other systems. Syntactic interoperability requires a common encoding format. For example, can a MARC record be used and understood in an XML environment?
- **Structural interoperability**: This refers to how metadata statements are expressed. Are both sets of metadata statements following the same structure (e.g., an entity-relationship model) or are the structures different?

Without interoperability on all three levels, metadata cannot be shared effortlessly, efficiently, or beneficially.

Flexibility refers to the ability of "metadata creators to include as much or as little detail as desired in the metadata record, with or without adherence to any specific cataloging rules or authoritative lists."[10] Some information professionals seek to create flexible metadata schemas that leave decisions about how much detail to include in the description to the individual institution or community. Flexibility, at least at some level, is seen in most metadata schemas, especially those that contain **optional elements** (i.e., metadata elements included at the discretion of the agency or the individual creating the metadata content).

Extensibility refers to the capacity to stretch or extend a schema; it refers to the ability to use additional metadata elements and qualifiers to meet the specific needs of various communities. Qualifiers may be used to identify an

- *Element refinement*: an additional term used to refine or sharpen the focus of an element (e.g., the element *title* could have a qualifier to specify that the data recorded is a subtitle, alternative title, earlier title, or another variant form of title), or
- *Encoding scheme*: an addition to specify the list of controlled terms or data types that supplied the value entered in a metadata element (e.g., the term entered in the *subject* element is identified as coming from the *Sears List of Subject Headings*). This is commonly used in Dublin Core.

An example of extensibility can be found in the education community. To meet their specific needs, a standard element set was extended by adding *instructional method* and *audience* as elements. There is a note of caution about extensibility, though. As extensibility increases, interoperability can decrease, because as the schema moves further away from its original design (through additional elements or qualifiers), it becomes less understandable to other systems using the base schema. In other words, there is an inverse relationship between extensibility and interoperability. This trade-off must be considered carefully before extensibility is employed.

6.5 Categories of Metadata

As mentioned earlier in this chapter, there are three broad categories of metadata: *descriptive*, *administrative*, and *structural*. For much of its history, discussions of metadata in the library and information science (LIS) professions have primarily focused on descriptive metadata. This is unsurprising given that description is a common activity; catalogers, indexers, archivists, and museum registrars describe resources regularly. Although administrative metadata is not new—recordkeeping has been around for ages—traditionally, it has not received as much attention as descriptive metadata. It is only in the last few decades that structural metadata needs have been recognized, or at least acknowledged, as a metadata issue. Each category of metadata is described below.

6.5.1 Descriptive Metadata

Descriptive metadata contains the most important identifying characteristics of an information resource and the analysis of its contents for the purposes of discovery, identification, selection, acquisition, and exploration. It includes the following kinds of information:

- **Identifying data**: titles, statements of responsibility, dates of publication or distribution, languages, formats, resource types, identifiers
- **Relationship data**: creators, contributors, publishers, sources, related works, other relationships
- **Content data**: subjects, abstracts, coverage, tables of contents, scope and content notes, genre/form, classification notations

This section is intentionally brief, as Chapters 8–13 examine various aspects of descriptive metadata in greater depth.

6.5.2 Administrative Metadata

If an institution creates a digital resource, where is it held? How is it stored? What type of object is it? When does it need to be updated? How are updates accomplished? How did the object come into the collection? Was it born digital? Was it digitized in-house, by a vendor, or by another organization? Who can access it and for what purposes? These questions can be answered with administrative metadata.

Administrative metadata is created for the purposes of management, decision making, and recordkeeping. It provides information about the technical, preservation, and storage requirements of information resources, particularly digital objects. Administrative metadata assists with the monitoring, accessing, reproducing, digitizing, and backing up of digital resources. It includes the following kinds of information:

- **Hardware and software requirements**: creation software, creation hardware, operating system requirements
- **Acquisition information**: dates when the resource was created, modified, and/or acquired; the physical source from which a digital object was derived
- **Ownership, rights, permissions, legal access, and reproduction information**: rights the organization has to the material, who may use the material and for what purposes, what reproductions exist and their current status

File and Information
- Name: 530541_10200170393760766_1093851742_n.jpg
- Kind: JPEG image
- Size: 880 KB (879,746 bytes)
- Created: Nov 03, 2023, 04:11:59 pm
- Modified: Nov 03, 2023, 04:11:59 pm
- Image size: 3072 × 2304
- Image DPI: 300 pixels/inch
- Color model: RGB
- ColorSync profile: sRGB IEC61966-2.1

Exif and Image Description
- Color Space: sRGB
- Components Configuration: 1, 2, 3, 0
- Compressed Bits Per Pixel: 4
- Contrast: Normal
- Custom Rendered: Normal process
- Digital Zoom Ratio: 1
- Exif Version: 2.2
- Exposure Bias Value: 0
- Exposure Mode: Auto exposure
- Exposure Program: Normal program
- Exposure Time: 1/13
- File Source: DSC
- Flash: Off, did not fire
- FlashPix Version: 1.0
- FNumber: 3.3
- Focal Length: 6.3
- Focal Length In 35mm Film: 38
- Gain Control: Low gain up
- ISO Speed Ratings: 200
- Light Source: unknown
- Max Aperture Value: 3.4
- Metering Mode: Pattern
- Pixel X Dimension: 3,072
- Pixel Y Dimension: 2,304
- Saturation: Normal
- Scene Capture Type: Standard
- Scene Type: A directly photographed image
- Sharpness: Normal
- Subject Distance Range: unknown
- White Balance: Auto white balance
- Make: NIKON
- Model: COOLPIX S50
- Orientation: 1 (Normal)
- Software: Adobe Photoshop CS2 Macintosh

Figure 6.1 An Example of Automatically Generated Technical Metadata for a Digital Photograph.

- **Use information**: how the materials may be used, when, in what form, and by whom; use and user tracking; circulation statistics; content re-use; exhibition records
- **File characteristics**: file size, bit-length, format, presentation rules, sequencing information, running time
- **Version control**: existing versions and the status of the resource being described; alternate digital formats, such as HTML or PDF for text, and GIF or JPG for images
- **Digitization information**: compression ratios, scaling ratios, date of image capture, resolution
- **Authentication and security data**: inhibitor, encryption, and password information
- **Preservation information**: integrity information, physical condition, preservation actions, refreshing data, migrating data, conservation actions for physical artifacts

Some administrative metadata elements, particularly technical metadata such as file sizes and compression rates, may be generated automatically when the object is created or digitized. A familiar example is the Exchangeable Image File Format (Exif) metadata automatically created by a digital camera when a photograph is taken (see Figure 6.1). Other administrative metadata elements, however, may need to be recorded manually.

Unlike most descriptive metadata, administrative metadata is not standardized. There is no single administrative metadata schema that has been adopted widely among institutions. The metadata captured for management purposes tends to be repository-specific and stored in a variety of forms, in a variety of places (e.g., administrative metadata may or may not be incorporated into a record primarily comprising descriptive metadata). Though there is no ubiquitous general administrative metadata schema, some separate schemas have been created to address specific sub-types of administrative metadata, such as Preservation Metadata: Implementation Strategies (PREMIS)[11] and NISO Metadata for Images in XML Schema (MIX)[12] for technical metadata.

Administrative metadata has several sub-types. These include technical metadata, preservation metadata, rights and access metadata, and meta-metadata. Each is discussed below.

6.5.2.1 Technical Metadata

If an information institution receives a digital resource, would they know what it is? Where it comes from? Would they understand what it can do? Could they interact with it or make it work? Without technical metadata, they might not be able to make use of the object. ***Technical metadata*** describes the characteristics, origins, and lifecycles of digital documents, and is key to the preservation of the resource for future use. According to PREMIS, "Technical metadata describes the physical rather than intellectual characteristics of digital objects."[13] Basic technical information is needed to understand the nature of the resource, the software and hardware environments in which it was created, and what is needed to make the resource accessible to users.

Technical metadata is format specific, thus different schemas are used for different resource types. For example, a streaming video requires different technical metadata than a digital image because they do different things and have distinct characteristics. As mentioned above, a typical example of technical metadata is Exif metadata, which is automatically attached to a digital photograph when it is taken (see Figure 6.1).

6.5.2.2 Preservation Metadata

Technology changes rapidly. Data files from years ago—WordStar documents and VisiCalc spreadsheets—are now no longer functional. Data has been lost because there were no plans to keep the data usable and there was no real understanding of how quickly technology would change. With this in mind, we must consider how much we are doing to preserve the information we create today. Will the Google documents and Excel spreadsheets that we rely upon today be usable in 500 years? What about fifty years? Or ten years, even? To save this information from oblivion, we must consider several questions. Should we preserve the look and feel of the software, or are we concerned with content only? One hundred years from now, will users still know what a PDF or a TIFF is? Will they be decipherable? When we preserve an information resource, how do we determine which version of that resource needs to be preserved? These questions are preservation metadata concerns.

Preservation metadata is the information needed to ensure the long-term storage and usability of digital content. It may include information about reformatting, migration, emulation, conservation, file integrity, and provenance. In 2015 the third version of the *PREMIS Data Dictionary for Preservation Metadata* was published; it is the standard for preservation metadata used in the United States. It contains a data model identifying four entities important to digital preservation activities.

- **Object**: a discrete unit of information subject to digital preservation; it has four subcategories:
  - **Intellectual entity**: a distinct intellectual or artistic creation
  - **Representation**: the set of files needed for a complete rendition of the intellectual entity
  - **File**: a named and ordered sequence of bytes that is known to an operating system
  - **Bitstream**: contiguous or non-contiguous data within a file that has meaningful common properties for preservation purposes
- **Event**: an action that involves or affects at least one Object or Agent associated with or known by the preservation repository
- **Agent**: a person, organization, or software program/system associated with Events in the life of an Object or with Rights attached to an Object
- **Rights statement**: an assertion of one or more Rights or permissions pertaining to an Object and/or Agent

Each entity has an extensive list of properties and relationships.[14]

6.5.2.3 Rights and Access Metadata

Rights and access metadata is information about who has access to information resources, who may use them, and for what purposes. It deals with issues of creators' intellectual property rights and the legal agreements that govern user access. It addresses questions such as: Who owns or manages the rights to the material? Are there different categories of information objects in the collection? Are there different categories of users who can access different combinations of those objects? Who can make copies of the resource? May the resource be leased and under what conditions?

In rights and access metadata, information about parties, contents, and transactions can be found. Some typical rights metadata elements include the following:

- Access categories
- Identifiers
- Names of creators
- Names of rights holders
- Dates of creation
- Copyright status

- Terms and conditions
- Access restrictions
- Periods of availability
- Usage information
- Payment options

An example of a rights metadata schema is the Open Digital Rights Language (ODRL) information model.

> The primary aim of the ODRL Information Model is to provide a standard description model and format to express permission, prohibition, and obligation statements to be associated to content in general. These statements are employed to describe the terms of use and reuse of resources. The model should cover as many permission, prohibition, and obligation use cases as possible, while keeping the policy modelling easy even when dealing with complex cases.[15]

The model's top-level classes include Policy, Asset, Party, Action, Rule, and Constraint.

6.5.2.4 Meta-Metadata

Not only can metadata track administrative data about a resource, but it can also track administrative information about its metadata. So, if metadata is "data about data," then data about metadata can be (and has been) called *meta-metadata*, although many just refer to it as administrative metadata. Meta-metadata is important for ensuring the authenticity of the metadata and tracking internal processes. Although meta-metadata may reside within some types of descriptive records (e.g., record creation and modification dates in a MARC record), other meta-metadata must be tracked in other ways. As is the case with general administrative metadata, few schemas for meta-metadata exist, but in 2003 the Dublin Core Metadata Initiative's (DCMI) Administrative Metadata Working Group approved the "AC-Administrative Components,"[16] a metadata element set to describe and manage metadata. This schema, created by Hytte Hansen and Leif Andresen, is loosely based on an administrative metadata element set proposed four years earlier. AC focuses on elements that describe attributes of the metadata record, changes and updates, and information for the interchange of records. Its elements include the following:

- Handling
- Action
- Database

- Contact
- Affiliation
- Transmitter

At this writing, however, there is no visible evidence that the schema has been widely implemented.

6.5.3 Structural Metadata

If an information institution received a digital object, one that it had no part in creating, could the object be opened? If the resource were a complex, multi-file object, would the pieces fit together? Would users be able to interact with the resource? Without structural metadata, probably not.

Structural metadata refers to the makeup or internal arrangement of a digital object, dataset, or other information resource being described. It is the data needed to ensure that a digital resource functions properly, can be used by patrons, and can be navigated easily. It refers to how individual related files are bound together to create a working digital object, how the object can be displayed on a variety of systems, and how it can be stored and disseminated. Structural metadata addresses what the resource is, what it does, and how it works. It captures the following kinds of information:

- Document types and their structures
- File types
- Object behaviors or functionality
- Associated search protocols
- Hierarchical relationships
- Sequencing and grouping of files
- Parent objects
- Paging information
- Associated files

Structural metadata can be included in the headers or bodies of some types of electronic documents, but in most metadata schemas, structural elements are not well represented. For most schemas focusing on descriptive metadata, it is simply unnecessary or inappropriate for the type of resource being represented. For example, with a single digital image, extensive structural metadata is not needed; however, if that individual image is part of a larger, more complex multimedia object that must operate as a single digital resource, then structural metadata becomes necessary. Sometimes structural metadata is referred to as *display metadata*, and sometimes it is mistaken for technical metadata. Although some metadata elements may overlap, technical metadata is not the same as structural metadata. The biggest difference between the two is that structural metadata is primarily machine readable and machine processable, while technical metadata is for humans to read and understand.

The use of structural metadata is not new, but the terminology used to describe it was not always referred to as metadata. An early, successful implementation of structural metadata is the page-turner model. A page-turner is used for materials with a defined internal structure and content that is meant to be viewed in a prescribed sequence (e.g., an e-book). It provides structure for the contents to be displayed and for the user to navigate through the information resource as one normally pages through a book. The page-turner may allow the user to navigate through the resource on more than one level, for example at the section level, the chapter level, and at the page level. The page-turner uses structural metadata to bind together individual images of pages to form a complete object (again, this may be on the level of an e-book, a volume of a set, or a chapter). It may also use structural metadata to associate a text file with each image of individual pages, so that the intellectual contents of the page image are searchable. Structural metadata can also associate these images with thumbnail images of the pages, images of greater or lesser resolution, HTML or XML-formatted pages associated with the web interface (though this may be done on-the-fly), a separate image file (or files) for an illustration on the page, or some other file or link. Some other early examples of structural metadata schemas included the Electronic Binding DTD (Ebind)[17] and the Making of America II project (MOA2),[18] both of which have since been replaced by METS.

6.5.3.1 METS (Metadata Encoding & Transmission Standard)

Structural metadata is at the heart of the ***Metadata Encoding & Transmission Standard*** (METS), developed as an initiative of the Digital Library Federation and maintained by the Library of Congress.[19] METS is an XML schema for encoding structurally complex digital objects into a single document that includes descriptive, administrative, and structural metadata. It provides metadata aimed at managing, preserving, displaying, and exchanging digital objects in a digital library environment. Although descriptive and administrative metadata are included in METS documents, the primary focus of the schema is on the structure of digital objects. It is extensible and modular in its approach.

METS Version 1 contains seven sections, of which, only the structural map is required.

- METS header
- Descriptive metadata
- Administrative metadata
- File section
- Structural map
- Structural links
- Behavior metadata

The METS header contains meta-metadata such as the creator and the creation date of the METS document. For the descriptive and administrative metadata sections, METS does not define the elements to be included. For the descriptive metadata section, it allows the creators to choose from a few extension schemas:

- **MARC Bibliographic Format**: standard bibliographic metadata found in library catalogs
- **MODS (Metadata Object Description Schema)**: an XML-encoded adaptation of MARC
- **EAD**: an encoded record format for archival finding aids
- **Dublin Core (DC)**: a general descriptive metadata schema primarily used with online resources
- **VRA (Visual Resource Association) Core**: a specialized metadata schema used to describe art and images
- **TEI (Text Encoding Initiative) Header**: metadata used to describe textual scholarly and literary works
- **Data Documentation Initiative (DDI)**: an international schema used to describe statistical and social science data

The administrative metadata section can be divided into four subgroupings: technical, intellectual property rights, source, and digital provenance metadata. For these areas, PREMIS, AudioMD Schema, VideoMD Schema, and MIX have been endorsed as extension schemas that may be used to complete the section. Both administrative and descriptive metadata can be held internally or externally. In other words, the metadata can be included inside a METS document or the METS object can point to a separate metadata record stored externally. Both approaches can be used within the same METS document.

The next component, the file section, is an inventory of all the files used to create the digital object. Files may be divided into hierarchically subordinate groups. For example, in a digital object that consists of images accompanied by text, there might be file groups for the thumbnail images, for the primary images, for TEI encoded text, and for PDF versions. The structural map specifies the ways in which all the files fit together to create the digital object. The map is hierarchically structured and allows the user to navigate from one part of the digital object to another (e.g., from track one to track two to track three on a digitized sound recording). The structural links section keeps a record of the hyperlinks and lateral relationships among individual files in the structural map. The behavior section describes how the object is to function or perform. Examples of METS documents can be seen at the Library of Congress's METS website.[20]

In March 2025, METS 2, a major revision of the standard, was released. The revision, which is not backward compatible with METS 1, is intended to make the standard easier to adopt and use. Major changes include: (1) the removal of the structural links and behavior sections entirely; (2) the integration of descriptive and administrative metadata into a single metadata section; and (3) the addition of a new structure section that includes one or more iterations of the structural map. Other more technical changes have been incorporated as well.[21] Both versions of METS will be supported for the foreseeable future.

6.6 Metadata Management Tools

As metadata applications have become more common and more schemas flourish, tools and systems have been developed to help deal with this proliferation. Three of these tools are application profiles, metadata registries, and crosswalks.

6.6.1 Application Profiles

As stated earlier, there is no one-size-fits-all metadata schema. Different schemas have been developed for different purposes, different communities, and different types of resources. All these schemas have strengths and weaknesses. When looking for a metadata schema to meet the needs of a particular project, it is sometimes discovered that no single schema satisfies all the metadata requirements of that project, but that parts of a few existing schemas would work well if they could be combined in a new way. A mechanism to allow metadata creators to use various elements from different schemas is the application profile.

An ***application profile*** is a formally developed specification that limits and clarifies the use of the components of one or more schemas for a particular metadata project. "Whether informal guidelines or formal profiles, additional rulesets are generally needed to supplement metadata schemas as published."[22] Application profiles, therefore, are a form of documentation that describes a project's recommended best practices for metadata creation. They contain policies, guidelines, and metadata elements drawn from one or more namespaces. A ***namespace*** is a formal collection of element types and attribute names; it is the authoritative place for information about the metadata schema that is maintained there. The namespace allows metadata elements to be unambiguously identified and used across communities, promoting semantic interoperability.

The elements selected for an application profile may be a small subset of the elements from a single schema, or they may be elements drawn from two or more schemas combined. An application profile is a formal way to declare which elements from which namespaces are used in a particular application or project or by a particular community. An example is the application profile proposed by the Dublin Core Libraries Working Group (DC-Lib) for describing library materials. It adds domain-specific elements (*date captured, edition,* and *location*) from the MODS metadata schema to the basic DC terms and elements.[23]

Application profiles, unlike metadata schemas, do not create or introduce new metadata elements; they simply mix and match existing elements from various schemas if one schema is not sufficient. Application profiles may also specify what values are permitted by selecting data value standards to be used in certain elements in the record. This is done to instill consistency in certain fields so that similar resources can be retrieved together. Application profiles may also refine the definitions of elements by using qualifiers to make them more specific. For example, an application profile may specify that the element *edition* from MODS will be available for use, that a particular list of values should be used for the DC *type* element, and that the DC *date* element may be made more specific with the following element refinements: *available, captured, created, issued, modified,* and *valid.*

6.6.2 Metadata Registries

Another tool helpful to the metadata creator is the ***metadata registry*** (MDR). An MDR is a database used to organize, store, manage, and share metadata schemas. It provides information about schemas and their elements, controlled vocabularies, application profiles, definitions, relationships, labels, and encoding schemes using a standard structure as outlined in ISO/IEC 11179, "Information Technology–Metadata Registries (MDR)."[24]

MDRs promote standardization, reuse, and interoperability among metadata schemas. They are used to exchange information, clarify meaning and usage, map elements across schemas, and prevent duplication of effort. Marcia Zeng and Jian Qin playfully refer to them as "shopping centers" to find existing metadata elements and application profiles so as not to reinvent the wheel.[25] Zeng and Qin identify several types of MDRs: cross-domain and cross-schema registries, organization-centered registries, domain-specific registries, and schema-specific registries.[26] It is hoped that metadata registries may be a source of machine-understandable information about schemas to support online agents and activities. A widely known example of an MDR is the Open Metadata Registry.[27]

6.6.3 Crosswalks

Crosswalks, too, are tools used to achieve interoperability, specifically semantic interoperability. Without a one-size-fits-all schema, crosswalks are needed so that users and creators understand equivalence relationships among metadata elements in different communities. A crosswalk could show, for example, that the 100 field in a MARC record for the primary (or first named) creator is roughly equivalent to the *Creator* field in a Dublin Core record. According to Margaret St. Pierre and William LaPlante, "A crosswalk is a specification for mapping one metadata standard to another. Crosswalks provide the ability to make the contents of elements defined in one metadata standard available to communities using related metadata standards."[28] They go on to observe that creation and maintenance of a crosswalk is difficult and susceptible to error. One needs expertise in each metadata schema included in the crosswalk. But because each standard is developed by experts in a particular field with inherent specialized terminology, persons with expertise in several standards are rare.

A key difficulty in creating and maintaining crosswalks is the element-mapping process. The mapping might not be too difficult if the schemas are relatively simple, are for the same types of materials, or have many overlapping concepts. It is far more complex, however, when the mapping is cross-domain, between schemas of various levels of granularity, or between schemas with great semantic differences. Generally, the more metadata schemas that are included in the crosswalk, the more difficult it is to do the mapping.

It is important to remember that the conversion process from one schema to another is not always precise. Few metadata crosswalks provide round-trip conversion with no loss of data. Some data can be lost in one direction or the other (or both). However, until technology that allows machines to understand and link the meanings of various metadata elements is developed further, crosswalks are still useful tools for semantic interoperability.

The following is a small portion of a crosswalk, which can be found in full on the LC website.[29] In each row, equivalent elements are provided. These are suggestions as to which MODS element may be used when converting from a Dublin Core record to MODS.

Dublin Core	MODS
Description	<note> <tableOfContents>
Date	<dateIssued> <dateCreated> <dateCaptured> <dateOther>
Rights	<accessCondition>

One can see that in some cases one element of a schema is equivalent to more than one element in another. For others, though, there may be a one-to-one correlation, or there may be no correlation.

6.6.4 Other Tools

Other tools currently in use include *harvesting* technologies, which use automated agents to collect metadata on the web at a minimal level of complexity. The harvested metadata is stored and retrieved as needed. The most widely known harvesting project is the Open Archives Initiative Protocol for Metadata Harvesting (OAI–PMH) in which data providers expose their metadata primarily in the form of Dublin Core–based XML documents for collection by harvesters.[30] This metadata, once collected, can then be added to large, searchable metadata indexes.

In addition, metadata creation tools, software, and templates (i.e., forms with blank fields that serve as guides for different metadata schemas) are among the other instruments available to improve productivity and consistency in metadata creation.

6.7 Conclusion

This chapter has provided an elementary introduction to metadata. Over the years some information professionals have debated whether metadata was a new concept in the online age or whether it was simply a recasting of activities performed in libraries for centuries. Although some see metadata creation as little more than the activities of traditional library cataloging applied to new formats, there are additional considerations. The complexity, quantity, and variety of metadata required to organize digital information is often greater than that needed for traditional resources, and different approaches are employed.

Parallels between the two processes certainly exist. The objectives of descriptive metadata and cataloging are alike—to allow users to navigate information systems to find, identify, select, obtain, and explore the information they need. These objectives are met by recording the important attributes of resources and their relationships to other entities (persons, corporate bodies, other resources). In that sense, cataloging and metadata creation are essentially the same—but only when focused on descriptive metadata.

Metadata creation has other facets that traditional library cataloging simply does not address. For example, an e-book requires more and different types of metadata than does a physical book sitting on a shelf. The digital object requires extensive structural metadata for it to be displayed and to function properly in an online environment. It will also require administrative metadata (such as technical, preservation, rights, and meta-metadata) as appropriate. This is in addition to the descriptive metadata needed. Compared to the structure of physical resources, the structure of digital objects is much more complex and requires additional documentation, technical infrastructure, and description.

As discussed in this chapter, the various conceptual components comprising metadata are highly intertwined. Consequently, when information professionals use the term *metadata*, they must be careful to clarify what they are referring to. One person's metadata may be another person's element, value, schema, controlled vocabulary, content standard, or encoding format.

Some Important Terms in This Chapter
(Definitions Provided in the Glossary)

Administrative metadata	Extensibility	Optional element
Application profile	Flexibility	Preservation metadata
Content standard	Granularity	Rights and access metadata
Controlled vocabulary	Harvesting	Schema
Crosswalk	Interoperability	Semantics
Descriptive metadata	Metadata	Structural metadata
Element	Metadata registry	Structure
Element refinement	Meta-metadata	Syntax
Encoding scheme (Dublin Core)	Namespace	Technical metadata

Some Important Acronyms in This Chapter

DACS:	*Describing Archives: A Content Standard*
DC:	Dublin Core
DCMI:	Dublin Core Metadata Initiative
DDI:	Data Documentation Initiative
EAD:	Encoded Archival Description
Exif:	Exchangeable Image File Format
HTML:	Hypertext Markup Language
ISBD:	*International Standard Bibliographic Description*
MARC:	Machine-Readable Cataloging
MDR:	Metadata Registry
METS:	Metadata Encoding & Transmission Standard
MIX:	NISO Metadata for Images in XML Schema
MODS:	Metadata Object Description Schema
OAI-PMH:	Open Archives Initiative Protocol for Metadata Harvesting
ODRL:	Open Digital Rights Language
PREMIS:	Preservation Metadata: Implementation Strategies
RDA:	*Resource Description & Access*
RDF:	Resource Description Framework
TEI:	Text Encoding Initiative
VRA:	Visual Resource Association
XML:	Extensible Markup Language

6.8 Discussion Questions and Exercises

- What are the different types of metadata, and what purposes do they serve?
- How does metadata for digital resources differ from metadata for print resources? What commonalities do they share?
- How might ideas about metadata differ between different information communities (e.g., libraries, archives, museums, digital libraries, scientific data repositories, etc.)?

6.9 Suggested Readings

Baca, Murtha, ed. *Introduction to Metadata*. 3rd ed. Los Angeles: Getty Research Institute, 2016. http://www.getty.edu/publications/intrometadata/.

Caplan, Priscilla. *Metadata Fundamentals for All Librarians*. Chicago: American Library Association, 2003.

Gartner, Richard. *Metadata in the Digital Library: Building an Integrated Strategy with XML*. London: Facet, 2021.

Haynes, David. *Metadata for Information Management and Retrieval*. 2nd ed. Chicago: ALA, 2018.

Liu, Jia. *Metadata and Its Applications in the Digital Library: Approaches and Practices*. Westport, CT: Libraries Unlimited, 2007.

Miller, Steven J. *Metadata for Digital Collections: A How-To-Do-It Manual*. 2nd ed. Chicago: Neal-Schuman, 2022.

Mitchell, Erik T. *Metadata Standards and Web Services in Libraries, Archives, and Museums*. Santa Barbara, CA: Libraries Unlimited, 2015.

Riley, Jenn. *Understanding Metadata*. Bethesda, MD: National Information Standards Organization, 2017. http://groups.niso.org/higherlogic/ws/public/download/17446/Understanding%20Metadata.pdf.

Zeng, Marcia Lei, and Jian Qin. *Metadata*. 3rd ed. Chicago: ALA Neal-Schuman, 2022.

6.10 Notes

All URLs accessed April 2025.

1. "Metadata," *FOLDOC: Free On-line Dictionary of Computing*, edited by Denis Howe, http://foldoc.org/metadata.
2. Anne J. Gilliland, "Setting the Stage," *Introduction to Metadata*, 3rd ed., edited by Murtha Baca (Los Angeles: Getty Research Institute, 2016), http://www.getty.edu/publications/intrometadata/setting-the-stage/.
3. U.S. National Archives and Records Administration (NARA), *Technical Guidelines for Digitizing Archival Materials for Electronic Access: Creation of Production Master Files–Raster Images*, June 2004, http://www.archives.gov/preservation/technical/guidelines.pdf.
4. Katherine M. Wisser, "Introduction to the Special Issue: Contextual Metadata," *Journal of Library Metadata* 11, no. 3-4 (2011): 101–3; Joan E. Beaudoin, "A Framework for Contextual Metadata Used in the Digital Preservation of Cultural Objects," *D-Lib Magazine* 18, no. 11-12 (2012), https://www.dlib.org/dlib/november12/beaudoin/11beaudoin2.html.
5. Lynne C. Howarth, "Metadata and Bibliographic Control: Soul-Mates or Two Solitudes?" *Cataloging & Classification Quarterly* 40, no. 3-4 (2005): 37–56.
6. Sherry L. Vellucci, "Metadata and Authority Control," *Library Resources & Technical Services* 44, no. 1 (2000): 33–43.

7. Stuart Weibel, "Metadata: Semantics; Structure; Syntax," *Weibel Lines: Ruminations on Libraries and Internet Standards*, https://web.archive.org/web/20190923040500/http://weibel-lines.typepad.com/weibelines/2008/02/metadata-semant.html.
8. Weibel.
9. Vellucci, 36–7.
10. Vellucci, 36.
11. "PREMIS: Preservation Metadata Maintenance Activity," Library of Congress, https://www.loc.gov/standards/premis/.
12. "MIX: NISO Metadata for Images in XML Schema: Technical Metadata for Digital Still Images Standard," Library of Congress, http://www.loc.gov/standards/mix/.
13. *PREMIS Data Dictionary for Preservation Metadata*, Version 3.0, Library of Congress, 32, http://www.loc.gov/standards/premis/v3/premis-3-0-final.pdf.
14. *PREMIS*, 6–7.
15. "ODRL Information Model 2.2," W3C, https://www.w3.org/TR/odrl-model/.
16. Jytte Hansen and Leif Andresen, "AC-Administrative Components: Dublin Core DCMI Administrative Metadata," Dublin Core Metadata Initiative, October 28, 2003, http://dublincore.org/groups/admin/.
17. Although the Ebind site is down, a mirror site is still available. "Digital Page Imaging and SGML: An Introduction to the Electronic Binding DTD (Ebind)," Berkeley Digital Library SunSITE, https://xml.coverpages.org/ebind.html.
18. Although the old MOA2 site is down, it is discussed at "Technology Reports: The Making of America II Project," *Cover Pages*, January 7, 2002, http://xml.coverpages.org/moa2.html; "The Making of America, Part 2," Digital Library Federation, 2004, https://old.diglib.org/standards/dlfmoaii.htm.
19. "METS: Metadata Encoding & Transmission Standard," Library of Congress, http://www.loc.gov/standards/mets/.
20. "METS Example Documents," Library of Congress, http://www.loc.gov/standards/mets/mets-examples.html.
21. "Metadata Encoding and Transmission Schema (METS) Version 2." Library of Congress, https://mets.github.io/METS2_whitepaper.html.
22. Priscilla Caplan, Metadata Fundamentals for All Librarians (Chicago: American Library Association, 2003), 7.
23. DCMI-Libraries Working Group, "Library Application Profile," Dublin Core Metadata Initiative, https://www.dublincore.org/specifications/dublin-core/library-application-profile/.
24. International Organization for Standardization, *Information Technology–Metadata Registries* (MDR), ISO/IEC 11179:2023, https://www.iso.org/standard/78915.html.
25. Marcia Lei Zeng and Jian Qin, *Metadata*, 3rd ed. (Chicago: ALA Neal-Schuman, 2022): 126.
26. Zeng and Qin, 312–16.
27. Open Metadata Registry, http://metadataregistry.org/.
28. Margaret St. Pierre and William P. LaPlante, "We Used to Call it Publishing—Issues in Crosswalking Content Metadata Standards," *Against the Grain* 11, no. 4 (1999): 74. https://docs.lib.purdue.edu/cgi/viewcontent.cgi?article=3551&context=atg.
29. "Dublin Core Metadata Element Set Mapping to MODS Version 3," Library of Congress, Network Development and MARC Standards Office, August 1, 2012, http://www.loc.gov/standards/mods/dcsimple-mods.html.
30. "Open Archives Initiative Protocol for Metadata Harvesting," Open Archives Initiative, http://www.openarchives.org/pmh/.

Chapter 7

Conceptual Models

Around the time of the new millennium, as more metadata schemas were being developed, there was interest in developing a shared vision of metadata to help unify diverse information communities in their approaches. There were concerns that the various metadata schemas that were being developed would not be interoperable and that some sort of overarching model or set of policies was needed to make resources discoverable on a wider scale. This notion was never fully realized—there is no single metadata schema or policy manual or conceptual model that satisfies the needs of all metadata creators, communities, and stakeholders. As time has passed, thoughts about our approaches to metadata have changed. There is a better understanding now that not every community needs to be grounded in a single conceptual model or schema. Instead, the focus is on how to share our individualized, community-specific metadata efficiently and effectively with little loss of data. There is continuing interest, however, in a shared understanding of the process of resource description within each of the various information communities. To achieve this common vision, individual information communities have designed their own metadata models. For example, there is a model specifically created to address the universe of bibliographic resources, one for cultural heritage resources in museums, and so on. In addition, the work being done to develop the Semantic Web has led to the creation of a data structure model that is key to sharing metadata of all types across communities.

7.1 What is a Model?

So, what exactly is a *model*? The *Free On-line Dictionary of Computing* states that it is "a description of observed or predicted behaviour of some system, simplified by ignoring certain details. Models allow complex systems, both existent and merely specified, to be understood and their behaviour predicted."[1] Merriam-Webster defines it as "a miniature representation of something; a description or analogy used to help visualize something ... that cannot be directly observed."[2] Models may be used for several reasons, including specifying a broad conceptual framework for the entire bibliographic universe or prescribing specific structural requirements for metadata statements.

It has been said, "All models are wrong," but this is often expanded to, "All models are wrong, but some are useful."[3] All models fall short in some way; the complexities of reality are not easily reduced to a simplified representation, but models may still be of use for understanding, predicting, communicating, and so on. With that in mind, the chapter will examine some current and earlier conceptual frameworks/models from the library and information science (LIS) landscape.

7.2 Entity-Relationship Models

Many, but not all, of the models used in the LIS discipline are **entity-relationship models** (E-R models).[4*] In E-R models, there are three classes of concern: *entities*, *relationships*, and *attributes*. Although entities and relationships provide the skeleton of the model, attributes give the description flesh and color. They help fill out the picture. A generic E-R model is presented in Figure 7.1.

Entities are things. They are objects of interest about which information is sought. Entities are capable of being distinctly identified. A person, a creative work, a corporate body, an event, and a concept are all examples of entities. An entity is often a focal point for gathering data.

Relationships are reciprocal associations or connections between entities. These connections are usually expressed in a way that indicates that the relationship flows in each direction between the entities. An entity may have one or more relationships, but only relationships of significance are usually documented. Among many others, relationships include creation relationships, whole-part relationships, appellation relationships, sequential relationships, and so on.

Attributes are characteristics of entities or relationships. Attributes are identifying features that help in understanding the essence of what is being described. Examples of attributes may include nature of content, language, duration, media type, pagination, format, dimensions, profession, address, and so on.

To provide a loose analogy, one might equate the components of E-R models to basic grammar. One could look at entities as nouns, relationships as verbs, and attributes as adjectives and adverbs. This is not an exact correlation, however, because conceptual models may apply the elements differently.

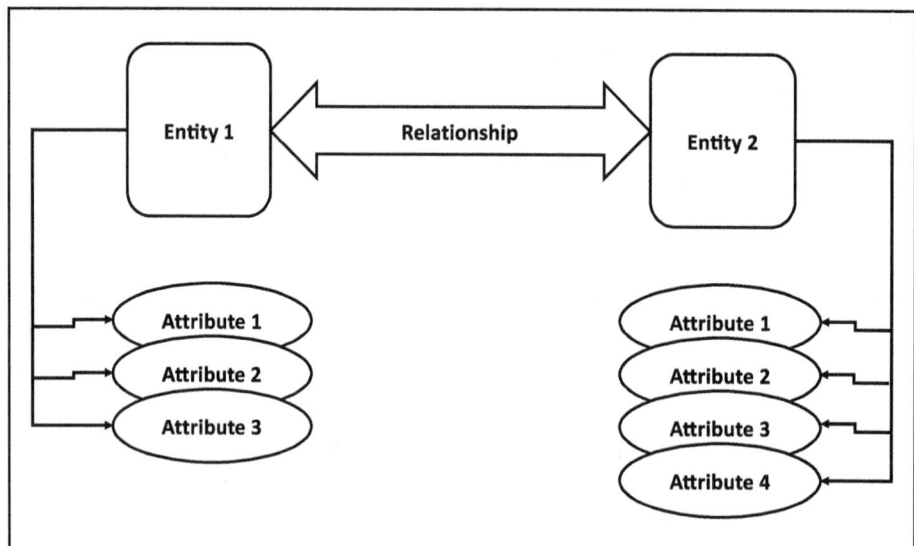

Figure 7.1 A Simple E-R Model.

---

*E-R models were first proposed by Peter Chen in 1976 in the context of database design.

7.3 Specific Conceptual Models

7.3.1 Libraries: IFLA's *Library Reference Model* (LRM)

In 2017, the International Federation of Library Associations and Institutions (IFLA) published its latest conceptual model of the bibliographic universe: *Library Reference Model* (LRM).[5] It is an E-R model used to help LIS professionals understand why patrons seek information, the components that make up information resources, and the relationships among the various components of the model. LRM is a harmonization of three earlier models:

- *Functional Requirements for Bibliographic Records* (FRBR),[6]
- *Functional Requirements for Authority Data* (FRAD),[7] and
- *Functional Requirements for Subject Authority Data* (FRSAD).[8]

In this section, we will cover the history of these four models and the relationships among them.

It is important to point out that LRM is an abstract conceptual model; it is not a system design, a metadata schema, a record structure, a content standard, or an encoding format. "The IFLA LRM model aims to make explicit general principles governing the logical structure of bibliographic information, without making presuppositions about how that data might be stored in any particular system or application."[9] It is a model that enumerates the entities found in the bibliographic universe and gathers them into a tripartite hierarchical structure, which allows for inheritance relationships. LRM identifies a limited number of attributes associated with each entity; its emphasis is on the importance of relationships among the entities. In addition, the conceptual model identifies five **user tasks**—tasks that users perform while using information retrieval tools and interacting with bibliographic data. These tasks inform the entire conceptual model, helping readers to remember end-users—the reason why the bibliographic universe is organized in the first place.

7.3.1.1 History of LRM

In 1998, IFLA published *Functional Requirements for Bibliographic Records*. This report and the conceptual model it details are often referred to as FRBR, which is pronounced "Ferber" by some and as the initials "F.R.B.R." by others. It applied an E-R model to the components of the bibliographic universe. FRBR contained three groups of entities, extensive lists of attributes for each entity, and lists of possible relationships among the entities. The model also mapped each attribute and relationship to four user tasks,[†] which demonstrated the significance of each element in bibliographic descriptions. FRBR helped to answer some important questions about what metadata might be of the most value to library users and how that metadata could be used. Finally, the model provided the international cataloging community with recommendations regarding a minimal set of required elements necessary to include in resource descriptions to support the user tasks.

A little over a decade after FRBR's publication, IFLA produced two related reports: FRAD in 2009 and FRSAD in 2010. FRAD, too, was an attempt to model the bibliographic universe, but instead of focusing on bibliographic records, FRAD was concerned with authority control. It extended the FRBR model by adding new entities, attributes, relationships, and user tasks.

[†]The fifth user task was added later in LRM.

When FRAD was first published, readers noticed there were differences between it and FRBR. This was not surprising, considering the length of time that had passed and the different foci of the reports (i.e., bibliographic data versus authority data), but the discrepancies were of concern to many. The following are some of the changes that were introduced in FRAD:

- New entities were included (e.g., *families*, *names*, *rules*).‡
- Two user tasks were replaced.
- A new type of user (metadata creators) was considered in the model.
- New types of relationships were introduced (e.g., person-to-person relationships, family-to-corporate body relationships).

When FRSAD was published, more incongruities were evident. FRSAD was designed as a high-level conceptual model of the subject relationships existing in the bibliographic universe. It increased the types of users considered, it modified the user tasks, but most significantly, it disregarded both FRBR's and FRAD's approaches to subjects in favor of a much more abstract, high-level conceptual framework. These discrepancies were starting to create tensions in the cataloging community. When the three conceptual models underpinning contemporary cataloging disagree on something as fundamental as subject access, something must be done. The reasons for creating LRM are well summarized in its background statement.

> Inevitably the three FR models, although all created in an entity-relationship modelling framework, adopted different points of view and differing solutions for common issues. Even though all three models are needed in a complete bibliographic system, attempting to adopt the three models in a single system required solving complex issues in an ad hoc manner with little guidance from the models. Even as FRAD and FRSAD were being finalized in 2009 and 2010, it became clear that it would be necessary to combine or consolidate the FR family into a single coherent model to clarify the understanding of the overall model and remove barriers to its adoption.[10]

Work on LRM began in 2010, the same year that FRSAD was published. As was the case with the original FRBR model, LRM is a high-level conceptual model. It is not a content standard; it does not provide specific rules or guidelines. It is not only a consolidation (or reconciliation or harmonization) of the three models, but also a broadening or generalization of the overall conceptual model. It has been influenced by the conceptual reference model developed by the International Committee for Documentation of the International Council of Museums. It has eliminated administrative focus and some of the more specific details found in the three models. After it was formally adopted by IFLA in 2017, LRM replaced the three FR conceptual models. For a more extensive discussion of the earlier models, please see the 11th edition of *Introduction to Cataloging and Classification* by Daniel N. Joudrey, Arlene G. Taylor, and David P. Miller.[11]

7.3.1.2 User Tasks

One of the primary purposes of creating metadata is to help users (e.g., patrons in a library) find the information resources they need. It is therefore advantageous, when creating metadata, to

---

‡Following a typographic convention used in the LRM documentation, the names of entities are italicized throughout these sections.

consider the objectives that users may have when approaching an information retrieval system so that their goals and needs may be met. The following is the list of user tasks identified in LRM (based on those first enumerated in FRBR).[12] Upon examination, it becomes clear that these tasks are also closely related to Cutter's objects of the catalog[13] and the Paris Principles.[14]§

LRM posits that users approach information systems to accomplish the following activities:

- *Find*: "To bring together information about one or more resources of interest by searching on any relevant criteria. The *find* task is about searching."[15] For example, a user might approach a retrieval system to search for articles published in *Cataloging & Classification Quarterly* in 2025, books about Minnie Earl Sears, or DVDs of Sondheim musicals.

- *Identify*: "To clearly understand the nature of the resources found and to distinguish between similar resources. The user's goal in the *identify* task is to confirm that the instance of the entity described corresponds to the instance sought, or to distinguish between two or more instances with similar characteristics."[16] Perhaps a user may wish to find the resources by Michael Gorman on cataloging. The user will depend upon the system to (1) collocate all the resources by each creator named Michael Gorman, and (2) distinguish the Michael Gorman who wrote about cataloging from the Irish fiddler named Michael Gorman, the Navajo artist named Michael Gorman, and the Michael Gorman who wrote about German history.

- *Select*: "To determine the suitability of the resources found, and to be enabled to either accept or reject specific resources. The *select* task is about reacting to possible options."[17] Systems help users to choose resources that are appropriate for their needs. This may involve attributes such as content, format, language, edition, or system requirements. For example, a user in Spain may need a copy of *Hamlet* in Catalan, but not in Spanish, Basque, Galician, Aranese, or the original English.

- *Obtain*: "To access the content of the resource. The user's goal in the *obtain* task is to move from consulting a surrogate to actually interacting with the library resources selected."[18] Users approach systems to gain access to information resources whether that is through call numbers, the names of journals containing articles sought, or direct links to internet resources.

- *Explore*: "To discover resources using the relationships between them and thus place the resources in a context. The *explore* task is the most open-ended of the user tasks. The user may be browsing, relating one resource to another, making unexpected connections, or getting familiar with the resources available for future use."[19] Users want to find resources that are known to them, but also to find unfamiliar materials. Exploration takes advantage of the hyperlinks in systems and browsable displays among other features.

As mentioned above, the earlier models had different configurations of the user tasks. FRBR, for example, contained only the first four listed above. Reflecting its orientation toward authority data, FRAD included another type of user in its model: metadata creators. This addition supplemented

---

§Both of which are discussed in Chapter 2.

the general users of bibliographic data addressed in FRBR. Consequently, the user tasks identified in FRAD were different. The first two tasks (i.e., find and identify) were identical to FRBR and LRM. The latter two, however, were quite different: *contextualize* and *justify*—tasks performed by those creating authority data.[20]

The FRSAD model had yet another variation on its users and user tasks. FRSAD recognized four sets of users: end-users, metadata creators, subject authority data creators (i.e., catalogers and the creators of controlled vocabularies), and reference librarians and other professionals who search on behalf of general end-users. FRSAD included the first three user tasks above, but its fourth task was *explore*.[21] The different versions of the user tasks are presented side-by-side with the current list from LRM in the first column.

LRM 2017	FRBR 1998	FRAD 2009	FRSAD 2010
Find	Find	Find	Find
Identify	Identify	Identify	Identify
Select	Select		Select
Obtain	Obtain		
Explore			Explore
		Contextualize	
		Justify	

To meet the needs of all users, metadata should be created with the users and their tasks in mind. The metadata created should include descriptions of the various entities of interest in the bibliographic universe, their attributes, and the relationships among those entities. Every piece of the description should be useful in meeting one of the user tasks outlined above. If an attribute or relationship does not support a user task, then metadata creators should consider whether that information is necessary.

7.3.1.3 Entities

Entities, as a reminder, are key objects of interest that can be described directly. They are things (agents, resources, subjects) that users search for in retrieval tools. LRM identifies 11 entities.** Each entity is provided in the table below, along with their official definitions.[22]

Entities	Tier	Definition
Res	1	Any entity in the universe of discourse.
Work	2	The intellectual or artistic content of a distinct creation.
Expression	2	A distinct combination of signs conveying intellectual or artistic content.
Manifestation	2	A set of all carriers that are assumed to share the same characteristics as to intellectual or artistic content and aspects of physical form. That set is defined by both the overall content and the production plan for its carrier or carriers.

**This is a reduction in the number of entities found in the three earlier IFLA conceptual models.

Entities	Tier	Definition
Item	2	An object or objects carrying signs intended to convey intellectual or artistic content.
Agent	2	An entity capable of deliberate actions, of being granted rights, and of being held accountable for its actions.
Person	3	An individual human being.
Collective Agent	3	A gathering or organization of persons bearing a particular name and capable of acting as a unit.
Nomen	2	An association between an entity and a designation that refers to it.
Place	2	A given extent of space.
Time-Span	2	A temporal extent having a beginning, an end, and a duration.

The LRM entities are structured into three hierarchical tiers (Figure 7.2). The hierarchical structure allows for ***inheritance relationships*** (i.e., "the transfer of attributes and relationships from the superclass to its subclasses").[23]

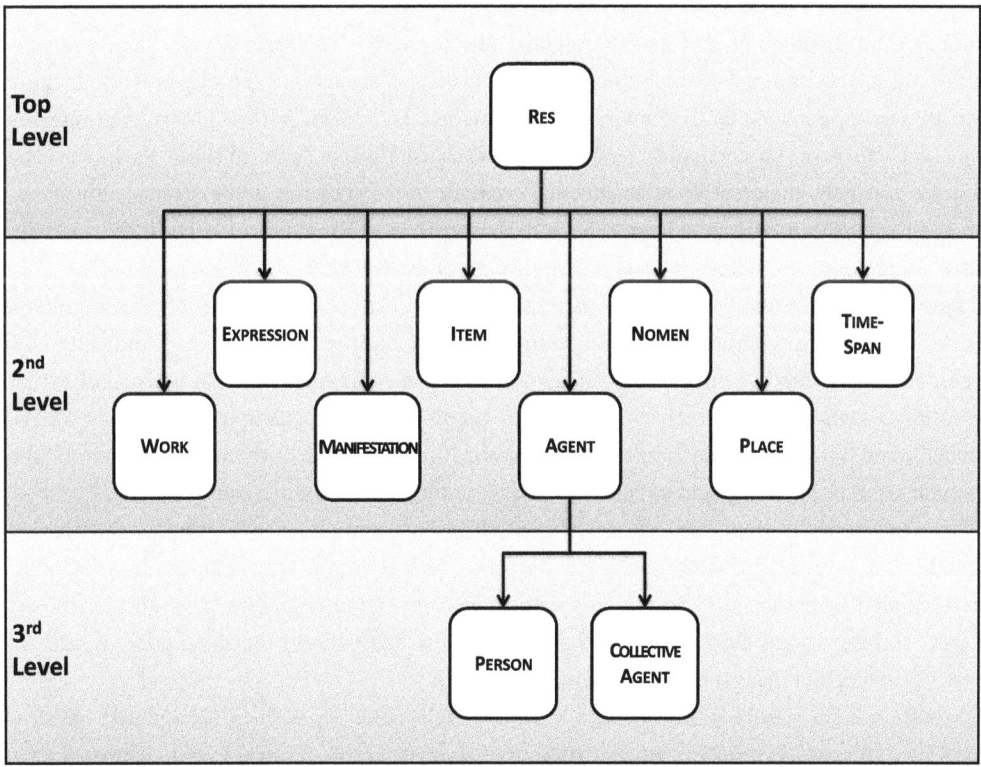

Figure 7.2 Entities in the *IFLA Library Reference Model*.

This forms part of the structure of enhanced entity-relationship models and can be expressed as "is a" (or isA). For example, the entity *person* is a subclass of the entity *agent*, this can be expressed as: *person* isA *agent*. Since all *persons* are *agents*, any relationship or attribute that applies to the entity *agent* also applies to the entity *person*, without needing to be explicitly declared for the entity *person*. The reverse direction does not hold; relationships or attributes explicitly defined for subclass entities do not apply to the whole superclass. Thus, for example, the entity *person* has a relationship to the entity *place* such as "is place of birth of," this relationship does not hold for those *agents* which are *collective agents*.[24]

A notable feature of LRM is that the top level is populated by only a single entity. **Res** is a very generic concept; it means "thing." Any given thing is a *res*, named as such because *res* is the Latin word for *thing* (*matter, issue, object*). Every other entity in the model, therefore, is a form or type of *res*, but with more specificity.

7.3.1.3.1 Resource Entities (WEMI)

The second level of the hierarchy includes what can be referred to as **resource entities**: entities that are components of an information resource (i.e., *work, expression, manifestation*, and *item*). These are also known by the widely adopted acronym WEMI (pronounced "Wemmy").

The entity **work** can be described as the distinct ideas or the artistic or intellectual vision of a creator. It is an abstract concept that represents content; there is no single physical object associated with it. It is recognized through individual *expressions* of the *work*. Examples of *works* include Pablo Picasso's *Guernica*, Dolly Parton's "I Will Always Love You," and William Shakespeare's *Romeo and Juliet*—not a particular version, edition, translation, or form of these works, just the ideas, the concepts, the creative or intellectual content. "A *work* comes into existence simultaneously with the creation of its first *expression*, no *work* can exist without there being (or there having been at some point in the past) at least one *expression* of the *work*."[25]

Expression, the next resource entity, is a realization of a *work* in the form of text, numbers, musical notation, choreographic symbols, sounds, movement, images, and so on. It indicates *how* the content of the *work* is being communicated. It is "the specific intellectual or artistic form that a *work* takes each time it is 'realized.' *Expression* encompasses, for example, the specific words, sentences, and paragraphs that result from the realization of a *work* in the form of a text, or the particular sounds, phrasing, and so on, resulting from the realization of a musical *work*."[26]

There can be more than one *expression* of a work. For example, a *work* might be expressed originally in the form of French text, but it may also have a Somali translation, a translation in American Sign Language, a spoken-word performance, a version expressed through French text but with accompanying illustrations, and so on; all of which contain the same content, artistic vision, or intellectual ideas (i.e., the same *work*).

Expression is also an abstract, intangible content-related entity with no designated physical carrier (i.e., you cannot touch or buy a textual *expression*; only the physical item that contains it). *Expressions* are reflected in translations, updated editions, new or revised versions, and augmented versions of a resource. Minor variations (spelling corrections, punctuation changes) are not considered significant enough to warrant identifying a new *expression* in most cases.

To start interacting with a material form, the previous two resource entities must be embodied in a ***manifestation***, which is a set of physical resources that contain a *work* and its *expression(s)*. For example, when a book is published, we have a set of physical objects (e.g., a print run).†† It is the situation in which the same content is reproduced, even though the format may be different. When a musical *work* is expressed in a studio performance, it can be recorded and then transferred onto compact discs, vinyl, magnetic tape, electronic sound files, and so on; each of these ***carriers*** (i.e., physical or electronic instantiations) represents a different *manifestation*. A *manifestation* comprises a set of individual *items*, resulting from the same production process. In some cases, though, a singleton *manifestation* may exist (e.g., a single sculpture by an artist).

The final resource entity, ***item***, is a single exemplar, instance, or representative unit of a *manifestation*. It is the individual copy of an information resource. An *item* is something that is purchased and put on a shelf (e.g., my copy of this textbook, your boxed set of *The Wire* DVDs). It is the physical or electronic resource that is being organized and integrated into a collection. As a rule, *items* are identical to each other, but occasionally they can differ in interesting ways. For example, there might be a damaged copy, a copy signed by the author, or a copy bound by a library's rebinding department.

7.3.1.3.2 Agent Entities

The second tier of the hierarchy also includes the entity, *agent*, which has two subclasses, *person* and *collective agent* (found in the third level of the hierarchy). Together, these comprise the **agent entities**—a set of entities that have responsibility for the creation, manufacture, distribution, ownership, or modification of resources, among other possible actions. An **agent** is a generic entity "capable of deliberate actions, of being granted rights, and of being held accountable for its actions."[27] As a superclass, the relationships and attributes associated with *agent* are inherited by its two subclasses.

In LRM, ***person*** is defined as a real human being, living or dead. This is a change from the earlier conceptual models that allowed fictitious and legendary persons, real non-human entities (e.g., Koko the gorilla), biblical figures, deities, mythological characters, and spirits to be treated as persons. Under LRM, Kermit the Frog is no longer considered to be a person. Kermit is simply a name used by an actual person with some sort of responsibility for a resource.

Collective agent is a group of two or more persons identifying themselves with a collective name and acting as a unit. *Collective agent* has subsumed two entities from the previous IFLA conceptual models. *Family* and *corporate body* are no longer considered entities, but they may be identified as specific types of a *collective agent*, along with the following bodies usually identified as corporate bodies in contemporary Anglo-American cataloging traditions.

- Corporations and other businesses
- Associations
- Non-profit organizations
- Educational institutions
- Musical and performing groups
- Governments
- Religious bodies
- Meetings, conferences, and congresses

---

††The word *physical* should be interpreted rather loosely; it might consist of electronic signals in a computer.

- Expeditions
- Exhibitions
- Festivals, fairs, and other events
- Art collectives

7.3.1.3.3 Other Entities

The last of the LRM entities include *nomen, place,* and *time-span*. Both *place* and *time-span* are essentially new entities (thanks to a generalization of FRBR's *place* entity). Obviously, **place** is a geographic location or space that is related to an event, a subject, a resource, or an agent. **Time-span** is another self-evident entity; it represents a period of time that can be identified through a beginning and an end. "The resulting duration can be associated with actions or occurrences that happened during that period of time."[28] Typical uses of *time-span* include identifying dates associated with various agents, publication dates, and subject-related dates.

The final entity, **nomen**, is the association between a name, label, or appellation and a *res* (or any of the other entities in LRM). "In a library context, the *nomens* for *persons, collective agents* ... or *places* have been traditionally referred to as names, the *nomens* for *works, expressions,* and *manifestations* as titles, while the *nomens* for *res* used in a subject context are variously referred to as terms, descriptors, subject headings, and classification notation."[29] Every entity in the bibliographic universe is named through at least one *nomen*, and more than one can be associated with any given entity. Horror author Stephen King, for example, is a *person*, and he is known by multiple *nomens* (Stephen King, Richard Bachman, Beryl Evans).

Although the concept of having a name, title, or label is rather straightforward, LRM introduces complicating aspects. Of all the concepts in the model, *nomen* is one that often leads to confusion. Much of this stems from explanations like this:

> The *nomen* entity can be understood as the reification of a relationship between an instance of *res* and a string. The string itself does not constitute an instance of the *nomen* entity but is modelled as the value of the *nomen string* attribute of an instance of the *nomen* entity.[30]

A *nomen* is defined as a separate entity, not as an attribute of a *res*. It is not a name given to a *res*. If it were an attribute of a *res* (or whatever more specific entity is being examined), it would be simpler. As an attribute, though, a name is nothing more than a **literal** (i.e., a literal string of characters that provides information); literals cannot have attributes of their own, only entities and relationships can. To allow for relationships between names and the entities they represent, LRM needed a *nomen* entity: a relationship "between an entity and a designation that refers to it."[31] To be able to describe more fully the designation associated with an entity, additional attributes are needed, such as the *nomen string* used to name, title, or label the entity, *language* of the nomen string, *category, script, context of use,* and so on.

So, a *nomen* is the association between an entity and what it is called, typically the *nomen string*. To go back to the example of Stephen King, we have a *person* (or, more generally, a *res*) with relationships to more than one *nomen*. The situation is illustrated in Figure 7.3.

A *nomen* is a highly abstract concept, but the **nomen string** (an attribute of the *nomen*) is what we use, view, and disambiguate to keep our entities clearly and unambiguously identified.

Conceptual Models

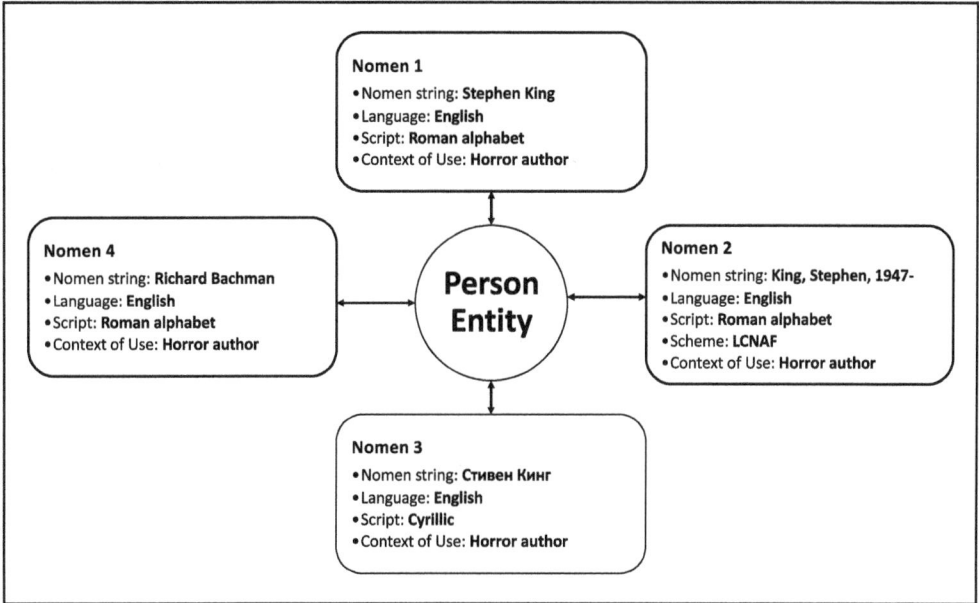

Figure 7.3 Nomens Illustrated.

In current library practice, name authority records are generally created for each bibliographically significant cluster of *nomens* that refer to the same instance of an entity, and record both the *nomen string* representing the preferred form of the access point (a *nomen*) and the *nomen strings* corresponding to any variant access points or identifiers (additional *nomens*). Although an authority record controls *nomens*, as a shortcut information about the instance of an entity referred to by the *nomens* is generally recorded in the same authority record along with information about the *nomens*, blurring the distinction between the entities *res* and *nomen*.[32]

The division between *nomen* and *nomen string* may be theoretically sound, and being able to describe the characteristic of a name can be useful, but to many information professionals, *nomens* and *nomen strings* are more than a little befuddling.

Additional entities appeared in the earlier FR-models, including

- two agent entities (*family, corporate body*) that have been subsumed into *collective agent*;
- four subject entities (*concept, object, event, thema*) that have been replaced by *res* (any thing can be a subject!); and,
- five entities specifically related to the authority control process (*name, identifier, controlled access point, agency,* and *rules*). *Name, identifier,* and *controlled access point* are now incorporated into the *nomen* entity, while *agency* and *rules* have been completely removed.

All were deemed out of scope for the revised vision of LRM.

7.3.1.4 Attributes and Relationships

Changes are also seen in how attributes and relationships in LRM are handled. **Attributes** are characteristics or traits used to describe a particular instance of an entity. They help to describe the entity by providing identifying details about it. **Relationships** are essential components of the bibliographic universe. They connect entities and provide context for them. In the harmonization process that resulted in LRM, there was significant effort made to focus on relationships rather than attributes. This was not unexpected, as one of the goals of revising the conceptual models was to ensure that the bibliographic universe was more in line with developments in web technologies. With LIS professionals prioritizing the development of clearly defined metadata using linked data principles (discussed in more detail below), the move to emphasize relationships over descriptive attributes makes sense.‡‡ Consequently, the number of attributes in LRM has been reduced and characteristics that were considered attributes in previous models are now treated as relationships.

Attributes continue to describe entities, and relationships continue to connect entities, but due to the strict hierarchical structure introduced in LRM, both attributes and relationships are now transferable from a superclass to its subclasses. In many cases, what applies to the larger class above (e.g., *agent*) trickles down to entities below it (e.g., *person* and *collective agent*). So, attributes and relationships defined at higher levels are generally not repeated at lower levels. For example, if an *agent* can have a creation relationship to a *work*, that relationship is also applicable to *person* and *collective agent*. An exception, however, was made for the attribute *category*, which is repeated in many places due to variations in how that attribute is defined under the different entities.

7.3.1.4.1 Attributes

In FRBR and FRAD, each entity had its own extensive set of highly specific attributes. Many of those myriad attributes are not listed in the consolidated LRM where attributes are fewer in number and more generic. Only essential attributes have been retained, and some new attributes have been introduced. The table below provides a small sampling of how some attributes in the earlier models have changed in LRM.[33]

FRBR/FRAD entities	Attributes	LRM implementation
Work	Title of work	Appellation relationship
	Date of work	Time-span associated with work relationship
	Form of work	Category of work attribute
	Subject of work	Subject relationship between work and res
	Context of work	(1) Place or Time-span associated with work relationship, (2) Category of work, or (3) Note attribute
Expression	Summarization of content	(1) Subject relationship, (2) Abridgement relationship, or (3) Note attribute

---

‡‡Or it will make sense when you read more about it. In short, the RDF structural model emphasizes relationships between entities, or in some cases, relationships between an entity and a literal. Preference is given to using unambiguously identifiable entities whenever possible.

FRBR/FRAD entities	Attributes	LRM implementation
Manifestation	Title of manifestation	(1) Merged into sub-type of Manifestation statement attribute or (2) Appellation relationship
	Statement of responsibility	Merged into sub-type of Manifestation statement attribute
	Edition	Merged into sub-type of Manifestation statement attribute
	Place of publication	(1) Manifestation was created by agent and Place associated with agent relationship or (2) Sub-type of Manifestation statement attribute
	Form of carrier	Category of carrier attribute
	Extent of carrier	Extent attribute
	Dimensions of carrier	Merged into Extent attribute
	Physical medium	Merged into Category of carrier attribute
	Typeface	Removed as too specific
Item	Item identifier	Appellation relationship
	Provenance of item	Ownership relationship
Person	Name of person	Appellation relationship
	Dates of person	Time-span associated with person relationship
	Title of person	Membership relationship
	Place of birth	Place associated with person relationship

In the harmonization process, many attributes have been

- removed because they were out of scope or too specific (e.g., *typeface*);
- replaced by a relationship (e.g., *names* and *titles*);
- merged into other similarly focused attributes (*dimensions*); or
- renamed and/or redefined more generically (e.g., *category* is now used extensively throughout the model and subsumed many former attributes such as *form of work*, *form of carrier*, etc.).

LRM includes 37 attributes, which are listed in Table 7.1. The attributes listed in LRM are representative of what may be useful in describing bibliographic resources, but they are not prescribed, and the list is not exhaustive. Differing implementation of cataloging rules may choose to ignore some and add others. "An application can define additional attributes to record additional relevant data or to record data at a greater level of granularity than is illustrated."[34]

Table 7.1 Attributes Specified in LRM

Entity	Attribute	Entity	Attribute
Res	Category	Item	Location
	Note		Use Rights
Work	Category	Agent	Contact Information
	Representative Expression		Field of Activity
Expression	Category		Language
	Extent	Person	Profession/Occupation
	Intended Audience	Nomen	Category
	Use Rights		Nomen String
	Cartographic Scale		Scheme
	Language		Intended Audience
	Key		Context of Use
	Medium of Performance		Reference Source
Manifestation	Category of Carrier		Language
	Extent		Script
	Intended Audience		Script Conversion
	Manifestation Statement	Place	Category
	Access Conditions		Location
	Use Rights	Time-span	Beginning
			Ending

7.3.1.4.2 Relationships

The final major component in an E-R model is relationships. As mentioned, there is a greater emphasis on relationships in LRM than in the original FRBR report (with its greater focus on attributes). There are 36 declared relationships. The top-level, most general relationship is RES *is associated with* RES. "All other relationships declared in the model are specific refinements of this relationship. … Any additional relationships needed by a particular implementation can be defined as refinements of the additional relationships defined in the model, or of the top relationship."[35]

The three integral relationships between the WEMI entities remain intact from FRBR.[§§]

- WORK *is realized through* EXPRESSION
- EXPRESSION *is embodied in* MANIFESTATION
- MANIFESTATION *is exemplified by* ITEM

Some of the inherent relationships found in the original model, however, have been deprecated. LRM identifies some other widely applicable, general relationships among entities.

- WORK *was created by* AGENT
- EXPRESSION *was created by* AGENT

[§§]In this section, I am invoking another typographical convention of LRM. In this section's examples, I present the entities in all capital letters. I am using italics to emphasize the types of relationships.

- MANIFESTATION *was created by* AGENT
- MANIFESTATION *was manufactured by* AGENT
- MANIFESTATION *was distributed by* AGENT
- ITEM *was modified by* AGENT
- ITEM *is owned by* AGENT

For the *res* entity, several relationships have been identified. These are unique to LRM because *res* never existed in any of the earlier models.

- WORK *has as subject* RES
- RES *has appellation* NOMEN
- RES *is associated with* PLACE
- RES *is associated with* TIME-SPAN

The relationships are understood to flow in both directions. Therefore, if an *agent* created a *work*, then we also understand that the *work* was created by the *agent*. All the relationships specified in LRM are found in Table 7.2.

Table 7.2 Relationships Specified in LRM

Focus	Relationships	Focus	Relationships
Res	• RES *is associated with* RES • RES *has association with* PLACE • RES *has association with* TIME-SPAN	Agents	• AGENT *is a member of* COLLECTIVE AGENT • COLLECTIVE AGENT *has part* COLLECTIVE AGENT • COLLECTIVE AGENT *precedes* COLLECTIVE AGENT
High-Level WEMI Relationships	• WORK *is realized through* EXPRESSION • EXPRESSION *is embodied in* MANIFESTATION • MANIFESTATION *is exemplified by* ITEM	Whole-Part Relationships	• WORK *has part* WORK • EXPRESSION *has part* EXPRESSION • EXPRESSION *was aggregated by* EXPRESSION • MANIFESTATION *has part* MANIFESTATION • PLACE *has part* PLACE • TIME-SPAN *has part* TIME-SPAN

WEMI and Agents	• WORK *was created by* AGENT • EXPRESSION *was created by* AGENT • MANIFESTATION *was created by* AGENT • MANIFESTATION *was manufactured by* AGENT • MANIFESTATION *is distributed by* AGENT • ITEM *is owned by* AGENT • ITEM *was modified by* AGENT	**Specific WEMI Relationships**	• WORK *precedes* WORK • WORK *accompanies / complements* WORK • WORK *is inspiration for* WORK • WORK *is a transformation of* WORK • EXPRESSION *is derivation of* EXPRESSION • MANIFESTATION *has reproduction* MANIFESTATION • MANIFESTATION *has alternate* MANIFESTATION • ITEM *has reproduction* MANIFESTATION
Subject and Name Relationships	• WORK *has as subject* RES • RES *has appellation* NOMEN • AGENT *assigned* NOMEN • NOMEN *is equivalent to* NOMEN • NOMEN *has part* NOMEN • NOMEN *is derivation of* NOMEN		

LRM, as mentioned earlier, contains hierarchical/inheritance relationships (e.g., X isA Y) but it also contains multi-step relationships. For example, to relate a person's pseudonym to the title of a work, several relationships must be identified.

1. WORK *was created by* AGENT (PERSON)
2. AGENT (PERSON) *isA* RES
3. NOMEN1 *is appellation* of RES
4. RES *has appellation* NOMEN2

In summary, these four relationships indicate that the creator of a work is a person who is known by more than one name.

In the final chapters of the model, additional components are addressed, including the following:

- E-R diagrams
- Nomens in a library context

- Bibliographic identities
- Representative expression attributes
- Aggregates
- Serials
- Alignment of user task to entities, relationships, and attributes

Although these are important topics, they are more detailed than needed for a simple introduction to the conceptual model. For more detail, please see the LRM documentation.[36]

The family of FR-models, from FRBR to LRM, has had a transformative effect on the information profession's thinking about bibliographic metadata—pushing it toward an entity-relationship model, which naturally points us toward linked data structures. It should be kept in mind that the FR-family of models was designed to reflect the bibliographic universe. Although that universe, in theory, includes all types of resources, it has been observed that FRBR and LRM do not address all types of information resources as well as they do print materials. For example, according to art librarians Murtha Baca and Sherman Clarke, the FRBR model did not apply to many types of resources collected by museums;[37] nor does it easily apply to collections in archives, historical societies, and other similar institutions. That is why other communities have developed their own conceptual models.

7.3.2 Archives: *Records in Contexts* (RiC)

In late 2012, the International Council on Archives (ICA) charged their Expert Group on Archival Description (EGAD) with the development of a conceptual framework for archival description that would merge four existing archival standards:[38]

- *General International Standard for Archival Description*
- *International Standard Archival Authority Records–Corporate Bodies, Persons, and Families*
- *International Standard Description of Functions*
- *International Standard Description of Institutions with Archival Holdings*

The conceptual framework developed, *Records in Contexts* (RiC), reconciles these four standards and re-conceptualizes archival description. It is presented as an E-R model, similar to LRM in the library world. In 2016, EGAD released a draft of RiC for comment. As of 2025, after more than a decade of work, the RiC framework comprises four new standards, not all of which are complete at the time of this writing.

- *Records in Contexts: Foundations of Archival Description* (RiC-FAD), a foundational document enumerating the principles and purposes of archival description.
- *Records in Contexts: Conceptual Model* (RiC-CM), a high-level, E-R model of archival information (e.g., archives, records, creators, users, and activities).
- *Records in Contexts: Ontology* (RiC-O), an implementation of the RiC conceptual model expressed in the W3C's Web Ontology Language (OWL), to provide the archival community with the ability to use linked data techniques with archival description.

- *Records in Contexts: Application Guidelines* (RiC-AG), a practical guide with examples for implementing RiC-CM and RiC-O.

Official versions of the first three components have been released, but the application guidelines are still under development.

The first completed document, RiC-FAD, provides an overview and brief history of archival description. It discusses the need for recordkeeping; the importance of key archival principles, such as provenance, *respect des fonds*, and original order,*** and the purpose of record description, including management, preservation, and use/reuse of records. In other words, RiC-FAD attempts to provide some context for archival description. (Context being a priority for archivists!)

The conceptual model, RiC-CM, "differs from the existing ICA standards [which] ... model a finding aid, whereas RiC-CM models the entities as such, as a basis for describing but without anticipating any particular end product."[39] It is intended to provide a new foundation for the design, creation, and implementation of standardized archival and record management systems. This approach will entail "transitioning from the prevailing approach of records description (the single, stand-alone fonds-based hierarchical description) to a more flexible, open, graph- or network-based approach."[40] In other words, the RiC framework is attempting to revise how archivists think about their records in a more globally connected society.

Table 7.3 Hierarchical Structure of the RiC-CM Entities

Level 1	Level 2	Level 3	Level 4
E01 *Thing*			
	E02 *Record Resource*		
		E03 *Record Set*	
		E04 *Record*	
		E05 *Record Part*	
	E06 *Instantiation*		
	E07 *Agent*		
		E08 *Person*	
		E09 *Group*	
			E10 *Family*
			E11 *Corporate body*
		E12 *Position*	
		E13 *Mechanism*	
	E14 *Event*		
		E15 *Activity*	
	E16 *Rule*		
		E17 *Mandate*	
	E18 *Date*		
	E22 *Place*		

Note: Numbering jumps from E18 to E22 in the current model due to deprecated elements.

***These concepts are discussed in Chapter 1.

7.3.2.1 Entities

The entities in RiC-CM are distributed among four hierarchical levels (see Table 7.3). Like LRM, the first level contains only a single entity: *thing* (*res* in LRM). Every entity in the model is a type or kind of thing, and so is any entity that is *not* specified in RiC-CM (e.g., entities that may be the subject of the records being described). In the levels that follow, there are four entities that are considered core: *record resource*, *instantiation*, *agent*, and *activity*. The following is a list of the RiC entities along with brief definitions based on the model's documentation.[41]

- **Thing**: Any idea, material thing, or event within the realm of human experience.
  - **Record resource**: Information produced or acquired and retained by an agent in the course of life or work activity. *Record resource* is a generalization of the next three entities.
    - **Record set**: One or more records that are grouped together by an agent based on the records sharing one or more attributes or relationships (e.g., an archival collection).
    - **Record**: Discrete information content formed and inscribed, at least once, by any method on any carrier in any persistent, recoverable form by an agent in the course of life or work activity (e.g., a single document).
    - **Record part**: A component of a record with independent information content that contributes to the intellectual completeness of the record (e.g., a part of a record, like an attachment to a saved email).
  - **Instantiation**: The inscription of information made by an agent on a carrier in any persistent, recoverable form as a means of communicating information through time and space. It is like the manifestation entity in LRM. You can have one or more instantiations for any of the three specific types of record resources (e.g., a printed policy document along with a PDF version represent two instantiations of a record).
  - **Agent**: A thing that performs activities in the world. While performing activities, agents may generate or use record resources. *Agent* is a generic entity comprising person, group, position, and mechanism. An agent may have one or more identities.
    - **Person**: An individual human being. A person may have an alternative identity (e.g., a pseudonym).
    - **Group**: Two or more agents that act together as an agent. Large groups may comprise myriad smaller units. Corporate bodies and families are types of groups, though other kinds of groups are possible.
      - **Family**: Two or more persons related by birth, marriage, adoption, civil union, or other conventions that bind them together as a socially recognized familial group.
      - **Corporate body**: An organized group of persons that act together as an agent, and that has a recognized legal or social status. This entity may be a government, legal, military, or religious body; a corporation, business enterprise,

agency, or non-profit organization; a cultural, educational, or some other form of institution; a musical or performing group, etc.
- **Position**: The functional role of a person within a group. It is the intersection between person and group. Examples might include presidents and other world leaders, corporate officials, heads of churches, educational institutions, and so on.
- **Mechanism**: A process or system created by a person or group that performs an activity. Mechanisms may include software agents, robots, and space and underwater probes that generate data.
- **Event**: Something that happens or occurs in time and space. "*Events* may be natural, such as earthquakes, storms, floods, or pandemics; or be caused by an *agent*, such as elections, wars, protests, building a home, monitoring water quality, converting a Word document into a PDF document, or managing *records*. ... Events have temporal and spatial boundaries."[42] A sub-type of event is activity.
  - **Activity**: The doing of something for an agent-designed purpose. "Purpose and process are complementary understandings of *activity*. Together the two perspectives address why the *activity* is performed, the expected ends or outcomes; and how the *activity* fulfils the purpose."[43] Activity in a corporate or government setting may be referred to as a "function."
- **Rule**: Conditions that govern the existence, responsibility, or authority of an agent; or the performance of an activity by an agent; or that contribute to the distinct characteristics of things created or managed by an agent. Rule has one sub-type, mandate.
  - **Mandate**: Delegation of responsibility or authority by an agent to another agent to perform an activity.
- **Date**: Chronological information associated with an entity that contributes to its identification and contextualization.
- **Place**: A bounded, named geographic area or region.

7.3.2.2 Attributes

There are more than three dozen attributes listed in RiC-CM. Among these, there are three common characteristics shared by all entities in the model. These are listed under the entity *thing*, but because every entity is a thing, these attributes can be used to describe all 19 RiC entities. The baseline attributes, with definitions provided by the RiC-CM documentation, are General Description, Identifier, and Name. In other words, every *thing* in the model may be described, have a unique identifier, and be called by an appellation.

The broad *record resource* entity, being a thing, repeats the three common attributes above, but then provides 13 specific attributes for record resource:

- Authenticity Note
- Classification

- Conditions of Access
- Conditions of Use

Conceptual Models

- Content Type
- History
- Integrity Note
- Language
- Legal Status
- Record Resource Extent
- Scope and Content
- State
- Structure

These, in turn, can also be used to describe the entities that are hierarchically subordinate to *record resource*. Because of inheritance relationships, the third-tier entities *record set*, *record*, and *record part* can be described using: (1) the three attributes of *thing*, (2) the 13 attributes of *record resource*, and (3) a few attributes of their own. All three list Documentary Form Type as an attribute, but *record set* has Accrual and Record Set Type as well.

Agent has three attributes that are also applicable to its four sub-types (and their sub-types as well):

1. History: a summary of the development of an entity throughout its existence
2. Language: a spoken or written human language represented in a record resource or used by an agent
3. Legal Status: a status defined by law

Among its sub-types, the entity *group* lists Demographic Group as an attribute. Its sub-types, *family* and *corporate body*, receive one new attribute apiece (Family Type and Corporate Body Type). *Person* lists both Demographic Group and Occupation, *mechanism* adds Technical Characteristics, but *position* can only be described using the attributes inherited from *thing* and *agent*.

The final entities and their attributes are listed in the table below. For more detailed information on the model's attributes, please see the RiC-CM documentation.[44]

Entity	Subordinate Entity	Additional Attributes
Instantiation		Authenticity Note
		Carrier Extent
		Carrier Type
		Conditions of Access
		Conditions of Use
		History
		Instantiation Extent
		Physical Characteristics Note
		Production Technique
		Quality of Representation Note
		Representation Type
		Structure

Entity	Subordinate Entity	Additional Attributes
Event		Event Type
		History
	Activity	Activity Type
Rule		Rule Type
		History
	Mandate	Mandate Type
Date		Date Qualifier
		Date Type
		Expressed Date
		Normalized Date
Place		Coordinates
		History
		Location
		Place Type

7.3.2.3 Relationships

Relationships indicate connections between the model's entities. The most fundamental relationships in RiC are addressed in Figure 7.4. The inherent relationships in RiC-CM start with the idea that every entity is a *thing*, and a thing can be related to any other thing. With that understood,

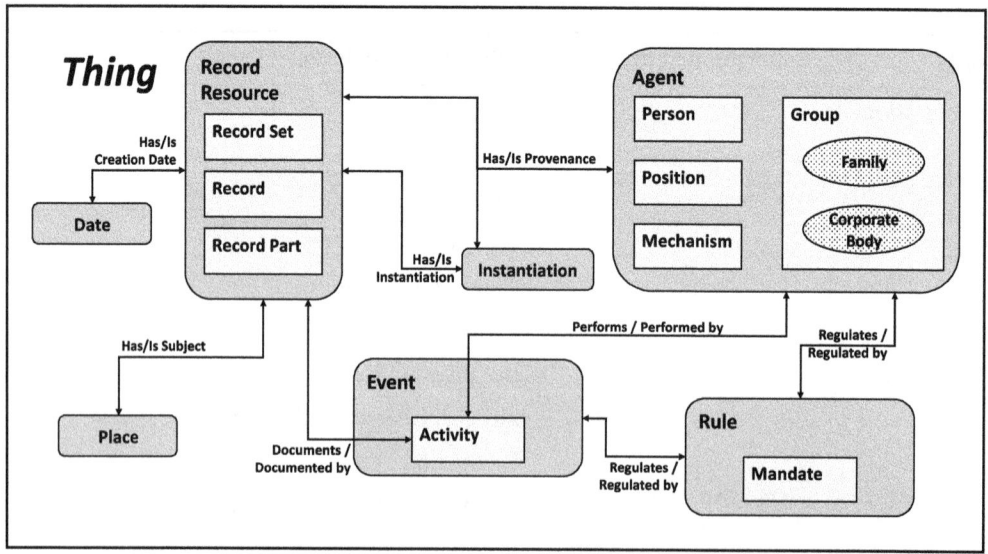

Figure 7.4 High-Level Relationships Specified in RiC-CM.

some basic high-level relationships can be identified for the individual entities. A *record resource*, for example, has the following relationships listed:

- *Record resource* documents an *Activity*
- *Record resource* has provenance *Agent*
- *Record resource* has as subject *Thing* or *Place*
- *Record resource* has creation date *Date*
- *Record resource* has an instantiation *Instantiation*.

In other words, a collection originates with an agent, documenting some activities in an agent's life or existence, and contains information about one or more subjects. The collection originated at a specific time and has been manifested into some form of physical or digital instantiation. Further, the entity *activity* is performed by an agent, which may be regulated by rules, and is documented in a record resource (which, in turn, has the relationships already identified).

In addition to the inherent relationships, RiC-CM includes other, more specific relationships, organized into thirteen broad categories.

- Whole-part
- Sequential
- Subject
- Record resource to record resource
- Record resource to instantiation
- Provenance
- Instantiation to instantiation
- Management
- Agent to agent
- Event
- Rule
- Date
- Spatial

Although it is not feasible to address all the myriad relationships in the model, exploring one or two of the categories can illustrate the types of relationships found in RiC-CM. The provenance category includes "Any relation that describes the provenance or origin of a *record resource* or *instantiation*, for example the relation between a *record resource* and the *agent* which created it or the *activity* from which it resulted."[45] This includes the following eight relationships.

- has provenance
- has creator
- has accumulator
- has sender
- has addressee
- has author
- has receiver
- has collector

A more robust category is the agent-to-agent relationships. It includes agent-oriented relationships, but also relationships for the entities that are subordinate to agent. They range from the very generic (e.g., *Agent* is associated with another *Agent*) to the highly specific (e.g., *Person* has teacher *Person*, *Person* has sibling *Person*).

- *Agent* is associated with *Agent*
- *Agent* has subordinate *Agent*
- *Agent* has successor relation with *Agent*
- *Agent* has work relation with *Agent*
- *Agent* was controller of *Agent*
- *Agent* was leader of *Group*
- *Group* has member *Person*
- *Group* has subdivision *Group*
- *Person* has spouse *Person*
- *Person* has child *Person*
- *Person* has sibling *Person*
- *Person* has family association with *Person*
- *Person* has descendent *Person*
- *Person* has correspondent *Person*
- *Person* has teacher *Person*
- *Person* knows of *Person*
- *Person* knows *Person*
- *Person* occupies *Position*
- *Position* exists in *Group*

A complete list of relationships is available in ICA's *Records in Contexts: Conceptual Model*, Version 1.0.[46]

The last section of the report, "Documenting Description," addresses the activity of archival description. It recognizes that the act of describing record resources leads to the creation of additional records. The archivist is performing an activity (description) that results in a new descriptive record (e.g., a finding aid). RiC-CM notes that it does not provide specialized components for documenting archival descriptions. Examples of how the existing entities, attributes, and relationships can be used to model archivists' processes can be found in Chapter 6 of the model.[47]

7.3.3 Museums: CIDOC Conceptual Reference Model (CRM)

The International Committee on Documentation (CIDOC) has worked for over twenty years on the development of a general data model focusing specifically on improving the exchange of information among museums and other cultural heritage institutions. Within the context of the CIDOC Conceptual Reference Model (CRM), **cultural heritage institution** is a broad term that refers to the organizations that acquire, preserve, and provide access to resources, bringing together libraries, archives, and museums. In 1999, the first complete edition of the CIDOC CRM was released by the CIDOC Documentation Standards Working Group. CIDOC CRM was subsequently submitted to the International Organization for Standardization (ISO) and was designated an official standard (ISO 21127) in 2006, with a recent update published in 2024, and additional revisions under development.[48]

Although called a *model*, the CRM does not exactly fit the definitions provided earlier in this chapter. It is certainly not a simplified description of a system. CIDOC CRM is, instead, an extraordinarily complex and thoroughly developed **ontology**—a formal representation of the reality of a knowledge domain—comprising hundreds of components. It is intended to promote the efficient and effective exchange of cultural heritage information by providing a common semantic framework to which heterogeneous sources of cultural heritage data can be mapped.

The CIDOC CRM has been developed in a manner that is intended to promote a shared understanding of cultural heritage information by providing a common and extensible semantic framework for evidence-based cultural heritage information integration. It is intended to be a common language for domain experts and implementers to formulate requirements for information systems and to serve as a guide for good practice of conceptual modelling. In this way, it can provide the "semantic glue" needed to mediate between different sources of cultural heritage information, such as that published by museums, libraries and archives.[49]

The CRM provides definitions and a formal structure for the description of nearly 100 entities (referred to as *classes* in CRM) and nearly 200 relationships (referred to as *properties*) used in cultural heritage documentation. Classes are the core components of the CIDOC CRM. A *class* is a "category of items that share one or more common traits serving as criteria to identify the items belonging to the class," and a *property* "serves to define a relationship of a specific kind between two classes."[50] A hierarchical understanding of classes and properties has been built into CRM allowing for subclasses, superclasses, subproperties, superproperties, and inheritance relationships among them. One entity sits at the top of the hierarchy of classes: *CRM Entity*, defined as "all things in the universe of discourse of the CIDOC Conceptual Reference Model"[51] (i.e., a thing or *res*). It contains several subclasses:

- Temporal Entity
- Time-Span
- Place
- Dimension
- Primitive Value
- Persistent Item
- Spacetime Volume

Some of these have additional subclasses. In some cases, the class hierarchies can get quite deep:

CRM Entity
  Persistent Item
    Thing
      Man-Made Thing
        Conceptual Object
          Symbolic Object
            Appellation
              Title

Classes and properties can also be divided into the following thirty-four functional units:[52]

- Acquisition Information
- Appellation Information
- Attribute Assignment
- Changing Thing
- Collection Information
- Condition Information
- De-accession and Disposal Information
- Description Information
- Documentation and References

- Existence Information
- Group Dynamics
- Image Information, Objects and Carriers
- Institution Information
- Location Information
- Mark and Inscription Information
- Material and Technique Information
- Measurement Information
- Object Association Information
- Object Collection Information
- Object Entry Information
- Object Name and Classification Information
- Object Number Information
- Object Production Information
- Object Title Information
- Part and Component Information
- Person Nationality Information
- Planned Activities (design, purpose, use)
- Recorder Information
- Reference Information
- Reproduction Rights Information
- Spatial–Temporal Relationship
- Subject Depicted Information
- Taxonomic Discourse
- Time-Span Information

These categories reflect possible uses for classes and properties within the realm of cultural heritage data. The functional categories are not mutually exclusive. For example, the class *Event* appears in thirteen different functional units. Each functional unit has a visual model showing how the classes and properties may connect.

CIDOC CRM is a complex system designed to represent and share cultural heritage metadata. Although it employs a somewhat different underlying structure (it is based on an object-oriented model rather than on an E-R model), it can be mapped to other metadata standards. To further explore this ontology, please consult the extensive documentation available on the CIDOC CRM website.[53]

7.3.4 The Semantic Web and Linked Data

As much as the conceptual models discussed up to this point differ from one another, they are alike in that they are primarily concerned with modeling information resources (and the entities related to them) that are described by metadata statements. In contrast, the Semantic Web, linked data, and the closely related standard RDF are concerned with modeling how metadata statements should be structured and related to one another.

In 1999, Sir Tim Berners-Lee first described his dream that someday computers would be able to analyze all the data on the web (including transactions between computers and people),[54] and that when that became possible, machines talking to machines would bring about the Semantic Web. The **Semantic Web** is a proposed extension to the traditional World Wide Web in which statements about resources are linked in a way that is semantically meaningful to computers. Different scholars have expressed its goals in a variety of ways:

- "The Semantic Web will bring structure to the meaningful content of Web pages, creating an environment where software agents roaming from page to page can readily carry out sophisticated tasks for users.... [It] will usher in significant new functionality as machines become much better able to process and 'understand' the data that they merely display at present."[55]
- "The general vision of a 'semantic web' can be summarized in a single phrase: *to make the web more accessible to computers*."[56]
- "The basic idea of a semantic web is to provide cost-efficient ways to publish information in distributed environments." [57]
- "The vision of the Semantic Web is to extend principles of the Web from documents to data. Data should be accessed using the general Web architecture using, e.g., URIs; data should be related to one another just as documents (or portions of documents) are already."[58]
- "The goal of the Semantic Web is to make Internet data machine-readable."[59]

What these statements indicate is that the current web is somewhat lacking in structure, semantics, and focus. The goal of the Semantic Web is to move from a document-based web that is understandable only to humans to a web of linked data that can be understood and processed by machines on a more granular level.

There are some significant differences between the Semantic Web and the traditional document-based web. At first, in the document-based web, we typically thought of a resource as a web page—a document encoded in HTML that contained information; it was a static, unidirectional transaction. Over time, this model has evolved; web resources are now more than just sites and documents, they include news outlets, commercial services (e.g., Amazon), technology products and services, interactive features (e.g., Facebook, TikTok), and so on. On the Semantic Web, however, the term *resource* is defined broadly; it can refer to information sources such as websites and online databases, but *resource* can also refer to real-life objects (e.g., a physical book, a painting, a chalice) as well as people, places, ideas, and so on. In other words, anything, electronic or not, can be represented on the Semantic Web as long as there is a **Uniform Resource Identifier** (URI) or an **Internationalized Resource Identifier** (IRI) that can be unambiguously connected to it. "A Uniform Resource Identifier (URI) is a compact sequence of characters that identifies an abstract or physical resource."[60] In other words, it is a character string that identifies something unambiguously. The familiar URL—what we see in a web browser's address bar—is one type of URI. An IRI is a URI that works with an expanded, international character set.

In the traditional document-based web, pages are containers of information. That information is marked up in HTML to indicate some major features (e.g., title, headings, paragraphs) and to denote how the content should be displayed, but little semantic structure is found. There is little to no indication of what types of data are found in a resource, who is responsible for it, what it is about, or that there are thousands of other resources that exist on the same topic (or are connected to it in some other way). The Semantic Web, on the other hand, hopes to supply better semantic structures in the data to improve understandability and to increase connections.

Linked data is the bedrock for the Semantic Web. **Linked data** is an approach to encoding data from a wide range of different sources and publishing it on the web in such a way that it may be understood by computers as related to the same resource or concept.

This approach is based on Berners-Lee's four rules of linked data.[61]

1. "Use URIs as names for things."—Identify everything using URIs (or IRIs).
2. "Use HTTP URIs so that people can look up those names."—Use standard internet protocols to make things as accessible as possible.
3. "When someone looks up a URI, provide useful information, using the standards (RDF, SPARQL)."—Make the sought information easily accessible.
4. "Include links to other URIs so that they can discover more things."—Make links!

In short, linked data

- is machine-readable,
- has meaning explicitly defined,
- is linked to other external data sets, and
- is linked to *from* external data sets.[62]

So, what does this mean in practical terms? If the Semantic Web's data is marked up more effectively and more thoroughly using standard protocols and IRIs that identify all the important persons, places, things, ideas, and so forth, computers can use that metadata to make links between related resources. For example, if two different resources contain metadata statements that say each of those resources is about *cataloging* (with each resource pointing to an IRI for an authorized description of that concept), then the machine will "understand" that both of those resources are about cataloging and thus are related to each other. The machine can exploit the connections and infer that if one of these resources were of interest, the other would be of interest to users as well.

When many resources are linked to the same or equivalent IRIs, those resources become connected. All of the connected resources are potentially of interest to users searching for materials about a particular topic, by a particular creator, from a particular place or year, and so on. These connections can be traversed automatically, allowing machines to offer a wider variety of, but also more accurately pinpointed, resources as part of search results (i.e., they will not be reliant solely on matching keywords in documents to words in search boxes). This will allow not just better search results but also information collections that can be created by automatic means and updated dynamically without human intervention. This brings together diverse resources that, in many cases, human beings would be unlikely to find. Linked data makes possible the discovery of information about entities that would otherwise have been separated by disassociated means of encoding or by different data silos.

With some intellectual effort, the often-tacit relationships between resources represented on the web (e.g., creators, subjects, locations) can be made more explicit and more easily machine actionable using linked data. This means that documents need to be described using metadata in a structured form, so that machines can process that data and get a better "understanding" of the content. To this end, linked data uses RDF as its structural standard to ensure interoperability and clarity in meaning.

7.3.4.1 Resource Description Framework (RDF)

Resource Description Framework (RDF), a metadata specification developed by the World Wide Web Consortium (W3C) in 1999, is a structural model for metadata statements.[†††] According to the W3C, RDF

> is a standard model for data interchange on the Web. RDF has features that facilitate data merging even if the underlying schemas differ, and it specifically supports the evolution of schemas over time without requiring all the data consumers to be changed. RDF extends the linking structure of the Web to use URIs to name the relationship between things as well as the two ends of the link (this is usually referred to as a "triple"). Using this simple model, it allows structured and semi-structured data to be mixed, exposed, and shared across different applications.[63]

It is a framework that allows us to make statements about resources. ***Resources*** are anything (documents, books, people, tangible objects, abstract concepts) found online or in the physical world; in RDF, the term *resource* is synonymous with *entity* or *thing* or *res*.[64] "RDF is intended for situations in which information on the Web needs to be processed by applications, rather than being only displayed to people. RDF provides a common framework for expressing this information so it can be exchanged between applications without loss of meaning. … RDF can be used to publish and interlink data on the Web."[65]

RDF enables the exchange and reuse of metadata in ways that are semantically unambiguous; in other words, RDF allows machines to "understand" what is being communicated by the metadata. This is accomplished by structuring all metadata statements in the form of triples. An ***RDF triple*** contains three components: a *subject*, a *predicate*, and an *object*.

- **Subject**: This is the topic of the RDF statement; it is the resource being described. Resources have properties (i.e., attributes) and relationships. In an RDF statement, an IRI is used to unambiguously identify the subject.[‡‡‡]

- **Predicate**: Properties and relationships are represented by the predicate. The predicate is an indication of the connection between the subject and the object, or it denotes the type of attribute that is expressed in the object. Predicates, too, are identified by IRIs.

- **Object**: This is another resource that is connected in some way to the subject, or it is a value associated with the predicate. The object may be the IRI for another resource, or it may be a literal (a string of alpha-numeric characters) providing the value for the attribute.

[†††] In this section, we are primarily concerned with the conceptual model rather than full implementations of RDF. Since the original version of RDF was published, the framework has been expanded considerably to include specific recommendations on syntax and vocabulary.

[‡‡‡] As described earlier in the chapter, an IRI is a Uniform Resource Identifier (URI), but with Unicode characters, not just ASCII characters. It is an improvement to the URI.

A generic representation of an RDF triple is presented in Figure 7.5.

In Figure 7.6 we have an RDF triple expressing a single relationship between two resources. The subject of our metadata statement is an online text with the title *A Very Brief Review of the MARC 21 Bibliographic Format*, and it has a creator whose name is known. The unique identifier for the web resource (a URL in this case) represents the subject, the predicate is a creation relationship that might be expressed in any number of ways (here, by using the Dublin Core element

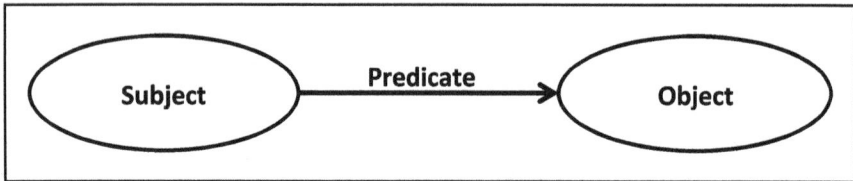

Figure 7.5 A Graphic Representation of an RDF Triple.

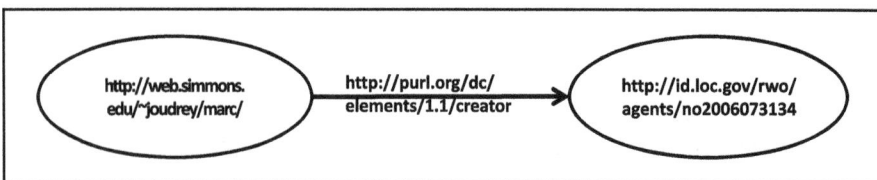

Figure 7.6 A Graphic Representation of an RDF Triple Using IRIs.

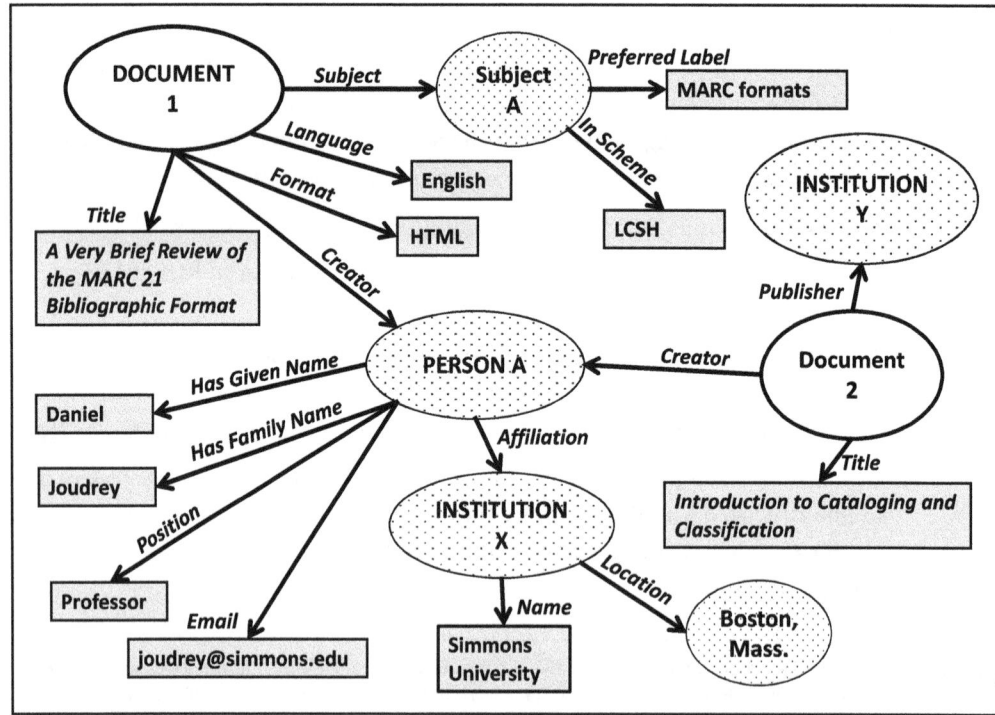

Figure 7.7 Entities Linked with RDF Triples.

Conceptual Models

Creator), and the object is represented by an IRI that identifies the author. Although an object can be expressed as a literal, in the RDF model an IRI is preferable whenever possible. The statement in Figure 7.6 is only one piece of a larger description of the document. A full description requires multiple RDF triples to give a complete picture. A set of RDF triples is referred to as an ***RDF graph***.

If the object is another resource, then the second resource could also have properties, which would have values, many of which could be other resources. There is no limit to the number of connections or links that may exist among the entities. The RDF triple is the basis for linked data, which is the foundation of the Semantic Web. Figure 7.7 is an illustration of the links that can exist using RDF.

In Figure 7.7 a resource, called *Document 1*, has properties such as Title, Creator, Format, Language, and Subject. Each property has a value. Sometimes, the value is a literal (in grey rectangles), and sometimes the value is another entity (polka-dotted ovals). The value of the Creator attribute is another resource called *Person A*. This resource has properties such as Given Name, Family Name, Position, E-mail, and Affiliation. The value of the Affiliation property is yet another resource called *Institution X*, which has its own properties (Name and Location). The links continue to amass as additional documents are connected to Person A—in this case, through creation relationships, but it could be through any number of other relationships as well. And those documents might link to publishers, manufacturers, distributors, and other creators and contributors. As you might imagine, a publisher entity could link to many thousands of documents, as could subject entities. The notion of the Semantic Web depends on massive amounts of data being linked.

For this model to be implemented practically, however, it must be expressed concretely. RDF may be encoded in XML[66] or in some other syntax such as Notation3[67] or the Terse RDF Triple Language (Turtle).[68] Using XML, an RDF description identifies the fact that it is using RDF, identifies the namespaces to be used for the property names, and provides the description. As mentioned above, the statement in Figure 7.6 contains only one RDF triple. This does not reflect the true nature of contemporary metadata description. Using RDF, a more complete description of this resource could look like the set of triples found in Table 7.4. Please note that even though this description is more complete, it is still a rather small description of the resource. Generally, additional statements would be needed to describe the resource more robustly. Although the display in Table 7.4 is illustrative, it is much more common to see metadata statements encoded

Table 7.4 An RDF Dataset in Tabular Form

#	Subject	Predicate	Object
1	http://web.simmons.edu/~joudrey/marc/index.html	http://www.w3.org/1999/02/22-rdf-syntax-ns#type	http://www.w3.org/2001/XMLSchema#CreativeWork
2	http://web.simmons.edu/~joudrey/marc/index.html	http://purl.org/dc/elements/1.1/title	"A Very Brief Review of the MARC 21 Bibliographic Format"
3	http://web.simmons.edu/~joudrey/marc/index.html	http://purl.org/dc/elements/1.1/creator	http://id.loc.gov/authorities/names/no2006073134

#	Subject	Predicate	Object
4	http://web.simmons.edu/~joudrey/marc/index.html	http://purl.org/dc/elements/1.1/language	"en"
5	http://web.simmons.edu/~joudrey/marc/index.html	http://purl.org/dc/elements/1.1/format	"text/html"
6	http://web.simmons.edu/~joudrey/marc/index.html	http://purl.org/dc/elements/1.1/subject	http://id.loc.gov/authorities/subjects/sh85080966
7	http://id.loc.gov/authorities/names/no2006073134	http://schema.org/familyName	"Joudrey"
8	http://id.loc.gov/authorities/names/no2006073134	http://schema.org/givenName	"Daniel"
9	http://id.loc.gov/authorities/subjects/sh85080966	http://www.w3.org/2004/02/skos/inScheme	"LCSH"
10	http://id.loc.gov/authorities/subjects/sh85080966	http://www.w3.org/2004/02/skos/prefLabel	"MARC formats"
11	http://id.loc.gov/authorities/subjects/sh85080966	http://www.w3.org/2004/02/skos/altLabel	"Machine-Readable Cataloging formats"

in one of the syntaxes mentioned above, such as XML (see Figure 7.8). In this view, the descriptive metadata is highlighted with boldface type, while the encoding and structural elements are in plain type.

In Figure 7.8, the first two lines state that this description is in XML, using RDF as the metadata structure. The next four lines indicate that the tags used throughout the description come from RDF itself, but also from the Schema.org vocabulary, the Dublin Core Metadata Element Set, and the Simple Knowledge Organization System (SKOS); IRIs for their namespaces are included. The next line, beginning with "rdf:Description rdf:about," indicates which resource is being described (i.e., the subject). It provides the IRI for *A Very Brief Review of the MARC 21 Bibliographic Format* and the type of resource that it is. What then follows is the description of the resource using five Dublin Core elements as predicates as was seen in the triples listed in Table 7.4. The first "</rdf:Description>" closing tag designates the end of the metadata describing the website. Please note that this website is not the only thing being described in the metadata; two smaller RDF graphs follow. The first enhances the description of the creator, providing a given and a family name to supplement the standard identifier used. The second provides more information about the subject matter of the original resource, showing the preferred term and

```
<?xml version="1.0"?>
<rdf:RDF
    xmlns:rdf="http://www.w3.org/1999/02/22-rdf-syntax-ns#"
    xmlns:schema="http://schema.org/"
    xmlns:dc="http://purl.org/dc/elements/1.1/"
    xmlns:skos="http://www.w3.org/2004/02/skos/">
<rdf:Description rdf:about="**http://web.simmons.edu/~joudrey/marc/ index.html**">
<rdf:type rdf:resource="http://www.w3.org/2001/XMLSchema#
    CreativeWork"></rdf:type>
    <dc:title>**A Very Brief Review of the MARC 21 Bibliographic Format**</dc:title>
    <dc:creator rdf:resource="**http://id.loc.gov/authorities/names/no2006073134**"/>
    <dc:language>**en**</dc:language>
    <dc:format>**text/html**</dc:format>
    <dc:subject rdf:resource="**http://id.loc.gov/authorities/subjects/sh85080966**"/>
</rdf:Description>
<rdf:Description
rdf:about="**http://id.loc.gov/authorities/names/no2006073134**">
    <schema:familyName>**Joudrey**</schema:familyName>
    <schema:givenName>**Daniel**</schema:givenName>
</rdf:Description>
<rdf:Description
rdf:about="**http://id.loc.gov/authorities/subjects/sh85080966**">
    <skos:inScheme>**LCSH**</skos:inScheme>
    <skos:prefLabel>**MARC formats**</skos:prefLabel>
    <skos:altLabel>**Machine-Readable Cataloging formats**</skos:altLabel>
</rdf:Description>
</rdf:RDF>
```

Figure 7.8 An RDF Dataset in XML.

an alternative term, as well as the source vocabulary that was used. A group of RDF graphs such as this is referred to as an ***RDF dataset***. This RDF dataset can be represented graphically, as seen in Figure 7.9.

As stated, RDF is considered one of the major building blocks in the vision for the Semantic Web. The Semantic Web is intended to provide more structure to the web that will allow computers to deal with its content in meaningful ways. It is intended that information will be defined in such a way that its meaning can be discerned, shared, and processed by automated tools as well as by people. This data, formatted as RDF triples, is stored on the web in ***triplestores***, databases specifically designed to house RDF structured data for Semantic Web queries.[69] "For the semantic web to function, computers must have access to structured collections of information and sets of inference rules that they can use to conduct automated reasoning."[70] The RDF metadata model provides this structure. Several groups within W3C are working toward realization of the Semantic Web, including several working on RDF-related specifications.[71] For more complete information about the Semantic Web, linked data, and the RDF family of standards, please consult the ample, but dense, documentation provided by the W3C on the web.[72]

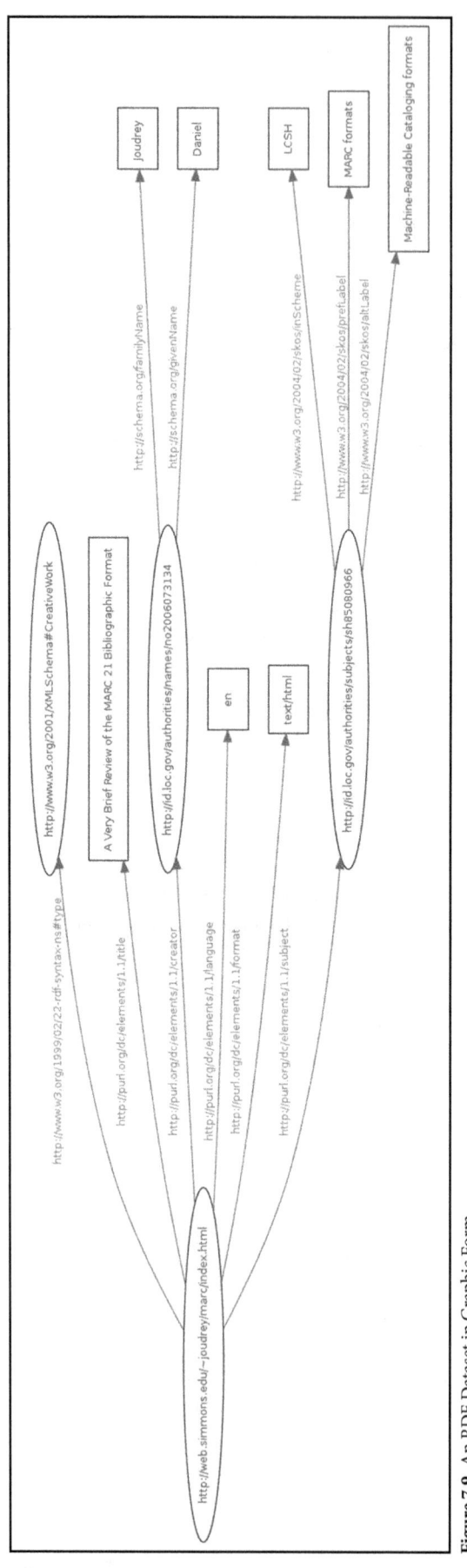

Figure 7.9 An RDF Dataset in Graphic Form.

7.3.4.2 Microdata

Whole documents can be described using Semantic Web principles, but so can individual pieces of content within documents through the use of additional attributes. To increase understanding of individual chunks of content, **microdata**, an HTML specification used to nest metadata within the content of web resources, can be embedded into a web page.[73] For example, using a vocabulary for marking up electronic content defined by Schema.org (a project to help "improve the web by creating a structured data markup schema supported by major search engines"[74]), the following statement could be added to the HTML code of the Library of Congress homepage:

```
<div itemscope itemtype="http://schema.org/Government Organization">
    <h1 itemprop="name">Library of Congress</h1>
    <span itemprop="alternateName">@librarycongress</span>
</div>
```

This states that the web resource is for a government agency, that its name is Library of Congress, that it is also known by its Instagram username @librarycongress, and that the two names are roughly equivalent.

Using embedded microdata or RDF structured metadata, all the following information could be added to improve machine understandability of the content:

- LC is the creator of the page.
- LC is a library.
- LC is part of the legislative branch of the United States government.
- *www.loc.gov* is the web address of a document that is created by, but is also about, LC.
- *www.loc.gov* may be used to represent the real-world entity named *Library of Congress*.
- LC has a general contact phone number of (202) 707-5000.
- LC is in Washington, DC (a geographic location, which could also be described extensively).
- LC is specifically located at 101 Independence Ave, SE, Washington, DC 20540.

In today's web of documents, though, the HTML encoding provides little more instruction than the following, primarily limited to the format and document structure of the web page:

- present the document using HTML
- identify this string of text as the title of the document
- present these other strings as headings (and, therefore, larger)
- format most content into paragraphs
- use a particular style sheet for details on how things are to be presented
- provide a link to the library catalog where *Search and browse records* is written

According to Tom Heath and Christian Bizer, "While most Web sites have some degree of structure, the language in which they are created, HTML, is oriented towards structuring textual documents rather than data. As data is intermingled into the surrounding text, it is hard for software applications to extract snippets of structured data from HTML pages."[75]

7.3.4.3 The Future of the Semantic Web

For many years, pages on the traditional web provided a limited number of hand-selected links to other web pages. Creators chose to point to other documents that they considered to be relevant to the information they were presenting—generally at the level of the whole resource or a discrete part of it. As the web developed, technologies emerged that allowed links to be automatically generated. A goal of the Semantic Web is to increase technology's abilities to connect an even wider variety of related resources through automatic means, but we are not quite there yet. Despite first being described at the beginning of the twenty-first century,[76] the practical aspects of Semantic Web development are still in relatively preliminary stages. While its foundations are being laid, there are few well-developed concrete products to demonstrate proof of concept.

The current activities in place to embrace linked data may eventually bring a full Semantic Web to fruition, but much work must be completed for that to happen. Adding more metadata and microdata to the web is an enormous task. For it to succeed, metadata must be created in a more collaborative fashion. In other words, the responsibility for creating the needed metadata must be shared among many, many institutions. The diversity attained by using metadata from multiple sources and multiple perspectives can help to create a more robust picture of the entities described for machines and for humans. And the fuller that picture is, the more connections can be made.

Many see the development of linked data and the Semantic Web as the next frontier of information organization, and concrete steps are being taken to help the LIS profession on this journey. One such project is the Library of Congress's Bibliographic Framework Initiative (BIBFRAME), which is an attempt to replace the MARC encoding format used in catalogs with a linked data approach to representing and exchanging bibliographic data on the web and in the networked world.[77][§§§] This project, like many others, is still in development and should be watched carefully by anyone interested in information organization. Other projects to incorporate linked data into library descriptive practices include the Program for Cooperative Cataloging (PCC) pilot projects aimed at incorporating URIs into MARC[78] and using Wikidata (a collaboratively edited database based on linked data principles and hosted by the Wikimedia Foundation) as an identity management hub.[79]

Among some, there is excitement about the potential of the Semantic Web and the changes that could occur as a result of its maturation. If it occurs, there will be far-reaching effects on information organization and cataloging, but exactly how things will change is not completely evident at this time. Although some have expressed hope about this journey, there are still plenty of naysayers who cannot imagine the Semantic Web vision being manifested—some because they do not believe that the needed metadata infrastructure is possible, some because they think the idea sounds like a pipe dream, and some because they feel the technology is already outdated and unnecessary.[80] With the rapid development of generative artificial intelligence (AI), the assumption that machines cannot understand unstructured data strings (e.g., text) is now being challenged. This assumption has long served as a foundational justification for the need for Semantic Web technologies, linked data principles, and RDF.

[§§§]For a fuller discussion of BIBFRAME, see Chapter 5,

7.3.5 DCMI Abstract Model (DCAM)

RDF influenced the DCMI Abstract Model, published in 2007 by the Dublin Core Metadata Initiative (DCMI). The primary purpose of the DCAM is to provide a conceptual model of metadata that is independent of any specific approach to encoding or semantics. By specifying the components and offering a generic model, the DCAM allows for better communication about metadata and interoperability across information environments. It describes how the syntax-independent model's entities are related to create complete metadata structures. The model "is primarily aimed at the developers of software applications that support Dublin Core metadata, people involved in developing new syntax encoding guidelines for Dublin Core metadata and people developing metadata application profiles based on DCMI vocabularies or on other compatible vocabularies."[81]

The DCAM comprises three related information models: a resource model, a description set model, and a vocabulary model. The three information models contain entities of various types. The DCMI Resource Model includes entities such as resources, properties, and values (which should seem familiar after reading about RDF and entity-relationship models). As is the case with RDF, a resource can be any single thing in the universe: a document, a person, an abstract concept, and so on. Resources are described using the same basic model, which is summarized entirely by a few simple statements in the DCAM.

- Each *described resource* is described using one or more *property-value pairs*.[****]
- Each *property-value pair* is made up of one *property* and one *value*.
- Each *value* is a *resource*—the physical, digital or conceptual entity or *literal* that is associated with a *property* when a *property-value pair* is used to describe a *resource*. Therefore, each *value* is either a *literal value* or a *non-literal value*:
    - A *literal value* is a *value* which is a *literal*.
    - A *non-literal value* is a *value* which is a physical, digital or conceptual entity.
- A *literal* is an entity which uses a Unicode string as a lexical form, together with an optional language tag or datatype, to denote a resource.[82]

The DCMI Resource Model states that Dublin Core metadata consists of statements describing resources and each description refers to properties and values (a second resource). This is analogous to the subject–predicate–object structure found in RDF triples. The concept of the *described resource* is equivalent to the subject in the RDF model. The importance of the property–value (i.e., predicate–object) relationship cannot be overstated. It is not enough to know either the property or the value in isolation; it is the combination that makes that metadata useful. For example, it is not enough to know that the resource is associated with Tokyo in some fashion. It is important to understand that Tokyo is the place of distribution or that it is the topic of the resource. The meaning of that geographic name is different depending on the context. The context is provided by identifying the property unambiguously and associating it clearly with the value "Tokyo."

[****]This can also be referred to as an *attribute-value pair*.

The DCMI Description Set Model introduces additional entities: *descriptions* and *description sets*. So, if a metadata statement is analogous to the RDF triple, then a **description** is analogous to an RDF graph for a single resource. It is a compilation of metadata statements used to describe a single resource. This is based on the Dublin Core "One-to-One Principle," which states that a description should be focused on one (and only one) resource at a time. For example, the metadata for *A Very Brief Review of the MARC 21 Bibliographic Format* outlined in lines 1–6 of Table 7.4 is a *description* in DCAM. A **description set**, then, is two or more metadata *descriptions* (similar to an RDF dataset). Thus, the complete Table 7.4 (lines 1–11) is a *description set*. In the DCAM, a *record* contains one or more description sets.

The final component is the DCMI Vocabulary Model, which introduces the concepts:

- Vocabularies
- Terms
- Properties
- Classes
- Vocabulary encoding schemes
- Syntax encoding schemes

In short, terms are components of vocabularies. Terms may be in the form of properties, classes, syntax encoding schemes, or vocabulary encoding schemes. For more about the vocabulary model or any other part of the DCAM, please consult the Dublin Core website.

The role and purpose of the DCAM is not particularly clear. It has seen little further development since it was originally presented, and its reception has not been particularly enthusiastic. In a blog post back in 2008, library technologist Karen Coyle expresses this sentiment clearly:

> Few outside of the small group that worked on the DCAM profess to understand it. I myself have read and re-read the DCAM document dozens of times and have still failed to have the "aha!" moment in which I would see how the DCAM explains everything of importance to metadata creation.[83]

Part of the problem may be that much of the ground it covers is already found in the more familiar and more widely implemented RDF model. In fact, some discussions within the DCMI in 2009–2010 proposed, among other things, deprecating the DCAM in favor of RDF. Others proposed removing two of the three components of the abstract model (leaving only the Description Set Model) again in favor of RDF.[84]

7.4 Conclusion

This chapter has provided an introduction to some of the conceptual models and frameworks that information professionals might encounter in their careers. Although some of these models may seem rather abstract and divorced from the reality of practice, they are key to understanding why and how professionals organize information. The models provide a foundation for understanding how users are served by information practices and individual components of metadata.

These frameworks create a space in the information professions to develop more concrete principles, standard practices, and consistent outputs to serve users. In the next chapter, the topics of description and access are discussed, some general principles of organizing are introduced, and points of convergence among various organizing traditions are reviewed.

Some Important Terms in This Chapter
(Definitions Provided in the Glossary)

Agent	Inheritance relationship	RDF (Resource Description Framework)
Agent entities	Internationalized Resource Identifier	
Attribute		RDF dataset
Carrier	Item	RDF graph
Class	Linked data	RDF triple
Collective agent	Literal	Relationship
CRM entity	Manifestation	Res
Cultural heritage institution	Microdata	Resource
Description (metadata)	Model	Resource entities
Description set	Nomen	Select
Entity	Nomen string	Semantic Web
Entity–Relationship model	Obtain	Time-span
Explore	Ontology	Triplestore
Expression	Person	Uniform Resource Identifier
Find	Place	User tasks
Identify	Property	Work

Some Important Acronyms in This Chapter

CIDOC:	International Committee on Documentation
CRM:	Conceptual Reference Model
DCAM:	DCMI Abstract Model
DCMI:	Dublin Core Metadata Initiative
EGAD:	Expert Group on Archival Description
FRAD:	*Functional Requirements for Authority Data*
FRBR:	*Functional Requirements for Bibliographic Records*
FRSAD:	*Functional Requirements for Subject Authority Data*
ICA:	International Council on Archives
IFLA:	International Federation of Library Associations and Institutions
IRI:	Internationalized Resource Identifier
ISO:	International Organization for Standardization

LRM:	*IFLA Library Reference Model*
OWL:	Web Ontology Language
RDF:	Resource Description Framework
RiC:	*Records in Contexts*
RiC-AG:	*Records in Contexts: Application Guidelines*
RiC-CM:	*Records in Contexts: Conceptual Model*
RiC-FAD:	*Records in Contexts: Foundations of Archival Description*
RiC-O:	*Records in Contexts: Ontology*
URI:	Uniform Resource Identifier
W3C:	World Wide Web Consortium
XML:	Extensible Markup Language

7.5 Discussion Questions and Exercises

- What are conceptual models, and what purpose do they serve in the information organization community?
- The WEMI entities (work, expression, manifestation, and item) are central to IFLA LRM's modeling of the bibliographic universe. Do you find WEMI to be a useful way of thinking about information resources? Consider:
    - How easy are the concepts to understand?
    - How are various aspects of information resources (e.g., titles, creators, publication information, physical dimensions, shelf numbers, subject headings, and so on) connected to the different components of WEMI?
    - Does WEMI apply to all types of information resources equally well?
- Select two of the conceptual models discussed in this chapter and compare them. What do they have in common, and how do they differ? How does each reflect the needs of the information communities that they were created for?
- What issues with the current document-based web is the Semantic Web intended to address?
- How might a shift towards greater use of linked data principles and technologies affect the practice of information organization?

7.6 Suggested Readings

Antoniou, Grigoris, Paul Groth, Frank van Harmelen, and Rinke Hoekstra. *A Semantic Web Primer*. 3rd ed. Cambridge, MA: MIT Press, 2012.

Berners-Lee, Tim, James Hendler, and Ora Lassila. "The Semantic Web." *Scientific American* 284, no. 5 (May 2001): 34–8, 40–3.

DeWeese, Keith P., and Dan Segal. *Libraries and the Semantic Web*. San Rafael, CA: Morgan & Claypool, 2015.

Guerrini, Mauro, and Tiziana Possemato. "Linked Data: A New Alphabet for the Semantic Web." *Italian Journal of Library, Archives, and Information Science* 4, no. 1 (2013). https://www.jlis.it/index.php/jlis/article/view/256.

Heath, Tom, and Christian Bizer. *Linked Data: Evolving the Web into a Global Data Space*. San Rafael, CA: Morgan & Claypool, 2011.

International Council on Archives. *Records in Contexts: Conceptual Model*. Version 1.0. November 2023. https://github.com/ICA-EGAD/RiC-CM/.

International Federation of Library Associations and Institutions, IFLA Study Group. *Functional Requirements for Bibliographic Records: Final Report*. Munich: Saur, 1998. http://www.ifla.org/publications/functional-requirements-for-bibliographic-records.

International Federation of Library Associations and Institutions, Working Group on Functional Requirements and Numbering of Authority Records. *Functional Requirements for Authority Data: A Conceptual Model*. The Hague: IFLA, 2009. https://www.ifla.org/publications/functional-requirements-for-authority-data.

International Federation of Library Associations and Institutions, Working Group on the Functional Requirements for Subject Authority Records (FRSAR). *Functional Requirements for Subject Authority Data: A Conceptual Model*. The Hague: IFLA, 2010. https://www.ifla.org/functional-requirements-for-subject-authority-data/.

Joudrey, Daniel N., Arlene G. Taylor, and David P. Miller. *Introduction to Cataloging and Classification*. 11th ed. Santa Barbara, CA: Libraries Unlimited, 2015.

Maxwell, Robert L. *FRBR: A Guide for the Perplexed*. Chicago: American Library Association, 2008.

Mitchell, Erik T. *Library Linked Data: Early Activity and Development*. Chicago: ALA TechSource, 2016.

Riva, Pat, Patrick Le Boeuf, and Maja Žumer. *IFLA Library Reference Model: A Conceptual Model for Bibliographic Information*. The Hague: IFLA, 2017. https://www.ifla.org/resources/?oPubId=11412.

Taylor, Arlene G., ed. *Understanding FRBR: What It Is and How It Will Affect Our Retrieval Tools*. Westport, CT: Libraries Unlimited, 2007.

Van Hooland, Seth, and Ruben Verborgh. *Linked Data for Libraries, Archives and Museums: How to Clean, Link and Publish Your Metadata*. Chicago: American Library Association, 2014.

7.7 Notes

All URLs accessed April 2025.

1. "Model," *FOLDOC: Free On-line Dictionary of Computing*, edited by Denis Howe, http://foldoc.org/model.
2. "Model," Merriam-Webster.com, http://www.merriam-webster.com/dictionary/model.
3. George E. P. Box, "Science and Statistics," *Journal of the American Statistical Association* 71, no. 356 (1976): 792.
4. Peter Pin-Shan Chen, "The Entity-Relationship Model: Toward a Unified View of Data," *ACM Transactions on Database Systems* 1, no. 1 (1976): 9–36.
5. Pat Riva, Patrick Le Boeuf, and Maja Žumer, *IFLA Library Reference Model: A Conceptual Model for Bibliographic Information* (The Hague: IFLA, 2017), https://www.ifla.org/resources/?oPubId=11412. [Henceforth cited as LRM.]
6. International Federation of Library Associations and Institutions, IFLA Study Group, *Functional Requirements for Bibliographic Records* [FRBR]: *Final Report* (Munich: Saur, 1998), 8, https://www.ifla.org/publications/functional-requirements-for-bibliographic-records. [Henceforth cited as FRBR.]

7. International Federation of Library Associations and Institutions (IFLA), Working Group on Functional Requirements and Numbering of Authority Records (FRANAR), *Functional Requirements for Authority Data: A Conceptual Model* (The Hague: IFLA, 2009), https://www.ifla.org/publications/functional-requirements-for-authority-data. [Henceforth cited as FRAD.]
8. IFLA Working Group on the Functional Requirements for Subject Authority Records (FRSAR), *Functional Requirements for Subject Authority Data (FRSAD): A Conceptual Model* (The Hague: IFLA, 2010), https://www.ifla.org/functional-requirements-for-subject-authority-data/. [Henceforth cited as FRSAD.]
9. LRM, 9.
10. LRM, 5.
11. Daniel N. Joudrey, Arlene G. Taylor, and David P. Miller, *Introduction to Cataloging and Classification*, 11th ed. (Santa Barbara, CA: Libraries Unlimited, 2015), 51–124.
12. LRM, 15–16; FRBR, 79.
13. Charles A. Cutter, *Rules for a Dictionary Catalog*, 4th ed. (Washington, DC: Government Printing Office, 1904), 12.
14. International Conference on Cataloguing Principles, Paris, 9th–18th October, 1961, *Report* (London: International Federation of Library Associations, 1963), 91–6.
15. LRM, 15–16.
16. LRM, 15–16.
17. LRM, 15–16.
18. LRM, 15–16.
19. LRM, 15–16.
20. FRAD, 46.
21. FRSAD, 33–4.
22. LRM, 20–36.
23. Pat Riva, Patrick Le Boeuf, and Maja Žumer, "Transition Mappings: User Tasks, Entities, Attributes, and Relationships in FRBR, FRAD, and FRSAD Mapped to Their Equivalents in the IFLA Library Reference Model," August 2017, 2, https://www.ifla.org/resources/?oPubId=11412.
24. LRM, 18.
25. LRM, 21.
26. LRM, 23.
27. LRM, 28.
28. LRM, 36.
29. LRM, 88.
30. LRM, 31–2.
31. LRM, 31.
32. LRM, 89.
33. Riva, Le Boeuf, and Žumer, "Transition Mappings," 14–56.
34. LRM, 37.
35. LRM, 61.
36. LRM.
37. Murtha Baca and Sherman Clarke, "FRBR and Works of Art, Architecture, and Material Culture," in *Understanding FRBR: What It Is, and How It Will Affect Our Retrieval Tools*, ed. Arlene G. Taylor (Westport, CT: Libraries Unlimited, 2007), 103–10.
38. Gretchen Gueguen et al., "Toward an International Conceptual Model for Archival Description: A Preliminary Report from the International Council on Archives' Expert Group on Archival Description," *American Archivist* 76, no. 2 (2013): 567–84.

39. International Council on Archives [ICA], *Records in Contexts: Conceptual Model*, Version 1.0, November 2023, 2, https://github.com/ICA-EGAD/RiC-CM/. [Henceforth cited as RiC-CM.]
40. RiC-CM, 13.
41. RiC-CM, 19–38.
42. RiC-CM, 32.
43. RiC-CM, 33.
44. RiC-CM, 39–73.
45. RiC-CM, 75.
46. RiC-CM, 74–115.
47. RiC-CM, 125–9.
48. International Council of Museums, International Committee for Documentation [ICM CIDOC], "Versions of the CIDOC-CRM," CIDOC-Conceptual Reference Model (website), https://www.cidoc-crm.org/versions-of-the-cidoc-crm.
49. ICM CIDOC, "What Is the CIDOC CRM?" CIDOC-Conceptual Reference Model (website), http://cidoc-crm.org/.
50. ICM CIDOC, "Terminology," *Volume A; Definitions of the CIDOC Conceptual Reference Model*, 12–13, http://cidoc-crm.org/Version/version-7.1.3. [Henceforth cited as *CIDOC-CRM Definitions*.]
51. *CIDOC-CRM Definitions*, 57.
52. ICM CIDOC, "Functional Overview," CIDOC-Conceptual Reference Model (website), http://cidoc-crm.org/functional-units.
53. ICM CIDOC, "The CIDOC CRM Home Page," CIDOC-Conceptual Reference Model (website), http://cidoc-crm.org/.
54. Tim Berners-Lee with Mark Fischetti, *Weaving the Web: The Original Design and Ultimate Destiny of the World Wide Web by Its Inventor* (New York: Harper-Collins, 1999), Chapter 12.
55. Tim Berners-Lee, James Hendler, and Ora Lassila, "The Semantic Web," *Scientific American* 284, no. 5 (2001): 34.
56. Grigoris Antoniou, Paul Groth, Frank van Harmelen, and Rinke Hoekstra, *A Semantic Web Primer*, 3rd ed. (Cambridge, MA: MIT Press, 2012), 1. [Italics added.]
57. Florian Bauer and Martin Kaltenböck, *Linked Open Data: The Essentials*, 2nd ed. (Vienna, Austria: DGS, 2016), 33, https://reeep.org/wp-content/uploads/2023/10/LOD-TheEssentials2016.pdf.
58. W3C, "W3C Semantic Web Frequently Asked Questions," https://www.w3.org/2001/sw/SW-FAQ.
59. "Semantic Web," Wikipedia, https://en.wikipedia.org/wiki/Semantic_Web.
60. Tim Berners-Lee, Roy Fielding, and Larry Masinter, "Uniform Resource Identifier (URI): Generic Syntax," IETF [Internet Engineering Task Force] Documents, January 2005, http://tools.ietf.org/html/rfc3986.
61. Tim Berners-Lee, "Linked Data," W3C Design Issues, July 2006, https://www.w3.org/DesignIssues/LinkedData.
62. Christian Bizer, Tom Heath, and Tim Berners-Lee, "Linked Data: The Story So Far," *International Journal on Semantic Web and Information Systems* 5, no. 3 (2009): 2.
63. "Resource Description Framework (RDF)," W3C, February 25, 2014, https://www.w3.org/RDF/.
64. "RDF 1.1 Concepts and Abstract Syntax," W3C, February 25, 2014, https://www.w3.org/TR/rdf11-concepts/.
65. "RDF 1.1 Primer," W3C, June 24, 2014, https://www.w3.org/TR/rdf11-primer/.
66. "RDF 1.1 XML Syntax," W3C, February 25, 2014, http://www.w3.org/TR/rdf-syntax-grammar/.
67. "Notation 3 (N3): A Readable RDF Syntax," W3C, March 28, 2011, https://www.w3.org/TeamSubmission/n3/.
68. "RDF 1.1 Turtle—Terse RDF Triple Language," W3C, February 25, 2014, https://www.w3.org/TR/turtle/.
69. Jack Rusher, "Triple Store," SWAD-Europe Workshop on Semantic Web Storage and Retrieval Position Papers, 13–14 November 2003, Vrije Universiteit, Amsterdam, Netherlands, https://www.w3.org/2001/sw/Europe/events/20031113-storage/positions/rusher.html.

70. Berners-Lee, Hendler, and Lassila, 34.
71. "Building the Web of Data," W3C, https://www.w3.org/2013/data/.
72. "W3C Standards and Drafts," W3C, https://www.w3.org/standards/techs/rdf#w3c_all.
73. Web Hypertext Application Technology Working Group (WHATWG), "Microdata," HTML Living Standard, https://html.spec.whatwg.org/multipage/microdata.html#microdata.
74. "About Schema.org," https://schema.org/docs/faq.html.
75. Tom Heath and Christian Bizer, *Linked Data: Evolving the Web into a Global Data Space* (San Rafael, CA: Morgan & Claypool, 2011), 2.
76. Berners-Lee, Hendler, and Lassila, 34–43.
77. "BIBFRAME: Bibliographic Framework Initiative," Library of Congress, https://www.loc.gov/bibframe/.
78. Program for Cooperative Cataloging, "PCC URIs in MARC Pilot," https://www.loc.gov/aba/pcc/pilots/URIs-in-MARC-Pilot.html.
79. "Wikidata:WikiProject PCC Wikidata Pilot," Wikidata, https://www.wikidata.org/wiki/Wikidata:WikiProject_PCC_Wikidata_Pilot.
80. Seth Grimes, "Semantic Web Business: Going Nowhere Slowly," *InformationWeek*, January 7, 2014, http://www.informationweek.com/software/information-management/semantic-web-business-going-nowhere-slowly/d/d-id/1113323; Kyle Banerjee, "The Linked Data Myth," *Library Journal*, August 13, 2020, https://www.libraryjournal.com/story/the-linked-data-myth; Rafe Brena, "What Happened to the Semantic Web?" *Towards Data Science*, August 3, 2023, https://towardsdatascience.com/what-happened-to-the-semantic-web-cbaaf547a09f. [behind paywall]
81. Andy Powell, Mikael Nilsson, Ambjörn Naeve, Pete Johnston, and Thomas Baker, "DCMI Abstract Model," Dublin Core Metadata Initiative, issued June 4, 2007, http://dublincore.org/documents/abstract-model/.
82. Powell et al.
83. Karen Coyle, "DCAM Explained … or, An Attempt to Unravel Key Concepts," Karen Coyle's Home Page, 2008, http://kcoyle.net/dcam.html.
84. Thomas Baker and Pete Johnston, "A Review of the DCMI Abstract Model with Scenarios for Its Future," written October 15, 2010, revised May 12, 2011, https://github.com/dcmi/repository/blob/master/wikis_pre2016/architecture/mediawiki/Review_of_DCMI_Abstract_Model.md.

Chapter 8

Description and Access

Loosely speaking, there are four parts to creating metadata for an information resource:

1. providing a description of the resource,
2. adding access points to this description,
3. analyzing the subject content of the resource, and
4. encoding all the metadata.

This chapter discusses the basics of resource description and access points (subject analysis is covered in Chapters 11–13 and encoding is discussed in Chapter 5).

For many years in libraries, the term **bibliographic record** has been applied to the recorded description of a resource. At times, the term *surrogate record* has been used instead to avoid the use of the word *bibliographic* (*biblio-* means *book*) in acknowledgment that information resources take many forms other than books. More recently, as the longstanding focus on the record structure has lessened due to the profession's explorations into linked data, some have begun to refer to our bibliographic data as *descriptive data, descriptions, metadata, descriptive metadata, resource descriptions,* or *metadata statements.* All these terms may be used somewhat interchangeably in this and the following chapters, as well as in the information professions at large.

After introducing so many terms, some definitions are in order before discussing the creation of resource descriptions. As stated several times already, an **information resource** is an instance of recorded information (e.g., a book, article, streaming video, sound recording, online journal). **Descriptive data** is information derived from a resource and used to represent it; it is an account of the resource's most important characteristics (i.e., **attributes**) that can help users with activities collectively referred to as the **user tasks** (i.e., find, identify, select, obtain, and explore). The attributes include both descriptive data (dates, extent, resource types, standard numbers, etc.) and access points (such as creator and contributor names, subjects, work titles). A **resource description** contains full descriptive and access information for a resource; it comprises a set of metadata statements referring to the same resource. A **metadata statement** is a standalone description of a single attribute of a resource.

<dc:title>Cataloging and Acquisitions Home</dc:title>

A resource description is contained in a **surrogate record**, a somewhat self-contained collection of metadata. Such a record stands in place of (i.e., is a surrogate for) a resource in retrieval tools such as catalogs, indexes, and bibliographies, while metadata statements may be encoded in documents directly or kept in triplestores on the web. Both metadata statements and surrogate records contain descriptive metadata. In metadata records or statements, a particular piece of descriptive data may be referred to as the *value* (or content) assigned to an element. An *element* is a field in a metadata schema that represents an important attribute. An *access point* is a term (word, heading, prescribed string, etc.) in a surrogate record that is used to retrieve that record. Access points are often singled out from other descriptive data and placed under authority control.* Access points reflect relationships between the information resource and creators, subjects, titles, genres, and so on.

A file of surrogate records serves as a filter to keep a user from having to search through myriad irrelevant resources. The descriptions must be distinctive enough that each resource is distinguishable from the others. A surrogate record's most important function is to assist the user in evaluating whether the resource it represents will be useful and contain information that the user wishes to explore further. Resource descriptions are most helpful when they are predictable in both form and content. Adherence to standards ensures such predictability. At the very least, most descriptive standards dictate which metadata elements are required and which are optional. Some are quite extensive in their guidance, while others provide only minimal instruction. Specific standards for description and access are discussed in greater detail in Chapter 9.

8.1 Creation of Metadata Descriptions

The process begins with a short examination of the resource to be described. This examination is meant to provide a sense of what is in hand (what the resource is, who is responsible for it, what its basic attributes are, etc.). Once the nature of the resource has been determined, a description is created by selecting important pieces of data (e.g., title, creator, date) from the information resource, determining certain characteristics of the resource (e.g., size, mode of issuance), and then placing those pieces of information in a certain order, usually dictated by a set of rules or conventions for description. These rules or conventions (i.e., *content standards*) are created by different communities, so that those communities can appropriately describe the resources for which they are responsible. Content standards serve as style manuals for metadata, identifying the elements to be included, providing definitions of each element, and sometimes providing rules for exactly what information to include in a description, for the structure of that information, and occasionally for its punctuation and order. Some standards also provide information about where to find the metadata and how to address metadata in different languages or scripts; some address issues related to capitalization, initials, numbers, and dates; and some provide instructions on the use of symbols, diacritical marks, abbreviations, and acronyms, among other topics.

Several of today's metadata standards are outgrowths of rules once known as *cataloging codes*. Such rules were essentially content standards, first for records in print retrieval tools and later for records to be entered into online systems. As online retrieval tools came into being, separate standards for the encoding of surrogate records were developed to create online records. The conceptual pieces necessary for online records are

- *Elements*: identification of which types of information (i.e., attributes) are to be included,

---

*Authority control is discussed in Chapter 10.

- ***Content***: metadata values, which may be prescribed with formatting instructions or may be loosely described in the standard, and
- ***Syntax***: encoding for machine manipulation using an encoding standard or a markup language.

A standard may dictate elements only (e.g., Dublin Core), content only (e.g., *Cataloging Cultural Objects*), or syntax only (e.g., XML schemas). Some metadata standards, however, have been created that combine the conceptual pieces in different ways. The Metadata Object Description Schema (MODS) used by libraries, for example, specifies what elements are available for use (i.e., it is a data structure standard), dictates the content and form of some elements (as does a content standard), and specifies the syntax to use (i.e., it dictates the encoding standard to use). Increasingly, metadata standards address more than one of the various components of metadata outlined in Table 6.1 on page 204.

Description is often begun by filling in a template that contains elements defined by the content standard. For example, in the library context, catalogers start a basic bibliographic description by transcribing or recording values in each applicable metadata element. This might be done using a template found in the cataloging module of an integrated library system, in a template used in a bibliographic network such as OCLC Online Computer Library Center, or by typing out the metadata on a card. Prior to starting a metadata description, however, it is important to understand the principles that inform the descriptive process, the nature of the resource being described, and the basic relationships that need to be identified to provide access to the resource. These issues are addressed in the following sections.

8.2 Principles of Description and Access

Metadata creators must have a basic understanding of the values and principles that inform the process of resource description. Awareness of these foundational principles can make the rationale for individual guidelines within a given descriptive standard easier to understand. Such principles can also act as a decision-making aid to the metadata creator in those inevitable situations when a descriptive standard's guidelines are ambiguous or do not provide adequate guidance for a specific situation—in other words, principles provide a foundation for cataloger's judgment. Some of the principles described below are freestanding, while others are part of a larger descriptive standard.

8.2.1 IFLA's *Statement of International Cataloguing Principles* (ICP)

Although IFLA's ICP[1] is not a description standard per se, it is an important document in international cataloging and is particularly notable for its influence on the current library cataloging content standard, *RDA: Resource Description & Access*.[2] The following is a modified excerpt from Daniel N. Joudrey, Arlene G. Taylor, and David P. Miller's 11th edition of *Introduction to Cataloging and Classification*:

> After a series of five meetings held around the world between 2003 and 2007, the IFLA Meeting of Experts on an International Cataloguing Code (IME ICC)

disseminated a document called the *Statement of International Cataloguing Principles* (ICP) in 2009, and it has since been revised and republished in 2016. The ICP arose from concerns about the future of cataloging that had been fodder for discussions over the previous decade or longer. The purpose of the ICP was to update and expand upon the previous statement of cataloging principles produced by the International Conference on Cataloguing Principles held in Paris in 1961. These "Paris Principles," based largely on the work of Seymour Lubetzky, have long been acknowledged as a guiding force in the development of cataloging codes around the globe, particularly concerning the choice and form of access points. From this point into the foreseeable future, the ICP is to be the basis for the international standardization of cataloging, having been built on earlier cataloging traditions and on the foundations of the FRBR and FRAD conceptual models, which were also created by IFLA working groups. The idea is that the *Statement of International Cataloguing Principles* can serve as a prefatory document to ensure a degree of consistency among the cataloging codes created by various countries.[3]

The ICP contains 13 basic principles. The following is a brief interpretation of each:

1. **Convenience of the User**: Think of the user first!
2. **Common Usage**: Use the language of everyday users.
3. **Representation**: The description should reflect how a resource describes itself.
4. **Accuracy**: Get the description right!
5. **Sufficiency and Necessity**: Require the data needed to make the resource findable and understandable.
6. **Significance**: Stick with the most relevant attributes to describe the resource.
7. **Economy**: Prefer ways to describe something quickly and efficiently.
8. **Consistency and Standardization**: Standardize as much data as possible, whenever possible.
9. **Integration**: Start with widely applicable rules, rather than specialized rules for specific resource types.
10. **Interoperability**: Work towards the sharing and re-use of data as much as possible.
11. **Openness**: Make data as available as possible. Do not place unnecessary restrictions on it.
12. **Accessibility**: Make it accessible to all. Comply with international standards for accessibility.
13. **Rationality**: Rules should make sense; they should be logical, not arbitrary.

In addition to these general principles, there are sections of the ICP on entities, attributes, and relationships; bibliographic descriptions; access points; objectives and functions of the catalog; and foundations for search capabilities, among others.

The most extensive section of the ICP is called "Access Points." It notes that access points may be controlled or uncontrolled, the latter being such things as the title proper or keywords found anywhere in a bibliographic record. Names, titles, and other metadata needed for consistency in locating resources should be controlled, with variant forms used as references. The principles discuss choice of access points to include in a bibliographic description. They suggest that the titles of works and expressions should be controlled, as well as the names of the creators of works. The ICP also states that corporate bodies may be considered to be creators if works are expressions of the collective thought or activity of the body or if the wording of the title, in combination with the nature of the work, clearly indicates that the corporate body is responsible for the content. "Additional authorized access points for persons, families, corporate bodies, and subjects should be provided to bibliographic data, when deemed important for finding and identifying the bibliographic resource being described."[4]

When RDA was being developed, its creators explicitly acknowledged the ICP as one of the primary foundations for the content standard (along with the IFLA conceptual models),[5] and the ICP provided the basis for many of RDA's guidelines on description, access points, and authority control. Many of the objectives and principles listed in the introduction of Original RDA (e.g., cost efficiency, accuracy, sufficiency, representation, common usage or practice) directly mirror principles from the ICP.

8.2.2 *General International Standard Archival Description* (ISAD(G))

There are some major differences between describing archival materials and describing library resources. Aside from focusing on aggregate descriptions, archival materials usually do not have established or given titles, so the archivist must assign one. Additionally, archives generally contain a wide variety of different material types, including correspondence, photographs, newspaper clippings, reports, and so on. One set of principles for describing archival materials is provided by the *General International Standard Archival Description* (ISAD(G)),[6] an international standard for archival description that provides a content model for finding aids and is intended to serve as the basis for the development of national archival standards. In addition to outlining 26 metadata elements for use in finding aids, ISAD(G) outlines four principles intended to guide archival description:

- Description proceeds from the general to the specific.
- Information should be relevant to the level of description.
- Descriptions should be linked between levels.
- Information should not be repeated.

These principles are subsequently found in many archival descriptive standards that are considered to be ISAD(G) compliant, such as *Describing Archives: A Content Standard* (DACS) in the United States and *Rules for Archival Description* (RAD) in Canada, or are used directly as the basis for archival description (e.g., the Archives Hub in the United Kingdom).[7]

8.2.3 *Describing Archives: A Content Standard* (DACS)

Another set of principles for the description of archival materials is provided by DACS, a standard maintained by the Society of American Archivists (SAA). DACS's guidelines for description and authority control are discussed in Chapters 9 and 10 of this text, respectively. Over its history, DACS has offered two sets of principles, each of which provides context for the process of archival description. The original DACS principles contained the following statements.

1. Records in archives possess unique characteristics.
2. The principle of *respect des fonds* is the basis of archival arrangement and description.
3. Arrangement involves the identification of groupings within the material.
4. Description reflects arrangement.
5. The rules of description apply to all archival materials, regardless of form or medium.
6. The principles of archival description apply equally to records created by corporate bodies, individuals, or families.
7. Archival descriptions may be presented at varying levels of detail to produce a variety of outputs.
    7.1. Levels of description correspond to levels of arrangement.
    7.2. Relationships between levels of description must be clearly indicated.
    7.3. Information provided at each level of description must be appropriate to that level.
8. The creators of archival materials, as well as the materials themselves, must be described.[8]

These are very similar to the principles enumerated in RAD, the Canadian archival content standard, with seven of the eleven statements being identical.[9†]

Although there was nothing inherently wrong with the original set of DACS principles, in 2019 SAA approved a substantial revision to the statement of principles to bring them into better alignment with the values and objectives of the archival community.[10] The revised principles are

1. Archival description expresses professional ethics and values.
2. Users are the fundamental reason for archival description.
3. Because archival description privileges intellectual content in context, descriptive rules apply equally to all records, regardless of format or carrier type.
4. Records, agents, activities, and the relationships between them are the four fundamental concepts that constitute archival description.
5. Records must be described in aggregate and may be described in parts.
6. Record creators and other agents must be described sufficiently to understand the meaning of records.
7. Activities that are essential to understanding records must be described.

---

†Numbers 1, 3, 7, and 7.1 are not in RAD; instead, RAD includes: P1.0. Archival description should be undertaken with attention to requirements for use. P2.0. The description of all archival material (e.g., fonds, series, collections and discrete items) should be integrated and proceed from a common set of rules. P5.1. Levels of arrangement and description constitute a hierarchical system. P5.2. Descriptions should proceed from general to specific.

Description and Access

8. Archival description must be clear about what archivists know, what they don't know, and how they know it.
9. Archivists must document and make discoverable the actions they take on records.
10. Archival description is accessible.
11. Archival description should be easy to use, re-use, and share.
12. Each collection within a repository must have an archival description.
13. Archivists must have a user-driven reason to enhance existing archival description.
14. Archival description is a continuous intellectual endeavor.[11]

There are certainly some similarities between the two sets of principles, but the differences are more evident. There is an apparent shift from addressing more technical processes toward emphasizing archival description's context, use, impact, and audience. Notably, **respect des fonds**, the principle that the records of a given creator should be kept separate from other records, has been removed from the revised DACS principles. Although the introduction to the principles acknowledges the importance of *respect des fonds* as a foundation of archival practice, it also cautions that the application of the principle can "flatten existing complexity" in collections created or collected by multiple agents, and encourages archivists to look for ways to "document the web of activities by which records are collected and created, and by whom, from within and outside of the organization."[12]

8.2.4 *Cataloging Cultural Objects* (CCO)

Cataloging Cultural Objects (CCO) is a descriptive standard for art and cultural heritage collections. It includes guidelines for describing works (visual art, structures, objects, etc.) and images (visual representations) of those works. The following are the ten key principles of CCO.

1. Establish the logical focus of each Work Record, whether it is a single item, a work made up of several parts, or a physical group or collection of works. Clearly distinguish between Work Records and Image Records.
2. Include all the required CCO elements.
3. Follow the CCO rules. Make and enforce additional local rules to allow information to be retrieved, repurposed, and exchanged effectively.
4. Use controlled vocabularies, such as the Getty vocabularies and Library of Congress authorities.
5. Create local authorities that are populated with terminology from standard published controlled vocabularies as well as with local terms and names. Structure local authorities as thesauri whenever possible. Record and document decisions about local authorities.
6. Use established metadata standards, such as the VRA Core Categories or *Categories for the Description of Works of Art*.
7. Understand that cataloging, classification, indexing, and display are different but related functions.
8. Be consistent in establishing relationships between works and images, between a group or collection and works, among works, and among images.

9. Be consistent regarding capitalization, punctuation, and syntax. Avoid abbreviations, but when necessary, use standard codes and lists for abbreviations (for example, the ISO abbreviations for countries).

10. For English-language information systems and users, use English-language data values whenever possible.[13]

CCO's element set and guidelines for cataloging works and images are discussed in Chapter 9.

8.2.5 Cataloguing Code of Ethics

The "Cataloguing Code of Ethics" differs from some of the other principles discussed in this section in that, rather than focusing on general descriptive practices, it focuses on the ethical implications of metadata, with a goal of providing "an intentional decision-making framework for those who work in cataloguing or metadata positions."[14] The Cataloging Ethics Steering Committee began work on the code in 2019 and released a final version in January 2021. Its principles are informed by *critical cataloging*, a movement in the metadata community that focuses on understanding oppressive knowledge organization structures and making metadata more inclusive. The code includes ten ethical principles that are intended to guide and improve descriptive practice:

1. We catalogue resources in our collections with the end-user in mind to facilitate access and promote discovery.

2. We commit to describing resources without discrimination whilst respecting the privacy and preferences of their associated agents.

3. We acknowledge that we bring our biases to the workplace; therefore, we strive to overcome personal, institutional, and societal prejudices in our work.

4. We recognise that interoperability and consistent application of standards help our users find and access materials. However, all standards are biased; we will approach them critically and advocate to make cataloguing more inclusive.

5. We support efforts to make standards and tools financially, intellectually, and technologically accessible to all cataloguers, and developed with evidence-based research and stakeholder input.

6. We take responsibility for our cataloguing decisions and advocate for transparency in our institutional practices and policies.

7. We collaborate widely to support the creation, distribution, maintenance, and enrichment of metadata in various environments and jurisdictions.

8. We insist on diversity, equity, and inclusion in the workplace. We promote education, training, equitable pay, and a fair work environment for everyone who catalogues so that they can continue to support search and discovery.

9. We advocate for the value of cataloguing work within our organisations and with external partners.

10. We work with our user communities to understand their needs in order to provide relevant and timely services.

In the introduction to the code, it is noted that the Cataloging Ethics Steering Committee intends to publish a separate document containing case studies that demonstrate how the principles could be used to navigate ethical issues. However, at the time of this writing, this supplementary material has not yet been issued.

8.3 Some Preliminary Considerations

As mentioned above, the process of description, no matter the environment in which it is undertaken, begins with an examination of the resource to be described. This examination helps organizers get their bearings and gain an understanding of the tasks ahead. Getting a sense of the scope, size, form, and contents of a resource is good preparation for describing it. Joudrey, Taylor, and Miller state that the description process begins with a series of decisions or considerations.[15] For example, in libraries, a cataloger might begin by asking some of the following questions:

- What type of resource is this?
- How was it issued?
- Is the whole resource, or just a part of it, being described?
- From which sources should the metadata be taken?
- Is this a new resource?
- Is it related to other resources?
- What characteristics are important to describe?

It is necessary to determine exactly what is to be described. In CCO, the general guidelines encourage organizers to think about the resource systematically: "To catalog a work is to describe what it is, who made it, where it was made, how it was made, the materials of which it was made, and what it is about."[16] This directive is applicable to all information resources in all information environments. The organizer must always start with a simple question: "What am I describing?"

8.3.1 Resource Types

Until recently, catalogers began the description process by determining the resource type. A ***resource type*** is a category that reflects the nature or overall form of the resource (a book, a map, a serial, etc.). This designation determined the instructions to be followed when creating metadata for that resource (e.g., there were separate rules for maps and other non-book formats). The emergence of electronic resources, to some extent, threw many traditional resource-type designations into chaos. For example, it was no longer quite as straightforward to describe an online map published in parts over periods of time. Catalogers were not always sure which instructions to follow when a resource fell outside the parameters of a single well-defined resource type.

Although organizers are still concerned with identifying the type of resource in hand, it is no longer the primary determining factor in how something is described. In the early 2010s, the library cataloging content standard, *RDA: Resource Description & Access* (hereafter referred to as *Original RDA*) changed the focus so that the basis of description is no longer centered on resource types. Instead, RDA simplified the situation by looking at common characteristics across all resource types and by organizing the description around the different components of the IFLA conceptual models (e.g., *IFLA Library Reference Model* (LRM)).[17] RDA contains guidelines for describing a resource, regardless of whether it is a sound recording, manuscript, three-dimensional object, or some other type.

In other information environments, resource types also play a role. In cultural heritage collections using CCO, *work type* is an equivalent concept to *resource type*. "Work Type typically refers to a work's physical form, function, or medium (for example, sculpture, altarpiece, cathedral, storage jar, painting, etching)."[18] It is one of the required elements in a description. In archives using DACS, material types may be brought out in the title devised for the collection if one or two specific forms predominate.[19]

8.3.2 Resource Entities from LRM

Another concern, particularly in libraries, is whether organizers should describe a *work* (the intellectual creation) or an *item* (the physical resource). This is not a new concern; it has been around for decades. This issue was a source of debates between two cataloging giants, Seymour Lubetzky and Michael Gorman, before the publication of *Anglo-American Cataloguing Rules, Second Edition* (AACR2) in 1978. AACR2 and its editor, Gorman, came down firmly on the side of describing the item in hand. Lubetzky, whose work on the Paris Principles influenced the first edition of the *Anglo-American Cataloging Rules* (AACR), believed that the work should be the prime focus.

In the 1990s, IFLA took on the challenge of identifying whether to describe works, items, or something else. In 1998, it released its *Functional Requirements for Bibliographic Records* (FRBR) report, which addressed the issue.[20‡] The FRBR model identified four resource entities that are the products of creation and, therefore, may be described in metadata: *work, expression, manifestation,* and *item* (often referred to collectively as WEMI). LRM, the replacement for FRBR, changed many parts of the conceptual model, but the WEMI entities remain at the core of its representation of information resources. In contemporary library cataloging, the entity that is usually chosen as the starting point for cataloging is the manifestation, because the catalog record should reflect the characteristics of all the items in a set, not just those of a single item. For example, no one wants to create, "from scratch," a record for every copy of a book collected by tens of thousands of libraries across the country when one record for the manifestation can apply to them all. Although the starting point is the manifestation level, metadata elements specifically related to the work and expression are also included in resource descriptions, often as access points. In the case of rare materials, the physical characteristics of the item are described explicitly.

FRBR and LRM are library-centric conceptual models. They do not apply particularly well to the archival environment or to art and other cultural heritage materials. Concepts like *work, expression, manifestation,* and *item* may be useful for describing published resources—which may be issued in various versions or editions, each with identical or near-identical copies—but they are not as relevant to the unique items that archives and museums typically collect. The museum and

---

‡Please see Chapter 7 for a more complete review of FRBR and LRM concepts.

archives communities have their own conceptual models: CIDOC CRM and RiC, respectively. Both are discussed in Chapter 7.

8.3.3 Mode of Issuance

To create a description, organizers must determine the resource's mode of issuance. *Mode of issuance*[§] refers to

- how the resource is issued (e.g., Is the resource published in separate parts or issues? Is it distributed as one unit?),
- how the resource is updated (e.g., Are there supplements, and if so, are supplements discrete or integrating?), and
- whether there is an expected conclusion to the resource's publication (e.g., Is it an ongoing publication?).

Mode of issuance can be complicated to describe and has been represented in a variety of ways by different descriptive metadata standards. Before RDA was adopted, AACR2 divided resources into two mutually exclusive groups: (1) *finite resources*, those that are complete or have a predetermined conclusion, and (2) *continuing resources*, those that are ongoing (i.e., those which will have additions made to them without a predetermined end in sight). These two categories have also been referred to as **monographs** and **serials**, and they have had an organizational impact on technical services divisions for years. The monograph versus serial distinction has been used to set up working departments in many large academic libraries. In some cases, technical services units have been divided so that separate cataloging and acquisitions departments handle monographs, while serials departments handle both the acquisition and cataloging of serials. In other cases, technical services units have been divided into acquisitions and cataloging, with each of those departments further divided into serials and monographs sections.

When Original RDA was first adopted, it refined the traditional monograph versus serial distinction by introducing four categories to describe mode of issuance:

- ***Single Unit***: One physical resource that is complete unto itself is described as a *single unit*. For example, the textbook *Introduction to Cataloging and Classification* is a single unit. A single unit also may be referred to as a *monograph*.
- ***Multipart Monograph***: There are resources that are distributed in volumes or parts. Often, they follow one another in succession and have the same title. If these resources are limited in duration (i.e., they are meant to end), then they are known as *multipart monographs*. For example, volume 1 of *The Works of Shakespeare in Two Volumes* is probably not a describable unit by itself, but volumes 1 and 2 together are. Together they make up a multipart monograph. Or, in some cases, there are resources that come in a larger set with the same overarching title (although each can also have its own title); they may also be described as a unit. For example, *Great Books of the Western World* is a set where each volume has its own, often famous, author and title. It might

---

[§]The following definition reflects the common usage of the term *mode of issuance* in libraries. The RDA element of the same name has a somewhat more restricted scope, which is defined below.

be cataloged as one resource with multiple volumes (i.e., as a multipart monograph), or each volume might be cataloged separately (i.e., each as a single unit).

- *Serial*: There are also resources that are issued in successive volumes or parts, are known by the same title, are often numbered, and are meant to continue indefinitely. These resources are called *serials*. Serials include scholarly journals, newspapers, popular magazines, and other periodicals. For example, all volumes and issues of the journal *Library Resources & Technical Services* are described together in one catalog record as a serial.

- *Integrating Resource*: Finally, there are some resources that are considered single units, but their content is updated periodically. New material is inserted seamlessly into an existing resource in such a way that the discrete update disappears. These are referred to as *integrating resources* and include loose-leaf publications, databases, and websites.

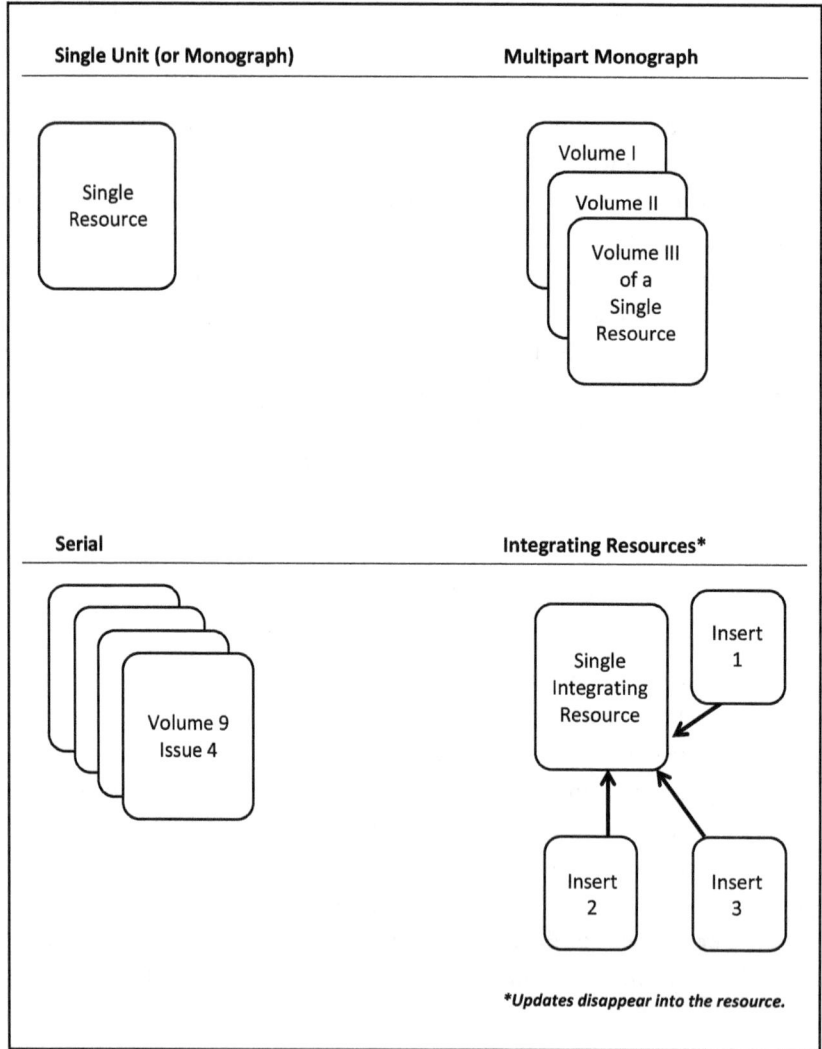

Figure 8.1 Modes of Issuance in Original RDA.

These modes are illustrated in Figure 8.1. Although RDA has since changed its approach to mode of issuance (as described below), these terms from the earlier version of the standard are still in common use; they continue to be a part of cataloging practice and remain useful for thinking through the characteristics of a resource being described.

A new, significantly revised version of RDA was published in 2020 (hereafter referred to as *Official RDA*),** which included a new way of modeling works issued over time. Instead of the four modes of issuance described above, RDA now defines only two modes of issuance: **single unit** (a resource issued as a single physical or logical unit) and **multiple unit** (a resource issued in multiple parts). A new term, ***diachronic work***, has been introduced to describe works that are intended to be embodied over time. Diachronic works include works traditionally thought of as serials and integrating resources, as well as multipart monographs that are issued over time. A ***static work***, in contrast, is intended to be embodied in a single act of production or publication. This category includes most monographs, including multipart monographs in which all the parts are intended to be issued simultaneously.

Official RDA also introduces a new element, ***extension plan***, which specifies whether a work is intended to be extended or changed over time, as well as how and when it is planned to end. RDA defines five types of extension plan:

- ***Static plan***: a resource in which all the content is embodied simultaneously, such as a novel or a photograph. Single-unit monographs and multipart monographs in which all the parts are issued at once are included in this category.

- ***Successive determinate plan***: a resource that is accumulated over time and has a definite planned end or termination point, such as a dictionary with multiple volumes that are published over several years. Multipart monographs that are issued over time are included in this category.

- ***Successive indeterminate plan***: a resource with content that is accumulated at intervals, with no predetermined end, such as a magazine, journal, or newspaper. Most serials fall into this category.

- ***Integrating determinate plan***: a resource where content is replaced, updated, or integrated over time with a definite intended endpoint; this includes some integrating resources, such as a project wiki or a conference website (assuming that the website will no longer be updated after the conference).

- ***Integrating indeterminate plan***: a resource with content that is replaced, updated, or integrated on an ongoing basis with no intended endpoint; this includes many integrating resources, such as a loose-leaf publication or a library website.

This new modeling is intended to allow catalogers to describe resources that are issued over time with greater precision. Official RDA's representation of different types of work by mode of issuance and extension plan is summarized in Figure 8.2.

**The development of RDA is discussed in Chapter 9.

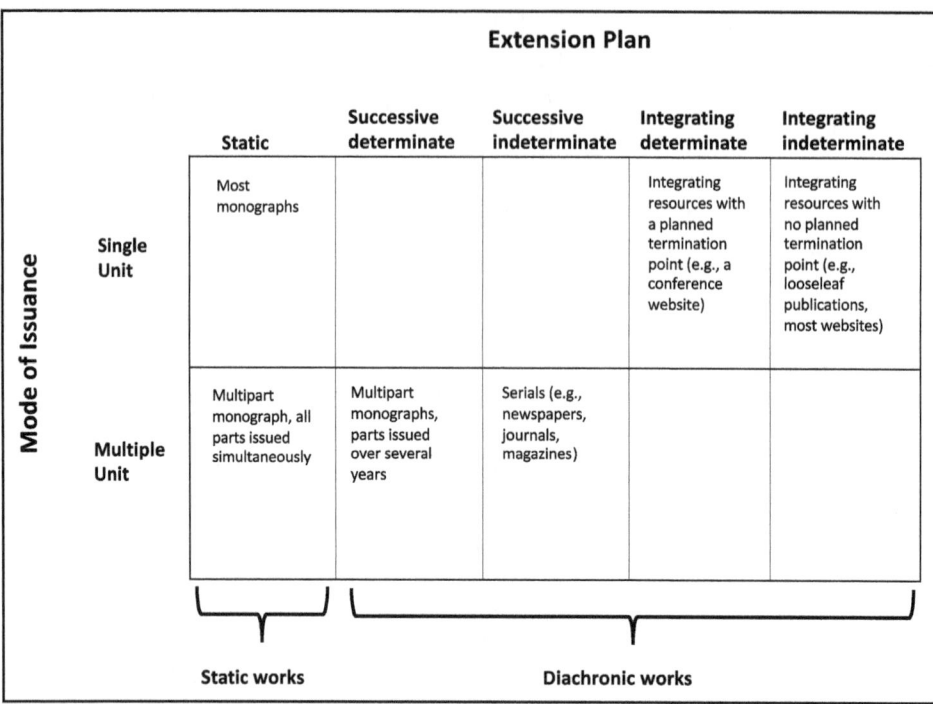

Figure 8.2 Mode of Issuance and Extension Plan in Official RDA.

8.3.4 Level of Description

Once a resource's mode of issuance and its extension plan have been determined, organizers must decide at which level to describe the resource. In libraries, typically there are three choices for a single resource.

- *Comprehensive Description*: This level entails describing the resource as a whole. The entire resource—not just a part—is described in the metadata. A single unit, a multipart monograph, a serial, and an integrating resource can be described comprehensively. For example, a 24-volume set of encyclopedias should be described comprehensively; creating separate records for each volume would not be especially helpful.

- *Analytical Description*: An analytical description means that only a part or a portion of the resource is described in the metadata. Again, this can be true of any resource, no matter its mode of issuance. Creating separate bibliographic records for each short story in a compilation of nine short stories is an example of creating analytical descriptions. As Original RDA states, "It is possible to prepare separate analytical descriptions for any number of parts of a larger resource (i.e., for one part only, for two or more selected parts, or for all parts of the resource)."[21] In indexing and abstracting services, this approach is used with journal indexing, where the article is the unit of description.

- *Hierarchical Description*: This entails describing the whole resource (made up of two or more parts) and the individual parts. It combines comprehensive and analytical descriptions. This level is not used in most libraries but dominates the descriptive approach in archives. The finding aid, the primary tool for description of and access to archival materials, is based on a hierarchical structure, in which the collection as a whole is described and then its parts.

Although these three categories are no longer present in Official RDA, the Library of Congress's RDA Metadata Guidance Documentation (MGDs)[††] acknowledges the need to ask the same types of questions.

> These three terms no longer exist in RDA. Instead, there is a decision about the level at which a cataloger can describe a work. Are you describing the complete work? Are you describing a part of [a] work? Are you describing the work at different levels of detail? How many records does that require? What relationships exist between those works and how should you express them?[22]

As mentioned previously, the three levels listed above are focused on the description of a single resource (i.e., manifestation- or item-level description). This, however, is not the only option for description. In many information environments, collection-level description (or collective description) may be preferable. ***Collection-level description*** entails creating metadata to describe more than one individual resource. This is the approach used in archives, where documents are described in the aggregate. In archives, collection-level description is used for both practical and intellectual reasons. On the practical side, many archival collections contain thousands of individual items; it would be very time consuming, expensive, and, at times, counterproductive to create an individual description for each piece of correspondence or each financial record in a collection. More importantly, on the intellectual side, archival documents may be understood and used more effectively in the aggregate, because the value of an archival record is enhanced by the relationships that connect it to the other records within the collection.

Collective description is used in libraries also. Sometimes, it is appropriate for special collections of unusual materials that are not traditionally described at the individual resource level (e.g., a collection of theater programs); sometimes, it may be used for low-priority resources (e.g., a box of donated paperbacks); and at other times, a library may use collection-level description as a temporary measure until full cataloging can be performed. In digital libraries, some collections of resources might be described in the aggregate (e.g., a collection of 500 digital photographs of postal scales), either permanently or temporarily. For some institutions, collection-level description is used to make some basic information about the collection available on the web. Museums, for instance, may provide rudimentary information about their entire collection (or parts thereof) on their websites to ensure some level of retrieval for the public through search engines.[23]

8.3.5 Sources

Another preliminary consideration is determining where to look for the most useful metadata. In library cataloging, much of the basic descriptive metadata about a resource is transcribed directly

---

[††]RDA Metadata Guidance Documentation is used in conjunction with the Official RDA Toolkit and the accompanying LC-PCC Policy Statements to provide examples and lengthier, narrative guidance than can be found in the policy statements. These supplementary materials to RDA are discussed in Chapter 9.

Table 8.1 Preferred Sources of Information According to Official RDA and the Library of Congress-Program for Cooperative Cataloging Policy Statements

Category of resource types	Examples	Preferred sources of information	If those are unavailable, then...
Resources comprising **pages**, **leaves**, **sheets**, or **cards** (or images of these)	Books, printed music, maps, manuscripts, posters, printed serials, sheets of microforms, flashcards, etc.	Title page, title sheet, or title card (or an image of these)	A cover/jacket issued with the resource, a caption, a masthead, or a colophon (or an image of these) or, if those are unavailable, then another source within resource.
Resources comprising **moving images**	Film reel, a DVD, a video game, an MPEG video file, etc.	Title frame or title screen	*If a tangible moving image resource:* (1) a label permanently affixed to the resource, (2) a container of the resource, (3) a digital menu, or (4) another source on any part of the resource. *If an online moving image resource:* (1) textual content, (2) embedded metadata in textual form that contains a title, or (3) another source within resource.
Other resources	Digital images, databases, globes, CDs, MP3 files, audio cassettes, objects, puppets, kits, websites, etc.	*If a tangible resource:* (1) a textual source on the resource or a label permanently affixed to resource (e.g., a label on an audio CD or a model), (2) an internal source, such as a title screen, (3) a container of the resource, or (4) another source on any part of the resource. *If an online resource:* (1) textual content, (2) embedded metadata in textual form that contains a title, or (3) another source on any part of the resource.	

from a ***preferred source of information***—the location in a resource where catalogers expect to find plentiful, rich metadata about that resource. RDA and supplemental resources such as the Library of Congress-Program for Cooperative Cataloging Policy Statements (LC-PCC PS) provide lists of preferred sources of information, based on broad categories of resources. If needed information is not found in one of the preferred sources, then alternative locations or features are consulted. Their guidelines for determining sources are summarized in Table 8.1.[24]

Archival and museum descriptive standards also articulate valid sources of information. DACS, the content standard used in the United States to guide archival description, states:

> All the information to be included in archival descriptions must come from an appropriate source, the most common of which is the materials themselves. In contrast to library practice, archivists rarely transcribe descriptive information directly from archival materials; rather, they summarize or interpolate information that appears in the materials or devise information from appropriate external sources, which can include transfer documents and other acquisition records, file plans, and reference works. Each element has one or more prescribed sources of information.[25]

In CCO, the object being described is the primary source of information about that object. Works of art, however, are not always complete in the information they contain about their origins, provenance, history, and so on. To supplement this, CCO expects catalogers to rely on outside scholarly sources to enhance descriptions—an approach similar to DACS's accompanying documentation. The sources used, when describing a resource according to the CCO guidelines, should be cited clearly in the metadata.[26]

8.3.6 Relationships

As the description process begins, organizers must also determine the relationships that a resource has to other entities, such as other resources, agents involved in the development of the resource, subjects discussed, and so on. It is important to identify who or what created, developed, presented, and disseminated the resource. Organizers must ask questions such as:

- Does this resource contain a new work or a new expression?
- Is it a new manifestation of a previously existing resource?
- Is this resource related to other resources? (e.g., Is it based on another work? Does it continue another work?)
- Is this resource part of a larger resource?

These questions will help organizers identify important bibliographic relationships and the necessary access points to supplement the basic descriptive data. These topics are addressed in the next section.

8.4 Access

In most online systems, keyword searching is available. If a user knows exactly what words or names have been used in a description, then keyword searching is successful. But users who do not know exact words or names must guess. This is sometimes successful and sometimes not. Why are keywords a problem in search systems? For a variety of reasons:

- Most words in the English language have more than one meaning, and most concepts have more than one word that represents them.
- Different users do not think of the same word(s) to express a concept, and different creators do not necessarily use the same word(s) to write about a concept.
- Persons and families do not necessarily retain the same name or same form of name throughout their existences, and corporate bodies do not necessarily use the same name or form of name in their documents, nor are they known by the same form of name by everyone.
- Different people, families, and corporate bodies have the same name, and many different corporate bodies use the same acronym.
- Titles of works that are reproduced, edited, or adapted are not always the same in the original and the new version.
- Titles are not unique; the same title can be given to very different works.

For all these reasons and more, libraries, archives, and museums prefer systematic consistency and predictability to the luck of keyword searching in their retrieval systems. An alternative to relying on keywords is to have specific formal ***access points*** (i.e., names, titles, subjects, etc.) that are chosen by the cataloger to provide retrieval of the metadata description.

One of the primary functions of access points is to represent relationships. Few information resources exist in total isolation. The majority have various kinds of relationships to other resources. For example, a resource may:

- have a creator who has also written other resources.
- have the same publisher or be in the same series as other related resources.
- originate in an institution where a research project has produced multiple reports concerning the same data.
- be a manifestation of the same work but in a different format or medium.
- have intellectual content that is the same or similar to that of another resource.
- be an adaptation, a translation, a commentary, a supplement, a sequel, or a teacher's guide to another work.
- be a part of a larger work, or conversely, contain a number of expressions of smaller works within it.
- be a performance of a work that also appears in written form.

Relationships abound in the bibliographic universe. Information systems operate on the presumption that if a user is interested in one resource, then they may be interested in others that are related to it. Therefore, successful document retrieval relies on having such relationships identified, at least implicitly, and retrieval is improved when such relationships are made explicit. When relationships are merely described (e.g., mentioned in a note)—or not even described—a user might discover those relationships only by chance. Access points make relationships explicit.

Access points need to be expressed consistently across records when the same word or name is used as an access point. To achieve this consistency, access points may be placed under **authority control** (the process of maintaining consistency in the strings used to represent persons, topics, etc.). A standardized string used to represent an entity consistently in bibliographic descriptions is called an **authorized access point** (AAP).‡‡ AAPs in bibliographic records allow for collocation and separation. A standardized access point brings together all the resources

- by a particular creator,
- containing a particular work or expression,
- on a particular subject, or
- in the same genre/form.

In other words, AAPs assist in meeting Cutter's objects of a catalog (described in Chapter 3) and the IFLA user tasks (introduced in Chapter 1). AAPs provide users with a greater understanding of the relationships among entities and the roles that various agents play in the development of resources.

The rest of the metadata world has also begun to see a need for access points, either with consistent form from record to record or with links to external resources that uniquely identify a person, corporate body, concept, and so forth. Much energy over the last three decades has been spent determining what descriptive metadata is needed for particular forms of information resources and how these descriptions can be encoded for display. As metadata accumulates to the massive numbers that library catalogs have been dealing with, the need for attention to problems of access to all this metadata becomes more apparent.

8.4.1 Types of Access Points

Typically, name access points are AAPs of the agents associated with a resource. Each agent has some type of relationship to the resource, which may be identified through a relationship designator (e.g., *author, artist, choreographer*) and, when MARC coding is used, through the MARC tag (e.g., 1XX for a primary creator; 7XX for subsequent creators and contributors). Title access points include both controlled and uncontrolled titles. A **controlled title** is one that has been established as part of authority work; it is used for work, expression, and series titles. An **uncontrolled title** is one that appears on a manifestation, such as a transcribed title proper. It can also include variant forms of a title proper (e.g., spine title, cover title, corrected title proper). Although **title proper** (i.e., the main title by which a manifestation is known) is an attribute for a resource, it can also be viewed as a relationship between the resource and the name(s) that it has been given. Controlled subject access points also represent relationships; for example, a subject heading reflects the relationship between a work and the thing(s) the work is about.

---

‡‡AAPs and authority control are discussed more fully in Chapter 10.

These relationships—these access points—make resources findable in the catalog in a consistent manner and provide collocation of related materials. In the future, it is likely that each AAP will be replaced by or at least supplemented with a standard identifier or an IRI rather than relying on a structured text string alone.

8.4.2 Relationships between Agents and Resources

Organizers typically provide name access points for **agents** (including people, corporate bodies, and families) who contributed to the intellectual or creative content of the resource. In WEMI terms, this means that access points are made for agents who have a relationship at the work or expression level. On the work level, access points are used to identify **creators** who play a primary role in the creation of the resource's content, such as authors, composers, and artists. There is no restriction on the number of creators that can be recorded. Additional access points may also be made for other agents associated with the work (e.g., recipients of correspondence, supervisors of theses and dissertations). On the expression level, access points are made for agents who contributed to the realization of the resource (commonly referred to as **contributors**), such as editors, illustrators, translators, performers, and so on.

There are other possible relationships between agents and the WEMI entities, but these relationships are usually not, at this time, identified through controlled access points. These roles include publishers, producers, manufacturers, distributors, owners, custodians, and others who may be related to manifestations and items in some other fashion. In a typical bibliographic description today, this type of data is transcribed as an attribute (e.g., publisher's name) or is recorded as a note rather than being treated as an access point. Access points tend to focus on entities that are considered bibliographically significant—those who made important contributions to the content, as opposed to the physical production or dissemination of the resource. This, however, may change in the future.

8.4.3 Relationships between Resources

In addition to representing relationships between resources and the agents who created them, access points identify relationships between information resources. Library cataloging has long provided rules for such access points; however, research to formally identify and categorize relationships began only in the 1980s. In her research, Barbara Tillett developed a taxonomy of bibliographic relationships.[27]

- **Equivalence relationships**: found in exact reproductions of the resource's content; these include copies, issues, facsimiles, reprints, photocopies, microforms, audiotapes of sound recordings on disc (if it is the same content), and other such reproductions
- **Derivative relationships**: found in modifications based on particular expressions or works; include new editions, revisions, adaptations, changes of genre (e.g., dramatization of a novel), new works based on the style or thematic content of other works, and the like

- **Descriptive relationships**: found in descriptions, criticisms, evaluations, or reviews of a work; include book reviews, annotated editions, critiques, commentaries, and so forth
- **Whole-Part relationships**: found in a component part of a larger work or in the relationship between a work and each of its various parts; include selections from anthologies or collections, articles from journals, maps in atlases, series that contain independent works, and so on
- **Accompanying relationships**: found in bibliographic resources that are created for the purpose of complementing particular works; they can complement equally, or one work can be the principal or predominant work; include resources with supplements (e.g., teacher's manual for a textbook), software manuals or help programs, concordances, indexes, parts of a kit, and other such complementary relationships
- **Sequential relationships**: found in bibliographic resources that continue or precede other resources; include successive titles of a serial, sequels and prequels of a movie, parts in a numbered series, and the like
- **Shared characteristic relationships**: found in any resources that coincidentally share characteristics in common, such as common creators, titles, dates, subjects, language, country of publication, and so on

Following upon Tillett's research, others have used empirical research to refine definitions and further delineate ways in which such relationships could be explicitly linked in retrieval tools.[28] For example, Richard Smiraglia presented the following taxonomy of Tillett's derivative relationships:[29]

- **Simultaneous derivations**: works published in two editions nearly simultaneously, such as a British edition and a North American edition of the same work; may have different titles, different sizes, or other differing characteristics
- **Successive derivations**: works revised one or more times and issued anew with statements indicating revision, as well as those issued successively without such statements
- **Translations**: works presented in languages other than the original
- **Amplifications**: original works that have been augmented by illustrations, musical settings, commentaries, and so forth
- **Extractions**: works presented in smaller forms, such as abridgments, condensations, and excerpts
- **Adaptations**: resources that modify original works; for example, simplifications, screenplays, librettos, arrangements of musical works, and so on
- **Performances**: sound or visual recordings of works, each of which may differ in such things as tone, amplification, and interpretation

Making such relationships explicit requires formalized rules for creating and applying a unique identifier for a work and, possibly, connecting devices such as cross-references.[30] This, of course, requires a consistent definition of *work*, which eluded organizers and researchers until the end of the twentieth century.³¹ Original RDA's identifier, in most cases, is a standardized *name/title access point*, consisting of the name of the work's primary creator and the preferred title for the work. In cases where a creator's name is unknown, a title-only access point suffices. These work identifiers often require the addition of qualifiers or relationship designators to make relationships explicit, and references are required to bring together variant forms of creators' names and titles.

8.4.4 Describing Relationships

To facilitate precise searching in an online environment, it is necessary to not only identify entities that have a relationship to the resource being described, but also to specify the nature of the relationship between entities. Original RDA addressed this with relationship designators. A *relationship designator* is a device (i.e., a label, phrase, or term) that clearly identifies the specific nature of the relationship that exists between entities; it provides additional context. Original RDA offered several long lists of relationship designators in its appendices, including designators to describe relationships between related works, expressions, manifestations, and items; relationships between WEMI entities and associated agents; and relationships between agents. Lists of relationship designators typically contain two reciprocal forms of each relationship type so that the relationships can be seen from either direction (e.g., *contained in / container of*).

In Official RDA, relationship designators have been replaced with relationship elements. A *relationship element* is an element that relates two RDA entities and specifies the nature of the relationship between them. This change, like many others connected to Official RDA, was made to facilitate more efficient processing by machines in a linked data environment. The new RDA relationship elements allow relationships to be described with more precision and to explicitly specify the types of entities connected by the relationship. For example, whereas Original RDA used the relationship designator *artist* to identify the creator of a visual work, Official RDA defines five possible relationship elements, depending on what type of agent created the work.

- artist agent
- artist person
- artist collective agent
- artist corporate body
- artist family

Although these relationship elements provide great precision for machine processing, they do not always function well as labels for catalog records and other displays intended to be read by humans. To address this need, the LC-PCC Metadata Guidance Documents (MGDs) include a set of relationship labels that provide more user-friendly terms that can be used for display of RDA metadata.³² A small sample of relationship designators, elements, and labels can be found in Table 8.2.

Description and Access

Table 8.2 Relationship Descriptors from Original RDA, Official RDA, and the LC-PCC MGDs

Original RDA Relationship Designator	Official RDA Relationship Element	LC-PCC Relationship Label
author *Inverse*: author of	**author agent** *Inverse*: author agent of **author person** *Inverse*: author person of **author collective agent** *Inverse*: author collective agent of **author corporate body** *Inverse*: author corporate body of **author family** *Inverse*: author family of	**author** *Inverse*: author of
translator *Inverse*: translator of	**translator agent** *Inverse*: translator agent of **translator person** *Inverse*: translator person of **translator collective agent** *Inverse*: translator collective agent of **translator corporate body** *Inverse*: translator corporate body of **translator family** *Inverse*: translator family of	**translator** *Inverse*: translator of
contained in (expression) *Inverse*: container of (expression)	**part of expression** *Inverse*: part expression	**part of** *Inverse*: part
video game adaptation of (work) *Inverse*: adapted as video game (work)	**video game adaptation of work** *Inverse*: adapted as video game work	**video game adaptation of** *Inverse*: adapted as video game

In the following excerpt from a MARC record for a 2018 English edition of *The Oresteia*, a trilogy of plays by Aeschylus originally written in Ancient Greek, one can see the relationship designators in use (highlighted in bold):§§

100	0#	$a Aeschylus, $e **author**.
240	10	$a Aeschylus. $t Oresteia. $l English
245	14	$a The Oresteia / $c a verse translation by David Mulroy, with introduction and notes.
264	#1	$a Madison, Wisconsin : $b The University of Wisconsin Press, $c [2018]
490	1#	$a Wisconsin studies in classics
700	1#	$a Mulroy, David D., $d 1943- $e **translator**, $e **writer of supplementary textual content**.
700	02	$i **Container of (expression)**: $a Aeschylus. $t Agamemnon. $l English.
700	02	$i **Container of (expression)**: $a Aeschylus. $t Choephori. $l English.
700	02	$i **Container of (expression)**: $a Aeschylus. $t Eumenides. $l English.
830	#0	$i **In series**: $a Wisconsin studies in classics.

AAPs, with relationship designators attached, provide a standardized way of representing the relationship between various agents and expressions and the resource being cataloged. The relationship designator *author* identifies Aeschylus as the primary author; relationship designators for *translator* and *writer of supplementary content* precisely denote the role played by David Mulroy in the realization of the resource. The relationship designator *container of (expression)* indicates that the resource contains the three separate translated plays listed in the data (each identified by a name/title access point), and the designator *in series* indicates a whole-part relationship with a publisher's series.

Once the agents responsible for the resource and any important bibliographic relationships have been identified and included as access points, the cataloger considers additional access points. These include titles proper, work titles, series titles, and variant titles (including cover titles, caption titles, running titles, titles on containers, title-bar titles, corrected titles, spine titles, and parallel titles). Subjects, as stated earlier, are also access points and are discussed in Chapter 12. The inclusion of access points makes resources findable in the catalog in a consistent and predictable manner. For an example of access points included in a full MARC bibliographic record, please see Figure 5.3 on page 175.***

Libraries are not the only information environment in which relationships are described. DACS encourages archivists to add access points for names, places, subjects, documentary forms (e.g., reports, diaries, correspondence, minutes), occupations, and functions (that is, activities, transactions, or processes) that are related to the materials being described.[33] DACS does not include

---

§§This example contains relationship designators from Original RDA. At the time of this writing, Official RDA has not yet been implemented.

***In Figure 5.3, personal name access points are found in the 100 and the first two 700 fields. The title proper access point appears in subfield a ($a) of the 245 field. Subject access points are in the four 6XX fields. The series access point is in the 830 field, and a name/title access point for a related work appears in the third 700 field.

a controlled set of terms to describe the nature of relationships beyond these general categories, though it does provide an option to describe the type of role played by a creator entity using terms from controlled vocabularies such as those found in RDA.[34]

In CCO, *creator role*, a required element, is used to describe "the role or activity performed by the creator in the conception, design, production, or alteration of the work."[35] CCO recommends that role terms should be drawn from a controlled list or authority file, such as the *agents* facet of the *Art & Architecture Thesaurus* (AAT). In addition to *creator role*, a CCO record may contain additional fields that provide information about the nature of the relationship, such as *creator display*, which can include a free-text account of the creator's role, and *attribution qualifier*, which indicates when the creator's role is uncertain in some way. It is also recommended to include a link to the creator's authority record when possible. For example:

Creator display: attributed to Michelangelo Merisi da Caravaggio (Italian, 1571–1610)
Role: painter
Qualifier: attributed to
Controlled Creator: Caravaggio, Michelangelo Merisi da, 1573–1610

This combination of fields makes it possible to provide nuanced information about relationships between creators and cultural heritage objects.

8.5 Common Attributes across Resource Types

Information resources have numerous attributes associated with them. Many attributes are useful in fulfilling the user tasks (i.e., find, identify, select, obtain, and explore). Other attributes, however, may not be important or necessary. Guided by metadata standards, organizers supply the most essential attributes in resource descriptions. What is considered most essential, however, varies among information communities, content standards, and schemas. What may be important to one community may not be important to another. For example, although a publishing company may find the name of the copy editor for a particular project to be important metadata in their record-keeping system, the same information is not considered significant when describing a book for a library. It all depends on the context. Although metadata may look somewhat different depending on the type of resource being described and the community that creates that description, there are consistencies to be found—that is, there are points of convergence among the various information environments. In the next sections, attributes common to many different resource types are enumerated and described.

8.5.1 Title, or, What Is It Called?

Most resources have a title. A *title* is a name that has been assigned to a resource by a creator, contributor, producer, owner, or, perhaps, someone else (e.g., an archivist). Identifying and finding a resource is much easier when the resource is called something. Some titles are descriptive (e.g., *Alternate Endings: Six New Ways to Die in America*, *Portrait of Cornelis van der Geest*, *Franklin D. Roosevelt Library Photographs, 1870–2004*), but some are less so (e.g., *Nope*, *Me Talk Pretty One*

Day, *Leviathan Wakes*), and others may be fairly unhelpful (e.g., *Untitled*). There are many kinds of titles, including but not limited to, the following:

- **Title Proper**: The main or primary title by which the resource is known (e.g., *The Brief Wondrous Life of Oscar Wao*).
- **Subtitle**: An additional title, subordinate to the title proper, that augments the title proper (e.g., *Tess of the D'Urbervilles: A Pure Woman, Faithfully Presented*).
- **Other Title Information**: An additional title, phrase, or statement that helps to qualify or amplify the title. All subtitles are a form of other title information, but not all examples of other title information are subtitles. For example, some other title information explains the form of the work (e.g., *A Moon for the Misbegotten: A Play in Four Acts*).
- **Devised Title**: The title provided by an archivist for a collection or by another information professional for an untitled resource (e.g., *Paul Hibbet Clyde and Mary Kestler Family Papers*).
- **Parallel Title**: A title proper that is repeated on the resource in another language or script (e.g., *Ma Vie en Rose = My Life in Pink*).
- **Alternative Title**: A second title for a resource that is joined to the first title with the word *or* (e.g., *Frankenstein, or, The Modern Prometheus*). Both titles together are considered to constitute the title proper of a resource.
- **Collective Title**: An inclusive title that represents a compilation (e.g., *Ten Days That Shook Scotland*) that contains two or more individually titled parts (e.g., ten essays about key moments in the history of Scottish football).
- **Conventional Collective Title**: A collective title referring to the form of the work used for a compilation containing two or more works by a person, family, or corporate body (e.g., *Plays, Works, Speeches*) or used for two or more parts of a work (e.g., *Selections*).

In addition, other titles exist, such as cover titles, corrected titles, spine titles, and so on. In CCO, rather than creating different elements for distinct types of titles, an additional element—Title Type—"provides a way to distinguish between the various types of titles (e.g., repository title, inscribed title, creator's title, descriptive title)."[36]

When recording titles, any number of issues may arise. Among other questions, organizers might ask: Where are titles found? If there is more than one, which title should be treated as the title proper? How are inaccuracies or typos addressed? Are introductory words or phrases recorded (e.g., Disney presents *Sleeping Beauty*)? If the archivist or cataloger must supply a title, what words, names, or concepts should be included? What if there are changes in a title over time (e.g., changes in a journal's title)? The answers to these questions may vary depending on the content standard used to guide the description.

8.5.2 Edition, or, Which Version Is It?

Once the name of the resource is understood, it is important to determine whether the resource has appeared in different versions. An ***edition*** is a particular version of a resource; it is all copies of a resource produced at the same time by the same entity using the same materials. Print materials, moving images, sound recordings, online resources, and other resource types might have version information associated with them. An *edition statement* is a declaration of the version; it is usually transcribed exactly as it appears on the resource itself, but may be taken from outside sources if needed. In art and cultural heritage collections, *edition* and *state* are elements that are used with artworks produced in multiples. *Edition* identifies a specific print in a limited run of identical artworks (e.g., 12/30, indicating this piece is the 12th of 30 identical pieces), and *state* refers to alterations or variations of the original version of a print or another work of art. Some examples of version metadata include the following:

- Eleventh edition
- 4th ed.
- Household edition
- Version 10.9.3
- Interactive version
- 22/400
- 7th of 10 states

When recording edition or version information, several issues may arise. Among other questions, organizers might ask: Where do I find edition information? How do I record statements of responsibility associated with an edition? Should I use abbreviations and numerals? What do these numbers mean? What are the equivalent concepts in other languages? For example, do *edition* and *edición* mean the same thing or are there differences between them?

8.5.3 Dissemination Information, or, Where Did It Come from and When?

Resource descriptions typically include information about the publication, distribution, presentation, manufacturing, or production of the resource. In short, our main concerns are

- Where is the resource from?
- Who or what published (manufactured, distributed, etc.) it?
- When was it made available?

The description, therefore, includes information about chronological periods associated with the dissemination of the resource, bodies responsible for the production of it, and geographic locations where the responsible parties are located.

In library cataloging, for tangible materials such as books and maps, the name of the publisher and the date and location of publication are included, whenever they are available. Additionally, manufacturing, production, and distribution information, as well as copyright dates, may be included if deemed important. For example, in a catalog record for a book, one might see something like the following publication statement:

> 264 #1 $a New York : $b Bloomsbury Libraries Unlimited, $c 2025.

In a Dublin Core description for the same resource, one might instead find this:

> <dc:publisher>Bloomsbury Libraries Unlimited</dc:publisher>
> <dc:date>2025</dc:date>

Aside from the display and encoding differences, the data is abbreviated because Dublin Core does not have a specific element for publication location.

In archives, publishers' names and locations (or those of a manufacturer or a distributor) are not likely to be recorded because archival collections are typically not considered published resources (although published materials may be part of the collection). On the other hand, dates are important pieces of data to be included. Dates may be associated with the collection as a whole (e.g., dates of creation, dates of acquisition) or with individual parts of the collection (e.g., dates for a particular series). In addition, locations associated with the collection (where it was created, assembled, accumulated, and/or maintained) and locations associated with those responsible for the collection are included in the description.

There are, as might be expected, numerous issues that can arise when recording dissemination information. Organizers may ask: What if there are multiple places of publication (distribution, manufacture, or production)? How much of the place name should be recorded? What if there are two or more corporate bodies listed as publishers? What is recorded for a self-produced resource? Can an individual person be a publisher? What if no dissemination information is provided at all? What do I do with all these dates?

In any repository type, date elements can be confounding. This is because there are so many kinds of dates. For example, one might encounter dates associated with

- Publication
- Distribution
- Manufacturing
- Construction
- Copyright
- Production
- Creation
- Design
- Presentation
- Performance
- Modification
- Alteration
- Access
- Activity
- Availability
- Recordkeeping activity
- Broadcast
- Display
- Exhibition

In addition to sorting through all the different kinds of dates, recording dates can be challenging. In a resource, any of the following forms of dates may be recorded.

- single years (1965)
- exact dates (15 January 1973)
- open dates (1941–)
- date ranges (1973–1981)
- approximate dates (2012?)
- approximate ranges (early sixteenth century)
- earliest and latest dates (1500 to 1530)
- uncertain or unknown dates

When confronted with problems related to dissemination information, one must remember that each metadata standard has its own set of elements and instructions for their use. How these problems are addressed varies among standards.

8.5.4 Physical Description, or, What Does It Look Like?

For all tangible resources and for many online resources, organizers are expected to describe the physical or electronic form of the resource. Usually, the organizer creates this metadata after examining the resource (e.g., counting, measuring, skimming). This metadata helps users to understand exactly what is being described. It tells them, for example, whether the latest Sufjan Stevens recording that they are seeking is available as an mp3 file, an AAC file, a wav file, a compact disc, a long-playing record album, or a reel-to-reel tape. In general, organizers want to know the following information about a resource:

- How many pages, volumes, documents, boxes, discs, objects, etc., are included?
- How big is the resource? What are its measurements?
- What does the resource look like, sound like, feel like, etc.? Is there color or sound? Are there illustrations? Is it digital? What are the techniques used to create it? What is it made of?
- What are the resource's content, carrier, and media types? What is its format?

The physical description of the resource, of course, varies depending on the type of material in hand. For example, a website and an archival collection require different kinds of data. Examples from a library, the web, an archives, and a museum follow:

> 300 ## $a 1 hand puppet : $b red and blue ; $c 20 cm + $e
> 1 teacher's booklet (14 pages ; 15 cm)
>
> <dc:type>image</dc:type>
> <dc:format>jpeg</dc:format>
> <dcterms:extent>1 photograph</dcterms:extent>
>
> **Extent**: 10 boxes
> **Extent**: 45 linear feet, including 200 photographs and 16 maps
> **Extent**: 1 box, 15 folders
>
> **Materials and Techniques**: pot-metal glass with vitreous paint
> **Dimensions Description**: 63.5 × 71.5 cm (25 × 28 1/8 inches)
>   **Value**: 63.5 **Unit**: cm **Type**: height
>   **Value**: 71.5 **Unit**: cm **Type**: width

8.5.5 Creator, or, Who Is Responsible for It?

Not only do resources need to be described, they also need to be connected with the agents responsible for their creation and development. Organizers, therefore, need to understand who or what is responsible for creating and contributing to a resource. The names and activities associated with creators and contributors are important pieces of information that should always be included in a resource description, if they are knowable and available. In some organizing traditions, this area of the description overlaps with the provision of access points for creators and contributors.

Creators and contributors may appear as part of the descriptive data and as access points added to the description. This is not, however, duplicate information. There are two different functions being addressed in these two forms of data. When the names of persons, families, and corporate bodies are included in the descriptive data, these are commonly included as part of a statement of responsibility. A *statement of responsibility* names the agents responsible for the intellectual or artistic content of a work, contributions to an expression, performances of the content, revisions of a work, and so on. A statement of responsibility is transcribed exactly as it appears on the resource. This allows the resource to be matched precisely to the description, helping to fulfill the user task *identify*. When these agents are also recorded as access points, their names are placed under authority control, and are, therefore, standardized. They do not necessarily reflect the form of name appearing on the resource itself, but they are necessary in the catalog for collocation of agents that may have used different forms of name at different points in their existences. For example, the title page of a book might provide the information shown in Figure 8.3.

A Modern Herbal:

The Medicinal, Culinary, Cosmetic and Economic Properties, Cultivation and Folk-Lore Of Herbs, Grasses, Fungi, Shrubs & Trees, With All Their Modern Scientific Uses With a New Service Index

by M. Grieve

with an introduction by
the editor Mrs. C. F. Leyle

New York
Hafner
1967

Figure 8.3 An Example of a Title Page.

From it, we could derive the following metadata:

> **Statement of Responsibility**: by M. Grieve
> **Subsequent Statement of Responsibility**: with an introduction by the editor Mrs. C.F. Leyle

The authority-controlled access points, however, for the same agents look a bit different:

> **Creator**: Grieve, Maud, Mrs.
> **Contributor**: Leyle, C. F., Mrs., 1890-1957.

In each case, the name is somewhat changed in the access point. The creator's name includes a first name and a term of address (Mrs.), and the name is entered in indirect order (i.e., it is inverted so that the last name or family name comes first). In the contributor's name, the order and the spacing are different, and birth and death dates have been added in the access point. Both museums and archives have similar issues in that they may include data from the resources being described as well as access points under authority control; that is, both controlled and uncontrolled forms of the same name may appear in the metadata for a resource.

8.5.6 Other Common Characteristics

In addition to those enumerated above, other characteristics common across resource types and communities include those reflecting the content of works, such as subject headings, thesaurus terms, classification notations, abstracts or summaries, scope and contents notes, tables of contents, genre/form descriptions, and culture, style, and language information. Subject matter and related characteristics are addressed in more detail in later chapters.

Many resources also have relationship and/or contextual information included in the description. This category includes attributes such as series information, accompanying materials, publication history, source and other relations, numbering information, biographical information or corporate history, provenance information, accession information, and custodial history. This data helps users to better understand the connections among resources and relevant background information.

Finally, every resource may have some administrative or identifying metadata that helps to locate and access the resource. This includes call numbers, shelf addresses, accession numbers, and standard identifiers (such as an Internationalized Resource Identifier [IRI], Uniform Resource Locator [URL], International Standard Book Number [ISBN], and so on). The common attributes described in this section are only just scratching the surface of descriptive elements. They are presented here at a very high level. More specific information about each of these and other areas can be found in the metadata standards themselves.

8.6 Conclusion

This chapter has addressed the descriptive part of metadata, which we have called *resource description*, including the use of formal access points to enhance discoverability. Libraries, archives, and museums have developed principles to inform resource description, support cataloger judgment, and guide the creation of descriptive standards. Although the creation of resource descriptions is somewhat dependent on the community for which the records are being created, some basic descriptive attributes are shared across different resource types.

In its discussion of the value of resource descriptions, the chapter concludes that they are most helpful when they are predictable in both form and content. Consistency in resource description is achieved by using shared standards. Whereas this chapter has provided a general introduction to resource description and the issues that accompany it, the next chapter addresses individual descriptive metadata standards that define descriptive elements and, in some cases, prescribe the form of content for those descriptions.

Some Important Terms in This Chapter
(Definitions Provided in the Glossary)

Access point	Diachronic work	Relationship designator
Agent	Edition	Relationship element
Alternative title	Element	Resource description
Analytical description	Extension plan	Resource type
Attribute	Hierarchical description	*Respect des fonds*
Authority control	Information resource	Serial
Authorized access point	Integrating determinate plan	Single unit
Bibliographic record		Static plan
Cataloging code	Integrating indeterminate plan	Static work
Collection-level description		Statement of responsibility
Collective title	Integrating resource	Subtitle
Comprehensive description	Metadata statement	Successive determinate plan
Content	Mode of issuance	Successive indeterminate plan
Content standard	Monograph	
Contributor	Multipart monograph	Surrogate record
Controlled title	Multiple unit	Syntax
Conventional collective title	Name/Title access point	Title
Creator	Other title information	Title proper
Critical cataloging	Parallel title	Uncontrolled title
Descriptive data	Preferred source of information	User tasks
Devised title		Value

Some Important Acronyms in This Chapter

AACR:	*Anglo-American Cataloging Rules*
AACR2:	*Anglo-American Cataloguing Rules, Second Edition*
AAP:	Authorized Access Point
AAT:	*Art & Architecture Thesaurus*
CCO:	*Cataloging Cultural Objects*
DACS:	*Describing Archives: A Content Standard*
DOI:	Digital Object Identifier
FRAD:	*Functional Requirements for Authority Data*
FRBR:	*Functional Requirements for Bibliographic Records*
ICP:	*Statement of International Cataloguing Principles*
IFLA:	International Federation of Library Associations and Institutions
IRI:	Internationalized Resource Identifier
ISAD(G):	*General International Standard Archival Description*
ISBD:	*International Standard Bibliographic Description*
ISO:	International Organization for Standardization
LC:	Library of Congress
LC-PCC:	Library of Congress-Program for Cooperative Cataloging
LC-PCC PS:	Library of Congress-Program for Cooperative Cataloging Policy Statements
LRM:	*IFLA Library Reference Model*
MGD:	Metadata Guidance Documentation
MODS:	Metadata Object Description Schema
RAD:	*Rules for Archival Description*
RDA:	*Resource Description & Access*
SAA:	Society of American Archivists
URI:	Uniform Resource Identifier
URL:	Uniform Resource Locator
VRA:	Visual Resources Association
WEMI:	Work-Expression-Manifestation-Item
XML:	Extensible Markup Language

8.7 Discussion Questions and Exercises

- How do principles of description and access differ across information communities?
- Select one of the preliminary considerations from section 8.3 and discuss:
  - What is the issue? How might it impact resource description?
  - How have different information communities approached this issue?
- What purpose do access points serve in the online environment? Why designate access points when keyword searching is available?
- What descriptive attributes are common across different resource types?

8.8 Suggested Readings

Baca, Murtha. "A Picture Is Worth a Thousand Words: Metadata for Art Objects and Their Visual Surrogates." In *Cataloging the Web: Metadata, AACR, and MARC 21*, edited by Wayne Jones et al., 131–8. Lanham, MD: Scarecrow Press, 2002.

Baca, Murtha, Patricia Harpring, Elisa Lanzi, Linda McRae, and Ann Whiteside. *Cataloging Cultural Objects: A Guide to Describing Cultural Works and Their Images*. Chicago: American Library Association, 2006. Also available at: https://www.vraweb.org/cco.

Chan, Lois Mai, and Athena Salaba. *Cataloging and Classification: An Introduction*. 5th ed. Lanham, MD: Rowman & Littlefield, 2023.

Describing Archives: A Content Standard: 2019.0.3. Chicago: Society of American Archivists, 2020. https://saa-ts-dacs.github.io/.

Dublin Core Metadata Initiative. https://www.dublincore.org/.

Guenther, Rebecca S. "MODS: The Metadata Object Description Schema." *Portal: Libraries and the Academy* 3, no. 1 (2003): 137–50.

International Federation of Library Associations and Institutions, Meetings of Experts on an International Cataloguing Code. *Statement of International Cataloguing Principles (ICP)*. 2016 edition. The Hague: IFLA, 2016. http://www.ifla.org/files/assets/cataloguing/icp/icp_2016-en.pdf.

Joudrey, Daniel N., Arlene G. Taylor, and David P. Miller. *Introduction to Cataloging and Classification*. 11th ed. Santa Barbara, CA: Libraries Unlimited, 2015.

Moulaison, Heather Lea, and Raegan Wiechert. *Crash Course in Basic Cataloging with RDA*. Santa Barbara, CA: Libraries Unlimited, 2015.

Svenonius, Elaine. *The Intellectual Foundation of Information Organization*. Cambridge, MA: The MIT Press, 2000.

Tillett, Barbara B. "Bibliographic Relationships." In *Relationships in the Organization of Knowledge*, edited by Carole A. Bean and Rebecca Green, 9–35. Dordrecht, The Netherlands: Kluwer Academic, 2001.

Wilson, Patrick. "The Catalog as Access Mechanism: Background and Concepts." In *Foundations of Cataloging: A Sourcebook*, edited by Michael Carpenter and Elaine Svenonius, 253–68. Littleton, CO: Libraries Unlimited, 1985.

8.9 Notes

All URLs accessed April 2025.

1. International Federation of Library Associations and Institutions (IFLA), Meeting of Experts on an International Cataloguing Code, *Statement of International Cataloguing Principles (ICP)*, 2016 edition (The Hague: IFLA, 2016), http://www.ifla.org/files/assets/cataloguing/icp/icp_2016-en.pdf. [Henceforth cited as ICP.]
2. *RDA: Resource Description & Access* (Chicago: American Library Association, 2010). Primarily accessed in the subscription product RDA Toolkit, http://www.rdatoolkit.org/. [Henceforth cited as RDA.] In lieu of page numbers, any references to specific parts of RDA are made using instruction or citation numbers (depending on which version is being discussed).
3. Daniel N. Joudrey, Arlene G. Taylor, and David P. Miller, *Introduction to Cataloging and Classification*, 11th ed. (Santa Barbara, CA: Libraries Unlimited, 2015), 52–61.
4. ICP, 8.
5. Joint Steering Committee for the Development of RDA, "Historic Documents: Outcomes of the Meeting of the Joint Steering Committee Held in Washington, DC, 16–20 October 2006," https://www.rdatoolkit.org/archivedsite/0610out.html.
6. International Council on Archives, *ISAD(G): General International Standard Archival Description*, 2nd ed. (Ottawa: International Council on Archives, 2000), https://www.ica.org/app/uploads/2024/01/CBPS_2000_Guidelines_ISADG_Second-edition_EN.pdf.
7. "ISAD(G)," JISC Archives Hub, https://archiveshub.jisc.ac.uk/isadg/.
8. *Describing Archives: A Content Standard*, 2nd ed. (Chicago: Society of American Archivists, 2013), xv–xix.
9. *Rules for Archival Description*, Revised version (Ottawa: Bureau of Canadian Archivists, 2008), xxiii–xxv.
10. Society of American Archivists, "May 20–22, 2019, Council Meeting Agenda," https://www2.archivists.org/groups/saa-council/may-20-22-2019-council-meeting-agenda.
11. *Describing Archives: A Content Standard*, 2019.0.3 version (Chicago: Society of American Archivists, 2022), xiii–xvii, https://mysaa.archivists.org/productdetails?id=a1B5a00000heUDGEA2. [Henceforth cited as DACS.]
12. DACS, xii.
13. Murtha Baca, Patricia Harpring, Elisa Lanzi, Linda McRae, and Ann Whiteside, on behalf of the Visual Resources Association, *Cataloging Cultural Objects: A Guide to Describing Cultural Works and Their Images* (Chicago: American Library Association, 2006), 2–3, https://www.vraweb.org/cco. [Henceforth cited as CCO.]
14. Cataloging Ethics Steering Committee, "Cataloguing Code of Ethics," 2021 version, American Library Association Institutional Repository, https://alair.ala.org/handle/11213/16716.
15. Joudrey, Taylor, and Miller, 161.
16. CCO, 3.
17. Pat Riva, Patrick Le Boeuf, and Maja Žumer, *IFLA Library Reference Model: A Conceptual Model for Bibliographic Information* (The Hague: IFLA, 2017), https://www.ifla.org/resources/?oPubId=11412. [Henceforth cited as LRM.]
18. CCO, 48.
19. DACS, 17–18.
20. International Federation of Library Associations and Institutions, IFLA Study Group, *Functional Requirements for Bibliographic Records* [FRBR]: *Final Report* (Munich: Saur, 1998), https://www.ifla.org/publications/functional-requirements-for-bibliographic-records. [Henceforth cited as FRBR.]

21. RDA 1.5.3 Analytical Description.
22. Program for Cooperative Cataloging, "*Resource Description & Access* (RDA) Metadata Guidance Documentation: Basic Cataloging Decisions," Library of Congress, updated May 30, 2024, https://www.loc.gov/aba/rda/mgd/index.html.
23. Heather Dunn, "Collection Level Description: The Museum Perspective," *D-Lib Magazine* 6, no. 9 (2000), http://www.dlib.org/dlib/september00/dunn/09dunn.html.
24. RDA, "Data Provenance" and accompanying LC-PCC Policy Statements (citation number 25.29.25.23, accessed July 10, 2024), https://access.rdatoolkit.org/Home/. [Accessible by subscription only.]
25. DACS, 1.
26. CCO, 248.
27. Barbara B. Tillett, "A Taxonomy of Bibliographic Relationships," *Library Resources & Technical Services* 35, no. 2 (April 1991): 156.
28. For more in-depth treatments of bibliographic relationships, see: Elaine Svenonius, *The Intellectual Foundation of Information Organization* (Cambridge, MA: MIT Press, 2000), 98–106; and Richard P. Smiraglia, *The Nature of "A Work": Implications for the Organization of Knowledge* (Lanham, MD: Scarecrow, 2001), 35–52.
29. Smiraglia, 42.
30. Svenonius, 95–7.
31. See Martha M. Yee, "What Is a Work?" *Cataloging & Classification Quarterly* 19, nos. 1–2 (1994) and *Cataloging & Classification Quarterly* 20, nos. 1–2 (1995); Smiraglia, *The Nature of "A Work"*; and FRBR.
32. Program for Cooperative Cataloging, "*Resource Description & Access* (RDA) Metadata Guidance Documentation: Relationship Labels," Library of Congress, updated April 25, 2024, https://loc.gov/aba/rda/mgd/relationshipLabels/index.html.
33. DACS, xix–xxii.
34. DACS, 28.
35. CCO, 96.
36. CCO, 50.

Chapter 9

Standards for Description and Access

Information resources may be described according to community-specific or project-related schemas. Several examples of metadata standards from different communities are discussed in this chapter. The emphasis of this chapter is on the content component of each schema. The selection is not exhaustive, but illustrative. It must be remembered that metadata standards are frequently being revised, updated, and re-imagined. It is therefore important that readers consult official documentation for each standard to find the most current information.

The following standards are addressed.

- **Bibliographic and General Metadata Standards**
    - *RDA: Resource Description & Access* (2020)
    - *RDA: Resource Description & Access* (2010)
    - *International Standard Bibliographic Description* (ISBD)
    - *Anglo-American Cataloguing Rules, Second Edition* (AACR2R)
    - Dublin Core (DC)
    - Metadata Object Description Schema (MODS)
- **Archives Metadata Standards**
    - *General International Standard Archival Description* (ISAD(G))
    - *Describing Archives: A Content Standard* (DACS)
- **Other Domain-Specific Metadata Standards**
    - *Cataloging Cultural Objects* (CCO)
    - VRA Core
    - *Categories for the Description of Works of Art* (CDWA)
    - ONIX (Online Information Exchange)
    - Index and bibliography records

9.1 Bibliographic and General Metadata Standards

Metadata standards in the library field were developed long before the term *metadata* was ever uttered. Some of our modern guidelines for description and access can be traced back to rules developed by Anthony Panizzi of the British Museum in the first part of the nineteenth century.

Cataloging codes, however, existed before that, with the first national code having been developed in France in the aftermath of the French Revolution. Examples of such cataloging standards discussed here are RDA and AACR2. ISBD, a long-established metadata element set and content standard, is also described, although ISBD's influence has diminished in recent years with the advent of RDA. Machine-Readable Cataloging (MARC), the standard currently used to disseminate much bibliographic metadata in libraries, is discussed in detail in Chapter 5, as it is an encoding schema. As the need for metadata for other communities, especially for electronic resources in those communities, became apparent in the mid-1990s, the Dublin Core was conceived and developed as a general-purpose schema. MODS, another general-purpose schema, followed in 2002; it was offered by the Library of Congress (LC) as an alternative to Dublin Core and to MARC-encoded cataloging records.

9.1.1 *RDA: Resource Description & Access* (2020)[*]

RDA: Resource Description & Access is the latest in a long line of descriptive cataloging content standards.[†] The official version of RDA (hereafter referred to as *Official RDA*), released in 2020, is the result of a major restructuring project that began in 2017.[1] The RDA Toolkit Restructure and Redesign Project, known colloquially as "3R," was intended to overhaul the conceptual structure of the original RDA standard (hereafter referred to as *Original RDA*), which was first published in 2010. Original RDA was based on the IFLA conceptual models, particularly *Functional Requirements for Bibliographic Records* (FRBR) and *Functional Requirements for Authority Data* (FRAD); with the deprecation of those earlier models in favor of the *IFLA Library Reference Model* (LRM), it became necessary to restructure RDA to bring it into alignment with LRM's revised modeling of bibliographic entities. The 3R project also aimed to overhaul the technological infrastructure of the RDA Toolkit,[2] the online interface used to access RDA. Whereas the Original RDA Toolkit has a book-like chapter structure and a sequential numbering system, the Official RDA Toolkit is essentially a collection of entities, elements, and guidance documents, with no beginning, middle, or end. The Official RDA Toolkit is optimized for the Semantic Web and is fully integrated with the RDA Registry, which contains linked data representations of all the entities, elements, and controlled vocabularies associated with RDA.[3]

The restructured Official RDA Toolkit is divided into four sections:

- **Entities**: This section contains a page for each of the thirteen RDA entities (described in greater detail below), along with a list of data elements for each entity. Each element is described by a separate page that provides additional information about using the element to record data. The Entities tab, together with the Guidance section, contains the main content of the standard.

---

[*] This section was written by Emily Baldoni, M.A., M.S., Metadata Librarian, Milner Library, Illinois State University.
[†] As discussed in Chapter 6, content standards specify how metadata values should be recorded in a resource description. Content standards provide instructions for populating metadata content.

- **Guidance**: This section focuses on instructions that affect multiple RDA elements, and contains explanations and guidance that provide additional context for describing entities. This includes chapters on aggregates, data provenance, fictitious persons and non-human entities, recording methods, transcription guidelines, and user tasks, among others.
- **Policies**: These are policy statements developed by various national libraries and cataloging communities to supplement Official RDA and guide catalogers in which options to apply. Individual policy statements are also interlinked throughout the Toolkit and can be viewed side by side with the entity and element pages that they apply to.
- **Resources**: Additional documentation that does not fall into the entities, elements, or guidance categories can be found here. Among other resources, this section includes a glossary, a link to the Original RDA Toolkit, and *vocabulary encoding schemes* (that is, controlled vocabularies) defined by RDA. There are over 40 RDA vocabulary encoding schemes, including lists of controlled terms to express carrier type, content type, font size, frequency of continuing resources, mode of issuance, recording source, and type of binding, among many others.

In line with its objective of supporting the creation of RDF-compliant linked data, Official RDA's entities, elements, and instructions can be used to create both *metadata statements* and *metadata description sets*. A *metadata statement* is simply a piece of metadata that describes an entity using an RDA element, such as

Manifestation <has title proper> Sense and Sensibility

As can be seen from this example, RDA metadata statements can be easily mapped onto the RDF triple structure (subject-predicate-object): in this example, the manifestation being described is the subject, *has title proper* (the element) is the predicate, and the title *Sense and Sensibility* is the object.

A *metadata description set* is a collection of one or more metadata statements, such as the set of statements that constitutes a catalog record for an information resource, an authority record for a person, corporate body, or place, or a Wikidata entry for any of these entities. Metadata description sets may contain metadata statements for a variety of entities. For example, a metadata description set for the 2018 Penguin edition of *Sense and Sensibility* might include some of the following statements:

Subject	Predicate	Object
Work	<has author agent>	Austen, Jane, 1775-1817
Expression	<has language of expression>	English
Manifestation	<has title proper>	Sense and Sensibility
Manifestation	<has place of publication>	New York
Manifestation	<has publisher agent>	Penguin Books
Manifestation	<has date of publication>	2018

The statements that make up this metadata description set may be stored in a MARC record, a relational database, as linked data in an RDF triplestore, or some other format; Official RDA, like Original RDA before it, is **schema-neutral**—it can be used with any encoding standard. Official RDA further stipulates that a metadata statement or metadata description set constitutes a **metadata work**. This allows RDA elements to be used to create further statements about the metadata descriptions themselves—in other words, to create meta-metadata.

9.1.1.1 Entities

RDA defines thirteen entities that are the focus of bibliographic description. As previously stated, RDA's overall structure has changed based on revisions made to the LRM conceptual model,[4] and individual entity pages for most of the discrete LRM entities (agent, collective agent, expression, item, manifestation, nomen, person, place, time-span, and work) are now the basic structure of the standard. The top-level entity from LRM, *res*, has been replaced by **RDA Entity**, defined as "an abstract class of key conceptual objects in the universe of human discourse that are a focus of interest to users of RDA metadata in a system for resource discovery."[5] In other words, an RDA Entity is any entity that is a focus of bibliographic description. RDA Entity has eight sub-types, several of which have additional sub-types below them:

- *Work*: A distinct intellectual or artistic creation.
- *Expression*: A realization of a work in the form of alphanumeric symbols, musical notation, sound, image, movement, etc., or some other form.
- *Manifestation*: A physical embodiment of an expression of a work.
- *Item*: A single exemplar or instance of a manifestation.
- *Agent*: An entity who is capable of deliberate actions, or being granted rights, and of being held accountable for its actions. *Agent* has two sub-types:
    - *Person*: An individual human being who lives or is assumed to have lived.
    - *Collective Agent*: A gathering or organization of two or more persons that bears a particular name and can act as a unit. *Collective Agent* has two sub-types:
        - *Corporate Body*: A collective agent composed of persons organized for a common purpose or activity.
        - *Family*: A collective agent composed of persons related by birth, marriage, adoption, civil union, or similar legal status, or who otherwise present themselves as a family.
- *Nomen*: A label for an RDA entity, such as a name, title, access point, or identifier.
- *Place*: A given extent of space.
- *Timespan*: A finite period of time.

Almost all of these entities are drawn directly from LRM, with the exception of *corporate body* and *family*, which have been added as sub-types of *collective agent*. The resource elements (that is, WEMI) are very similar to those found in Original RDA. Dates and time periods were previously treated as **attributes** (that is, descriptive characteristics) used to describe other entities in Original

RDA; in Official RDA, *timespan* has been promoted to an entity that can itself be the subject of descriptions. The *nomen* entity is also new. Because it is closely related to authority control concepts, it will be discussed in greater detail in Chapter 10.

Each entity page in the RDA Toolkit begins with a brief definition and scope note for the entity, followed by a prerecording section that provides general information that must be considered before beginning a new description of an entity, including required elements for a minimum or effective description of the entity (levels of description are discussed in greater detail in section 9.1.1.5 below). The prerecording section also includes criteria for determining the **entity boundary** between two instances of the entity—that is, it defines what differences between entities necessitate a new description. For example, for the *person* entity, a significant difference in place or date of birth or death indicates a new description is necessary. The prerecording section is followed by a recording section, which includes lists of applicable recording methods (discussed in greater detail in section 9.1.1.3) and elements that can be used to describe the entity.

9.1.1.2 Elements

An **element** in RDA is "a specific aspect, characteristic, attribute, or relationship used to describe an RDA entity."[6] RDA defines over 3,000 elements to describe its thirteen entities, representing a significant increase from Original RDA. The specificity with which elements are scoped is in large part responsible for the high number of elements in Official RDA. For example, to express the relationship between a translator and an expression, RDA defines not just one element, but five separate elements each depending on the type of agent acting as translator:

- translator agent
- translator collective agent
- translator corporate body
- translator person
- translator family

Due to the specificity of elements in Official RDA, and the standard's preference for element names that reflect the entity they apply to, element names can sometimes be quite lengthy (e.g., *adapted as video screenplay expression*, which refers to an expression that is a screenplay of a video based on an expression of another work).

For each element, RDA defines a specific *domain* and *range*. **Domain** refers to the RDA entity that an element is used to describe. Elements can only have one domain; in other words, an element can only be used to describe *one* of the thirteen RDA entities. It cannot be reused with entities outside of that domain. **Range** refers to the type of RDA entity that is reflected in the value for that element. In the context of an RDF triple (or linked data statement), the domain reflects the subject, the element is the predicate, and the range is the object. A range, however, is not defined for every element, because not all objects of an RDF triple are entities; sometimes they are literals (i.e., strings of text).

Elements fall into two categories: *relationship elements* and *attribute elements*. A **relationship element** connects two RDA entities; both the domain and the range refer to an RDA entity. For example, the domain of the element *place of publication* is a *manifestation*; its range is *place*. An

Table 9.1 Selected Official RDA Elements for WEMI Entities

Entity	Elements	Notes
Work	access point for work	
	adaption of work	
	author agent	Also has sub-elements for various agent types (author collective agent, author corporate body, author family, author person)
	director agent	Also has sub-elements for various agent types
	inspired by	
	remake of work	
	subject	Also has sub-elements for various entity types (e.g., subject person, subject place, subject timespan)
Expression	access point for expression	
	colour	
	editor agent	Also has sub-elements for various agent types
	intended audience of expression	
	performer agent	Also has sub-elements for various agent types
	translation of	
	translator agent	Also has sub-elements for various agent types
Manifestation	digital file characteristic	
	dimensions	
	extent of manifestation	
	place of publication	
	publisher agent	Also has sub-elements for various agent types
	statement of responsibility	
Item	binder agent	Also has sub-elements for various agent types
	donor agent	Also has sub-elements for various agent types
	restriction on use of item	
	seller agent	Also has sub-elements for various agent types

attribute element, in contrast, is an element that simply describes an RDA entity by connecting it to a value, rather than to another RDA entity. For example, the element *biographical information* is used to provide information about the life or history of a person. Its domain is *person*, but it does not have a range, since its value is simply the biographical note, rather than another RDA entity. There are far too many elements to cover all of them here; readers are encouraged to consult the Official RDA Toolkit for a full list. A small sample of RDA elements for WEMI entities is available in Table 9.1.‡

Each element is described by its own element page in the RDA Toolkit. Element pages are structured similarly to entity pages, though there are a few differences. In addition to a brief definition, the definition and scope section contains an element reference block that includes the IRI from the RDA Registry for the element, its domain and range, and mappings to equivalent concepts or fields from Dublin Core, LRM, and the MARC 21 bibliographic and authority formats. The element reference section also includes one or more alternate labels for the element that are intended to be somewhat more user-friendly than the official element name. For example, the relationship element *adaptation of work* has the alternate label *is adaptation of work*; the element *translator agent* has the alternative labels *has translator agent* and *translator*. Instructions for recording data using the element are provided through a series of conditions and options, described in greater detail below.

9.1.1.3 Data Recording Methods

In Official RDA, four different data recording methods are identified. Not all of the recording methods, however, apply to every data element in RDA (e.g., you would not likely use an access point or an IRI for a copyright date). Individual element pages identify which recording methods may be used for the element. When there is a choice between several possible recording methods, it is expected that application profiles will provide additional guidance on which method to apply for a given element. The four recording methods include

- *Unstructured description*: An unstructured description is an informal string of narrative data. It could be a free-text note or a straightforward transcription of data directly from the source. "A significant expansion of the tenth edition published in 2006 by Arlene G. Taylor" is an unstructured description, as is "edited by Susan Hill" in a statement of responsibility. Official RDA outlines several possible transcription methods in its Guidance section, and also allows catalogers to use an alternative transcription method from an outside source.

- *Structured description*: A structured description is a formal string of organized or controlled data. This may include
  - Structured notes constructed using a string encoding scheme that prescribes the order of elements and their punctuation. A ***string encoding scheme*** is a set of rules or instructions used to convert two or more metadata values into a structured string (e.g., *International Standard Bibliographic Description* or ISBD).

---

‡Elements for *nomen*, *place*, *timespan*, and the *agent* entities will be discussed in greater detail in Chapter 10.

- Access points for names, titles, and subjects that are constructed according to a string encoding scheme or drawn from a vocabulary encoding scheme (a structured list of controlled terms, also known as a *controlled vocabulary*), such as the Library of Congress/NACO Authority File (LCNAF) or *Library of Congress Subject Headings* (LCSH).[§]
- Terms for concepts drawn from a controlled vocabulary, such as the RDA vocabulary encoding schemes.
- Values associated with a structured data type, such as numbers, dates, and times.

- **Identifiers**: An identifier is a machine-readable string that is uniquely associated with an entity and can be used to differentiate that entity from others within a particular domain or context. Identifiers can be locally or externally assigned. For example, **n 79151500** is a standard identifier attached to an authority record for a person; it can be used to represent that person. Other common examples include ISBNs, notations for controlled vocabulary terms, and system control numbers.
- **Internationalized Resource Identifiers (IRIs)**: An IRI is similar to an identifier in that it is a machine-readable string that is uniquely assigned to an entity to identify the entity and disambiguate it from others. But whereas identifiers are designed to be unique only within their local system, IRIs are globally unique identifiers that are intended to be used in the context of RDF semantics and linked open data.[**]

An example of how the four recording methods might be used to represent a single RDA entity is provided in Table 9.2. Depending on the requirements of the application profile and the system being used to input metadata, a cataloger could populate the *author person* element using any of the four recording methods.

Table 9.2 Different Recording Methods to Represent an RDA Entity

Recording Method	Example	Data Source
Unstructured description	Miguel de Cervantes	Transcribed from title page
Structured description	Cervantes Saavedra, Miguel de, 1547–1616	Authorized access point from LCNAF
Identifier	n 79100233	LCNAF control number
IRIs	http://id.loc.gov/rwo/agents/n79100233	LC Linked Data Service (id.loc.gov)
	https://www.wikidata.org/wiki/Q5682	Wikidata

[§] An ***access point*** is a word or phrase representing a name, title, or subject that is used to retrieve a resource. Access points are often placed under authority control. Types of access points are discussed in Chapter 8; construction of authorized access points is discussed in Chapter 10.

[**] For a fuller discussion of IRIs in the context of the Semantic Web and linked data, see Chapter 7.

9.1.1.4 Conditions and Options

Official RDA's instructions for recording data are presented in terms of *options*, *conditions*, and *condition options*, which may appear on entity pages, element pages, or within individual guidance chapters. This marks a significant change from Original RDA, which provides more conventionally structured instructions followed by a series of exceptions, alternatives, and optional additions/omissions. In contrast, in Official RDA, each individual instruction is presented as an ***option***—that is, a suggested way to record metadata, which the cataloger can choose to apply or not. In some cases, there may only be one option; in others, multiple options are provided. For example, Figure 9.1 shows the options for recording the script of an expression using an unstructured description.

These options provide three different ways of recording the script that the resource is written in (e.g., Latin, Cyrillic, Kanji, Arabic): a term indicating the script can be transcribed directly from the resource; details regarding the script can be recorded in an unstructured note; and/or details about the script can be recorded using the element *details of script*. More than one option can be applied. For example, a cataloger may choose to apply both the first and third options from Figure 9.1 by transcribing a term for the script from the resource and recording that information in the *details of script* element. RDA does not provide any guidance on which options to apply.

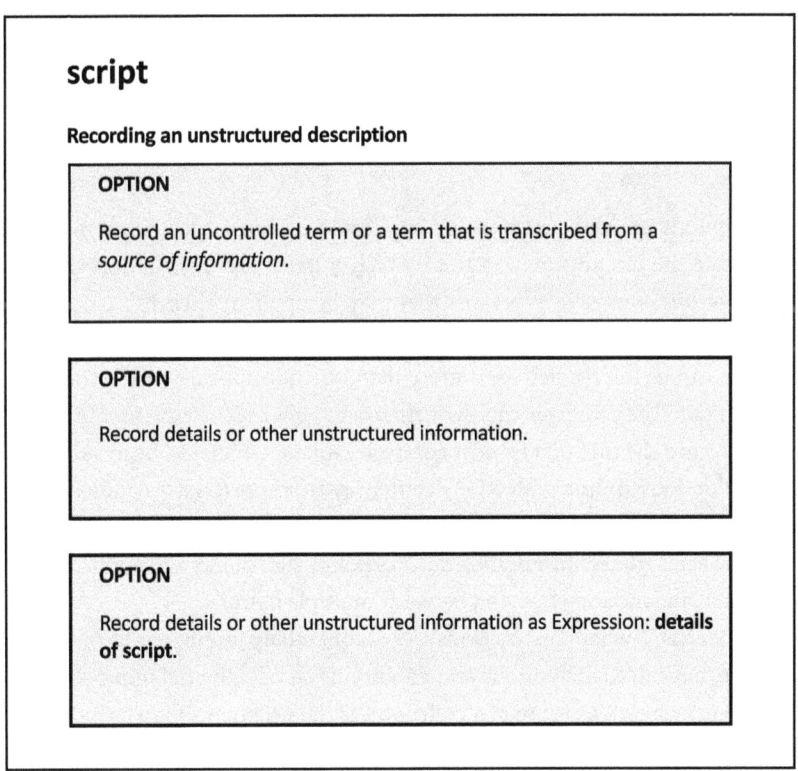

Figure 9.1 Options for Recording an Unstructured Description for Script.

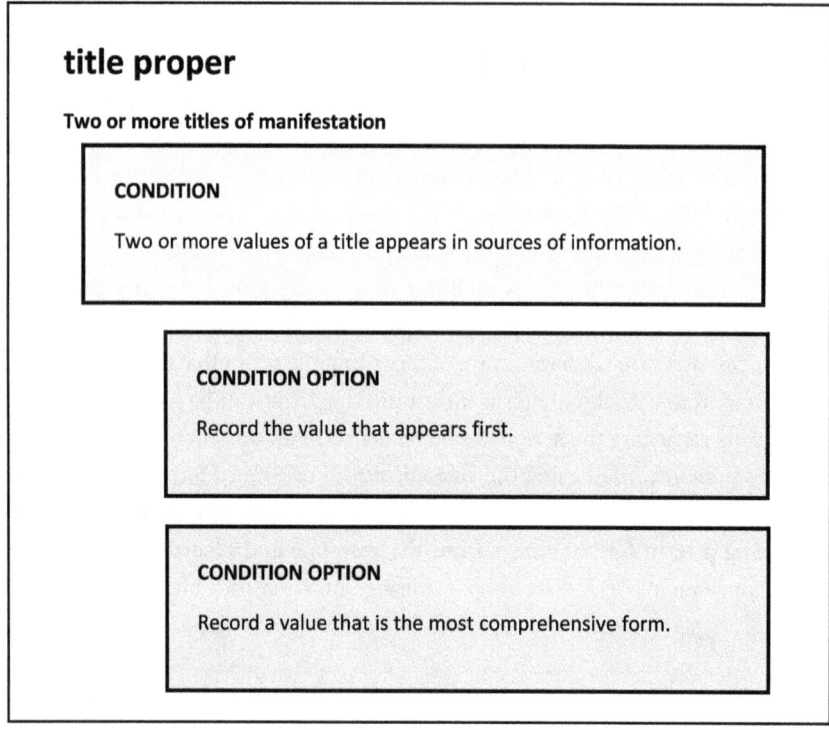

Figure 9.2 Conditions and Options for Recording Title Proper.

Sometimes options are only relevant or applicable under a specific scenario. In this case, **conditions** indicate the circumstances under which a particular instruction should be applied, and **condition options** convey instructions that may be applied when those conditions are met. Figure 9.2 shows an example of a condition and its condition options for the element *title proper*.

The condition can be interpreted as: if more than one title appears on the source, apply one of the following options. The cataloger can then choose to either record the first title that appears on the source or to record the title that is most complete. Again, Official RDA indicates no preference between the two options; in line with RDA's shift away from prescriptive guidelines, the standard offers many options, but few requirements. Supplementary materials produced by national libraries and individual cataloging communities, such as policy statements and application profiles, may provide additional guidance on choosing between multiple options.

Unlike Original RDA, where instructions were sequentially numbered to reflect the standard's chapter structure, Official RDA's options and conditions lack sequential numbering, reflecting the new standard's reorientation as more of a collection of data elements than a traditional cataloging code. Though the Official RDA Toolkit does have a mechanism for generating citation numbers for individual instructions, the citation numbers are randomly generated and do not reflect the overall structure of the Toolkit (e.g., the guidelines for recording the title proper of a manifestation with multiple titles are assigned the citation number 99.39.48.43, while the guidelines for recording the title proper of a multipart manifestation are assigned 66.01.29.53, even though the two sections are immediately adjacent to one another).

9.1.1.5 Levels of Description

Original RDA defined a set of key descriptive elements as *core*. Though Official RDA no longer uses this terminology, it defines several levels of description for describing information resources:

- **Coherent Description**: A description of an information resource that is well-formed (that is, it follows a basic subject-predicate-object structure) and conforms with RDA's guidance for relating its component entities (*work, expression, manifestation, item*). In other words, a coherent description conforms to the RDF data structure and is compatible with RDA's modeling of the WEMI entities.

- **Minimum Coherent Description**: A description of an information resource that meets the criteria for a coherent description and includes a description of at least one of its WEMI entities. That entity must be described by at least one **appellation element** (that is, an element that provides some kind of label for the entity, such as a name, title, access point, or identifier).

- **Effective Description**: A description that meets the criteria for minimum coherent description and includes additional elements or descriptions of related entities that are considered useful for identification or access.

RDA also defines criteria for a minimum description of individual entities (e.g., work, expression, manifestation, item, person, corporate body). The minimum description criteria vary from entity to entity, but in general consist of only one or two required elements, one of which is always an appellation element. For example, a metadata description set for a manifestation must contain at least one *appellation of manifestation* element or sub-element (e.g., a title, access point, or identifer) and must contain at least one *expression manifested* or *work manifested* element; a metadata description set for a person must contain at least one *appellation of person* element or sub-element (e.g., a name, access point, or identifier).

Official RDA contains little guidance on what constitutes an effective description. It is, in this sense, significantly less prescriptive than Original RDA, which included an extensive list of core elements for description. Instead, Official RDA shifts the responsibility to application profiles and other supplementary materials to determine additional criteria for what constitutes an effective description.

9.1.1.6 Supplementary Materials and Implementation Considerations

Official RDA is not intended to be used in isolation; instead, it is understood that individual metadata communities will design their own application profiles, policy statements, and metadata guidance documentation to guide implementation of the standard. An **application profile** is a document that specifies a community's best practices for metadata creation. It indicates which RDA elements are to be used, and whether they are required or repeatable; an application profile may also specify which recording method to use or prescribe a specific controlled vocabulary for use with individual elements. A metadata community may choose to create multiple application profiles to specify procedures for different types of materials (e.g., one for moving image works, another for early printed resources). One example is the *Music Library Association RDA Application Profile*, which defines best practices for describing musical resources using Official RDA.[7]

Policy statements are supplemental information sources that provide catalogers with guidance on how to interpret RDA instructions. Like application profiles, policy statements are developed by individual metadata communities to foster consistency in description. Policy statements were also developed for Original RDA; however, given the less prescriptive nature of Official RDA, policy statements are expected to play an even larger role in the implementation of the revised standard. Policy statements are particularly important for guiding catalogers in the choice of which options to apply. As of 2025, policy statements created by the British Library, Library and Archives Canada, the Library of Congress and the Program for Cooperative Cataloging (LC-PCC), the Music Library Association, and the National Library of New Zealand have been integrated into the Official RDA Toolkit. Policy statements can be accessed through the *Policies* tab of the Toolkit, or they can be viewed side by side with the RDA instructions to which they apply.

Figure 9.3 shows an excerpt of the guidelines for the *place of publication* element along with the LC-PCC Policy Statements (LC-PCC PS) that apply to them. In this example, RDA provides several options for how to record an unstructured description: catalogers may record the place of publication using basic or normalized transcription (both outlined in the Guidance section of the RDA Toolkit), or they can use some other set of transcription guidelines ("any transcription guidelines"). The associated LC-PCC PS indicates that catalogers should use normalized transcription and not apply the other transcription options; the final PS directs catalogers to record additional words or phrases under the circumstances specified in the statement.

In addition to policy statements, catalogers following LC-PCC practice have another resource for RDA cataloging in the RDA Metadata Guidance Documentation (MGDs).[8] The MGDs were developed to provide additional guidance and more detailed instructions that could not easily fit into the condition-option structure of the Official RDA Toolkit. The MGDs include narrative MGDs that provide instructions on describing specific entities and explain new concepts introduced by Official RDA, as well as 1:1 MGDs that are mapped to a specific LC-PCC PS and provide additional information about applying the policy statement. This supplementary documentation is intended to serve as a bridge between Official RDA's generalized, non-prescriptive instructions and the very specific guidelines often needed for everyday cataloging practice—not only for LC and members of the PCC, but also for the many U.S. libraries that follow LC-PCC practice for consistency and interoperability in shared databases like OCLC.

At the time of this writing, PCC plans to have a rolling implementation from May 1, 2024 to April 30, 2027.[9] In spite of the robust supplementary documentation, there are a number of barriers to implementation for libraries of all sizes, including cost (the Official RDA Toolkit, like the Original Toolkit before it, is a subscription-based tool), time needed to train staff to use the

Standards for Description and Access 317

place of publication

Recording an unstructured description

Record an unstructured description for a related place as a value of Place: **name of place**.

OPTION	LC-PCC
Record an unstructured description by transcribing text and spoken word content from a manifestation using Guidance: Transcription guidelines. **Guidelines on basic transcription.**	LC/PCC practice: Do not apply the option.
Record an unstructured description by transcribing text and spoken word content from a manifestation using Guidance: Transcription guidelines. **Guidelines on normalized transcription.**	LC/PCC practice: Apply the option.
Record a word or phrase that appears with a place name.	LC/PCC practice: Apply the option if the word or phrase is required to make sense of the place name.

Figure 9.3 An Excerpt from the LC-PCC PSs for Place of Publication.

new standard, and the often abstract language used by the Official Toolkit. Given these challenges, some libraries may delay implementation past the PCC date or may choose to forgo switching from Original RDA to Official RDA entirely. The cataloging community is likely to find itself in a hybrid environment for some time, where both Official and Original RDA are in active use for metadata production. Original RDA is described in detail in the following section. Table 9.3 summarizes some of the differences between Official and Original RDA. An example of Official RDA metadata created using guidance from the LC-PCC MGDs and policy statements is shown in Figure 9.4.

Table 9.3 Key Differences between Official RDA and Original RDA

	Original RDA	**Official RDA**
Conceptual Model	Based on FRBR and FRAD	Based on LRM

Entities	Follows FRBR's organization into three groups of entities:
	• WEMI resource entities
	• Agents: Persons, Families, and Corporate Bodies
	• Subjects: Concepts, Objects, Events, and Places (never fully developed)
		RDA Entity is a general entity supertype for all the other entities
		
		Revised organization of agent entities:
		• agent
		  ○ person
		  ○ collective agent
		    ▪ corporate body
		    ▪ family
		
		Timespan has been promoted from attribute to entity
		
		New *nomen* entity provides more robust modelling for appellation elements
		
		Subject entity group removed (only a revised *place* is retained as an entity)

Instructions	Instructions are sequentially numbered and follow a book-like chapter structure	Instructions lack sequential numbering (though the RDA Toolkit can generate citation numbers, they do not reflect structure)
	Instructions provide guidelines for cataloging practice, core elements, and are qualified by exceptions, alternatives, and optional additions and omissions	Instructions are significantly less prescriptive, presented as a series of conditions and options with no preference expressed for which options should be applied
Policy Statements	Policy statements are separate from the RDA text; links to policy statements appear alongside the relevant instructions	Policy statements can be viewed inline with relevant instructions or via separate Policies tab For catalogers following LC/PCC practice, LC-PCC PSs are supplemented by MGDs
Relationships *(discussed in Chapters 8 and 10)*	Relationship designators, provided in appendices, describe relationships between WEMI entities, between WEMI and agents, and between agents	Relationship elements are used to represent relationships between RDA entities and are integrated into the main text of the standard

	Original RDA	**Official RDA**
Mode of Issuance *(discussed in Chapter 8)*	Four modes of issuance are defined: • Single unit • Multipart monograph • Serial • Integrating resource	Works issued over time are modeled as *diachronic works* Two modes of issuance are defined: • Single unit • Multiple unit Five *extension plan* types specify whether a work is intended to be updated over time: • Static plan • Successive determinate plan • Successive indeterminate plan • Integrating determinate plan • Integrating indeterminate plan
Names, Titles, and Access Points *(discussed in Chapter 10)*	Names and titles are attributes of persons, families, corporate bodies, and WEMI entities Syntax (order of elements, punctuation, spacing) for access points is provided in Appendix E	*Nomen* (a label for any RDA entity) is a freestanding entity that can itself be the subject of metadata statements Appellation elements (*name, title, access point, identifier*) connect entities with the nomens that represent them Access point syntax is considered a type of string encoding scheme and is not prescribed
Fictitious Persons and Real Non-Human Entities *(discussed in Chapter 10)*	Fictitious persons and real non-human entities can be credited as creators and contributors of resources and can have access points and authority data created for them	The scope of the *person* entity is restricted to human beings who live or are assumed to have lived, excluding fictitious characters and non-human entities Fictitious persons credited with authorship are to be treated as pseudonyms of the agent responsible; non-human entities are external to RDA

Entity	Element	Metadata Content
Manifestation	title proper	Introduction to cataloging and classification
	statement of responsibility relating to title proper	Daniel N. Joudrey, Arlene G. Taylor, and David P. Miller
	designation of edition	Eleventh edition
	place of publication	Santa Barbara, California
	name of publisher	Libraries Unlimited
	date of publication	[2015]
	title of series	Library and information science text series
	mode of issuance	single unit
	identifier for manifestation	9781598848571 (hardback : acid-free paper) 9781598848564 (pbk : acid-free paper)
	media type	unmediated
	carrier type	volume
	extent of manifestation	xxv, 1048 pages
	illustrative content	illustrations
	dimensions	27 cm
	supplementary content	Includes bibliographical references (pages 1001-1022) and index.
Expression	content type	text
	language of expression	English
	summarization of content	This new edition reintroduces the topic of library cataloging from a modern perspective. This textbook delineates the new cataloging landscape; shares a principles-based perspective; provides introductory text for beginners and intermediate students; emphasizes descriptive and subject cataloging, as well as format-neutral cataloging, and covers new cataloging rules and RDA
	expanded version of expression	Expanded version of: Introduction to cataloging and classification. Tenth edition / Arlene G. Taylor ; with the assistance of David P. Miller.
Work	author person	Joudrey, Daniel N., author Taylor, Arlene G., 1941- author Miller, David P. (David Peter), 1955- author
	preferred title of work	Introduction to cataloging and classification
	identifier for work	https://id.oclc.org/worldcat/entity/E39PCGqjgm9CTXftWhtwXYjkCP
	part work	Cataloging in context -- Development of catalogs and cataloging codes -- Underlying principles and conceptual models -- Resource Description and Access (RDA) basics -- Manifestations and items ... [*Table of contents continues*] ... Appendix B: ICC11 RDA book template.
	based on work	Based on: Taylor, Arlene G., 1941- Introduction to cataloging and classification.
		Subject headings and classification data would also be included in the final metadata record.

Figure 9.4 An Example of Official RDA Metadata Recorded in a Template.

9.1.2 *RDA: Resource Description & Access* (2010)[††]

At the beginning of the twenty-first century, some catalogers felt that a new approach to describing resources was needed. The *Anglo-American Cataloguing Rules, Second Edition* (AACR2), the cataloging standard in use since 1981, was showing its age; its handling of electronic resources was awkward at best. Cataloging experts, also, believed there was a greater need to embrace principles-based cataloging, rather than continuing to use a standard that was rules based. (See Andrew Osborn's description of a legalistic approach to cataloging on page 69.)[10] No one, however, wished to completely dismantle the decades of work that had come before. A balance between approaches was needed.

RDA: Resource Description & Access[11] (aka Original RDA), published in 2010, was based on earlier cataloging standards. It represented an attempt to create a global approach to cataloging built upon

1. Anglo-American cataloging traditions as illustrated in AACR2,
2. IFLA's conceptual models, *Functional Requirements for Bibliographic Records* (FRBR)[12] and *Functional Requirements for Authority Data* (FRAD),[13] and
3. IFLA's *Statement of International Cataloguing Principles* (ICP).[14]

Much of Original RDA's content was based on the previous standard, AACR2, with which RDA was to remain backward compatible. Many of the actual cataloging instructions were the same, but the order and presentation of the instructions changed dramatically. From FRBR and FRAD, RDA employed their underlying entity-relationship model, the user tasks, and many of their entities, attributes, and relationships. From the ICP, RDA embraced basic principles, such as the Principle of Representation and the Principle of Convenience of the User. RDA combined the conceptual models and the principles into a foundation that allowed for greater use of cataloger's judgment in the creation of bibliographic metadata.

Although Original RDA appeared briefly in print, it was always intended to be a subscription-based electronic tool. The Original RDA Toolkit includes the text of the content standard, along with other features such as search functionality, workflows, policy statements, mappings, examples, archives of superseded instructions, and links to other related resources. After a period of thorough and rigorous testing, the U.S. national libraries (LC, the National Library of Medicine, and the National Agricultural Library) implemented it in early 2013.[15] Numerous academic, special, and public libraries in the United States also implemented RDA (though some libraries chose to remain using AACR2). By the mid-2010s, national (or other notable) libraries in nearly two dozen countries had adopted Original RDA.[16] Seven translations of the content standard are included in the Original RDA Toolkit: Catalan, Finnish, French, German, Italian, Norwegian, and Spanish. A Chinese translation is also available in print.

[††] Though Official RDA is intended to eventually replace Original RDA, at the time of this writing, Original RDA remains a predominant descriptive standard used for cataloging in the United States and other parts of the world. The following section therefore presents extensive background on the development, structure, and content of the earlier RDA standard.

Original RDA was intended to be more international in scope and to be schema-neutral. In other words, it was not meant to be as entirely Anglo-centric as AACR2, and it was meant to be implemented independently from any particular encoding standard or display format. Individual libraries can make choices about the scripts and languages used in bibliographic metadata, the transliteration approaches used, and the calendar and numeric systems employed. Being schema-neutral, RDA is not specifically tied to MARC, ISBD, BIBFRAME, or any other system. Thus, the instructions in RDA can be used to formulate descriptive metadata compatible with any chosen encoding format. Original RDA is not concerned with how data should be displayed. In the United States and other countries, the punctuation from ISBD is often used to create groupings of different elements in cataloging data. RDA does not require this type of display, but many libraries chose to implement it based on LC's decision to retain ISBD punctuation in its MARC records. In 2016, the PCC announced strategies to eliminate ISBD punctuation from MARC-encoded bibliographic metadata.[17] In January 2020, guidelines were released to address the creation of minimally punctuated MARC bibliographic records.[18] In short, the omission of the punctuation is considered optional. For more on ISBD, see section 9.1.3.

As a content standard, Original RDA provides guidelines on how to describe a resource. In previous content standards, the focus was primarily on creating descriptive data for a resource and on the choice and form of access points. In RDA, the description of other types of entities is included. There are individual chapters, for example, that address how to describe persons, families, and corporate bodies. These chapters list myriad attributes that can be used to create authority data for each of these types of agents. RDA also provides guidance for identifying relationships between entities.

The FRBR model's entities and relationships act as the skeleton for Original RDA. The content standard begins with a general introduction, with the rest of the chapters divided up into ten sections:

- Section 1: Recording Attributes of Manifestation & Item
- Section 2: Recording Attributes of Work & Expression
- Section 3: Recording Attributes of Agents
- Section 4: Recording Attributes of Concept, Object, Event, & Place
- Section 5: Recording Primary Relationships between Work, Expression, Manifestation, & Item
- Section 6: Recording Relationships to Agents
- Section 7: Recording Relationships to Concepts, Objects, Events, & Places
- Section 8: Recording Relationships between Works, Expressions, Manifestations, & Items
- Section 9: Recording Relationships between Agents
- Section 10: Recording Relationships between Concepts, Objects, Events, & Places

As can be seen, Sections 1–4 are dedicated to describing entities (i.e., works, expressions, manifestations, items, different agents, and subjects), and Sections 5–10 are focused on recording relationships. Most sections contain between one and five chapters. For example, Section 1 contains the following chapters:

- Section 1: Recording Attributes of Manifestation & Item

  1: General Guidelines on Recording Attributes of Manifestations and Items

  2: Identifying Manifestations and Items

  3: Describing Carriers

  4: Providing Acquisition and Access Information

The sections related to subjects, however, are mostly empty.

The chapters are broken down into logical components based on the nature of the chapter. Chapter 2, for example, begins with three introductory sections focused on the chapter's scope, the basis for identifying the resource, and sources of information, followed by an enumeration of the major attributes used to describe manifestations and items.

2.0   Purpose and Scope
2.1   Basis for Identification of the Manifestation
2.2   Sources of Information
2.3   Title
2.4   Statement of Responsibility
2.5   Edition Statement
2.6   Numbering of Serials
2.7   Production Statement
2.8   Publication Statement
2.9   Distribution Statement
2.10 Manufacture Statement
2.11 Copyright Date
2.12 Series Statement
2.13 Mode of Issuance
2.14 Frequency
2.15 Identifier for Manifestation
2.16 Preferred Citation
2.17 Note on Manifestation
2.18 Custodial History of Item
2.19 Immediate Source of Acquisition of Item
2.20 Identifier for Item
2.21 Note on Item

Each attribute may include a single metadata element or multiple sub-elements, each with one or more associated instructions. For example, under 2.8 Publication Statement there are entries for

2.8.1 Basic Instructions on Recording Publication Statement
2.8.2 Place of Publication
2.8.3 Parallel Place of Publication
2.8.4 Publisher's Name
2.8.5 Parallel Publisher's Name
2.8.6 Date of Publication

For each element, RDA provides a definition and the sources of information to consult, followed by basic instructions for recording the element.

Some elements are identified in RDA as core. A *core element* is one that is required in all descriptions (if the information is applicable and discernible). Some elements are always core, but others are considered *core-if*, meaning that the element is required only in certain circumstances. For example, the element *extent* is required, but only if the resource is complete or if the total extent is known. In the RDA Toolkit, a label identifies individual core elements in the instructions.

Carrier Type
CORE ELEMENT

RDA identifies nineteen manifestation-level elements as core. These are

- Title proper
- Statement of responsibility relating to title proper
- Designation of edition
- Designation of a named revision of edition
- Numeric/alphabetic designation of first issue or part of sequence
- Chronological designation of first issue
- Numeric/alphabetic designation of last issue
- Chronological designation of last issue
- Date of production
- Place of publication
- Publisher's name
- Date of publication
- Title proper of series
- Numbering within series
- Title proper of subseries
- Numbering within subseries
- Identifier for the manifestation
- Carrier type
- Extent

There are, of course, additional core elements for works, expressions, agents, and other entities. The complete list can be found in the instructions at RDA 0.6. It should be remembered that core elements represent the bare minimum for description. Conscientious catalogers record all the data needed to make a resource findable, identifiable, and understandable.

An instruction, unsurprisingly, is a statement that tells the cataloger what to do when transcribing or otherwise formulating the metadata. An example of a multipart instruction appears in Figure 9.5. Illustrative examples typically follow instructions or parts of instructions. In the Toolkit, examples are placed in textboxes to ensure that they are noticeable on the screen.

You may notice that an exception appears in Figure 9.5. *Exceptions* describe situations where the cataloger is expected to deviate from standard practice; exceptions are usually made for

---

2.12.2.3 Recording Title Proper of Series   LC-PCC PS

Record the title proper of series by applying the basic instructions on recording titles at 2.3.1.

> **EXAMPLE**
> Bartholomew world travel series
> Great sacred choruses
> Allstate simulation film library
> . . .

Record an alternative title proper of series as part of the title proper of series.

If the title proper of series includes numbering as an integral part of the title, transcribe the numbering as part of the title proper of series.

> **EXAMPLE**
> Publication #122 of the Social Science Education Consortium
> The twenty-sixth L. Ray Buckendale lecture
> Cuaderno número G del instituto

Exception
If:
    the resource being described consists of two or more issues or parts
  and
    numbering that is an integral part of the title proper of series differs from issue to issue or part to part
then:
    omit the numbering from the title proper of series. Use a mark of omission (…) to indicate such an omission. Record the numbering as numbering within the series (see 2.12.9).

> **EXAMPLE**
> Publication … of the Indiana University Research Center in Anthropology, Folklore, and Linguistics

---

Figure 9.5 An Example of an Original RDA Instruction. (Based on the layout of RDA 2.12.2.3 in the RDA Toolkit.)

specific situations or for particular resource types. Exceptions are always applied whenever the circumstances warrant it. In addition to exceptions, catalogers might also encounter alternatives and options. *Alternatives* provide a different approach to what was specified in the immediately preceding instruction. Options come in two flavors: optional additions and optional omissions. Obviously, *optional additions* allow catalogers to supplement the information required by the previous instruction with more data; *optional omissions* allow catalogers to omit some information called for in the preceding instruction when it is not absolutely essential for identifying the resource. Whether to apply alternatives and options is based on cataloger's judgment, local policies, or an existing policy statement (see below). In the Toolkit, exceptions, options, and alternatives are labeled with italicized lettering and a vertical bar in the left margin, as can be seen in Figure 9.5.

Also seen in Figure 9.5, next to the instruction number and its caption, is an icon that reads *LC-PCC PS*. In the Original RDA Toolkit, this is a link to a *policy statement*, which contains an interpretation of an instruction, guidance on applying alternatives and options, or a supplemental policy that applies to an instruction. Policy statements also identify additional core elements. The PS icon in the figure is a link to the Library of Congress-Program for Cooperative Cataloging Policy Statements (LC-PCC PSs). Many U.S. libraries that use RDA also follow the LC-PCC PSs so that their cataloging is consistent with that of LC and PCC libraries. This means that catalogers at these libraries not only include RDA's core elements in their descriptions but also the additional elements that LC and the PCC have determined should be required (if applicable and discernible). For example, the LC-PCC PSs add 19 more core elements for the description of manifestations:

- Parallel title proper
- Other title information
- Earlier title proper
- Later title proper
- Key title
- Abbreviated title
- ISSN of series
- ISSN of subseries
- Mode of issuance
- Frequency

- Note on title
- Note on issue/part
- Media type
- Dimensions
- Layout
- Digital file characteristic
- Note on changes in carrier
- Restrictions on use
- Uniform Resource Locator

In addition to the links to the LC-PCC PSs, there are also icons in the Toolkit that link to policy statements produced by the national libraries of Australia, Canada, Finland, Germany, Sweden, and the United Kingdom, as well as those provided by the Music Library Association.

Original RDA, like Official RDA, is not used in isolation. As discussed above, policy statements might be followed, although this is not required. Following LC practices, libraries in the United States implementing RDA are doing so using MARC as an encoding standard and ISBD punctuation as a display standard—at least for the time being. This should make it clear that library cataloging is a complex process that requires several different standards in order to be complete (and this does not even begin to address the subject analysis!). For a comprehensive overview of the process of descriptive cataloging using Original RDA, please see Joudrey, Taylor, and Miller's *Introduction to Cataloging and Classification*.[19]

RDA	Element	Metadata Content	MARC	ISBD
Manifestations and Items				
2.3.2	Title proper (T)	Introduction to cataloging and classification	245 $a	n/a
2.4.2	Statement of responsibility for title proper (T)	Daniel N. Joudrey, Arlene G. Taylor, and David P. Miller	245 $c	/
2.5	Designation of edition (T)	Eleventh edition	250 $a	n/a
2.8.2	Place of publication (T)	Santa Barbara, California	264 #1 $a	n/a
2.8.4	Publisher's name (T)	Libraries Unlimited	264 #1 $b	:
2.8.6	Date of publication	[2015]	264 #1 $c	,
2.12.2	Title proper of series (T)	Library and information science text series	490 $a	n/a
2.13	Mode of issuance	single unit	Ldr/07Value=m	
2.15	Identifier for manifestation	9781598848571 (hardback : acid-free paper)	020 $a	n/a
		9781598848564 (pbk : acid-free paper)		
Carriers				
3.2	Media type	unmediated	337 $a	n/a
3.3	Carrier type	volume	338 $a	n/a
3.4	Extent	xxv, 1048 pages	330 $a	n/a
3.5	Dimensions	27 cm	300 $c	;
Works and Expressions				
6.9	Content type	text	336 $a	n/a
Content				
7.10	Summarization of the content	This new edition reintroduces the topic of library cataloging from a modern perspective. This textbook delineates the new cataloging landscape; shares a principles-based perspective; provides introductory text for beginners and intermediate students; emphasizes descriptive and subject cataloging, as well as format-neutral cataloging, and covers new cataloging rules and RDA.	520 $a	n/a

Figure 9.6 An Example of Original RDA Metadata Recorded in a Template.

7.12	Language of the content	**English**	008/35-37 546	n/a
7.15	Illustrative content	**illustrations**	300 $b	:
7.16	Supplementary content	**Includes bibliographical references (pages 1001-1022) and index.**	500 $a 504 $a	n/a
Persons, Families, and Corporate Bodies (PFCs) Associated with Resource				
19.2	Principal or First-named Creator	**Joudrey, Daniel N., author.**	1XX $a	n/a
19.2	Additional creators	**Taylor, Arlene G., 1941- author.** **Miller, David P. (David Peter), 1955- author.**	7XX $a	n/a
Related Resources				
25.1	Related work	**Cataloging in context -- Development of catalogs and cataloging codes -- Underlying principles and conceptual models -- Resource Description and Access (RDA) basics -- Manifestations and items ...** [*Table of contents continues*] **... Appendix B: ICC11 RDA book template.**	500/505/7XX/490	
		Based on (work): Taylor, Arlene G., 1941- Introduction to cataloging and classification. **Library and information science text series.**		
26.1	Related expression	**Significant expansion of: Introduction to cataloging and classification. Tenth edition / Arlene G. Taylor ; with the assistance of David P. Miller.**	500/7XX	
Other Needed Metadata				
Subject headings and classification data would also be included in the final metadata record.				

Key: RDA: RDA instruction number
    Element: RDA element name; includes *Core*, *Core-if*, *LC Core*, and *ICC11 Core* for books
    (T): Transcribed data
    Metadata content: Place to record the data
    MARC: Typical MARC fields and subfields
    ISBD: Preceding ISBD punctuation when used in MARC

Figure 9.6 (*Continued*)

9.1.3 *International Standard Bibliographic Description* (ISBD)

Around the world, the *International Standard Bibliographic Description* (ISBD) has long been known as an internationally agreed upon cataloging standard that has been used as a format for the creation and sharing of bibliographic data.[20] ISBD was designed in the early 1970s to facilitate the international exchange of cataloging records by (1) standardizing the elements to be used in the description, (2) assigning an order to these elements, and (3) specifying a system of symbols to be used in punctuating the elements. Historically, there have been several ISBDs based upon different resource types.[21] Previously there were separate ISBDs for monographs, rare materials, serials, cartographic materials, electronic resources, and so on. Efforts to consolidate these separate ISBD standards began in 2003, and the consolidated edition was finalized and published in 2011. The most recent update, issued in 2021, is the current version of the standard (at least in 2025).[22] Translation efforts and harmonization with LRM and RDA are ongoing initiatives of the IFLA ISBD Review Group.[23]

When ISBD was adopted as an international standard, it was expected that national cataloging agencies would incorporate it into their cataloging rules. It has been widely adopted for use in many countries and incorporated into several sets of national cataloging rules, including AACR2. Joudrey, Taylor, and Miller state, "In countries without a national content standard, ISBD provides order out of what could be chaos."[24] It provides basic rules for recording the information needed for a sharable bibliographic record. It does not necessarily go into the level of detail found in national or international cataloging codes (like Official RDA), but it provides enough guidance to get the work done. In countries where a national or international cataloging code has been implemented, the role and importance of ISBD has been somewhat diminished. For example, because RDA has not adopted most of the substantial features of ISBD, it has largely been relegated to a system of punctuation with which online catalogs display their data.[25] As more countries show interest in Official RDA, it is unclear just what ISBD's significance will be in the future; perhaps one day it will disappear altogether from modern cataloging. As mentioned above, the PCC in the United States has discussed strategies to optionally eliminate ISBD from MARC-based cataloging.[26]

When used as a descriptive cataloging standard, ISBD requires that an information resource be totally identified by the description, independent of any access points. It contains nine areas of description:

> **Area 0**—Content form and media type
> **Area 1**—Title and statement of responsibility
> **Area 2**—Edition
> **Area 3**—Material or type of resource specific details
> **Area 4**—Publication, production, distribution, etc.
> **Area 5**—Physical description
> **Area 6**—Series
> **Area 7**—Notes
> **Area 8**—Resource identifier and terms of availability

There are two things to consider when using ISBD for creating resource descriptions. First, ISBD punctuation is prescribed, and it precedes and predicts the data element that comes next. For example, a space-slash-space in Area 1 says that the statement of responsibility is coming next. Second, each area contains more than one element, so the order of data is prescribed. For example, in Area 1 the prescription for content and punctuation includes the following:

> **Title : other title information / 1st statement of responsibility ; subsequent statement of responsibility**

It should be noted that prescribed punctuation is both preceded and followed by a space (except for commas and periods).

Area 0 identifies the form of the content and type of carrier that contains the resource being described. It comprises three elements: content form, content qualification, and media type. These elements provide an overview of what the resource is in terms of form of expression and carrier (storage or housing unit). Some of the elements are mandatory and populated with terms from prescribed lists. The following is an example of metadata recorded in Area 0:

> **Music (performed) : audio**

Area 1 contains titles and statements of responsibility. There may be more than one type of title needed (e.g., subtitle, part title, parallel title), as well as other supplementary information related to the title (e.g., information about the place and date of a conference). A statement of responsibility contains the names of agents responsible for the intellectual content of the resource, but not necessarily those responsible for presentation and packaging. For example, the name of the artist performing on a music CD would be included in Area 1, but not the name of the company that manufactured the CD. An example for a sound recording might look like this:

> **Acoustic Sondheim : live from Brooklyn / Eleri Ward**

Area 2 contains a statement about the version of the resource. It might be a new edition of a book, a new iteration of a software package, or a regional version of a resource (e.g., the city edition of a newspaper). Area 2 may contain a statement of responsibility relating only to the version being described (e.g., a person who has worked on the edition in hand but did not work on earlier editions).

> **Sixth edition / revised by Richard L. DeGowin**

Area 3 contains information that is unique to particular classes of resources. ISBD currently gives rules and examples only for serials, mathematical data for cartographic resources, and music format statements for notated music. For example, in describing serials, it is important to identify the date and the volume number of the first issue of the serial.

> **Vol. 1, no. 1 (Fall 1980)-**

Area 4 contains dissemination information, including the name of the publisher, producer, and/or distributor that is responsible for issuing the resource, along with the geographic location of the publisher, producer, or distributor. An important element in Area 4 is the date of the public appearance of the resource. This area may also contain data regarding manufacturing the resource.

Such data is given separately from the publication data if manufacturing is the work of a separate entity.

Burbank, CA : DC Comics, 2025

Area 5 contains a physical description of an information resource. The physical description includes the extent of the resource (e.g., 2 sound discs, 365 p., 4 videocassettes), the dimensions (often height, but also sometimes width, diameter, etc.), and other physical details such as information about illustrations or about material from which an object is made. Area 5 is also used to describe *accompanying material*, which is a physically separable part of the resource that is issued (or intended to be issued) at the same time.

xxxiii, 535 p. : ill., maps ; 25 cm + 1 answer book

Please note that the example above contains abbreviations. Using abbreviations for *pages* and *illustrations* is recommended practice in ISBD; in RDA cataloging, however, these abbreviations are not allowed.

Area 6 contains the title of a larger bibliographic resource of which the resource is part. This might be a series, subseries, or multipart monographic work. A series can be a group of separate works that are related in subject or form and/or are published by the same entity (e.g., *Library and Information Science Text Series*). There may also be information other than the title: a series title can have the same kinds of additional title information as in Area 1 and a series may have statements of responsibility that relate only to the series. If a series has an ISSN (International Standard Serial Number), it may appear in Area 6. Numbering of the resource within the larger resource set is also given in Area 6.

(CIHM/ICMH Microfiche series = CIHM/ICMH collection de microfiches ; no. 72002)

Area 7 contains notes relating to the resource being described. Notes may describe the nature, scope, or artistic form of the work; give the language or the audience of the text; identify the source of the title if there is no chief source of information; or explain relationships of this work to others. This area relies heavily on free text.

Includes index.

Originally published by Henmar Press as individual pieces; original copyright dates: 1960, 1977.

Illustrations colored by hand.

Area 8 contains a standard number that is used as a resource identifier. Typically, this is defined as a designation assigned by a publisher, or a number recognized as an international standard—which is often the International Standard Book Number (ISBN). The area may be repeated if more than one identifier may be important to users. The area also contains information about the terms of availability of the resource (e.g., free to members, but others must pay; unavailable to the public until fifty years after the death of the creator).

978-1-63715-072-6 (hardback)

Finally, we should say a few words about the formats that ISBD records take. In the ISBD standard, each area (after Area 0) may be set off from the next area by a point-space-dash-space.

> Text (visual) : unmediated
>
> Introduction to cataloging and classification / Daniel N. Joudrey, Arlene G. Taylor, and David P. Miller. — 11th edition. — Santa Barbara, California : Libraries Unlimited, 2015. — xxv, 1048 p. : ill. ; 26 cm. — (Library and information science text series). — Includes bibliographical references and index. — Significant expansion of: Introduction to cataloging and classification. 10th ed. / Arlene G. Taylor ; with the assistance of David P. Miller. — ISBN 978-1-598-84857-1

Or the areas may be set off by a new line or paragraph.

> Text (visual) : unmediated
>
> Introduction to cataloging and classification / Daniel N. Joudrey, Arlene G. Taylor, and David P. Miller. — 11th edition. — Santa Barbara, California : Libraries Unlimited, 2015.
> xxv, 1048 p. : ill. ; 26 cm. — (Library and information science text series). Includes bibliographical references and index.
> Significant expansion of: Introduction to cataloging and classification. 10th ed. / Arlene G. Taylor ; with the assistance of David P. Miller.
> ISBN 978-1-598-84857-1

Or ISBD information may be found in tabular form as seen in Table 9.4.

Table 9.4 Tabular Display of ISBD Metadata

ISBD Area	Metadata Content
Area 0	Text (visual) : unmediated
Area 1	Introduction to cataloging and classification / Daniel N. Joudrey, Arlene G. Taylor, and David P. Miller
Area 2	11th edition
Area 3	n/a
Area 4	Santa Barbara, California : Libraries Unlimited, 2015
Area 5	xxv, 1048 p. : ill. ; 26 cm
Area 6	(Library and information science text series)
Area 7	Includes bibliographical references and index. — Significant expansion of: Introduction to cataloging and classification. 10th ed. / Arlene G. Taylor ; with the assistance of David P. Miller
Area 8	ISBN 978-1-598-84857-1

In most instances, unless a card catalog is still in use, full ISBD formatting is rarely seen because the metadata is usually placed into MARC records. Displays that are based on MARC records are much more likely to have patron-friendly labels (e.g., **TITLE:** for Area 1). For more information on ISBD, please see the ISBD documentation found on IFLA's website[27] and Joudrey, Taylor, and Miller's *Introduction to Cataloging and Classification*.[28]

9.1.4 *Anglo-American Cataloguing Rules, Second Edition* (AACR2)

Until 2010, the *Anglo-American Cataloguing Rules, Second Edition*[29] was the descriptive cataloging standard for more than thirty years in the United States and other Anglo-American countries. If Official RDA replaces Original RDA, which replaced AACR2, you may be wondering why the earlier content standard is still being addressed in this book. At this time, even into the second iteration of RDA, not all libraries have switched from AACR2. For a variety of reasons—financial concerns, philosophical differences, simple intransigence—some libraries have chosen to continue using AACR2 rather than make the switch. Brief coverage of AACR2 may help newer information professionals understand some of the legacy data they may encounter.

Differences exist between AACR2 and both versions of RDA, especially in terms of overall structure and in the addition of access points to descriptions. AACR2's structure was not based on an IFLA conceptual model like LRM or FRBR. Instead, Part I: Description was based on an earlier version of ISBD. It closely follows ISBD's list of elements, their order, and the system of punctuation developed for interoperability. AACR2, though, was an expansion of ISBD, which supplied little more than definitions and examples at that time. AACR2 provided detailed rules on recording each of the elements and sub-elements.

Another major difference between the current RDA standards and AACR2 involves access points. The older rules call for access points for persons, corporate bodies, geographic names, and titles, as well as combinations of names and titles. Some specific access points called for by AACR2 include collaborators, editors and compilers, corporate bodies, titles (including titles of series), related works, and sometimes translators and illustrators. Yet, AACR2 also limited the number of access points in each category. For example, if there were four primary authors, only the first would be listed in the statement of responsibility and only the first would get an access point. Original RDA, on the other hand, simply calls for access points for all creators and contributors of importance, without limits on the number that may be used. AACR2's list of access points are book-oriented choices, reflecting the origins of AACR2, whereas in fact, many access points are for performers, choreographers, programmers, and cartographers, among others.

Another notable difference in AACR2 is the explicit use of the *main entry* concept.[‡‡] According to Seymour Lubetzky's Paris Principles—the foundation for AACR2's Part 2: Headings, Uniform Titles, and References—one of the access points chosen for a resource is selected to be the primary access point. This ***main entry*** is used to clearly and unambiguously identify the intellectual work found in the resource. This means the cataloger must identify the creator with the greatest responsibility for the development of the resource. For example, if a professor asks you

---

[‡‡] See Chapter 2.

to purchase the textbook *Introduction to Social Anthropology* for their class, it is helpful to know *whose* book you are looking for. It is much clearer which work is being referred to when they are distinguished by their main entries.

- Mair, Lucy, 1901-1986. Introduction to Social Anthropology
- Piddington, Ralph. Introduction to Social Anthropology
- Wissler, Clark, 1870-1947. Introduction to Social Anthropology

Identifying the primary creator, however, is not always possible. In those cases, AACR2 provides guidance in the choice of main entry. Sometimes, for example, the main entry is the first-named creator (for a work with up to three creators) or in some cases the main entry is the title; it all depends on the circumstances of creation. Often it is quite simple (e.g., if there is only a single creator, that creator is the main entry).

Although RDA does not use the term *main entry*, the concept persists. The reasons for establishing main entry include the following:

- to provide a standard citation to show relationships among resources, identify works about other works, and identify works contained in larger works
- to provide sub-arrangement under subjects and classification numbers
- to provide for collocation in the catalog of all manifestations containing the same work, even though the resources may be published with different titles (e.g., translations) or even when editions of a work have different authors
- to ensure selection of the most important and most predictable access point in situations where cataloging time has been reduced.

In a catalog record, a main entry is not enough to ensure that users will be able to retrieve the information they need. Additional access points, called **added entries** in AACR2, supplement the primary access point. For a comparison of some major differences between AACR2 and Original RDA, see Table 9.5.

For a more complete overview of AACR2, please see the third edition of *The Organization of Information* by Taylor and Joudrey.[30] For extensive guidance on using AACR2, please see the 10th edition of Arlene G. Taylor's *Introduction to Cataloging and Classification*.[31]

Table 9.5 Key Differences Between Original RDA and AACR2

AACR2	Original RDA
General material designations (GMD) provide an early warning that a resource is in a non-book format. The GMD is provided immediately after the title proper in square brackets.	Descriptions contain three elements that replace the GMD: • *Content Type* • *Media Type* • *Carrier Type*

AACR2	Original RDA
Often, the description requires the use of abbreviations (e.g., ill., ed., col., port., min., in., ft., b., d.), including Latin abbreviations, such as *et al.*, *s.l.*, and *s.n.* (for *et alia*, *sine loco*, and *sine nomine*).	In descriptions, RDA restricts the use of all abbreviations. Only abbreviations that appear on the resource may be transcribed. Typically, only abbreviations of dimensions and duration are recorded.
AACR2 employs the *rule of three*, meaning that if a resource has four or more names listed for any one activity in a statement of responsibility or as access points, only the first name gets included in the description. For example, "by Lois Lane … [et al.]."	RDA allows the description to contain as many names in the statement of responsibility as deemed appropriate. There is an option to limit the names and to be selective of which to include. For example, "by Lois Lane, Clark Kent, Jimmy Olsen, Lana Lang, Perry White [and twelve others]." As many access points as deemed necessary may be added to the bibliographic description.
AACR2 often encourages manipulating basic descriptive data. For example, typos are corrected in titles, words are omitted from statements of responsibility, and so on.	RDA's principle of representation means catalogers transcribe exactly what is seen on the resource without altering it.
AACR2 is used to describe the item in hand. Properties of the intellectual or artistic work are also addressed.	RDA is based on the FRBR model and addresses not only works and items, but is also used to describe manifestations, expressions, persons, families, corporate bodies, and places.
The term *author* is often used for those responsible for the creation of works.	When identifying those responsible for the creation of works, the more neutral term *creator* is used instead.
The term *heading* is used to refer to the standardized name established for an entity.	An *authorized access point* (AAP) is established for entities under the instructions in RDA.
Under the rules in AACR2, catalogers choose a *main entry* and a limited number of *added entries* as access points for the description.	In RDA, catalogers choose the *agents* responsible for a resource (e.g., creators and contributors). One agent is identified as the *primary* creator of the work (or the first-named, if primary responsibility is unclear or shared), when creating a name/title access point to cite a work.
There are no rules for families as creators.	Families can be considered creators of resources.
The relationship between an access point and the resource may be unclear.	Relationship designators (e.g., narrator, illustrator) may be applied to the access point to clarify the role played by the agent.

AACR2	Original RDA
When a compilation of individual works (e.g., short stories) lacks a collective title, the resource is entered under the author of the first work.	A compilation is usually entered in the catalog under its title, but if there is no collective title the cataloger constructs separate access points for *each* of the works in the compilation.
Authority work primarily consists of establishing an authorized name for an entity and its cross-references (with some additional data that may be needed to resolve conflicts).	Under RDA, besides establishing a name and cross-references, there are many additional elements about an entity that may be recorded (e.g., occupation, birthplace).

9.1.5 The Dublin Core (DC)

The Dublin Core[32] (shortened form of the Dublin Core Metadata Element Set [DCMES]) was born out of a workshop on metadata semantics held in Dublin, Ohio, in 1995. "At this event, called simply the 'OCLC/NCSA Metadata Workshop,' more than 50 people discussed how a core set of semantics for Web-based resources would be extremely useful for categorizing the Web for easier search and retrieval. They dubbed the result 'Dublin Core metadata' based on the location of the workshop."[33] The idea was to create an internationally agreed-upon set of metadata elements that could be completed by the creators of electronic documents, particularly web resources, which seemed particularly troublesome at the time.[34] The participants in the annual workshops and conferences that have developed and expanded DC are experts from many different fields (e.g., publishers, computer specialists, librarians, information scientists, software producers, text-markup experts). Therefore, it is a cross-domain standard and can be the basis for metadata for any type of resource in any field. It is meant for simple description at low cost; it provides just enough metadata to discover a resource, rather than an extensive or perfect description. It has been approved as ANSI/NISO Standard Z39.85-2012[35] and ISO standard 15836.[36] It is used internationally, and a number of application profiles have been developed for specific domain applications that use basic DC as a starting point. "Application profiles provide the rules that govern the creation and reuse of metadata instances. Their function is both to explain the metadata but also to potentially constrain the metadata so that correct usage can be determined."[37] DC can also be used as an exchange format between institutions that use differing metadata approaches.

The Dublin Core Metadata Initiative (DCMI), which is a project of the Association for Information Science and Technology (ASIS&T),[38] oversees the development of the standard. In its early years DC had been implemented primarily using HTML, but it is now implemented using RDF and XML. Templates have been developed that anyone can use to create DC metadata. Such templates can be filled in and previewed, and then XML-formatted data can be displayed for copying and pasting into a document header.[39]

The DCMES consists of 15 repeatable, optional elements.

- **Contributor**: an agent responsible for adding to or enhancing the content of the resource (e.g., editors, illustrators); the contributions, however, are secondary to those made by creators

- **Coverage**: identification of spatial locations, temporal periods, and/or jurisdictions reflected in the content of the resource
- **Creator**: an agent primarily responsible for developing the content of the resource (e.g., authors, researchers, artists, composers)
- **Date**: a date of an event in the lifecycle of the resource (such as creation date, availability date, or date of revision); it is recommended that a formal encoding scheme be used, such as the W3CDTF profile of ISO 8601 (Date and Time Formats)[40]
- **Description**: a textual statement of the content of the resource; this could be an abstract, a table of contents, a free-text account, or a combination of these
- **Format**: a designation of the physical medium, file format, or dimensions of the resource, such as the size or duration; recommended best practice is to select a value from a controlled vocabulary such as the Internet Media Types (also known as MIME types)[41]
- **Identifier**: a string or number that uniquely identifies the resource (e.g., URL, URI, IRI, DOI, ISBN); recommended best practice is to conform to a formal identification system
- **Language**: an indication of the language of the content of the resource; recommended best practice is to use the language tags defined in RFC 4646[42]
- **Publisher**: a name of the agent, institution, or repository responsible for making the resource available (e.g., person, publishing house, university)
- **Relation**: a reference to related resources along with an indication of their relationships to the described resource (e.g., a work that the described resource is part of, is referenced by); recommended best practice is to use a string or number from a formal identification system to identify the referenced resource (e.g., URL, URI, IRI, DOI, ISBN)
- **Rights**: a statement, link, or identifier that gives information about rights held in and over the resource (e.g., statement about intellectual property rights)
- **Source**: the related resource from which the present one is derived in whole or in part; as with *Relation*, recommended best practice is to use a string or number from a formal identification system to identify the referenced resource (e.g., URL, URI, IRI, DOI, ISBN)
- **Subject**: a topic reflected in the resource; use of controlled vocabularies and formal classification schemes is encouraged
- **Title**: the name of the information resource
- **Type**: a designation of the nature or genre of the content of the resource; recommended best practice is to select a value from a controlled vocabulary such as the DCMI Type Vocabulary (e.g., Dataset, Event, MovingImage, Text)[43]

A Dublin Core description is provided in Figure 9.7.

The general principles for using the DCMES include the following:

- the core set can be extended with further elements needed by a particular community,
- all elements are optional,

DC Element	Qualifier	Metadata Content
Identifier		ISBN: 9781598848571
	Citation	Joudrey, Daniel N., et al. Introduction to Cataloging and Classification. 11th ed. Santa Barbara, CA: Libraries Unlimited, 2015.
Title		Introduction to cataloging and classification
Title	Alternative	Introduction to cataloging and classification, 11th ed.
Creator		Daniel N. Joudrey
		Arlene G. Taylor
		David P. Miller
Contributor		
Subject	LCSH	Resource description & access
		Descriptive cataloging
		Subject cataloging
		Classification—Books
	DDC	025.3
	LCC	Z693 .W94 2015
Description		This new edition reintroduces the topic of library cataloging from a modern perspective ... [*Summary continues*].
	Table of Contents	Cataloging in context -- Development of catalogs and cataloging codes -- Underlying principles and conceptual models -- Resource Description and Access (RDA) basics -- Manifestations and items ... [*Table of contents continues*] ... Appendix B: ICC11 RDA book template.
Publisher		Libraries Unlimited
Date	Issued	2015
Type	DCMI Type	Text
		Image
Format	Medium	Book
	Medium	Volume
	Extent	xxv, 1048 pages
	Extent	27 cm
Source		Taylor, Arlene G. Introduction to cataloging and classification. 10th ed. Westport, CT: Libraries Unlimited, 2006.
Relation	IsPartOf	Library and information science text series.
	Replaces	Taylor, Arlene G. Introduction to cataloging and classification. 10th ed.
Language		eng
Coverage	Spatial	United States
	Temporal	21st century
Rights		Copyright © 2015 by Daniel N. Joudrey, Arlene G. Taylor, and David P. Miller

Figure 9.7 An Example of Dublin Core Data Recorded in a Template.

- all elements are repeatable,
- any element may be refined by *qualifiers* (that is, refinements that make the scope of the element more specific or identify a controlled vocabulary to be used with the element), but
- qualifiers cannot change the meaning of the element.

Additionally, DC embraces the *one-to-one principle*, which states that a description should refer to only one resource. Each element should be focused on the resource being described, not entities associated with that resource (e.g., the creator). The form of the content of each element, however, is not prescribed by Dublin Core. This means that those creating the descriptions can, in fact, do what they like. Although best-practice recommendations may be made, there is no agency enforcing compliance with these principles or other recommendations.

For a time, there were two competing camps within the DCMI community, each with strong advocates. The Minimalist camp wanted just the fifteen elements with no qualifiers. The Qualifiers camp insisted that refinements are useful and necessary. In a sense, both camps have won. The NISO standard contains just the 15 basic elements, but refinements (identified as *dcterms*) may be used as part of the system.[44] There are two broad classes of refinements now used.

- *Element Refinements*: qualifiers that sharpen the focus of an element, that is, they make the meaning of an element narrower or more specific
- *Encoding Schemes*: qualifiers that identify a controlled vocabulary or a data type that aids in the interpretation of an element value; these are referred to as *Vocabulary Encoding Schemes* and *Syntax Encoding Schemes*

A list of refinements is provided in the *dcterms* namespace. Some are used to qualify one of the 15 elements in the DCMES, but some may be used alone or in place of an element. Table 9.6 shows the DCMES, with qualifiers that apply to each element.[45]

Dublin Core is used worldwide. The DCMI currently supports several "communities" that bring together interest groups for people in a particular domain or who are engaged in specific topics within the DCMI framework.[46] In addition, the standard is used to organize resources ranging from simple websites to complex government information. It has been used in catalogs, databases, and digital collections. Application profiles based on DC have been created over the years. An example is the Library Application Profile, which defines required elements, permitted qualifiers and dcterms, permitted encoding or vocabulary schemes, additional elements from other metadata schemas (such as MODS), and so on.[47]

9.1.6 Metadata Object Description Schema (MODS)

The Metadata Object Description Schema (MODS) is a hybrid metadata standard that incorporates both an encoding scheme and a metadata structure standard. It was developed as an XML schema by the LC Network Development and MARC Standards Office in consultation with other experts.[48] It can be used to create original non-MARC bibliographic metadata records, or it can

Table 9.6 Some Refinements Used with the Dublin Core

DC Element	Refinements / Additional DC Terms	Encoding Schemes (Vocabulary or Syntax)
Contributor	n/a	n/a
Coverage	spatial	DCMI-Box; DCMI-Point; ISO 3166; TGN
	temporal	DCMI-Period; W3C-DTF
Creator	n/a	n/a
Date	available; created; dateAccepted; dateCopyrighted; dateSubmitted; issued; modified; valid	DCMI-Period; W3C-DTF
Description	abstract; tableOfContents	n/a
Format	extent; medium	Internet Media Types (IMT)
Identifier	bibliographicCitation	URI
Language	n/a	ISO 639-2; ISO 639-3; RFC 1766; RFC 3066; RFC 4646
Publisher	n/a	n/a
Relation	conformsTo; hasFormat; hasPart; hasVersion; isFormatOf; isPartOf; isReferencedBy; isReplacedBy; isRequiredBy; isVersionOf; references; replaces; requires	URI
Rights	accessRights; license	n/a
Source	n/a	URI
Subject	n/a	DDC; LCC; LCSH; MeSH; NLM; UDC
Title	alternative	n/a
Type	n/a	DCMIType
DC terms associated with educational materials	audience educationLevel instructionalMethod mediator	
DC terms associated with collections	accrualMethod accrualPeriodicity accrualPolicy	
Additional DC terms	provenance rightsHolder	

carry metadata from existing MARC 21 records into an XML environment. It includes a subset of MARC fields but uses language-based tags rather than numeric ones (e.g., <title> is used rather than 245 $a). Its language-based tags can be understood by any English-speaking person, although as with all language-based tagging, international use by non-English readers could be problematic.

MODS provides an alternative "between a very simple metadata format with a minimum of fields and no or little substructure (for example, DC) and a very detailed format with many data elements having various structural complexities such as MARC 21."[49] In other words, it is richer than DC but simpler than a MARC record containing RDA or AACR2 metadata. MODS was designed with a strong affinity to MARC. When MODS was designed some MARC elements were combined into a single MODS element, and some MARC fields were dropped altogether. Because it is only a subset of MARC, records converted to MODS cannot be fully converted back to MARC 21 without some loss of data. In addition, some MARC elements recur in more than one element as sub-elements. For example, *name*, *identifier*, and *titleInfo* can be used as both elements and sub-elements with the same definition for each. *Name*, for example, can be the name of a person, organization, or event associated with the primary resource, or it can be a name associated with another related resource.[50]

MODS has top-level elements followed by sub-elements. The twenty top-level elements are

- abstract
- accessCondition
- classification
- extension
- genre
- identifier
- language
- location
- name
- note
- originInfo
- part
- physicalDescription
- recordInfo
- relatedItem
- subject
- tableOfContents
- targetAudience
- titleInfo
- typeOfResource

An example of sub-elements follows, showing the sub-elements under *originInfo*:

- agent
- copyrightDate
- dateCaptured
- dateCreated
- dateIssued
- dateModified
- dateOther
- dateValid
- displayDate
- edition
- frequency
- issuance
- place
- publisher

MODS has been available since June 2002, and the current version of MODS is the MODS 3.8 schema (released in 2022). As with preceding versions, an accompanying list of approved changes from MODS 3.7 is provided.[51] See Figure 9.8 for a sample MODS bibliographic record.

9.2 Archives Metadata Standards

The archival community was relatively late in developing community metadata strategies. Tremendous progress, however, has been made over the past fifty years on the international and national fronts. A few metadata standards related to archives are discussed here as examples.

9.2.1 *General International Standard Archival Description* (ISAD(G))

General International Standard Archival Description (ISAD(G))[52] is a standard created by the International Council of Archives (ICA) that provides guidance for archival description. Like ISBD in the library world, it has been used as the basis to develop national archival description standards (e.g., DACS, see section 9.2.2 below). It was designed to facilitate the creation of archival descriptions that "identify and explain the context and content of archival material in order to promote its accessibility."[53] ISAD(G), however, is expected to be supplanted by ICA's conceptual framework known as *Records in Contexts* (described on pages 241–48). Although much information is acquired and recorded at every stage of the management of archival resources, the ISAD(G) rules are for description of materials starting at the point that it has been decided to preserve and control them. The rules in the standard do not explain how to describe special materials such as sound recordings, maps, and so on. Manuals that already exist for such materials are to be consulted as needed.

There are 26 elements identified in ISAD(G). Each has rules that include the name of the element, a statement of the purpose of the element in a description, the rules that apply to the element, and examples, if possible. The elements are organized into seven areas of descriptive information:

- **Identity Statement Area**: information essential to identify the unit being described (e.g., title, dates, level of description)
- **Context Area**: information about the origin and custody of the unit (e.g., creator names, biographical history)
- **Content and Structure Area**: information about the subject matter and the arrangement (e.g., scope and content, system of arrangement)
- **Conditions of Access and Use Area**: information about availability and uses of the materials (e.g., conditions governing reproduction, conditions governing access)
- **Allied Materials Area**: information about related resources (e.g., existence and location of copies, publication note)

```xml
<mods xmlns="http://www.loc.gov/mods/v3" xmlns:xsi="http://www.w3.org/2001/XMLSchema-instance" xsi:schemaLocation="http://www.loc.gov/mods/v3 http://www.loc.gov/standards/mods/v3/mods-3-5.xsd" version="3.5">
    <titleInfo>
        <title>Introduction to cataloging and classification</title>
    </titleInfo>
    <name type="personal" usage="primary">
        <namePart>Joudrey, Daniel N.</namePart>
        <role><roleTerm type="text">author.</roleTerm></role>
    </name>
    <name type="personal">
        <namePart>Taylor, Arlene G.</namePart>
        <namePart type="date">1941-</namePart>
        <role><roleTerm type="text">author.</roleTerm></role>
    </name>
    <name type="personal">
        <namePart>Miller, David P. (David Peter)</namePart>
        <namePart type="date">1955-</namePart>
        <role><roleTerm type="text">author.</roleTerm></role>
    </name>
    <typeOfResource>text</typeOfResource>
    <genre authority="marcgt">bibliography</genre>
    <genre authority="rdacontent">text</genre>
    <originInfo>
        <place>
            <placeTerm type="code" authority="marccountry">cau
            </placeTerm>
        </place>
        <dateIssued encoding="marc">2015</dateIssued>
        <edition>Eleventh edition.</edition>
        <issuance>monographic</issuance>
    </originInfo>
    <originInfo eventType="publication">
        <place>
            <placeTerm type="text">Santa Barbara, California :
            </placeTerm>
        </place>
        <publisher>Libraries Unlimited,</publisher>
        <dateIssued>[2015]</dateIssued>
    </originInfo>
    <language>
        <languageTerm type="code" authority="iso639-2b">eng
        </languageTerm>
    </language>
    <physicalDescription>
        <form authority="marcform">print</form>
        <extent>xxv, 1048 pages : illustrations ; 27 cm.</extent>
        <form type="media" authority="rdamedia">unmediated</form>
        <form type="carrier" authority="rdacarrier">volume</form>
    </physicalDescription>
    <note type="statement of responsibility" altRepGroup="00">Daniel N. Joudrey, Arlene G. Taylor, and David P. Miller.</note>
    <note>Significant expansion of: Introduction to cataloging and classification. Tenth edition / Arlene G. Taylor ; with the assistance of David P. Miller.</note>
    <note type="bibliography">Includes bibliographical references (pages 1001-1022) and index.</note>
```

Figure 9.8 An Excerpt from a MODS Record. (MODS coding shown in bold.)

```xml
            <subject authority="lcsh">
                    <titleInfo><title>Resource description & access</title></titleInfo>
            </subject>
            <subject authority="lcsh">
                    <topic>Descriptive cataloging</topic>
            </subject>
            <subject authority="lcsh">
                    <topic>Subject cataloging</topic>
            </subject>
            <subject authority="lcsh">
                    <topic>Classification</topic>
                    <topic>Books</topic>
            </subject>
            <subject authority="bisacsh">
                    <topic>LANGUAGE ARTS & DISCIPLINES / Library & Information Science /
                    Cataloging & Classification</topic>
            </subject>
            <subject authority="bisacsh">
                    <topic>LANGUAGE ARTS & DISCIPLINES / Study & Teaching</topic>
                    </subject>
            <classification authority="lcc">Z693 .W94 2015</classification>
            <classification authority="ddc" edition="23">025.3</classification>
            <classification authority="bisacsh">LAN025030 LAN020000</classification>
            <relatedItem type="series">
                    <titleInfo><title>Library and information science text series</title>
                    </titleInfo>
            </relatedItem>
            <relatedItem>
                    <titleInfo><title>Introduction to cataloging and classification</title>
                    </titleInfo>
                    <name type="personal">
                            <namePart>Taylor, Arlene G.,</namePart>
                            <namePart type="date">1941-</namePart>
                    </name>
            </relatedItem>
            <identifier type="isbn">9781598848571 (hardback : acid-free paper)</identifier>
            <identifier type="isbn">9781598848564 (pbk : acid-free paper)</identifier>
            <identifier invalid="yes" type="isbn">9781440837456 (ebook)</identifier>
            <identifier type="lccn">2015012911</identifier>
            <recordInfo>
                    <descriptionStandard>rda</descriptionStandard>
                    <recordContentSource authority="marcorg">DLC
                    </recordContentSource>
                    <recordCreationDate encoding="marc">150616</recordCreationDate>
                    <recordChangeDate encoding="iso8601">20160818094544.0
                    </recordChangeDate>
                    <recordIdentifier>18660797</recordIdentifier>
                    <recordOrigin>Converted from MARCXML to MODS version 3.5 using
                    MARC21slim2MODS3-5.xsl (Revision 1.106 2014/12/19)</recordOrigin>
                    <languageOfCataloging>
                            <languageTerm type="code" authority="iso639-2b">eng
                            </languageTerm>
                    </languageOfCataloging>
            </recordInfo>
</mods>
```

Figure 9.8 (*Continued*)

- **Note Area**: information that cannot be accommodated in any of the other areas (e.g., notes)
- **Description Control Area**: information about the preparation of the archival description (e.g., archivist's notes, rules, date of description)

Six elements are considered essential for international exchange of descriptive information:

- **Reference code**: code made up of standardized country code, repository code, and local repository specific numbers
- **Title**: concise title conveying authorship, subject matter, and form of material
- **Creator**: originator of a particular collection
- **Date(s)**: dates of creation or subject matter, depending upon the nature of the unit being described
- **Extent of the unit of description**: statement of the bulk, quantity, or size
- **Level of description**: statement of the grouping being described (e.g., fonds or sub-fonds; series, subseries, file, or item)

Five of the six core elements are derived from the Identity Area, with only the Creator element coming from the Context Area. The standard does not dictate the encoding that is to be used, although there has been much cooperation with the development of the Encoded Archival Description (EAD) standard.

9.2.2 *Describing Archives: A Content Standard* (DACS)

DACS[54] is a standard for the description of archival materials that has been accepted by much of the U.S. archival community. It supersedes *Archives, Personal Papers, and Manuscripts* (APPM),[55] a content standard developed by Steve Hensen while at LC that was based on AACR2 and was used by the archival community as a standard for the creation of MARC catalog records.[55] DACS is based on the international standard for archives, ISAD(G), and can be used to create any type or level of description of archival and manuscript materials, including catalog records and full finding aids.[56]

The DACS standard has two parts—one for describing archival materials and one for archival authority records. The second part is discussed in Chapter 10 of this text. In its preliminary sections, DACS includes a preface, which contains information about revisions, implementation neutrality, and its relationships to other standards; a statement of principles that restate generally accepted archival theory and constitute the basis for the standard (the principles are reviewed on pages 273–75); and an overview of archival description and access.

---

[55] AACR2 has only a skeletal chapter for manuscripts; it is geared toward illuminated manuscripts and itself acknowledges the need for other content standards to be used for archival descriptions.

The first chapter of DACS discusses levels of description, including guidelines for single-level description (only one level of description) and multilevel description (one level of description with at least one subordinate level of description). Like other content standards, it also contains guidelines for required (minimum), optimum, and added value descriptions. Chapters 2–8 present rules for the 25 elements of archival description.

2. **Identity Elements**
   2.1 Reference Code (Required)
   2.2 Name and Location of Repository (Required)
   2.3 Title (Required)
   2.4 Date (Required)
   2.5 Extent (Required)
   2.6 Name of Creator(s) (Required, if known)
   2.7 Administrative/Biographical History (Optimum)

3. **Content and Structure Elements**
   3.1 Scope and Content (Required)
   3.2 System of Arrangement (Added value)

4. **Conditions of Access and Use Elements**
   4.1 Conditions Governing Access (Required)
   4.2 Physical Access (Added value)
   4.3 Technical Access (Added value)
   4.4 Conditions Governing Reproduction and Use (Added value)
   4.5 Languages and Scripts of the Material (Required)
   4.6 Finding Aids (Added value)

5. **Acquisition and Appraisal Elements**
   5.1 Custodial History (Added value)
   5.2 Immediate Source of Acquisition (Added value)
   5.3 Appraisal, Destruction, & Scheduling Information (Added value)
   5.4 Accruals (Added value)

6. **Related Materials Elements**
   6.1 Existence and Location of Originals (Added value)
   6.2 Existence and Location of Copies (Added value)
   6.3 Related Archival Materials (Added value)
   6.4 Publication Note (Added value)

7. **Notes Elements**

    7.1 Notes (Added value)

8. **Description Control Elements**

    8.1 Description Control Element (Added value)

    8.2 Rights Statements for Archival Description (Single-level miminum required)

Although DACS is a schema-neutral content standard that does not prescribe any particular method of output, it provides examples encoded with EAD and with MARC 21.

9.3 Other Domain-Specific Metadata Schemas

Many metadata schemas have been developed by different communities for use in specific situations for specialized resources. They support description that allows for details needed by users searching for resources in a particular domain. A few are discussed here as examples.

9.3.1 *Cataloging Cultural Objects* (CCO)

Cataloging Cultural Objects (CCO) is a content standard like RDA and DACS, but one that has been designed for communities that describe works of art, architecture, cultural artifacts, and images of these things.[57] Similar to Dublin Core's one-to-one principle, CCO instructs catalogers to create separate records for works and for images of those works. Although the VRA Core and CDWA (discussed below) provide lists and descriptions of elements or categories for metadata element sets, CCO prescribes the data values and defines the order, syntax, and form in which the values are to be entered into a data structure. Similar to RDA and DACS, CCO concentrates on principles of good cataloging and documentation, not on rigid rules. Catalogers are expected to make informed judgments.

CCO is divided into three parts. Part One: General Guidelines deals with such issues as what unit is being cataloged, what is a work and what is an image, the relationships between works and images, specificity and exhaustivity of cataloging, and the kinds of relationships that may be delineated. Although CCO does not discuss administrative and technical metadata, Part One includes a discussion of database design issues and what may be needed for such designs. Lastly, Part One discusses authority files and controlled vocabularies.

Part Two: Elements is divided into nine chapters.

- Object naming
- Creator information
- Physical characteristics
- Stylistic, cultural, and chronological information
- Location and geography
- Subject

- Class
- Description
- View information

Each chapter contains discussion of the concept, the rules for the elements covered by that chapter, and ways for presenting the data for display and indexing. Some elements are marked as required. These are expected to appear in the description if the element is applicable and discernible. These include the following:

- **Object Naming**
  - Work Type
  - Title
- **Creator Information**
  - Creator display
  - Controlled Creator
  - Role
- **Physical Characteristics**
  - Measurements display
  - Materials and Techniques display
- **Stylistic, Cultural, and Chronological Information**
  - Display Date
  - Earliest Date
  - Latest Date
- **Location and Geography**
  - Current Location display
- **Subject**
  - Controlled Subject
- **View Information**
  - View Description
  - View Type
  - View Subject Controlled

Additional required elements are listed for Part Three of CCO, which covers authorities for personal and corporate names, geographic places, concepts, and subjects.

9.3.2 VRA Core

According to the Visual Resources Association's website, the VRA Core element set provides a categorical organization for "the description of works of visual culture as well as the images that document them. Works of visual culture can include objects or events such as paintings, drawings, sculpture, architecture, photographs, as well as book, decorative, and performance art. It is an internationally recognized metadata standard that is used both as a standalone format, and as an approved extension schema to METS for objects that contain cultural heritage resources."[58] The current version (4.0) was released in 2007 and last updated in 2014.[59] There are three main supporting documents (in English): an introduction, an element outline, and the element descriptions with tagging examples. (Documentation is also available in Chinese, Italian, and Greek.)

The element description document includes the names of the categories, each followed by a definition, information about attributes and sub-elements, recommendations for use of controlled vocabularies or standardized lists, whether or not the element is required and repeatable, and mappings to the previous version of the VRA Core elements, the *Categories for the Description of Works of Art* (CDWA) (see below), CCO, and DC elements. A VRA Core 4.0 XML schema was developed along with Core 4.0, and in the document of element descriptions examples encoded with XML are provided. There are nineteen basic categories of elements:

- **Work, Collection, or Image**: identifies the record as being for a work (a physical or created object or an event), for an image (a visual surrogate of a work), or for a collection (an aggregate of works or images)

- **Agent**: identifies the names of entities that have contributed to the design, creation, or production of the work or image; has sub-elements for *name, culture, role, dates*, and *attribution*; use of authority files recommended

- **Cultural Context**: identifies a culture, people, or country from which a work, image, or collection originates or with which it has been associated; use of controlled terms recommended

- **Date**: identifies dates associated with appearance of the work or image, such as creation, design, production, alteration, and restoration dates; has sub-elements for *earliest date* and *latest date*; use of standard date presentations recommended

- **Description**: a free-text note that may include comments, description, interpretation, and any other information not recorded in other elements

- **Inscription**: identifies marks or written words (e.g., signature, date, dedication) added to the object either at its production or later in its history; has sub-elements for *author, position*, and *text*

- **Location**: identifies geographic location and/or a specific site location of the work or image; has sub-elements for *name* and *refid* (an identifying number or code); use of controlled terms recommended

- **Material**: identifies the substance that composes a work or image; may be repeatable to accommodate mount, base, and applied materials (e.g., paper and ink, oil paint and canvas); use of *Art & Architecture Thesaurus* (AAT) terms recommended

- **Measurements**: identifies the size, shape, scale, dimensions, or format of the work or image; has attributes for *types* and *units*

- **Relation**: identifies a related work or image and the relationship that exists between the described and the related works or images; includes a lengthy list of recommended relationships for the relationship *type* attribute (e.g., partOf, modelFor, mateOf, copyAfter)
- **Rights**: identifies copyright information, intellectual property statements, or other information needed for rights management; has sub-elements for *rights holder* and *text* (of the rights statement)
- **Source**: identifies the source of the information recorded about the work or image (e.g., a bibliographic citation to a book that describes the work or image); has sub-elements for *name* and *refid*
- **State Edition**: identifies the number or name of a state, edition, or impression of a work that exists in more than one form; has sub-elements for *name* and *description*; has attributes that identify the number of known states, editions, or impressions and which one this is
- **Style Period**: identifies a defined style, historical period, group, movement, etc., characteristics of which appear in the work or image; use of AAT terms recommended
- **Subject**: gives terms or phrases that describe or interpret the work or image and that represent what it depicts or expresses; use of controlled terms recommended
- **Technique**: identifies the processes, techniques, or methods used in making or altering the work or image; use of AAT terms recommended
- **Textref**: gives identification values derived from textual references (e.g., catalog number) that are not associated with a particular repository or other location; has sub-elements for *name* and *refid*
- **Title**: the identifying phrase given to the work or image; use of data content rules for titles of artworks recommended
- **Work Type**: identifies the specific type of work, image, or collection being described; use of AAT terms recommended

Guidelines for description using the VRA Core are included in CCO.***

9.3.3 *Categories for the Description of Works of Art* (CDWA)

Categories for the Description of Works of Art (CDWA) is another metadata element set that, like the VRA Core, is used for describing and accessing information about works of art, architecture, material culture, and related images.[60] CDWA comprises around 540 categories and sub-categories. Of these, thirty-six are considered core (i.e., required if applicable); these categories are required to describe a work in a unique and unambiguous way. The CDWA core categories are divided into six groupings based on their purpose or focus. These include categories for the following:[61]

*** The instructions in CCO can be applied to VRA Core or to CDWA.

- Objects, architecture, or group
- Related textual references
- Creators
- Places
- Generic concepts
- Subjects

The core categories under *Object, architecture, or group* are

- Catalog Level
- Object/Work Type
- Classification Term
- Title or Name
- Measurements Description
- Materials and Techniques Description
- Creator Description
- Creator Identity
- Creator Role
- Creation Date
    - Earliest Date
    - Latest Date
- Subject Matter
- Current Location Repository Name/Geographic Location
- Current Repository Numbers

The remaining core categories are for access and authority control and are discussed in Chapter 10. CDWA, like VRA Core, recommends encoding records with XML.

9.3.4 ONIX (Online Information Exchange)

The publishing world has also developed standards that can be used for the description of resources by their publishers. ONIX (Online Information Exchange) is a family of XML standards that publishers and others in the book trade can use to distribute ***ONIX messages***—electronic information about books, serials, and other publications.[62] ONIX is maintained by EDItEUR (an international organization that coordinates standards for digital publishing and book commerce) jointly with several book industry and user groups. In the online environment, ONIX messages contain highly detailed metadata about resources. ONIX addresses both the metadata structure (the elements) and the encoding of the metadata. XML was chosen as the encoding format because it is optimized for data exchange between computers, the tags are human readable, and XML software is inexpensive enough even for small publishers.

ONIX for Books, the most widely used metadata standard for describing print and electronic books, is now available in Release 3.1.[63] "In March 2023, EDItEUR released ONIX 3.1, a relatively small update building on the 3.0.8 version of ONIX but sacrificing a little backward compatibility—half a dozen data elements have been removed, after having been 'deprecated' for up to a decade."[64] Further revisions are expected to build upon 3.1 as it continues to develop. An excerpt from an ONIX for Books message is presented in Figure 9.9.

```xml
<ONIXMessage release="3.0">
   <Header>
      <Sender>
              <SenderName>ABC-CLIO</SenderName>
              <ContactName>Jane Doe</ContactName>
              <EmailAddress>Jane_Doe@abc-clio.com</EmailAddress>
      </Sender>
   </Header>
   <Product>
      <RecordReference>9781598848571</RecordReference>
      <NotificationType>03</NotificationType>
      <ProductIdentifier>
              <ProductIDType>15</ProductIDType>
              <IDValue>9781598848571</IDValue>
      </ProductIdentifier>
      <Barcode>
              <BarcodeType>01</BarcodeType>
              <PositionOnProduct>00</PositionOnProduct>
      </Barcode>
      <DescriptiveDetail>
              <ProductComposition>00</ProductComposition>
              <ProductForm>BB</ProductForm>
              <NoCollection/>
              <TitleDetail>
                     <TitleType>01</TitleType>
                     <TitleElement>
                            <TitleElementLevel>01</TitleElementLevel>
                            <TitleText>Introduction to Cataloging and Classification
                            </TitleText>
                     </TitleElement>
              </TitleDetail>
              <Contributor>
                     <SequenceNumber>1</SequenceNumber>
                     <ContributorRole>A01</ContributorRole>
                     <PersonName>Daniel N. Joudrey</PersonName>
                     <PersonNameInverted>Joudrey, Daniel</PersonNameInverted>
              </Contributor>
              <Contributor>
                     <SequenceNumber>2</SequenceNumber>
                     <ContributorRole>A01</ContributorRole>
                     <PersonName>Arlene G. Taylor</PersonName>
                     <PersonNameInverted>Taylor, Arlene</PersonNameInverted>
              </Contributor>
              <EditionNumber>11</EditionNumber>
              <Extent>
                     <ExtentType>00</ExtentType>
                     <ExtentValue>1048</ExtentValue>
                     <ExtentUnit>03</ExtentUnit>
              </Extent>
              <Subject>
                     <MainSubject/>
                            <SubjectSchemeIdentifier>10</SubjectSchemeIdentifier>
                            <SubjectCode>LAN025030</SubjectCode>
                            <SubjectHeadingText>LANGUAGE ARTS & DISCIPLINES /
                            Library & Information Science / Cataloging & Classification</
                            SubjectHeadingText>
              </Subject>
      </DescriptiveDetail>
```

Figure 9.9 An Excerpt from an ONIX for Books Message. (ONIX coding shown in bold.)

```xml
<CollateralDetail>
    <TextContent>
        <TextType>03</TextType>
        <ContentAudience>00</ContentAudience>
        <Text textformat="02"> A new edition of this best-selling textbook reintroduces the topic of library cataloging from a fresh, modern perspective. <br/> • Delineates the new cataloging landscape• Shares a principles-based perspective • Provides introductory text for beginners and intermediate students • Emphasizes descriptive and subject cataloging, as well as format-neutral cataloging • Covers new cataloging rules and RDA</Text>
    </TextContent>
    <TextContent>
        <TextType>03</TextType>
        <ContentAudience>00</ContentAudience>
        <Text>Not many books merit an eleventh edition, but this popular text does. Newly updated, <i>Introduction to Cataloging and Classification</i> provides an introduction to descriptive cataloging based on contemporary standards, explaining the basic tenets to readers without previous experience, as well as to those who merely want a better understanding of the process as it exists today. The text opens with the foundations of cataloging, then moves to specific details and subject matter such as Functional Requirements for Bibliographic Records (FRBR),.... </Text>
    </TextContent>
    <TextContent>
        <TextType>12</TextType>
        <ContentAudience>00</ContentAudience>
        <Text textformat="02"><b>Daniel N. Joudrey</b>, MLIS, PhD, is associate professor, School of Library and Information Science, Simmons College, Boston, MA. <b>Arlene G. Taylor</b>, MSLS, PhD, is professor emerita, School of Information Sciences, University of Pittsburgh, ....
        </Text>
    </TextContent>
    <TextContent>
        <TextType>06</TextType>
        <ContentAudience>00</ContentAudience>
        <Text textformat="02">"I recommend this book to instructors and students, to practicing professionals and paraprofessionals, and to selectors for libraries that support library science curricula. Ideally, this text would be used in conjunction with a wide variety of practical exercises in original cataloging and the creation of authority records." - <strong>Technical Services Quarterly </strong></Text>
    </TextContent>
</CollateralDetail>
            ... [MUCH MORE DETAIL] ...
</Product>
</ONIXMessage>
```

Figure 9.9 (*Continued*)

ONIX for Books defines hundreds of metadata elements with accompanying code lists. The elements allow a publisher to present online the information that was previously contained on book jackets and in publishing brochures and catalogs—information such as synopses, quotations from reviews, author biographies, intended audience, and so on. The standard comprises several parts.

- **Product Information Format Specification**: a comprehensive guide to the complete ONIX for Books format. It includes overviews of the ONIX product record, the XML data elements and tags, the top-level XML message structure, and the message header; it also provides sample messages.
- **Acknowledgment Specification**: a format for sending response messages to confirm receipt of ONIX data.
- **Implementation and Best Practice Guide**: a content standard that guides users to minimize variation in ONIX data.
- **Code lists**: ONIX code lists are available in a variety of forms. These lists control the values that are entered into certain metadata elements.[65]

ONIX uses XML to transmit ONIX messages. ONIX for Books may be encoded in two different XML applications: an XML schema and RELAX NG (RNG), another XML schema language. Although a DTD was available for earlier versions of ONIX, it is not recommended; the XML and RNG schemas are the preferred methods for structuring ONIX messages. All these components are found on the EDItEUR website. An ONIX message contains both (1) a header with information about the sender, addressee, and administrative metadata, and (2) a product record with information about the resource being described. The product record may contain eight blocks of data:

1. Product description
2. Marketing collateral detail
3. Content detail
4. Publishing detail
5. Related material
6. Product supply
7. Promotion detail
8. Production detail

Block 1, *Product description*, contains information similar to traditional library cataloging data found in RDA, AACR2, or ISBD. It contains 11 data groups to describe the form and content of the resource.

P.3 Product form
P.4 Product parts
P.5 Collection
P.6 Product title detail
P.7 Authorship
P.8 Event
P.9 Edition
P.10 Language
P.11 Extents and other content
P.12 Subject
P.13 Audience

Within each data group, one or more elements is used to provide the necessary detail. For example, under P.6 *Product title detail* the following elements are provided.

P.6.1	Title type code	P.6.7	Title without prefix
P.6.2	Title element level	P.6.8	Subtitle
P.6.3	Part number	P.6.9	Thesis type code
P.6.4	Year of annual	P.6.10	Thesis presented to
P.6.5	[Deprecated element]	P.6.11	Year of thesis
P.6.6	Title prefix		

A mapping from ONIX to MARC facilitates the use of ONIX data in library catalogs.[66] There are also projects that link MARC records in catalogs to ONIX data held in XML-encoded databases.

For P.6.1, *Title type code*, ONIX provides a code list of 15 values that can be entered into that data element.

Value	Description
00	Undefined
01	Distinctive title (book); Cover title (serial); Title on item or collection (serial content item or reviewed resource)
02	ISSN key title of serial
03	Title in original language
04	Title acronym or initialism
05	Abbreviated title
06	Title in other language
07	Thematic title of journal issue
08	Former title
10	Distributor's title
11	Alternative title on cover
12	Alternative title on back
13	Expanded title
14	Alternative title
15	Alternative title on spine

A partnership between EDItEUR and NISO has been responsible for the production of ONIX for Subscription Products, a family of XML formats for information about serial products and subscription information.[67] This has led to the development of additional ONIX formats, such as SPS (Serials Products and Subscriptions), SOH (Serials Online Holdings), and SRN (Serials Release Notification). The ONIX Serials Coverage Statement is an XML structure for use in the three formats.

9.3.5 Index and Bibliography Records

For nearly forty years, there was no official standard for the descriptive content of index records in the United States. The ANSI standard, *Basic Criteria for Indexes* (Z39.4-1984),[68] was woefully out of date and had no mention of the data to be included in the description of an item. The National Information Standards Organization (NISO) tried to update this standard, but committees could not come to agreement with the American Society for Indexing, and so a proposed revision of Z39.4 was withdrawn in 1996. In 1997, the rejected replacement for Z39.4 was instead released as a NISO technical report: TR-02, *Guidelines for Indexes and Related Information Retrieval Devices*. Although its author, James Anderson, presented useful, updated information in TR-02 to help fill the void, it was not an official NISO standard.[69] "While this publication was very robust, it was twenty years out of date and did not address more modern techniques such as embedded indexing and indexes designed for electronic searching."[70]

A second edition of ISO 999 *Information and Documentation—Guidelines for the Content, Organization and Presentation of Indexes* was released as an international standard in 1996.[71] It was intended to update, clarify, and exemplify basic indexing methods that were presented in its original 1975 edition. It contains additional information on the organization of indexes, quality control, and arrangement. It was reviewed and reconfirmed in 2015. The standard contains sections that address the following areas:

- Scope
- Associated standards
- Definitions
- Functions
- Types of indexes (Subject, Author, Name, Geographic, Title, and Number/Code indexes)
- Quality control (Length, Detail, Consistency, etc.)
- Content and organization (Construction, Concepts, Proper names, Locators, References, etc.)
- Arrangement (Filing order, Word-by-word versus Letter-by-letter, Alphanumeric arrangement, Subheadings, etc.)
- Presentation (Notes, Search aids, Style, etc.)

Creators of indexes have their own standards for information to be included in an index record. Agencies like H. W. Wilson that publish several different indexes in different subject areas have some consistency from index to index. Electronic index records tend to include more information than do paper versions. Similar to OPACs, electronic index records tend to use labels, which are not included in paper versions. (For an example of a labeled index record, refer back to Figure 3.10 on page 126.)

In 2015, the American Society for Indexing published the *Best Practices for Indexing* guide. It addresses issues important in back-of-the-book indexing. It is structured into 11 chapters:

- Metatopic
- Entry Array
- Main Headings
- Subheadings
- Locators
- Cross-references
- Double-posting
- Headnote
- Alphabetization
- Usability
- Characteristics of a Quality Index

The chapters are followed by seven appendices addressing specific types of resources (e.g., children's books, cookbooks). Each appendix addresses the topics of the 11 chapters for these specialized resource types.[72]

In 2021, NISO published *Criteria for Indexes* (Z39.4-2021), which "provides guidelines for the content, organization, and presentation of indexes used for the retrieval of documents and parts of documents. It deals with the principles of indexing regardless of the type of material indexed, the indexing method used, the medium of the index, or the method of presentation for searching. It emphasizes three processes essential for all indexes: comprehensive design, vocabulary management, and syntax."[73] It is now the de facto standard for indexing activities in the United States.

There is one standard for bibliographic references, ISO 690:2021,[74] guiding the content that is to be included in entries in bibliographies. It developed as an ISO Technical Report and replaced two earlier standards with more up-to-date guidance on creating bibliographic references and citations for a wide range of information resources, both tangible and electronic.

9.4 Conclusion

From the preceding sections, one can see that resource description and access are dependent upon the community for which the data is being created. Some communities have long histories of using standards. The library community has the longest traditions, being based upon principles that have been developing for centuries. Other communities have recognized the experience of libraries and have patterned their guidelines for creation of surrogate records after ISBD or another library standard. The creators of DC, VRA Core, CDWA, CCO, and others have included librarians, along with other people with organizing experience, in their planning committees. The most widely used content standards in the United States are RDA, DACS, and CCO. The remaining standards discussed in this chapter rarely prescribe the form of content, but instead they prescribe and define metadata structures (i.e., element sets) and display. All these standards are necessary to provide consistency in the process of describing and providing access to information resources.

Some Important Terms in This Chapter
(Definitions Provided in the Glossary)

Accompanying material
Added entry
Agent
Alternative
Application profile
Attribute
Attribute element
Coherent description
Collective agent
Condition
Condition option
Core element
Core-If element
Corporate body
Domain
Effective description
Element
Element refinement
Encoding scheme

Entity boundary
Exception
Expression
Family
Identifier
Internationalized Resource Identifier
Item
Main entry
Manifestation
Metadata description set
Metadata statement
Metadata work
Minimum coherent description
Nomen
One-to-one principle
ONIX message
Option

Optional addition
Optional omission
Person
Place
Policy statement
Qualifier
Range
RDA entity
Relationship element
Schema-neutral
String encoding scheme
Structured description
Timespan
Unstructured description
Vocabulary encoding scheme
Work

Some Important Acronyms in This Chapter

AACR:	*Anglo-American Cataloging Rules*
AACR2:	*Anglo-American Cataloguing Rules, Second Edition*
ANSI:	American National Standards Institute
APPM:	*Archives, Personal Papers, and Manuscripts*
ASIS&T:	Association for Information Science and Technology
CCO:	*Cataloging Cultural Objects*
CDWA:	*Categories for the Description of Works of Art*
DACS:	*Describing Archives: A Content Standard*
DC:	Dublin Core
DCMES:	Dublin Core Metadata Element Set
DCMI:	Dublin Core Metadata Initiative
DOI:	Digital Object Identifier
DTD:	Document Type Definition
EAD:	Encoded Archival Description

FRAD:	*Functional Requirements for Authority Data*
FRBR:	*Functional Requirements for Bibliographic Records*
HTML:	Hypertext Markup Language
ICP:	*Statement of International Cataloguing Principles*
IFLA:	International Federation of Library Associations and Institutions
IRI:	Internationalized Resource Identifier
ISAD(G):	*General International Standard Archival Description*
ISBD:	*International Standard Bibliographic Description*
ISBN:	International Standard Book Number
ISSN:	International Standard Serial Number
ISO:	International Organization for Standardization
LC:	Library of Congress
LCNAF:	Library of Congress/NACO Authority File
LC-PCC:	Library of Congress-Program for Cooperative Cataloging
LC-PCC PS:	Library of Congress-Program for Cooperative Cataloging Policy Statements
LCSH:	*Library of Congress Subject Headings*
LRM:	*IFLA Library Reference Model*
MARC:	Machine-Readable Cataloging
MGD:	Metadata Guidance Documentation
MLA:	Music Library Association
MODS:	Metadata Object Description Schema
NISO:	National Information Standards Organization
ONIX:	Online Information Exchange
RDA:	*Resource Description & Access*
RDF:	Resource Description Framework
URI:	Uniform Resource Identifier
URL:	Uniform Resource Locator
WEMI:	Work-Expression-Manifestation-Item
VRA:	Visual Resources Association
XML:	Extensible Markup Language

9.5 Discussion Questions and Exercises

- How do the descriptive standards discussed in this chapter reflect the different information communities that they were designed for? Are there elements that are common across different standards?

- How have library descriptive cataloging standards changed in recent decades, from AACR2 to Original RDA and finally to Official RDA? What changes in the information landscape have shaped the development of new cataloging standards?

- ONIX, like many library descriptive metadata standards, focuses primarily on published materials, but was designed by the publishing community. Select one of the library metadata standards discussed in this chapter and compare it to ONIX.
  - What is similar about the standards?
  - What is different?
  - What does this suggest about the different information environments that produced them?

9.6 Suggested Readings

Baca, Murtha, and Patricia Harpring, eds. *Categories for the Description of Works of Art*. Revised 2024 by Emily Benoff. Los Angeles: The Getty, 2024. http://www.getty.edu/research/publications/electronic_publications/cdwa/.

Baca, Murtha, Patricia Harpring, Elisa Lanzi, Linda McRae, and Ann Whiteside. *Cataloging Cultural Objects: A Guide to Describing Cultural Works and Their Images*. Chicago: American Library Association, 2006. Also available at: https://www.vraweb.org/cco/.

Describing Archives: A Content Standard (DACS). 2nd ed. Chicago: Society of American Archivists, 2013. http://www2.archivists.org/groups/technical-subcommittee-on-describing-archives-a-content-standard-dacs/dacs.

Dublin Core Metadata Initiative. http://dublincore.org/.

EDItEUR. "ONIX: Overview." http://www.editeur.org/83/Overview/.

Godby, Carol Jean. *Mapping ONIX to MARC*. Dublin, OH: OCLC Research, 2010.

International Standard Bibliographic Description (ISBD). Consolidated ed. Berlin: De Gruyter Saur, 2011. http://www.ifla.org/files/assets/cataloguing/isbd/isbd-cons_20110321.pdf.

Maxwell, Robert L. *Maxwell's Handbook for RDA, Resource Description & Access: Explaining and Illustrating RDA: Resource Description and Access Using MARC21*. Chicago: American Library Association, 2013.

"MODS: Metadata Object Description Schema." Library of Congress. https://www.loc.gov/standards/mods/.

RDA: Resource Description & Access. Chicago: American Library Association, 2010– . Available by subscription at: http://www.rdatoolkit.org/.

"VRA Core: A Data Standard for the Description of Images and Works of Art and Culture." Library of Congress. https://www.loc.gov/standards/vracore/.

9.7 Notes

All URLs accessed April 2025.

1. Chris Oliver, *Introducing RDA: A Guide to the Basics After 3R* (Chicago: ALA Editions, 2021), 2–3.
2. *RDA: Resource Description & Access* (Chicago: American Library Association, 2020–). Primarily accessed in the subscription product RDA Toolkit, http://www.rdatoolkit.org/. [Henceforth cited as Official RDA.]
3. *RDA Registry*, https://www.rdaregistry.info/.
4. Pat Riva, Patrick Le Boeuf, and Maja Žumer, *IFLA Library Reference Model: A Conceptual Model for Bibliographic Information* (The Hague: IFLA, 2017), https://www.ifla.org/resources/?oPubId=11412.
5. Official RDA, "RDA Entity" (citation number 18.99.62.29, accessed April 25, 2025), https://access.rdatoolkit.org/Home/.

6. Official RDA, "Element" (no citation number, accessed April 25, 2025), https://access.rdatoolkit.org/en-US_rdaregistry.info-termList-RDATerms-1041.
7. *MLA RDA Application Profile*, https://musiclibraryassociation.github.io/mla-rda-mg/Content/Intro/intro_mla_application_profile.html.
8. Program for Cooperative Cataloging, *Resource Description & Access (RDA) Metadata Guidance Documentation*, https://www.loc.gov/aba/rda/mgd/.
9. Program for Cooperative Cataloging Policy Committee, "Update on the PCC's implementation of the Official RDA Toolkit," Library of Congress, June 13, 2023, https://www.loc.gov/aba/pcc/rda/update-on-PCC-implementation-of-Official-RDA.pdf.
10. Andrew Osborn, "The Crisis in Cataloging," *Library Quarterly* 11, no. 4 (October 1941): 393–411.
11. *RDA: Resource Description & Access* (Chicago: American Library Association, 2010–). Primarily accessed in the subscription product RDA Toolkit, https://original.rdatoolkit.org/. [Henceforth cited as Original RDA.]
12. International Federation of Library Associations and Institutions, IFLA Study Group, *Functional Requirements for Bibliographic Records: Final Report* (Munich: Saur, 1998), https://www.ifla.org/publications/functional-requirements-for-bibliographic-records. [Henceforth cited as FRBR.]
13. International Federation of Library Associations and Institutions (IFLA), Working Group on Functional Requirements and Numbering of Authority Records (FRANAR), *Functional Requirements for Authority Data: A Conceptual Model* (The Hague: IFLA, 2009), https://www.ifla.org/publications/functional-requirements-for-authority-data. [Henceforth cited as FRAD.]
14. International Federation of Library Associations and Institutions (IFLA), Meeting of Experts on an International Cataloguing Code, *Statement of International Cataloguing Principles (ICP)*, 2016 edition (The Hague: IFLA, 2016), http://www.ifla.org/files/assets/cataloguing/icp/icp_2016-en.pdf. [Henceforth cited as ICP.]
15. Beacher Wiggins, "Library of Congress Announces Its Long-Range RDA Training Plan," Library of Congress, March 2, 2012, https://www.loc.gov/catdir/cpso/news_rda_implementation_date.html.
16. European RDA Interest Group [EURIG] 2016 Annual Meeting, "EURIG Minutes of the Members' Meeting, 2016," https://www.rdatoolkit.org/sites/default/files/rsc/2016_EURIG_Minutes_rev.pdf; Alan Danskin, "EURIG Annual Report: 2016–2017: Presented on 8 May 2017 at University of Florence," http://www.casalini.it/eurig2017/presentations/danskin.pdf.
17. Program for Cooperative Cataloging (PCC) ISBD and MARC Task Group, "Revised Final Report," 2016, http://www.loc.gov/aba/pcc/documents/isbdmarc2016.pdf.
18. Program for Cooperative Cataloging, "PCC Guidelines for Minimally Punctuated MARC Bibliographic Records," Policy effective January 2020, https://www.loc.gov/aba/pcc/documents/PCC-Guidelines-for-Minimally-Punctuated-MARC-Data-v.1.2.docx.
19. Daniel N. Joudrey, Arlene G. Taylor, and David P. Miller, *Introduction to Cataloging and Classification*, 11th ed. (Santa Barbara, CA: Libraries Unlimited, 2015), Chapters 4–9.
20. *International Standard Bibliographic Description* (ISBD), recommended by the ISBD Review Group, approved by the Standing Committee of the IFLA Cataloguing Section, Consolidated ed. (Berlin: De Gruyter Saur, 2011), http://www.ifla.org/files/assets/cataloguing/isbd/isbd-cons_20110321.pdf.
21. "Superseded ISBDs," International Federation of Library Associations and Institutions, http://www.ifla.org/isbd-rg/superseded-isbd-s.
22. *ISBD International Standard Bibliographic Description: 2021 Update to the 2011 Consolidated Edition*, approved by the IFLA ISBD Review Group, 2022, https://repository.ifla.org/handle/123456789/1939.
23. "ISBD Review Group," International Federation of Library Associations and Institutions, http://www.ifla.org/isbd-rg.

24. Joudrey, Taylor, and Miller, 887.
25. Joudrey, Taylor, and Miller, 887.
26. PCC ISBD and MARC Task Group, "Revised Final Report," http://www.loc.gov/aba/pcc/documents/isbdmarc2016.pdf.
27. "ISBD Review Group," IFLA.
28. Joudrey, Taylor, and Miller, Chapter 23.
29. *Anglo-American Cataloguing Rules, Second Edition, 2002 Revision* (AACR2R), prepared under the direction of the Joint Steering Committee for Revision of AACR (Ottawa: Canadian Library Association; Chicago: American Library Association, 2002, loose-leaf, with updates), D-2. Available by subscription to the RDA Toolkit, http://www.rdatoolkit.org.
30. Arlene G. Taylor and Daniel N. Joudrey, *The Organization of Information*, 3rd ed. (Westport, CT: Libraries Unlimited, 2009).
31. Arlene G. Taylor, *Introduction to Cataloging and Classification*, 10th ed., with the assistance of David P. Miller (Westport, CT: Libraries Unlimited, 2006).
32. "DCMI Home," Dublin Core Metadata Initiative, http://dublincore.org/.
33. "History of the Dublin Core Metadata Initiative," Dublin Core Metadata Initiative, http://dublincore.org/about/history/.
34. "Dublin Core Metadata Element Set, Version 1.1: Reference Description," Dublin Core Metadata Initiative, 2012, http://dublincore.org/documents/dces/.
35. *The Dublin Core Metadata Element Set*, ANSI/NISO Z39.85-2012 (Baltimore, MD: NISO, 2013), https://www.niso.org/publications/ansiniso-z3985-2012-dublin-core-metadata-element-set.
36. *Information and Documentation—The Dublin Core Metadata Element Set—Part 1: Core Elements*, ISO 15836:2017 (Geneva: ISO, 2017). Available for purchase at: https://www.iso.org/standard/71339.html.
37. Karen Coyle, "DC Tabular Application Profiles," Dublin Core Metadata Initiative, 2020, https://www.dublincore.org/blog/2020/dc_tabular_application_profiles/.
38. "ASIS&T: Association for Information Science and Technology," https://www.asist.org/.
39. Dublin Core Generator, created by Nick Steffel, http://dublincoregenerator.com/.
40. Misha Wolf and Charles Wicksteed, "Date and Time Formats," W3C, 1997, http://www.w3.org/TR/NOTE-datetime.
41. "Media Types," Internet Assigned Numbers Authority (IANA), https://www.iana.org/assignments/media-types/media-types.xhtml.
42. "RFC4646: Tags for Identifying Languages," IETF [Internet Engineering Task Force] Documents, https://www.ietf.org/rfc/rfc4646.txt.
43. See DCMI Type Vocabulary at: "DCMI Metadata Terms," Dublin Core Metadata Initiative, 2020, http://dublincore.org/documents/dcmi-terms/.
44. "DCMI Metadata Terms."
45. "DCMI Metadata Terms."
46. "DCMI Community Groups," Dublin Core Metadata Initiative, http://www.dublincore.org/groups/.
47. DCMI-Libraries Working Group, "Library Application Profile," Dublin Core Metadata Initiative, https://www.dublincore.org/specifications/dublin-core/library-application-profile/.
48. Library of Congress, Network Development and MARC Standards Office (NDMSO), "MODS: Metadata Object Description Schema," http://www.loc.gov/standards/mods/.
49. Rebecca S. Guenther, "MODS: The Metadata Object Description Schema," *Portal: Libraries and the Academy* 3, no. 1 (2003): 139.
50. Guenther, 140.
51. Library of Congress NDMSO, "Approved Changes for MODS 3.8," Library of Congress, 2022, http://www.loc.gov/standards/mods/changes-3-8.html.

52. International Council on Archives, *ISAD(G): General International Standard Archival Description*, 2nd ed. (Ottawa: International Council on Archives, 2000), https://www.ica.org/app/uploads/2024/01/CBPS_2000_Guidelines_ISADG_Second-edition_EN.pdf. [Henceforth cited as ISAD(G).]
53. ISAD(G), 7.
54. *Describing Archives: A Content Standard*, Version 2022.0.1.1. (Chicago: Society of American Archivists, 2022), http://www2.archivists.org/groups/technical-subcommittee-on-describing-archives-a-content-standard-dacs/dacs. [Henceforth cited as DACS.]
55. Steven L. Hensen, comp., *Archives, Personal Papers, and Manuscripts: A Cataloging Manual for Archival Repositories, Historical Societies, and Manuscript Libraries*, 2nd ed. (Chicago: Society of American Archivists, 1989).
56. DACS, Preface.
57. Murtha Baca, Patricia Harpring, Elisa Lanzi, Linda McRae, and Ann Whiteside, *Cataloging Cultural Objects: A Guide to Describing Cultural Works and Their Images* (Chicago: American Library Association, 2006), 4, https://www.vraweb.org/cco/.
58. "An Introduction to VRA Core," Library of Congress, http://www.loc.gov/standards/vracore/VRA_Core4_Intro.pdf.
59. "VRA Core: A Data Standard for the Description of Images and Works of Art and Culture," Library of Congress, http://www.loc.gov/standards/vracore/.
60. *Categories for the Description of Works of Art*, ed. Murtha Baca and Patricia Harpring; revised 2024 by Emily Benoff (Los Angeles: The Getty, 2024), http://www.getty.edu/research/publications/electronic_publications/cdwa/.
61. Patricia Harpring, "Overview of Categories," *Categories for the Description of Works of Art*, ed. Murtha Baca and Patricia Harpring; revised 2024 by Emily Benoff (Los Angeles: The Getty, 2024), https://www.getty.edu/publications/categories-description-works-art/overview-categories/.
62. "ONIX," EDItEUR, http://www.editeur.org/8/ONIX.
63. "ONIX for Books," EDItEUR, http://www.editeur.org/11/Books/.
64. "Overview," EDItEUR, https://www.editeur.org/83/Overview/.
65. "Release 3.0 and 3.1 Downloads," EDItEUR, https://www.editeur.org/93/Release-3.0-and-3.1-Downloads.
66. Jean Godby, *A Crosswalk from ONIX Version 3.0 for Books to MARC 21* (Dublin, OH: OCLC Research, 2012), http://www.oclc.org/research/publications/library/2012/2012-04.pdf (report) and http://www.oclc.org/research/publications/library/2012/2012-04a.xls (crosswalk).
67. "ONIX for Subscription Products," EDItEUR, http://www.editeur.org/17/ONIX-for-Serials/.
68. American National Standards Institute, *American National Standard for Library and Information Sciences and Related Publishing Practices—Basic Criteria for Indexes*, ANSI Z39.4-1984 (New York: American National Standards Institute, 1984).
69. James D. Anderson, *Guidelines for Indexes and Related Information Retrieval Devices* (Bethesda, MD: NISO Press, 1997), https://www.niso.org/publications/tr02-1997-guidelines-indexes.
70. "Criteria for Indexes (Z39.4) Working Group," National Information Standards Organization, https://www.niso.org/standards-committees/criteria-indexes.
71. International Organization for Standardization, *Information and Documentation: Guidelines for the Content, Organization and Presentation of Indexes*, ISO 999:1996 (Geneva: ISO, 1996).
72. American Society for Indexing, *Best Practices for Indexing Guide* (Tempe, AZ: ASI, 2015), v.
73. American National Standards Institute and National Information Standards Organization, *Criteria for Indexes*, ANSI/NISO Z39.4-2021 (Baltimore, MD: National Information Standards Organization, 2021).
74. International Organization for Standardization, *Information and Documentation—Guidelines for Bibliographic References and Citations to Information Resources*, ISO 690:2021 (Geneva: ISO, 2021).

Chapter 10

Authority Control

10.1 Authority Control

In libraries, archives, museums, and other cultural heritage institutions, authority control is an important function for efficient retrieval. **Authority control** has three major concerns: consistency, relationships, and uniqueness. It is achieved through the following processes:

1. maintaining consistency in the forms of names used to represent entities as access points* (e.g., persons, corporate bodies, families, places, works, expressions, genres, and subjects),

2. identifying the network of relationships among entities (particularly agents, works, and subjects), and

3. disambiguation of identically named entities; ensuring that entities are identified uniquely, and the access points chosen to represent them cannot be used for any other entity.

In other words, authority-controlled access points are consistently presented, they are explicitly linked to other related access points, and they are unique because similarly named entities have been disambiguated, all for the purpose of **collocation** in retrieval (i.e., bringing together related resources).

The goals for authority control are to assist users to

- find an entity using their own vocabulary (e.g., to find books by Hans Christian Andersen, even if he used H.C. Andersen on the title page; to find resources about *stamp collecting* using the search term *philately*);

- identify entities (e.g., to identify the Michael Gorman who is a librarian, as opposed to the artist, architect, the fiddle player, or the fly-fishing enthusiast; to determine if Vincent Willem van Gogh is the same person as the artist Vincent van Gogh);

- collocate resources, persons, and other entities regardless of terminology used (e.g., to bring together all resources that are or are related to the opera *La Traviata*, including Verdi's score, resources using an alternative title such as *Violetta*, or *The Lost One*, a separately published libretto by Piave, various sound recordings, and so on);

---

*As discussed in Chapter 8, an access point is a word or phrase chosen by the cataloger to allow for the retrieval of a resource description.

- select an appropriate resource based on the access point (e.g., Is the use of *bridge* in a search limited to the card game, or will resources about structures across rivers or about dental work be retrieved? Is this the version of *Introduction to Sociology* that I want?);

- explore relationships among names and entities (e.g., How are Mark Twain, Samuel Langhorne Clemens, Quintus Curtius Snodgrass, and Louis de Conte related?); and

- provide a syndetic structure to aid in subject searching or to provide variant forms of name for persons, families, corporate bodies, or works (e.g., to show how the terms *designer dogs, boutique dogs, mixed breed dogs, cockapoo*, and *goldendoodle* are related).

Authority control is the result of the process of doing authority work (described below). It is so named because for many years it was thought necessary to determine an authorized name, title, or subject for every entity known by more than one form of name. For example, the Library of Congress (LC) has established **Confucius** as the English form of the name to be used consistently in the United States; this means that the names given to this person in many other languages, including his Chinese names (孔子, 孔丘), have been relegated to positions of variant forms of name that act as cross-references to the authorized form. If every variant name, title, or subject term were to be given equal status, however, then one would not need to be *the* authorized form used in every record. One name, of course, might need to be chosen as the default for display, but that would not necessarily be the same in every library, archives, or museum. As the profession continues to invest in a linked data future, the importance of textual strings will likely lessen and the importance of connections to authoritative sources of information about an entity will increase. In the future, which name is used will likely play a less significant role in information retrieval; a searcher may be able to use any of the forms of name to gain access to information related to the entity sought.

10.1.1 Authority Control of Names

In today's information environment, however, we still rely on authority control to determine a preferred form of name for a person, at least on the national level. If a person has been identified by different names and/or different forms of name (e.g., Jacqueline Bouvier, Jackie Kennedy, Jacqueline Kennedy Onassis, and Jackie O.), and if that person's name is brought under authority control, then one version of the person's name is chosen as the preferred one and the others are documented as cross-references to it. Thus, a search for one form of the name will retrieve information resources related to the person regardless of which name or form of name appears in a particular resource. For example, a user can search either **Kennedy, Jackie** or **Onassis, Jacqueline Kennedy**, and still receive relevant search results. This may be accomplished by using a direct reference, such as

> Kennedy, Jackie
> *See*: **Onassis, Jacqueline Kennedy, 1929-1994**

or the retrieval tool may be configured to go to the preferred name automatically and seamlessly when one of the cross-references is used in the user's search. If a search system does not employ authority-controlled access points, however, then the searcher may retrieve nothing at all, despite relevant resources being available in the collection.

A *preferred name* is a name or form of name that is selected to represent an entity in a particular context. That preferred name is the basis for an *authorized access point* (AAP); an AAP is a human-readable, established string of alphanumeric characters used to represent an entity. It is generally documented in an *authority record*—a record containing information about an entity that is entered into an information system to help ensure consistency in retrieval.[†] *Variant names*— names for an entity other than the one that has been selected as preferred—are the basis for *variant access points* (VAPs), which are also found in authority records as cross-references. VAPs are strings that represent an entity, but they are *not* authorized for use as access points in bibliographic metadata. The following is an example of some of the data found in an authority record.

AAP:	**Shakespeare, William, 1564-1616**
VAPs:	Shakspeare, William, 1564-1616
	Shakspere, William, 1564-1616
	Szekspir, Wiliam, 1564-1616
	Saixpēr, Gouilliam, 1564-1616
	Šekspyras, 1564-1616
	Şēkspiyar, Villiyam, 1564-1616
	Tsikinya-chaka, 1564-1616
	Шекпир, Вильям, 1564-1616
	沙士北亞威廉姆, 1564-1616
	Hākipia, Wiremu, 1564-1616
	[many others]

If this data is included in a retrieval tool, it means that any search on an alternate form of name will cause a reference to be displayed to the searcher. For example, a search for *Szekspir, Wiliam* could retrieve the following message:

"Szekspir, Wiliam, 1564-1616" is not used in this library's catalog.
Try a search for **Shakespeare, William, 1564-1616**.

Authority control is needed for collocation—for bringing together everything related to a person, family, corporate body, place, work, or expression, regardless of what names have been used. One has only to look at some websites that do not have authority control to see that there is value to this process. For example, a recent search for *Bob Smith* in the books category at Amazon[1] resulted in the following first 10 out of over 3,000 results sorted by Amazon's default arrangement of results:

1. *Dear **Bob** and Sue* (Book 1) by Matt and Karen **Smith**
2. ***Bob Smith**'s 27th Dream* by **Bob Smith**
3. *Dear **Bob** and Sue* (Book 2) by Matt and Karen **Smith**
4. ***Bob Smith**'s Key West* by Hornbuckle

[†]Authority records may be encoded in a variety of formats, including the MARC authority format and MADS. Many examples in this chapter use language-based labels rather than MARC tags. But later in the chapter there are some examples with MARC coding. For more information about the MARC authority format, please see Table 10.1 for a quick overview. For more extensive documentation, see the Library of Congress website: https://www.loc.gov/marc/authority/.

5. *Dear **Bob** and Sue* (Book 3) by Matt and Karen **Smith**
6. *Openly **Bob*** by **Bob Smith**
7. *Alcoholics Anonymous Big Book* by Alcoholics Anonymous
8. *Initial Experiences with The Kabbalah* by Mr. **Bob Smith** and Mr. Rordan Phobos
9. *Silent **Bob** Speaks: The Collected Writings of Kevin **Smith*** by Kevin **Smith**
10. *Throne of Grace: A Mountain Man, an Epic Adventure, and the Bloody Conquest of the American West* by Tom Clavin and **Bob** Drury

One can see that out of the first ten results, only three were authored by individuals named Bob Smith and one is implied in the data (a co-founder of Alcoholics Anonymous was named Dr. Bob Smith). There is a mixture of different types of keywords that were used to retrieve these results (e.g., parts of names, titles proper).

When an author search was performed in Amazon's advanced search screen, the results still lacked consistency and useful collocation:

1. *L. Ron Hubbard Presents Writers of the Future Volume 40* by L. Ron Hubbard, Nancy Kress, S. M. Stirling, Gregory Benford, **Bob** Eggleton … [no reference to Smith found on the page]
2. *The Big Book of Alcoholics Anonymous* (2nd ed.) by Bill Wilson, Bill W, Dr. **Bob Smith**, Alcoholics Anonymous
3. *Courage and Calling: Embracing Your God-Given Potential* by Gordon T. **Smith** [no reference to Bob found on page]
4. *Marvel Masterworks: The Uncanny X-Men 8* by Chris Claremont, Dave Cockrum, Paul **Smith**, Brent Anderson, **Bob** Wiacek
5. *X-Men Mutant Massacre Prelude Omnibus* by Chris Claremont, Marvel Various, John Romita, Jr., Barry Windsor-**Smith** [no reference to Bob found on page]
6. *Fly Fishing Maine* by **Bob** Mallard and George **Smith**
7. *Big Plans* by **Bob** Shea and Lane **Smith**
8. *Theology and the Avett Brothers* by Alex Sosler, **Bob** Crawford, and James K. A. **Smith**
9. *Spider-Man: Clone Saga Omnibus Vol. 1* by Terry Kavanagh, Marvel Various, Steven Butler, Mark Bagley [no reference to Bob or Smith found on page]
10. *Winning the Cancer Battle* by **Bob** Phillips, Louis **Smith**

In the first thirty results of this search, only five items were written by authors actually named Bob Smith.

On the other hand, an author search for *Smith, Bob* in the LC catalog[2] on the same day yielded 47 much more focused results; some of which are listed here.

Smith, Bob
Smith, Bob, 1910-
Smith, Bob, 1914-

Smith, Bob, 1917-1998
>See: **Smith, Buffalo Bob, 1917-1998**

Smith, Bob, 1920-

Smith, Bob, 1927-2016
>See: **Smith, Robert J. (Robert John), 1927-2016**

Smith, Bob, 1939-1995
>See: **Wolfman Jack, 1939-1995**

Smith, Bob, 1941-

Smith, Bob, 1948-

Smith, Bob, 1948 August 26-
>See: **Smith, Bob (Bob W.), 1948-**

Smith, Bob, 1949-

Smith, Bob, 1950-

Smith, Bob, 1951 November 18-
>See: **Smith, Bob (Bob A.), 1951-**

Smith, Bob, 1955 August 21-
>See: **Smith, Robert L. (Robert Lee), 1955 August 21-**

Smith, Bob, 1957 April 6-

Smith, Bob, 1958-2018

Smith, Bob (Bob A.), 1951-

Smith, Bob (Bob W.), 1948-

Smith, Bob D. (Bob David), 1932-

The preceding results were retrieved by using the browse function for creators; other search functions will yield different results. The entries above show the AAPs in boldface type, VAPs in plain type, with *see* instructions in italics. One may not know, at first, which Bob Smith is which, but once a needed Bob Smith has been identified, then all titles relating to that person are found together, and it is not necessary to look at any of the other entries.

10.1.2 Authority Control of Works and Expressions

Authority control is also concerned with identifying works and expressions. Why do catalogers create metadata about works and expressions? Generally, there are two reasons:

- Expressions and manifestations of a work are not always known by the same title, and
- Different works may be known by the same title.

The AAP is the primary mechanism by which catalogers unambiguously

- represent a work or expression embodied in a resource, or
- represent a relationship between one work or expression and another (i.e., a related work).

By creating a unique AAP, various resources containing the same intellectual or artistic content can be collocated in the catalog, no matter their individual titles proper. And resources with identical titles but with different content can be differentiated through the use of an AAP. AAPs not only bring together the like, they separate the unlike, or, more accurately, AAPs collocate entities that are the same, and disambiguate entities that are different.

A favorite example to illustrate the necessity for authority data for works and expressions is William Shakespeare's *Hamlet*. This work has been known by different titles over the years—across various languages, scripts, and transliterations. The following are just a few of the variations that can be found.

- *Hamlet*
- *Hamlet, Prinz von Dännemark*
- *Gamlet*
- *Khamleot*
- *Shakespeare's Hamlet*
- *Tragedien om Hamlet, Prins av Danmark*
- *The Tragedy of Hamlet*
- *The Tragicall Historie of Hamlet, Prince of Denmarke*

All these resources are brought together in the catalog under a single preferred title, *Hamlet*, which when combined with the authorized access point for Shakespeare provides a standard citation for the work in the form of a name/title access point:

Shakespeare, William, 1564-1616. Hamlet.

To identify particular expressions of *Hamlet* in the authority file, additional metadata elements are appended to the name/title access point to differentiate them. This requires the creation of a new authority record for each expression. For example, there is an authority record that has an AAP for translations of the play into another language:

Shakespeare, William, 1564-1616. Hamlet. Esperanto.

10.1.3 Authority Work

In order to have authority control, it is necessary for someone to do authority work. In this process, information professionals create authority data about an entity. **Authority data** is the result of a cataloger gathering information about an entity that is part of the bibliographic universe. Authority data helps information professionals to better understand the agents that are responsible for the creation and enhancement of works and expressions. It also helps catalogers better understand the content and the origins of works (and their varying expressions) that appear in resources. Current practice dictates the establishment of a unique identifier and an AAP for each entity that is intended to be used as an access point. The authority work process requires identifying all variants for the names of agents or titles of works, and making the necessary decisions about which variants represent the same names or works, which should be the authorized form, and which should be cross-references.

Most systems still require the choice of one name as the authorized access point (formerly known as the *heading*). The term **heading** came from the print catalog days when each access point was printed at the top (head) of the copy of the description and was called the heading for the record (see Figure 10.1). In the online catalog, the AAP no longer appears at the head of each record, although sometimes it is at the head or the side of a list of records in a catalog display (see Figure 10.2).

Although there is still an emphasis on establishing a standardized name or title for agents, works, and expressions, the process of authority work may involve more than just determining the authorized access point. With the publication of *Functional Requirements for Authority Data* (FRAD) in 2009,[3] and its subsequent influence on *RDA: Resource Description & Access* (2010),[4] many attributes for describing persons, families, and corporate bodies were introduced. For example, these changes allowed those creating authority data for a person to add attributes such as place of birth, affiliation, field of activity, and profession to the authority record. Although these elements are not required, some authority data creators regularly include this descriptive information to assist with the identification of an entity (see Figure 10.3).[‡]

Some information professionals, however, have questioned the need for including personal data about individuals as part of authority work. Some have questioned whether this data is *truly*

```
Z693
.W94        Introduction to cataloging and classification.
2015        Joudrey, Daniel N.
               Introduction to cataloging and classification / Daniel N. Joudrey, Arlene
            G. Taylor, and David P. Miller. – 11th ed. – Santa Barbara, Calif. : Libraries
            Unlimited, 2015.
               xxv, 1048 p. : ill. ; 26 cm. – (Library and information science text
            series)
               Includes bibliographical references (p. 1001-1022) and index.
               Significant expansion of: Introduction to cataloging and classifica-
            tion. 10th ed. / Arlene G. Taylor ; with the assistance of David P. Miller.
               ISBN 978-1-598-84857-1


               1. Resource description & access. 2. Descriptive cataloging. 3. Subject
            cataloging. 4. Classification—Books. I. Taylor, Arlene G., 1941-  II. Miller,
            David P. (David Peter), 1955-  III. Title. IV. Series.
```

Figure 10.1 Catalog Card Showing the Title Placed at the Top of the Record as the Heading for the Card.

[‡]Please note that this is a MARC record. For information about the various MARC fields in the authority format, please see Table 10.1 for a quick overview. For more extensive documentation, see the Library of Congress website: https://www.loc.gov/marc/authority/.

Number	Author / Titles	Media	Year
1	**Smith, Bob, 1910-**		
	Farthest reach : Oregon & Washington	Book	1941
	My first book	Book	1942
2	**Smith, Bob, 1914-**		
	Basics of Bible interpretation	Book	1978
	Dying to live	Book	1976
	Love story … the real thing	Book	1975
	When all else fails … read the directions	Book	1974
3	**Smith, Bob, 1920-**		
	Seven steps in the dark	Book	1991
4	**Smith, Bob, 1941-**		
	Hamlet's dresser : a memoir	Book	2002
5	**Smith, Bob, 1948-**		
	Yoga for a new age	Book	1986
	Yoga for a new age	Book	1982
6	**Smith, Bob, 1949-**		
	Stunt flying with paper airplanes	Book	1992
7	**Smith, Bob, 1950-**		
	Salt and light	Sound recording	2015
8	**Smith, Bob, 1957 April 6-**		
	Do you? : business the Yahoo! way	Book	2001
9	**Smith, Bob, 1958-2018**		
	Growing up gay : from left out to coming out	Book	1995
	Gay comedy jam : "freedom tour" live!	Sound recording	1997
	Openly Bob	Book	1997
	Remembrance of things I forgot : a novel	Book	2011
	Selfish and perverse	Book	2007
	Treehab : tales from my natural, wild life	Book	2016
	Way to go, Smith!	Book	1999
10	**Smith, Bob (Bob A.), 1951-**		
	Archie's favorite Christmas comics	Book	2014
	Batman adventures. Batgirl : a league of her own	Book	2020

Figure 10.2 Search Results Showing the Authorized Access Points for Various Persons Named Bob Smith.

necessary and have raised concerns about the privacy of the individuals being described.⁵ Kelly J. Thompson, for example, has discussed how the *gender* attribute in Original RDA raised ethical issues in general, and discussed how it can be problematic for the trans community. Thompson demonstrated that the power to name and assign labels to individuals' gender identities has resulted in the outing of transgender authors in 65 percent of NARs that they had examined.⁶ These concerns led some to reconsider how much additional personal data should be included in authority records. In 2022, the Program for Cooperative Cataloging (PCC) Ad Hoc Task Group on Recording Gender in Personal Name Authority Records released recommendations stating that catalogers should no longer record the *gender* attribute in personal name authority records.⁷

Authority work also includes identification of relationships between variant names and titles and their corresponding authorized forms, or between two or more related names or titles (e.g., the relationship between the pseudonym *Mark Twain* and the birth name *Samuel Langhorne Clemens*). For example, in a catalog, the MARC-encoded authority data

> 100 1# $a Twain, Mark, $d 1835-1910
> 500 1# $a Clemens, Samuel Langhorne, $d 1835-1910
> 500 1# $a Snodgrass, Quintus Curtius, $d 1835-1910
> 500 1# $a Conte, Louis de, $d 1835-1910

generates the following *see also* reference based on an author search for **Twain, Mark, 1835-1910**:

> For works of this author written under other names, *see also*:
> **Clemens, Samuel Langhorne, 1835-1910**;
> **Snodgrass, Quintus Curtius, 1835-1910**; and
> **Conte, Louis de, 1835-1910**.

Once decisions about the entity have been made, authority work then involves the process of documenting, in an authority record, the work done along with the decisions made. An authority record is a compilation of metadata about a person, a family, a corporate body, a place, a work, an expression, or a subject. It includes evidence of all the decisions made and all the relationships among variants that have been identified.

Doing authority work in concert with many other people is very helpful, saving hours of work for individual catalogers. One such cooperative project is NACO, the Name Authority Cooperative Program of the PCC (Program for Cooperative Cataloging).⁸ Participants in NACO follow a common set of standards and guidelines when creating or updating authority records so that consistency is maintained in the Library of Congress/NACO Authority File (LCNAF), a large, shared authority file.

10.1.4 Authority Files

The product of authority work is an authority record. A collection of authority records compiled in a retrieval system or a database is known as an ***authority file***.§ Various types of authority records are accumulated and stored in authority files (e.g., subjects, names, titles), which are separate from

---

§It should be noted that in the card catalog days, authority files were also in the form of cards.

ID:		n 79117152	Entered:	800602	Replaced:	20221026
008/06 Geo Subd:	n-Not applic	008/11 SH System:	a-LCSH	008/29 Ref Eval:	b-Not eval
008/07 Roman:	|-No attempt	008/15 Subj Use:	a-Appropriate	008/31 Rec Upd:	a-Can be used
008/09 Kind Rec	a-Estab hdg	008/17 Type Subd:	n-Not applic	008/33 Level Estab:	a-Fully

010	$a n 7911715
024 7#	$a Q185696 $2 wikidata $1 http://www.wikidata.org/entity/Q185696
024 7#	$a 29528997 $2 viaf $1 http://www.viaf.org/viaf/29528997
040	$a DLC $b eng $e rda $c DLC $d DLC $d MWA $d DLC $d OCoLC $d InNd $d UPB ...
046	$f 18321129 $g 18880306 $2 edtf
053 #0	$a PS1015 $b PS1018
100 1#	$a Alcott, Louisa May, $d 1832-1888
368	$c Americans $2 lcdgt
368	$c Bay Staters $2 lcdgt
370	$a Germantown (Philadelphia, Pa.) $b Boston (Mass.) $c United States $2 naf
372	$a Fiction $2 lcsh
372	$a Novels $2 lcsh
372	$a Short stories $2 lcsh
372	$a Poetry $2 lcsh
374	$a Authors $2 lcsh
374	$a Novelists $2 lcsh
374	$a Poets $2 lcsh
377	$a eng
400 1#	$a Alcott, Lou, $d 1832-1888
400 1#	$a Alcott, Louy, $d 1832-1888
400 1#	$a Alcott, L. M. $q (Louisa May), $d 1832-1888
400 1#	$a Alcott, Louisa M. $q (Louisa May), $d 1832-1888
400 1#	$a Alkūt, Luwīzā, $d 1832-1888
400 0#	$a Author of Kitty's class-day, $d 1832-1888
400 0#	$a Author of Little men, $d 1832-1888
400 0#	$a Author of Little women, $d 1832-1888
400 1#	$a Barnard, A. M., $d 1832-1888
400 1#	$a Little men, Author of, $d 1832-1888
400 1#	$a Little women, Author of, $d 1832-1888
400 1#	$a Олкотт, Луиза Мэй, $d 1832-1888
400 1#	$a אלקוט, לואיזה מיי, $d 1832-1888
400 1#	$a ألكوت، لويزا مي
400 1#	$a アルコツトルイザメイ, $d 1832-1888
400 1#	$a オルコツトルイザメイ, $d 1832-1888
667	$a Non-Latin script references not evaluated.
670	$a Gulliver, L. Louisa May Alcott, a bibliography ... 1932.
670	$a Her Jo's boys, 1983: $b t.p. (Louisa M. Alcott)
670	$a MWA/NAIP files $b (hdg.: Alcott, Louisa May, 1832-1888; usage: Louisa M. Alcott; author of Little women; author of An old-fashioned girl; author of Little men; author of Hospital sketches; author of Kitty's class-day; author of Moods; author of Aunt Jo's scrap-bag; author of Work; author of Aunt Kipp; author of Eight cousins; author of Psyche's art)
670	$a Wikipedia, Dec. 9, 2010 $b (Louisa May Alcott; b. Nov. 29, 1832 in Germantown (Philadelphia), Pa.; d. Mar. 6, 1888 in Boston, Mass.; American novelist)
670	$a Selected letters of Louisa May Alcott, 1995, via WWW, viewed April 20, 2022 $b (letters signed: Lou, Louy, Louisa, L. M. Alcott, L. M. A.)
678 0#	$a Louisa May Alcott (1832-1888) was an American novelist.

Figure 10.3 An Excerpt of an Authority Record. (Source: Library of Congress, *Classification Web Plus*—Record Number n79117152.)

Table 10.1 A Selection of Tags in the MARC Authority Format

MARC Tag Blocks	Notable Fields
00X Control Fields	008 Fixed field
0XX Number and Code Fields	010 Library of Congress Control Number (LCCN)
	046 Special Coded Dates
	053 LC Classification Number
1XX Heading Fields	100 Heading – Personal Name
	110 Heading – Corporate Name
	111 Heading – Meeting Name
	130 Heading – Uniform Title
3XX Heading Information Fields	336 Content Type
	370 Associated Place
	372 Field of Activity
	373 Associated Group
	374 Occupation
	377 Associated Language
	378 Fuller Form of Name
	380 Form of Work
	386 Creator/Contributor Characteristics
4XX See References **(Unauthorized Names/Terms)**	400 Personal Name
	410 Corporate Name
	...
5XX See Also References **(Other Related Authorized Names/ Terms)**	500 Personal Name
	510 Corporate Name
	...
64X Series Treatment Fields	644 Series Analysis Practice
	645 Series Tracing Practice
	646 Series Classification Practice
667-68X Notes	667 Nonpublic general note
	670 Source data found
	675 Source data not found
	678 Biographical or historical data
	680 Public general note

bibliographic files (the collection of records which contain metadata for individual resources). In many library management systems, bibliographic records are linked to the authority records that describe agents, works, and subjects (refer to Figure 4.4 on page 153 for an example of linkages). If linked, cross-references housed in the authority records can be displayed to users in the results of their searches of the bibliographic file, such as:

> Smith, Bob, 1939-1995
> *See*: **Wolfman Jack, 1939-1995**

In the United States, one of the most widely used authority files is the aforementioned Library of Congress/NACO Authority File (LCNAF). Other authority files (or data value standards) in use include subject heading lists, thesauri, and classification schemes, which are discussed in later chapters. Several standards exist for name control, including the LCNAF and the Getty vocabularies, which are primarily used in the art and museum communities. In recent years, many data value standards have been made available in linked-data-compatible formats. This entails providing the same authority data but with *Internationalized Resource Identifiers* (IRIs) that provide unambiguous identification. For example, the following are just a few of the more than 100 authority files and controlled vocabularies in LC's Linked Data Service:[9]

- *American Folklore Society Ethnographic Thesaurus*
- Code List for Cultural Heritage Organizations
- Extended Date/Time Format Datatypes Scheme
- ISO 639-1: Codes for the Representation of Names of Languages
- Library of Congress/NACO Authority File
- *Library of Congress Classification* (LCC)
- *Library of Congress Demographic Group Terms* (LCDGT)
- *Library of Congress Genre/Form Terms for Library and Archival Materials* (LCGFT)
- *Library of Congress Subject Headings* (LCSH)
- MARC Relator, Country, Language, and Geographic Area codes
- RDA Content, Media, and Carrier types

To be useful as broadly as possible, the data is provided in a variety of formats (e.g., RDF in XML, N-Triples, JSON) using two data structure schemas—Metadata Authority Description Schema (MADS) and Simple Knowledge Organization System (SKOS). This freely available service, with its focus on linked data implementations, allows authority control concepts to be applied beyond the library and information science communities of practice—even into the general web environment—but this will happen only if online content creators take advantage of this authoritative and trustworthy data.

10.1.5 International Authority Control Efforts

Authority work is done all over the world. National bibliographic agencies have independent authority files, each of which contains data about entities that also appear in other authority files. This highly trusted authoritative data, however, is scattered around the world. To harness the collective knowledge of the international information community, work has been done to develop an international authority file known as the Virtual International Authority File (VIAF).

> VIAF's goal is to make library authority files less expensive to maintain and more generally useful to the library domain and beyond. To achieve this, VIAF seeks to include authoritative names from many libraries into a global service that is available via the Web. By linking disparate names for the same person or organization, VIAF provides a convenient means for a wider community of libraries and other agencies to repurpose bibliographic data produced by libraries serving different language communities. More specifically, the VIAF service:
>
> - Links national and regional-level authority records, creating clusters of related records
> - Expands the concept of universal bibliographic control by (1) allowing national and regional variations in authorized form to coexist; and (2) supporting needs for variations in preferred language, script and spelling
> - Plays a role in the emerging Semantic Web.[10]

At the turn of the century, the VIAF project began to aggregate this data in one interface. In the design phase, there were several suggestions as to how to bring this data together. The method chosen was a distributed model, based on a suggestion by Barbara Tillett, instead of creating one massive authority file.[11] The Library of Congress, OCLC, and the German national library established VIAF as a joint project; OCLC maintains the service and provides open access to the data for everyone.[12] In 2025, VIAF contains authority data from more than fifty agencies in over thirty countries and territories for agents, works, expressions, meetings, and geographic names.[13] It displays national and regional variations in authority data based on differences in language, character sets, and spelling.[14]

International authority control requires standards, and there are several that may be used to good advantage. In the international library community, the International Federation of Library Associations and Institutions (IFLA) issued its second edition of *Guidelines for Authority Records and References (GARR)* in 2001.[15] *Functional Requirements for Authority Data* (FRAD)[16] and *Functional Requirements for Subject Authority Data* (FRSAD)[17] also address authority control issues; both, however, have been superseded by the *IFLA Library Reference Model* (LRM).[18]

10.2 Bibliographic Standards For Authority Control

As mentioned in Chapter 8, the creation of metadata in a broad sense requires description of the resource, attention to access points for the description, and encoding. Encoding is discussed in Chapter 5, and Chapter 8 addresses description and access. The next step after description and access is to ensure that the access points are under authority control.

Several models and standards address issues of authority control in libraries to varying degrees. Bibliographic models and standards are discussed first; standards that exist for archives and for the art and museum communities are described in later sections. The library-oriented standards include

- *IFLA Library Reference Model* (LRM)
- *Statement of International Cataloguing Principles* (ICP)
- *RDA: Resource Description & Access* (2020)
- *RDA: Resource Description & Access* (2010)
- *Anglo-American Cataloguing Rules, 2nd ed.* (AACR2)
- Metadata Authority Description Schema (MADS)

10.2.1 IFLA's *Library Reference Model* (LRM) and Its Precursors

Although IFLA LRM is the current conceptual model influencing library cataloging standards (e.g., RDA), its earlier incarnations have had considerable influence on where the model stands today. In this section, the earlier models, *Functional Requirements for Bibliographic Records* (FRBR) and FRAD, are reviewed before discussing LRM.

10.2.1.1 *Functional Requirements for Bibliographic Records* (FRBR)

FRBR was IFLA's original attempt to create a conceptual model that formalized the entities, attributes, and relationships observed in the bibliographic universe. FRBR defined three groups of entities. Group 1 focused on information resources—products of creation or intellectual endeavor. Resources comprise four entities: *work*, *expression*, *manifestation*, and *item* (WEMI).** FRBR also identified Group 2 entities—agents responsible for creating the content of resources or otherwise contributing to them. This group included *person* and *corporate body*, with *family* later added by FRAD.[19] The third group in the original FRBR model identified entities that can be subjects of works—this third group contained *concept*, *object*, *event*, and *place*, plus the entities from Groups 1 and 2. The results of an investigation focused on subject entities was published as the FRSAD model in 2010.[20] This third model did not address individual entities for specific kinds of subjects (e.g., *concept*, *place*, *person*), focusing instead on a more generic level (see discussion below).

In FRBR, works, expressions, and the Group 2 and Group 3 entities could all be recorded as authority-controlled access points, but the model did not describe how those entities and relationships are reflected in access points in bibliographic records, nor did it delineate how a cataloger was to determine the name or AAP that was to be used for these entities.[21] The task of addressing authority-controlled data was assigned to the IFLA Working Group on Functional Requirements and Numbering of Authority Records, which devised FRAD, and the Working Group on Functional Requirements for Subject Authority Records, which designed the FRSAD model.

**This is one aspect of FRBR that remains in the LRM conceptual model.

10.2.1.2 *Functional Requirements for Authority Data* (FRAD)

FRAD, like FRBR, is a deprecated conceptual model. Its purpose was to provide a framework for the authority data necessary to support authority control locally, nationally, and internationally. It was never meant to be a practical application or an implementation plan. FRAD, like FRBR, was centered on users, defined as both the creators of authority records and end users who benefit from controlled access points and cross-reference structures. Four user tasks were identified in FRAD: *find, identify, contextualize,* and *justify.* The tasks *find* and *identify* are the same as in FRBR and LRM. The tasks *contextualize* and *justify* applied to authority record creators, not to end users. *Contextualize* addressed placing authority data in context and clarifying relationships; *justify* addressed documenting, through citations, the choice of the form of name to be used in a controlled access point.

The FRAD model, as mentioned already, added *family* to FRBR's Group 2 entities, but it also added five entities that were needed for a complete model of authority control:

- **Name**: the word, character, group of words, or character string that an entity is known by (e.g., a personal name, a title); known in FRSAD as *nomen* and in LRM as a *nomen string* used to identify a *nomen*.

- **Identifier**: anything that uniquely identifies an entity, such as a number, a code, a word or phrase, a logo, or other such device (e.g., no2006073134); can be correlated to a *nomen string* in LRM.

- **Controlled access point**: a character string to be used for retrieval found in a bibliographic record, authority record, or reference record (e.g., **Dickinson, Emily, 1830-1886**).

- **Rules**: a set of instructions for formulating controlled access points (e.g., RDA).

- **Agency**: an organization that has responsibility for applying rules to the construction and/or modification of controlled access points (e.g., LC or another library).

FRBR identified some attributes for each of the entities in its model. FRAD added attributes of its own. For example, the attributes enumerated in FRBR and FRAD for *person* are listed below. These attributes can be used to more fully describe an individual in an authority record, rather than just simply creating an authorized form of name.

FRBR	FRAD
- Dates associated with the person - Title of person - Other designation associated with the person	- Gender - Place of birth - Place of death - Country - Place of residence - Affiliation - Address - Language of person - Field of activity - Profession/Occupation - Biography/History

FRAD also used entity-relationship modeling to define how different entities are connected. FRAD provided an extensive relationships section focused on (1) relationships that operate at a generic level between the entity types, (2) relationships that are commonly shown in the reference structure of the authority record, and (3) relationships between one controlled access point and another.[22] For example, the following table illustrates relationships between entity types:[23]

Entity Type	Sample Relationship Types
Person to Person	• Pseudonymous relationship • Attributive relationship • Collaborative relationship • Sibling relationship • Parent/child relationship
Person to Family	• Membership relationship
Person to Corporate Body	• Membership relationship
Family to Family	• Genealogical relationship
Corporate Body to Corporate Body	• Hierarchical relationship • Sequential relationship
Work to Work	• Equivalence relationship • Derivative relationship • Descriptive relationship • Whole-Part relationship • Accompanying relationship • Sequential relationship • Shared characteristic relationship

Part II of FRAD delineated, in some detail, the practice of providing authority data—mostly within the library sector, although brief mention is made of the archives, art, cultural heritage, and museum communities.

10.2.1.3 *IFLA's Library Reference Model* (LRM)

It can be difficult to keep two or more related models in sync when they have been developed and published over an extended period of time and were completed by different committees with different charges. This was the case with FRBR, FRAD, and FRSAD. Although they were part of the same family of "Functional Requirements" models, they had different approaches to some concepts. For example, they each approached names and subjects differently. FRBR identified *name* as an attribute of an entity, and for subjects, it provided Group 3 entities (*concept, object,* etc.) that had relationships to the Group 1 entity *work*. FRAD treated names as separate entities (e.g., a person has a relationship to a name or names) but treated subject matter as an attribute of *work*. FRSAD, which addressed subjects only, approached the concept at a more abstract level. It introduced two terms for familiar entities: ***nomen***, meaning a name or label, and ***thema***, meaning subject matter. For conceptual consistency within the cataloging world, these types of discrepancies had to be addressed. This was the purpose of developing LRM: to address inconsistencies and harmonize the models.

As discussed in Chapter 7, changes were introduced in LRM. Although it is still an entity-relationship model of the bibliographic universe, it is narrower in scope. Distinctions between bibliographic and authority data are de-emphasized, as articulated in LRM's scope statement:

> The IFLA LRM model aims to make explicit general principles governing the logical structure of bibliographic information, without making presuppositions about how that data might be stored in any particular system or application. As a result, the model does not make a distinction between data traditionally stored in bibliographic or holdings records and data traditionally stored in name or subject authority records. For the purposes of the model, all of this data is included under the term bibliographic information and as such is within the scope of the model.[24]

Some basic entities have changed in the harmonized model. FRBR and FRAD's specific Group 2 entities are simply referred to as *agents* in LRM. Agents play roles in creating, distributing, manufacturing, owning, and modifying resources. Agents, therefore, are logical entities to be included as access points in bibliographic descriptions. An agent may be a **person** (an individual human being) or a **collective agent** (an entity that subsumes both *family* and *corporate body*). Another change is that the definition of *person* no longer allows for fictitious, legendary, and mythological characters, as well as individual non-human entities (e.g., Lassie, the dog; Keiko, the whale) to be viewed as persons (which was possible previously). Agents, and the nomen strings that are used to identify them, are typically under authority control.

LRM also changes how subjects are addressed. It has eliminated the four unique subject entities from FRBR—*concept, object, event,* and *place*—in favor of the more generic approach found in FRSAD, but with some additional changes. *Thema* has been replaced in LRM with an even more generalized entity, ***res*** (i.e., *thing* in Latin); everything in the universe is a *res*. The model explicitly identifies two key relationships involving subject matter: (1) a *res* can be the subject of a *work*, and (2) a *res* has an appellation (a *nomen*). Subjects and their associated nomen strings are also likely candidates to be placed under authority control.

Two resource entities, *work* and *expression*, may also be described in authority data. Not only can a standard AAP be established for a work (or an expression), but an authority record can be created to document its other attributes. For example, the work Shakespeare's *Hamlet* has been known by different titles across various editions and translations. Establishing a consistent AAP, such as **Shakespeare, William, 1564–1616. Hamlet**, ensures reliable identification of the work and its expressions. The authority record also contains, in addition to the AAP, the form of work (**Play; Drama; Tragedies (Drama)**), beginning date created ([**1599 … 1602**]), place associated with the work (**England**) and any cross-references needed for variant access points for the work (e.g., **Shakespeare, William, 1564-1616. Tragicall historie of Hamlet Prince of Denmarke**).

The LRM revision process has not been kind to FRAD. Most of the FRAD entities have been deprecated. *Rules* and *agency* are considered out of scope because of their administrative focus. FRAD's *name, identifier,* and *controlled access point* entities have been merged into *nomen*.

The FRAD-specific user tasks (*contextualize* and *justify*) were removed from LRM because they are administrative in nature and thus fall outside its scope.[25]

Many of the FRAD relationships identified in the previous section have been generalized in LRM. For example, a pseudonymous person-to-person relationship is represented by two res/nomen relationships (**RES** *has appellation* **NOMEN1**; **RES** *has appellation* **NOMEN2**) and a descriptive work-to-work relationship is now represented by a work/res relationship (**WORK** *has subject* **RES**). The list of relationships specified in LRM is found in Table 7.2 on pages 239–40. More details on specific relationships and the rest of the changes in the harmonized model can be found in the LRM documentation.

Original RDA (2010) was greatly influenced by the FRBR and FRAD models (FRBR more so than FRAD). The changes brought forth in LRM are reflected in Official RDA (2020), especially in its revised structure. The changes in user tasks, entities, attributes, and relationships have found their way into the current version of RDA, transforming what was once a narrative content standard into something more akin to a data dictionary.

10.2.2 IFLA's *Statement of International Cataloguing Principles* (ICP)

The *Statement of International Cataloguing Principles* (ICP),[26] published in 2009 and updated in 2016, is IFLA's revision of its 1961 Paris Principles. The ICP provides guidelines that are applicable to the online library catalogs of today as well as to the retrieval tools of the future. The revision process consisted of a series of IFLA Meetings of Experts on an International Cataloguing Code, the fifth and last of which was held in 2007. The ICP broadens the Paris Principles from covering primarily textual works to covering all types of materials, and in addition to choice and form of entry covered by the Paris Principles, these new principles cover all aspects of bibliographic and authority records used in library catalogs. It also provides "guiding rules that should be included in cataloguing codes internationally, as well as guidance on search and retrieval capabilities. [The] 2016 edition takes into consideration new categories of users, the open access environment, the interoperability and the accessibility of data, features of discovery tools and the significant change of user behaviour in general."[27] The principles were built on the FRBR and FRAD conceptual models in addition to other cataloging traditions from the past (e.g., Cutter, Ranganathan, Lubetzky).[††]

The principles echo the user tasks in the "objectives and functions" of the catalog: to find resources in a collection, to identify a resource or agent, to select a resource that is appropriate, to obtain access to a resource, and to navigate and explore a catalog. The ICP states that the "highest principle for the construction of cataloguing codes should be the convenience of the users of the catalogue."[28] The general principles are enumerated in Chapter 8 (see page 272).

The most extensive section of the ICP is called "Access Points." As mentioned in Chapter 8, the ICP notes that access points may be controlled or uncontrolled, the latter being such things as the *title proper* or *keywords* found anywhere in a bibliographic record. Names, titles, and other

---

[††] At the time of this writing no plans have been announced, but with LRM having replaced FRBR and FRAD, it would not be surprising to see IFLA start the revision process for the ICPs in the next few years.

metadata needed for consistency in locating resources should be normalized, with variant forms used as references. The principles discuss choice of access points to include in a bibliographic description. They suggest that the titles of works and expressions should be controlled, as well as the names of the creators of works.[29] Section 5.3 of the principles addresses authorized access points (AAPs). It begins with some general principles on the use of standards, on how to address different language and scripts, and on transliteration. Following those are principles that pertain to the choice and form of AAPs for various entities. These include the following:[30]

- Names (and the forms of those names) used in AAPs are to be represented consistently. The preferred names should be the ones found predominantly on manifestations or well-accepted conventional names.
- If more than one name is used by an entity, then one must be chosen as the basis of the AAP. If the variations are not representing different personas, then preference is given first to a commonly known or conventional name, but finally to an official name if a commonly known or conventional name is not found.
- Successive different names for a corporate body that are more than minor variations are treated as names of new entities connected with references to earlier/later names.
- If needed, further identifying characteristics should be added to distinguish the entity from others with the same name.
- In all cases, variant forms not selected as the AAP should be included in the authority data as references or alternate display forms.
- Names of persons or families that consist of several words should be arranged in the order that follows the conventions of the country and language that is most associated with that person or family.
- Corporate names should be given in direct order unless they are part of a jurisdiction or the name implies subordination, in which case the authorized form should begin with the name of the jurisdiction or the superior body.
- A name for a work/expression may be a title that can stand alone, a name/title combination, or a title with qualifiers added. The preferred work/expression title should be the title found in the first manifestation of the work in the original language, or, if not available, the title most commonly used.

When the creators of RDA began developing a new content standard, they affirmed the role of the ICP as the basis for the cataloging principles used throughout Original RDA.[31] It has not only embraced the principles but also clearly follows the general guidelines for description, access points, and authority control. The following sections address approaches to authority control in both versions of RDA.

10.2.3 *RDA: Resource Description & Access* (2020)

The latest content standard intended for use in libraries, *RDA: Resource Description & Access* (2020),[32] provides elements and options for describing entities that are the focus of authority work, including persons, families, corporate bodies, places, works, and expressions. As with the rest of the standard, the elements and instructions relevant to authority records are presented in terms of *conditions* and *options*.‡‡ Official RDA does not prescribe which options should be applied in authority work; instead, this is the domain of application profiles and policy statements, such as the Library of Congress-Program for Cooperative Cataloging Policy Statements (LC-PCC PS).§§ In light of Official RDA's less prescriptive orientation, the sections that follow primarily focus on the elements that the standard defines for access points and authority data, rather than specific policies or procedures for authority work. For catalogers following LC/PCC practice, the content and format of access points created with Official RDA are expected to remain largely the same as those created with Original RDA (discussed at length later in this chapter), though the terminology, element set, and underlying conceptual model have changed.

In addition to the traditional subjects of authority work (agents, works, and expressions), Official RDA also provides elements for describing timespans, which could open the door to creating authority records for time periods or even for specific years (e.g., the Renaissance, the period of Queen Victoria's reign, 1975). At this time, however, authority records are not created for timespans in descriptive cataloging. Although all kinds of dates appear in both bibliographic and authority records (e.g., dates of publication, authors' birth dates), these dates are simply provided as strings; there is no access point or authority record for the date.

Though Official RDA does provide options for the construction of access points, it does not specify a string encoding scheme (i.e., a standard syntax) to determine the order of elements, spacing, or punctuation of access points. Whereas Original RDA included instructions for access point syntax in Appendix E, Official RDA leaves the choice of a string encoding scheme for access points up to the discretion of individual metadata communities, another example of Official RDA's move away from the prescriptive guidelines of a traditional content standard. To fill this gap, the LC-PCC Metadata Guidance Documentation (MGDs) provide instructions on access point syntax, which, in combination with the data elements from RDA, can be used to construct AAPs and VAPs.[33]

10.2.3.1 Nomens and Appellations

Official RDA uses the *nomen* entity to model the relationship between entities and the names, access points, and identifiers that represent them. **Nomen**, like most other Official RDA entities, is derived from LRM and is defined as "a label for any RDA entity except a nomen."[34] Examples of nomens include titles for works and expressions, names of corporate bodies, families, and persons, and access points and identifiers for any of these entities. The basic relationship between any entity in RDA and its label(s) can be modeled as

RDA ENTITY<*has appellation*>**NOMEN**

Because nomens are defined as entities in Official RDA (rather than simple attributes of other entities), they can themselves be the subject of additional metadata statements. Some of the elements available for describing nomens include

---

‡‡For an overview of the format of Official RDA instructions, see Chapter 9.
§§Other policy statements in the RDA Toolkit include the British Library PS, Library and Archives Canada PS, National Library of New Zealand PS, and the Music Library Association Best Practices.

- **Category of nomen**: A type to which a nomen belongs. For example, for personal names, this could be an indication of the type of name (e.g., pseudonym, married name, nickname, stage name).
- **Context of use**: The circumstances in which a nomen is used.
- **Intended audience of nomen**: The type of users for whom the nomen is intended (e.g., grade school students, Spanish speakers).
- **Language of nomen**: The language that the nomen is expressed in.
- **Nomen string**: The combination of symbols that forms the label for the entity. This is the actual string of characters that makes up the name, title, access point, or identifier.
- **Note on nomen**: An unstructured note about the nomen.
- **Part nomen**: A nomen that is a component part of another nomen (e.g., *Cervantes Saavedra* is the surname part of the personal name access point **Cervantes Saavedra, Miguel de, 1547-1616**).
- **Scheme of nomen**: The *vocabulary encoding scheme* (that is, controlled vocabulary) or string encoding scheme in which a nomen is established. For example, the AAP for Cervantes provided above is established in the LCNAF (a vocabulary encoding scheme).
- **Script of nomen**: The script (e.g., Roman, Cyrillic, Arabic) used to express the nomen.

These nomen elements have the potential to express rich information about the names, titles, and access points recorded in authority records. Not all of these can currently be expressed in the MARC 21 authority format, though this could change in the future.

Official RDA defines a number of appellation elements that connect entities with nomens. An ***appellation element*** records the relationship between an entity and a label that it is known by. Basic categories of appellation elements based on type of nomen include

- **Access point**
  - Authorized access point
  - Variant access point
- **Identifier**
- **Name**
  - Preferred name
  - Variant name
- **Title**
  - Preferred title
  - Variant title

Relationship elements in Official RDA allow relationships to be described with more precision and explicitly specify the types of entities connected by the relationship; for this reason, there are numerous individual elements defined for each of the general appellation types listed above. For example, in the case of AAPs, there are individual elements for *authorized access point for work*, *authorized access point for expression*, *authorized access point for person*, and *authorized access point for corporate body*, among others. Though the terminology of appellation elements may be new, the basic concepts (identifiers, access points, preferred names and titles, etc.) have long been the subject of authority work and can be seen in the existing structure of AAPs and VAPs in authority records. The table below provides an example of appellation elements in a metadata description set for a work.

Work	
has preferred title of work	Don Quixote
has variant title of work	Ingenioso hidalgo don Quijote de La Mancha
has variant title of work	Don Quijote de la Mancha
has authorized access point for work	Cervantes Saavedra, Miguel de, 1547-1616. Don Quixote
has variant access point for work	Cervantes Saavedra, Miguel de, 1547-1616. Ingenioso hidalgo don Quijote de La Mancha
has variant access point for work	Cervantes Saavedra, Miguel de, 1547-1616. Don Quijote de la Mancha

10.2.3.2 Describing Agents

Official RDA's guidelines for describing those who create, realize, distribute, own, or modify information resources are organized around the entity pages for the five agent entities: *agent*, *collective agent*, *corporate body*, *family*, and *person*. Though *agent* and *collective agent* are both described by a full complement of elements, these generic entities (which mainly exist to provide hierarchical structure for the *agent* group) are not generally employed in current cataloging. Each agent entity is described by

- *Appellation elements**** that record the names, access points, and identifiers that the entity is known by,
- *Relationship elements* that relate the entity to other RDA entities, and
- *Attribute elements* that are used to describe important characteristics of the entity not represented by a relationship.

The following sections focus on elements for describing and creating access points for persons as an example of authority work. There may be additional considerations for describing families and corporate bodies, but the basic set of elements associated with them is similar.

One notable change to the treatment of agents in Official RDA is that fictitious persons and real, non-human entities (such as animals) are no longer considered persons, and responsibility for resources cannot be attributed to them. Original RDA allowed fictitious characters (e.g., Sherlock Holmes) and non-human entities (e.g., Koko the gorilla) who were credited with authorship to

---

***Appellation elements, introduced in the previous section, are treated separately here because of their importance for authority work but note that appellations are also technically a type of relationship element, because they express a relationship between the entity being described and a *nomen*.

be recorded as creators in bibliographic records, and provided instructions for creating AAPs for them; in contrast, Official RDA, following changes in LRM, defines *person* more narrowly as "an agent who is an individual human being who lives or is assumed to have lived."[35] In cases where a fictitious person appears in a statement of responsibility, Official RDA directs catalogers to treat the fictitious person as a pseudonym of the agent responsible for the resource; non-human entities are considered entities outside the scope of RDA. The PCC, however, has stated that it will not follow the Official RDA policy in this area. Instead, catalogers following LC/PCC practice may continue to create authority records for fictitious persons and non-human entities and credit them with the creation of works and expressions in bibliographic records.[36]

10.2.3.2.1 Persons: Appellation Elements

In the context of authority work for persons, appellations include names, access points, and identifiers that are used to represent the person. The basic relationship between a person and their name is expressed by the element *name of person*, which in turn has several sub-elements for more specific types of names:

- fuller form of name
- given name
- preferred name of person
- surname
- variant name of person

Because the name selected as the *preferred name of person* is also used as the basis for the authorized access point in current cataloging practice, some guidance may be needed when choosing between different names or forms of name used by a person to ensure consistency. Official RDA provides over two dozen conditions (many with several optional approaches) for selecting a preferred name, including some that address very specific scenarios such as terms of rank, persons identified by surnames only, saints, names in multiple languages, names consisting of a word or phrase, among others. General LC/PCC practice is to apply the option to record (in this order of preference)

1. the name that appears most frequently on manifestations,
2. the predominant name used in outside sources, or
3. the most recently used name.[37]

This practice is similar to that followed under Original RDA. In general, most LC-PCC PSs direct catalogers to apply options that are consistent with current cataloging practice when possible.

The relationship between a person and an access point that represents them is expressed by the element *access point for person*, which has two sub-elements: *authorized access point for person* and *variant access point for person*. Official RDA contains numerous conditions and options for constructing access points for persons, such as options for names containing compound surnames, patronymics, initials, names of royal houses, and names consisting of a phrase. The general instructions under *access point for person* provide additional elements and designations that may be added to the base name for a person to form a complete access point, such as

- date of birth
- date of death
- fuller form of name
- period of activity of person
- profession or occupation
- term of rank or honour or office
- terms associated with a person named in sacred scripture or an apocryphal book

The element *identifier for person* records a code, number, or other string that is used to uniquely identify a person in a certain application or setting. The primary identifier in the context of the LCNAF is the Library of Congress Control Number (LCCN) associated with the person's authority record, but other identifiers for personal names may also be relevant, such as Open Researcher and Contributor ID (ORCID), International Standard Name Identifier (ISNI), or an identifier from another national authority file. An example of appellation elements in the metadata description set for a person is included in Table 10.2.

10.2.3.2.2 Persons: Relationship Elements

Official RDA provides numerous relationship elements that connect a person to other related RDA entities. These elements further describe and contextualize the person, and in a system configured to display linkages could be used to allow a user to navigate and explore relationships between entities. In Original RDA, relationships with other persons or corporate bodies were indicated by relationship designators; in Official RDA, they are modeled as relationship elements.[†††] Information about related places and dates is also represented as a relationship element, since place and timespan have been fully developed as entities in Official RDA. A small sample of relationship elements for persons includes

Relationship Type	Selected Relationship Elements
Person to Person	• assistant • coworker • friend • student • teacher
Person to Corporate Body	• employee • graduate of • officer of • person member of corporate body of
Person to Place	• place of birth • place of death
Person to Timespan	• date of birth • date of death • period of activity of person

---

[†††]See section 10.2.4.3 below for further discussion of relationship designators in Original RDA.

Table 10.2 Selected Official RDA Elements Describing a Person

Element Type	Element	Value	Source of Value	MARC Encoding
Appellation Elements	authorized access point for person	Milner, Ange V. (Angeline Vernon), 1856-1928	AAP formed by combining preferred name and birth and death dates	100 1_ $a Milner, Ange V. $q (Angeline Vernon), $d 1856-1928
	identifier for person	no2021058037	Identifier from LCNAF	010 $a no2021058037
	variant access point for person	Milner, Angeline, 1856-1928	VAP formed by combining variant name and birth and death dates	400 1_ $a Milner, Angeline, $d 1856-1928
Relationship Elements	date of birth	1856-04-09	Date of birth recorded using a string encoding scheme	046 $f 1856-04-09
	date of death	1928-01-13	Date of death recorded using a string encoding scheme	046 $g 1928-01-13
	place of birth	Bloomington (Ill.)	AAP for place from LCNAF	370 $a Bloomington (Ill.)
	place of death	Normal (Ill.)	AAP for place from LCNAF	370 $b Normal (Ill.)
	person member of corporate body of	Illinois Library Association. War Service Committee	AAP for related corporate body from LCNAF	510 2_ $w r $i Member of: $a Illinois Library Association. War Service Committee
Attribute Elements	profession or occupation	Librarians	Term from LCDGT	374 $a Librarians $2 lcdgt

This data would be recorded in the authority record for the person in the current cataloging environment. As noted in Chapter 8, LC and the PCC have issued a list of relationship labels to be used to indicate Official RDA relationships in authority records.[38] The LC-PCC relationship labels are mapped to the applicable RDA relationship element and provide a more concise and user-friendly label for display (e.g., *member of* instead of *person member of corporate body of*). These relationship labels are recorded in conjunction with the AAP for the related entity to indicate the nature of the relationship being described. In the example below (using MARC encoding), the relationship label in bold shows the relationship between the Italian writer Italo Calvino and the university from which he graduated.

> 100 1# $a Calvino, Italo
> 510 2# $w r $i **Graduate of**: $a Università di Torino

Official RDA also enumerates many relationships between persons and the WEMI entities (e.g., *artist person of, author person of, translator person of*). However, in the current cataloging environment, these relationships are more commonly recorded in the opposite direction (from WEMI entity to person) in the bibliographic record. Relationships between WEMI entities and agents as a component of description and access are discussed in Chapter 8.

10.2.3.2.3 Persons: Attribute Elements

Attribute elements provide additional information about the person that cannot be represented as a relationship to another RDA entity. Attributes defined by Official RDA to describe persons include

- address of person
- biographical information
- category of person
- field of activity of person
- gender
- language of person
- note on person
- profession or occupation
- term of rank, honour, or office

These attribute elements continue Original RDA's expansion of authority data, including not only basic information necessary to establish AAPs and VAPs but also broader background information that may be helpful in contextualizing a person. Most of these elements first appeared as attributes in Original RDA, and many already have dedicated fields in the MARC 21 authority format. None of these attribute elements are required, and some (e.g., address of person) may not be advisable to include in records for living persons because of privacy concerns. As noted previously, LC-PCC policy is to not record gender in personal name authority records. An example of a metadata description set for a person using Official RDA appellation, relationship, and attribute elements can be found in Table 10.2, along with the MARC tags that would be used to encode the metadata in the current cataloging environment.

10.2.3.3 Describing Works and Expressions

In addition to agents, Official RDA also contains elements for describing and creating access points for resource entities—not just works and expressions, but also manifestations and items. However, in current cataloging practice, authority records are not typically created for manifestations and items. Instead, most authority work for WEMI entities focuses on works and expressions, which carry the intellectual and creative content of resources.

10.2.3.3.1 Works and Expressions: Appellation Elements

The elements for works and expressions, like those for agents, can be divided into three general groups:

- **Appellation elements** that indicate the titles, access points, and identifiers used to name the entity,
- **Relationship elements** that describe relationships with other RDA entities (agents, other WEMI entities, etc.), and
- **Attribute elements** that describe other characteristics of the work or expression.

Most of the appellation elements for works and expressions follow the general pattern discussed in section 10.2.3.1, with individual elements defined for preferred and variant titles, preferred and variant access points, and identifiers. In addition, a few more specialized appellation elements are defined on the work level, such as specific appellation elements for musical works (e.g., *opus number, numeric designation of musical work*) and serials (e.g., *ISSN, key title*).

Constructing an AAP for a work or expression begins with selecting one title as the preferred one; this preferred title then becomes the basis of the access point, with other elements added to the access point as needed to identify the resource being described and disambiguate it from other similarly named resources if necessary. In Official RDA, the primary instructions for choosing preferred titles for works and expressions appear under the elements *preferred title of work* and *preferred title of expression*, respectively; instructions for using the preferred title to create access points are found under the elements *authorized access point for work* and *authorized access point for expression*.

In line with Official RDA's move away from prescriptive guidelines, many options are offered for choosing preferred titles and constructing access points, some of which align with current cataloging practice and some of which do not. Catalogers following the LC-PCC PSs and MGDs for construction of AAPs will apply options that result in largely the same practice as that followed under Original RDA, which is described in section 10.2.4. For example, the guidelines for *access point for work* include numerous options for additional elements or designations that can be added to the title to form a complete access point, including *category of work, date of work, place of origin of work*, and *authorized access point for agent*.[39] No order of preference is indicated between the various options. Without guidance on which options to apply, this could result in any of the following authorized access points being created for Miguel de Cervantes' *Don Quixote*:

> **Don Quixote (Novel)**
> **Don Quixote (1605)**
> **Don Quixote (Spain)**
> **Cervantes Saavedra, Miguel de, 1547-1616. Don Quixote**
> **Cervantes Saavedra, Miguel de, 1547-1616. Don Quixote (Novel, 1605)**

How are catalogers to determine which option to apply? The RDA guidelines remain neutral, so catalogers must apply policy statements and/or local application profiles, if they exist and if they address these issues. In the United States, the associated LC-PCC policy statement directs catalogers to apply the option to include an authorized access point for an agent associated with the work (the fourth example) and includes a link to an MGD containing additional guidance on constructing the access point. The LC-PCC PSs note that some of the other options can be applied in cases of conflict, but in line with practice under Original RDA, the basic format for work access points remains the preferred title of the work combined with the authorized access point for the creator (if applicable). This example illustrates how policy statements supplement Official RDA to create consistent access points and ensure continuity of practice.

10.2.3.3.2 Works and Expressions: Relationship Elements

Official RDA defines many relationships between works and expressions and other RDA entities—far too many to list here. Works and expressions can have relationships with any other RDA entity, including people, corporate bodies, families, other WEMI entities, and places. Dates, which were previously treated as attributes of works and expressions, are now within the scope of the timespan entity and can also be represented via work and expression relationship elements. A small sample of Official RDA relationship elements for works and expressions is provided in Table 10.3.

Table 10.3 Selected Official RDA Relationship Elements for Works and Expressions

Relationship Type	Selected Relationship Elements	
Work-to-Work	• abridgement of work • abstract of • adapted as graphic novel work • music for work • parody of work	• prequel work • remake of work • sequel work • subject work • supplement to work
Work-to-Expression	• commentary on expression • representative expression	• review of expression • subject expression
Work-to-Person (*similar elements defined for other agents*)	• academic supervisor • addressee person • author person • artist person	• director person • lyricist person • screenwriter person • subject person
Work-to-Place	• coordinates of cartographic content • description of place	• place of capture of representative expression • place of origin of work • subject place

Relationship Type	Selected Relationship Elements	
Work-to-Timespan	• date of representative expression • date of work • subject timespan	
Expression-to-Work	• expression analyzed in • expression commentary in	• expression reviewed by • representative expression of
Expression-to-Expression	• abridgement of expression • adaptation of expression • arrangement of	• dubbed version of • revised as • translation of
Expression-to-Person *(similar elements defined for other agents)*	• abridger person • actor person • conductor person	• performer person • translator person
Expression-to-Place	• place of capture	
Expression-to-Timespan	• date of capture • date of expression	

The LC-PCC MGDs recommend relationship labels for denoting work- and expression-level relationships to persons and other RDA entities. As with relationship labels for agents, these are intended to be included within authority records in conjunction with the AAP for the related entity, to indicate the nature of the relationship between the entities. For example, a metadata description set for Jane Austen's novel *Pride and Prejudice*, using LC-PCC relationship labels (formatted in bold below) and encoded in MARC, might include the following:

> 100 1# $a Austen, Jane, $d 1775-1817. $t Pride and prejudice
>
> 530 #0 $w r $i **Adapted as motion picture**: $a Pride and prejudice (Motion picture: 1940)
>
> 500 1# $w r $i **Parodied as**: $a Grahame-Smith, Seth. $t Pride and prejudice and zombies
>
> 500 1# $w r $i **Sequel**: $a Tennant, Emma. $t Pemberley

In the example above, the relationship labels are used to indicate the Official RDA relationship elements *adapted as motion picture work*, *parodied as work*, and *sequel work*, respectively.

10.2.3.3.3 Works and Expressions: Attribute Elements

Like other RDA entities, works and expressions also have attribute elements that further describe their characteristics. Attributes of works focus on the content of the resource. A few of the more general attribute elements for works include

- category of work
- coverage of content
- history of work
- nature of content

- note on work
- subject
- system of organization

Note that some of these (such as *subject*) are likely to appear in bibliographic records, instead of or in addition to authority records, but they are still work-level attributes. There are also a number of specialized attribute elements for specific resource types, such as theses and dissertations (e.g., *academic degree*) and serials (e.g., *frequency*).

Attribute elements for expressions focus on characteristics related to the realization of the work through text, sound, image, or some other form. Some expression attributes apply to many resource types (e.g., *designation of version, language, content type*), while others are applicable only to particular resource types. For example, *key of expression* and *medium of performance of musical content* describe musical content; *scale* and *relief representation* apply to maps; *form of tactile notation* provides information about resources written in braille.

Official RDA also introduces a new concept called *representative expression* which, while not widely implemented in current cataloging practice, could potentially impact the description of works and expressions in the future. A **representative expression** is a canonical realization of a work that contains attributes considered to be essential in characterizing the work. This reflects the idea that some expressions of a work are more primary in identifying the work than others; the expression considered to be the most representative may often be the first or earliest known expression (e.g., the 1605 Spanish text of *Don Quixote* by Cervantes), but not necessarily. The concept allows some attributes that are technically defined on the expression level to also be recorded as representative expression attributes for the work, if considered important for identification. For example, the metadata element set describing *Don Quixote* on the work level could now contain attribute elements such as *date of representative expression* (1605), *content type of representative expression* (text), and *language of representative expression* (Spanish). While determining representative expression attributes may be straightforward for some works, it is likely to be highly subjective for others. Like many new concepts introduced with Official RDA, it remains to be seen how fully representative expression attributes will be implemented in cataloging practice.

10.2.4 *RDA: Resource Description & Access* (2010)

Original RDA not only provides guidelines for the description of resources (based on the WEMI entities) but also for the following activities:

- describing and establishing access points for agents that may act as creators, contributors, others associated with resources, and the subjects of works;
- describing and establishing access points for works and expressions that may be contained in resources; and
- describing relationships between a variety of entities.

Each of these activities is addressed in the sections that follow.

10.2.4.1 Describing and Establishing Access Points for Agents

Original RDA contains four chapters for describing the agents responsible for creating, contributing to, disseminating, or owning resources. In earlier content standards (e.g., AACR2), the focus was typically on establishing name headings for persons, geographic jurisdictions, and corporate bodies, as well as uniform titles for works and expressions. In Original RDA the emphasis goes beyond establishing just authorized access points; the focus is on describing entities more robustly with a wide variety of attributes. As mentioned above, this has been under scrutiny in recent years, but Original RDA provides the means for a fuller description of agents.

Original RDA provides general guidelines for describing agents. These guidelines address, among other topics, definitions, objectives and principles, languages and scripts, capitalization, diacritical marks, spacing of initials and acronyms, abbreviations, and the construction of authorized and variant access points. The general guidelines apply to each of the chapters that address the various kinds of agents.

The following section examines how to describe *persons* because it is a good illustration of the overall authority work process. Although not covered in this section, there are different and additional considerations unique to corporate bodies, families, and places that must be considered when describing those types of entities.

10.2.4.1.1 Describing Persons: Names

In the guidelines for describing persons, the initial focus is on establishing a *preferred name for the person*, which is the basis for an AAP and reflects the name most commonly associated with the person. The preferred name could be a person's real name, a pseudonym, a stage name, a title of nobility, a nickname, initials, or a word, phrase, or other appellation by which a person is known. Some persons use one name for their whole lives, but sometimes they may use different forms of that name. Thus, there are instructions on choosing the preferred name for a person when different forms of the same name have been used. For example, there may be variations in fullness:

Michèle Valerie Cloonan versus **Michèle Cloonan**

The general rule for variations in fullness is to use the form most commonly found, and if that is not possible, to use the latest form of name, or if that is not clear, to use the fullest form of name. There may also be language variations:

Joan of Arc versus **Juana de Arco**

The general rule for forms in different languages is to use the form commonly found in most resources. If that is not clear, use the form of name most commonly found in reference sources from the person's home country. Additional rules are given for more complex scenarios. There also may be situations where the same name appears in different scripts:

Peter Ilich Tchaikovsky versus **Петр Ильич Чайковский**

In general, if the name appears in a script that is not used by the agency creating the metadata, then the name should be transliterated to the agency's preferred script, or, as an alternative, another form commonly found in reference sources may be used. Spelling variations may also be encountered:

Joanne A. Quitmeyer versus **Joann Quitmeyer**

If two or more different spellings of the same name are encountered, the general rule is to use the form of name that appears in the resource that was received first.

Some persons may use different names during their lifetimes. Sometimes, persons use real names in everyday life, but publish their works under different names; some use separate names for different *bibliographic identities* (i.e., different personas to write in different genres); and some change their names at various points in their lives. There are instructions for these situations as well. In general, choose the most well-known name for the person; if this is unclear, choose, in this order,

1. the most frequently used name in resources,
2. the name appearing most frequently in references sources, or
3. the latest name used.

For names that have changed, use the latest name adopted by the person (e.g., use **Arlene G. Taylor** not **Arlene Taylor Dowell**). For those with more than one bibliographic identity, establish each identity separately (e.g., use **Charles L. Dodgson** for his works on mathematics and **Lewis Carroll** for his literary works).

Numerous instructions follow on how to record the name chosen as the preferred form. The guidelines are divided into instructions for:

- surnames (including compound surnames, hyphenated surnames, persons known by a surname only, married persons known by a partner's name, etc.),
- names containing titles of nobility,
- patronymics,
- given names only,
- names comprising words, phrases, or initials, and
- variant names.

The general rule for recording variant names is simple. It states that the cataloger should record variant names when they differ from the preferred name. Specific variant name instructions are provided for real names, names in religion, secular names, earlier or later names of a person, alternative linguistic forms of names, and other alternative monikers. As noted previously, variant names are documented in authority records to provide cross-references in the catalog.

10.2.4.1.2 Creating Access Points for Persons

After a preferred name is determined, an authorized access point can be established. An AAP is the standardized string of characters used to represent a person, place, corporate body, subject, or family in metadata. Although many believe the use of textual character strings is an antiquated approach to identity management (it is), it is still the most human-friendly approach available at this time. In the future, when Official RDA is widely adopted, more machine-processable approaches may be employed (e.g., the use of IRIs), but for now catalogers establish a unique AAP for the entity and use it consistently in all metadata associated with that entity to allow for collocation in retrieval.

When constructing an AAP, catalogers begin with the preferred name chosen for the person. Most names contain multiple parts, so the cataloger must determine the entry element. The *entry element*, the part of the name entered first, should be chosen according to the conventions used with the person's native language or in the person's country of origin or residence. In many parts of the world that means the first element in the AAP should be the family name (also referred to as *surname* or *last name*), followed by a comma and the rest of the name. For example, in the United States, the name *Rebecca Green* would be entered as **Green, Rebecca**. In Spain, where persons have compound surnames (i.e., two family names), a person is typically entered under the first of the family names. For example, librarian Jesús Alonso Regalado's preferred name would be established as **Alonso Regalado, Jesús**. In Portugal, however, a person with two surnames would typically be entered under the second family name because that is the tradition in that country (e.g., **Ferreira, José Gomes**). In other parts of the world, surnames are less common or less important, and persons may be entered under their given names instead (e.g., **Björk Ingimundardóttir**). If the preference of the person is known or discernible, that preference should take precedence over standard practices.

When the preferred name is unique, it can stand alone as an AAP, but many names are rather common. In these cases, additional data elements are required to identify the entity precisely. The following are the most typical additions to a personal name:

- middle initials
- fuller forms of name
- birth and death dates
- periods of activity
- titles associated with the person (e.g., royal titles, titles of nobility, religious titles, *Saint*, *Spirit*)
- professions or occupations (e.g., Notary, Composer, Veterinarian)
- terms of rank, terms of honor, terms of office (e.g., Captain, Ph.D.)
- other designations associated with the person

For example, there is more than one Rebecca Green in the world. Thus, the name needs additional elements to formulate unique AAPs to differentiate the different Rebecca Greens. The following are the Rebecca Greens currently in the LCNAF:

- **Green, Rebecca, 1743-1806**
- **Green, Rebecca, 1952-**
- **Green, Rebecca, 1963-**
- **Green, Rebecca, 1975-**
- **Green, Rebecca, 1978-**
- **Green, Rebecca, 1979-**
- **Green, Rebecca, 1986-**
- **Green, Rebecca E. (Rebecca Erin), 1972-**

- **Green, Rebecca J. (Rebecca Jane), 1949-**
- **Green, Rebecca L.**
- **Green, Rebecca L. (Rebecca Lynn)**
- **Green, Rebecca Meade, 1795-1867**
- **Green, Rebecca, RN**

Each Rebecca Green has an authority record. Each authority record contains the established AAP, any variant forms of name used by that Rebecca Green, and possibly some additional identifying information.

10.2.4.1.3 Other Attributes for Describing Persons

The Original RDA metadata elements for describing persons are listed below. Some elements or sub-elements are identified as core; they are presented here in boldface type. *Core elements* are always recorded, if they are applicable to the entity being described and the information is found in sources. The rest of the elements are recorded in the authority data based on cataloger's judgment.

- 9.2 Name of Person, particularly **Preferred Name of Person**
- 9.3 Date Associated with Person, including **Date of Birth** and/or **Date of Death**, if available
- 9.4 **Title of Person**, if applicable
- 9.5 Fuller Form of Name
- 9.6 **Other Designation Associated with Person**, required for specific categories of persons
- 9.7 Gender
- 9.8 Place of Birth
- 9.9 Place of Death
- 9.10 Country Associated with Person
- 9.11 Place of Residence, Etc.
- 9.12 Address of Person
- 9.13 Affiliation
- 9.14 Language of Person
- 9.15 Field of Activity of Person
- 9.16 **Profession or Occupation**, required for some unusual names
- 9.17 Biographical Information
- 9.18 **Identifier for Person**

This list shows the most obvious contribution of the FRAD conceptual model to contemporary cataloging practices (nearly all the elements were originally enumerated in FRAD rather than in FRBR). Most of the elements are self-explanatory. Most authority records in the LCNAF contain few of these elements for a variety of reasons. It may be because some records were created under earlier sets of cataloging guidelines; some records are less than complete because additional metadata was unavailable or not applicable; or it could be that, in some cases, the cataloger simply chose not to.

10.2.4.2 Describing and Creating Access Points for Works and Expressions

Original RDA also provides guidelines on how to record authority data for works and expressions. Establishing an AAP is usually the most pressing reason for creating authority data for a work or an expression, but metadata other than the name/title AAP is also recorded. There are a dozen work-related and expression-related elements, two of which are considered core in Original RDA: *preferred title for work* and *identifier for work*. Four additional elements are considered core *if* a preferred title is not unique and needs disambiguation: *form of work*, *date of work*, *place of origin of work*, and *other distinguishing characteristic of work*. In addition, there are specific instructions and elements aimed at establishing authority data for musical works, legal works, treaties, religious works, and official communications; each may require one or more core elements to be recorded.

As is the case with establishing names for agents, establishing titles for works and expressions entails choosing one title to be the preferred one, while the other titles are recorded as variant forms. The primary consideration in choosing the preferred title is the creation date. For works created after 1500, catalogers are to choose the best-known title in the original language as the preferred title. For works created before 1501, catalogers are to choose the best-known title in the original language that is found in reference sources. If those instructions cannot be easily followed, alternative approaches are provided. There are specific instructions for special cases (e.g., how to record a preferred title for parts of a work) and guidelines for recording variant titles as well.

With all the metadata about a work or expression collected, the AAP can be established. There are sets of guidelines for establishing AAPs for five distinct types of resources:

- general works and expressions
- musical works
- legal works
- religious works
- official communications

The general instructions can also be used to create authority data for series (a series can be considered a work in its own right).

Authorized access points for works come in two basic forms:

- name/title access points
- title-only access points

The first is used when there is an identifiable creator(s) for the work; the second is used for anonymously created works and a few other types. Determining the agent most responsible for creating a work is a longstanding practice in cataloging. Until the advent of RDA, this was known as choosing the main entry (discussed under AACR2 in Chapter 9). This terminology has been omitted from RDA, but the basic concept has lived on as the first step in establishing a name/title AAP to identify a work.

The basic Original RDA guidelines for establishing an AAP are organized around several conditions of creation (as seen in the following table).

Situation	Basic Instruction	Example
Works created by one agent	The AAP for the work comprises the AAP for the agent and the preferred title for the work.	**Cassatt, Mary, 1844-1926. Children playing with a dog**
Collaborative works	The AAP for the work comprises the AAP for the agent with principal responsibility for the work and the preferred title for the work. If the agent with principal responsibility is not clear, the first-named agent is used.	**Bernstein, Leonard, 1918-1990. Candide**
Compilations of works by different agents	For compilations with contributions by different creators, no single agent is chosen as the primary creator; the AAP is for the title only.	**Norton anthology of world masterpieces**
Adaptations and revisions	If the work is presented as a new expression of a work, the AAP is identical to that of the original expression of the work. If this is a significant transformation of the content, the agent responsible for the new content is the name used in the AAP.	For the first three editions of a book, the same name/title AAP was used: **Immroth, John Phillip. A guide to Library of Congress classification**. But, due to large-scale revisions, its fourth edition is known as: **Chan, Lois Mai. Immroth's Guide to the Library of Congress classification**
Commentary, Annotations, Illustrations etc., added to an existing work	If the commentary, annotations, or illustrations are the focus of the resource, then an AAP reflecting these features is created.	**Mategrano, Terri. Shakespeare's Hamlet** is used for work where the focus is on the commentary or criticism, rather than on the original text of Shakespeare's *Hamlet*
	If the resource is presented as little more than a new edition of a previously existing work with some extra content, then the AAP is identical to the original work.	**Carroll, Lewis, 1832-1898. Alice's adventures in Wonderland** is used for the original edition as well as for the 150th anniversary edition featuring illustrations by Salvador Dalí
Works of uncertain or unknown origin	If there is no agreement among scholars as to the agent responsible for creating a work or the creator is truly unknown, then only the title is used as the AAP.	**Beowulf**
	If reference sources generally concur on a probable creator, that creator's name is used as the beginning part of the AAP for the work.	**Aneirin. Gododdin**

There are, of course, some exceptions, options, and alternatives for specific resource types and conditions.

Although in many cases there is little difficulty in determining the agent primarily responsible for the creation of the work, for some resources it can be challenging. Some resource types, such as sacred scripture, compilations, motion pictures, television programs, and other aggregate works, typically do not have a single identifiable creator. These types of work are usually known by title only.

There are special instructions for certain types of material (musical works, legal works, etc.) to address some difficulties in determining the creator. For example, works created by corporate bodies may seem challenging at first. Original RDA, however, gives guidance for this with its listing of eight categories into which a resource must fall for a corporate body to be considered its creator. The list includes categories such as works about the administration of the body itself, works that reflect the collective thought of the body, hearings conducted by the body, reports of a conference or other such event, and works of art or musical performances created by two or more artists/musicians acting as a group. If a work is created by a corporate body, but does not fall into one of the categories, the AAP is based on the title only, if there is no person or family also involved in its creation.

In some cases, no matter the type of creator, additional data elements may be added to make the AAP unique. These include the elements listed in the following table.

Element	Example
Form of work	**Gale, Zona, 1874-1938. Miss Lulu Bett (Novel)**
Date of work	**Wilson, Lanford, 1937-2011. Works. 1996**‡‡‡
Place of origin	**Maryland gazette (Annapolis, Md.: 1727)**
Other distinguishing characteristics	**Bulletin (Alaska State Council on the Arts)**

Expressions of a work can also have AAPs established for them. For each expression, the AAP for the work is duplicated and additional data elements are added to the AAP to distinguish that particular expression—perhaps using *language, content type, date, other distinguishing characteristics*, or a combination of these, if needed.

100 1# $a Shakespeare, William, $d 1564-1616. $t Hamlet

100 1# $a Shakespeare, William, $d 1564-1616. $t Hamlet. $l Romanian

As with other types of entities, variant access points may be recorded in the authority data. For example, in the authority record for **Shakespeare, William, 1564-1616. Hamlet** in the LCNAF, there are variant access points for the variant titles *The Tragedy of Hamlet* and *Shakespeare's Hamlet*.

---

‡‡‡"Works" is what is referred to as a *conventional collective title*. It is used for the complete works of an author. Other conventional collective titles include headings such as **Plays, Poems, Correspondence, Speeches, Selections**, and so on.

10.2.4.3 Describing Relationships

As discussed in Chapter 8, access points in bibliographic records are a way to identify relationships between a resource and agents, works, expressions, and subjects. This, however, is not the only way to identify and describe relationships. Relationships can also be described in authority records. There are numerous relationships that can be documented, including those between

- authorized and variant access points for the same entity,
- between two different AAPs for the same agent, and
- relationships among different entities (e.g., two different persons, two works, a family and a corporate body).

The nature of the relationship may take many forms, for example there could be a sequential relationship, a whole-part relationship, and so on. The point of documenting these relationships is to clarify how entities (works, persons, etc.) are connected to other entities.

The first type of relationship discussed is the most common: the relationship between an AAP and its VAPs. This reflects the basic *See* relationship discussed at the beginning of this chapter. Here is an example of a well-known author that has been known by many different names during their career.[§§§]

100 1# $a Eliot, George, $d 1819-1880
400 1# $a Cross, Marian Evans, $d 1819-1880
400 1# $a Cross, Mary Ann, $d 1819-1880
400 1# $a Ėliot, Dzhordzh, $d 1819-1880
400 1# $a Evans, Marian, $d 1819-1880
400 1# $a Evans, Mary Ann, $d 1819-1880
400 1# $a Lewes, M. E. $q (Marian Evans), $d 1819-1880
400 1# $a שזדראשזד, טאילע, $d 1819-1880

At times, a creator might use different names (i.e., separate identities) when creating different sorts of works. A well-known example is **Charles L. Dodgson**, who wrote about mathematics, but also wrote literary works using his alternate identity, **Lewis Carroll**. This reciprocal *see also* relationship is recorded in the authority records for each identity.

Authority Record 1
100 1# $a Dodgson, Charles Lutwidge, $d 1832-1898
500 1# $a Carroll, Lewis, $d 1832-1898

Authority Record 2
100 1# $a Carroll, Lewis, $d 1832-1898
500 1# $a Dodgson, Charles Lutwidge, $d 1832-1898

Sometimes the situation is simpler: some authors write under more than one name for whatever reasons they choose, with no concerns about establishing different bibliographic identities.

[§§§]Table 10.1, on page 375, contains a selection of MARC tags for authority records.

No matter how this comes about, the creators of authority data try to connect different names and identities/personas used by the same actual person in their authority data. For example, one finds this information in Isaac Asimov's authority record:

> 100 1# $a Asimov, Isaac, $d 1920-1992
> 500 1# $a French, Paul, $d 1920-1992
> 500 0# $a Dr. "A", $d 1920-1992

Sometimes the relationship goes beyond just a single entity. It can be important to record the connections among different entities, whether they are individuals, corporate bodies, families, or places. An example of a connection between two people can be found in the *see also* reference in the record for Caroline Hennell Bray, a children's author, indicating that she was a friend of George Eliot.

> 100 1# $a Bray, Charles, $c Mrs., $d 1814-1905
> 400 1# $a Bray, Caroline, $d 1814-1905
> 500 1# $w r $i Friend: $a Eliot, George, $d 1819-1880

The relationship may also be between entities of another type. For example, John Lennon was a member of the musical group The Beatles. In his authority record, the following is recorded.

> 100 1# $a Lennon, John, $d 1940-1980
> 510 2# $w r $i Corporate body: $a Beatles

Corporate bodies change their names for a variety of reasons (positive, negative, or neutral). And they may do it more than once. Name changes for a corporate body are recorded in the entity's authority records (one for each name the company uses). The example below indicates that an infamous corporation is now known by a less recognizable (and less inflammatory) name.

> 110 2# $a Philip Morris Incorporated
> 510 2# $w r $i Predecessor: $a Philip Morris and Company
> 510 2# $w r $i Successor: $a Altria Group

Another case where multiple entities are connected in the authority file might occur when there is a partnership underlying a joint pseudonym. For example, science fiction author James S. A. Corey is in fact two individuals. This is recorded in the authority record for Corey.

> 100 1# $a Corey, James S. A.
> 500 1# $a Abraham, Daniel
> 500 1# $a Franck, Ty
> 663 ## $a Joint pseudonym of Daniel Abraham and Ty Franck. For works of these authors written under their own names, search also under: $b Abraham, Daniel $b Franck, Ty

In Chapter 8, an extract from a MARC record describing a trilogy of plays by Aeschylus (*The Oresteia*) is used to illustrate ***relationship designators*** (terms that identify the nature of a relationship between entities) in a bibliographic record (see page 292). In that example, there are access points for

- creator (100 field),
- title proper (245 field in $a),
- individual plays (three 700 fields),
- translator (700 field),
- series (830 field), and
- *uniform title* (i.e., the name/title AAP for the work in 240 field) with the language of the expression included ($l).

In the authority record for the work, you will find the following information:

> 100 0# $a Aeschylus. $t Oresteia
> 380 ## $a Plays $2 lcac
> 380 ## $a Drama $2 lcsh
> 380 ## $a Trilogy
> 400 0# $a Aeschylus. $t Orestea
> 400 0# $a Aeschylus. $t Ορεστειακά
> 500 0# $w r $i Author: $a Aeschylus
> 500 0# $w r $i Container of (work): $a Aeschylus. $t Agamemnon
> 500 0# $w r $i Container of (work): $a Aeschylus. $t Choephori
> 500 0# $w r $i Container of (work): $a Aeschylus. $t Eumenides

Because this information is at the work level, it does not include metadata about title proper (manifestation level), translator (expression level), or series (manifestation level). The relationship designator *container of (work)* indicates that *The Oresteia* contains the three separate works listed in the authority data. Reciprocal relationships are found in the authority records for each of the three individual plays.

> 100 0# $a Aeschylus. $t Agamemnon
> 500 0# $w r $i Contained in (work): $a Aeschylus. $t Oresteia

Other *related work* relationships—such as successor, supplement, complement, summarization, adaptation, transformation, and imitation—can also be identified in authority data. The following are examples of some of these relationships.

> 130 #0 $a Star wars (Motion picture)
> 500 1# $w r $i Film director: $a Lucas, George, $d 1944-
> 530 #0 $w r $i Sequel: $a Empire strikes back (Motion picture)
>
> 100 1# $a James, P. D. $t Death comes to Pemberley
> 500 1# $w r $i Based on (work): $a Austen, Jane, $d 1775-1817. $t Pride and prejudice

> 100 1# $a Thomas, Ambroise, $d 1811-1896. $t Hamlet
>
> 500 1# $w r $i Opera adaptation of (work): $a Shakespeare, William, $d 1564-1616. $t Hamlet

In each of these examples, there is an explicit relationship codified by a formal AAP in a 5XX field. In older MARC records, relationships may not be formalized, relying on notes rather than additional access points. For example, the next three examples show different approaches to recording the relationship among three related works. Users, who usually cannot see authority data, may miss that there is a direct relationship between the film *A Christmas Story* and its source material, Jean Shepherd's novel, *In God We Trust: All Others Pay Cash*. In the record for *Christmas Story, The Musical*, however, the relationship between the musical and the two works it is based on is made explicit through formal references in the 5XX fields.

> 130 #0 $a Christmas story (Motion picture)
>
> 670 ## $a IMDb, April 7, 2003 $b (Christmas story, A; 1983, directed by Bob Clark; writing credits: Leigh Brown, Bob Clark, Jean Shepherd (also novel: In God we trust, all others pay cash))

> 100 1# $a Shepherd, Jean. $t In God we trust, all others pay cash
>
> 670 ## $a Pasek, B. A Christmas story, the musical, 2013: $b t.p. (based upon the motion picture A Christmas story ... and upon In God we trust: all others pay cash, written by Jean Shepherd)

> 100 1# $a Pasek, Benj. $t Christmas story, the musical
>
> 500 1# $w r $i Based on (work): $a Shepherd, Jean. $t In God we trust, all others pay cash
>
> 530 #0 $w r $i Based on (work): $a Christmas story (Motion picture)
>
> 670 ## $a A Christmas story, the musical, 2013: $b t.p. (based upon the motion picture A Christmas story ... and upon In God we trust: all others pay cash, written by Jean Shepherd)

In addition to agents and works, relationships can also be identified in subject authority files, but that is discussed in Chapter 12.

10.2.5 *Anglo-American Cataloguing Rules, Second Edition* (AACR2)

Prior to the release of Original RDA, the second edition of the *Anglo-American Cataloguing Rules* was the content standard used in many English-speaking countries for over three decades. One might ask, "If RDA has replaced AACR2, why is the earlier content standard still being addressed in this book?" As stated in Chapter 9, not all libraries switched from AACR2 to RDA for a variety of reasons, such as financial concerns, philosophical differences, and/or simple intransigence. Like RDA, AACR2 provides instructions for creating authority-controlled headings for persons, corporate bodies, and other entities, which are presented in Chapters 22–25. Although the terminology is somewhat different, the processes for determining headings are quite like those for creating access points using Original RDA. The following is an outline of the major concerns addressed by catalogers when establishing the heading for a person.

I. **Choice of name**: Choose the most well-known name for the person.
    a. **Choice among different names**: Choose the name that is most clearly the predominant name. If that is unclear, choose:
        i. the name that appears most frequently in the person's works,
        ii. the name that appears most frequently in reference sources, or
        iii. the latest name.
    b. **Pseudonyms**: If the person has one or more pseudonyms, apply the following:
        i. One pseudonym only for works: Use the pseudonym.
        ii. Separate bibliographic identities: Establish all identities.
        iii. Contemporary authors using different names: Establish all names.
    c. **Change of names**: Use the latest name (usually).

II. **Choice among different forms of the same name**
    a. **Fullness**: Choose the most well-known name.
    b. **Language**: Choose the form corresponding to the language of most of the person's works.
    c. **Names in non-Roman scripts**:
        i. Entered under given name: Use the form found in English-language reference sources.
        ii. Entered under surname: Romanize the name.
    d. **Spelling**: Choose the predominant spelling.

III. **Entry element**: Select as the entry element that part of the name under which the person would normally be listed in authoritative alphabetic lists in their language or country of residence or activity. There are specific rules addressing:
    a. Order of elements
    b. Entry under surname
    c. Entry under titles of nobility
    d. Entry under Romanian patronymics
    e. Entry under given name
    f. Entry under other names
    g. Entry under initials, letters, or numerals
    h. Entry under phrases

IV. **Additions to names**: includes rules for titles of nobility, saints, spirits, additions for surname entries, additions for given-name entries, dates, fuller forms, distinguishing terms, and undifferentiated names.

V. **Special rules for names in certain languages**: Arabic, Burmese and Karen, Chinese, Indic, Indonesian, Malay, and Thai names.

For more detail about how to establish headings and uniform titles, please see AACR2, which is available in the RDA Toolkit. Or, for a guide to cataloging using AACR2, please consult Arlene G. Taylor's tenth edition of *Introduction to Cataloging and Classification*, published in 2006.[40]

10.2.6 Metadata Authority Description Schema (MADS)

Metadata Authority Description Schema (MADS) is an XML schema for an authority element set that may be used to provide metadata about agents (people, organizations), events, and terms (topics, geographic names, genres, etc.).[41] MADS was created to serve as a companion to the Metadata Object Description Schema (MODS) described in Chapter 9. It is intended to be a simpler way to encode authority data than the MARC 21 Authority Format, while remaining compatible with MARC-based authority data. The latest version, at the time of this writing, is MADS 2.1 published in 2016.

Each MADS record must contain the schema's main element, <authority>, that contains the authoritative form of the name or term covered by the record. The record may have any number of the additional main elements labeled <related> and/or <variant>. Elements marked <variant> represent references from an alternative name or term to the authorized access point (e.g., from Knowles, Beyoncé to **Beyoncé, 1981-**). Elements marked <related> serve as references from other authorized forms of name or term to the authorized access point (e.g., from **Dodgson, Charles Lutwidge, 1832-1898** to **Carroll, Lewis, 1832-1898**).

Each of these top-level elements (<authority>, <related>, and <variant>) can have one or more of the following descriptor elements:

- name
- titleInfo
- topic
- temporal
- geographic
- hierarchicalGeographic
- genre
- occupation

The following are additional miscellaneous elements that might be added to a MADS record:

- affiliation
- classification
- extension
- fieldOfActivity
- identifier
- language
- note
- recordInfo
- URL

A MADS record can be as basic or extensive as required and can be customized according to the level of description desired for the type of system in which it is intended to be used. An excerpt from a MADS record is shown in Figure 10.4.

```xml
<mads:mads xmlns:mads="http://www.loc.gov/mads/v2"
xmlns:xlink="http://www.w3.org/ 1999/xlink"
xmlns:mods="http://www.loc.gov/mods/v3" xmlns:xsi="http://www.w3.org/
2001/XMLSchema-instance" xsi:schemaLocation="http://www.loc.gov/mads/
http://www.loc.gov/standards/mads/mads.xsd http://www.loc.gov/mods/v3
http://www.loc.gov/standards/mods/v3/mods-3-2.xsd">
    <mads:authority lang="eng">
        <mads:name type="personal" authority="naf" >
            <mads:namePart>Abbott, Elizabeth</mads:namePart>
            <mads:namePart type="date">1942-</mads:namePart>
        </mads:name>
    </mads:authority>
    <mads:variant type="other" lang="eng">
        <mads:name type="personal">
            <mads:namePart>Namphy, Elizabeth Abbott</mads:namePart>
            <mads:namePart type="date">1942-</mads:namePart>
        </mads:name>
    </mads:variant>
    <mads:note type="source">Tropical obsession, 1986: title page (Elizabeth Abbott Namphy)
        </mads:note>
     <mads:note type="source">Penguin.ca website, viewed 25 June 2014: author page (Elizabeth
        Abbott is the former Dean of Women at the University of Toronto and the bestselling author
        of A History of Celibacy and A History of Mistresses)</mads:note>
    <mads:identifier type="lccn">nb2014014243</mads:identifier>
    <mads:fieldOfActivity>Authorship</mads:fieldOfActivity>
    <mads:fieldOfActivity>History</mads:fieldOfActivity>
    <mads:extension>
        <mads:profession>
            <mads:professionTerm>Authors</mads:professionTerm>
            <mads:professionTerm>Historians</mads:professionTerm>
        </mads:profession>
    </mads:extension>
    <mads:recordInfo>
        ....
    </mads:recordInfo>
</mads:mads>
```

Figure 10.4 An Excerpt from a MADS Record, Based on LC MARC Authority Record nb2014014243. (MADS coding shown in bold.)

10.3 Standards for Archives

The archival community has long recognized the need for authority-controlled access points and contextual information about the creators and contributors to archival collections. In the mid-1990s they began to develop their own guidelines. This section addresses the following standards for authority data.

- *International Standard Archival Authority Record for Corporate Bodies, Persons, and Families* (ISAAR(CPF))
- *Describing Archives: A Content Standard* (DACS)
- Encoded Archival Context for Corporate Bodies, Persons, and Families (EAC-CPF)

10.3.1 *International Standard Archival Authority Record for Corporate Bodies, Persons, and Families* (ISAAR(CPF))

In 1996, the International Council on Archives (ICA) published the *International Standard Archival Authority Record for Corporate Bodies, Persons, and Families* (ISAAR(CPF)), with a substantially revised second edition following in 2004.[42] This standard, however, will likely be supplanted in the near future due to the work done by ICA to develop a conceptual framework known as *Records in Contexts* (described in Chapter 7).

ISAAR(CPF) provides guidance on creating archival authority records for corporate bodies, persons, and families who have created and maintained the records, documents, and other resources that comprise archives. The principle behind this work is that the creation of separate descriptions of creators of archival collections, which are then linked to descriptions of those collections (e.g., finding aids, web pages), provides an efficient means of capturing and managing contextual information that is vital to the discovery, use, and understanding of archival collections. The second edition aligns more closely with related international standards, such as *General International Standard Archival Description* (ISAD(G)), the ICA standard for archival description (see pages 342 and 345). The Encoded Archival Context for Corporate Bodies, Persons, and Families (EAC-CPF) provides a complementary data structure standard for the machine-readable interchange of ISAAR(CPF)-compliant data. Part II of DACS (see below) is derived from ISAAR(CPF).

The bulk of ISAAR(CPF) consists of a listing of elements needed for an archival authority record. A purpose is given for each element, followed by the rule for transcribing it and examples of its application. Elements are divided into four areas:

- **Identity area**: includes type of entity; authorized form(s) of name; parallel forms of name; standardized forms of name according to other rules; other forms of name; and identifiers for corporate bodies
- **Description area**: includes dates of existence; history; places; legal status; functions, occupations, and activities; mandates/sources of authority; internal structures/genealogy; and general context
- **Relationships area**: includes names/identifiers of related corporate bodies, persons, or families; category of relationship; description of relationship; and dates of the relationship
- **Control area**: includes authority record identifier; institution identifiers; rules and/or conventions; status; level of detail; dates of creation, revision, or deletion; languages and scripts; sources; and maintenance notes

Relationships to resources are also accommodated in ISAAR(CPF). Chapter 6 of the standard outlines the type of information that should be included to describe adequately the relationships between agents and archival materials. The description of a relationship may include identifiers, titles, resource types, the nature of the relationship, and dates associated with those resources and/or relationships.

10.3.2 *Describing Archives: A Content Standard* (DACS)

Describing Archives: A Content Standard (DACS) is a standard that has been accepted and used by the U.S. archival community to describe collections and associated agents. DACS has two parts—one for describing archival materials and one for creating archival authority records. The first part is discussed in section 9.2.2 of this text. The introduction to the second part emphasizes that to understand archival materials completely, one must have some knowledge of the context in which they were created. The three steps required for establishing context are

- identifying agents that played important roles in the creation of the materials;
- assembling biographical information about the individuals and families and collecting historical data about the corporate bodies, including their structure, functions, and relationships; and
- providing standardized forms of the names of the agents to facilitate retrieval.[43]

Chapter 9 in DACS, "Archival Authority Records," covers the first step, and Chapter 10, "Form of Name," provides guidance on the use of companion standards for the third step. Chapters 11–14 describe the elements of archival authority records, the management of those records, and related archival materials and other resources.

Chapter 9 identifies the necessity to establish archival authority records, levels of description, and the minimum elements that need to be included in an authority record: the authorized form of name, the type of entity, dates of existence, and an authority record identifier.[44] In addition to guidelines for the authorized form of name, Chapter 10 provides guidelines for recording the type of entity, variant forms of names, and identifiers for corporate bodies (including the jurisdiction that assigned the identifier). Chapter 11 provides the descriptive elements for corporate bodies, persons, and families; Chapter 12 attends to relationships between the entity being described in the authority record and other corporate bodies, persons, and families; Chapter 13 lays out the information necessary for authority record management; and Chapter 14 deals with relationships between the entity being described in the authority record and archival materials and other resources. DACS clearly maps its elements to those in the international standard, ISAAR(CPF).

10.3.3 Encoded Archival Context for Corporate Bodies, Persons, and Families (EAC-CPF)

Encoded Archival Context for Corporate Bodies, Persons, and Families (EAC-CPF),[45] a standard for encoding data in archival authority records, was released in 2010 and formally adopted by the Society of American Archivists (SAA) in 2011. EAC-CPF, like Encoded Archival Description (EAD), uses XML for encoding, but while EAD describes archival collections, EAC-CPF describes agents who may be creators or subjects of archival collections. EAC-CPF records do more than just control the different forms of name used by a person, corporate body, or family. According to Daniel Pitti, they also describe "their essential functions, activities, and characteristics, and the dates and places they were active."[46] Pitti goes on to explain that creator descriptions facilitate interpretation of archival records in addition to facilitating access. Understanding the lives and work of people and groups who created archival collections is essential to understanding the archival records that are the byproducts of those lives and activities. In other words, EAC-CPF records attempt to place creators in context.

Data encoded with EAC-CPF is intended for use in federated database applications and collaborative research across a broad range of domains, including prosopography[****] and genealogical studies. The designers intended that the intellectual content of EAC-CPF records comply with ISAAR(CPF) and be compatible with EAD, though the members of the SAA Technical Subcommittee on Encoded Archival Standards are aware that changes may be needed to comply with the still developing RiC conceptual framework. The EAC-CPF format complements other authority structures from a variety of domains. While coming from the archival community its structure does not provide any limitation as to the types of resources to which it may be connected.

Several archives-related projects have implemented the EAC-CPF standard. These range from single-institution projects focused on specific topic areas to national and international efforts. One of the most developed is Trove from the National Library of Australia.[47] The foundations of the Trove dataset were harvested from existing database projects developed by various communities. After harvesting and aggregating the data, Trove provides access not only to records about entities but also to various resource types. Archives Portal Europe is an online research tool developed collaboratively from 2009 to 2015 and funded by the European Commission.[48] It contains EAD and EAC-CPF records contributed by institutions throughout Europe. Social Networks and Archival Context (SNAC) is a collaborative project in the United States that aggregates information about entities to provide access to distributed archival resources.[49] SNAC began as a research project on the viability of harvesting existing data sources and storing that information in the EAC-CPF format. With projects such as these, the use of EAC-CPF has gained momentum.

10.4 Standards for Art and Museums

The art and museum community also has addressed the need for control of names and titles in descriptions of objects. The Getty Research Institute has created a set of controlled vocabulary tools, including, among others, one for terminology in the fields of art and architecture (*Art & Architecture Thesaurus*) and one for artist names, including biographical information as

---

[****]Prosopography, sometimes referred to as *collective biography*, is an investigation of the common characteristics of a group of people; it is research that identifies and relates a group of persons or characters within a particular historical or literary context.

well as variations in names (*Union List of Artist Names*).[50] The art and museum community has also created standards that provide for consistency in its metadata. The following standards are addressed in this section.

- *Cataloging Cultural Objects* (CCO)
- *Categories for the Description of Works of Art* (CDWA)
- VRA Core

10.4.1 *Cataloging Cultural Objects* (CCO)

Cataloging Cultural Objects (CCO)[51] is discussed in Chapter 9 as being a content standard rather than a prescription of metadata elements. The authors of CCO believe that authority control is a critical aspect of effective description, especially in the online environment. They recommend using authority files for certain metadata elements. Part three of CCO, "Authorities," covers guidelines for the elements that the authors believe are the most important to be controlled: *personal and corporate names*, *geographic places*, *concepts*, and *subjects*. Each is discussed separately, with sections under each group for introductory material, "Editorial Rules," and "Presentation of the Data."

The chapter on personal and corporate name authorities covers artists, architects, studios, architectural firms, patrons, repositories, and "others responsible for the design and production of cultural works."[52] The following elements are required for name authority records:

- **Names** (preferred, alternates, and variants)
- **Display Biography**
- **Birth Date** (or **Start Date** for corporate bodies)
- **Death Date** (or **End Date** for corporate bodies)
- **Nationality** (or **National Affiliation** for corporate bodies)
- **Life Roles** (or **Functions** for corporate bodies)
- **Sources**

Other elements are recommended for inclusion:

- **Notes**
- **Gender**
- **Date of Earliest Activity**
- **Date of Latest Activity**
- **Place/Location**
- **Related People**
- **Related Corporate Bodies**
- **Relationship Type**

- **Events**
- **Record Type** (Person or Corporate Body)

Some of the elements are free-text fields, while some suggest prescribed formatting (e.g., date fields should use the ISO standard for dates), and others recommend the use of controlled vocabulary. Figure 10.5 presents an excerpt from a CCO authority record.

Names:	**Meléndez, Luis** (preferred, inverted)
	Luis Meléndez (preferred, natural order) Meléndez, Luis Egidio (variant) Meléndez de Rivera Durazo y Santo Padre, Luis Egidio (variant) Rivera Durazo y Santo Padre, Luis Egidio Meléndez de (variant) …
Display Biography:	Spanish painter, 1716-1780
Nationality:	Spanish
Birth Date:	1716
Death Date:	1780
Life Roles:	painter miniaturist
Gender:	male
Place of Birth:	Naples (Campania, Italy)
Place of Death:	Madrid (Comunidad de Madrid, Spain)
Related People:	
Relationship Type: child of	Meléndez, Francisco Antonio (Spanish painter, 1682-1752)
Relationship Type: student of	Meléndez, Francisco Antonio (Spanish painter, 1682-1752)
Relationship Type: nephew of	Menéndez, Miguel Jacinto (Spanish painter, 1679-1734)
Relationship Type: assistant of	Loo, Louis Michel van (French painter, 1707-1771)
Note:	Luis Meléndez (1715–1780) is now recognized as the premier still-life painter in 18th-century Spain, indeed one of the greatest in all of Europe, though his reputation had long been eclipsed by the achievements of his Spanish contemporary, Francisco Goya. …
Sources:	Union List of Artist Names (1988-).
	National Gallery of Art, "Luis Melendez: Master of the Spanish Still Life: May 17 – August 23, 2009." https://www.nga.gov/exhibitions/luis-melendez.

Figure 10.5 An Example of a CCO-based Authority Record for Luis Meléndez.

The geographic names authority section covers places that are both physical features and administrative geographic entities. Geographic place names are used primarily for the location of works but are also used in authority records for personal and corporate names. The following table includes the elements for geographic place authority records.

Required	Recommended
Names	Coordinates
Broader Context	Note
Place Type	Related Places
Sources	Relationship Types
	Dates

Some elements are controlled, some are free-text, and for *Coordinates* and *Dates*, especially, it is recommended that consistent formatting be used.

Concept authority includes terms used to describe works or images that are not covered by the other authorities (e.g., terms that are not names of persons, organizations, geographic places, events, or subjects). Concepts may describe the type of work (e.g., painting), its material (e.g., canvas), activities associated with a work (e.g., oil painting [technique]), its style (e.g., Art Nouveau), the role of the creator or other persons (e.g., painters [artists]), and other attributes or various abstract concepts (e.g., contrast). The following are elements used for concept authority records.

Required	Recommended
Terms (preferred, alternates, and variants)	Qualifiers
Broader Context	Dates
Note	Related Concepts
Sources	Relationship Types

Concept authority records, in particular, are created in such a way that the terms in them can be displayed in a hierarchical arrangement.

CCO lists several sources for authority files for names, geographic places, and concepts. Among the most important in the world of art, architecture, and museums are the previously mentioned Getty Vocabularies, including *Union List of Artist Names* (ULAN), *Getty Thesaurus of Geographic Names* (TGN), *Art & Architecture Thesaurus* (AAT), and *Cultural Objects Name Authority* (CONA).[53]

In addition to its emphasis on authority control for some fields, CCO puts a premium on identifying relationships between works.[54] CCO distinguishes between intrinsic and extrinsic relationships. An **intrinsic relationship** is one that is essential to identifying the work being cataloged. Whole-part relationships, for example, are intrinsic. Examples of whole-part relationships include architectural complexes (e.g., the statues atop a building described separately from the building), manuscripts (e.g., the illustrations described separately from the text), triptychs (e.g., separate description of one panel of a tripartite altarpiece), works in collections, and items in a series. An **extrinsic** relationship is one that is informative but not essential. Examples of extrinsic relationships include a work copied after another, a preparatory sketch or model, a work referenced within another work (e.g., a famous painting on the wall behind the main object in another painting), or two works that are intended to be seen together (e.g., separate portraits of spouses). Attention is also given to the concept of database design and to the display of relationships when designing and constructing databases.[55]

10.4.2 *Categories for the Description of Works of Art* (CDWA)

Categories for the Description of Works of Art (CDWA)[56] was introduced in Chapter 9 as an element set for describing and accessing works of art, architecture, and other material culture. Fifteen of the thirty-six core categories of CDWA are listed in Chapter 9. The remaining twenty-one are listed here, grouped according to CDWA's organization for authority data:

- **Creator Identification Authority**
    - Name
    - Name Source
    - Display Biography
    - Birth Date
    - Death Date
    - Nationality/Culture/Race
    - Life Roles
- **Place/Location Authority**
    - Place Name
    - Place Name Source
    - Place Type
    - Broader Context
- **Related Textual References Authority**
    - Brief Citation
    - Full Citation
- **Generic Concept Authority**
    - Term
    - Term Source
    - Broader Context
    - Scope Note
    - Note Source
- **Subject Authority**
    - Subject Name

- Source
- Broader Context

These elements are much like the ones listed in CCO. Each of the five groupings contains a much larger list of elements that may be used to specifically describe that entity type. For example, under *creators* one finds the following elements:

- 28.1. Person Authority Record Type
- 28.2. Person/Corporate Body Name
- 28.3. Display Biography
- 28.4. Birth Date
- 28.5. Death Date
- 28.6. Birth Place
- 28.7. Death Place
- 28.8. Person Nationality/Culture/Race
- 28.9. Gender
- 28.10. Life Roles
- 28.11. Person/Corporate Body Event
- 28.12. Related Person/Corporate Body
- 28.13. Person/Corporate Body Broader Context
- 28.14. Person/Corporate Body Label/Identification
- 28.15. Person/Corporate Body Descriptive Note
- 28.16. Remarks
- 28.17. Citations
- 28.18. Person Authority Record ID

Additional sub-elements appear under more than a few of those listed.

CDWA also recommends maintaining separate authority files for visual works, textual materials, persons/corporate bodies, locations/places, generic concepts, and subjects so that such information is recorded once and then linked to all appropriate work records.

10.4.3 VRA Core

The VRA Core[57] was discussed in Chapter 9 as a "data standard for the description of works of visual culture as well as the images that document them."[58] The 19 individual metadata elements of the VRA Core were listed in the previous chapter, along with suggestions as to which elements could take their values from an authority file or controlled vocabulary list.

VRA Core, like CCO, emphasizes relationships. Its basic data model stresses that descriptions may focus on one of three primary divisions—works, images of those works, and collections. Thus, the primary types of relationships between records in VRA Core 4.0 are work-to-work, image-to-work, and work-to-collection or image-to-collection relationships. The documentation for VRA Core explains that in order to give meaning to an image record, it is necessary to show its relationship to the work from which it was derived. The link is made via the *relation* element, and the nature of the relationship is defined by the *type* attribute. A work may have several images associated with it, or an image may represent more than one work; such multiple relationships should be identified. In VRA Core, *collection* is defined as an aggregate of works or images. Therefore, it may be necessary to show image-to-collection relationships or work-to-collection relationships. Typically, VRA Core is not used to create authority data for agents. *Agent* is provided as an attribute for a work or an image. Sub-elements under agent, however, include *name*, *culture*, *dates*, *role*, and *attribution*.

10.5 Standards and Projects in Online Settings

During the last three decades several research projects have looked at ways to describe agents in such a way as to avoid duplication of effort and to link identical and complementary identities. A research project that began in the late 1990s and ended in 2003 was called InterParty.[59] Even though it did not produce an active namespace, it had some interesting characteristics that are thought provoking for anyone contemplating future uses of authority files. The project defined *party* as any one of the disparate types of identities responsible for creation of intellectual property or content (e.g., authors, composers, performers, producers, directors, publishers, libraries). The project brought together people from the book industry, music recording industry, rights management, libraries, the technology community, and the identifier community. InterParty looked at the fact that databases containing metadata about people and organizations already exist and identify parties in their own context (e.g., publisher databases of authors, editors; music industry databases of composers, directors; library authority files of authors, editors, composers). InterParty suggested that such databases could be linked with a common functional goal of unique identification and disambiguation of parties. Each database would agree to make available common non-confidential metadata. InterParty envisioned adding a new linking layer to assert, for example, that "Person X in Namespace A is the same as Person Y in Namespace B" (or to indicate they are not the same). The owner of Namespace B would then need to verify such an assertion by agreeing or disputing. Although this research effort did not yield a separate standard to reflect its findings, much of what was uncovered has found expression in standards and schemas developed in the past twenty years, particularly VIAF.

Another project, begun in 1998 and conducted by the Dublin Core community, recognized the need for *agent metadata* to complement and be linked to metadata for information resources. The DCMI Agents Working Group[60] was working toward developing functional requirements for describing agents. Their goal was to identify existing conventions for agent description, including the InterParty project discussed earlier. They intended to develop a recommendation for an agent element set, but the work never came to fruition. The DCMI Agents Working Group was deactivated in 2009.

The *International Standard Name Identifier* (ISNI)[61] initiative, begun in 2011, is another effort to create persistent identifiers for persons and corporate bodies and facilitate identity management and disambiguation. ISNI is a standard, adopted by ISO, for the unique identification of public identities in all fields of creative activity. ISNI has three related objectives. It aims to create identifiers that

- are relevant across domains,
- serve all the needs of the various information industry stakeholders, and
- support a high level of interoperability.

ISNI is currently supported through a membership model and is governed by the ISNI International Agency.

ORCID (originally standing for Open Researcher and Contributor ID) was organized in 2010. It is a separate initiative "to enable transparent and trustworthy connections between researchers, their contributions, and their affiliations by providing a unique, persistent identifier for individuals to use as they engage in research, scholarship, and innovation activities."[62] It is a nonprofit organization focused on individuals engaged in scholarly communication, providing persistent unique identifiers to resolve issues of name ambiguity in scholarly publications. ORCID contains information not only about scholars but also their affiliations and relationships to scholarly products.[63]

10.6 Conclusion

The massive amounts of data managed by libraries, archives, and museums have led to the development of authority control. Searchers must be able to find works related to specific persons, corporate bodies, places, or other works. As the number of names and titles increases, the ability to find specific names and titles and sort them out from similar and identical ones becomes difficult without authority control. The building of the Semantic Web has the promise of enhancing the advantages of authority work by linking authority files with a diverse range of other resources and data sources, such as biographical dictionaries, genealogical databases, telephone directories, and official websites for named entities, as well as with the information resources created by those entities.

As stated in various places in this chapter, authority control also applies to subjects. The next three chapters address providing access to subject content.

Some Important Terms in This Chapter
(Definitions Provided in the Glossary)

Appellation element	Core element	Relationship element
Attribute element	Entry element	Representative expression
Authority control	Extrinsic relationship	Res
Authority data	Heading	Thema
Authority file	Intrinsic relationship	Uniform title
Authority record	Nomen	Variant access point
Authorized access point	Person	Variant name
Bibliographic identities	Preferred name	Vocabulary encoding
Collective agent	Relationship designator	scheme
Collocation		

Some Important Acronyms in This Chapter

AACR2:	*Anglo-American Cataloguing Rules, Second Edition*
AAP:	Authorized Access Point
AAT:	*Art & Architecture Thesaurus*
CCO:	*Cataloging Cultural Objects*
CDWA:	*Categories for the Description of Works of Art*
CONA:	*Cultural Objects Name Authority*
DACS:	*Describing Archives: A Content Standard*
EAC-CPF:	Encoded Archival Context for Corporate Bodies, Persons, and Families
FRAD:	*Functional Requirements for Authority Data*
FRBR:	*Functional Requirements for Bibliographic Records*
FRSAD:	*Functional Requirements for Subject Authority Data*
GARR:	*Guidelines for Authority Records and References*
ICA:	International Council on Archives
ICP:	*Statement of International Cataloguing Principles*
IFLA:	International Federation of Library Associations and Institutions
IRI:	Internationalized Resource Identifier
ISAAR(CPF):	*International Standard Archival Authority Record for Corporate Bodies, Persons, and Families*
ISAD(G):	*General International Standard Archival Description*
ISNI:	International Standard Name Identifier
ISO:	International Organization for Standardization
LC-PCC PS:	Library of Congress-Program for Cooperative Cataloging Policy Statements

LCC:	*Library of Congress Classification*
LCCN:	Library of Congress Control Number
LCDGT:	*Library of Congress Demographic Group Terms*
LCGFT:	*Library of Congress Genre/Form Terms for Library and Archival Materials*
LCNAF:	Library of Congress/NACO Authority File
LCSH:	*Library of Congress Subject Headings*
LRM:	*IFLA Library Reference Model*
MADS:	Metadata Authority Description Schema
MARC:	Machine-Readable Cataloging
MGD:	Metadata Guidance Documentation
NACO:	Name Authority Cooperative Program
ORCID:	Open Researcher and Contributor ID
PCC:	Program for Cooperative Cataloging
RiC:	*Records in Contexts*
RDA:	*Resource Description & Access*
SAA:	Society of American Archivists
SNAC:	Social Networks and Archival Context
TGN:	*Getty Thesaurus of Geographic Names*
ULAN:	*Union List of Artist Names*
URI:	Uniform Resource Identifier
VAP:	Variant Access Point
VIAF:	Virtual International Authority File
VRA:	Visual Resources Association
WEMI:	Work-Expression-Manifestation-Item

10.7 Discussion Questions and Exercises

- What problems in information retrieval is authority control intended to address? Consider potential issues related to names for
    - Persons
    - Corporate bodies
    - Works and expressions
- How does searching in systems with authority control differ from searching in systems without authority control?

- How have general bibliographic standards for authority control changed in recent decades, from AACR2 to Original RDA to Official RDA?
- In both Original and Official RDA, catalogers have the option of recording extensive authority data about persons who create or contribute to resources. In recent years, some have questioned whether too much data is being recorded in personal name authority records. What are the potential issues with recording personal information in authority records, and how should catalogers deal with them?
- How have other communities (e.g., archives, museums, online settings) approached authority control? How do these approaches compare to library standards for authority control?

10.8 Suggested Readings

Baca, Murtha, and Patricia Harpring, eds. *Categories for the Description of Works of Art*. Revised 2024 by Emily Benoff. Los Angeles: The Getty, 2024. http://www.getty.edu/research/publications/electronic_publications/cdwa/.

Baca, Murtha, Patricia Harpring, Elisa Lanzi, Linda McRae, and Ann Whiteside. *Cataloging Cultural Objects: A Guide to Describing Cultural Works and Their Images*. Chicago: American Library Association, 2006. Also available at: https://www.vraweb.org/cco.

Describing Archives: A Content Standard. Version 2022.0.1.1. Chicago: Society of American Archivists, 2022. http://www2.archivists.org/groups/technical-subcommittee-on-describing-archives-a-content-standard-dacs/dacs.

Getty Research Institute. "Getty Vocabularies." http://www.getty.edu/research/tools/vocabularies/index.html.

International Federation of Library Associations and Institutions, IFLA Study Group. *Functional Requirements for Bibliographic Records: Final Report*. Munich: Saur, 1998. https://www.ifla.org/publications/functional-requirements-for-bibliographic-records.

International Federation of Library Associations and Institutions, Meetings of Experts on an International Cataloguing Code. *Statement of International Cataloguing Principles*. 2016 edition. The Hague: IFLA, 2016. http://www.ifla.org/files/assets/cataloguing/icp/icp_2016-en.pdf.

International Federation of Library Associations and Institutions, Working Group on Functional Requirements and Numbering of Authority Records. *Functional Requirements for Authority Data: A Conceptual Model*. The Hague: IFLA, 2009. https://www.ifla.org/publications/functional-requirements-for-authority-data.

Joudrey, Daniel N., Arlene G. Taylor, and David P. Miller. *Introduction to Cataloging and Classification*. 11th ed. Santa Barbara, CA: Libraries Unlimited, 2015.

Pitti, Daniel V. "Creator Description: Encoded Archival Context." *Cataloging & Classification Quarterly* 39, no. 1/2 (2004): 201–26.

RDA: Resource Description & Access. Chicago: American Library Association, 2010– . Available by subscription at: http://www.rdatoolkit.org/.

Sandberg, Jane, ed. *Ethical Questions in Name Authority Control*. Sacramento, CA: Library Juice Press, 2018.

Smiraglia, Richard P. *The Nature of "A Work": Implications for the Organization of Knowledge*. Lanham, MD: Scarecrow, 2001.

10.9 Notes

All URLs accessed April 2025.

1. Amazon, www.amazon.com.
2. Library of Congress Online Catalog, https://catalog.loc.gov/.
3. International Federation of Library Associations and Institutions (IFLA), Working Group on Functional Requirements and Numbering of Authority Records (FRANAR), *Functional Requirements for Authority Data: A Conceptual Model* (The Hague: IFLA, 2009), https://www.ifla.org/publications/functional-requirements-for-authority-data. [Henceforth cited as FRAD.]
4. *RDA: Resource Description & Access* (Chicago: American Library Association, 2010). Primarily accessed in the subscription product RDA Toolkit, http://www.rdatoolkit.org/. [Henceforth cited as Original RDA.]
5. Amber Billey, "Just Because We Can, Doesn't Mean We Should: An Argument for Simplicity and Data Privacy with Name Authority Work in the Linked Data Environment," *Journal of Library Metadata* 19, no. 1/2 (2019): 1–17; Amber Billey, Emily Drabinski, and K. R. Roberto, "What's Gender Got to Do with It? A Critique of RDA 9.7," *Cataloging & Classification Quarterly* 52, no. 4 (2014): 412–21.
6. Kelly J. Thompson, "More Than a Name: A Content Analysis of Name Authority Records for Authors Who Identify as Trans," *Library Resources & Technical Services* 60, no. 3 (2016): 140–55.
7. PCC Ad Hoc Task Group on Recording Gender in Personal Name Authority Records, "Revised Report on Recording Gender in Personal Name Authority Records," Library of Congress, https://www.loc.gov/aba/pcc/documents/gender-in-NARs-revised-report.pdf.
8. "NACO: Name Authority Cooperative Program," Program for Cooperative Cataloging, Library of Congress, http://www.loc.gov/aba/pcc/naco/index.html.
9. "Linked Data Service: Authorities and Vocabularies," Library of Congress, http://id.loc.gov/.
10. "VIAF: The Virtual International Authority File," OCLC Research, OCLC, http://www.oclc.org/research/activities/viaf.html.
11. Barbara Tillett, "Authority Control: State of the Art and New Perspectives," *Cataloging & Classification Quarterly* 38, no. 3/4 (2004): 23–42; also published in *Authority Control in Organizing and Accessing Information: Definition and International Experience*, eds. Arlene G. Taylor and Barbara B. Tillett (New York: Haworth Information Press, 2004), 23–42.
12. "VIAF: The Virtual International Authority File," OCLC Research.
13. "VIAF Virtual International Authority File," VIAF [website], https://viaf.org/.
14. "VIAF," OCLC, https://www.oclc.org/en/viaf.html.
15. International Federation of Library Associations and Institutions, Working Group on GARE Revision, *Guidelines for Authority Records and References*, 2nd ed. (Munich: K. G. Saur, 2001), https://www.ifla.org/resources/?oPubId=8079.
16. FRAD.
17. International Federation of Library Associations and Institutions, Working Group on the Functional Requirements for Subject Authority Records (FRSAR), *Functional Requirements for Subject Authority Data (FRSAD): A Conceptual Model* (The Hague: IFLA, 2010), http://www.ifla.org/node/5849. [Henceforth cited as FRSAD.]
18. Pat Riva, Patrick Le Boeuf, and Maja Žumer, *IFLA Library Reference Model: A Conceptual Model for Bibliographic Information* (The Hague: IFLA, 2017), https://www.ifla.org/resources/?oPubId=11412. [Henceforth cited as LRM.]
19. FRAD.
20. FRSAD.

21. For more about the FRBR model, see: Daniel N. Joudrey, Arlene G. Taylor, and David P. Miller, *Introduction to Cataloging and Classification*, 11th ed. (Santa Barbara, CA: Libraries Unlimited, 2015); *Understanding FRBR: What It Is and How It Will Affect Our Retrieval Tools*, ed. Arlene G. Taylor (Westport, CT: Libraries Unlimited, 2007); and Robert L. Maxwell, *FRBR: A Guide for the Perplexed* (Chicago: American Library Association, 2008).
22. FRAD, 30–49.
23. FRAD, 31–2.
24. LRM, 9.
25. LRM, 9.
26. International Federation of Library Associations and Institutions (IFLA), Meeting of Experts on an International Cataloguing Code, *Statement of International Cataloguing Principles (ICP)*, 2016 edition (The Hague: IFLA, 2016), http://www.ifla.org/files/assets/cataloguing/icp/icp_2016-en.pdf. [Henceforth cited as ICP.]
27. ICP, 4.
28. ICP, 5.
29. ICP, 8.
30. ICP, 8–10.
31. "Historic Documents: Outcomes of the Meeting of the Joint Steering Committee Held in Washington, DC, 16–20 October 2006," Joint Steering Committee for Development of RDA, https://www.rdatoolkit.org/archivedsite/0610out.html.
32. *RDA: Resource Description & Access* (Chicago: American Library Association, 2020–). Primarily accessed in the subscription product RDA Toolkit, http://www.rdatoolkit.org/. [Henceforth cited as Official RDA.]
33. Program for Cooperative Cataloging, "LC-PCC Metadata Guidance Documents: Access Point Syntax," Library of Congress, https://www.loc.gov/aba/rda/mgd/mg-accessPointSyntax.pdf.
34. Official RDA, "Nomen" (no citation number, accessed July 7, 2024), https://access.rdatoolkit.org/Home/.
35. Official RDA, "Person" (no citation number, accessed July 9, 2024), https://access.rdatoolkit.org/Home/.
36. Program for Cooperative Cataloging, "LC-PCC Metadata Guidance Document: Fictitious and Real Non-Human Entities," Library of Congress, January 31, 2022, https://www.loc.gov/aba/rda/mgd/mg-fictitiousRealNonHumanEntities.pdf.
37. Official RDA, "Preferred Name of Person" (citation number 81.10.19.84, accessed July 8, 2024), https://access.rdatoolkit.org/Home/.
38. Program for Cooperative Cataloging, "*Resource Description & Access* (RDA) Metadata Guidance Documentation: Relationship Labels," Library of Congress, updated April 25, 2024, https://loc.gov/aba/rda/mgd/relationshipLabels/index.html.
39. Official RDA, "Additional Elements and Designations in Access Points for Work" (citation number 13.98.40.08, accessed July 9, 2024), https://access.rdatoolkit.org/Home/.
40. Arlene G. Taylor, *Introduction to Cataloging and Classification*, 10th ed. with the assistance of David P. Miller (Westport, CT: Libraries Unlimited, 2006).
41. "MADS: Metadata Authority Description Schema," Library of Congress, http://www.loc.gov/standards/mads/.
42. International Council on Archives, *International Standard Archival Authority Record for Corporate Bodies, Persons, and Families* (ISAAR(CPF)), 2nd ed. (Paris: International Council on Archives, 2004).
43. "Introduction to Archival Authority Records," *Describing Archives: A Content Standard*, Version 2022.0.1.1 (Chicago: Society of American Archivists, 2022), http://www2.archivists.org/groups/technical-subcommittee-on-describing-archives-a-content-standard-dacs/dacs.
44. DACS, Chapter 9.

45. "Encoded Archival Context: Corporate Bodies, Persons, and Families (EAC-CPF)," Society of American Archivists, http://eac.staatsbibliothek-berlin.de/.
46. Daniel V. Pitti, "Creator Description: Encoded Archival Context," *Cataloging & Classification Quarterly* 39, no. 1/2 (2004): 201–26.
47. "Trove," National Library of Australia, http://trove.nla.gov.au/.
48. "Archives Portal Europe Homepage," Archives Portal Europe, https://www.archivesportaleurope.net/.
49. Social Networks and Archival Context (SNAC), https://snaccooperative.org/.
50. "Getty Vocabularies," Getty Research Institute, http://www.getty.edu/research/tools/vocabularies/.
51. Murtha Baca, Patricia Harpring, Elisa Lanzi, Linda McRae, and Ann Whiteside, on behalf of the Visual Resources Association, *Cataloging Cultural Objects: A Guide to Describing Cultural Works and Their Images* (Chicago: American Library Association, 2006), https://www.vraweb.org/cco. [Henceforth cited as CCO.]
52. CCO, 279.
53. "Getty Vocabularies," Getty.
54. CCO, 13–19.
55. CCO, 20–7.
56. *Categories for the Description of Works of Art*, eds. Murtha Baca and Patricia Harpring; revised by Emily Benoff (Los Angeles: The Getty, 2024), http://www.getty.edu/research/publications/electronic_publications/cdwa/.
57. "VRA Core: A Data Standard for the Description of Images and Works of Art and Culture," Library of Congress, https://www.loc.gov/standards/vracore/.
58. "An Introduction to VRA Core," Library of Congress, https://www.loc.gov/standards/vracore/VRA_Core4_Intro.pdf.
59. Andrew MacEwan, "Project InterParty: From Library Authority Files to E-Commerce," *Cataloging & Classification Quarterly* 39, no. 1/2 (2004): 429–42; also published in *Authority Control in Organizing and Accessing Information: Definition and International Experience*, eds. Arlene G. Taylor and Barbara B. Tillett (New York: Haworth Information, 2004), 429–42.
60. "DCMI Agents Working Group," Dublin Core Metadata Initiative, http://www.dublincore.org/groups/agents/.
61. International Standard Name Identifier, http://www.isni.org/.
62. "About ORCID," ORCID, https://orcid.org/about/what-is-orcid/mission.
63. ORCID, https://orcid.org/.

Chapter 11

Subject Analysis

11.1 Subject Analysis and Aboutness

In libraries, archives, museums, and indexing environments, subject analysis is performed to determine what an information resource is about, what the resource is, and which concepts should be represented in the resource's metadata. Historically, subject access has been one of the most challenging aspects of organizing information because identifying and describing what a resource is and what it is about can be difficult and time-consuming even with seemingly simple resources; with non-textual, imaginative, or complex scholarly materials, the process can be all the more demanding. Yet information professionals still see the value inherent in the process, despite the ambiguity, subjectivity, and high costs associated with it.

"For library and information science (LIS) practitioners and students ... it is important to develop an understanding of the concept of *aboutness*. The term refers to the subject matter (i.e., topics, themes, content) and the structure of a resource (i.e., its genre, its form)."[1] Although LIS researchers have been prolific in exploring the usefulness and limitations of *subject languages* (i.e., controlled vocabularies and classification schemes), they have produced little research on how to determine aboutness. Ironically, the task most dependent on human brainpower is the one least explored and understood! Consequently, many information professionals have only had instruction in the application of various controlled vocabularies and not in the process of determining aboutness. This can lead to difficulties, especially when the topics of the resource are not self-evident, or the resource has several meanings or purposes. Those who lack an understanding of the multiple components, difficulties, and approaches to determining aboutness may not identify necessary concepts and thus may omit useful controlled vocabulary terms when describing a resource.

One of the most influential articles on the topic is Robert Fairthorne's 1969 subject analysis literature review. He is generally recognized as having coined the term *aboutness* as an attempt to avoid dealing with the philosophical complexities associated with the term *subject*.[2] What he succeeded in doing, however, was to change the name of the concept, that is, to provide a synonym for *subject* in LIS literature. The complexities inherent in the concept *subject* quickly attached themselves to the new term because no real distinction between the terms *subject* and *aboutness* is generally acknowledged in the field. In addition, Fairthorne is also credited with making a distinction between two types of aboutness.

- ***Extensional aboutness*** addresses the inherent subject properties of the work; it is a relatively stable, recognizable subject matter.
- ***Intensional aboutness*** addresses subject properties that are associated with users, their requests, or the reasons for which the document has been acquired; it is a meaning-based, changing, interpretive aboutness.[3]

Over the years, writers have pointed out that aboutness is more than just the words found in the resource and the creator's aim or purpose (i.e., extensional aboutness).[4] Determining aboutness may also involve thinking about who may use the resource and for what purposes, considering what questions the document may answer, and various other aspects (i.e., intensional aboutness). It can be a tricky mixture of fact gathering and interpretation. Fairthorne notes

> *Moby Dick* is about a whale, *Othello* is about a handkerchief, and about other things. The difficulties are to identify which of the things mentioned refer to relevant topics, and how to deal with topics of the document that are not mentioned explicitly. ... Parts of the document are not always what the entire document is about, nor is a document usually about the sum of the things it mentions.[5]

F. W. Lancaster, a leading authority on indexing and abstracting, went so far as to say that the same resource *could* be described in various ways in different institutions, and that it *should* be, if the intended users would be interested in the resource for different reasons.[6] Fairthorne disagreed, arguing that "an indexer does not and cannot index all the ways in which a document will interest all kinds of readers, present and future."[7] Tore Olafsen and Libena Vokac also weighed in on this issue: "The indexer has to make guesses at what questions the future user of the system will put. Regardless of how cleverly the guesswork is constructed, they are still guesses, while the user approaches the system with his own concrete question, and his associations may be different from those of the indexer."[8]

Due to concerns related to costs, efficiency, and interoperability, most information institutions focus their subject analysis activities on the most visible and universal aspects of a resource's aboutness, rather than attempting to describe all possible uses of the resource or all possible interpretations or meanings. In short, for the purposes of providing subject access in LIS institutions, we focus on what a resource is *about* rather than what a resource *could mean*. This is true of texts, where individual readers may take away a variety of meanings from the same work, and it is certainly a major concern when it comes to providing access to creative works, such as photographs, music, and sculpture.

11.2 What is Subject Analysis?

Subject analysis is the part of the metadata creation process that identifies and articulates the subject matter and genre/form properties of information resources. The process includes three important steps:

1. examining a resource to determine what it is about,
2. describing the aboutness in a written statement, and
3. using that statement to assign controlled vocabulary terms and/or classification notations.

The first step, the ***conceptual analysis***, is a comprehensive examination of the physical properties and the intellectual or creative contents of an information resource. This is done to understand

- what the resource *is about* (i.e., its subject matter), and
- what the resource *is* (i.e., its genre or form); sometimes this is referred to as ***is-ness*** when compared to *aboutness*.

When analyzing a book, for example, one must review the myriad bibliographic features found in it (e.g., title page, table of contents, introduction, various chapters, illustrations) to determine the book's form as well as its subject matter. Throughout the analysis, notes are taken so that details are not lost. If we were performing a conceptual analysis of *Teenagers from the Future*, we might start with the title page (Figure 11.1), the table of contents (Figure 11.2), and the back cover (Figure 11.3) before moving on to more content-rich features of the resource (such as the introduction and the actual text).

In the second step, after the analysis is complete, an ***aboutness statement*** is written based on the notes that were taken. This may be a single sentence or a short paragraph describing and summarizing one's understanding of the topical matter, the genre/form, and the relationships among the important subject concepts. The aboutness statement is used to identify the terms or concepts to be searched in the controlled vocabulary. The statement can also help the information professional to construct a rudimentary hierarchy to get a better understanding of how the concepts fit together and how they might fit into a classification scheme. The following is an example of an aboutness statement (with significant concepts highlighted):

> This resource is a collection of scholarly **essays** about the **Legion of Super-heroes**, a fictitious organization that exists in **DC Comics**. The **science-fiction** comic books are about a group of **30th-century teenage superheroes** dedicated to protecting the universe. The book contains critical essays about the depiction of **superheroes** and **teenagers** in comic books as well as the **history of the comic book series**.

The third and final step entails translating the aboutness statement into the specific symbols and/or terminology found in the subject languages employed. For example, in the third step, one

Figure 11.1 Title Page from *Teenagers from the Future: Essays on the Legion of Super-Heroes*, edited by Timothy Callahan (Edwardsville, IL: Sequart Research & Literacy Organization, 2011).

Table of Contents

Foreword	1
Introduction by Timothy Callahan	4
The Perfect Storm: The Death and Resurrection of Lightning Lad by Richard Bensam	9
Liberating the Future: Women in the Early Legion by John G. Henry	36
The Silver Age Legion: Adventure into the Classics by Christopher Barbee	48
The (Often Arbitrary) Rules of the Legion by Chris Sims	58
Shooter's Marvelesque by Jeff Barbanell	63
The Legion's Super-Science by James Kakalios	84
Bridging Past and Present with the Future: The Early Legion and JLA by Scipio Garling	98
Decades Ahead of Us to Get It Right: Architecture and Utopia by Sara K. Ellis	111
Those Legionnaires Should Just Grow Up! by Greg Gildersleeve	124
Thomas, Altman, Levitz, and the 30th Century by Timothy Callahan	133
The Amethyst Connection by Lanny Rose	162
Revisionism, Radical Experimentation, and Dystopia in Giffen's Legion by Julian Darius	175
Coming Out of Future Closets: Gender Identity and Homosexuality in the Legion by Alan Williams	226
Diversity and Evolution in the Reboot Legion by Matthew Elmslie	242
Fashion from the Future, or "I Swear, Computo Forced Me to Wear This!" by Martin A. Pérez	261
Generational Theory and the Waid Threeboot by Matthew Elmslie	284
A Universe in Adolescence by Paul Lytle	295
The Racial Politics of the Legion by Jae Bryson	309
Afterword by Barry Lyga	320

Figure 11.2 The Table of Contents from *Teenagers from the Future*.

> **For half a century, the Legion of Super-Heroes** has occupied its own, vital corner of the DC Universe – and comics fandom. The Legion's expansive cast, bizarre characters, futuristic setting, extended storylines, and elaborate continuity all set it apart from other super-hero comics. From the 1980s onward, revisions and reboots have reinterpreted the Legion, proving the continued vitality of the concept.
>
> This essay collection, from fans and scholars alike, is as diverse as Legion history. Essays examine significant runs (by Jim Shooter, Paul Levitz, and Keith Giffen); the Legion's science, architecture, and fashion; the role of women, homosexuality, and race; the early Legion's classical adaptations, teenage cruelty, and relation to the early Justice League; Lightning Lad's death and resurrection; whether the Legion should be allowed to age; the Amethyst saga; the themes of the reboot Legion; and the so-called Threeboot's relationship to adult adolescence and generational theory.
>
> This book, edited by Timothy Callahan, boasts a foreword by Matt Fraction, an afterword by Barry Lyga, and essays by Jeff Barbanelli, Christopher Barbee, ….
>
> No Legion fan or comics scholar should go without this critical celebration of the Legion.
>
> PRICE: $26.95 U.S.
>
> FILE UNDER: COMIC BOOKS / GRAPHIC NOVELS
>
> SEQUART JOURNAL #3
>
> **LEGAL**: The Legion of Super-Heroes and related characters are trademarks of DC Comics. This book is not endorsed by DC Comics.

Figure 11.3 Blurb from Back Cover of *Teenagers from the Future*.

would assign appropriate, authorized terms found in *Library of Congress Subject Headings* (LCSH), *Sears List of Subject Headings, Art & Architecture Thesaurus* (AAT), *Library of Congress Genre/Form Terms* (LCGFT), or another such list, and classification notation(s) from *Dewey Decimal Classification* (DDC), *Library of Congress Classification* (LCC), *Universal Decimal Classification* (UDC), or another scheme. The subject-related metadata for *Teenagers from the Future* might include

LCSH:	Legion of Super-Heroes (Fictitious characters)—In comics
	Comic books, strips, etc.—History and criticism
	Science fiction comic books, strips, etc.—History and criticism
	Superheroes in comics
	Teenagers in literature
LCGFT:	Essays
	Comics criticism
DDC:	741.5973
LCC:	PN6728.L44

Throughout this process, the goals are not only to identify the intellectual and creative contents of information resources but also to ensure that individual resources are carefully and purposefully positioned within a collection. In other words, subject analysis is performed to

- provide users with subject access to information,
- collocate resources of a like nature,
- provide a logical location for similar tangible resources on the shelves,
- alleviate retrieval problems associated with keywords and natural language through the predictable use of controlled terminology and classification notation, and
- save the users' time by providing an intellectual framework for finding similar resources together.

If we once again look at Cutter's objects of the catalog (illustrated in Figure 3.1 on page 104), we see that he considered subject and genre/form access to be essential functions of a catalog. Not only did he want users to be able to find a known work on a certain subject, but he also wanted users to be able to find all the works that the library could offer on a particular subject or in a particular genre or form. Subject analysis makes this possible.

11.3 Challenges in Subject Analysis

Determining what an information resource is about can be difficult, and not everyone agrees on how it should be done or even where the difficulties lie. In *Two Kinds of Power*, Patrick Wilson discusses many of the challenges in the subject analysis process. He believes that one difficulty was imposed upon us by Cutter's second object of the catalog, which states that a catalog should show what a library has on a given subject. Wilson suggests that it is problematic to take Cutter's statement to mean that there is an obvious subject in every information resource and that we should be able to identify it as *the* subject of the work.[9]

Although some resources may have a single, easily determined subject, others may not be quite so clear; they may have several multifaceted themes, with complex relationships among the subtopics. The aboutness of a college textbook titled *An Introduction to Sociology* is straightforward to analyze and describe, but another text such as *An Encyclopedia of Nineteenth Century Sociology* is a bit more complex, and a third text, *Comparing Methods in Sociological Research in Panama, Peru, and Spain*, is even more so. All three are about sociology per se, but the second text is more specifically a resource that is about sociology in the nineteenth century in a particular bibliographic form (an encyclopedia). Because the content is focused on the origins and early development of sociology, it is obviously written from a historical perspective, while not being *about* history. This distinction has a certain subtlety that is learned through education in our present-day Western tradition; in other places and other times, history would have been considered the subject of anything historical regardless of the specific topic. The third resource is a more complex subject that involves not only the discipline of sociology but also a specific aspect of it: research. The work, however, is not just about sociological research; it compares the methods used in sociological research in three separate places. This resource involves a discipline, a subtopic, several geographic areas, and a comparative relationship (and possibly a chronological element and other content characteristics that are not evident from the title). Although this resource is more complex than the first (*An Introduction to Sociology*), it is still relatively simple to analyze.

The burgeoning relationships among various fields, topics, and ideas in this increasingly interdisciplinary world can result in some challenging materials to analyze. This increased level of complexity may affect one's ability to understand certain resources and to articulate what they are about. For example, a highly technical dissertation may be more difficult to analyze than a work of popular science, and a complex literary analysis that demonstrates the confluence of social, religious, and economic factors in altering the portrayal of wealthy families in eighteenth-century English fiction is considerably more difficult to analyze than a book introducing a new diet regimen.

11.3.1 Cultural Differences

Numerous factors influence the subject analysis process, including the nature of the resource being analyzed, the background of the person performing the analysis, and the characteristics of the subject languages used for translation. An understanding of the place of one's culture as well as one's education in determining subject matter is important. Some researchers, such as social psychologist Richard E. Nisbett, believe that even our most basic cognitive processes are culturally influenced.[10] Nisbett's research indicates that persons from different parts of the world are likely to interpret concepts or situations differently based on historical cultural differences. Although his research has focused on differences between Eastern and Western societies, his theories could apply to other geographic and cultural divisions. George Lakoff, a cognitive linguist, has written about the research of anthropologists Brent Berlin and Paul Kay on the understanding of color depending upon one's language. Berlin and Kay found that there are 11 basic color categories in English, but in some other languages there are fewer categories. In languages that have only two basic color terms, the terms are the equivalent of *black* and *white*, or *cool* and *warm*.[11] In other words, their research shows that something as basic as identifying colors can be influenced by culture and language.

When persons doing subject analysis have grown up in different cultures with different languages, they might not comprehend the world around them in quite the same way, which influences their perceptions of aboutness. D. W. Langridge provides another example when he comments upon the unconscious effect that must occur in the mind of a person accustomed to the former arrangement of the library in the People's University of China (now Renmin University of China), where all knowledge was divided into three groups: theory of knowledge, knowledge of the class struggle, and knowledge of the productive struggle.[12] Although differences among Western cultures are perhaps not quite so dissimilar as those between Western and non-Western cultures, we should remember that we may see things differently than the person next to us, depending upon such things as education, language, and cultural background. For example, one indexer might refer to a group of persons as *revolutionaries*, while another might refer to that same group as *terrorists*, and yet another might refer to them as *freedom fighters*. This illustrates how our subject languages may affect a user's understanding of the world and its information.

Like other social constructs, subject access tools are shaped by cultural biases. Despite the best efforts of those who maintain subject languages, general classification schemes and controlled vocabularies primarily reflect the perspectives of dominant cultural groups. For example, an American classification system, such as the *Dewey Decimal Classification* (DDC), will dedicate far more space to Christianity than to Jainism in the Religion class. This emphasis on the dominant culture—often defined as that of white, Christian, middle-class, educated, English-speaking, married, straight, cisgendered men—can make it difficult to accurately describe resources created by, for, and about those outside the so-called cultural mainstream. When catalogers and indexers are constrained by biased vocabularies, the resulting descriptions can limit discovery, reduce visibility, and ultimately diminish access to diverse voices and perspectives. It can also marginalize individuals from underrepresented groups, undermining their trust in libraries, archives, and museums as inclusive institutions, discouraging their engagement with information services, and perpetuating systemic inequities in information access. Achieving accurate and respectful representation of diverse groups remains one of the most critical ongoing challenges in subject analysis.

11.3.2 Consistency

Another challenge associated with the subject analysis process is consistency. Evidence of the difficulty in consistently determining and articulating aboutness is found in a few studies in which people have been asked to list terminology that they would use to search for specific resources. For example, in a 1954 study by Oliver Lilley, 340 students looked at six books and suggested an average of 62 different terms that could be used to search for each book.[13] In a 1992 study, Lourdes Collantes found "an average of 25.6 [topical] names per object or concept."[14] It is important to note that this is not a failure of controlled vocabulary. It is a failure of individuals to come up with the same natural language terms to describe the resource or to determine the same aboutness from a document. There is evidence that information professionals using the same controlled vocabulary and the same rules for applying it will produce consistent subject headings if they share a common understanding of aboutness.[15]

Langridge believes that inconsistencies in subject analysis are the result of confusing aboutness with purpose, that is, mixing up the questions, "What is it about?" and "What is it for?"[16] Langridge thinks that if those questions remain clear and separate, then determining aboutness should be fairly straightforward. Even if one does not agree with his assessment that determining aboutness can be straightforward, his question—*What is it for?*—provides a valuable insight into the conceptual analysis process. At first glance, Richard W. Unger's *The Art of Medieval Technology: Images of Noah the Shipbuilder* appears to be about the biblical figure Noah and his ark.[17] However, upon examining the author's purpose, the table of contents, and the captions with the illustrations, one learns that the work is really about changes in the techniques used in shipbuilding during the Middle Ages, as documented through medieval religious art, noting that artists' depictions of Noah building the ark changed as the technology and shipbuilding techniques advanced through the centuries.

Another case can be seen in the sociology examples mentioned earlier. In our culture, we consider the subject of *An Encyclopedia of Nineteenth Century Sociology* and *An Introduction to Sociology* to be the same: sociology. One resource, however, is written from the perspective of history. The two resources convey distinct types of information, and their purposes, perspectives, and forms affect our understanding of the aboutness. A user looking for one of these treatments would likely not be satisfied with the other. Addressing the resource's form, the creator's point of view, or the question "What is it for?" helps us to distinguish among different treatments of the same subject. Addressing these types of issues, however, does not solve all the challenges in the subject analysis process.

11.3.3 Non-textual Information

Determining the topics of non-textual information resources is even less clear-cut than the process for textual ones. For visual resources, several levels of conceptual analysis are possible. In 1939, art historian Erwin Panofsky identified three levels of meaning in works of art.[18]

1. **The primary or natural subject matter**: This is the pre-iconographic or factual level in which objects and events are identified (e.g., this is a painting of 13 long-haired men in robes gathered around a long table for a meal).

2. **The secondary or conventional subject matter**: This is the iconographic level, in which some cultural knowledge of themes and concepts manifested in stories, images, and allegory is needed (e.g., this is not just an image of 13 men gathered for a meal, it is a representation of the Last Supper).

3. **The intrinsic meaning or content**: This is the iconological level, in which the work is interpreted, based on an understanding of the "basic attitudes of a nation, a period, a class, a religious or philosophical persuasion—unconsciously qualified by one personality [the artist] and condensed into one work"[19] (e.g., this painting is Leonardo da Vinci's *Last Supper* from 1498, a mural in the Convent of Santa Maria delle Grazie in Milan, Italy. It depicts the internal confusion of the 12 disciples after Jesus announced one of them would betray him—each one wondering if it would be him). On this level, meaning depends upon an understanding of the two previous levels. This level requires a sophisticated understanding of world cultures, symbolism, and the significance of the work and its context in art history.

More than eighty years later, Panofsky's categories remain useful for analyzing the content of visual images. With artworks it is certainly easiest to describe them at the pre-iconographic level, that is, to enumerate objects and scenes represented in the image, rather than any literary themes or intrinsic meaning. In some cases, it may be possible to identify a subject concept (e.g., a depiction of a battle scene) but also to determine from a work's title a specific instance of the concept (e.g., the Battle of Gettysburg). Sara Shatford Layne relates Panofsky's first level of meaning to the *of-ness* of the resource (i.e., what an image is depicting, what it is of) and his second level to aboutness. The utility of the third level, however, is less clear. She states that the third level cannot be used to analyze visual images with any degree of consistency.[20] With musical works, identifying concepts and enumerating themes and topics is even more difficult. If one wants true conceptual analysis of non-textual information resources, such analysis would be at the interpretive thematic level. It is fairly easy to describe how an object looks, but the identification of intrinsic meaning or iconological significance for a non-textual resource requires special study and training.

11.3.4 Exhaustivity

When examining documents for subject content, one must have a clear idea about the level of exhaustivity that is required. **Exhaustivity**, the number of concepts that will be considered in the analysis and the subject description, may be guided by any of the following:

- local policy (e.g., use no more than three main concepts),
- type of material (e.g., archival collections require more depth of indexing), or
- published guidelines (e.g., the *Subject Headings Manual* limits the number of LCSH terms that may be applied to a resource).

A. G. Brown identifies two basic degrees of exhaustivity: *summarization* and *depth indexing*.[21] **Summarization** identifies a dominant overall subject of the resource, recognizing only concepts embodied in the main theme. **Depth indexing** aims to extract all the main concepts addressed in a resource, recognizing subtopics and lesser themes.

In library cataloging, subject analysis has traditionally been carried out at the summarization level, relinquishing depth indexing to other enterprises. In the cataloging of books and serials in libraries, the cataloger generally attempts to find the overall subject concepts that encompass the whole resource. Depth indexing has traditionally been used for parts of resources (e.g., articles in journals, chapters in books) and has usually been done by commercial indexing enterprises. In the case of a journal such as the *Journal of Statistics Education*,[22] the subject at the summarization level can be no more in depth than *statistics education* and *data science education*, even though the subjects of individual articles are much more specific.

In libraries, whole resources could be indexed more deeply, but it raises questions about how accurate, precise, or helpful the resulting descriptions would be. One must consider the users' needs. If a 900-page resource contains only a few paragraphs or a few pages on a particular topic, is it worth the users' time to be directed to that resource? For example, in the book *Teenagers from the Future*, a look at the table of contents (see page 429) shows various concepts that might be included if this resource were indexed at a more granular level.

Summarization	Depth Indexing
Legion of Super-Heroes (Fictitious characters)—In comics	**Legion of Super-Heroes (Fictitious characters)—In comics**
Comic books, strips, etc.—History and criticism	**Comic books, strips, etc.—History and criticism**
Science fiction comic books, strips, etc.— History and criticism	**Science fiction comic books, strips, etc.— History and criticism**
Superheroes in comics	**Superheroes in comics**
Teenagers in literature	**Teenagers in literature**
	Women in comics
	Justice League of America (Fictitious characters)
	Architecture in literature
	Dystopias in literature
	Gay men in comics
	Lesbians in comics
	Gender identity in comics
	… and many more!

Instead of just the summarization level subject headings enumerated earlier in the chapter, additional terms representing topics and subtopics found in the individual essays could be added. Although portions of the resource are about these concepts, the library has generally focused on pointing users to resources that are entirely or primarily about the topics listed as subject headings in the metadata.

Many books (though certainly not all) have extensive back-of-the-book indexes, and this has been one of the justifications for subject cataloging at the summarization level. That is, there is a difference in degree between *document retrieval* and *information retrieval* (see Figure 11.4). Summarization allows for document retrieval, after which many users consult the document's internal index (which, for electronic resources, may mean conducting a word search within the text) to retrieve the relevant information they need from the document. Depth indexing, however, enables retrieval at a much finer granularity, down to individual sections, paragraphs, or even sentences within a document.

Exhaustivity affects both precision and recall in retrieval. **Precision** is the measurement of how many of the documents retrieved are relevant. **Recall** is the measurement of how many of the relevant documents in a system are retrieved. Depth indexing is likely to increase precision because more specific terminology is used. Summarization is likely to increase recall because the search terms are broader and more sweeping in their application of terminology.

Figure 11.4 Continuum of Exhaustivity.

The summarization approach is very useful in retrieving tangible resources (e.g., books, DVDs, print journals). With intangible digital resources (e.g., online zines, datasets, websites), we must think carefully about summarization versus depth indexing. Search engines perform the ultimate depth indexing (although through automatic rather than intellectual means). Often, the occurrence of a word anywhere in an online resource means that the site will be retrieved by a search on that word, whether or not the word accurately reflects the topics covered in the resource. However, because this retrieval approach is based on matching specific strings of characters, rather than searching for the concepts signified by those strings, full text indexing increases recall while greatly decreasing precision.

In addition to considering exhaustivity, information professionals also must determine what is an analyzable unit. Traditionally, whole resources have been the analyzable units in libraries, collections are described in archives, individual works of art are depicted in museums, and individual articles are the units described in commercial indexing enterprises (along with individual poems, stories, or essays published in collections). In digital libraries and other online spaces there is, so far, no definition for an analyzable unit. It could be a single image, a collection of 500 scanned images, or something in between.

11.3.5 Objectivity

The challenges addressed above (levels of complexity, difficulty, consistency, etc.) raise questions as to whether the subject analysis process can be an objective or impartial one. For example, some find it much easier to analyze resources about topics with which they are already familiar or those that they simply enjoy; some find it difficult to analyze resources they dislike or disagree with on a philosophical, moral, social, religious, or political basis. Information professionals are expected to remain objective and impartial in all their work-related activities, but is this realistic?

Subject analysis is performed by catalogers (and will continue to be for at least the near future, notwithstanding developments in artificial intelligence [AI]), thus the analysis occurs within the human mind, which is an imperfect instrument. Text, images, sounds, and other forms of communication can only be viewed and processed through the lens of the individual; their perception and cognitive processing are distinct and specific to that individual. "It is not hard, therefore, to conclude that no two analyses of the same resource are going to be exactly alike. We must remember that we perceive the world uniquely, and that our interpretation of that world (i.e., our perceived reality) may be very different than that of other people, depending upon such things as education, language, cultural background, intellectual interests, knowledge, and our assumptions about the world around us."[23] Any of these things can contribute to how we interpret an information resource. Acknowledging that these differences exist is a necessary first step to performing the work of subject analysis.

Daniel N. Joudrey found that 75 percent of the LIS students who participated in his study of aboutness determination questioned the validity of the creator's premise in at least one of the three information resources they were analyzing.[24] Is this surprising? Information professionals (and LIS students) are only human after all. Although information professionals are expected to remain impartial, there is a human tendency to judge the information that we encounter, whether it is a bad first impression from cover art or lasting doubts about a creator's evidence to support their claims. With controversial resources or resources representing an opposing point of view, judgments and preconceptions may be unavoidable. In such cases, it is important to be aware of and to acknowledge one's biases, prejudices, and beliefs when conducting the conceptual analysis, and to seek the opinions of others when needed.

Those with vastly different understandings of the world might vehemently disagree as to how objective the subject analysis process is or can be. Although some with a more positivist, empirical view of the world might believe that there is an innate, identifiable aboutness in each information resource just waiting to be discovered, others disagree. Those with a more constructivist understanding may view the process as one that can only be performed through the lens of the analyst's own background, responsibilities, and even mood. In other words, they see conceptual analysis as a highly subjective, interpretive process that is dependent on human skills of observation, interpretation, and analysis. Whatever one's epistemological orientation, the work of subject analysis must provide subject access to information resources in a systematic, deliberate fashion. Consequently, information professionals often forego long philosophical debates over the nature of reality, aboutness, and subject determination, and instead focus on completing the task at hand—with an understanding that although cataloging is not a neutral act, we should attempt to keep our biases in check as much as possible while performing the process and remember that self-awareness is crucial.

11.4 Some Methods Used to Determine Aboutness

Not everyone agrees on how to approach the determination of aboutness, so there is no single process used by everyone. Over the years, various methods have been offered. Some are simply lists of bibliographic features that can be consulted, whereas others provide questions and concepts to consider while examining a resource. Some view the process as comprising two activities, while others believe there are three or four discrete steps. Some, however, do not conceive of the process in terms of discrete steps at all. This section discusses the most familiar and useful approaches to determining aboutness.

11.4.1 Langridge's Approach

Langridge views the subject analysis process as a series of discrete activities.[25] He also stresses that conceptual analysis must be performed independently from any particular classification scheme or controlled vocabulary, and that the analysis should be written down so as to avoid muddled notions of aboutness.[26] In addition to examining the various parts of the text, he states that the information professional must keep three basic questions in mind in order to determine the aboutness of an information resource.

- What is it?
- What is it for?
- What is it about?[27]

According to Langridge, the first question is answered by one of the fundamental forms of knowledge. In other words, one must ask: Is this resource a work of history? Is it science? Is it art? Langridge identifies twelve distinct forms of knowledge under which he believes all resources can be classified:

- Philosophy
- Natural science
- Technology
- Human science
- Social practice
- History
- Moral knowledge
- Religion
- Art
- Criticism
- Personal experience
- Prolegomena (logic, mathematics, grammar—the foundations of knowledge)[28]

Langridge's second question looks at the purpose of the document. Why was it created? How might it be used? Examining the discipline it falls within may help to answer this question. Is it for a specific audience? Is this book on cows meant for a zoologist? Is it for a veterinarian? Is it for a vegetarian, or a researcher studying the place of cows in spirituality? Is it for a dairy farmer? Is it for a child or a chef? These reflect different perspectives that might affect our understanding of the resource and its aboutness. Langridge sees disciplines as ever-evolving areas of interest or specialization nested within the twelve forms of knowledge.

The answer to the third question is one or more topics. Topics are the everyday phenomena that we perceive: concepts, objects, places, events, people, groups, and so on. Langridge points out that topics are not specific to any one form of knowledge or discipline. For example, the topic *clothing* can appear in any number of disciplines or sub-disciplines, such as clothing design, clothing manufacturing, home economics, social customs, psychological or religious aspects of clothing, and so on. In his approach to subject analysis, Langridge also includes some other characteristics as part of the process, such as examining the nature of the text (bibliographic structures and mediums of communication) and the nature of the thought (point of view, type of writing, audience, intellectual level, etc.); these help to bring out additional aspects or perspectives of the aboutness.

11.4.2 Wilson's Approaches

Wilson has described four possible methods that one may use to come to an understanding of what a resource is about.[29] The first might be called the *Purposive Method*.* In this approach, one tries to determine the creator's aim or purpose in creating the information resource. If the creator provides a statement of purpose, then we may presume to know what the work is about. But some creators give no such statement, others seem to aim at several things at once, and others provide multiple statements indicating different purposes or objectives in each. If no statement is provided, one might assume or guess at the author's purpose; if multiple statements are provided, then one may have to discern between primary and secondary purposes or aims.

Wilson's second method might be called the *Figure-Ground Method*. Using this method, one tries to determine a central figure that stands out from the background of the rest of the information resource. This might be an idea, a person, an object, a place—whatever is the central aspect of the subject. What stands out, however, depends on the observer of the resource as well as on its creator. What catches one's interest is not necessarily the same from person to person and may not even be constant for the same person over time. Education, background knowledge, intellectual interests, and initial assumptions about the information resource can also influence what stands out.

Wilson's third method is the *Objective Method* (which is the method used in most attempts at automated conceptual analysis). One tries to be objective by counting references to various terms to determine which concepts predominate the text. Unfortunately, something constantly referred to in the resource might be a background idea (e.g., Germany in a work about the Second World War). The primary concept may be signified by different words throughout the resource, so the information professional must recognize that these variations refer to the same idea. It is also possible that the concept that is central to the aboutness might not be expressed explicitly in the text. Wilson gives the example of a work being about a person's political career without those exact words ever appearing in the text. Collantes found that when people were asked to read abstracts and then write down subject words or phrases that they believed conveyed the meaning in the abstracts, eight percent of the readers used words that did not appear anywhere in the abstract.[30]

The last of Wilson's methods is the *Cohesion Method*, an approach that looks at the unity of the content. When using this method, one tries to determine what holds the work together, what content has been included, and what has been left out. The observer of the information resource must know quite a lot about the subject to recognize what was omitted. In addition, there may be several ways in which the work can appear to be unified, and creators do not always reach the ideal of a completely unified presentation.

11.4.3 Use-Based Approaches

Over the years, a few other approaches to subject analysis have been discussed in the LIS literature. Some can be described as *use-based* approaches. The main idea is that aboutness can be determined by looking at how a resource could be used or what questions a resource could answer.

---

*The authors of this text have added more consistent and descriptive names for each of the methods.

Lancaster, concerned about users and how the resource might be used, suggests asking three questions to determine aboutness:

- What is it about?
- Why has it been added to our collection?
- What aspects will our users be interested in?[31]

Concerns about use, purpose, or patrons' interests, though informative, will not suffice as the only approach to aboutness determination because the information professional is being asked to perform an impossible task: to predict all the possible (present and future) uses for a document. No matter how skilled one may be, this approach amounts to little more than guessing why an information resource may be needed. Therein lie the difficulties associated with use-based approaches to aboutness. This is not to say that asking how a document could be used has no place in aboutness determination. On the contrary, it is an important question; it just cannot be the only question.

As this discussion indicates, there is no single correct way to determine aboutness. Different approaches to identifying relevant aboutness data may be used by different analysts, or by the same analyst with different resources or on different days. One can use any or all these methods, but the different methods will not necessarily lead to the same result. If they give the same result, as they often could, it would appear that the subjects have been identified. However, a single person might arrive at three or four different subjects using different methods, and several persons might arrive at different results using the same method. In the following section, an approach to conceptual analysis that considers some of the important components described above is offered.

11.5 Conceptual Analysis Process

Conceptual analysis comprises three interconnected components:

- an examination of the physical resource (or the display of a digital resource),
- an examination of the intellectual or creative content, and
- numerous stages of aboutness determination performed simultaneously.

In the following sections, these components are addressed.[32]

11.5.1 Resource Examination

The conceptual analysis process begins with an examination of the resource, particularly its bibliographic features and visual elements. Like the process of descriptive cataloging, in which both content and carrier are considered when creating metadata, the conceptual analysis of a resource requires an examination of both the intellectual content and the physical resource (if the resource is in a tangible form). The examination starts with the parts of the resource that stand out. In many instances this begins with the information resources themselves, but in other instances it begins with accompanying materials (e.g., manuals, containers, inserts, cases, labels). Somewhat different techniques must be used for textual resources versus those containing non-textual information. Concentrating first on the textual resources, the following parts should be considered.

11.5.1.1 Cover, Jacket, or Container

Generally, the cover (or jacket or container) is the first thing one sees when examining a tangible resource. It kicks off the input process. Without even realizing it, a person seeing the cover gets a first impression of the resource. For that reason alone, this source must be considered. This may be where the title information and the creator's name are first encountered (which may or may not be identical to the information found on the title page or other preferred sources of information). In addition to basic information about title and creator, one may encounter a great deal of visual information from this source. Whether this information is helpful depends upon many factors. A cover may be explicitly designed to include meaningful imagery, or it may be designed to catch the eye; its illustrations may be subtle, symbolic, literal, apparently random, or simply a clever marketing strategy. Although there are no guarantees that this information will be useful, it should be considered a potential source of aboutness data.

11.5.1.2 Title and Subtitle

A title can be helpful in giving an immediate impression of the topic of a document, but titles can also be misleading. Occasionally, more than one form of title or subtitle may be found on an information resource. The title *Introduction to Cataloging and Classification* is quite straightforward. On the other hand, the title *What the Thunder Said* is not so clear; it is a website devoted to the life and works of T. S. Eliot. Although a straightforward title might convey what is needed to start the analysis, subject analysts need to be cautious of relying on titles that are meant to be humorous, ironic, clever, obfuscating, and so on.

11.5.1.3 Tables of Contents

A list of contents can help to clarify the main topic and identify subtopics. It can be especially helpful for resources that are collections of articles, papers, reports, and the like, by different creators. A table of contents can show the variety of specific topics covered in a resource. Individual chapter titles, like titles proper, are not always helpful or clear, though. Some creators prefer to use tongue-in-cheek or cryptic chapter titles; so, the table of contents is only one of the sources consulted during the conceptual analysis.

11.5.1.4 Introductions or Prefaces

Introductions, prefaces, opening essays, or some equivalent feature may contain some of the most useful, concrete, and straightforward aboutness data in the entire resource. Unfortunately, these features are not always present in resources. Often, an introduction is an aid in determining the creator's overall purpose or objective in creating the work (as suggested by Wilson)[33] and may also serve to indicate a creator's point of view or perspective on the topic (as recommended by Langridge).[34]

11.5.1.5 Illustrations and Other Visual Features

Illustrations and their captions are particularly important in assessing subjects in fields such as art, where in many cases, illustrations make up most of the content and therefore must be examined in order to determine aboutness. The captions for illustrations often are quite descriptive of subject content. In some resources, however, the illustrations may provide little helpful aboutness information or may even be distracting.

11.5.1.6 Other Bibliographic Features

Some information professionals also consult dedications and acknowledgements, hyperlinks, abstracts (if present), and indexes. These elements may confirm or contradict impressions gained from examining the title, table of contents, introduction, and so on. Like Wilson's objective method, a back-of-the-book index can show which topics receive the most attention, as indicated by the number of pages devoted to each;[35] what it does not provide, however, is context to show which topics are related and how so.[36]

11.5.1.7 The Text

In addition to examining the bibliographic and visual features, the text itself should be examined to get a more complete understanding of the information resource. In looking through the text, one may encounter helpful information in the introductory sections, opening paragraphs, conclusions, chapter summaries, and bolded section headings throughout a resource. Section headings, if used, can provide a quick overview of the content found in individual parts of a chapter.

There are several approaches that may be taken to examining the text, the most common being skimming, which allows the analyst to quickly get a sense of what the creator has written and of the topics covered in the document. This process can be used to help reinforce, refine, or refute emerging aboutness assumptions. In addition to skimming, some may choose occasionally to sample paragraphs or to read longer passages when needed.

While examining the text, some may choose to work in a linear fashion from the beginning to the end of the resource, while others may choose to focus only on the beginning and the end of the information resource, under the assumption that the richest aboutness data will be found in the introductory and concluding chapters, sections, or features. Still others may flip randomly through a resource stopping only at what catches the eye. Individuals must find the approach that works best for them and best for the resource they are examining at that moment. No single approach will work equally well for every resource.

11.5.1.8 Non-textual Information

For tangible non-textual resources, one must examine the object, picture, or other representation itself. Some non-textual resources include accompanying materials such as boxes with text, booklets, instruction sheets, labels, and so on. Intangible electronic resources that are basically images or other forms of artistic work quite often have captions that explain something about them. For individual works or objects with no accompanying text, however, one must examine the resources themselves and translate those ideas into words (which can be quite difficult, if not impossible, without special training or education).

11.5.2 Content Examination

During the examination of the physical resource, one must also be concerned with various aspects of the intellectual and creative contents of the resource. In this section, identifying concepts of interest, important content characteristics useful in aboutness determination, and some content examination strategies are addressed.

11.5.2.1 Identification of Concepts

Different types of concepts can be used as the subjects of information resources, including topics, names, and chronological elements.

11.5.2.1.1 Topics

Most people think of topical terms when asked to identify the subject of a resource. A topic can represent a principal object of attention or a theme running through an information resource. Topics can be concrete or abstract. Ideas, objects, phenomena, activities, processes, structures, groups, substances, and more, can be the topics of works. In short, an information resource can be about anything imaginable.

11.5.2.1.2 Names

In the process of determining what a document is about, it may be found that the subject, or one aspect of the subject, is a person, a corporate body, a geographic area, a title, or some other named entity.

Personal Names. An individual person, living or dead, can be the topic of a book, a movie, or some other form of resource. It may be primarily biographical, or it may cover aspects of a person's career (e.g., the aforementioned site dedicated to T. S. Eliot). Such a work is also, in a sense, about one representative of a group of persons (e.g., literary authors). The Library of Congress, in applying LCSH, for example, has the policy of assigning a subject heading for a group to which a person belongs, as well as for the individual person, on the assumption that if an information seeker wants to learn about literary authors, then a site about one such person may be of use. A work can be about deities, biblical figures, legendary and fictitious characters, and named animals as well.

Corporate Body Names. A corporate body is an organization or group of persons who are identified by a name and who act as an entity. A corporate body may be the subject of a resource about an organization, a musical group, a company, a legislative body, a church group, a vessel, and so forth (e.g., a book may be about Exxon-Mobil, The Beatles, or the Worcester Public Library). There are also entities whose names resemble corporate bodies, but that are not. Sometimes such bodies have the same name as the building they work in. This is often true of churches, for example, and then one must be certain whether the building or the corporate entity is the topic of the work.

Geographic Names. Geographic names can take different roles in the determination of subject content. In some cases, a document may be about a specific place (e.g., a work about the history of Amherst, Massachusetts). However, much of the time, a work is not about the place per se, but the geographic location provides a context for the topical content, as in a work about the projects and life of architect Julia Morgan, who did virtually all her work in California. Falling between these extremes is the case where a geographic area is the subject of the topic. An example is the exhibition catalog, *"A Sweet Foretaste of Heaven": Artists in the White Mountains, 1830–1930*. The exhibition consisted of landscape paintings of the White Mountains of New Hampshire, but the book itself is not about that geographic area.

Titles. Titles are another type of entity that may be used as a subject concept. A resource can be about one or more scholarly, literary, musical, or artistic works. Reviews, adaptations, critical essays, histories, and parodies are some examples of resources that might reference the title of another work in their subjects. For example, the book *Butterfly in the Typewriter* is about John Kennedy Toole and how his book *The Confederacy of Dunces* came to be published after his death.

Other Named Entities. Some named entities resemble both corporate names and geographic names but are neither. Entities such as named buildings, structures, cemeteries, bridges, and archaeological sites fall into this category. An example is the subject heading **Megiddo (Extinct city)**, which is used to represent the archaeological site.

11.5.2.1.3 Chronological Elements

The time period can be an important aspect of the subject content of information resources. Time periods limit the coverage of the topic and therefore dictate content in subtle ways. For example, resources about computer access to information in the 1970s will not include information about the Semantic Web or Open Access journals. Time can be expressed in several ways. Named periods (e.g., Bronze age) and styles (e.g., Rococo) often act as surrogates for chronology. These are of particular importance in the fields of art, architecture, music, history, and literature, but they have not been particularly well handled by controlled vocabularies or by the Machine-Readable Cataloging (MARC) format. Only specific dates or date ranges are usually treated as separate chronological elements, because named periods and styles generally have been treated as adjectival qualifiers to topical information.

11.5.2.2 Content Characteristics

Just as topics, names, and chronological elements are important to understanding the aboutness of information resources, so are some additional characteristics that are related to the content and the creator. These characteristics include what Langridge discussed as "the nature of the text" and "the nature of the thought."[37] According to Langridge,

> There remain a number of very important characteristics requiring identification which have always been treated as part of the process of subject analysis. I shall refer to these as formal characteristics to distinguish them from the real subject features. Though none of these formal elements alters the subject of a document, some of them can make a considerable difference to its treatment or presentation.[38]

For some resources, a few of these content characteristics may be relevant in the conceptual analysis process, but with others, perhaps none will be useful at all. Like so many other factors in the conceptual analysis process, it will depend on the nature of the resource being analyzed. The following characteristics should be considered if they are applicable.

11.5.2.2.1 Research Methods

Although this characteristic will not be appropriate for most popular or creative works, some academic research materials, scientific articles, technical reports, and the like might benefit from considering the methods used to examine the issue, hypothesis, or research questions. This characteristic might be useful in helping to better understand the aboutness, the form, and the level of the work, as well as the means used to reach conclusions. It also may be particularly useful in the indexing of scientific datasets, papers, and articles.

11.5.2.2.2 Point of View

Except for Langridge, point of view is rarely mentioned in discussions of conceptual analysis. Although not all resources have a specialized or identifiable point of view, some are written from a particular perspective, which could be of special interest to some users and could be anathema to others. This content characteristic can be helpful when analyzing some types of resources and necessary when describing those works from a particular viewpoint. For resources that may be controversial in some fashion (e.g., political works; religious works; cultural treatises; works on sexuality, gender, age, or wealth inequality), the point of view may be an important piece of metadata that will help the users to find, identify, and select the resources that they need. This content characteristic, however, is rarely if ever translated into controlled vocabulary terms or classification notations; instead, it may be addressed in summary statements or abstracts.

11.5.2.2.3 Language, Tone, Audience, and Intellectual Level

These characteristics are addressed together because they are interrelated. The relationships among them are multifaceted and myriad. For example, the language chosen by the creator helps to set the tone of the work. The language and tone are shaped by the intellectual level that the creator is striving for and by the creator's intended audience for the work. In examining the work, the language and tone are particularly helpful in understanding the audience and intellectual level (e.g., whether it is an academic or a popular work). Although none of these directly affects aboutness, they may help to establish some context for understanding the information resource.

These characteristics may also affect the resource examination process. The analyst may need to treat a scholarly intellectual work differently than a popular work. For example, a scholarly resource may need more exploration of the content, more reading of the introduction and conclusion, and more time to complete the analysis than a work of popular culture.

Of those writing on aboutness determination, few address these issues. Langridge addresses one of the four—*audience*—in his discussion of "form of thought." Audience may also appear as the answer to his conceptual analysis question: *What is it for?*[39] Joudrey found that 92 percent of the participants in his qualitative study of aboutness were concerned with audience. Although the study participants found audience helpful in the aboutness determination process, some were reluctant to include the concept in their final descriptions of the resource. He notes, "the participants included audience [in their aboutness statements] when the book was written for and directed toward one particular audience, and they excluded the concept when the item could appeal to multiple audiences or a more general audience."[40]

Language and tone are almost never addressed in the subject analysis process. Audience and intellectual level are sometimes addressed in the translation stage of subject analysis (e.g., in subject headings), but audience may also appear in other places in metadata descriptions. For example, in MARC bibliographic records, headings from *Library of Congress Demographic Group Terms* can be placed in the 385 field for audience characteristics; *audience* is also sometimes used as a supplemental element in some implementations of Dublin Core.

11.5.2.2.4 Genre and Form

The final characteristic to examine in the conceptual analysis process is the ***genre*** and ***form*** of both the overall resource and its parts. Genre and form are not subject features. They describe what a resource *is* rather than what it is about. They are concepts, however, that have been associated with subject analysis from the inception of the idea that books could be entered in catalogs and placed on shelves according to categories to which they belonged. Early categories included forms such as encyclopedias, biographies, and histories, as well as subjects such as chemistry and religion. Later, as subject headings evolved to mean what a resource is *about* instead of a category to which the book belonged, the idea of form and genre remained as part of the subject analysis process. Because it was often difficult to separate the idea of genre/form from aboutness, as in the case of history (which seems to incorporate elements of both), the concept of genre/form began to be treated separately in metadata descriptions only in the last few decades.

To aid in the process of separating genre and form from subject, the Subject Analysis Committee (SAC) of the American Library Association (ALA) published a definition for form in January 1993.

> Form data are those terms and phrases that designate specific kinds or genres of materials. Materials designated with these terms or phrases may be determined by an examination of:
>
> - their physical character (e.g., videocassettes, photographs, maps, broadsides)
> - the particular type of data that they contain (e.g., bibliographies, questionnaires, statistics)
> - the arrangement of information within them (e.g., diaries, outlines, indexes)
> - the style, technique, purpose, or intended audience (e.g., drama, romances, cartoons, commercials, popular works) or a combination of the above (e.g., scores)
>
> A single term may be modified by other terms, in which case the whole phrase is considered to be form data (e.g., aerial photographs, French dictionaries, conversation and phrase books, wind ensemble suites, telephone directories, vellum bound books, science fiction).[41]

More recently, the Library of Congress (LC) has been paying additional attention to this content characteristic, going so far as to create a thesaurus of terms just for genre/form concepts. Its introduction states,

> Genres and forms may be broadly defined as categories of resources that share known conventions. More specifically, genre/form terms may describe the purpose, structure, content, and/or themes of resources. Genre/form terms describing content and themes most frequently refer to creative works and denote common rhetorical devices that usually combine elements such as plot and setting, character types, etc. Such terms may be closely related to the subjects of the creative works, but are distinct from them.[42]

Separating genre/form from subject became increasingly important as retrieval systems became more advanced and the information professions became more attuned to organizing information that is not just in textual form. In the discipline of music, for example, identifying genre/form has always been critical and has been accommodated by treating it as subject. Now more users are looking for other kinds of information (e.g., city ordinances, chalk drawings, digital maps, sculpture reproductions). By separating genre/form from subject, it is possible to take advantage of system design to allow searching for resources in specific genres or forms. Some metadata schemas have elements that are defined specifically for this concept (e.g., *Form of work* in RDA; *Type* and *Format* in Dublin Core; *worktype* and *material* in VRA Core).

11.5.2.3 Content Examination Strategies

As discussed earlier, different approaches to identifying relevant aboutness data may be used by different analysts, or by the same analyst with different resources or on different days. Some may use Langridge's or Lancaster's questions, while others may use one or more of Wilson's approaches, and still others may use no organized method at all. Answering a series of questions, whether formally or informally, can help streamline the subject analysis process. A sample set of questions and an example of the process is found in Appendix E of this textbook.

In his research, Joudrey found that LIS students with no previous experience or coursework in organizing information mostly used the same approaches to conceptual analysis. The most commonly used approaches are three of the four described by Wilson: *Purposive Method*, *Figure-Ground Method*, and *Objective Method*. The participants rejected some of the other strategies described in the LIS literature by either using them infrequently (or not at all) or by stating that they were not approaches they had considered, or they would consider. For example, although the participants explored the creator's purpose in writing a document, overall, they did not consider how patrons would use the documents, what questions the documents would answer, or how someone would search for the documents. Based on Joudrey's research, it seems that Patrick Wilson got it right back in the late '60s.[43] Joudrey concludes:

> Because of the interpretive nature of all of the processes that the participants used (and those that they did not use), it is recommended that each content examination strategy should be used in conjunction with other strategies. Wilson was accurate when he stated that each of the approaches that he described was *a* method, and not *the* method, to analyze aboutness. No one approach to the content was observed in isolation, nor should they be used in isolation. Similar to conducting good qualitative

research, the content examination strategies need be triangulated. Getting as many perspectives as possible on the items is the best strategy for determining aboutness.[44]

11.5.3 Stages in Aboutness Determination

To better understand what happens during the conceptual analysis process, Joudrey analyzed the activities that were being performed while study participants were attempting to determine what information resources were about. While the physical resources were being examined and the participants were considering things like the creator's purpose and what topics were mentioned most often, they were also advancing through several simultaneous stages: *input, assumption making, revisions, interpretation*, and *stopping*.

The conceptual analysis process begins with an input phase in which data is collected by encountering content in some form or manner (seeing, noticing, etc.). This may occur through simple visual examination, more in-depth exploration of general content, or through seeking specific desired chunks of data. Shortly after the input process begins (sometimes as early as viewing the cover), assumptions about the resource's aboutness start to form. These assumptions may be about macro-level, micro-level, or chapter-level aboutness, or they may be about other characteristics of the resource. These assumptions then undergo a revision process, in which assumptions are refined, reinforced, and/or refuted. Concurrently with the input, assumption making, and revision processes, the multifaceted process of interpretation begins.[†] This entails several individual activities, including finding context, analyzing, comparing, and reasoning. After the first moments of the input process, all these other processes are performed simultaneously and continuously until an understanding of the resource's aboutness is reached. The final process centers on how and when one decides to stop the examination of the resource.[45]

11.6 Next Steps in Subject Analysis

Once the conceptual analysis is complete, it is helpful to write an aboutness statement that begins, "This resource is about …" It may be one or two sentences, or it could be a short paragraph. As Langridge states, the conceptual analysis should be written down to avoid muddled notions of aboutness.[46] It helps the information professional to keep track of all the major concepts and to relate them to each other. Depending on the degree of exhaustivity that is being followed, the concepts included may be limited to the main idea of the entire work or to all the major subtopics found in the resource.

Once the aboutness statement is complete, the aboutness concepts that have been identified must then be translated into the subject languages being used. The information professional identifies the key concepts and chooses terms from the aboutness statement to be searched in the controlled vocabulary. Specific rules for using controlled vocabularies are found in their introductions, as well as, in some cases, manuals that accompany them (e.g., LCSH's *Subject Headings*

[†]In Joudrey's original work, the process was referred to as *sense making*. To avoid confusion with Brenda Dervin's sense-making methodology, the term has been changed here.

Manual). To translate an aboutness statement into classification notations, it is necessary to understand the hierarchy or the facets of the classification scheme being used. It is helpful to determine the discipline into which the information resource falls because most classification schemes begin with a disciplinary division of the areas of knowledge. For example, a history of Spain is usually considered to fall within the discipline of history and the sub-discipline of European history, while a history of chemistry is generally thought to fall within the broad area of the sciences, specifically in the discipline of chemistry. Creating a string for discipline, sub-discipline, topics and sub-topics within the discipline, accompanied by concepts of treatment, place, time, and form is helpful in translating the aboutness into a classification scheme.

11.7 Future of Subject Analysis

In recent years, with advances in search engine technology and generative AI, as well as the high costs of original cataloging, the necessity for subject analysis has been questioned. Some have suggested that information resources no longer need to be analyzed because when users are searching for information, computers (through automatic indexing) can identify *some* documents relevant to users' needs, and therefore the time and money spent on humans performing subject analysis could be diverted to other activities such as digitization projects. Others have suggested that computers can analyze documents and assign classification numbers and/or descriptors. Despite improvements in search engines and AI, the development of *microdata*, the introduction of user tagging, and other activities meant to improve online retrieval, many LIS professionals are reluctant to turn over subject analysis activities to machines. There is still a preference in our discipline for reflective subject analysis over algorithmic approaches to subject access.

Why is there still such reluctance? Despite advances, technology thus far has not proved itself up to the tasks of subject analysis. Machines are not yet adept at identifying the aboutness of information resources and they still cannot, with any satisfactory degree of accuracy, assign concepts from controlled vocabularies and classification notation. Although a computer can determine what words are used in a document and the frequency of those words, aboutness is more than just the words found in a resource. Machines simply do not yet provide thoughtful analysis; they lack insights into what content is most significant or meaningful, and they cannot prioritize subject concepts, other than ranking them based on word-frequency (i.e., a process that is computational, not conceptual).

At this time, generative AI is improving at an astonishing, and sometimes alarming, rate; however, it cannot yet understand or intuit some complex, multifaceted, or nuanced concepts represented in a body of text, in images, and other forms of communication. Even the most sophisticated systems cannot yet replace the human mind for its efficiency and efficacy in understanding the deeper meanings of texts and being able to represent those meanings using subject languages. Moreover, two significant problems remain: (1) the tendency of AI systems to "hallucinate"—generating incorrect or misleading information when they do not have an answer—and (2) the intellectual property rights concerns related to granting AI systems access to protected resources.

Beyond technical limitations, generative AI systems are incapable of performing the ethical, interpretive, and contextually sensitive work that true subject analysis demands. Cultural competence, moral reasoning, and awareness of power dynamics are human capabilities that machines cannot replicate. AI systems struggle to discern layered or implied meanings, and their dependence on biased, incomplete, or skewed training data can amplify existing problems rather than address them. Identifying surface-level topics is not enough; subject analysis requires deep analytical skills and critical human judgment—not pattern-matching algorithms or predictive text generation. Until generative AI can demonstrate genuine ethical reasoning and contextual understanding, it will remain unfit for the complex intellectual work of subject analysis.

Although AI tools—now being integrated into information systems (e.g., LSPs)—may offer suggestions to assist subject analysts, they must be treated as supplements, not substitutes, for human judgment. Just because AI can be deployed in information organization tasks does not mean it should be, especially without critical reflection on its consequences (e.g., amplification of bias, environmental costs, and erosion of professional expertise). When used thoughtfully and judiciously, AI may serve as a useful support tool—but the core work of subject analysis must remain firmly rooted in human insight, expertise, and ethical responsibility.

Until these issues are addressed and until generative AI technology improves further, humans will continue to perform this vital task despite its drawbacks. As stated by the Working Group on the Future of Bibliographic Control: "Subject analysis—including analyzing content and creating and applying subject headings and classification numbers—is a core function of cataloging; although expensive, it is nonetheless critical."[48]

11.8 Conclusion

This chapter has examined the nature of subject and the process of determining the aboutness of resources—a critical first step in providing subject access. It addressed the ethical challenges inherent in assigning subject metadata, including bias, cultural subjectivity, and the limitations of automated systems like AI in capturing nuanced meaning. Before applying subject access tools, it is important to understand the general principles and structures that underlie them. With a solid understanding of aboutness now established, we turn next to two specific approaches to representing subjects: controlled vocabularies and classification schemes—tools that transform subject analysis into structured, actionable metadata.

Some Important Terms in This Chapter
(Definitions Provided in the Glossary)

Aboutness	Form	Precision
Aboutness statement	Genre	Recall
Conceptual analysis	Intensional aboutness	Subject analysis
Depth indexing	Is-ness	Subject language
Exhaustivity	Of-ness	Summarization
Extensional aboutness		

	Some Important Acronyms in This Chapter
AAT:	*Art & Architecture Thesaurus*
AI:	Artificial Intelligence
ALA:	American Library Association
DDC:	*Dewey Decimal Classification*
LC:	Library of Congress
LCC:	*Library of Congress Classification*
LCGFT:	*Library of Congress Genre/Form Terms for Library and Archival Materials*
LCSH:	*Library of Congress Subject Headings*
LIS:	Library and Information Science
LSP:	Library Services Platform
MARC:	Machine-Readable Cataloging
SAC:	Subject Analysis Committee
UDC:	*Universal Decimal Classification*

11.9 Discussion Questions and Exercises

- Select a book (preferably one you have not read yet) and try applying at least two of the methods for determining aboutness discussed in this chapter to the resource. What works well, and what doesn't? Did you receive the same results from the two different methods?

- How does subject analysis for non-textual materials differ from subject analysis for textual materials?

- What are the barriers to objectivity in subject analysis? Should catalogers strive for objectivity? Is objectivity in subject analysis possible?

11.10 Suggested Readings

Chan, Lois Mai, Phyllis A. Richmond, and Elaine Svenonius, eds. *Theory of Subject Analysis: A Sourcebook*. Littleton, CO: Libraries Unlimited, 1985.

Cleveland, Donald B., and Ana D. Cleveland. *Introduction to Indexing and Abstracting*. 4th ed. Santa Barbara, CA: Libraries Unlimited, 2013.

Holley, Ralph M., and Daniel N. Joudrey. "Aboutness and Conceptual Analysis: A Review." *Cataloging & Classification Quarterly* 59, no. 2/3 (2021): 159.

Joudrey, Daniel N. "Building Puzzles and Growing Pearls: A Qualitative Exploration of Determining Aboutness." PhD diss., University of Pittsburgh, 2005. https://d-scholarship.pitt.edu/10357/.

Joudrey, Daniel N., Arlene G. Taylor, and David Miller. *Introduction to Cataloging and Classification*. 11th ed. Santa Barbara, CA: Libraries Unlimited, 2015.

Lakoff, George. *Women, Fire, and Dangerous Things: What Categories Reveal about the Mind.* Chicago: University of Chicago Press, 1987.

Lancaster, F. W. *Indexing and Abstracting in Theory and Practice.* 3rd ed. Champaign: University of Illinois, Graduate School of Library and Information Science, 2003.

Lancaster, F. W. *Vocabulary Control for Information Retrieval.* 2nd ed. Arlington, VA: Information Resources Press, 1986.

Langridge, D. W. *Subject Analysis: Principles and Procedures.* London: Bowker-Saur, 1989.

Pettee, Julia. "The Subject Approach to Books and the Development of the Dictionary Catalog." In *Theory of Subject Analysis: A Sourcebook*, edited by Lois Mai Chan, Phyllis A. Richmond, and Elaine Svenonius, 94–8. Littleton, CO: Libraries Unlimited, 1985.

Wellisch, Hans H. "Aboutness and Selection of Topics." *Key Words* 4, no. 2 (March/April 1996): 7–9.

Wilson, Patrick. *Two Kinds of Power: An Essay on Bibliographical Control.* Berkeley: University of California Press, 1968.

11.11 Notes

All URLs accessed April 2025.

1. Ralph M. Holley and Daniel N. Joudrey, "Aboutness and Conceptual Analysis: A Review," *Cataloging & Classification Quarterly* 59, no. 2/3 (2021): 159.
2. Robert A. Fairthorne, "Content Analysis, Specification, and Control," chap. 3 in *Annual Review of Information Science and Technology*, Vol. 4, ed. by Carlos A. Cuadra and Ann W. Luke (Chicago: Encyclopedia Britannica, 1969), 79.
3. Fairthorne, 79.
4. Patrick Wilson, *Two Kinds of Power: An Essay on Bibliographical Control* (Berkeley: University of California Press, 1968), 81–5.
5. Fairthorne, 79.
6. F. W. Lancaster, *Indexing and Abstracting in Theory and Practice*, 3rd ed. (Champaign: University of Illinois, Graduate School of Library and Information Science, 2003), 9.
7. Fairthorne, 77.
8. Tore Olafsen and Libena Vokac, "Authors' reply to R Moss's Letter to the Editor," *Journal of the American Society for Information Science* 34, no. 4 (1983): 294.
9. Wilson, 69–92.
10. Richard E. Nisbett, *The Geography of Thought: How Asians and Westerners Think Differently. . . and Why* (New York: Free Press, 2004).
11. George Lakoff, *Women, Fire, and Dangerous Things: What Categories Reveal about the Mind* (Chicago: University of Chicago Press, 1987), 24–6.
12. D. W. Langridge, *Subject Analysis: Principles and Procedures* (London: Bowker-Saur, 1989), 4.
13. Oliver L. Lilley, "Evaluation of the Subject Catalog: Criticisms and a Proposal," *American Documentation* 5, no. 2 (1954): 41–60.
14. Lourdes Y. Collantes, "Agreement in Naming Objects and Concepts for Information Retrieval" (PhD diss., Rutgers University, 1992), 154.
15. For example: Regene C. Ross, Chair, Task Force on Copy Cataloging, *Report of the Task Force on Copy Cataloging*, May 12, 1993, cited by Thomas Mann, in "'Cataloging Must Change!' and Indexer Consistency Studies: Misreading the Evidence at Our Peril," *Cataloging & Classification Quarterly* 23, nos. 3/4 (1997): 37–8.

16. Langridge, 9.
17. Richard W. Unger, *The Art of Medieval Technology: Images of Noah the Shipbuilder* (New Brunswick, NJ: Rutgers University Press, 1991).
18. Erwin Panofsky, *Studies in Iconology: Humanistic Themes in the Art of the Renaissance* (New York: Harper & Row, 1972), 5–17.
19. Panofsky, 7.
20. Sara Shatford, "Analyzing the Subject of a Picture: A Theoretical Approach," *Cataloging & Classification Quarterly* 6, no. 3 (1986): 45.
21. A. G. Brown, in collaboration with D. W. Langridge and J. Mills, *An Introduction to Subject Indexing*, 2nd ed. (London: Bingley, 1982), frames 48, 51.
22. *Journal of Statistics and Data Science Education*, https://amstat.tandfonline.com/journals/ujse21.
23. Holley and Joudrey, 181.
24. Daniel N. Joudrey, "Building Puzzles and Growing Pearls: A Qualitative Exploration of Determining Aboutness" (PhD diss., University of Pittsburgh, 2005), 165–71, https://d-scholarship.pitt.edu/10357/.
25. Langridge, 73–98, 136.
26. Langridge, 57.
27. Langridge, 8–10.
28. Langridge, 33–7.
29. Wilson, 78–88.
30. Collantes, 154.
31. Lancaster, *Indexing and Abstracting*, 9.
32. Some of this section appeared in an earlier form in Arlene G. Taylor, "Books and Other Bibliographic Materials," in *Guide to Indexing and Cataloging with the Art & Architecture Thesaurus*, eds. Toni Petersen and Patricia J. Barnett (New York: Oxford University Press, 1994), 101–19. Some materials are derived from Daniel N. Joudrey's dissertation, "Building Puzzles and Growing Pearls."
33. Wilson, 78–88.
34. Langridge, 73–98, 136.
35. Wilson, 78–88.
36. Joudrey, 127.
37. Langridge, 55–7.
38. Langridge, 45.
39. Langridge, 45.
40. Joudrey, 198.
41. ALA Subject Analysis Committee, "Definition of Form Data," *Arlene G. Taylor Homepage*, http://www.pitt.edu/~agtaylor/ala/form-def.htm.
42. "Introduction to Library of Congress Genre/Form Terms for Library and Archival Materials," *Library of Congress Genre/Form Terms for Library and Archival Materials*, 2022 edition (Washington, DC: Library of Congress, 2022), 3, https://www.loc.gov/aba/publications/FreeLCGFT/freelcgft.html.
43. Joudrey, 357–60.
44. Joudrey, 361.
45. Joudrey, 351–2.
46. Langridge, 57.
47. "What Are AI Hallucinations?" IBM, https://www.ibm.com/topics/ai-hallucinations.
48. Working Group on the Future of Bibliographic Control, *On the Record: Report of the Library of Congress Working Group on the Future of Bibliographic Control* (Washington, DC: Library of Congress, 2008), http://www.loc.gov/bibliographic-future/news/lcwg-ontherecord-jan08-final.pdf.

Chapter 12

Systems for Vocabulary Control

In the digital age, subject searching remains a vital approach to finding information resources. Users search catalogs, indexes, and other retrieval tools to find resources that match their interests. In this increasingly web-centric information environment, a search engine is often the first retrieval tool that users approach to find information about a topic they want to explore. Yet some are frustrated with the millions of results from *keyword** searches performed using Google and other search engines. With the massive increase in availability of recorded information, it has become more evident that keyword searching alone—the approach primarily used by search engines—will not suffice for all information retrieval tools in all information environments. One reason that problems occur is the semantic ambiguity inherent in natural language: virtually every common word in the English language has more than one meaning or sense,[1] and many of those senses have more than one nuance; many words can be used as nouns, verbs, adjectives, and/or adverbs. Search systems that purport to respond to natural language cannot always successfully distinguish among different meanings or various parts of speech in large general systems, although progress has been made in search systems that focus on specific subject areas. Recent advances in artificial intelligence, including large language models, are improving search systems' ability to handle natural language ambiguities, although challenges remain in broad, general-purpose environments.

In addition, there is evidence that people writing about the same concepts often do not use the same words to express them, and people searching for the same concept do not think of the same words to search for it. Many of the inter-indexer consistency studies in the second half of the twentieth century asked participants to think up words in their heads, not to take vocabulary from a list; therefore, although these studies have been used by some authors to "prove" that subject indexing is worth little because indexers are inconsistent, what the studies really showed was that people do not think of the same terms to express the same aboutness concepts. Thomas Mann has given an excellent analysis of some inter-indexer consistency studies that support these observations.[2] The clear implication is that controlled vocabulary—usually in the form of a list of authorized terms with their accompanying cross-references and other relationships—helps to reconcile all the various possible words that can be used to express a concept and to differentiate among all the possible meanings that can be attached to certain words.

In recent years, however, it has also become clearer that controlled vocabularies are not necessarily appropriate for all information environments. Controlled vocabularies work best

---

*A keyword is a term that is representative of the content of a resource; it can be considered "key" to finding information. It may be a term that is extracted from a document or chosen by the searcher.

in contained systems. It is only feasible to create, maintain, and apply them in systems such as indexes, databases, or catalogs, which rely on human expertise for success. A controlled approach to terminology does not yet work well for a large-scale, distributed system like the current internet, where no one is responsible for identifying the subjects of works and assigning authorized descriptors, and where the number of resources is enormous.

12.1 What are Controlled Vocabularies?

A ***controlled vocabulary*** is a list or database of terms (or phrases) in which all terms representing a concept are brought together. In other words, it is a ***data value standard***—a list of controlled values that can be used to populate a metadata element. In this chapter, we focus mostly on controlled vocabularies that reflect the subjects of information resources, but a controlled vocabulary can contain many types of terms. For example, it might be a list of resource types, languages, media types, demographic terms, or genre/form headings. The term *controlled vocabulary* is another way of expressing the idea of authority control, but usually for entities other than names and titles. As with name authority control, there are three major concerns in establishing a controlled vocabulary: consistency, relationships, and uniqueness.

If a retrieval system uses controlled vocabulary to represent subject concepts, a search for a word with more than one meaning often will offer differentiation among various meanings. For example, if one searches the term *bridges*, the results could contain many different topics. Users, therefore, might find it helpful to have authority control in place to distinguish among the uses of the term.

> **Bridges**
> **Bridges (Computer networks)**
> **Bridges (Dentistry)**
> **Bridges (Graph theory)**

An authority-control-enhanced online retrieval tool, like a catalog, may direct a searcher to broader, narrower, and/or related terms when a subject search is conducted.

> **Bridges—Foundations and piers**
>   *Broader Term*: **Hydraulic structures**
>   *Related Term*: **Caissons**
>   *Narrower Term*: **Scour at bridges**

It can also bring together, under one authorized term (e.g., **Periodicals**), all the synonymous and nearly synonymous terms that may be used to express a concept (e.g., Magazines, Journals).

In a controlled list, one of the terms representing the same concept is designated as the *authorized* or *preferred term* to be used in metadata descriptions. Choosing a preferred term is an attempt to control synonyms and nearly synonymous terms. It ensures consistency, which allows for greater collocation of concepts in a retrieval tool. For example, in *Library of Congress Subject Headings* (LCSH), the term **Private investigators** has been chosen for use instead of any of several other alternative terms marked UF (Used for) such as *Gumshoes, Private detectives*, or *Private eyes*. Using the authorized term consistently means that all resources about this profession can be retrieved together by searching for that term. The alternatives act as cross-references that point to the chosen term.

> Gumshoes
> USE **Private investigators**

Identifying relationships among terms, therefore, is another key function of many, but not all, controlled vocabularies. The network of relationships is referred to as a vocabulary's ***syndetic structure*** (i.e., its web of interconnected relationships). Relationships among the authorized terms may be identified as *used for* (UF) references, *broader terms* (BT), *narrower terms* (NT), or *related terms* (RT).[‡] As seen above, the terms that are not designated as preferred have references from them to the chosen terms or phrases. The authorized term, **Private investigators**, also has other relationships that are specified in the vocabulary.

> **Private investigators**
> UF Gumshoes
>   Investigators, Private
>   Private detectives
>   Private eyes
>   Private I's
> BT Police, Private
> RT Detectives
> NT Gay private investigators
>   House detectives
>   Lesbian private investigators
>   Store detectives
>   Women private investigators

Even though a word chosen as the authorized heading may have multiple meanings, in a controlled list each term should represent a single concept only. In other words, a controlled vocabulary usually requires homograph control or disambiguation among different meanings of the same word. For example, one controlled vocabulary includes two specific uses of the word *plates*, but each is given a parenthetical qualifier to separate them:

> **Plates (Engineering)**
> **Plates (Tableware)**

Each term in a controlled list should be unique and unambiguous. Definitions, scope notes, creation dates, identifier codes, associated classification numbers, categories, and other features can also assist with this.

[‡]More information about relationships is in section 12.3 of this chapter.

12.2 Types of Controlled Vocabularies

According to *ANSI/NISO Z39.19-2005 (R2010): Guidelines for the Construction, Format, and Management of Monolingual Controlled Vocabularies* (henceforth referred to as Z39.19), controlled vocabularies fall into four major categories:

- **Simple Term Lists**
- **Synonym Rings**
- **Taxonomies**
- **Thesauri** (including **Subject Heading Lists**)

Each is described in the following sections with examples provided.

12.2.1 Simple Term Lists

A ***simple term list*** (sometimes called a *pick list*) is not a particularly sophisticated form of controlled vocabulary. It is a straightforward listing of limited values that may be used for a particular metadata element. There is no concern about semantic relationships in a simple term list. These lists are usually presented in alphabetical or in some other logically evident order (e.g., geographic contiguity, chronological order).

Simple term lists tend to be used with non-subject metadata, such as format, location, language, and so on, and they lend themselves to being placed in pull-down menus because they are usually finite in scope. An example is the controlled vocabulary for media types in *RDA: Resource Description & Access*.[3] It provides a straightforward alphabetical list of choices to describe the form of media a resource represents:

- **Audio**
- **Computer**
- **Microform**
- **Microscopic**
- **Projected**
- **Stereographic**
- **Unmediated**
- **Video**

This example also serves as a reminder that not all controlled vocabularies are subject-focused. They are also used in descriptive cataloging, encoding, and so forth.

12.2.2 Synonym Rings

According to Z39.19, a ***synonym ring***, also referred to as a *synset*, is a different kind of controlled vocabulary. Its function is not so much to provide a list of terms to assign to documents during the indexing or cataloging process; instead, it is used during retrieval activities. It is a behind-the-scenes instrument used in retrieval tools to connect equivalent terms. A synonym ring is made up of equivalence tables or lists. It is used specifically to broaden a search to enhance information retrieval, so that when a user searches one term within the cluster, all the terms can be searched. The equivalence relationships might include not only true synonyms and nearly synonymous

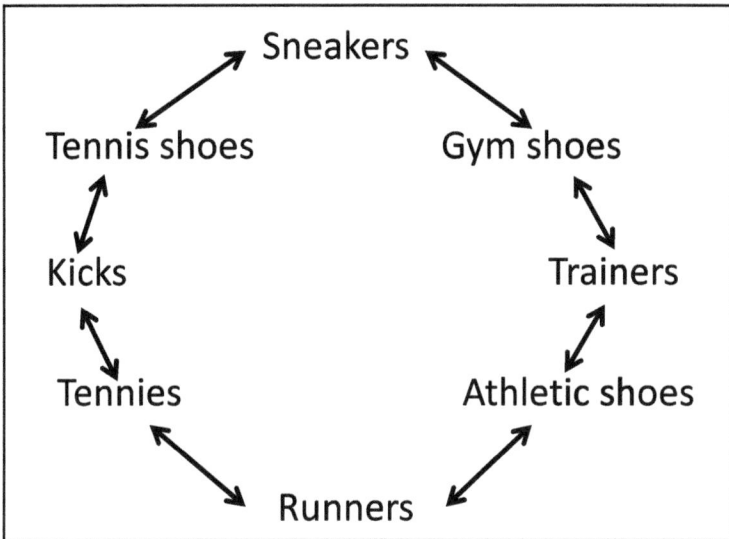

Figure 12.1 An Illustration of the Synonym Ring Concept.

terms, but also acronyms, variant spellings, and popular or scientific terms. One term may be the authorized one if the terms are from a thesaurus, but authority control is not the focus of this type of controlled vocabulary—it is about improving retrieval among natural language variants. An illustration of the concept is provided in Figure 12.1.

12.2.3 Taxonomies

The third type of vocabulary, a ***taxonomy***, is a hierarchically ordered list of terms. It is an orderly classification illustrating a defined knowledge domain. A taxonomy often contains preferred terms only; synonymous terms are not listed. A taxonomy may differ from a thesaurus (the fourth type of vocabulary) in that it generally has shallower hierarchies and a less complicated structure. Often the term is used for a scientific list, such as Linnaeus's eighteenth-century biological taxonomy, but it does not have to be. A taxonomy can contain terms from any discipline. For example, one can create a simple taxonomy of metadata types:

> **Metadata**
> *Administrative metadata*
> > Preservation
> > Recordkeeping
> > Rights
> > Technical
> > Use
>
> *Descriptive metadata*
> > Analytical
> > Contextual
>
> *Structural metadata*
> > Behavioral

Sometimes, the term *taxonomy* is used interchangeably with *classification* or *thesaurus*. Taxonomies are discussed further in the next chapter.

12.2.4 Thesauri and Subject Heading Lists

According to Z39.19, *thesauri* are the most complex type of controlled vocabulary in use in the library and information science professions. A **thesaurus** is an authority-controlled list of terms in which semantic relationships are identified. Often the focus of a thesaurus is on hierarchical structures, but other relationships are included. Thesauri are usually made up of single terms and bound terms representing single concepts (often called **descriptors**). Bound terms occur when a single concept must be represented by two or more words. For example, the words *type, A,* and *personality* cannot be separated into discrete units without losing the meaning. The entire phrase *Type A Personality* is necessary for expressing the concept.

Since the mid-twentieth century, numerous thesauri have been created for a vast number of different subject areas. Some thesauri are publicly available online, but others are proprietary products and cannot be accessed without a subscription to a particular database or service. Some thesauri comprise terms from multiple disciplines, such as the *UNESCO Thesaurus*[4] (which covers education, culture, natural sciences, social and human sciences, communication, and information) and the *American Folklore Society's Ethnographic Thesaurus*[5] (designed to provide access to resources about folklore, ethnomusicology, cultural anthropology, and other related fields). Other thesauri focus primarily on narrower subject areas, such as the *NASA Thesaurus*,[6] covering the aerospace industry. Later in this chapter, some representative thesauri are described briefly. The following example comes from the *Thesaurus of ERIC Descriptors* (ERIC),[7] which is used to index education materials:

Early Reading

Scope note: Reading by children before they reach school age
Category: Reading

Broader Terms	**Related Terms**
Reading	Beginning Reading
Narrower Terms	Early Experience
N/A	Emergent Literacy
	Prereading Experience
	Reading Readiness

A ***subject heading list*** is a specialized type of thesaurus that allows for more complexity in the structure of its authorized terms. For example, the LCSH equivalent to the ERIC term above is **Reading (Early childhood)**. In addition to single terms and bound concepts, subject heading lists may allow compound phrases and intricately constructed strings of terms. ***Subject heading strings*** append one or more subdivisions (based on geographic, chronological, form, or additional topical aspects) to an initial term or phrase to create additional context for the concept. The following is an example from LCSH of a string composed of a subject heading with three topical subdivisions added to bring out more specific aspects of the topic.

Railroads—Employees—Training of—Simulation methods

The first term in this string, **Railroads**, is referred to as a *subject heading*, but the entire string (subject heading and subdivisions) may also be referred to as a *subject heading*. Those new to LCSH may find this confusing, but individual terms, phrases, and strings that are established in the vocabulary may all be referred to by the same label.

Subject heading lists have been created primarily in library communities, while thesauri have been created largely in indexing communities. This does not mean, however, that libraries cannot or do not use thesauri or that an indexing service might not employ a subject heading list; it is simply a generalization about the origins of these tools. Both types attempt to provide subject access to information resources by providing terminology that can be consistent and reliable rather than uncontrolled and unpredictable. Both choose authorized terms and establish references from non-preferred terms. Both provide structural hierarchies so that terms are presented in relation to their broader, narrower, and related terms.

Although Z39.19 does not distinguish subject heading lists from thesauri, there are some distinctions worth noting. Thesauri are more strictly hierarchical because they are usually made up of single terms. The rules in Z39.19 that have to do with identifying broader, narrower, and related terms are much easier to follow when working with a single-term system than when working with a system that includes phrases, compound headings, and strings.[8] Thesauri are typically narrower in scope, comprising terms from one specific subject area. Subject heading lists may be more general in scope, covering a broad subject area or, indeed, the entire reach of knowledge. Thesauri are more likely to be multilingual than are subject heading lists. Again, because single terms are used, equivalent terms in other languages are easier to find and maintain.

Thesauri and subject heading lists are the most widespread forms of subject vocabularies used in libraries, archives, and museums. Among the best-known subject heading lists are *Library of Congress Subject Headings* (LCSH), *Sears List of Subject Headings* (*Sears*), and *Medical Subject Headings* (MeSH). A brief description of each is provided later in this chapter.[§]

12.3 Relationships in Controlled Vocabularies

A key feature of thesauri and subject heading lists is that they identify relationships among terms and make connections (i.e., references) between related concepts. The relationships identified among terms are organized into three primary types: (1) equivalence relationships, (2) hierarchical relationships, and (3) associative relationships.

[§]Some additional forms and structures of vocabularies (e.g., ontologies, folksonomies) are addressed in sections 12.8 and 12.9.

12.3.1 Equivalence Relationships

Thesauri (including many subject heading lists) operate by choosing a preferred way of expressing a concept and then making certain that alternative ways of expressing that concept will be connected to the preferred terminology. This practice identifies and addresses *equivalence relationships*. Traditionally, the unused (or unauthorized) terminology appears in the vocabulary listed under the preferred terminology and is often preceded by the abbreviation **UF** meaning *used for*. The unauthorized terms also appear in the list as *entry vocabulary* to act as pointers to the chosen terms as a **USE** reference. For example, under the heading **House plants**, two synonyms are listed.

> **House plants**
> UF   Houseplants
>   Indoor plants

Elsewhere in the vocabulary, two reciprocal references are made at the place in the list where the synonyms appear.

> Houseplants
>   USE **House plants**
>
> ...
>
> Indoor plants
>   USE **House plants**

Equivalence relationships address a variety of relationships among terms. These include synonymous terms, such as *clothing* and *clothes*, which represent the same concept without difference in nuance. The **House plants** example above illustrates this concept, as does the following.

> **Physicians**
> UF   Doctors
>   Doctors of medicine
>   MDs (Physicians)
>   Medical doctors

You will also find nearly synonymous terms; terms that are not truly equivalent, but they are close enough that it is deemed impractical to establish both terms in a controlled vocabulary.

> **Seawater** (May Subd Geog)
> UF   Ocean water
>   Sea-water [Former heading]
>   Sea waters
>   Seawaters

The concepts *seawater* and *ocean water* are not precisely identical (obviously the source of the water differs), but is there enough of a difference that some users would only want resources about ocean water but not about seawater or vice versa? In LCSH, **Seawater** was chosen as an authorized term and *ocean water* became a reference.

Lexical variants, another category of equivalence relationship, are "different word forms for the same expression. Lexical variants may result from spelling differences, grammatical variation, and abbreviations. Terms in inverted and natural order, plurals and singulars, and the use of punctuation may create lexical variants."[9] For example, in a controlled vocabulary one spelling must be chosen as the preferred form and the alternative spellings are included as references.

>   Catalogues
>   USE **Catalogs**

>   Art, Dakota
>   USE **Dakota art**

Some *antonyms*, terms with opposite meanings, are also treated as equivalents. This might seem surprising, but some antonyms are so interconnected that one cannot be understood without the other. For example, how does one write about *inequality* without also addressing *equality*? It is not necessary to assign both terms in that case, so the *taxonomists* (i.e., the creators of a controlled vocabulary) would choose one or the other.

>   Inequality
>   USE **Equality**

>   Deceleration
>   USE **Acceleration (Mechanics)**

There is one other type of equivalence relationship that might be found in a controlled vocabulary: the *upward reference*. This is used when a term that might be added to the vocabulary is considered too specific for the vocabulary in hand. In that case, the term is treated as a cross-reference to a broader concept that incorporates the more specific term.

>   Caricaturists
>   USE **Cartoonists**

Although there is a difference between the two (the two terms represent a hierarchical relationship rather than an equivalence relationship), the vocabulary treats them as equivalent terms.

>   **Food security** (May Subd Geog)
>   UF   Food deserts
>   Food insecurity
>   Insecurity, Food
>   Security, Food

In the final entry, you can see not only an upward reference (*Food deserts*) but also an antonym (*Food insecurity*) and lexical variants in the form of inverted headings (*Insecurity, Food*; *Security, Food*) appearing as UF references under the authorized heading.

12.3.2 Hierarchical Relationships

Thesauri also keep track of the *hierarchical relationships* of a concept. In most, these are designated as *broader term* (BT) and *narrower term* (NT) relationships, although some thesauri, such as AAT, may not use the traditional relationship indicators (relying on hierarchical displays instead). The relationship between BT and NT is like a parent–child relationship. The broader term is the parent; it has less specificity. The narrower term is the child term; it is more specific, more focused. The relationship is reciprocal. So, if a BT points to an NT, then the entry for the NT must point to the BT in the thesaurus.**

There are different kinds of hierarchical relationships that may be designated simply as broader and narrower terms in a general vocabulary but are designated more specifically in other thesauri. These include the following categories.

Genus-species relationships (also known as generic or class-class member relationships) indicate that the narrower terms are a type of or kind of whatever the broader term represents. In the following example, all the NTs are a type or kind of building.

Buildings
NT Auditoriums
    Church buildings
    Clubhouses
    Garages

The meaning of *whole-part relationships* is rather self-evident. The BT represents the whole, while the NTs represent the parts. In the following example, the NTs are parts of a head.

Head
NT Brain
    Ear
    Face
    Hair
    Mouth
    Nose

In *instance relationships* (or generic topic-named example relationships), the BT is a particular category of thing/entity, and each NT is an example or an instance of that thing/entity. For example, the **Aegean Sea** is not a type or kind of sea, it is a named example of a sea.

Seas
NT Adriatic Sea
    Aegean Sea
    Arabian Sea
    Baltic Sea
    Caribbean Sea

**References from narrower terms to broader terms typically do not appear in most catalogs.

12.3.3 Associative Relationships

The final type of relationship highlighted in many thesauri is the *associative relationship*. These are usually designated as *related term* (RT) relationships. These, too, are reciprocal. These are the least well-defined relationships. They indicate a relationship that might be of interest, which is not a hierarchical or equivalence-based relationship. Some controlled vocabularies do not enumerate specific types of RT relationships to include, whereas others might provide strict guidelines. In some thesauri, RT relationships are restricted to terms that are in different hierarchies. In other words, terms that share a common parent term are not labeled RTs. There are various kinds of related-term relationships, including when

- one term is needed to define another term (e.g., *stamps* is needed in the definition of *philately*),
- the meanings of two terms overlap, or two terms may be used interchangeably, yet are not synonyms (e.g., *carpets* and *rugs*), and
- linking persons to their fields of endeavor (e.g., *attorneys* and *law* or *midwives* and *midwifery*).

12.3.4 Displaying Relationships

In the following example of the subject heading **Maintenance**, the subject heading (the preferred term in boldface type) is shown in relation to its UFs, BT, NTs, and RTs. In addition, a see also note (SA) provides additional information about relationships with other headings of interest.

Maintenance
UF   Preventive maintenance
          Upkeep
BT   Maintainability (Engineering)
RT   Repairing
          Service life (Engineering)
SA   subdivision **Maintenance and repair** under kinds of objects, including machinery, vehicles, structures, etc., e.g., **Automobiles—Maintenance and repair**; **Dwellings—Maintenance and repair**; **Nuclear reactors—Maintenance and repair**
NT   Buildings—Repair and reconstruction
          Grounds maintenance
          Military bases—Maintenance
          Plant maintenance

All the relationships are reciprocal: under **Maintainability (Engineering)**, the narrower term **Maintenance** would be listed. Under **Repairing**, the related term **Maintenance** would be listed, and under **Grounds maintenance**, the broader term **Maintenance** would be listed.

Most controlled vocabularies display terms in alphabetical order with all their relationships enumerated below the entry, as seen in the **Maintenance** example, but some also provide a hierarchical display of the vocabulary terms (e.g., AAT).

Top of the AAT hierarchies
.... Activities Facet
.... Functions (hierarchy name)
.... functions (activities)
.... information handling functions
.... maintenance
.... environmental control
.... humidity control
.... noise control
.... pollution control
.... air purification
.... smoke abatement
.... housekeeping
.... preventing
.... migration (function)

In this format, the terms are placed in juxtaposition to each other so that one can visualize broader and narrower relationships. Such lists are helpful in seeing where a term fits within an entire hierarchy, not just its relationship to the terms immediately above and below it.

12.3.5 Lexical Relationships

Relationships can also be expressed in other ways. For example, the following are relationships shown in the general lexical database WordNet:[10]

- **Synonyms** are terms that have the same, or nearly the same, meaning and often can be substituted for each other. A synonym is like the UF relationships and USE references in traditional thesauri.

- **Coordinate terms** might be called siblings; they have the same parent term. Coordinate terms are not addressed in most traditional thesauri.

- **Hypernyms** are parent terms. It is a superordinate category comprising all the instances that are "kinds of" the hypernym (e.g., *family* is a hypernym for *nuclear family, extended family, foster family*). A hypernym is like some BT relationships in traditional thesauri.

- **Hyponyms** are child terms. A hyponym is a member of a class (e.g., *nuclear family* is a hyponym of the class *family*). A hyponym is like some NT relationships in traditional thesauri.

- **Holonyms** are the name of wholes of which the meronyms are the parts (e.g., a *family* has as its members: *children, parents, sister, siblings*). A holonym is like some BT relationships in traditional thesauri.

- **Meronyms** designate constituent parts or members of the whole (e.g., *sister* is a meronym of *family*). A meronym is like some NT relationships in traditional thesauri.

- ***Antonyms*** have opposite meanings (e.g., *hot* is an antonym of *cold*). Antonyms are not addressed in most traditional thesauri.

These lexical concepts describe relationships between terms at a greater level of specificity than most traditional thesauri, which usually focus on generalized hierarchical, equivalence, and associative relationships. For example, LCSH lists *Aunts* as an NT to *Families*, without indicating whether it is a hyponym or a meronym. These more specialized lexical relationships have, however, been used in some attempts to improve keyword searching and natural language processing.[††]

12.4 Controlled Vocabulary Challenges

In the process of creating a controlled vocabulary, there are certain difficulties that must be addressed. An understanding of these problems can enhance one's ability to use a particular existing vocabulary. This section addresses the following issues:

- Specific versus General Terms
- Synonymous Concepts
- Inclusive Terminology
- Word Form for One-Word Terms
- Sequence and Form for Multi-word Terms and Phrases
- Compound Concepts
- Homographs and Homophones
- Qualification of Terms
- Abbreviations and Acronyms
- Popular versus Technical Terms
- Pre-coordination versus Post-coordination (Subdivision of Terms)

Examples are provided to illustrate these challenges.

12.4.1 Specific versus General Terms

The level of specificity must be decided at the outset of establishing a controlled vocabulary. Various lists may have different thresholds for how specific the terminology will be. In the example below, the heading **Cats** is not as specific as **Longhair cats**.

> **Cats**
>   **Longhair cats**
>   **Persian cat**
>   **Himalayan cat**

[††]Described in section 12.9 below.

Longhair cats is not as specific as **Persian cat**, which in turn is not as specific as **Himalayan cat**. Varying levels of semantic depth may be found in different vocabularies because they serve institutions of different sizes and kinds, different audiences, different age levels, and so on. In LCSH, for example, the most specific term available is **Himalayan cat**; in *Sears,* a smaller vocabulary usually serving less extensive collections, the most specific term is **Cats**, although an instruction is given that, if needed, a term for a specific breed of cat may be created.

To some extent the decision on this matter is based on the types of users who are expected to search for headings from the list and upon the nature of the information resources that are to be assigned terms from the list. If the collection has mainly general kinds of information, then **Cats** is probably sufficient, even to cover a few more specific items. If the users are children likely to be looking for general kinds of information, then again **Cats** is probably sufficient as the most specific level. A vocabulary used to describe a collection in a veterinary school library, however, will need to be more specific.

12.4.2 Synonymous Concepts

The English language rarely has true synonyms—that is, situations where two words mean *exactly* the same thing and have no variations in nuance. However, there are multitudes of nearly synonymous words and phrases that mean so close to the same thing that they can be interchanged for each other in most contexts. Hans Wellisch wrote, "Authors have, therefore, great freedom in the choice of terms and may use several words for the same concept, which may be admirable from the point of view of style, but would be disastrous when transferred unchanged to an index."[11] These are the terms that make keyword searching so problematic and frustrating.

In the creation of a controlled vocabulary, it is necessary to identify all the synonymous and nearly synonymous terms that should be brought together under a single authorized term. For example, do the terms *apparel, clothes, clothing, costume, dress,* and *garments* all mean the same thing? If not precisely the same, are the differences important enough to warrant separate vocabulary terms for them? Is there enough of a logical distinction among them that some information resources should be placed under the term *garments*, others under *clothing*, and still others under *clothes*? Would users (or indexers and catalogers) understand the distinctions among them? If not, then perhaps they should be treated as synonyms despite their slight differences. When making such a determination, one should consider which of the terms is best known to intended users; but with regional, national, and international differences in vocabulary, the choice of the preferred term might be somewhat arbitrary.

12.4.3 Inclusive Terms

A challenge in choosing terms is ensuring that those chosen are unbiased and inoffensive. This seems like common sense, but over the years various controlled vocabularies have been criticized for their choices of terms. Most often, this has focused on the ways that various groups of people—predominantly marginalized groups of people—have been identified. At times, terms and cross-references that are now considered racist, sexist, anti-Semitic, Islamophobic, homophobic, transphobic, or otherwise offensive have been included as acceptable terms in vocabularies.

Much of the attention given to these problems stems from the writings of Sanford Berman,[12] Hope Olson,[13] and others who have been concerned about the representation of groups of people in controlled vocabularies and classification systems.[14] Although their important work is somewhat beyond the scope of this book, readers interested in exploring these issues are encouraged to start with Berman's foundational 1971 tract on LCSH, *Prejudices and Antipathies*, for an introduction to some of the problems.[15] In a review of Berman's work thirty years later, Stephen Knowlton found that nearly two-thirds of the problematic headings that Berman identified in *Prejudices and Antipathies* had been partially or fully revised to address Berman's concerns.[16] Of course, that left about one-third of the identified problems unresolved.

Despite progress, new issues continue to arise.[17] In recent years, much attention has been paid to the debate over the use of the pejorative and dehumanizing term *illegal aliens* in LCSH.[18] Some argued for its continued usage with the debate spilling into the chambers of the polarized U.S. Congress.‡‡ In 2021, seven years after the first request by students at Dartmouth College (supported by the Dartmouth Libraries) to make a change to the subject heading,[19] the Library of Congress (LC) finally replaced it with two new headings: **Noncitizens** and **Illegal immigration**.[20] This solution is not without its detractors. Many were (and still are) dissatisfied with the continued use of the term "illegal" in one of the headings; others were not happy with LC choosing a term (**Noncitizens**) that is not widely used—many advocates wanted to see the term *undocumented immigrants* chosen instead.

12.4.4 Word Form for One-Word Terms

Words in English often have more than one form that can mean the same thing (e.g., *clothing* and *clothes*). As language evolves, a concept may be expressed first as two words, then as a hyphenated word, then as one word (e.g., *meta data, meta-data, metadata*). Sometimes all three forms appear in use at the same time. British and American spellings give us another case of word form difference (e.g., *colour* and *color*). Adding a prefix to a word can create a new word with a different meaning. However, when the meaning is opposite, it often does not make sense to use both terms in the controlled vocabulary (e.g., *equality* and *inequality*).

A major word form difference is singular versus plural. There is no uniform rule on which form to use; each vocabulary may approach it differently, following the policies of the creating agency. Most of the time the plural has the broadest coverage (e.g., *videocassettes* rather than *videocassette*); but at times the singular is broader (e.g., *apple* can apply to both the fruit and the tree, while the term *apples* refers only to the fruit). Sometimes the singular and the plural forms of a word have different meanings (e.g., in *Sears*, the heading **Art** refers specifically to visual art; the heading **Arts** refers to a broader concept that includes visual arts, literature, and the performing arts).

---

‡‡ Although rare, this is not the first time a government body has involved itself in the details of cataloging. See the discussion of Anthony Panizzi in Chapter 2.

12.4.5 Sequence and Form for Multi-word Terms and Phrases

In some controlled vocabularies there are terms and phrases made up of two or more words. Some of these headings are modified nouns (e.g., **Environmental education**); others are phrases with conjunctions or prepositions (e.g., **Information theory in biology**); and a third group has qualifiers added in parentheses (e.g., **Bridges (Dentistry)**). A problem in constructing such terminology in a controlled way is being consistent in the order and form of the individual words used. For example, the phrases *energy conservation* and *conservation of energy resources* mean the same thing. The first phrase places the concept with other headings beginning with the word *energy*; the second phrase puts the concept with other topics having to do with conservation. If the list creates such phrases, it must be certain to have references from every possible construction of the phrase—referring from them to the construction that was chosen.

Some controlled vocabularies (notably LCSH) present certain multi-word terms and phrases in inverted order (e.g., **Education, Bilingual**; **Asylum, Right of**). Much of this was done in the past to collocate a group of headings on a broad concept with sub-concepts arranged alphabetically below it. Thus, instead of *bilingual education* being found in the Bs and *higher education* being found in the Hs, both were found in the Es as **Education, Bilingual** and **Education, Higher**. Research has shown that few users think of such phrases in inverted order but instead look for them in direct order. In LCSH few new inverted forms are being established, but previously established ones still exist. One therefore finds inconsistencies such as **Medical education** and **Communist education** juxtaposed with **Education, Humanistic** and **Education, Greek**.

12.4.6 Compound Headings

As mentioned earlier, most thesauri primarily comprise single words and bound terms representing single distinct concepts. Other controlled vocabularies, however, include multi-topic concepts in the form of phrases. When creating a controlled vocabulary, the taxonomists must determine whether ***compound headings*** are desirable or acceptable, when to employ them (rather than employing single terms), and what forms these phrases should take (discussed in the section above). The following are some examples of compound headings found in LCSH:

- **Animals, Prosecution and punishment of**
- **Comic strip characters in motion pictures**
- **Church work with cowgirls**
- **Diplomatic and consular service, Communist countries**
- **Marine invertebrates as pets**
- **Running races in rabbinical literature**

As you can see in the examples, multiple topics are being brought out in each heading. Multi-topic subject terms can create problems in organizing a controlled vocabulary; as more concepts are incorporated into a phrase, the relationships to other concepts in the vocabulary can become less clear. For example, how is **Animals, Prosecution and punishment of** related to **Animals** or to **Prosecution** or to **Punishment**? This is especially difficult to determine when one learns of the heading's broader term: **Superstition**.

12.4.7 Homographs and Homophones

Homographs are words that look the same but have different meanings. *Mercury* can be a liquid metal, a planet, a car, or a Roman god; *bridge* can be a game, a structure spanning a chasm, a device connecting two computer networks, a location on a ship, or a dental device, among other meanings. In a controlled vocabulary there must be some way to differentiate among the various meanings. Two common ways are either to use qualifiers to distinguish between the terms or to choose synonyms as the preferred terms. In the world of art and architecture, the term *structures* can be used in more than one way; consequently, AAT has created two separate qualified headings to address the different meanings: **structures (single built works)** and **structures (structural elements)**. Homographs may or may not be pronounced the same. For example, *mare* pronounced as one syllable with a silent *e* is a mature female horse; *mare* pronounced as two syllables is a large, dark area on the moon (derived from the Latin and Italian word *mare,* meaning *sea*). Traditionally, different pronunciations did not play a role in creating a controlled vocabulary, because the vocabulary was treated visually.

Homophones, which are words that are spelled differently but pronounced the same, have also been ignored in controlled vocabularies in a visual world (e.g., *moat* and *mote; fowl* and *foul*). However, because what appears on computer screens is now quite regularly read aloud electronically to people with visual impairments, we need to give attention to pronunciations of homographs and to distinguishing among homophones.

12.4.8 Qualification of Terms

As mentioned above, one of the ways of dealing with homographs is to add a ***qualifier***. A qualifier is an addition or annotation that is affixed to a term to clarify its meaning. For example, the homograph *tablets* is represented in LCSH in different ways to address some of its various meanings:

> Tablets (Computer)
>   USE **Tablet computers**
>
> Tablets, Cuneiform
>   USE **Cuneiform tablets**
>
> Tablets, Heraclean
>   USE **Heraclean tablets**
>
> **Tablets (Medicine)**
>
> Tablets, Memorial
>   USE **Sepulchral monuments**
>
> **Tablets (Paleography)**

Tablets (Medicine) and **Tablets (Paleography)** require qualifiers because no other commonly used word could easily replace *tablet* and creating a phrase heading would be awkward and not reflect common usage.

Qualifiers are also used to differentiate usages of a word in different settings. For example:

    Adultery (Aztec law)   **Adultery (Islamic law)**
    Adultery (Byzantine law)   **Adultery (Jewish law)**
    Adultery (Canon law)   **Adultery (Roman law)**
    Adultery (Germanic law)   **Adultery (Yanzi law)**
    Adultery (Inca law)

In addition, qualifiers can be used to identify the context of unfamiliar words. For example, the name *Yanzi* is identified as **Yanzi (African people)** in the authorized heading for that group.

12.4.9 Abbreviations, Acronyms, and Initialisms

Abbreviations, acronyms, and initialisms can cause problems in adding concepts to controlled vocabularies. ***Abbreviations*** are shortened forms of words. ***Acronyms*** are abbreviations made up of initial letters of words from a phrase, and the resulting group of letters is pronounced as a word (e.g., POTUS for *President of the United States*). ***Initialisms*** are abbreviations made up of initial letters of a phrase, but each letter is pronounced separately (e.g., ABC for the *American Broadcasting Company*). Traditionally, the determination whether to spell out abbreviations, acronyms, and initialisms was based on the intended users of the controlled vocabulary and their expected knowledge. With a move to more global retrieval, this practice has been reconsidered. Without the ability to assume a certain population, it is best to assume that they should be spelled out. A few, however, have global recognition. In the English version of the *UNESCO Thesaurus*, the acronym AIDS is the preferred term, but alternative forms—*Acquired Immunodeficiency Syndrome* and *HIV/AIDS*—are provided as cross-references. In the Spanish and French versions of the thesaurus, the acronym SIDA is the preferred form, with its own references.

12.4.10 Popular versus Technical Terms

When a concept can be represented by both technical and popular terminology, the creators of a controlled vocabulary must decide which will be used. For example, the National Library of Medicine's MeSH uses **Neoplasms**, whereas LCSH uses **Cancer**. If the list is intended to be used for information resources that will be retrieved by a specialized audience only, then specialized terminology is justified. Again, though, in a global information environment, one can no longer be certain of a particular audience; anyone with internet access can view MeSH terminology, not just medical specialists.

12.4.11 Pre-Coordination versus Post-Coordination (Subdivision of Terms)

Subdivisions are used in controlled vocabularies that pre-coordinate terms. A *subdivision* is a term or phrase appended to a subject heading to provide additional specificity and context. Subdivisions are an alternative to creating phrase headings with compound concepts. The following are some of the uses of subdivisions in LCSH:

- to show treatment of only a part of a larger subject (e.g., **Merchant marine—Officers**)
- to show special aspects of a larger subject (e.g., **Merchant marine—Watch duty**)
- to show various forms of material (e.g., **Chemistry—Bibliography**, **Chemistry—Dictionaries**, **Chemistry—Laboratory manuals**)
- to show geographical or chronological limitations (e.g., **Architecture—Great Britain—19th century**)

Controlled vocabularies can be pre-coordinated or post-coordinated. The term *coordination* (or *coordinated*) refers to the point at which terms are joined together to represent more complex concepts. Pre-coordination occurs when terms are combined in the vocabulary itself or are combined by the cataloger, archivist, or indexer when creating metadata for a resource. Thus, ***pre-coordination*** is the indexing process in which metadata creators or taxonomists combine multiple subject concepts into strings comprising a primary concept plus one or more additional facets (additional topical aspects, place names, time periods, forms). "Individual terms representing concepts may be precoordinated into semantically linked, heading-subheading [subdivision] combinations. These terms can be used during the indexing and searching processes. They are also very useful in browsing and navigation, especially by users who are not totally familiar with a controlled vocabulary and its structure."[21] Here is an example of a string with three different concepts combined by the cataloger at the time of metadata creation.

Diabetes in children—Diet therapy—Recipes

Some controlled vocabularies, particularly subject headings lists, allow for pre-coordination; but others do not, relying instead on post-coordination. ***Post-coordination*** is the indexing concept that complex concepts do not need to be brought together in the controlled vocabulary or the metadata description. Only single terms or phrases will be used to describe the resource, and users must combine multiple concepts during their search processes to find more complex topics. For example, it relies on users to create searches such as

Diabetes AND Children AND Diet AND Recipes

Here are some additional examples of pre-coordinated strings found in LCSH:

Gold mines and mining—Accidents—California

Cultural property—Protection—Law and legislation—Criminal provisions

Even when using a pre-coordinated indexing system, multiple subject strings are often needed because a single string cannot capture all the concepts that describe what a resource is about. Thus, most surrogate records contain multiple pre-coordinated strings, because the rules for applying controlled vocabularies may limit the length of strings. And too many concepts in the same string can be confusing for both catalogers and users.

To many, pre-coordination may seem like something of a relic from the card catalog era, but it is not without value. Pre-coordination provides context. It allows for precision in description, which allows users to see how the various concepts addressed in a resource are related. For example, it clarifies that one resource, which has the string **Science—Study and teaching—History**, is about the history of teaching science. And another resource, which has been assigned the string **Science—History—Study and teaching**, is about teaching the history of science. And, if these strings are used as searches in a catalog, users can find exactly the resources they need without cluttering up the results with irrelevant resources. This benefit, however, cannot be enjoyed in a post-coordinated approach or when using keyword searching.

Post-coordination of two or more discrete terms is an approach developed for the online search environment. In post-coordinated systems, which include many modern indexing and abstracting databases, each concept is entered into a surrogate record discretely, without stringing together sub-concepts, place names, and the like. Searchers must use Boolean operators to combine terms in a search box, to retrieve results that represent the intersection of multiple topics (AND), either or both topics (OR), or one topic while excluding others (NOT). Keyword searching is the ultimate form of post-coordinate indexing.

The following example represents concepts found in a resource that discusses money in colonial America for a young audience. The first is an LCSH string added to the record. The set of terms following are from FAST (Faceted Application of Subject Terminology),[§§] an alternative to LCSH that uses a mostly post-coordinated approach to subject representation:

> **LCSH**
> 650 #0 $a Money $z United States $x History $y Colonial period, ca. 1600-1775
> $v Juvenile literature
>
> **FAST**
> 648 #7 $a 1600-1775
> 650 #7 $a Money $x Colonial period. $2 fast
> 651 #7 $a United States. $2 fast
> 655 #7 $a History. $2 fast
> 655 #7 $a Juvenile works. $2 fast

This example shows only one topic for a straightforward resource. Each approach seems reasonable, supports information retrieval, and clearly explains what the resource is about. When several subjects are addressed in the same resource, however, it can be unclear how the separate concepts

---

[§§] The terms were found using the FAST Converter tool provided by OCLC Online Computer Library Center. For more about FAST, see section 12.8.8 in this chapter.

are connected in a post-coordinated approach. For example, the following strings could be created for a resource that compares gold mining in California in the nineteenth century to diamond mining in South Africa in the twentieth century:

> **Gold mines and mining—California—History—19th century**

> **Diamond mines and mining—South Africa—History—20th century**

The pre-coordinated strings make clear the places and times in which the major topics are addressed. With a post-coordinated approach though, this is not true:

- **Diamond mines and mining**
- **Gold mines and mining**
- **California**
- **South Africa**
- **History**
- **19th century**
- **20th century**

It may not be quite clear if this resource is about diamond mining in California, gold mining in the twentieth century, diamond mining in South Africa in the nineteenth century, gold mining in South Africa, or something else. Pre-coordinated strings provide context that the post-coordinated approach cannot reproduce.

With the use of most controlled vocabularies, the searcher must still do some post-coordination, even if the cataloger or indexer has already pre-coordinated some concepts. It is a matter of degree. LCSH, for example, has no pre-coordinated terminology for the concept *dancers and musicians*. It is up to the user who wants a work covering this concept to search the headings **Dancers** AND **Musicians** using Boolean operators.

12.5 Principles for Creating Controlled Vocabularies

There are some general principles that apply to the creation of controlled vocabularies. These are to be distinguished from principles that come into play when assigning vocabulary terms. The general principles discussed here for creating vocabularies are *specificity, literary warrant,* and *direct entry.*

12.5.1 Specificity

Specificity is the level of semantic depth found in a particular controlled vocabulary. Taxonomists designing controlled vocabularies must decide how many levels to include for any given area of knowledge. Vocabularies intended for a general audience may need far less detail than those designed for other more specific populations. For example, LCSH, which is often used in larger academic library systems, has greater specificity in its established subject headings than does *Sears*, which tends to be used in smaller, more general libraries. This is evident from the greater hierarchical depth in the concepts that are found in LCSH and is made obvious by the relative sizes of the vocabularies. The very specific term **Canned raspberries** is found in LCSH; it is a narrower term found under **Canned berries**, which is under the heading **Canned fruit**, which in turn is a narrower term of **Canned foods**.

> **Food**
>   **Canned foods**
>   **Canned fruit**
>   **Canned berries**
>   **Canned raspberries**

In *Sears,* the choices are

1. **Canning and preserving**, which is used for canned foods in general,
2. **Berries**, which is broader than the topic, or
3. **Fruit—Preservation**, which seems to be more about the process of preserving fruit than a particular product.

The instructions in *Sears* say that specific types of foods with the topical subdivision—**Preservation** can be added, as can more specific types of berries, when needed. This allows the vocabulary to be supplemented when more specificity is deemed necessary. Subject heading lists and thesauri created for specific subject fields or disciplines can be more specific in their headings than general vocabularies such as LCSH. For example, MeSH (Medical Subject Headings) offers greater specificity for the field of medicine.

12.5.2 Literary Warrant

Controlled vocabulary lists tend to be created using E. Wyndham Hulme's principle of ***literary warrant***. This means that terminology is added to a subject heading list or thesaurus only after a concept appears in the literature and therefore needs to have specific terminology established. New terms appearing in resources are used to expand the controlled vocabulary. Usually, no attempt is made to add new terminology to a list until it is needed for use in metadata records; otherwise, taxonomists would be predicting the future or basing new additions on what they think *should* be there, at least theoretically. In the twentieth century, purely theoretical approaches to creating subject languages have fallen out of favor. For example, in the *ERIC Thesaurus* there are headings for **Asian Americans, Students,** and **Librarians**. Although ERIC includes a heading for **Asian American students**, it does not contain a heading representing *Asian American librarians*, and it will not do so, unless there is educational literature related to that specific group, as there was for Asian American students.

Although literary warrant is useful in limiting the terminology added to controlled vocabularies, it is necessary to recognize that there are problems with this principle. For example, literary warrant relies on existing, "authoritative" literature, which may reflect the biases of dominant groups. Not everyone has equal access to sharing their knowledge or points of view; not everyone has access to publish in traditional academic or literary outlets. The principle of literary warrant can act as a gatekeeper, restricting representation of certain concepts or kinds of knowledge. It can marginalize or exclude underrepresented voices, perpetuating inequities in library collections and subject access systems.

12.5.3 Direct Entry

Another principle of creating controlled vocabulary terms is that of *direct entry*, which states that a concept should be entered into the vocabulary using the term that names it clearly and simply, rather than treating that concept as a subdivision of a broader concept. For example, in LCSH there is currently a preference for a modified term to express a concept (e.g., **Railroad stations**) over the use of a broader term subdivided by another aspect (e.g., **Railroads—Stations**). Direct entry is also an important component of the *Sears List of Subject Headings*, which outlines the concept in its guiding principles.

> The principle of direct entry holds that a subject heading should stand as a separate term rather than as a subdivision under a broader heading. If the reader wants information about owls, the direct approach is to consult the catalog under the heading **Owls**, not under the broader subject **Birds** subdivided by the narrower topic **Owls**. In other words, the cataloger has entered the book directly under **Owls**, not indirectly under "Birds—Owls," or under "Birds—Birds of prey—Owls." The latter two subject strings are both specific, but they are not direct.[22]

12.6 Principles for Applying Vocabulary Terms

The first step in applying controlled vocabulary terms takes place after the cataloger or indexer determines the aboutness of a resource. Once the nature of content is understood, and an aboutness statement has been written, choices must be made to determine which subject concepts are to be represented in the metadata record for the resource. Not every concept in an aboutness statement can be translated into the chosen controlled vocabulary. Although controlled vocabularies are useful in describing key concepts, places, events, time periods, and objects (often in the form of nouns and noun phrases), they are not always helpful in translating actions and relationships among those concepts. The indexer, therefore, must be familiar enough with the controlled vocabulary to know which ideas can be translated and which cannot.

In the aboutness statement, the most important concepts are selected as targeted searches in the controlled vocabulary. This may entail circling significant words in the statement or compiling a list of terms. Translating these words into authorized descriptors or subject headings, however, may be more difficult than one might initially expect. One may have to follow several paths established by cross-references in the vocabulary before finding the appropriate terms. In some cases, it may take a staggering effort to remain faithful to the aboutness of the resource, while following specific application rules in addition to following general principles. For example, subdivisions that look appropriate for the resource may be restricted in their use, leaving the cataloger or archivist feeling thwarted by the complex rules that accompany some controlled vocabularies (e.g., LCSH's *Subject Headings Manual*). In other cases, one may discover that there is simply no appropriate way to translate a particular concept. The following sections address some general principles focused on the application of controlled vocabulary terms.

12.6.1 Specific Entry and Coextensive Entry

The principle of *specific entry* states that a cataloger should use the most specific terms available in the vocabulary that closely match the aboutness of the resource. If a term is too broad or too narrow, it is misleading. For example, an information resource about musicians should be entered under **Musicians**, not under **Entertainers** or **Pianists**. If the work is about a variety of entertainers, rather than just **Musicians**, then the term **Entertainers** should be assigned. If the work is about pianists, and that term is in the vocabulary, then the entry should be **Pianists**, not **Musicians**. If the vocabulary does not get as specific as **Pianists** or does not allow the creation of such terms for specific categories of musicians, then the principle of specific entry calls for using **Musicians** as the most specific entry available from that vocabulary. Specific entry allows an experienced user to know when to stop searching for an appropriate controlled vocabulary term. One does not have to try broader terms unless information is not found under a specific term.

It once was true that *specific entry* could be treated in a relative way. In a small collection there might be only one or two items about musicians, although there might be several items about entertainers that include musicians as one type of entertainer; for that collection, there might be a decision that **Entertainers** would be the most specific heading used. Now that libraries are all essentially contributing to a global union catalog, organizers should follow the principle of specific entry in order for searching to be effective.[23] On the other hand, some have called for including broader terms in catalog records to assist less-experienced catalog users with navigating the system and finding the resources that they need[24] (e.g., a record could include headings for both **Persian cats** and **Cats**, even though the item focuses primarily on Persian cats). Or, if we could break out of tradition and make references in our retrieval tools from specific subject headings to broader ones, then "too specific" would not have to be a concern.

It should be noted that *specific entry* is not the same concept as *coextensive entry*—the principle that the subject headings applied to an information resource will cover all, but no more than, the concepts or topics covered in that resource. Coextensive entry is about matching as exactly as possible the subject entries to the limits and scope of the aboutness of the information resource. To have coextensive entry using LCSH, for example, an information resource about crocheting potholders requires two specific entries: one for **Crocheting** and another for **Potholders**. There is no one specific heading to cover these two concepts together. To have just one heading that is coextensive with the subject of such a resource, the heading would have to be *Crocheting potholders*, or *Potholders—Crocheting*, but these are not used in LCSH.

12.6.2 Number of Terms Assigned

There should be no arbitrary limit on the number of terms or descriptors assigned. If the conceptual analysis has been done at the summarization level, then the number of terms given should be the number that is needed to express that summary. Likewise, if the conceptual analysis has been performed in depth, the number of terms necessary to cover all the concepts should be allowed. This, however, is not always the case. Some information institutions have local policies that restrict the number of subject headings assigned to an information resource. Although this might help to cut down on the time spent indexing, it does users no favors. For example, if the local policy states,

"No more than three descriptors are to be added to a record," but the information resource is about four specific, discrete concepts, which one is to be left out of the record? The time spent deciding what topics to omit might in fact be lengthier than the time spent adding a fourth subject term. Some controlled vocabulary systems (e.g., LCSH) place limits on the number of terms that should be assigned. The LCSH *Subject Headings Manual* states that up to six headings should suffice, but catalogers should not assign more than ten subject headings to a resource.

12.6.3 Concepts Not in the Controlled Vocabulary

If a concept is not present in the controlled vocabulary, it should be represented temporarily by a more general concept, rather than simply adding unauthorized terms to the record (e.g., use **Artificial intelligence** until a new heading for *generative artificial intelligence* is established). The new concept should be proposed as a new addition to the subject list or thesaurus. And once (or if) the new concept is added to the vocabulary, a change in the metadata record should be made. This means that the cataloger or indexer should flag the record for updating; otherwise, it might be forgotten or lost among a sea of records. It should be noted, however, that some controlled vocabulary systems (e.g., *Sears*) allow the cataloger or indexer to add their own terms as needed.

12.7 Controlled Vocabulary Standards

In this section, thesauri and subject heading lists commonly used in libraries, archives, and museums are described. The list is not meant to be comprehensive, but is a sample that LIS professionals might encounter frequently. These include the following:

- *Library of Congress Subject Headings* (LCSH)
- *Sears List of Subject Headings* (*Sears*)
- *Medical Subject Headings* (MeSH)
- *Library of Congress Genre/Form Terms for Library and Archival Materials* (LCGFT)
- *Library of Congress Demographic Group Terms* (LCDGT)
- *Art & Architecture Thesaurus* (AAT)
- *Thesaurus of ERIC Descriptors* (ERIC)
- Faceted Application of Subject Terminology (FAST)
- Homosaurus: An International LGBTQ+ Linked Data Vocabulary

12.7.1 *Library of Congress Subject Headings* (LCSH)

Library of Congress Subject Headings (LCSH) is a list of authority-controlled terms that are used to represent the subject matter of resources. It is an all-purpose, multidisciplinary vocabulary; it is not restricted to a particular knowledge domain. LCSH comprises subject headings that have been established since 1898; it also contains references, scope notes, and subdivisions that may be used to make headings more specific. LCSH is the most comprehensive list of English-language subject headings in existence. It attempts to cover the world of knowledge and is the only subject heading list accepted as a worldwide standard.[25] It is used in libraries, archives, and cultural heritage institutions in many kinds of settings, including countries other than the United States. "LCSH has been translated into many languages and is used around the world by libraries large and small."[26] Some concepts that are useful in describing the contents of a resource are outside the scope of LCSH. Biographies, corporate histories, works about a place, or criticism of a literary work require authority-controlled names or titles, which are not included in LCSH. Consequently, other sources must be used. As discussed in Chapter 10, the Library of Congress maintains the LC/NACO Authority File (LCNAF) for names of persons, corporate bodies, geographic jurisdictions, titles of works, and name/title combinations.[27] The art world also has several name authority files maintained by the Getty Research Institute that might be used as well: the *Union List of Artist Names* (ULAN), the *Cultural Objects Name Authority* (CONA), and the *Getty Thesaurus of Geographic Names* (TGN).[28] These authority files and other controlled vocabularies are necessary to supplement LCSH.

LCSH is available in several formats. The longest-running format was the print version. For many years it was published in new editions every five years or so, but starting in 1988 with the 11th edition, new print versions of LCSH were typically produced once a year, most recently as a six-volume set. In 2013, however, LC changed its approach to providing access to cataloging documentation, announcing that it would no longer publish physical copies of the list. LCSH is still produced but only in electronic formats. A fully updated electronic version is available through

1. *Classification Web Plus* (by subscription),[29]
2. OCLC's authority files,[30]
3. the LC Authorities website,[31] and
4. the LC Linked Data Services.[32]

Most years a new edition of the list is also produced for distribution as print-ready PDFs on the LC website.[33] LCSH is, however, updated continuously. New headings and references are added regularly, and existing headings may be revised or removed.

In the subject cataloging process, LCSH is used in conjunction with the *Subject Headings Manual* (SHM).[34] The SHM is an essential tool for anyone who wishes to apply subject headings appropriately. It contains approximately 300 numbered instruction sheets all prefixed with the letter *H* (e.g., H 1095, H 180). **Instruction sheets** enumerate policies and practices employed by LC when applying or establishing subject headings. The manual was formerly issued in print form but is now freely available in PDF at LC's website.[35] The SHM is also available through LC's subscription-based *Classification Web Plus*. A sample from LCSH is shown in Figure 12.2. A MARC-encoded subject authority record (from *Classification Web Plus*) is displayed in Figure 12.3.***

***MARC authority records for subject terms do not contain narrower terms, because the narrower terms have their own MARC records containing the reciprocal broader terms.

Fascism (May Subd Geog)
[D726.5 (World history)]
[JC481 (Political theory)]
Here are entered general works on fascism including works on post-World War II fascist movements. Works on German fascism during the Nazi regime are entered under **National socialism**.
- UF Neo-fascism
- BT Authoritarianism
      Collectivism
- RT Corporate state
      National socialism
      Synarchism
      Totalitarianism
- NT Anti-fascist movements
      Fascist economics
      Fascist propaganda
      Labor unions and fascism
      Neo-Nazism

Fascism—Argentina
- NT Peronism
  ...

Fascism—Posters
- BT Political Posters

Fascism and architecture (May Subd Geog)
- UF Architecture and fascism
- BT Architecture
  ...

Fascism and labor unions
- USE Labor unions and fascism
  ...

Fascism and youth (May Subd Geog)
- UF Youth and fascism
- BT Youth

Fascism in art (Not Subd Geog)
  ...

Fascist propaganda (May Subd Geog)
- UF Propaganda, Fascist [Former heading]
- BT Fascism
      Propaganda, Italian

Fascists (May Subd Geog)
- NT Jewish fascists
      Neo-Nazis
      Women fascists

Figure 12.2 Sample Entries from *Library of Congress Subject Headings* (LCSH) as Displayed in *Classification Web Plus* (August 5, 2024). Available by Subscription at: https://classweb.org/.

> **Subject Record Fascism**
>
> ID: sh 85107461   Entered: 860211   Replaced: 19990331
> 008/06 Geo Subd: i-Indirect   008/11 SH System: a-LCSH   008/29 Ref Eval: a-Eval
> 008/07 Roman: |-No attempt   008/15 Subj Use: a-Appropriate   008/31 Rec Upd: a-Can be used
> 008/09 Kind Rec: a-Estab hdg   008/17 Type Subd: n-Not applic   008/33 Level Estab: a-Fully
>
> 010 $a sh 85047355
> 035 $a (DLC)sh 85047355
> 035 $a (DLC)45772
> 040 $a DLC $c DLC $d DLC
> 053 #0 $a D726.5 $c World history
> 053 #0 $a JC481 $c Political theory
> 150 $a Fascism
> 450 $a Neo-facism
> 550 $w g $a Authoritarianism
> 550 $w g $a Collectivism
> 550 $a Corporate state
> 550 $a National socialism
> 550 $a Synarchism
> 550 $a Totalitarianism
> 680 $i Here are entered general works on fascism including works on post-World War II fascist movements. Works on German fascism during the Nazi regime are entered under $a National socialism.
> 681 $i Note under $a National socialism

Figure 12.3 A Sample Authority Record for an LC Subject Heading Shown in Figure 12.2, as Displayed in *Classification Web Plus*. Available by Subscription at: https://classweb.org/. (Source: *Classification Web Plus*—LCCN: sh 85047355.)

12.7.2 *Sears List of Subject Headings* (*Sears*)

Sears is still published in print form with a new single-volume edition coming out every four years or so.[36] Since 2018, the *Sears* list has been available as an online database, in addition to its continuing publication in print.[37] The same basic information is provided in the online version, but the formatting of the entries is slightly different.

The *Sears* list is intended for small collections used by persons with general information needs. Its main users are school and small-to medium-sized public libraries. For most of its existence *Sears* has followed the lead of LCSH in format and in terminology choices. In its use of LCSH terminology, though, *Sears* has used only the more general terms and has not included the more specific terms or the ones geared for research audiences. In addition, *Sears* has fewer subdivisions.

In the last few editions, *Sears* has taken the initiative to make needed changes that LCSH was slow or reticent to make. For example, the change of **Afro-Americans** to **African Americans** was made first by *Sears*. In some cases, however, *Sears* has made changes that are not in alignment with LCSH. In 2002 the 17th edition of *Sears* replaced the heading **Indians of North America** with

Fascism		
	Geographic Note:	May subdivide geographically
	Dewey:	320.53; 321.9; 335.6
	Scope Note:	Use for materials on the political philosophy, movements, or regimes that advocate a centralized autocratic government, severe economic and social regimentation, and the exaltation of nation and race over the individual. Materials on fascism in Germany during the Nazi regime are entered under **National socialism**.
	Use For:	Authoritarianism; Neo-fascism
	Broader Term(s):	**Totalitarianism**
	Narrower Term(s):	**National socialism**
		Neo-Nazis
Fascism—Canada		
	Dewey:	320.53; 971.05
Fascism—United States		
	Geographic Note:	May subdivide geographically
	Dewey:	320.53; 973.9
Fashion		
	Geographic Note:	May subdivide geographically
	Dewey:	391
	Scope Note:	Use for materials on the prevailing mode or style of dress....

Figure 12.4 Subject Heading Entries from the *Sears List of Subject Headings*.

Native Americans; more than twenty years later, LCSH has yet to make a change of this nature.[†††] In 2016 *Sears* replaced the term *illegal aliens* with the heading **Unauthorized immigrants**, five years before LCSH addressed the issue. In 2008 a Spanish-language translation, *Sears Lista de Encabezamientos de Materia*, was published.[38] Although *Sears* remains a recognized resource for smaller libraries, its more limited scope (compared to LCSH) means that it may not meet all subject access needs. A sample from *Sears* is shown in Figure 12.4.

12.7.3 *Medical Subject Headings* (MeSH)

MeSH is the controlled vocabulary created and maintained by the National Library of Medicine (NLM) in the United States.[39] As in other controlled vocabularies, there is a listing for each term or concept giving its unique identifier, a scope note, related terms, classification numbers, and other relevant metadata. MeSH has a strict hierarchical arrangement (referred to as a *tree structure*). Although it does not specifically identify terms as BTs or NTs, the tree structures indicate the hierarchical relationships among the terms. For each term and phrase found in the list of main headings, MeSH provides a tailored list of allowable qualifiers (i.e., subdivisions).

[†††]In 2024, LC announced that it was developing a project to address the subject headings related to indigenous peoples.

MeSH, which is updated annually, is used to provide subject access points on every bibliographic record created at NLM, whether it is for the MEDLINE database or the NLM catalog. MeSH was first produced as a print product beginning in 1960 and became available in electronic form in 1975. Since 2008, MeSH has been available only as an online resource. The MeSH Browser is free for anyone who wishes to use it.[40] The vocabulary can be searched directly through the MeSH Browser or can be downloaded in XML, MARC 21, RDF, or ASCII formats.[41] A sample heading from MeSH, along with its allowable qualifiers, is shown in Figures 12.5 and 12.6. Figure 12.7 shows some of the locations in the hierarchical tree structure that contain the heading.

12.7.4 Library of Congress Genre/Form Terms for Library and Archival Materials (LCGFT)

Library of Congress Genre/Form Terms for Library and Archival Materials (LCGFT)[42] is used by libraries and archives to describe what a resource is, rather than what it is about. LCGFT contains **genre/form headings**, which generally represent the literary genre, artistic form, or publication format of a resource.

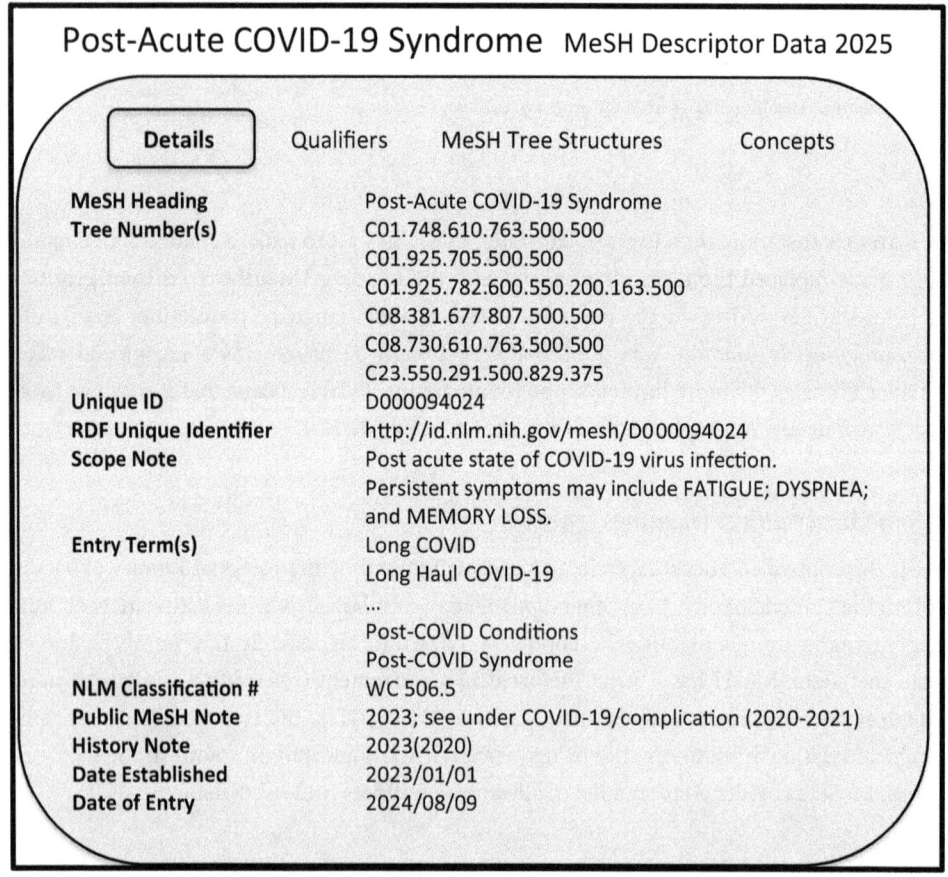

Figure 12.5 A MeSH Entry. (Source: MeSH Browser: https://meshb.nlm.nih.gov/record/ui?ui=D000094024.)

Systems for Vocabulary Control 485

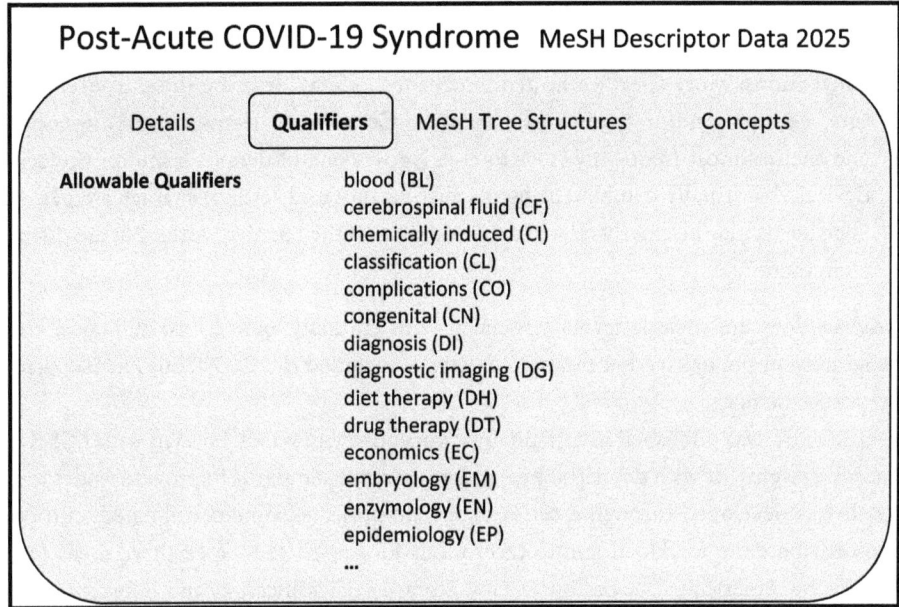

Figure 12.6 Allowable Qualifiers for MeSH Entry. (Source: MeSH Browser: https://meshb.nlm.nih.gov/record/ui?ui=D000094024.)

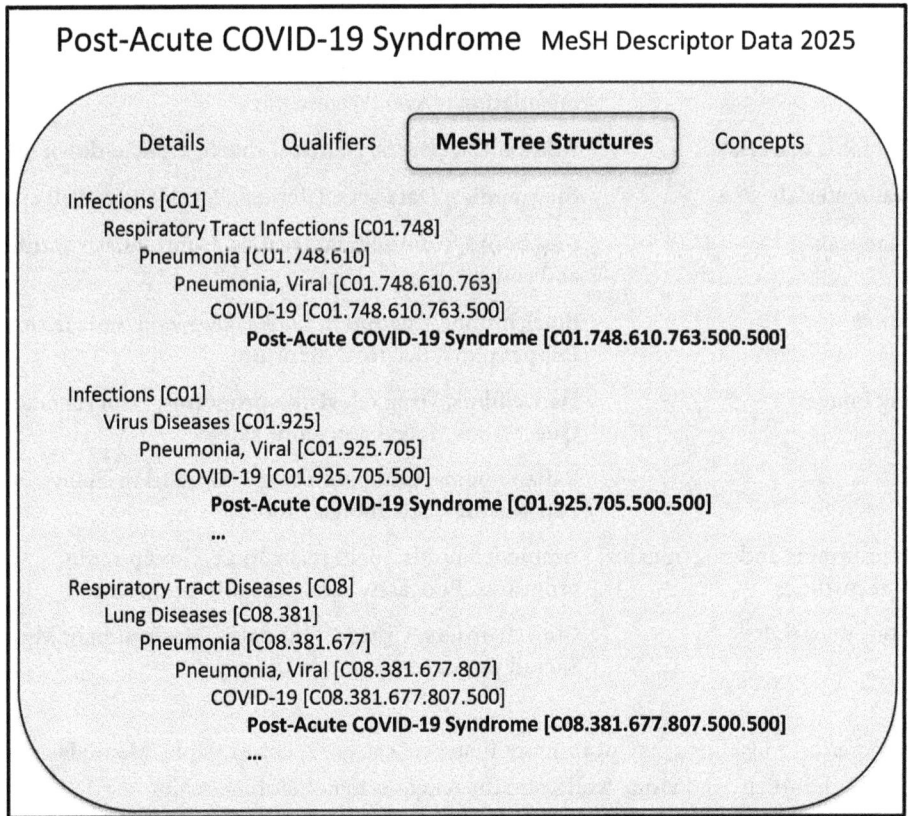

Figure 12.7 Tree Structures in MeSH for One Term. (Source: MeSH Browser: https://meshb.nlm.nih.gov/record/ui?ui=D000094024.)

> In 2007 the Library of Congress began a project to develop genre/form terms.... Genres and forms may be broadly defined as categories of resources that share known conventions. More specifically, genre/form terms may describe the purpose, structure, content, and/or themes of resources. Genre/form terms describing content and themes most frequently refer to creative works and denote common rhetorical devices that usually combine elements such as plot and setting, character types, etc. Such terms may be closely related to the subjects of the creative works, but are distinct from them.[43]

The thesaurus does not include terms associated with ethnicity, nationality, audience, creation dates, geography, or popularity. For example, **Poetry** is included in LCGFT, but *French poetry* and *Medieval poetry* are not.

In 2011 LCGFT was published as a standalone vocabulary that may be used with LCSH, other subject access systems, or with descriptive cataloging content standards to provide values for form elements. It was developed through a series of special projects, some coordinated with outside groups to distribute the workload and to receive outside expertise in specialized areas (e.g., LC worked with the American Association of Law Libraries' Classification and Subject Cataloging Policy Advisory Working Group on the terms for law materials). Currently, LCGFT contains genre and form terms from nine areas.

Area	Examples
Artistic and visual works	Jigsaw puzzles, Mandalas, Self-portraits, Video installations (Art), Watercolors
Cartographic materials	Atlases, Gazetteers, Nautical charts, Upside-down maps
General materials	Biographies, Data sets, Dictionaries, Menus, Wall charts
Law materials	Casebooks, Commercial treaties, Court rules, Statutes and codes
Literature	Black humor, Cartonera books, Doggerel, Epic fiction, Puppet plays, Satirical literature
Moving images	Dance films, Drag television programs, Film remakes, Queer films, Television game shows
Music	Ballad operas, Campaign songs, Gregorian chants, Peyote songs, Songbooks, Yodels
Radio programs and non-musical sound recordings	Ambient sounds, Field recordings, Gossip radio programs, Podcasts, Western radio programs
Religious materials	Church orders, Creeds, Mandalas, Mashyakhah, Myths, Sacred works

Some genre/form headings may fit in more than one category. For example, **Mandalas** appears under both the artistic and visual works and the religious materials hierarchies.

Unlike LCSH, LCGFT does not allow for subdivision of terms. It does, however, use many of the same formatting techniques and relationship indicators found in LCSH. It is likely that LCGFT will seem familiar to those who have used LCSH.

> **Educational films**
> Films that are intended to impart knowledge and information, including those for classroom viewing. For films that use a structured format to teach or train the audience see **Instructional films**.
> UF Informational films
> BT Documentary films
>   Instructional and educational works
> NT Science films
>   Social guidance films

12.7.5 *Library of Congress Demographic Group Terms* (LCDGT)

While developing LCGFT, the Library of Congress recognized that many genre and form terms, such as **Children's poetry** and **Swahili drama**, contained references to creator or audience characteristics. To create a structurally pure thesaurus that does not include outside concepts, LCGFT excluded all demographic characteristics from its list of terms. LC began work on developing a thesaurus of *demographic group* terms in 2013.

> A demographic group may be defined as a subset of the general population, and refers to the group's age, occupation, nationality, ethnic background, medical condition, etc. Individuals may belong to several demographic groups (e.g., an American (nationality) who is a librarian (occupation); a computer engineer (occupation) who is also a doctoral student (education level)). LCDGT is a stand-alone vocabulary that may be used in conjunction with any other controlled vocabulary and descriptive cataloging code.[44]

This thesaurus is called, unsurprisingly, *Library of Congress Demographic Group Terms* (LCDGT) and the first edition was published in 2015.[45] LCDGT includes nine categories of terms.

Category	Examples
Age groups	Boys, Middle-aged people, Older people, Preteens
Educational levels	College juniors, Eighth grade students, Doctoral students
Ethnic/Cultural group	Ashkenazim, Basques (European people), Cree (North American people), Hispanic Americans
Language groups	Central Khmer speakers, Marathi speakers, Spanish speakers
Medical, psychological, and disability category	Depressed people, Dyslexics, Leprosy patients

Category	Examples
National/Regional groups	Asians, Bay Staters, Bhutanese, Germans
Occupations and Fields of Activity	Book editors, Catalogers, Lighting designers, University and college faculty members
Religion groups	Ashkenazim, Benedictines, Sufis
Social groups (including gender and sexual orientation groups)	Bisexuals, Boys, Children of depressed people, Ecology students, Intersex people, Lesbians, Socialists, Transgender people

As was seen in LCGFT, some demographic group terms may also fall in more than one category. For example, **Ashkenazim** belongs in both the *religion* and *ethnic* categories; **Boys** belongs to both the *social* and *age* categories. Demographic terms may be used to represent audience or creator/contributor characteristics of a resource. The following is an example from LCDGT; it, too, is similar in structure to LCSH.

Two-spirit people
Established June 2022.
People who identify as two-spirit.
UF   Two-spirited people
         Two-spirits
         Twospirit people
         Twospirited people
BT   Gender minorities
         Indigenous people of America
RT   Indigiqueer people

12.7.6 *Art & Architecture Thesaurus* (AAT)

The *Art & Architecture Thesaurus* provides access to all kinds of cultural heritage information. Terms describe objects, textual materials, images, architecture, and material culture.[46] AAT is widely used in several communities: archives, libraries, museums, visual resources collections, and conservation agencies. It is arranged into eight high-level categories called *facets* that progress from the abstract to the concrete. The facets are divided into one or more hierarchies. For example, the *Activities* facet is broken down into five hierarchies, each of which may be broken down further into additional conceptual hierarchies or clusters of terms organized into tree structures of broader and narrower terms.

Facets	Hierarchies	Notes
Associated Concepts	Associated Concepts	Contains abstract concepts and phenomena, theoretical and critical concerns, ideologies, attitudes, and social or cultural movements.
Physical Attributes	Attributes and Properties Conditions and Effects Design Elements Color	Contains observable, measurable characteristics of artifacts and materials, such as size, shape, and properties.
Styles and Periods	Styles and Periods	Contains terms for styles, periods, movements, cultures, and nationalities.
Agents	People Organizations Living Organisms	Contains designations of people, organizations, animals, and plants.
Activities	Disciplines Functions Events Physical and Mental Activities Processes and Techniques	Contains areas of endeavor, actions, methods, and occurrences.
Materials	Materials	Contains substances (natural or synthetic) used to produce structures or artifacts.
Objects	Built Environments Components Furnishings and Equipment Object Genres Object Groupings and Systems Visual and Verbal Communications	Contains tangible or visible things.
Brand names	Brand Names	Contains objects, materials, and activities known by brand names.

AAT is available as a searchable web resource that provides full access to the preferred terms, alternative terms, and sources.[47] It can also be freely downloaded in two formats for incorporation into local retrieval tools, either as XML encoded records or as relational tables. The AAT dataset is also freely available in several linked data formats (e.g., RDF, JSON, Turtle). The electronic version is updated continually. Extensive online documentation is available to help new users. An example of the type of data found in an AAT record is shown in Figure 12.8. On the AAT website, terms also display additional scope notes, as well as extensive lists of sources and contributors. To get a better sense of the full display, see the record for "still life painters" in the *Art & Architecture Thesaurus* online database.[48]

Click the ■ icon to view the hierarchy.

Semantic View (JSON, RDF, N3/Turtle, N-Triples)

ID: 300266118   **Record Type:** concept
Page Link: http://vocab.getty.edu/page/aat/300266118

still life painters (still life artists, <artists by subject or style of work>, ... People (hierarchy name))

Note: Artists who specialize in painting inanimate objects such as bowls of fruit, bottles, and flowers, which are often arranged in an aesthetic composition.

Terms:
    still life painters (preferred,C,U,English-P,D,U,PN)
    still life painter (C,U,English,AD,U,SN)
    still-life painter (C,U,English,AD,U,N)
    still-life painters (C,U,English,UF,U,N)
    stillevenschilders (C,U,Dutch-P,D,U,U)
    pintores de naturaleza muerta (C,U,Spanish-P,D,U,PN)
    pintor de naturaleza muerta (C,U,Spanish,AD,U,SN)
    Stilllebenmaler (C,U,German-P,AD,U,MSN)
    Stilllebenmalerin (C,U,German,AD,U,FSN)
    Stillebenmaler (C,U,German,UF,U,U)

Facet/Hierarchy Code: H.HG

Hierarchical Position:
    Agents Facet
    .... People (hierarchy name) (G)
    .... people (agents) (G)
    .... <people by occupation> (G)
    .... <people in the humanities> (G)
    .... <people in the arts and related occupations> (G)
    .... <people in the arts> (G)
    .... <people in the visual arts and related occupations> (G)
    .... <people in the visual arts> (G)
    .... artists (visual artists) (G)
    .... <artists by subject or style of work> (G)
    .... still life artists (G)
    .... still life painters (G)

Additional Parents:
    Agents Facet
    .... People (hierarchy name) (G)
    .... people (agents) (G)
    .... <people by occupation> (G)
    .... <people in the humanities> (G)
    .... <people in the arts and related occupations> (G)
    .... <people in the arts> (G)
    .... <people in the visual arts and related occupations> (G)
    .... <people in the visual arts> (G)
    .... artists (visual artists) (G)
    .... <artists by medium or work type> (G)
    .... painters (artists) (G)
    .... <painters by subject of work> (G)
    .... still life painters (G)
...

Figure 12.8 A Partial Record for Still Life Painters (http://vocab.getty.edu/page/aat/300266118) from the *Art & Architecture Thesaurus* Online Database. (Contains information from the J. Paul Getty Trust, Getty Research Institute, the *Art & Architecture Thesaurus*, which is made available under the ODC Attribution License.)

12.7.7 Thesaurus of ERIC Descriptors

ERIC (Educational Resources Information Center) is a national information system designed to provide access to a large body of education-related literature. In addition to journal articles, ERIC indexes descriptions and evaluations of programs, book reviews, research reports, curriculum and teaching guides, resource materials, instructional materials, position papers, and computer files. These materials are indexed using terms from the *Thesaurus of ERIC Descriptors*. The last print version of the thesaurus was published in 2001.[49]

The most current version of the thesaurus is available as an online product. Its interface allows both searching[50] and browsing[51] the thesaurus. As of 2025, the *ERIC Thesaurus* "contains a total of 11,875 terms. There are 4,578 descriptors and 7,165 synonyms. There are also 132 dead terms, which are no longer used as descriptors but remain in the Thesaurus to aid in searching older records."[52] It displays the ERIC descriptors in alphabetical order as search results and in the browse interface. The browse interface also allows for browsing by 41 categories, including Arts, Counseling, Facilities, Learning and Perception, Mental Health, Reading, and Science and Technology.

Within each term's record, broader and narrower terms are hyperlinked, allowing users to explore hierarchical relationships. Conveniently, the interface also allows users to search for a descriptor in the ERIC index directly from that term's record via a hyperlink marked "Search collection using this descriptor." An entry from the online display of the ERIC thesaurus is shown below.

Metadata

Scope note: Information that characterizes data, or the individual elements that describe and are used to provide access to an object, most often an information resource

Category: Information/Communications Systems

Broader Terms	**Related Terms**
Data	Cataloging
Narrower Terms	Indexing
N/A	Information Retrieval
Use this term instead of	
Metainformation	

12.7.8 Faceted Application of Subject Terminology (FAST)

At the turn of the century, some catalogers began to express dissatisfaction with LCSH. Many felt that there was less need for complex subject heading strings, especially when cataloging web resources and digital objects. Their desire was for a controlled vocabulary that retained the rich semantics of LCSH but was, at the same time, intuitive and easy enough to apply without needing a master's degree in library and information science.[53] An OCLC research group explored the issue and began to develop a new schema derived from LCSH, but specifically designed for applications that go beyond the traditional library catalog; thus FAST (Faceted Application of Subject Terminology) was born.[54]

FAST is a *faceted vocabulary*, meaning that the terms are divided into defined categories representing specific aspects of the subject matter. For example, some terms are topical, some are chronological, and so on. This means that in FAST, the LCSH string **Microsoft Corporation—Employees—Biography** is converted to three separate headings, each representing a separate facet.

> *Corporate Names*: **Microsoft Corporation**
> *Topical*: **Employees**
> *Form/Genre*: **Biography**

FAST includes nine facets, which are identified in the following table.

Category	Description	Examples
Topical	General subject matter, objects, or concepts	**Cataloging; English language—Etymology**
Geographic Names	Place names (Continents, countries, localities, geographic features)	**Europe; Uruguay; Lake Erie**
Chronological	Time periods	**2001-2009; 1984**
Named Events	Occurrences or historical incidents	**Cannes Film Festival; War of 1812**
Personal Names	Names of persons	**Buttigieg, Pete, 1982- ; Posey, Parker, 1968-**
Corporate Names	Names of organizations or groups	**Human Rights Campaign (U.S.); Planetas (Musical group : Spain)**
Meetings	Conferences, congresses, sporting events, and other meetings	**Olympic Winter Games; American Library Association. Annual Conference**
Titles	Names associated with works	**Beowulf; Qur'an; Hamlet (Shakespeare, William)**
Form/Genre	Types or kinds of bibliographic structures, literary or artistic forms, and formats	**Science fiction television programs; Biography**

Although faceted, FAST *does* allow for some subdivisions, but each facet's main headings can be subdivided only by subdivisions from the same facet. Thus, topical headings may be subdivided only by topical subdivisions (e.g., **Hospitals—Administration**) but not by a chronological or any other type of subdivision. Each heading and heading-subdivision combination is established with its own authority record in the FAST authority file.

In recent years, FAST headings have become more prevalent in MARC bibliographic records, particularly those retrieved from OCLC's WorldCat database. FAST headings are added to bibliographic records in WorldCat automatically based on the LCSH headings in the record. There are several online tools developed to support the use of FAST. These include

- **FAST Converter**, which translates LCSH to FAST[55]
- **assignFAST**, which automates the selection of terms based on autosuggest technology, and
- **importFAST**, which converts LC personal or corporate names to the FAST system.

Although it was not originally intended to replace LCSH, in some libraries—most notably at the British Library—it has effectively done so. "In May 2022, the [British] Library announced its intention to change its preferred subject heading system from LCSH to FAST, starting in the summer of 2022. The British Library is the first (and perhaps only) national library to have taken this step."[56] In the coming years, some have predicted that the Library of Congress may follow suit. This view is supported by statements in 'Library of Congress Subject Headings: A Post-Coordinated Future,' an LC report in which the authors conclude that pre-coordination—a hallmark of LCSH—"may have served users well historically, but what comes next for LCSH should be dictated by the future not the past."[57] Whether that is hinting that a post-coordinated vocabulary like FAST will be adopted at LC or that LC may make significant changes to LCSH, we will just have to wait and see what happens.

12.7.9 Homosaurus

The Homosaurus is one of the newest notable controlled vocabularies. It is an international thesaurus of terms related to the lesbian, gay, bisexual, transgender, and queer (LGBTQ+) community that was created to improve access to LGBTQ-themed resources in libraries and other information institutions.[58] It has been designed to supplement larger, more general controlled vocabularies like LCSH. It is maintained by the Digital Transgender Archive and contains more inclusive, nuanced, and current terminology to represent subjects important to the LGBTQ+ community. Terms related to sexual orientation and gender have evolved over the last few decades and more general vocabularies often do not represent the most accurate or current usage of the community. The Homosaurus can be used to make resources findable using terms that may be more familiar to those seeking those resources.

The Homosaurus provides a structured, hierarchical network of terms, linking concepts through broader, narrower, and related-term relationships. It is available in linked data formats, enhancing its interoperability with contemporary metadata systems. The vocabulary is used not only in libraries, but also in archives, digital repositories, and community information projects committed to inclusive resource discovery. As of 2025, the Homosaurus includes approximately 4,000 terms and continues to expand through frequent updates.

> **Queer people** (https://homosaurus.org/v3/homoit0001195)
>
> **Identifier**
> : homoit0001195
>
> **Preferred Term**
> : Queer people
>
> **Description (Scope Note)**
> : Individuals who identify with non-normative gender and/or sexual identities, typically people who are not heterosexual and/or are not cisgender. Only use for people who identify as queer.
>
> **Issued (Created)**
> : 2019-05-14 07:04:18 UTC
>
> **Modified**
> : 2022-01-19 19:15:52 UTC
>
> **Broader Terms**
> : Bi+ people   LGBTQ+ people   Reclaimed terms
>
> **Related Terms**
> : Culturally queer   Genderqueer identity   Parents of queer people
>   Persecution of queer people Queer characters   Queer families
>   Queer identity   Queer parents   Queer people in fandom
>   Queercrip   Queerphobia
>
> **Narrower Terms**
> : Closeted queer people   Genderqueer people   Indigiqueer people
>   Queer college students   Queer men   Queer transgender people
>   Queer women   Queer youth
>
> **Replaces**
> : http://homosaurus.org/v2/queerPeople
>
> **Hierarchy Display:**
> Bi+ people
> LGBTQ+ people
> Reclaimed terms
> > **Queer people**
> > > Queer youth
> > > Closeted queer people
> > > Genderqueer people
> > > Indigiqueer people
> > > Queer men
> > > Queer transgender people
> > > Queer women
> > > Queer college students
>
> **Other Formats:** N-Triples, JSON-LD, Extended JSON, TTL, XML, MARC XML
> **Temporary Experimental Formats (includes language identifiers):** N-Triples, JSON-LD, TTL

Figure 12.9 An Entry from The Homosaurus. (https://homosaurus.org/v3/homoit0001195.)

12.8 Ontologies

Ontologies are not just another type of controlled vocabulary. Although they are similar to thesauri in that they address relationships among concepts, there are significant differences. The most notable is that the purpose of an ontology is farther reaching than that of a controlled vocabulary. A thesaurus, most often, is focused on addressing synonyms, homographs, hierarchy, and so on. Although an ***ontology*** is a formalized vocabulary of terms, an ontology's emphasis is not solely lexical; it is also an attempt to represent the reality or essence of a situation, knowledge domain, or conceptual framework through formal definitions and specific relationships (i.e., those going beyond simple hierarchy and synonymy). In its attempt to provide a detailed understanding of a particular knowledge domain or subject area, an ontology is like a cross between a controlled vocabulary and a conceptual model. LIS professor Elin Jacob states,

> Ontologies have been variously construed as classification schemes, taxonomies, hierarchies, thesauri, controlled vocabularies, terminologies and even dictionaries. While they may display characteristics reminiscent of each of these systems, to equate ontologies with any one type of representational structure is to diminish both their function and their potential in the evolution of the Semantic Web.[59]

Ontology is a word with many nuances, which is ironic considering the common purpose of the term. Definitions are not always in alignment nor are they always clear. In the field of philosophy, the term has a long and respectable history meaning a systematic account of existence. More recently the term has come to be used in the information science community for the categories of things that may exist in a particular domain and to refer to the knowledge shared by persons working in that domain; in other words, it is a systematic account of the entities and their relationships found in a particular shared reality that enables computers to make inferences or deductions based on clearly defined relationships among entities. According to computer scientist Thomas Gruber, "An ontology defines (specifies) the concepts, relationships, and other distinctions that are relevant for modeling a domain. The specification takes the form of the definitions of representational vocabulary (classes, relations, and so forth), which provide meanings for the vocabulary and formal constraints on its coherent use."[60] According to Marcia Lei Zeng and Jian Qin,

> By definition, an ontology is a formal model that allows knowledge to be represented for a specific domain. An ontology describes
> (a) the types of things that exist (*classes*),
> (b) the relationships between them (*properties*), and
> (c) the logical ways those classes and properties can be used together (*axioms*).[61]

Jacob states, "Following Gruber's lead, an ontology can be defined as a partial, simplified conceptualization of the world as it is assumed to exist by a community of users—a conceptualization created for an explicit purpose and defined in a formal, machine-processable language."[62]

The broadest usage of the term is for a formal representation or specification of what is common sense or "objective" reality to a human being. An ontology defines the nature of reality by identifying the classes, properties, individuals, and data values in a particular knowledge domain in order to model the relationships among them, with the ultimate goal of making web content more accessible to machines.[63] It is created to keep conceptual and semantic ambiguity at a minimum in an information and technological environment, which is something that is not always possible with traditional controlled vocabularies. For example, in the *NASA Thesaurus*,[64] a traditional controlled vocabulary, you find the following concepts to help describe resources about the first moon landing. The terms are placed in hierarchies, which represent broader and narrower term relationships:

>**celestial bodies**
>>**natural satellites**
>>>**moon**
>
>**personnel**
>>**flying personnel**
>>>**astronauts**
>
>**space flight**
>>**manned space flight**
>>>**Apollo flights**
>>>>**Apollo 11 flight**

You also find a small number of related terms.

>**Apollo 11 flight**
>>RT   Earth-Moon trajectory
>>   lunar flight
>>   lunar landing
>>   manned spacecraft
>
>**astronauts**
>>RT   astronautics
>>   crews
>>   pilots
>>   spacecrews

The controlled vocabulary's use of standardized terms and relationship indicators can be easily navigated by humans and used to retrieve resources within a database or catalog. However, if the goal is to systematically represent reality to help machines "understand" and process information about this knowledge domain, additional entities and relationships are necessary. Entities such as *Buzz Aldrin, Neil Armstrong, Michael Collins, command module, lunar module*, and so on, are needed to bring out a more robust, realistic, and accurate picture of the event (i.e., domain) being modeled. Not only that, but additional relationships, such as *commanderOf / commandedBy, componentOf / containsComponent, landedOn / landingSiteOf, pilotOf / pilotedBy*, and so forth, are necessary to achieve the specificity needed for machine processing and inferences.[65] This is an example of how ontologies are different from traditional controlled vocabularies in terms of scope and function.

A formal ontology is useful for enhancing interoperability among systems in different knowledge domains or for creating artificial intelligence (AI) tools or agents that can perform certain tasks; both of which are goals of the Semantic Web. Ontologies also serve as foundational structures for knowledge graphs, increasingly used in modern AI systems for reasoning and inference. To fulfill the vision of the Semantic Web, terms must have explicit meanings and relationships so that machines can automatically process and interpret online information. Ontologies provide the necessary structure for this kind of machine understanding. However, because the same term may carry different meanings in different contexts, and the same meaning may be represented by different terms, standardization is essential. To achieve this, the Web Ontology Working Group of the World Wide Web Consortium (W3C) developed the OWL Web Ontology Language.[66]

The relationships identified in OWL (and its second edition, OWL2) are somewhat different from those found in thesauri. According to the *OWL2 Primer*,[67] like any modeling language, OWL is concerned with ***individuals*** (i.e., entities, such as a person or a thing), ***classes*** (i.e., groups or categories of entities with something in common), and ***properties*** (i.e., attributes or relationships). In addition, there are other concerns brought out in OWL. These include class hierarchies (e.g., one class is subclass of another), which allow inferences to be made based on the relationships among groups. If Lassie (an individual) is a member of the class *dogs*, and *dogs* is a subclass of *animals* (another class), then a machine can deduce, based on class hierarchies, that Lassie is an animal, and what is true of all animals is true for Lassie, but what is true for Lassie is not necessarily true for all animals. Individuals can be members of multiple classes (e.g., Lassie is a dog, but Lassie is also a pet). Some classes may be equivalent (e.g., *animals* and *beasts*), but some are not (e.g., *cats* and *dogs*). When membership in one class (e.g., *dogs*) excludes the entity from memberships in another class (e.g., *cats*), those classes are said to be *disjoint classes* (i.e., incompatible classes).

Beyond the class structures enumerated, OWL also describes individuals and their relationships through properties (e.g., Lassie *hasSister* Sassie). These statements can be made both in positive and negative forms. Property statements also can be hierarchically structured. Some relationships provided for in OWL are

- **subClassOf**: x is a subset of the class y (e.g., the class *dogs* is a subset of the class *animals*)
- **one of**: the enumerated thing is an instance of the class (e.g., Lassie is one member of the class *dogs*)
- **equivalentClass**: two class descriptions have the same set of individuals (e.g., the class *animals* is equivalent to the class *beasts*)
- **intersectionOf**: a class can belong to two other classes (e.g., the class *dogs* can be both *animals* and *pets*)
- **disjointWith**: two classes have no individuals in common (e.g., the class *cats* does not include any individuals of the class *dogs*)

The relatively simple structures presented here are just the beginning and are intended only to illustrate some basic differences between ontologies and the other forms of controlled vocabularies discussed earlier. Ontologies can be quite complex, the details of which go beyond the scope of this book.

12.9 Natural Language Approaches to Subjects

In addition to controlled approaches to subject terminology, there are also natural language approaches. These uncontrolled approaches include the longstanding practices of keyword searching and natural language processing (NLP), as well as the development of tagging (also known as *user tagging* or *social tagging*), which has been incorporated into a variety of web-based environments and a small number of information retrieval tools.

12.9.1 Keywords

Keyword searching allows users to search records or documents using their own terms. Users can choose to search all parts of a record or focus on specific subsections of a record. For example, a subject keyword search queries not only controlled subject terms, but also other potentially relevant fields, such as the title, tables of contents, summaries, contents notes; this offers flexibility in retrieval. If full-text searching is available, the search can extend to the contents of the resource itself.‡‡‡ Some systems may also allow searching of author-supplied keywords, which is particularly common in institutional repositories that collect theses, dissertations, articles, and other scholarly outputs from academic institutions.

Although keyword searching can be an effective tool for conducting broad initial searches, it faces notable challenges. Issues such as synonymous concepts, word forms, and homographs often hinder retrieval accuracy. These challenges stem from the fact that keyword searching relies on two key assumptions:

1. Authors writing about the same concepts will use the same terms in their writings.
2. Searchers can guess the terms used by the authors.

A 1993 study of journal articles in the natural and social sciences found that even articles sharing common references—and therefore likely discussing related subjects—rarely used the same keywords.[68] Another study the same year highlighted difficulties in selecting keywords for literature searches, as multiple terms often represent the same concept.[69]

To address these issues, some systems implemented synonym rings (or synsets). Synonym rings are databases grouping synonymous terms. When a user performs a keyword search, the system taps into the synset to suggest synonyms, sparing the searcher from manually identifying alternative terms. For example, a search for *airplane* might automatically include *aircraft* and *plane*.

Early implementations of synonym rings faced limitations. Many lists were too small or specialized to cover broader fields. Some systems lacked the ability to distinguish between word roles, such as nouns and adjectives, which could lead to incorrect phrase substitutions (e.g., substituting *big airplane* for *gigantic aircraft*) without considering proper grammar and context.[70]

In modern information retrieval (IR) systems, full text analysis allows articles and other writings to be analyzed and indexed when they are added to the system. These systems retrieve

---

‡‡‡Keyword searching in the context of information retrieval systems is discussed in more detail in Chapter 4.

documents using keywords but face limitations when attempting to transmit large amounts of text (e.g., over distributed networks or the web). Furthermore, simple keyword searching often does not adequately address semantic challenges, such as synonymous terms and word relationships. In the 1990s, Sujata Banerjee and Vibhu Mittal proposed enhancing keyword searching with lexical databases like WordNet to address some of these issues.[71] Their approach used synonym substitution and hierarchical word relationships to improve search results. For example:

1. A search for *family crisis* might yield exact matches first.
2. If insufficient matches were found, the system would suggest alternative terms to the user, such as *household crisis* or *home crisis*, using synonymous adjectives.
3. Synonym substitution for nouns might suggest *family emergency*.
4. The system could generalize terms to hypernyms (e.g., *family situation* or *family state of affairs*) or suggest hyponyms (e.g., *foster home crisis* or *marriage crisis*).

This approach demonstrated the potential of large lexical databases to enhance keyword searching, though such tools remain uncommon in many systems today.

Recent advances in natural language processing (NLP) and machine learning have transformed keyword searching. Modern systems often incorporate machine-learning models like BERT (Bidirectional Encoder Representations from Transformers), which understand the context of words in a query. Unlike older approaches relying on static synonym rings, these models dynamically interpret word relationships, significantly improving search precision and recall.[72] User's intent and context are also factors considered in more recent search tool advancements.

While traditional keyword searching provides a foundation for information retrieval, its limitations underscore the need for advanced methods. Innovations such as synonym rings, lexical databases, and NLP-driven models like BERT have significantly improved retrieval accuracy and usability. As technology continues to evolve, further integrating these advancements will enhance the ability of IR systems to meet diverse user needs. While keyword searching emphasizes matching terms to documents, natural language processing seeks to interpret meaning, structure, and user intent more deeply.

12.9.2 Natural Language Processing

Natural language processing (NLP) research aims to enable computers to interpret and react to human languages. So far, most progress in this area has focused on spoken and written language, though research into sign language is also being conducted. Goals of NLP include machine translation, question answering, and creating conversational AI agents and dialogue systems.[73] A goal of NLP, related to question answering, is improved and enhanced information retrieval. The IR process can be described in three distinct steps:

1. to interpret users' information needs as expressed in free text,
2. to represent the complete range of meaning conveyed in documents, and
3. to "understand" when there is a match between the user's information need and all (and no more than) the documents that meet it.

To accomplish any NLP task, certain challenges must be addressed:[74]

- Sentences are often incomplete descriptions of what they mean. For example, "The door opened" does not tell whether the door was opened by a person, the wind, or its own weight. If the next sentence is, "Susan walked in," then the implication is that Susan opened the door, although that may or may not be the case.

- The same expression can mean different things in different contexts. For example, "Where's the water?" can mean that one is thirsty, or it can mean that one wants to know how to get to the beach.

- Natural languages are constantly gaining new words, usages, expressions, and meanings. An example is the creation and evolution of the word *blog*, which descended from *web log* or *weblog* and can be used as both a noun and a verb.

- There are many ways to say the same thing. For example, "Mary registered for two summer courses" and "Mary signed up for two courses in the summer term" mean essentially the same thing. This problem applies not only to natural language sentences, but also to individual words, as discussed above with the challenges related to synonymous concepts.

- Sentences that are constructed identically can mean different things. In the two sentences, "Jennifer took the course with Professor Jones" and "Jennifer took the course with Mary," the first sentence indicates that the professor taught the course that Jennifer took. But the second could mean that Jennifer and Mary are both students and took a course together, or it could mean that Professor Mary Jones likes to be addressed by her first name. Such ambiguities can often be sorted out through the context of surrounding sentences, but some cannot.

Successful NLP systems must contain information about the different areas of linguistics, as each area provides valuable information about how words, sentences, and dialogues are created and interpreted:[75]

- **Phonetics**: the study of how individual sounds are created and perceived. Not all languages have the same sounds; speech recognition systems need to be able to recognize different sounds depending on the language they are built for.

- **Phonology**: the study of patterns of sounds in languages, and how they combine to form syllables. Different languages have different rules for what phonemes can combine in what order and how a phoneme might change in different contexts. For example, in American English an *S* at the end of a word might be pronounced as a *Z*.

- **Morphology**: the study of *morphemes* (i.e., units of meaning) in a language, and how they combine. Morphemes are words, prefixes, suffixes, and other word structures that can modify meaning. For example, in English, adding an *S* at the end of a word often indicates plurality.

- **Syntax**: the study of how words combine to create phrases and sentences and what combinations are allowed in different languages. Syntactic analysis includes identifying parts of speech and creating representations of the underlying structure of sentences.
- **Semantics**: the study of meaning in language, and the relationship between words and what they represent. For example, "She wants to print a pdf" indicates a wanting event in which she wants a printing event to occur wherein she must have access to a computer and a printer, but in order to understand that sentence an NLP system must have access to a knowledge base (i.e., an ontology) that includes what printing and a pdf are.
- **Discourse analysis**: the study of how information is exchanged across sentences and how that context informs the semantic interpretation. For example, the meaning of pronouns such as *it, them,* and *her* can be given individual meanings only if what or who they refer to can be determined.
- **Pragmatics**: the study of how context affects interpretation. For example, the question "Do you have the time?" should not be answered with "Yes," but should be interpreted as a request to be told the time. In the case of an IR system, the result of such analysis should be a translation to a command to be executed by the system. If the system is asked a question such as "Do you have anything on artificial intelligence?" the response should be a list of sources on artificial intelligence, not "Yes."

Speech recognition systems must include knowledge of phonetics and phonology for the languages they are built for, in addition to the other linguistic fields. Text-based systems do not need to be concerned with the sounds of a language, but they have the additional tasks of identifying words and sentences, and interpreting punctuation, spelling, and other formatting or orthographic information that may add or change meaning in the text.

Recent breakthroughs in NLP have been largely driven by the development of large language models like GPT (Generative Pre-trained Transformer) and BERT. These models, which are trained on massive stores of textual data, serve as the cornerstone for many of the recent innovations in NLP, enabling more accurate and nuanced capabilities in understanding, generating, and manipulating language. As a result, tasks such as translation and question answering, and the development of conversational AI systems (e.g., ChatGPT) have seen significant improvements. Library and information science professionals are exploring how these advancements can transform retrieval, information organization, and research in general. As powerful as these tools have become, however, they also introduce ethical challenges, including concerns about algorithmic bias, data privacy, environmental costs, and the need for responsible deployment.

12.9.3 Tagging and Folksonomies

Tagging is another natural language approach used to describe the content of resources. It is a process by which a distributed mass of users applies keywords—referred to as *tags* or *hashtags* in this context—to resources for the purposes of collaborative information organization and retrieval.

Tagging is a populist approach to description within a contained system (such as a catalog) or out on the open web. Michalis Gerolimos states that the popularity of tagging "grew with the advent of social media and networking websites and brought an innovative element to what can generally be referred to as document description: users describing their own or someone else's documents or resources for personal (most of the time) purposes."[76]

Tagging allows individual users to group similar resources together by using their own terms or labels, with few or no restrictions. The tags assigned to a resource can be based on a variety of facets.

Facets	Examples
Subject Matter	cooking, Sigur_Rós, metadata, PattyGriffin
Form	images, humor, gossip, recipes
Purpose	reference, delivery, travel, howTo
Time	February, now, 2025, future
Location	box3, guest-bedroom, Normal-IL
Task or Status	toRead, toDo, toSort, mine, own
Affective or Critical Reactions	cool, fun, schlocky author, Questionable Literary Merit, yaas
Other/Indiscernible Reasons	I_am_morbid, woo-woo, G, 5, aargh

The tags applied are then either used for searching, or they may be displayed in the form of an alphabetical list or as a tag cloud for browsing. ***Tag clouds*** are visual representations of tags that have been assigned. In some systems, tag clouds display the tags used in the entire site, and in others, the tag clouds represent the tags of only one person, resource, or group. The tag cloud may look like a paragraph composed of individual words displayed in various font sizes, with the font size representing the relative popularity of the tag. The larger the font, the more frequently that tag has been used in the system (see Figure 12.10). The individual tags in the cloud may be arranged alphabetically or ranked by the popularity of the tags.

Tagging may be applied in numerous domains to various kinds of resources.

Types of Resources	Examples
Web Bookmarks	Bibsonomy, Diigo, Hatena
Digital Images and Videos	Instagram, Flickr, YouTube
Social Network or Blog Posts	X (Twitter), Facebook, WordPress, Blogger
Personal Library Resources	LibraryThing
Resources in Online Catalogs	Miami-Dade Public Library System Catalog, Villanova University Library Catalog

```
2017 2022 21ˢᵗ century 415 class book academic acquired_2009 ABM adult adult non-fiction
amazon_wishlist apartment archives Arlene back guest room bedroom Beth bibliotecologia books for
school books read-2022 books-i-own Box 5 butter room cataloging Catalogs catalogue
categorization ck class Class Reading classText Class Textbook classic classification
classification schemes classifying coding controlled vocabularies Course Reserve currently-
reading dad's office Daniel Daniel Jourdrey data dense Dewey Dominican Dublin Core
education encoding standards English FISOE for class for school FRBR goals grad
school great GSLIS have-read heavy helpful history indexing INFO527 information
information arrangement information organization information retrieval
information science information studies Joudrey Knowledge Organization
librarianship library and information science library school
library science LIS LIS 415 LIS-415 LIS415 LIS501 MARC marc21 Marc-21
metadata MLIS 7300 MLIS books MLIS textbooks organization organizing
information organizationOfInfo own purchased_2010 RatedOnAmazon rda read
reference required reading required text retrieval tools SAB:Ab-Biblioteksväsen Sarah
school books Simmons SLIS Spring 2011 Spring 2014 standards still have? stolen-from-tim
subject analysis subject cataloging summer-2013 Taylor technology text textbook
textbooks theory to-read toRead UAlbany Valdosta State University UnderTheStairs
vocabulary control WEMI wishlist work
```

Figure 12.10 An Example of a Tag Cloud.

According to Thomas Vander Wal, "The value in this external tagging is derived from people using their own vocabulary and adding explicit meaning. ... People are not so much categorizing, as providing a means to connect items ... to provide their meaning in their own understanding."[77]

When it was first introduced, tagging was seen by many as an exciting development because it is an approach to subject metadata by the people, for the people—without restrictions, unfamiliar jargon, and complex application rules. Users can assign as many tags as they like, and the terminology they use is their own. It can be done by non-experts, and it is primarily performed by volunteers. Tagging provides some added value to our current retrieval tools, but there are also some drawbacks associated with user tagging. These problems are familiar to anyone who has ever performed a keyword search: there is no synonym or homograph control, no control of word forms (e.g., singular versus plurals), impaired precision, and no hierarchical and associative relationships identified. For example, the genre *science fiction* has been represented by all the tags presented here:

- science fiction
- sciencefiction
- science_fiction
- ScienceFiction

- scifi
- SciFi
- sci-fi
- Sci/Fi
- syfy
- sy-fy
- Sy Fy
- fiction.sciencefiction
- ciencia ficción
- sf
- SF
- sff
- scifi/fantasy
- siensfixion

In other words, tagging lacks the benefits of controlled vocabularies. In addition, the tags assigned by some users may be so idiosyncratic or personal that they are of no real value to anyone else or may be misleading.

An aggregation of tags is referred to as a ***folksonomy*** (a blend of *folks* and *taxonomy*). Thomas Gruber argues that with folksonomies, "we now have an entirely new source of data for finding and organizing information: user participation. ... Tags introduce distributed human intelligence into the system."[78] Emanuele Quintarelli states folksonomy is an activity of "collaborative categorization using freely chosen keywords by a group of people cooperating spontaneously."[79] She goes on to identify both drawbacks and strengths of folksonomy, acknowledging that they lack precision in language, lack syndetic structures, do not work well in retrieval, and do not scale well. On the other hand, folksonomies do reflect the general populace's language and needs, and they are inclusive of everyone's input, helpful for understanding resources, and low cost.[80] Based on a study she conducted, Shuheng Wu states,

> Although folksonomies are known to have various issues (e.g. lack of accuracy, misspellings, ambiguity, and problems with polysemy) ... participants still found tags useful for making selection to fulfill their information needs, as tags provided them with insights into the subject matter of resources. As Participant 04 described, "tags further confirm that the subject matter in the book is aligned with what I am expecting, let me get a general sense of what the book will be about."[81]

For many years, it has been assumed that if enough users tag enough resources, sufficient data can be aggregated to achieve stability, reliability, and consensus. For this data to be useful in augmenting current approaches to subject access, though, a critical mass of tags must be accumulated. The idea is that many tags applied to discrete resources by myriad individuals (who are tagging for countless reasons) will provide sufficient information to understand the nature of the resource and to allow us to take technological advantage of an inexpensive way to organize web-accessible information resources. Without a sufficient volume of data, however, the benefits are limited. For example, one or two user tags assigned to a catalog record may not provide much insight into the resource being described or reliable supplementary access points; but 200 tags, similar in purpose, may provide additional, useful, meaningful machine-derived subject access points for the record. In libraries and other cultural heritage institutions, however, sufficient data is not often accumulated.

Although it is a popular approach to describing materials on the web, tagging is not a common feature in most retrieval tools found in LIS institutions. In 2012 Sharon Yang found that only 5 percent of integrated library systems and 47 percent of discovery interfaces allowed users to add tags to resources.[82] In 2015, in a small study of public libraries and tagging, Isola Ajiferuke, Jamie Goodfellow, and Adeola Opesade found that in the catalogs that had implement tagging, a large percentage of resources have remained untagged.[83] This is supported by the 2020 findings of Brinna Michael and Myung-Ja Han that tagging is not used in libraries as much as initially anticipated, and that only a small number of catalog records in the system they examined included user tags.[84] In 2021, Philip Hider and Gemma Steele stated, "The question remains how library catalogs can best harness this added value offered by social cataloging, noting that around half of the LT [LibraryThing] tags do not relate to subject or genre, and some of those that do might also be considered as 'noise.'"[85]

Despite its shortcomings, tagging appears likely to remain a staple of social media environments, where it is valued both for its utility and for the enjoyment users derive from it. With further research, information professionals may find inexpensive ways to leverage user-generated metadata to supplement and enhance expert-created subject metadata.

12.10 Conclusion

This chapter has addressed issues of vocabulary control. Controlled vocabularies are most often associated with subject access, but they also serve other functions. All controlled vocabularies deal with issues and problems during their construction; understanding these issues contributes to making the best use of the vocabulary, as does understanding the general principles of application. Controlled vocabularies may come in several different forms: simple term lists, synonym rings, taxonomies, thesauri (including subject heading lists), and ontologies. These tools will continue to be used far into the future, but it is important to recognize the fast-moving developments in natural language processing, particularly through generative AI, which has potential to reshape subject access methods.

For subject access, subject heading lists and thesauri are the most prevalent types of vocabularies in use in information institutions today. Subject heading lists created by libraries were the first to appear. Thesauri are more strictly hierarchical and, for the most part, are developed in subject-specific situations and/or commercial indexing services. The latest addition to verbal approaches to subject access is the folksonomy, which is made up of user tags assigned to web-based resources. The next chapter continues the discussion of subject access, shifting the focus to categorization and classification systems.

Some Important Terms in This Chapter
(Definitions Provided in the Glossary)

Abbreviation	Genus-Species relationship	Qualifier
Acronym	Hierarchical relationship	Related term
Antonym	Holonym	Simple term list
Associative relationship	Homograph	Specific entry
Broader term	Homophone	Specificity
Class	Hypernym	Subject heading list
Coextensive entry	Hyponym	Subject heading string
Compound heading	Individual	Subdivision
Controlled vocabulary	Initialism	Syndetic structure
Coordinate term	Instance relationship	Synonym
Coordination	Instruction sheet	Synonym ring
Data value standard	Keyword	Tag cloud
Demographic group	Literary warrant	Tagging
Descriptor	Meronym	Taxonomist
Direct entry	Narrower term	Taxonomy
Entry vocabulary	Natural language processing	Thesaurus
Equivalence relationship	Ontology	Tree structure
Faceted vocabulary	Post-coordination	Upward reference
Folksonomy	Pre-coordination	Whole-part relationship
Genre/Form heading	Property	

Some Important Acronyms in This Chapter

AAT:	*Art & Architecture Thesaurus*
AI:	Artificial Intelligence
BERT:	Bidirectional Encoder Representations from Transformers
BT:	Broader Term
CONA:	*Cultural Objects Name Authority*
CV:	Controlled Vocabulary
ERIC:	Education Resources Information Center
FAST:	Faceted Application of Subject Terminology
GPT:	Generative Pre-trained Transformer
IR:	Information Retrieval
JSON:	JavaScript Object Notation

LC:	Library of Congress
LCDGT:	*Library of Congress Demographic Group Terms*
LCGFT:	*Library of Congress Genre/Form Terms for Library and Archival Materials*
LCNAF:	Library of Congress/NACO Authority File
LCSH:	*Library of Congress Subject Headings*
MeSH:	*Medical Subject Headings*
NLM:	National Library of Medicine
NLP:	Natural Language Processing
NT:	Narrower Term
OWL:	Web Ontology Language
RDF:	Resource Description Framework
RT:	Related Term
SA:	See Also
SHM:	*Subject Headings Manual*
TGN:	*Getty Thesaurus of Geographic Names*
UF:	Used For
ULAN:	*Union List of Artist Names*
W3C:	World Wide Web Consortium

12.11 Discussion Questions and Exercises

- How is subject content expressed verbally in metadata?
- How are controlled vocabularies structured?
- Is a controlled vocabulary necessary or can natural language approaches suffice in some environments?
- How do ontologies assist in identifying concepts?
- How are tagging and keyword searching used with subject content?

12.12 Suggested Readings

Allemang, Dean, Jim Hendler, and Fabien Gandon. *Semantic Web for the Working Ontologist*. 3rd ed. New York: Association for Computing Machinery, 2020.

Berman, Sanford. *Prejudices and Antipathies: A Tract on the LC Subject Heads Concerning People*. Metuchen, NJ: Scarecrow, 1971.

Billey, Amber, Elizabeth Nelson, and Rebecca Uhl in collaboration with Core, eds. *Inclusive Cataloging: Histories, Context, and Reparative Approaches*. Chicago: ALA Editions, 2024.

Chan, Lois Mai. *Library of Congress Subject Headings: Principles and Applications*. 4th ed. Westport, CT: Libraries Unlimited, 2006.

Clark, Alexander, Chris Fox, and Shalom Lappin, eds. *The Handbook of Computational Linguistics and Natural Language Processing*. Malden, MA: Wiley-Blackwell, 2010.

Cleveland, Donald B., and Ana D. Cleveland. *Introduction to Indexing and Abstracting*. 4th ed. Santa Barbara, CA: Libraries Unlimited, 2013.

Eisenstein, Jacob. *Introduction to Natural Language Processing*. Cambridge, MA: The MIT Press, 2019.

Jacob, Elin K. "Ontologies and the Semantic Web." *Bulletin of the American Society for Information Science and Technology* 29, no. 4 (April/May 2003): 19–22. https://asistdl.onlinelibrary.wiley.com/doi/10.1002/bult.283.

Joudrey, Daniel N., Arlene G. Taylor, and David P. Miller. *Introduction to Cataloging and Classification*. 11th ed. Santa Barbara, CA: Libraries Unlimited, 2015.

Kao, Anne, and Stephen R. Poteet, eds. *Natural Language Processing and Text Mining*. London: Springer, 2007.

Lancaster, F. W. *Indexing and Abstracting in Theory and Practice*. 3rd ed. Champaign: University of Illinois, Graduate School of Library and Information Science, 2003.

Library of Congress, Catalogers Learning Workshop. "Library of Congress Subject Headings: Online Training." Janis L. Young and Daniel N. Joudrey, instructors. https://www.loc.gov/catworkshop/lcsh/.

Mann, Thomas. *The Oxford Guide to Library Research*. 4th ed. New York: Oxford University Press, 2015.

Noy, Natalya F., and Deborah L. McGuinness. *Ontology Development 101: A Guide to Creating Your First Ontology*. Stanford, CA: Knowledge Systems Laboratory, Stanford University, 2000. https://protege.stanford.edu/publications/ontology_development/ontology101.pdf.

Olson, Hope A. *The Power to Name: Locating the Limits of Subject Representation in Libraries*. Dordrecht, The Netherlands: Kluwer Academic, 2002.

Pustejovsky, James, and Amber Stubbs. *Natural Language Annotation for Machine Learning*. Sebastopol, CA: O'Reilly Media, 2013.

Quintarelli, Emanuele. "Folksonomies: Power to the People." Paper presented at the ISKO Italy-UniMIB Meeting, Milan, Italy, 2005 http://www.iskoi.org/doc/folksonomies.htm.

Sowmya, V. B. *Practical Natural Language Processing: A Comprehensive Guide to Building Real-World NLP Systems*. Sebastopol, CA: O'Reilly, 2020.

Svenonius, Elaine. *The Intellectual Foundation of Information Organization*. Cambridge, MA: MIT Press, 2000.

12.13 Notes

All URLs accessed April 2025.

1. David Crystal, *Internet Linguistics: A Student Guide* (London: Routledge, 2011), 98–103.
2. Thomas Mann, "'Cataloging Must Change!' and Indexer Consistency Studies: Misreading the Evidence at Our Peril," *Cataloging & Classification Quarterly* 23, nos. 3/4 (1997): 3–45.
3. "RDA Media Type: Concepts," Open Metadata Registry, http://metadataregistry.org/concept/list/vocabulary_id/37.html; *RDA: Resource Description & Access* (Chicago: American Library Association, 2010). Primarily accessed in the subscription product *RDA Toolkit*, http://www.rdatoolkit.org/.
4. "UNESCO Thesaurus," UNESCO, http://vocabularies.unesco.org/browser/thesaurus/en/.
5. "The American Folklore Society Ethnographic Thesaurus," Library of Congress Linked Data Service, https://id.loc.gov/vocabulary/ethnographicTerms.html.
6. NASA STI Program, *NASA Thesaurus* (Washington, DC: National Aeronautics and Space Administration, 2012), https://www.sti.nasa.gov/nasa-thesaurus/.
7. "Thesaurus," ERIC Educational Resources Information Center, https://eric.ed.gov/.

8. National Information Standards Organization, *ANSI/NISO Z39.19-2005 (R2010): Guidelines for the Construction, Format, and Management of Monolingual Thesauri* (Baltimore, MD: NISO Press, 2010), 43–57, http://groups.niso.org/higherlogic/ws/public/download/12591/z39-19-2005r2010.pdf.
9. Patricia Harpring, *Introduction to Controlled Vocabularies* (Los Angeles: Getty Research Institute, 2010), Section 3.1.1.1, https://www.getty.edu/research/publications/electronic_publications/intro_controlled_vocab/index.html.
10. "WordNet: A Lexical Database for English," Princeton University, http://wordnet.princeton.edu/.
11. Hans H. Wellisch, "Aboutness and Selection of Topics," Key Words 4, no. 2 (March/April 1996): 9.
12. Sanford Berman, *Joy of Cataloging* (Phoenix, AZ: Oryx, 1981); *Prejudices and Antipathies: A Tract on the LC Subject Heads Concerning People* (Metuchen, NJ: Scarecrow, 1971), http://www.sanfordberman.org/prejant.htm.
13. Hope A. Olson, *The Power to Name: Locating the Limits of Subject Representation in Libraries* (Dordrecht, The Netherlands: Kluwer Academic, 2002).
14. For example, Joan K. Marshall, *On Equal Terms: A Thesaurus for Nonsexist Indexing and Cataloging* (New York: Neal-Schuman, 1977); Doris H. Clack, *Black Literature Resources: Analysis and Organization* (New York: Marcel Dekker, 1975).
15. Berman, *Prejudices and Antipathies*.
16. Steven A. Knowlton, "Three Decades since Prejudices and Antipathies: A Study of Changes in the Library of Congress Subject Headings," *Cataloging & Classification Quarterly* 40, no. 2 (2005): 127–8.
17. For a variety of essays on equity, diversity, inclusion, and social justice efforts in cataloging, please see *Inclusive Cataloging: Histories, Context, and Reparative Approaches*, eds. Amber Billey, Elizabeth Nelson, and Rebecca Uhl (Chicago: ALA Editions, 2024)
18. *Change the Subject*, film by Sawyer Broadley, Jill Baron, Óscar Rubén Cornejo Cásares, Melissa Padilla, 2019, Dartmouth Digital Library Program, https://n2t.net/ark:/83024/d4hq3s42r.
19. Violet B. Fox, "Cataloging News," *Cataloging & Classification Quarterly* 54, no. 7 (2016): 506–20.
20. "ALA Welcomes Removal of Offensive 'Illegal aliens' Subject Headings," American Library Association, https://www.ala.org/news/2021/11/ala-welcomes-removal-offensive-illegal-aliens-subject-headings.
21. ANSI/NISO Z39.19-2005 (R2010), 37.
22. "Principles of the *Sears List of Subject Headings*," *Sears List of Subject Headings*, 23rd ed., ed. Violet B. Fox (Armenia, NY: H. W. Wilson/Grey House Publishing, 2022).
23. Mann, "'Cataloging Must Change!'" 9–10.
24. Working Group on the Future of Bibliographic Control, *On the Record: Report of the Library of Congress Working Group on the Future of Bibliographic Control* (Washington, DC: Library of Congress, 2008), http://www.loc.gov/bibliographic-future/news/lcwg-ontherecord-jan08-final.pdf.
25. James D. Anderson and Melissa A. Hofmann, "A Fully Faceted Syntax for Library of Congress Subject Headings," *Cataloging & Classification Quarterly* 43, no. 1 (2006): 8–9.
26. Library of Congress Cataloging Policy and Support Office, *Library of Congress Subject Headings Pre- vs. Post-Coordination and Related Issues* (Washington, DC: Library of Congress, 2007), http://www.loc.gov/catdir/cpso/pre_vs_post.pdf.
27. "Library of Congress Authorities," Library of Congress, http://authorities.loc.gov/.
28. All three authority lists can be found at: "Getty Vocabularies," Getty Research Institute, http://www.getty.edu/research/tools/vocabularies/.
29. *Classification Web Plus* (Washington, DC: Library of Congress, Cataloging Distribution Service), https://classweb.org/Menu/. [Requires subscription.]

30. For membership information, see "Get Involved with OCLC: Membership Resources," https://www.oclc.org/en/membership/member-resources.html. Subject headings are accessible through the OCLC WorldShare interface and through the OCLC Connexion client.
31. "Library of Congress Authorities," Library of Congress, http://authorities.loc.gov/.
32. "ID.LOC.GOV – Linked Data Services," Library of Congress, https://id.loc.gov/.
33. "Library of Congress Subject Headings PDF Files," Library of Congress, https://www.loc.gov/aba/publications/FreeLCSH/freelcsh.html.
34. *Subject Headings Manual*, 1st ed. (Washington, DC: Cataloging Distribution Service, Library of Congress, 2008).
35. "List of the Subject Headings Manual PDF Files," Library of Congress, https://www.loc.gov/aba/publications/FreeSHM/freeshm.html.
36. *Sears List of Subject Headings*, 23rd ed., ed. Violet B. Fox (Armenia, NY: H. W. Wilson/Grey House Publishing, 2022).
37. See https://www.hwwilsoninprint.com/sears.php for more information on print and subscription access to *Sears*.
38. *Sears: Lista de Encabezamientos de Materia: Nueva Traducción y Adaptación de la Lista Sears*, ed. Iván E. Calimano (New York: H. W. Wilson, 2008).
39. "Welcome to Medical Subject Headings," U.S. National Library of Medicine, https://www.nlm.nih.gov/mesh/meshhome.html.
40. "Medical Subject Headings Browser," U.S. National Library of Medicine, https://meshb.nlm.nih.gov/.
41. "Download MeSH Data," U.S. National Library of Medicine, https://www.nlm.nih.gov/databases/download/mesh.html.
42. Library of Congress, "Library of Congress Genre/Form Terms PDF Files," https://www.loc.gov/aba/publications/FreeLCGFT/freelcgft.html.
43. "Introduction to *Library of Congress Genre/Form Terms for Library and Archival Materials*," *Library of Congress Genre/Form Terms for Library and Archival Materials* (Washington, DC: Library of Congress, 2022), 1–3, https://www.loc.gov/aba/publications/FreeLCGFT/gftintro.pdf.
44. Library of Congress, "Introduction to *Library of Congress Demographic Group Terms*," *Library of Congress Demographic Group Terms Manual* (Washington, DC: Library of Congress, 2024), [2], https://www.loc.gov/aba/publications/FreeLCDGT/Introduction-to-LCDGT.pdf.
45. Library of Congress, "Library of Congress Demographic Group Terms PDF Files," https://www.loc.gov/aba/publications/FreeLCDGT/freelcdgt.html.
46. "*Art & Architecture Thesaurus* Online: About the AAT," Getty Research Institute, http://www.getty.edu/research/tools/vocabularies/aat/about.html.
47. "*Art & Architecture Thesaurus* Online," Getty Research Institute, http://www.getty.edu/research/tools/vocabularies/aat/.
48. "Still Life Painters," *Art & Architecture Thesaurus*, https://www.getty.edu/vow/AATFullDisplay?find=still+life+painters&logic=AND&note=&english=N&prev_page=1&subjectid=300266118.
49. Educational Resources Information Center (ERIC), *Thesaurus of ERIC Descriptors*, 14th ed. (Phoenix, AZ: Oryx, 2001).
50. "Thesaurus [Search]," ERIC Educational Resources Information Center, https://eric.ed.gov/.
51. "Thesaurus [Browser]," ERIC Educational Resources Information Center, https://eric.ed.gov/?ti=all.
52. "Purpose and Scope," ERIC Educational Resources Information Center, https://eric.ed.gov/?ti=all.
53. Rebecca J. Dean, "FAST: Development of Simplified Headings for Metadata," in *Authority Control in Organizing and Accessing Information: Definition and International Experience*, eds. Arlene G. Taylor and Barbara B. Tillett (New York: Haworth Information Press, 2004), 331–2.

54. "SearchFAST," OCLC Research, OCLC, http://fast.oclc.org/searchfast/.
55. "FAST Converter," OCLC Research, OCLC, https://fast.oclc.org/lcsh2fast/.
56. Alan Danskin, et al., "FAST the Inside Track: Where We Are, Where Do We Want to Be, and How Do We Get There?" *Cataloging & Classification Quarterly* 61, nos. 5/6 (2023): 506–24.
57. Nancy Cooey and Amy Phillips, "Library of Congress Subject Headings: A Post-Coordinated Future," *Cataloging & Classification Quarterly* 61, nos. 5/6 (2023): 491–505.
58. "Homosaurus: An International LGBTQ+ Linked Data Vocabulary," https://homosaurus.org/.
59. Elin K. Jacob, "Ontologies and the Semantic Web," *Bulletin of the American Society for Information Science and Technology* 29, no. 4 (April/May 2003): 19, https://asistdl.onlinelibrary.wiley.com/doi/10.1002/bult.283.
60. Tom Gruber, "Ontology," in *Encyclopedia of Database Systems*, eds. Ling Liu and M. Tamer Özsu (New York: Springer-Verlag, 2009), https://tomgruber.org/writing/definition-of-ontology.
61. Marcia Lei Zeng and Jian Qin, *Metadata*, 3rd ed. (Chicago: ALA, 2022), 127.
62. Jacob, "Ontologies and the Semantic Web," 19.
63. "OWL 2 Web Ontology Language Document Overview (Second Edition)," W3C, 2012, https://www.w3.org/TR/owl-overview/.
64. NASA STI, *NASA Thesaurus*, https://www.sti.nasa.gov/nasa-thesaurus/.
65. Example based on one mentioned briefly in Andreas Blumauer, "From Taxonomies over Ontologies to Knowledge Graphs," The Semantic Puzzle, blog posting, July 15, 2014, https://semantic-web.com/from-taxonomies-over-ontologies-to-knowledge-graphs/.
66. "OWL Web Ontology Language Overview," W3C, https://www.w3.org/TR/owl-features/.
67. "OWL 2 Web Ontology Language Primer (Second Edition)," W3C, 2012, https://www.w3.org/TR/owl2-primer/.
68. S. Nazim Ali, "Subject Relationship Between Articles Determined by Co-occurrence of Keywords in Citing and Cited Titles," *Journal of Information Science* 19, no. 3 (1993): 225–31.
69. Renee B. Bush, "A Bibliography of Monographic Works on Biomaterials and Biocompatibility," *Journal of Applied Biomaterials* 4, no. 2 (1993): 195–209.
70. Sujata Banerjee and Vibhu O. Mittal, "On the Use of Linguistic Ontologies for Accessing and Indexing Distributed Digital Libraries," in *Digital Libraries '94: Proceedings of the First Annual Conference on the Theory and Practice of Digital Libraries, June 19–21, 1994, College Station, Texas*, ed. John L. Schnase (College Station: Texas A&M University, 1994), https://www.jcdl.info/archived-conf-sites/dl94/paper/banerjee.html.
71. Banerjee and Mittal.
72. Cameron Hashemi-Pour, "BERT Language Model," TechTarget, https://www.techtarget.com/searchenterpriseai/definition/BERT-language-model.
73. Daniel Jurafsky and James H. Martin, *Speech and Language Processing*, 2nd ed. (Upper Saddle River, NJ: Pearson, 2009), 1–2.
74. Elaine Rich and Kevin Knight, *Artificial Intelligence*, 2nd ed. (New York: McGraw-Hill, 1991), 377–9.
75. Rich and Knight, 379–80; Jurafsky and Martin, *Speech and Language Processing*, 2–3; and James Pustejovsky and Amber Stubbs, *Natural Language Annotation for Machine Learning* (Sebastopol, CA: O'Reilly Media, 2013), 3–4.
76. Michalis Gerolimos, "Tagging for Libraries: A Review of the Effectiveness of Tagging Systems for Library Catalogs," *Journal of Library Metadata* 13, no. 1 (2013): 37.
77. Thomas Vander Wal, "Folksonomy Coinage and Definition," *Vanderwal.net* (blog), 2007, http://vanderwal.net/folksonomy.html.
78. Thomas Gruber, "Ontology of Folksonomy: A Mash-Up of Apples and Oranges," *International Journal on Semantic Web and Information Systems* 3, no. 1 (2007): 3–4, http://tomgruber.org/writing/ontology-of-folksonomy.htm.

79. Emanuele Quintarelli, "Folksonomies: Power to the People," ISKO Italia Documenti, 2005, http://www.iskoi.org/doc/folksonomies.htm.
80. Quintarelli.
81. Shuheng Wu, "Implementing Bibliographic Enhancement Data in Academic Library Catalogs: An Empirical Study," *Cataloging & Classification Quarterly* 61, nos. 3–4 (2023): 314.
82. Sharon Yang, "Tagging for Subject Access: A Glimpse into Current Practices by Vendors, Libraries and Users," *Computers in Libraries* 32, no. 9 (2012): 20–1.
83. Isola Ajiferuke, Jamie Goodfellow, and Adeola Opesade, "Characteristics and Effectiveness of Tags in Public Library Online Public Access Catalogues," *Canadian Journal of Information and Library Science* 39, nos. 3–4 (2015): 273.
84. Brinna Michael and Myung-Ja Han, "User Tagging Behaviors in an OPAC," *Library Resources & Technical Services* 64, no. 1 (2020): 10.
85. Philip Hider and Gemma Steele, "LibraryThing and Literary Works Revisited," *Library Resources & Technical Services* 65, no. 3 (2021): 123.

Chapter 13

Systems for Categorization

In this chapter, we discuss another approach to subject access—using categories or classification systems, rather than words or tags. Both approaches attempt to translate the aboutness of resources into artificial subject languages to bring together like materials, but each approach does this in its own way. When using verbal techniques, topical words or tags are assigned to a resource; in systems for categorization, a resource is placed into the most suitable group available. These groupings, which may or may not be represented by notations or symbols, are often based on disciplines or broad forms of knowledge.

Categorization has a much longer history than controlled vocabularies. Philosophers have tried to categorize knowledge for many centuries. Classification is a form of categorization, but over the last two centuries classification (particularly bibliographic classification) has come to be associated with assigning some kind of notation to physical information resources; this is reinforced by the tendency of many to confound the ideas of classification notations and call numbers. (Call numbers are not addressed in this chapter. For more information about call numbers, see Appendix B.) In the thinking of some, the connection to categorization has been lost. However, the categories devised by philosophers in past centuries are the bases for the major classification schemes still in use today.

Classification theory has not received as much attention in the United States as it has in India, the United Kingdom, and some other countries. There has been a tendency in the United States to see classification only as a location device for the arrangement of physical resources on a shelf (exemplified by the phrase "mark 'em and park 'em"). Nevertheless, categorizing resources, including online ones, is a useful and necessary part of the organizing process, whether or not full advantage of it is taken.

13.1 What are Categories, Classifications, and Taxonomies?

The concepts *classification* and *categorization* are often used interchangeably, but are they the same? The answer is not clear. This question is further complicated by the resurgence of the term *taxonomy* for systems of categorization that are used online and in intranet systems. Before moving on to various approaches to grouping similar resources or ideas, it may be helpful to discuss and distinguish among the terms: **categorization**, **classification**, and **taxonomy**.

Here are some definitions provided by the *Oxford English Dictionary*:[1]

- ***Categorization***: the action of categorizing; classification.

- *Category*: a class or division, in any general scheme of classification.
- *Classification*: the results of classifying; the action of classifying or arranging in classes, according to shared characteristics or perceived affinities; assignment to an appropriate class or classes; a category to which something is assigned; a class.
- *Class*: a set or category of things having some related properties or attributes in common, grouped together, and differentiated from others under a general name or description; a kind, a sort; an inclusive or general taxonomic category.

Merriam-Webster defines *classification* as the "the act or process of classifying; systematic arrangement in groups or categories according to established criteria; *specifically*: taxonomy; class, category."[2] Ultimately, neither source helps to distinguish between classification and categorization.

This lack of clarity is not confined to dictionaries. The two words *classification* and *categorization* are sometimes used interchangeably in the library and information science (LIS) literature. Some authors, however, are more rigorous in their use of the terms. Classification has specific connotations in libraries; thus, over the years some distinctions have been made. In general, categorization is broader and more abstract than classification; categorization is a cognitive function that is used to group concepts, rather than a structured process used to systematically arrange physical resources. Categorization can be seen as an amorphous or less well-defined grouping, whereas classification is a comprehensive hierarchical structure for organizing information resources on linear shelves. Elin Jacob points out that in the LIS field the term *classification* can have several senses. The term may refer to three distinct but related concepts:

- a system of classes, ordered according to a predetermined set of principles and used to organize a set of entities;
- a group or class in a classification system; and
- the process of assigning entities to classes in a classification system.[3]

Jacob also compares *categorization* and *classification*:

> While traditional classification is rigorous in that it mandates that an entity either is or is not a member of a particular class, the process of categorization is flexible and creative and draws nonbinding associations between entities—associations that are based not on a set of predetermined principles but on the simple recognition of similarities that exist across a set of entities.[4]

Christopher Dent also attempts to distinguish between the terms *classification* and *categorization* to countermand the lack of precision found in the LIS literature:

> In my view *classification* is an artificial (synthetic, non-fundamental) process by which we organize things for presentation or later access. It involves the arbitrary creation of a group of classes, which have explicit definitions and may be arranged in a hierarchy. In other words, a class is strictly defined and once inhabited the inhabitants

can be enumerated. *Categorization* on the other hand is a natural process in the sense that humans do it as part of their cognitive fundament. It is … an act of simplification to make apprehension and comprehension of the environment more efficient. Categories spring up out of necessity and because they are designed to replace the details of definition are themselves resistant to definition.[5]

To put it more succinctly, Dent concludes, a class "is a defined grouping of entities in which the members fulfill the definition of the class and can be listed" and a category "is a cognitive label applied to a non-enumerable grouping of entities wherein membership is determined by typicality amongst the members and not some overarching definition."[6] Although few are as precise as Dent or Jacob in differentiating between the two concepts, these distinctions are helpful in understanding the discussions of categories and classes that follow.

Complicating this discussion is the renewed popularity of the term *taxonomy*. Definitions of taxonomy abound in the literature, and some of those definitions contradict each other. Amy Warner says that the terms *taxonomies, thesauri,* and *classification systems* are synonyms. They are "organized lists of words and phrases, or notation systems, that are used to initially tag content, and then to find it through navigation or search."[7] Similar confusion with definitions is indicated in the *Montague Institute Review*: "A taxonomy is a system for naming and organizing things into groups that share similar characteristics."[8] These definitions do not include the necessity for hierarchy. However, others, such as Thomas Wason, argue that hierarchy remains typical: "A taxonomy is a knowledge map of a topic, typically realized as a controlled vocabulary of terms and or phrases. A taxonomy is an orderly classification of information according to presumed natural relationships. … The most typical form of a taxonomy is a hierarchy."[9] F. W. Lancaster, in decrying the "rediscovery of wheels" that he saw in "new" concepts, wrote:

> My biggest complaint, however, is the fact that the noun *classification* has virtually been replaced by (shudder!) *taxonomy*, (double shudder!!) *ontology*, or even (triple shudder!!!) *taxonomized set of terms*. The way these terms are defined in recent articles clearly shows that they are used synonymously with *classification scheme*.[10]

The word *taxonomy* comes from the Greek *taxis* (arrangement, order) and *nomos* (law). Taxonomies have existed in the strict hierarchical world of science since Aristotle, in *Historia Animalium*, created a taxonomy of the animal kingdom. The most famous scientific taxonomy, however, is Linnaeus's *Systema Naturae*, a classification of plants and animals from 1735. The taxonomies being constructed today for use, though, do not necessarily follow such strict rules, nor are they always hierarchical. What they do seem to have in common is categories. Therefore, the discussions of categorization in this chapter are also applicable to taxonomies.

Lists of taxonomies that one finds online often include traditional classification schemes, subject heading lists, folksonomies, and ontologies, as well as subject-specific tools that actually call themselves *taxonomies*. Examples of the last are the Taxonomy of Educational Technology[11] and GRIN Taxonomy[12] from the U.S. National Plant Germplasm System. Some taxonomies are proprietary to the organizations that created them and are under copyright, so they may not be freely used in other situations.

13.2 Theory of Categorization

It was mentioned in Chapter 1 that human beings seem to have a basic drive to organize and that children begin to categorize early in their development. For example, it is essential that children learn to distinguish between things that are and are not edible. At later stages, children begin to categorize toys and other objects by color, shape, purpose, their own notions of value, or some other criteria. Adults have a great need for categories too. Categories abound in daily life—from the grocery store to the office to our homes. Most people, although they may not even realize it, categorize the assorted items found in their homes and offices every day; for example, few would place their forks and knives in the living room, because eating utensils are associated with kitchens—not with couches, bookcases, or photos of grandma.

Theories of categories go back at least as far as the ancient Greeks. For example, the ancient philosopher and mathematician Pythagoras categorized the cycle of life as consisting of *birth, growth, decay, death, absorption*, and *metamorphosis*. Later, Empedocles placed every physical thing into one of four elements: *earth, air, fire*, and *water*. The most influential discussion of categories comes from Aristotle and his attempt to organize the objects and ideas of the world.

13.2.1 The Rise and Fall of the Classical Theory of Categories

The roots of contemporary classification systems can be traced back to Aristotle's "classical theory of categories." The word *category* comes from the Greek *kategorein*, meaning to accuse, to assert, to predicate.[13] Aristotle's theory reflected this definition; his categories were ten states of being or ten things that can be expressed about an object or an idea. His categories are

- Substance
- Quantity
- Quality
- Relation
- Place
- Time
- Position
- State
- Action
- Affection[14]

Aristotle's theory placed objects or ideas into the same category based on what they have in common. This approach went unchallenged until the mid-twentieth century because, as George Lakoff says, categories were thought to be well understood. Until then, a category was considered to be an abstract container with strict binary membership, that is, things belonged either inside or outside of the container; there were no grey or fuzzy areas. Categories were also defined as mutually exclusive groups, that is, things could belong to one and only one category, and the shared common attributes of the group members were what defined the category.[15] This narrow view of categories, however, began to change about seventy-five years ago.

13.2.2 Cracks in the Classical Theory of Categories

A brief history of the research of the second half of the twentieth century will serve to illuminate the process of categorizing and its relationship to classification. This history is summarized from

Lakoff's *Women, Fire, and Dangerous Things: What Categories Reveal about the Mind*.[16] Cracks began to appear in the classical theory of categories in 1953, when Ludwig Wittgenstein showed that a category like *game* does not fit the classical mold. This category has no single collection of common properties. For example, a game may be for education, amusement, or competition, and it may involve luck or skill. The category also has no fixed boundary because new kinds of games can be added to it. Wittgenstein proposed that since there is no one attribute that is common to all games, **family resemblances** (a complex network of similarities and relationships) unite *games* into what we call a category. Just as members of a family have similarities, so do games.

J. L. Austin, in a paper published in 1961, extended Wittgenstein's analysis to the study of words. He wondered why we call different things by the same name (e.g., foot of a mountain, foot of a list, person's foot). Should not *mountain*, *list*, and *person* be in the same category if they all have a foot? But there are times when words do belong in the same category even though they share no common properties (e.g., *ball*, *bat*, and *umpire* can all go into the category *baseball*). Austin, like Wittgenstein, helped to show that traditional views of categories were inadequate.

Lotfi Zadeh contributed **fuzzy set theory** to the chipping away of the classical theory of categories. He noted that some categories are well defined while others are not. One either is or is not a member of a club, but whether one is tall or not depends to some extent upon the observer. The category *tall* is graded—one may be neither clearly tall nor clearly short; and a shorter person, looking at someone of medium height, might say that the person is tall. In 1965, Zadeh devised a form of set theory to include gradations of membership in categories.

Floyd Lounsbury's studies of Native American kinship systems also chipped away at the classical theory. He found that among various groups the same name (category) is used to express the kinship relationships of several different types of relatives. For example, in one group, uncles, great-uncles, and nephews on one's mother's side of the family are all called by the same word. The challenge to classical theory is that what seem to be definite and distinct categories in one culture and language are not the same categories in another culture and language.

Brent Berlin and Paul Kay (also mentioned in Chapter 11) published their work on color in 1969. They found that there could be anywhere from 2 to 11 expressions for the basic colors in different languages. (In recent years, some have identified a 12th basic color in various languages, but the color is not always the same.)[17] Although most people around the world can physiologically perceive and conceptually differentiate all 11 or 12 basic colors, depending on their language, they may not be able to express all of them as separate words. For example, in traditional Welsh, the word *glas* was used for blue but also for some shades that English speakers might refer to as *green* or *grey*. Again, it is shown that language and culture can play a significant role in the establishment of categories. In 1978, drawing on work done in neurophysiology, Paul Kay and Chad McDaniel concluded that human biology influences perception of color. They drew on fuzzy set theory to determine that in all cultures that have fewer than 11 basic colors, cold colors always include green, blue, and black, whereas warm colors always include red, orange, yellow, and white. Thus, color categories are not quite as arbitrary as some might infer from the Berlin and Kay studies.

Roger Brown began the study of **basic level categories**. His work published in 1965 observed that there is a first level at which children learn categories (e.g., *flower* for any variety of flower). Yet, there are many names that can be used for such categories; some are more specific (e.g., *violet*, *daffodil*) and some more general (e.g., *plant*). Brown considered the children's level to be the "natural" level, whereas the more specific and more general levels were viewed as "achievements of the imagination." Brent Berlin and associates, in research on naming plants and animals published from 1969 to 1977, also showed that there seems to be a universal level at which humans name things, and for plants and animals it is more likely to be at the genus level (e.g., *oak*, not *tree* and not *Sawtooth oak*); although this might not hold true for someone with experience only in an urban environment or for someone whose training has led to a more precisely honed level. It can be suggested that certain basic levels of categories have to do with being human and are the same across cultures.

13.2.3 Prototype Theory

The major crack in the classical theory of categories came when Eleanor Rosch developed ***prototype theory*** with her work between 1973 and 1981. She theorized that if, as classical theory states, categories are defined only by properties that all members share, then no members should be better examples of the category than any other members. She further theorized that if categories are defined only by properties that all members share, then categories should be independent of the humans doing the categorizing. She found that, contrary to classical theory, categories do have best examples (i.e., prototypes). For example, Rosch found in her research that people thought that a robin was a better example of *bird* than was an ostrich. And she found that human capacities do play a role in categorization (e.g., for someone 5 feet tall, there are many more tall people in the world than there are for someone 6 feet tall); this is related to Zadeh's fuzzy set theory. Ad hoc categories also figure in here. Ad hoc categories are those that are made up spontaneously. Different people will put different things into a category such as *camping gear* depending upon their experience, where they are going, how they will camp, and so forth.

Because the most widely used classification schemes in the United States are based upon the classical theory of categories, classifiers using them are sometimes quite frustrated to find that they have a subject concept that does not fit neatly into one of the categories. Multifaceted, cross-disciplinary information resources are not easily accommodated by the structure and rigidity of classical categories.

13.3 Bibliographic Classification

Classification, as noted earlier, is a structured system of categories used to collocate similar ideas or objects. One type of classification is ***bibliographic classification***, which came into being for the purpose of arranging and retrieving information resources and later became used for arranging metadata records in library catalogs and other information retrieval tools. Bibliographic classification schemes (henceforth referred to as *classification schemes* or *classifications*) in the form that we know them are relatively new in the history of information organization.* Early depositories

---

* The following is a quick review of some material covered in Chapter 2.

of recorded information usually had some arrangement: title, broad subject, chronology, author, order of acquisition, or size. At the Alexandrian library, Callimachus's pinakes had at least 10 broad categories (or main classes). Arrangement within the classes tended to be by author. This seemed to be a model for arrangement of catalogs and bibliographies into the Early Middle Ages.

During the High Middle Ages, when monastery libraries became the keepers of books, there was little need for classification because libraries were so small. In the Late Middle Ages, the universities that developed began to divide their books according to the *Trivium* (Grammar, Rhetoric, Logic) and the *Quadrivium* (Arithmetic, Music, Geometry, Astronomy), the seven subjects taught in the medieval university. But within the seven classes, the books had fixed shelf locations.

Starting in the sixteenth century, librarians devised different classification schemes. Often these were based upon philosophers' systems of knowledge. However, none caught on, and fixed locations continued to predominate. With the rapid growth of libraries in the nineteenth century, librarians felt a need for better arrangement so that the content of the collections would be more apparent to users. Philosopher Francis Bacon in the early seventeenth century had divided knowledge into three basic "faculties": history (natural, civil, literary, ecclesiastical); philosophy (including theology); and works of imagination (poetry, fables, etc.). This scheme had widespread influence, and numerous classification schemes were based upon it. The most famous was that of Thomas Jefferson, who classified his own library before he eventually sold it to the Library of Congress as the basis of a new collection in 1815.

In 1876 Melvil Dewey published what later became known as the *Dewey Decimal Classification* (DDC), and shortly thereafter, Charles Ammi Cutter began work on his *Expansive Classification*. Paul Otlet and Henri La Fontaine began development of the *Universal Decimal Classification* (UDC) in 1895, based on the fifth edition of DDC. At the beginning of the twentieth century, Library of Congress created its own classification (LCC), based loosely on the main class outline of Cutter's *Expansive Classification*. S. R. Ranganathan created his *Colon Classification* (CC) in the early 1930s and adapted the word *facet* as a term to indicate the various subparts of the whole classification. From the early 1970s and continuing through today, the Bliss Bibliographic Classification Association has been developing the second edition of the *Bibliographic Classification* (BC2); it is a total reworking of the classification that was created by Henry Bliss in the first half of the twentieth century and published in four volumes in the United States between 1940 and 1953. BC2 is so thoroughly revised that it is an entirely new scheme, based on the faceting principles developed over much of the twentieth century by Ranganathan and, later, the Classification Research Group in the United Kingdom.

Although classification is mostly associated with arranging tangible resources on shelves, it is also a useful way to divide large databases. It offers an alternative to alphabetical subdivision. And if several databases choose the same classification scheme, it is possible to enable subject searching across systems. Classification can also be used as an intermediary between different languages. The notations of a classification are not tied to any specific language, so their meanings can be presented in whatever language is appropriate. The DDC, for example, has, or shortly will have, translations in Arabic, French, German, Greek, Icelandic, Indonesian, Italian, Norwegian, Russian, Spanish, Swedish, and Vietnamese. The UDC is also multilingual; there are recent printed full editions in English, French, Portuguese, and Spanish, with online partial editions in over 50 more languages. The United States-based LCC has not yet moved in a multilingual direction.

Traugott Koch has suggested that there are four broad varieties of classification schemes.[18]

- **Universal schemes**: schemes that cover the universe of knowledge (e.g., DDC, UDC, LCC, CC, BC2)
- **National general schemes:** like universal schemes, but designed for use in a single country (e.g., *Nederlandse Basisclassificatie* in the Netherlands and the *Sveriges Allmänna Biblioteksförening* in Sweden)
- **Subject specific schemes**: schemes that cover a particular subject area or knowledge domain (e.g., the *Xwi7xwa* (pronounced "whei-wha") *Classification Scheme* for Indigenous knowledge; *Iconclass* for art resources; and the *National Library of Medicine Classification* and the *Mathematics Subject Classification*, both covering their respective subject areas)
- **Home-grown schemes**: schemes created to address the needs of a particular service or institution

There are a few homegrown schemes in print that are interesting and useful in particular contexts. One example is "Metis: Library Classification for Children," a set of 26 broad categories labeled A to Z established by four librarians who worked at the Ethical Culture School in New York City.[19] Some others have adapted it, but the original site is down. Another example is *A Classification System for Libraries of Judaica*, now in its third edition.[20] It is kept up to date by people who use it. For example, after the publication of the third edition, a synagogue librarian created a Holocaust expansion that was posted online. Like many other home-grown schemes, this expansion seems to have disappeared from the web.[21]

13.3.1 Components of Classification Schemes

Classification schemes typically comprise four major components: schedules, notation, an index, and instructions. The ***schedules*** are lists of topics organized into a conceptual framework, where the topics are arranged in relation to other topics in the same discipline and subject area. Schedules are the heart of the classification; they comprise main classes and all the subtopics that fall within them, usually arranged from broader concepts to more specific concepts as you move further into a subject area. Hope Olson and John Boll state that schedules consist of the following:

- A verbal description, topic by topic, of the things and concepts that can be represented in or by the scheme.
- An arrangement of these verbal descriptions in classed or logical order that is intended to permit a meaningful arrangement of topics and that will be convenient to users.[22]

They include captions, notes, cross-references, footnotes, and notation. Some schemes also include ***tables***, which are independent listings of notations for concepts that can be appended or added to the notations from the schedules. Tables comprise listings of concepts such as forms/genres, geographic areas, chronological periods, and languages.

Notation refers to the symbols (most often alphanumeric) used to represent a topic in the classification scheme that provide a logical order. Notation may be referred to as either *pure* or *mixed*.

Pure Notation (DDC)	Caption	Mixed Notation (LCC)
394.2646	Halloween	GT4965

Pure notation uses only one type of symbol, either letters or numbers. For example, the DDC uses a pure notation of 0–9. That numerical base puts some limitations on the structure of the scheme; no part of the classification can contain more than 10 things unless special provisions allow for concepts to extend across multiple spans of numbers or additional hierarchical levels are introduced. Thus, using a purely numerical base may result in lengthier numbers to precisely express highly specific concepts. **Mixed notation** allows for multiple types of symbols to be used. In LCC, the combination of capital letters from the Roman alphabet and Arabic numbers (as both whole numbers and decimals) results in having much more room in which to place concepts. The alphabet has 26 letters. In most places in LCC, letters are doubled, giving the potential for up to 676 divisions versus the 100 available to DDC; if three letters are used, LCC could offer up to 17,576 sections versus DDC's 1,000 sections! LCC has not come close to using this amount of "real estate."

The benefit of using letters and/or numbers in the notation is the self-evident order of those symbols (0–9 and A–Z). It is therefore relatively easy to shelve items labeled with alphanumeric symbols. If other types of symbols are incorporated (such as punctuation marks, letters from other alphabets, use of both uppercase and lowercase letters) then extensive filing rules will be required to order the items. For example, without extensive documentation would you know that the following UDC classification numbers are in the correct filing order? I certainly wouldn't!

> 621+624
> 621/622
> 621
> 621:622
> 621(41)
> 621.1

An *index*, in this context, is the key to a classification scheme. It lists the topics represented in the scheme (along with synonyms) in alphabetical order and points to the notation in the classification system where a given topic may be found. Because topics are scattered across the schedules into different disciplinary approaches, there is often a one-to-many relationship between major topics and classification notations. The following is a brief excerpt from the DDC relative index.

Hallmarks	929.9
Halloween	394.2646
Handicrafts	745.5941646
Photographic images	779.93942646
Hallstatt period	936.02[23]

In addition, instructions for the schemes are needed. Every classification is more complicated than simply going to the list and finding a number. Instructions are needed to provide general principles of application, priorities, guidelines for making decisions among more than one notation, and more. Some major bibliographic classifications have separate manuals that give further instructions and examples. These may be written by the administrative organizations responsible for the maintenance of the schemes, by independent parties, or by both.

13.3.2 Hierarchical and Enumerative Classification

As most of the schemes mentioned above were devised before anyone challenged the classical theory of categories, these schemes are firmly based in hierarchical arrangements (even the faceted CC and BC2 can be somewhat hierarchical within their individual sub-categories). **Hierarchical classification** begins with broad, top-level categories, which branch into any number of subordinate levels, moving from the general to the specific (creating the familiar tree structure associated with hierarchies). The partitions from one level to the next are based on *characteristics of division*—a chosen attribute that allows a larger group of entities to be divided into smaller more specific categories. An illustration might be helpful to explain this concept.

Figure 13.1 depicts a simple literature class with three characteristics of division (period, form, and language). At the top, there is a class representing all of literature. This is a massive class containing everything considered to be literature; it is of little use to anyone except those with the tiniest collections of literature. For nearly every institution, literature needs to be divided further. A characteristic of division must be chosen and then applied. This results in the second level of the hierarchy. The characteristic of division used first is *language*. This results in the massive top-level class being divided into more manageable chunks. This means all literature written in the various languages of the world would be collocated together and thus separated from literatures in other languages. Division by language only goes so far; further division is usually needed. In the third level, the language classes are divided into various forms (poetry, drama, fiction, humor, letters, etc.). *Form* is the second characteristic of division, with the third being *time periods* (only applied

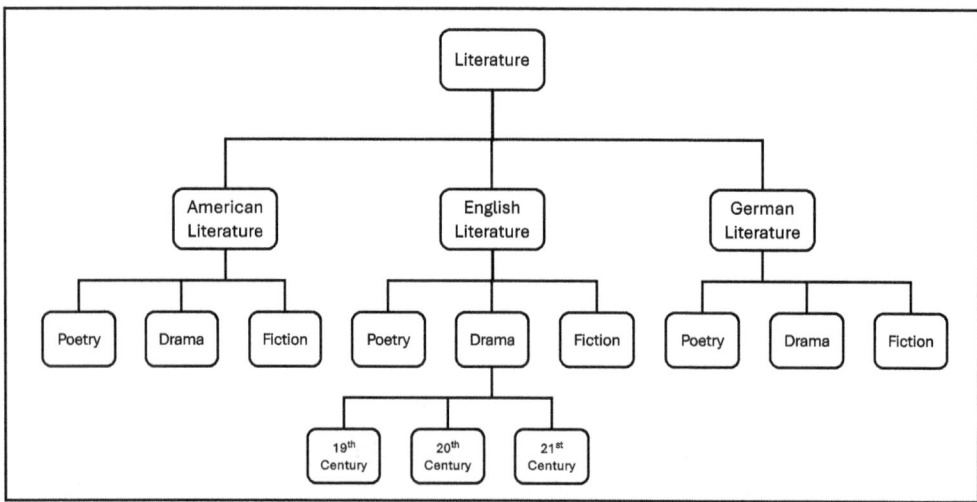

Figure 13.1 Literature Hierarchy Illustrating Three Characteristics of Division.

under English drama in the figure, but period would also be applied to every other grouping in the third level as well). As division continues, categories become increasingly specific as they get smaller.

To be consistent, the class requires a ***citation order***—a set sequence of the characteristics of division. The classification should not divide all American literature by form first and period second, but Italian literature by period first and then by form. In this example the established citation order is

1. Language
2. Form
3. Period

Citation order determines what characteristics get collocated and which end up being scattered. In this figure, preference is given to language groupings, meaning all literature in German is brought together, all literature in Russian is together, all Thai literature is collocated. This does mean, however, that not all poetry is together. There are clusters of poetry within each language, but no single place for *all* poetry. Likewise, there is no place for all twentieth-century literature (no matter the language or form). Period and form, as lesser priorities, are scattered to varying degrees depending on the citation order. This is why choosing a citation order is critical when designing a classification scheme; it affects what ultimately sits together on the shelves.

It is easy to see the hierarchical structures inherent in the DDC, which starts with 10 main classes, divides each of those by 10 (creating 100 divisions), divides each of the divisions into 10 more (creating 1,000 sections), divides each of those into 10 subsections (10,000), and so on into potential infinity (see Figures 13.2 and 13.3).

The same classification schemes are also enumerative. ***Enumerative classification*** attempts to assign a designation for every subject concept (both single and composite) needed in the system. All schemes have elements that are enumerative, but some have more than others. LCC is much more enumerative than DDC because it attempts to list a notation for every possible topic (or to allow for alphabetical arrangement of topics) within its 21 main classes (see Figure 13.4).

Although DDC lists basic numbers in its schedules, it allows for more complex numbers to be constructed through several other sources (tables, primarily); LCC, on the other hand, includes this level of detail directly in its schedules (see Figure 13.5). UDC, originally based on DDC, was hierarchical and enumerative at its base when it was designed; it has now developed into a scheme that is somewhat closer to what is called a *faceted classification* through the addition of number-building techniques.

Dewey Decimal Classification

10 Main Classes

000	Computer science, information & general works
100	Philosophy & psychology
200	Religion
300	Social sciences
400	Language
500	Science
600	Technology
700	Arts & recreation
800	Literature
900	History & geography

An Example of the Hundred Divisions

600	Technology
600	Technology
610	Medicine & health
620	Engineering
630	Agriculture
640	Home & family management
650	Management & public relations
660	Chemical engineering
670	Manufacturing
680	Manufacture for specific uses
690	Construction of buildings

An Example of the Thousand Sections

600	Technology
640	Home & family management
640	Home and family management
641	Food and drink
642	Meals and table service
643	Housing and household equipment
644	Household utilities
645	Household furnishings
646	Sewing, clothing, management of personal and family life
647	Management of public households (Institutional housekeeping)
648	Housekeeping
649	Child rearing; home care of people with illnesses and disabilities by family and friends

Figure 13.2 An Example of Hierarchical Arrangement in the *Dewey Decimal Classification* (DDC). (Source: WebDewey, OCLC.)

```
600         Technology
640                   Home & family management
641                              Food and drink
641.2                                   Beverages (Drinks)
641.3                                   Food
641.4                                   Food preservation and storage
641.5                                   Cooking
641.51                                          Beginner and gourmet cooking
641.52-641.54                                   Cooking specific meals
641.52                                                  First meal of the day
641.53                                                  Light meals
641.54                                                  Main meal of the day
641.55                                          Money-saving and timesaving cooking
641.56                                          Cooking for special situations, reasons, ages
641.57                                          Quantity, institutional, travel, outdoor cooking
641.58                                          Cooking with specific fuels, appliances, utensils
641.59                                          Cooking characteristic of specific geographic
                                                    environments, ethnic cooking
641.6                                   Cooking specific materials
641.7                                   Specific cooking processes and techniques
641.8                                   Cooking specific kinds of dishes and preparing beverages
```

Figure 13.3 An Example of Additional Subdivisions Found in the DDC. (Source: WebDewey, OCLC.)

Library of Congress Classification

Main Class Outline

A	General Works
B	Philosophy. Psychology. Religion
C	Auxiliary Sciences Of History
D	World History
E	History Of The Americas
F	History Of The Americas
G	Geography. Anthropology. Recreation
H	Social Sciences
J	Political Science
K	Law
L	Education
M	Music And Books On Music
N	Fine Arts
P	Language And Literature
Q	Science
R	Medicine
S	Agriculture
T	Technology
U	Military Science
V	Naval Science
Z	Bibliography. Library Science. Information Resources (General)

Figure 13.4 Main Classes in the *Library of Congress Classification* (LCC). (Source: Library of Congress.)

TX703-726.3	Cookbooks
TX703-713	Early to 1800
TX714-725	1800-
TX714	General recipe collections
	Class here works consisting of collected recipes not primarily of a regional, ethnic, or international nature, nor using a specific ingredient or method of cooking, in which the technique of cooking is not emphasized
	For treatises see TX651
	For ethnic or regional cooking see TX714-725
	For international cooking see TX725.A1
	American
	For French, German, etc., cookbooks published in America, see TX719, TX721, etc.
TX715	General works
TX715.2.A-Z	By style of cooking, A-Z
TX715.2.A47	African American cooking
TX715.2.C34	California style
	Hawaiian style see TX724.5.H3
TX715.2.L68	Louisiana style
TX715.2.M53	Midwestern style
TX715.2.N48	New England style
TX715.2.P32	Pacific Northwest style
	Pennsylvania Dutch style see TX721
TX715.2.S68	Southern style
TX715.2.S69	Southwestern style
TX715.2.W47	Western style
TX715.6	Canadian
TX715.8	Greenlandic
	Latin American
TX716.A1	General works
TX716.A3-Z	By region or country, A-Z
TX717	English
TX717.2	Celtic
...	[... other regions of the world]
	Other
TX725.A1	International
TX725.A3-Z	By region or country, A-Z
	Including Africa, Australia, Middle East, etc.
TX725.M628	Middle East
(TX725.N36)	Near East see TX725.M628
	Cooking using alcoholic beverages
TX726	Wine. Liquors
TX726.2	Cider
TX726.3	Beer

Figure 13.5 An Example of Hierarchical and Enumerative Arrangement Found in LCC. (Source: Library of Congress, *Classification Web Plus*.)

13.3.3 Faceted Classification

Faceted classification, like hierarchical/enumerative schemes, attempts to include all possible subjects, but it does not do this by creating a singular place in a hierarchy for each topic (with its own specified number). Faceted classification is made up of many discrete topics. It is an attempt to divide the universe of knowledge into its component parts and then to gather those parts into individual ***facets*** (or categories). Within each facet, topics are assigned an individual notation. When the cataloger assigns a classification notation to an information resource, the notations assigned to each subtopic in the resource are identified and then strung together, in the appropriate order, to create a multidimensional classification.

This concept of faceted classification was named first by Ranganathan in his explanation of his *Colon Classification* (CC). CC provides lists of symbols for single concepts, with rules for combining them into complex concepts. This approach is also referred to as *analytico-synthetic classification* because the classification is established through an analysis of topics into component parts and then notation is synthesized from those parts.

Ranganathan posited five fundamental categories that can be used to illustrate the facets of a subject. These categories are often referred to by the initialism ***PMEST***.

- **Personality (P)**: "the something in question";[24] an entity; the focal point or most specific aspect of the subject
- **Matter (M)**: what the entity is made of or a component part
- **Energy (E)**: an action, activity, change, operation, or process
- **Space (S)**: where the entity/personality is located or where something takes place
- **Time (T)**: a time frame for the entity or when something happens

To illustrate the fundamental categories, we can look at a topic like "wooden furniture design in eighteenth-century America," which contains all five. Furniture is the focal subject or entity. The furniture is made of wood; thus, it belongs in matter. Design is an action, so it constitutes the energy facet. Space is the United States, and the period is the eighteenth century. If each facet has a specific notation (e.g., perhaps 28 for furniture, 4 for wood), then these notations can be strung together, according to a designated formula.

Ranganathan developed facet formulas for each disciplinary area in CC, which may include multiple rounds and levels of some of the fundamental categories. These formulas provide a clearly defined citation order, preventing inconsistency. In CC, the following is an example of a facet formula for education topics: [P] [E] [2P] [2P2] [S] [T].

Fundamental Category	Facet
Personality [P]	Educand [i.e., ones to be educated]
Energy [E]	Problem
2nd Round Personality [2P]	Subject matter
2nd Round Personality 2nd level [2P2]	Method
Space [S]	Location
Time [T]	Period

As should be evident by this example, not every fundamental category is necessary in every facet formula, and some fundamental categories may appear multiple times (e.g., 2P for a second round of personality).

CC uses punctuation marks between the notations as *facet indicators*, which help to identify the relationships among the facets. In the earliest versions of the scheme, Ranganathan primarily used the colon (:) as the facet indicator, which gave the scheme its name. By the middle of the twentieth century, he realized that a more elaborate system of facet indicators was needed to avoid confusion, and additional pieces of punctuation were adopted for this purpose.

Fundamental Category	Facet Indicator
Personality [P]:	Comma (,)
Matter [M]:	Semicolon (;)
Energy [E]:	Colon (:)
Space [S]:	Dot/Period (.)
Time [T]:	Inverted comma/Single quotation mark (')

By using the facet formula for education (above), consulting the CC schedules for the various facets, and assigning the appropriate facet indicators, a classification number can be created. A topic such as "teaching library classification using exercises in 2025 for post-graduate education at a university in Massachusetts" is transformed into **T45:3(2:51),4.7385'P25**.

Notation	Meaning
T	Education
45	University; Post-graduate
:3	Teaching
(2:51)	Library Science; Classification
,4	Heuristic method
.7385	Massachusetts
'P25	2025

The typically long and complex notations created in faceted schemes are not easy to use for shelving physical resources. However, in online retrieval systems they have the potential to be quite helpful, as each facet may be searched independently. Some faceted schemes, such as BC2, do not use facet indicators; instead, the notations may be integrated, obscuring the individual parts.

Although many modern, special classification schemes are now faceted, the larger general schemes used in Anglo-American libraries are still primarily hierarchical. LCC has little faceting capability. There are tables in some schedules that can be used to identify the meaning of an exact number within a range of numbers, but those table numbers are added mathematically (not appended) to a base number in the schedule; the resulting notation does not show its components as separate facets. DDC has more faceting capabilities than LCC, but its schedules are primarily enumerative. There are six tables that can be used at various places in the classification. The notations from the tables are appended to the end of the notation from the schedules so that the facet generally remains intact. In some cases, the end of the schedule notation and the beginning of the table notation are not demarcated; but often, with the most common subdivisions, the table notation is preceded by the digit 0. For information about how DDC and LCC classification notations are incorporated into *call numbers* (combinations of classification notations and *cutter numbers*[†]), see Appendix B.

13.4 Classification Concepts

When implementing classification schemes, information professionals must navigate various theoretical concepts and practical issues. Some of these apply to the schemes regardless of how they are going to be used (e.g., as a way of arranging physical resources, as a way of identifying subject content). Others are issues particularly in the use of classification as a device for arranging physical resources.

13.4.1 Broad versus Close Classification

When beginning to use a classification scheme it is necessary to decide whether to use only the top levels of the scheme, whether to use the scheme at the deepest level possible, or something in between. *Broad classification* refers to the use of only main classes and primary divisions within a classification scheme, typically limited to one or two levels of subdivisions. *Close classification* involves the application of all available minute subdivisions for specific subjects, utilizing the full depth and specificity of the classification system. This distinction parallels the specific versus general concept found in controlled vocabularies.

If the intent of using the scheme is to collocate topics, then broad versus close may depend upon the size of the collection that is being classified. If the collection is large, then using only the top levels of the scheme means that a very large number of resources will be collocated at the same notation. On the other hand, if the collection is very small, then using close classification may

---

[†] Cutter numbers are specific notations that represent the primary creator, the first-named creator, or the title. They consist of the first letter of a last name or title and usually two or three numbers (decimals). In LCC, cutter numbers are also used to put subject concepts and geographic locations into alphabetical order as part of the classification number; this is usually followed by a creator or title cutter as well.

mean that most notations are assigned to only one or two resources, with the result that collocation is minimal, unless one is using a scheme like DDC where one can drop digits off the end of the notation to get to the next broader level of the concept being sought.

It should be noted that what is considered close classification for a small collection may be broad classification for a sizable collection. For a small public library, the DDC notation 612.1 (*Circulatory system in medicine*) is fairly specific; but in a medical library there may be thousands of information resources on the human circulatory system. For that collection, close classification would mean employing notation at a much more specific level, such as 612.1127 (*White corpuscle counts*), when needed.

Another issue has to do with the globalization of information organization. Even if a collection in a particular place is small, its metadata may be combined into a retrieval tool with that of other collections. If some of the metadata has been created using close classification, and some has been created using broad classification, the combined effect may be confusing and less helpful. It may be necessary in today's world to use the closest classification available in the scheme being used. This is problematic in some institutions where the classification is used for arranging physical resources. Close classification often produces long notations, which sometimes must be placed on small resources. Michael Gorman suggested that this problem be solved by using shorter notations for call numbers but using close classification for the purposes of intellectual retrieval.[25]

13.4.2 Classification of Knowledge versus Classification of a Particular Collection

Classification of knowledge is the concept that a classification system can be created that will encompass all knowledge that exists. DDC began as a classification of knowledge—at least Western knowledge as understood by Melvil Dewey in the 1870s. *Classification of a particular collection* is the concept that a classification system should only be devised for the information resources that are being added to collections, using **literary warrant**—the idea that new numbers should only be added to a classification scheme when a resource about a new concept exists.[‡] LCC began as a classification of a particular collection.

Even though DDC began as a classification of knowledge, it has been forced to use literary warrant for updates and revisions. Some areas of knowledge that have developed in the twentieth and twenty-first centuries needed significantly more space in the scheme than originally provided, if indeed they were given any space at all (e.g., computer science). Dewey devoted a whole division to the artificial waterways known as *canals*, but the concept has been moved and the "real estate" allotted to the concept has been reduced to allow expansion of other areas such as engineering. Why? Because canals no longer receive the attention that they did in Dewey's day.

13.4.3 Integrity of Numbers versus Keeping Pace with Knowledge

Integrity of numbers is the concept that in the creation and maintenance of a classification scheme, a notation, once assigned, should always retain the same meaning, and should never be used with

---

[‡] Literary warrant is used for both classification schemes and controlled vocabularies. Thus, the concept also appears in Chapter 12.

another meaning. *Keeping pace with knowledge*, in contrast, is the concept that it may be necessary to move concepts, insert new concepts, and change meanings of numbers as knowledge changes.

Dewey was a strong advocate of the integrity of numbers. He did not want the users of his system ever to have to change a number on a resource because the number's meaning had been changed in the classification. He wanted new concepts to be assigned to new numbers. As the twentieth century went forward, however, it became impossible to keep pace with new knowledge without sometimes changing the older notations. For example, in the field of mathematics the understanding of the field changed with new research. So, it became necessary to change Dewey's arrangement of the basic sections of mathematics, with the following result:

DDC 1st edition	DDC 23rd edition
510 Mathematics	510 Mathematics
511 Arithmetic	511 General principles of mathematics
512 Algebra	512 Algebra
513 Geometry	513 Arithmetic
514 Trigonometry	514 Topology
515 Conic sections	515 Analysis
516 Analytical geometry	516 Geometry
517 Calculus	517 Unassigned
518 Quaternions	518 Numerical analysis
519 Probabilities	519 Probabilities and applied mathematics

At the local level, reassignment of numbers always involves soul searching on the part of catalogers. As cost is an ever-present issue, there is a desire not to have to change notations because of time and, therefore, expense. On the other hand, if changes are not made, then the digits 513, as seen in the example above, would mean both *geometry* and *arithmetic,* and consequently, collocation would be compromised, making both searching for classification numbers in the catalog and browsing the shelves confusing for users.

Notation and structural changes also involve soul searching on the part of those designing and maintaining the classification. They worry about the impact of changes on those applying the system, but they must update the classification periodically or it will become irrelevant and out of date, and consequently the scheme will not continue to serve its purpose. If it is flexible enough, updates can be accomplished by inserting new notations. LCC, for example, accomplishes most of its updating in this fashion. If the scheme is less flexible, as with DDC, some inserting can be done, but sometimes the meanings of numbers must also be changed or more levels of hierarchical depth must be added. Areas of the classification where there has been tremendous growth (e.g., technology, computer science, medicine) often have lengthy base numbers in DDC, whereas some disciplines or topics may require many fewer digits (e.g., the entire logic division where only one subtopic goes beyond the first three digits).

It was mentioned earlier that some classification issues are general, but others are issues for the use of classification for arranging physical resources. Integrity of numbers versus keeping pace with knowledge is an issue that has both general and physical implications and gives us a transition into the issues regarding physical entities. In this case, reclassification of physical resources when meanings of numbers have been changed is an expensive process. In most collections complete reclassification is not done. Instead, there is often some kind of process set up to reclassify resources as they are returned following their first use after the change. Or sometimes, all the resources affected by a change of numbers in a whole section of the scheme are reclassified on a project basis. Changing only some of a collection, of course, ignores the use of classification as a search key in an online system. Searching a system where certain notations bring up surrogate records for information resources on different subjects is not satisfactory.

13.4.4 Closed versus Open Stacks

Patrons' direct access to resources on the shelves is sometimes assumed due to the prevalence of open stacks in most libraries in the modern Anglo-American library tradition. **Open stacks** means patrons of the facility have the right to go to the shelves themselves to browse and retrieve materials. Accordingly, **closed stacks** means that the resource storage areas are accessible only to the staff of the library, archives, or other place that houses information resources. In closed stack situations users must request resources at a desk and then wait for them to be retrieved and delivered. This eliminates any possibility of browsing in the stacks. In a closed stacks situation one can browse only in the catalog—not always an effortless process, depending upon system design.

Some large research libraries have had closed stacks for a long time. There are various reasons for this, including tradition, vandalism, and precedence of certain classes of users (e.g., faculty, graduate students) over others. In such libraries, a proposal to stop classifying resurfaces every so often. The question asked is, "Why classify if readers cannot browse?" Such a proposal includes data about how costs will be lowered if classification is stopped. However, classification is a form of subject access, and if browsing of the stacks is not allowed, then browsing of the classification notations in the catalog becomes even more important. Reference librarians often use classification to assist users in finding subject-related material.[26]

In archives, the storage areas are almost always closed. This hardly matters as far as classification goes because classification has not been found to be particularly useful for archives in any case. A collection of records can have individual pieces that are on diverse subjects, and dividing and separating these out to classify would violate the principle of *respect des fonds*.[§] It is conceivable that whole collections could be classified, but usually the classification in such a case would be so broad as to be nearly meaningless.

[§] *Respect des fonds* is the principle that archival materials created by an institution or individual should be kept together and not intermixed with the records of other creators.

13.4.5 Fixed versus Relative Location

The term *fixed location* signifies a set place where a physical information resource will always be found or to which it will be returned after having been removed for use. A fixed location identifier can be an accession number; a designation made up of room number, stack number, shelf number, and shelf position; or some other form of designation. The term *relative location* is used to indicate that an information resource will be or might be in a different place each time it is reshelved; that is, it is reshelved relative to what else has been acquired, taken out, returned, and so forth, while it was out for use. The method for accomplishing this is usually a call number with the top line or two being a classification notation. (See discussion of call numbers in Appendix B.)

13.4.6 Location Device versus Collocation Device

A persistent issue in the use of classification is whether it should primarily serve to bring related materials together (collocation) or simply to indicate where an individual resource can be found (location). A *location device* is a number or other designation on a resource to tell where it is located physically. It can be, among other designations, an accession number, a physical location number, or a call number. A *collocation device* is a number or other designation used to place it next to other resources that are like it. It is usually a classification notation.

Cost-conscious administrators often think of classification mainly as a location tool. Their argument is simple: if the call number on the item matches the number in the catalog record, users can find the resource. This, however, assumes that subject headings are sufficient for finding related materials in the catalog. Thomas Mann, cited above, and others have shown that both subject headings and classification are required for the most effective retrieval of subject-related material.[27]

It is not clear whether the same notation is adequate to serve both the collocation and the location functions. Gorman, as mentioned above, has suggested that a fully detailed classification be assigned for the purpose of collocation, while a shortened version of it be used for a location device.[28] (This would not really be helpful in the case of LCC, because most notations, even for complex subjects, are relatively short.) In most of the United States, one classification notation has served for both collocation and location for many decades. In other places though, especially where classified catalogs are used, the functions of collocation and location have been served by different notations for decades.

13.5 The Use of Categories and Taxonomies Online

The use of categories or taxonomies (the terminology seems to depend upon the site) is readily apparent online. On a commercial shopping site like Amazon[29] or a website for a large-scale retailer, such as the Wegmans grocery store,[30] a taxonomy is often found directly on the homepage or in a pull-down menu (or both). An information architect or a taxonomist created this taxonomy to provide shoppers with a quick, user-friendly set of links to the main divisions to improve navigation and the overall experience of the site, as well as the ability to find information and products quickly and efficiently. The following are the top-level categories provided in Wegmans' taxonomy:

- Baby & Toddler
- Bakery
- Bulk Foods
- Cheese
- Dairy
- Deli
- Frozen
- Grocery
- Health & Wellness
- Household Essentials
- Kitchen & Home
- Meat
- Party Celebrations & Gifts
- Personal Care & Makeup
- Prepared Foods
- Produce & Floral
- Seafood
- Seasonal Home
- Wine, Beer & Spirits

Under each of the top-level categories, a second level of hierarchy contains an additional set of headings. Taking *Bakery* as an example, the second level offers the following categories to explore:

- Artisan Bread & Rolls
- Breakfast
- Desserts
- Sandwich Breads & Rolls
- Special Diet

Under the category *Desserts,* a third layer of hierarchy is present. These sub-categories include

- Angel Food Cake/Dessert Cups
- Bars/Puffs/Eclairs
- Brownies
- Cannoli
- Cheesecakes
- Chocolate Shop
- Cookie Cakes
- Cookies
- Cupcakes
- Layer Cakes
- Mousse Desserts
- Pies/Crostata
- Puddings/Trifles
- Shortcakes
- Tarts
- Ultimate Cakes

In addition to these sub-categories, a Wegmans-specific search engine is also provided with additional facets to further narrow the results (e.g., brands, dietary restrictions, EBT eligible, new items). The taxonomy offers users, who may not know what they want, an option to browse, exploring the various products available in the commercial venture's inventory. The difficulty with taxonomies at some commercial sites like Amazon is the overwhelming size of the overall inventory, and the unpredictability of the hierarchies employed. Even at the deepest, most specific levels of a taxonomy, there still may be too many resources to browse and the user still may need to conduct a keyword search.

Taxonomies also are used by noncommercial sites, such as the National Center for Biotechnology Information's public databases.[31] But, perhaps, the most well-known example of using categorization online was the Yahoo! Directory, where, before it closed in 2014, websites were placed into categories created by Yahoo! indexers, and the categories were browsed in hierarchical fashion. The Yahoo! Directory is no longer in use, but there are some sites that still use this approach to organizing lists of internet resources. Two examples are the Best of the Web directory[32] of products and services and the WWW Virtual Library.[33]

As was seen at Wegmans, sub-categories in the WWW Virtual Library are hierarchically nested under these top-level categories:

- Agriculture
- The Arts
- Business and Economics
- Communication and Media
- Education
- Humanities and Humanistic Studies
- Information and Libraries
- International Affairs
- Law
- Natural Sciences and Mathematics
- Recreation
- Regional Studies
- Social and Behavioural Sciences
- Society

Hierarchies in these types of taxonomies, however, do not always represent genus-species relationships. The categories at the second level are not necessarily a type or kind of the broader concept at the first level. Nor are the sub-categories at the second level necessarily at equivalent levels of specificity with each other.

13.6 Conclusion

This chapter has addressed categorization and classification to provide subject access to information resources. One of the most critical factors in information retrieval is to have resources and metadata records arranged and displayed in a logical fashion. Classification often plays a significant role in this arrangement and display. Familiarity with the history of categories and the basics of classification theory can help with understanding and using the classification schemes employed today. Arrangement of classification schemes (i.e., hierarchical, enumerative, and faceted) is based on classification theory. Classification schemes are numerous, ranging from universal to home-grown systems. Regardless of which scheme is used, there are classification concepts and issues that must be addressed in the application of any scheme. Some concepts apply to the arrangement of physical resources, while others apply both to physical and intangible resources. A number of online sites use categories or classifications (often called taxonomies in this environment) to organize resources or products, although the arrangements are not always strictly hierarchical.

Some Important Terms in This Chapter
(Definitions Provided in the Glossary)

Basic level categories	Closed stacks	Literary warrant
Bibliographic classification	Collocation device	Location device
Broad classification	Cutter number	Mixed notation
Call number	Enumerative classification	Notation
Categorization	Facet	Open stacks
Category	Facet indicator	PMEST
Characteristic of division	Faceted classification	Prototype theory
Citation order	Family resemblance	Pure notation
Class	Fixed location	Relative location
Classification	Fuzzy set theory	Schedule
Classification scheme	Hierarchical classification	Tables
Close classification	Index	Taxonomy

Some Important Acronyms in This Chapter

BC2:	*Bibliographic Classification, 2nd ed.*
CC:	*Colon Classification*
DDC:	*Dewey Decimal Classification*
LIS:	Library and Information Science
LCC:	*Library of Congress Classification*
UDC:	*Universal Decimal Classification*

13.7 Discussion Questions and Exercises

- What is classification? How does it differ from categorization and taxonomy?
- How has the theory of categories changed over the past century? What implications might these theoretical changes have for bibliographic classification?
- What are the strengths and weaknesses of hierarchical, enumerative, and faceted classification? How are elements of hierarchical, enumerative, and faceted classification employed in the major bibliographic classification schemes currently in use?
- Define each of the following classification concepts and provide an example of how it might affect the practice of classification in a library or other information environment.
    - Broad versus close classification
    - Classification of knowledge versus classification of a particular collection
    - Integrity of numbers versus keeping pace with knowledge

- Closed versus open stacks
- Fixed versus relative location
- Location device versus collocation device

13.8 Suggested Readings

Bowker, Geoffrey C., and Susan Leigh Star. *Sorting Things Out: Classification and Its Consequences.* Cambridge, MA: MIT Press, 1999.

Broughton, Vanda. *Essential Classification.* Chicago: ALA Neal-Schuman, 2015.

Chan, Lois Mai, and Athena Salaba. *Cataloging and Classification: An Introduction.* 5th ed. Lanham, MD: Rowman & Littlefield, 2023.

Chan, Lois Mai, Sheila S. Intner, and Jean Weihs. *A Guide to the Library of Congress Classification.* 6th ed. Santa Barbara, CA: Libraries Unlimited, 2016.

Classification Research Group. "The Need for a Faceted Classification as the Basis of All Methods of Information Retrieval." In *Theory of Subject Analysis: A Sourcebook,* edited by Lois Mai Chan, Phyllis A. Richmond, and Elaine Svenonius, 154–67. Littleton, CO: Libraries Unlimited, 1985.

Hunter, Eric J. *Classification Made Simple: An Introduction to Knowledge Organisation and Information Retrieval.* 3rd ed. Farnham, UK: Ashgate, 2009.

Joudrey, Daniel N., Arlene G. Taylor, and David P. Miller. *Introduction to Cataloging and Classification.* 11th ed. Santa Barbara, CA: Libraries Unlimited, 2015.

Lakoff, George. *Women, Fire, and Dangerous Things: What Categories Reveal about the Mind.* Chicago: University of Chicago Press, 1987.

Langridge, D. W. *Classification: Its Kinds, Elements, Systems, and Applications.* London: Bowker-Saur, 1992.

Library of Congress, Catalogers Learning Workshop. "Library of Congress Classification: Online Training." Janis L. Young and Daniel N. Joudrey, instructors. https://www.loc.gov/catworkshop/lcc/.

Mann, Thomas. *The Oxford Guide to Library Research.* 4th ed. New York: Oxford University Press, 2015.

McIlwaine, I. C. *The Universal Decimal Classification: A Guide to Its Use.* Rev. ed. The Hague: UDC Consortium, 2007.

Ranganathan, S. R. *Prolegomena to Library Classification.* 3rd ed. London: Asia Publishing House, 1967.

Satija, M. P., and Alex Kyrios. *A Handbook of History, Theory and Practice of the Dewey Decimal Classification System.* London: Facet Publishing, 2023.

Snow, Karen. *A Practical Guide to Dewey Decimal Classification.* Lanham, MD: Rowman & Littlefield, 2024.

Snow, Karen. *A Practical Guide to Library of Congress Classification.* Lanham, MD: Rowman & Littlefield, 2017.

13.9 Notes

All URLs accessed April 2025.

1. OED: Oxford English Dictionary, https://www.oed.com/.
2. Merriam-Webster Online Search, http://www.merriam-webster.com/.
3. Elin K. Jacob, "Classification and Categorization: A Difference That Makes a Difference," *Library Trends* 52, no. 3 (Winter 2004): 522.
4. Jacob, 527.
5. Christopher J. Dent, "Old Stuff: Classification v Categorization," *Glacial Erratics* (blog), http://www.burning-chrome.com/~cdent/mt/archives/000401.html.

6. Dent.
7. Amy J. Warner, "A Taxonomy Primer," https://web.archive.org/web/20160305124415/http://www.ischool.utexas.edu/~i385e/readings/Warner-aTaxonomyPrimer.html.
8. "Ten Taxonomy Myths," Montague Institute Review (November 2002; updated January 7, 2012), https://www.montague.com/review/myths.html.
9. Thomas D. Wason, "Dr. Tom's Taxonomy Guide," The Dr. Tom Guides (website), http://www.tomwason.com/drtomtaxonomiesguide.html.
10. F. W. Lancaster, *Indexing and Abstracting in Theory and Practice*, 3rd ed. (Champaign: University of Illinois, Graduate School of Library and Information Science, 2003), xiii.
11. Bertram C. Bruce and James A. Levin, "Educational Technology: Media for Inquiry, Communication, Construction, and Expression," *Journal of Educational Computing Research* 17, no. 1 (1997): 79–102, https://www.ideals.illinois.edu/items/13507.
12. U.S. Dept. of Agriculture, Agricultural Research Service, "GRIN Taxonomy," U.S. National Plant Germplasm System, https://npgsweb.ars-grin.gov/gringlobal/taxon/taxonomyquery.aspx.
13. Douglas Harper, "Category," *Online Etymology Dictionary*, https://www.etymonline.com/word/category.
14. Aristotle, *Categories*, trans. E. M. Edghill (Urbana, IL: Project Gutenberg, 2000), https://www.gutenberg.org/cache/epub/2412/pg2412.txt.
15. George Lakoff, *Women, Fire, and Dangerous Things: What Categories Reveal about the Mind* (Chicago: University of Chicago Press, 1987), 6.
16. Lakoff, 16–57.
17. Stephen L. Zegura, "Genes, Opsins, Neurons, and Color Categories: Closing the Gaps," in *Color Categories in Thought and Language*, eds. C. L. Hardin and Luisa Maffi (Cambridge: Cambridge University Press, 1997), 289.
18. Traugott Koch and Michael Day, "Executive Summary," *The Role of Classification Schemes in Internet Resource Description and Discovery* (Bath, UK: UKOLN, 1997), iii, http://www.ukoln.ac.uk/metadata/desire/classification/classification.pdf.
19. Metis: Library Classification for Children, https://schoollibrarycatologing.weebly.com/metis.html.
20. David H. Elazar and Daniel J. Elazar, *A Classification System for Libraries of Judaica*, 3rd ed., with the assistance of Rachel K. Glasser and Rita C. Frischer (Northvale, NJ: Jason Aronson, 1997).
21. Carylyn Gwyn Moser, "Elazar Classification System Holocaust Expansion," https://web.archive.org/web/20220517002859/https://sites.google.com/site/mtevansco/elazar-classification.
22. Hope A. Olson and John J. Boll, *Subject Analysis in Online Catalogs*, 2nd ed. (Englewood, CO: Libraries Unlimited, 2001), 155–6.
23. *WebDewey*, https://dewey.org/webdewey/login/login.html. [subscription only]
24. Mohimer P. Satija, "Colon Classification (CC)," *Knowledge Organization* 44, no. 4 (2017): 305.
25. Michael Gorman, "The Longer the Number, the Smaller the Spine; or, Up and Down with Melvil and Elsie," *American Libraries* 12, no. 8 (September 1981): 498–9.
26. Thomas Mann, *The Oxford Guide to Library Research*, 4th ed. (New York: Oxford University Press, 2015), Chapter 3.
27. Mann, Chapter 3.
28. Gorman, "The Longer the Number," 498–9.
29. Amazon, http://www.amazon.com/.
30. Wegmans, https://www.wegmans.com/.
31. "Taxonomy," National Center for Biotechnology Information, National Library of Medicine, https://www.ncbi.nlm.nih.gov/taxonomy.
32. Best of the Web Directory, https://botw.org/.
33. The WWW Virtual Library, http://www.vlib.org/.

Appendix A

Arrangement of Metadata Displays

For most of the twentieth century, catalogs were in card, book, or microform formats. In card catalogs, the order of surrogate records was by a filing arrangement achieved by humans. Persons doing the filing had rules to follow that would lead to an arrangement intended to help users find what they were looking for. In early book catalogs, the same was true because book catalogs often were made from cards or slips created by catalogers and placed in order by filers.

As computers entered the picture, book and then microform catalogs began to be created in databases where the actual filing was done according to computer algorithms. Finally in the 1980s, online public access catalogs (OPACs) came into use. The records were stored sequentially or randomly within the computer, but to display the results of a search to a user, the subset of records retrieved had to be arranged and then displayed on the screen in some order. Early computer algorithms dictated an order of characters: sometimes numerals preceded letters, sometimes not; and there was great difficulty in even displaying diacritical marks, let alone arranging them to display in some meaningful order.

Search results in OPACs and other database-based retrieval tools continue to be arranged on screen by computer algorithm. A few systems have been developed to make use of MARC tags and subfield codes to create more logical arrangements. Whatever the algorithm, no computer can make up for a typographical error the way a filer can. In a card catalog, an alert filer would see a typo such as *Form one to zero* and file it properly as *From one to zero*. In a computer, which would see *form* as a properly spelled word, the title with the typo would be arranged before all other entries for the correctly spelled title. Intervening between *form* and *from* would be titles beginning with words such as *formal, formation, Franciscan, fraud, frock,* and many hundreds of others. Retrieval of known items is much more difficult when typographical errors are involved.

A.1 Filing History

Charles A. Cutter, in addition to his rules for description, name headings, and subject headings, included filing rules in his cataloging code.[1] There have been separate filing codes, not connected with cataloging rules, ever since Cutter. Earlier filing codes reflected the influence of the classified catalog. They pre-sorted catalog entries into categories. For example, entries beginning with the word *orange* were sorted into:

1. personal names—separating single surname entries (e.g., **Orange, Carolyn**) from compound surname entries (e.g., **Orange-Keysville, James**);
2. geographic entities (e.g., **Orange County (Calif.)**);

3. corporate bodies (e.g., **Orange and Rockland Utilities, Inc.**);
4. subject headings—separating the fruit (e.g., **Orange peel**) from the color (e.g., **Orange azalea**); and
5. titles (e.g., **Orange bear reader**).

Even though the rules were for dictionary catalogs, the categories were to be filed one after another instead of being interfiled alphabetically. The earlier codes also reflected the many variant local practices that existed.

The 1942 *A.L.A. Rules for Filing Catalog Cards*[2] had many rules with two or three correct alternatives for a particular filing dilemma. One library could use rules 1.a. and 2.b., while another library could use rules 1.b. and 2.a. Both could claim to be following the American Library Association (ALA) filing rules. Users going from one library to another could encounter different filing rules for each catalog.

By the mid-1960s frustration with the rules had peaked. People in ALA decided to create a consistent code of filing rules derived from one basic principle. The resulting 1968 *ALA Rules for Filing Catalog Cards*[3] recommended straight alphabetical order, but there were exceptions. For example, personal surname entries (for single surnames only) were to be arranged before other entries beginning with the same word (e.g., **Love, Harold G.** was filed before the title *Love and beauty*). Also, a filer had to spell out (mentally) numerals and abbreviations in the language of the item and then file the card in the place where the spelled-out form would go in the catalog (e.g., *1984* was filed as *Nineteen eighty-four*).

In 1980, ALA again published a code of filing rules,[4] and this time they were so different that they were not identified as a third edition. They called for straightforward filing according to principles, but still, alphabetical order was not absolute. A brief review of these rules serves to highlight some of the problems that keep people from finding what they want in computer displays, especially when a displayed set takes up more than one or two screens.

A.2 General Rules for Arrangement

Traditional arrangement in catalogs is *word-by-word*. This means that everything beginning with a particular word should precede other entries beginning with a word that has the same beginning letters as the first word (e.g., *New York* files before *Newark*). Not all information retrieval tools use this arrangement. Some encyclopedias and dictionaries, for example, use *letter-by-letter* arrangement. The difference is that in word-by-word arrangement, a space between words is treated according to the principle "nothing files before something." That is, a space is "nothing," and it should be filed before a character, which is "something." According to the *ALA Filing Rules*, spaces, dashes, hyphens, diagonal slashes, and periods are all considered to be "nothing." Arrangements using the letter-by-letter approach ignore spaces and some of the punctuation marks just mentioned, and the entry files as if it is all run together into one word (e.g., *New York* is treated as *Newyork* and follows *Newark*). A longer example may assist in clarifying the distinction:

Word-by-Word	Letter-by-Letter
A book about myself	A book about myself
Book bytes	Bookbinding
Book-making (Betting)	Book bytes
Book of bells	Booker, William, 1905-
Book reports	Bookfinder
Bookbinding	Bookkeeping made simple
Booker, William, 1905-	Book-making (Betting)
Bookfinder	Book of bells
Bookkeeping made simple	Book reports
Books that changed the world	Booksellers and bookselling
Booksellers and bookselling	Books that changed the world

Another principle of arrangement is that numerals precede letters. Formerly, numerals were filed as spoken and spelled out, for example,

> Twenty-four dramatic cases …
> 24 ways to …
> XXIVth Congress of …

However, in the 1980 filing rules the difficulties of mentally spelling out the number *24* in French, German, Russian, and so on, for both filers and users were recognized. Numerals were to go first, but in numerical order, and Roman numerals filed with Arabic numerals. Thus, *1/2* (the fraction) was to file before *1* (the first integer). But computers have difficulty with this. The computer sees *1/2* as one-slash-two, not as one-half. In the following example one can see that numerical order for a computer is based upon an arrangement of numerals by whatever is the first digit, then the second digit, and so on, rather than by the value of the number, and Roman numerals are seen as letters:

Manual Filing	Machine Arrangement
6 concerti grossi	10 times a poem
9 to 5	1984
10 times a poem	6 concerti grossi
XIXth century drawings	9 to 5
90 days to a better heart	90 days to a better heart
1984	XIXth century drawings

Among other principles of manual filing are

- letters in the English alphabet precede letters of non-Roman alphabets;
- an ampersand (&) may be ignored, or optionally, may be spelled out in its language equivalent; and
- punctuation, non-alphabetic signs, and symbols are ignored.

Computers generally treat these the same way except that they cannot follow the option of spelling out ampersands in their language equivalents. Ampersands are problematic for retrieval because a user who has heard a title, but has not seen it, does not know whether *and* is spelled out or represented by an ampersand and usually does not know to try the other way if one way does not work. To ensure access, however, catalogers often make additional title access points for the spelled-out form when ampersands or numerals have been used in titles.

A.3 Filing/Display Dilemmas

There are quite a few situations that cannot be resolved by human intellect as was done in the past. It seems impossible to program computers to handle all these situations so that the outcome is logical. For example, when titles are transcribed from preferred sources of information in the process of creating metadata, the title is taken character by character as it appears. In titles that start with names beginning with prefixes, for example, the names are sometimes written with a space following the prefix (e.g., DeGaulle and De Gaulle); or, titles may start with or contain words that began as two words and are in the process of becoming one word (e.g., *on line, on-line,* and *online*). This means that some titles that begin with or contain the same words according to human understanding appear to a computer to contain different words. Here is another case where a user, having heard a title spoken, would not know which way to look for it.

Another spacing problem comes from punctuation marks. As mentioned above, the *ALA Filing Rules* says that spaces, dashes, hyphens, diagonal slashes, and periods are all considered to be "nothing." However, this is not true in all computer systems. Such marks might be replaced by a space, or they might not even be replaced by a space, resulting in words being run together inappropriately (e.g., *surrogate/metadata records* might become *surrogatemetadata records*).

Computers also have difficulty with abbreviations. A human or a natural language processing system can usually tell whether *Co.* means *County* or *Company*; whether *St.* means *Street* or *Saint*; whether *Dr.* means *Doctor* or *Drive*. Most systems cannot tell the difference, however, and arrangement is simply done by the letters that are there. The resulting retrieval challenge is that even if users know the titles they are searching for word-for-word, if they have only heard the titles and have not seen them, they do not know if certain words are abbreviated or spelled out.

Dates in subject headings present yet another challenge. In traditional manual practice, dates are to be arranged in chronological order. With *Library of Congress Subject Headings* (LCSH), however, some dates are preceded by a phrase identifying a name for the particular period of time (e.g., **United States—History—Revolution, 1775-1783**). These headings can be placed in chronological order by a human, but a computer cannot see *1775-1783* until it has arranged *Revolution* preceding or following all other numerals. The following table contains a comparison of human versus machine arrangement as applied to dates:

Manual Filing	Machine Arrangement
United States—History—Revolution, 1775-1783	United States—History—1800-
United States—History—1800-	United States—History—1801-1809
United States—History—1801-1809	United States—History—1900-
United States—History—War of 1812	United States—History—1945-
United States—History—Civil War, 1861-1865	United States—History—Civil War, 1861-1865
United States—History—1900-	United States—History—Revolution, 1775-1783
United States—History—1945-	United States—History—War of 1812

Some machine systems place numerals after letters, but in any case, the letters would be together and the numerals would be together. How many users know whether in a long list of time periods for the history of a country, the named periods come last or the dates alone come last?

Initials and acronyms also present challenges. If they are written with periods or spaces between them, they are filed as if each letter is a word (e.g., *A B C* files as if the first word is *A*, the second is *B*, and the third word is *C*; while *ABC* files as a single word). For example:

>A.A.
>A.A.U.W.
>A apple pie
>A B C programs
>AAA
>Aabel, Marie
>Abacus calculating
>ABCs of collecting

Users are at a loss to know whether periods or spaces have been used. This kind of situation requires the assistance of catalogers and the software in retrieval systems to assist. Catalogers sometimes add access points both with and without spaces, and software programs for indexing these terms often normalize the data by stripping out punctuation so that retrieval is improved.

The final arrangement problem to be discussed here is the one surrounding initial articles and elisions. Articles (*a, an, the,* and their equivalents in other languages) that come at the beginning of an access point are supposed to be ignored in filing. This can only happen in all languages if the system is using an encoding scheme like MARC, wherein a human can provide in an indicator the number of characters that the computer should ignore before beginning the arrangement order. Even in the MARC format there is no provision for indicating articles for every possible title access point. In MARC 21, for example, uniform titles and titles in subfield *t* ($t) of several access point fields do not have indicators for articles. In addition, if a system is programmed to give access to subtitles, those beginning with articles will be arranged under the articles.

A system cannot just have a stopword list of all articles in all languages. First, some articles are ordinary words in other languages (e.g., the German *die* or the French *thé*). Second, if the article is part of a proper name, it should be arranged under the article. For example:

> **Los angeles custodios** [title filed under *A*]
> **Los Angeles in fiction** [title filed under *L*]
> **Los Angeles Bar Association** [corporate body name filed under *L*]

Elisions (substitution of an apostrophe for a letter or letters when running two words together, e.g., *they'll* for *they will*) present a similar problem, especially when they begin an access point. In the following example an elided article begins each access point:

> **L'enfant abandonné** [title filed under *E*]
> **L'Enfant, Edouard** [person's name filed under *L*]

The main concern in the issues discussed above is that in online systems, when searchers retrieve responses that take more than two screens to display, they have to understand the arrangement. If they think that responses are in alphabetical order, and if they expect, for example, an acronym to be at the beginning of the listing, they might not even go to the screen that actually has the entry. Although arrangement is done by computers, some programming can be done by humans to enable displays to be more predictable.

Arrangement of retrieved metadata in response to a search is still evolving. The first online catalogs were automated card catalogs, but they lacked the sophisticated filing arrangements that could be accomplished in card catalogs. Display of search results has had many improvements, but problems still exist. An appropriate display is highly dependent upon system design.

A.4 Notes

1. Charles A. Cutter, *Rules for a Dictionary Catalog*, 4th ed. (Washington, DC: Government Printing Office, 1904; reprint, London: Library Association, 1962), 12.
2. *A.L.A. Rules for Filing Catalog Cards* (Chicago: American Library Association, 1942).
3. *ALA Rules for Filing Catalog Cards*, 2nd ed. (Chicago: American Library Association, 1968).
4. *ALA Filing Rules* (Chicago: American Library Association, 1980).

Appendix B

Arrangement of Physical Information Resources in Libraries

Arrangement of physical resources has been of concern to libraries, archives, and other information centers for centuries. Clay tablets, papyrus scrolls, parchment, and eventually paper resources all had to be arranged. In the nineteenth and twentieth centuries, various new media (e.g., films, photographs, sound recordings) appeared, needing eventually to be arranged. Since the early 1980s, there has been concern about arrangement of electronic resources contained in physical packaging (e.g., CD-ROMs).

Physical resources are often arranged by **call number**.* A call number is a notation on a resource that matches the same notation in the metadata record. It is the number used to "call" for an item in closed stacks—thus, the source of the name *call number*. A call number usually consists of at least two lines on a label placed on the outside of the packaging. The top line is usually a classification notation. With long notations, the classification notation may continue onto a second line. The next line is usually for a *cutter number*.

Cutter numbers were devised by Charles A. Cutter in the late nineteenth century for the purpose of creating a logical sub-arrangement of resources under classification notations. In most instances, the most logical sub-arrangement is alphabetical by the primary access point, whether it is an author, creator, or title. In essence, cuttering alphabetizes all the works that fall under the same classification notation. Cutter devised a table in which letters of the alphabet were listed in one column and equivalent numerals were listed in an adjoining column (see Figure B.1).

Using the following example from "F" in Cutter's table,

Folq	669
Fols	671
Fom	672
Fon	673
Fonf	674
Fonn	675
Fons	676
Font	677
Fontai	678
Fontan	679
Fontani	681

---

*For more explanation of call numbers, see Chapter 19 of Daniel N. Joudrey, Arlene G. Taylor, and David P. Miller, *Introduction to Cataloging and Classification*, 11th ed. (Santa Barbara, CA: Libraries Unlimited, 2015).

Goetz	611	Goun	711	Greene J	811	Guald	911
Gof	612	Goup	712	Greene S	812	Gualt	912
Gog	613	Gour	713	Greenh	813	Guan	913
Goh	614	Gourd	714	Greenl	814	Guar	914
Goi	615	Gourg	715	Greeno	815	Guari	915
Gois	616	Gouri	716	Greenw	816	Guarn	916
Gol	617	Gous	717	Gref	817	Guas	917
Gold	618	Gout	718	Greg	818	Guat	918
Goldi	619	Gouv	719	Gregg	819	Guaz	919
Goldo	621	Gov	721	Gregori	821	Gub	921
Golds	622	Gow	722	Gregory	822	Gud	922
Goldsc	623	Gower	723	Gregory M	823	Gudm	923
Goldsm	624	Goy	724	Grei	824	Gue	924
Gole	625	Goz	725	Grel	825	Guel	925
Goli	626	Gr	726	Gren	826	Guen	926
Golo	627	Grab	727	Greni	827	Gueno	927
Golov	628	Graber	728	Grenv	828	Guep	928
Golt	629	Grac	729	Grep	829	Guer	929
Gom	631	Graci	731	Gres	831	Guere	931
...		...		...		...	

Figure B.1 An Excerpt from a Three-Figure Cutter Table.

a Cutter number for an author named Fontaine might be F678d. The lowercase "d" is a *work mark* assigned to help keep the resources of a particular creator who writes on the same subject in alphabetical order. The work mark usually stands for the first non-article word of the title of the work; although for biographies the work is usually cuttered for the name of the person the work is about, and the work mark stands for the last name of the biographer. This kind of Cutter number is most often used with *Dewey Decimal Classification* (DDC) notations.

Library of Congress Classification (LCC) also uses cutter numbers (with a small "c") to differentiate resources that share the same classification notation (see Figure B.2). LC borrowed Charles Cutter's idea but created its own table that takes only a few lines. With LCC, a third line for a call number is often the resource's date of publication. (Typically, dates are only used in DDC call numbers to sub-arrange more than one edition of the same work.) Examples of call numbers are

        DDC: 378.4
                    F678d

        LCC: QE22.D25
                    S65
                    1997

LC Cutter Table								
(1) After initial ***vowels***								
for the second letter:	b	d	l-m	n	p	r	s-t	u-y
use number:	2	3	4	5	6	7	8	9
(2) After initial letter ***S***								
for the second letter:	a	ch	e	h-i	m-p	t	u	w-z
use number:	2	3	4	5	6	7	8	9
(3) After initial letters ***Qu***								
for the third letter:	a	e	i	o	r	t	y	
use number:	3	4	5	6	7	8	9	
For initial letters ***Qa-Qt*** use numbers: **2-29**								
(4) After other initial ***consonants***								
for the second letter:	a	e	i	o	r	u	y	
use number:	3	4	5	6	7	8	9	
(5) For ***expansion***								
for the letter:	a-d	e-h	i-l	m-o	p-s	t-v	w-z	
use number:	3	4	5	6	7	8	9	
In most cases, Cutters must be adjusted to file an entry correctly and to allow room for later entries.								

Figure B.2 An Excerpt from the LC Cutter Table.

There are also alphabetical arrangements, accession order arrangements (i.e., numbers assigned to items in the order in which they arrive), and fixed location arrangements for physical information resources. In public and school libraries, in particular, fiction is often grouped together, sub-arranged in alphabetical order by author (sometimes with a prefix indicating *fiction*, such as **F** or **Fic**). Other uses for alphabetical order include arrangements of biographies and serials. Biographies may be arranged in alphabetical order by the last name of the biographee (sometimes with **B** as a prefix). Some materials, like physical copies of serials, newspapers, and DVDs, are often arranged in alphabetical order by title. Accession order arrangements may be used for materials waiting to be cataloged. They may also be used for fixed location settings, such as remote storage.

In most institutions there is more than one sequence of the classification scheme or other arrangement used (e.g., more than one A–Z sequence, if using LCC, or more than one 000–999 sequence, if using DDC). There is often a reference collection that gathers together information resources from all parts of the classification scheme. In some libraries the prefix **R** or **Ref** is used to indicate an item's inclusion in the reference collection. These are kept separately from regular circulating collections. In academic libraries there are often collections of reserve items for use for certain courses. In many libraries some kinds of information resources are separated by format.

Microforms, maps, DVDs, sound recordings, and the like, are arranged in their own groups with their own sequences. This is often for housing and preservation purposes. Some media centers have tried to interfile all formats in classification order, but the idea has never really caught on. Finally, some institutions that serve multilingual communities separate their resources first by the languages represented in the collection (e.g., the Spanish language section, the Tagalog language section, the Tamil section). Within each language division, the resources are arranged according to the library's preferred classification system.

Appendix C

EAD3-Encoded Finding Aid

This is the EAD Record for the collection described in Figure 3.8.

```xml
<?xml version="1.0" encoding="UTF-8"?>
<?xml-model href="ead3.rng" type="application/xml" schematypens="
http://relaxng.org/ns/structure/1.0"?>
<ead xmlns="http://ead3.archivists.org/schema/">
    <control>
        <recordid instanceurl="http://beatleyweb.simmons.edu/collectionguides /
        CharitiesCollection/ CC030.xml">CC030</recordid>
        <filedesc>
            <titlestmt>
                <titleproper>Guide to the Industrial School for Girls (Dorchester, Boston, Mass.)
                    records, 1873-1934</titleproper>
                <author>Processed by: Molly Tierney; supervised by: Jason Wood; machine-
                    readable finding aid created by: Katie Sallade</author>
            </titlestmt>
            <publicationstmt>
                <publisher>Simmons University Archives, Simmons University</publisher>
                <address>
                    <addressline>Boston, MA, U.S.A.</addressline>
                </address>
                <p>
                    <date>© 2012</date>
                    Simmons University. All Rights Reserved.
                </p>
            </publicationstmt>
            <notestmt>
                <controlnote>
                    <p>Part of the LEADS project, Simmons University Archives and the Simmons
                        University Graduate School of Library and Information Science.</p>
                </controlnote>
            </notestmt>
        </filedesc>
        <maintenancestatus value="new"/>
        <maintenanceagency>
            <agencyname>Simmons University. Archives</agencyname>
        </maintenanceagency>
        <languagedeclaration>
            <language langcode="eng"/>
            <script scriptcode="Latn"/>
        </languagedeclaration>
        <conventiondeclaration>
            <citation>DACS</citation>
        </conventiondeclaration>
        <maintenancehistory>
            <maintenanceevent>
```

```
                    <eventtype value="created"/>
                    <eventdatetime>2012</eventdatetime>
                    <agenttype value="human"/>
                    <agent>Katie Sallade</agent>
                </maintenanceevent>
            </maintenancehistory>
    </control>
    <archdesc level="collection" relatedencoding="MARC">
        <did>
            <head>Descriptive Summary</head>
            <unittitle encodinganalog="245">Industrial School for Girls (Dorchester, Boston,
                Mass.) records</unittitle>
            <unitdatestructured label="Dates:" unitdatetype="inclusive" encodinganalog ="245">
                <daterange>
                    <fromdate>1873</fromdate>
                    <todate>1934</todate>
                </daterange>
            </unitdatestructured>
            <unitid countrycode="US" repositorycode="MBSi-LS"
                encodinganalog="099">CC 30</unitid>
            <origination label="Creator:">
                <corpname rules="AACR" encodinganalog="110">
                    <part>Industrial School for Girls (Dorchester, Boston, Mass.)</part>
                </corpname>
            </origination>
            <langmaterial encodinganalog="546">
                <language langcode="eng">English</language>
            </langmaterial>
            <physdescstructured label="Quantity:" physdescstructuredtype="spaceoccupied"
                coverage="whole" encodinganalog="300">
                <quantity>0.5</quantity>
                <unittype>linear feet</unittype>
            </physdescstructured>
            <physdesc>1 manuscript box</physdesc>
            <repository>
                <corpname>
                    <part>Simmons University (Boston, Mass.).</part>
                    <part>Archives.</part>
                </corpname>
            </repository>
            <physloc>Collection may be stored offsite. Please contact Archives staff for more
                information.</physloc>
            <abstract encodinganalog="545">The Industrial School for Girls was established in 1853
                and incorporated 1855 in the names of Lucretia O. Everett and Maria Greenwood.
                It moved from Winchester, Massachusetts, to Dorchester, Massachusetts, in 1858,
                located at 232 Centre Street. It provided a home and training school for various
                branches of housework to develop the habits and principles to become upright, self-
                supported women. By the mid-1940s the Industrial School for Girls had evolved into
                the Everett House located at the same place, and in the 1950s the New England Home
                for Little Wanderers acquired it.</abstract>
            <abstract encodinganalog="520">The Industrial School for Girls collection contains
                the annual reports of the Board of Managers, arranged chronologically with a
                concentration of reports from 1873 to 1934. Also, there is a paper read at the 50th
                anniversary of the Dorchester Industrial School on June 7, 1904, as well as a bound
                copy of <title render="italic"><part>Suggestions to Visitors of Dependent Children
                </part></title>, 1874.</abstract>
        </did>
```

```xml
<accessrestrict encodinganalog="506">
    <head>Access Restrictions</head>
    <p>Collection is open.</p>
</accessrestrict>
<userestrict>
    <head>Copyright Notice</head>
    <p>Copyright for materials resides with the creators of the items in question, unless
        otherwise designated.</p>
</userestrict>
<prefercite>
    <head>Preferred Citation</head>
    <p>[Identification of item: description and date], Industrial School for Girls
        (Dorchester, Boston, Mass.) records, CC 30, Simmons University Archives, Boston, MA,
        USA.</p>
</prefercite>
<acqinfo encodinganalog="541">
    <head>Acquisitions Information</head>
    <p>Transferred from the Simmons University School of Social Work Library, 1991</p>
    <p>Accession number: 2002.178</p>
</acqinfo>
<processinfo>
    <head>Processing Information</head>
    <p>Processed by Molly Tierney, December 2002</p>
    <p>Supervised by Jason Wood</p>
    <p>This collection guide was encoded as part of the LEADS project by Katie Sallade,
        November 2012</p>
</processinfo>
<userestrict>
    <head>Publishing Permission</head>
    <p>Please contact the University Archivist with requests to publish any material from
        the collection.</p>
</userestrict>
<bioghist>
    <head>Organizational History</head>
    <p>The Industrial School for Girls was established in 1853 and incorporated 1855 in
        the names of Lucretia O. Everett and Maria Greenwood. It moved from Winchester,
        Massachusetts, to Dorchester, Massachusetts, in 1858, located at 232 Centre Street.
        It provided a home and training school for various branches of housework to develop
        the habits and principles to become upright, self-supported women. They accepted
        on average 25 students through an application process, … girls between 10 to 14
        years of age, whose family or friends are unable or unfit to care for them. The original
        age of acceptance was between the ages of 6 to 10, which gradually rose with modern
        social standards. Reductions of boarding charges were made when relatives could not
        pay. The girls attend public schools (this started in 1881) and Congregational church.
        They would go out to earn their living as soon as able under the immediate care of
        the head of household, usually in country families, and each one, unless returned
        to relatives, would be supervised under the care of one of the managers. By the
        mid-1940s the Industrial School for Girls had evolved into the Everett House located
        at the same place. And in the 1950s the New England Home for Little Wanderers
        acquired it.</p>
    <p>Information taken from <title render="italic"><part>Directory of Charitable and
        Beneficent Organizations</part></title>, Boston, 1907 and 1940 or the <title
        render="italic"><part>Report of the Board of Managers</part></title>, 1926 and the
        finding aid for CC 6,<title render="doublequote"><part>Guide to the New England
        Home for Little Wanderers records</part></title>.</p>
</bioghist>
```

```xml
<scopecontent>
    <head>Collection Overview</head>
    <p>The Industrial School for Girls records consist of the annual reports of the Board of
    Managers, arranged chronologically with a concentration of reports from 1873 to
    1934. Also, there is a paper read at the 50th anniversary of the Dorchester Industrial
    School June 7, 1904, which has a summation of the first 50 years of the School and a
    bound copy of Suggestions to Visitors of Dependent Children, 1874 which provides
    guidance for guardians of the girls.</p>
    <p>There has been an annual report printed every year except in 1858 when they were
    moving from Winchester to Dorchester. The reports cover officers' positions, brief
    history of the School, student population, admission application statistics, requests
    for student help placement, expense reports, list of subscribers for previous year,
    donations made and by-laws of the organization. Missing are the years: 1919, 1923,
    1925, 1928, 1930, and 1932.</p>
</scopecontent>
<arrangement>
    <head>Collection Arrangement</head>
    <p>Collection is arranged into 3 series:</p>
    <list listtype="unordered">
        <item><ref target="cc030s1">Annual Reports</ref></item>
        <item><ref target="cc030s2">Manual</ref></item>
        <item><ref target="cc030s3">50th Anniversary Paper</ref></item>
    </list>
</arrangement>
<controlaccess>
    <head>Online Catalog Headings</head>
    <p>These and related materials may be found under the following headings in online
    catalogs.</p>
    <list listtype="unordered">
        <item>
            <subject encodinganalog="650" source="lcsh">
                <part>Charities</part>
                <part>Massachusetts</part>
                <part>Boston</part>
            </subject>
        </item>
        <item>
            <geogname encodinganalog="651" source="lcsh">
                <part>Dorchester (Boston, Mass.)</part>
            </geogname>
        </item>
        <item>
            <corpname encodinganalog="610" source="lcnaf">
                <part>Industrial School for Girls (Dorchester, Boston, Mass.)</part>
            </corpname>
        </item>
        <item>
            <corpname encodinganalog="610" source="lcnaf">
                <part>New England Home for Little Wanderers</part>
                <part>History</part>
            </corpname>
        </item>
        <item>
            <geogname encodinganalog="651" source="lcsh">
                <part>Winchester (Mass.)</part>
            </geogname>
        </item>
    </list>
```

```xml
</controlaccess>
<relatedmaterial>
    <p>Part of the School of Social Work Library Charities Collection.</p>
</relatedmaterial>
<dsc dsctype="combined">
    <head>Detailed Description of the Collection</head>
    <c01 level="series" id="cc030s1">
        <did>
            <unittitle label="Series I">Annual Reports</unittitle>
            <unitdate>1873-1934 </unitdate>
            <physdesc>3 folders</physdesc>
        </did>
        <scopecontent>
            <p>This series contains the Industrial School for Girls' annual reports printed
                each year except in 1858. The reports cover officers' positions, brief history
                of the School, student population, admission application statistics, requests
                for student help placement, expense reports, list of subscribers for previous
                years, donations made, and by-laws of the organization. Missing years
                include: 1919, 1923, 1925, 1928, 1930, and 1932.</p>
        </scopecontent>
        <c02>
            <did>
                <container localtype="box">1</container>
                <container localtype="folder">1</container>
                <unittitle>Bound 1873-1885, 1886-1900</unittitle>
            </did>
        </c02>
        <c02>
            <did>
                <container localtype="folder">2</container>
                <unittitle>1874-1920</unittitle>
            </did>
        </c02>
        <c02>
            <did>
            <container localtype="folder">3</container>
            <unittitle>1921-1934</unittitle>
            </did>
        </c02>
    </c01>
    <c01 level="series" id="cc030s2">
        <did>
            <unittitle label="Series II">Manual</unittitle>
            <unitdate>1879</unitdate>
            <physdesc>1 folder</physdesc>
        </did>
        <scopecontent>
            <p>This series contains a bound copy of <title
                render="italic"><part>Suggestions to Visitors of Dependent Children
                </part></title>, 1874 which provides guidance for guardians of the girls.
                </p>
        </scopecontent>
        <c02>
            <did>
                <container localtype="folder">4</container>
                <unittitle>1879</unittitle>
            </did>
```

```xml
            </c02>
        </c01>
        <c01 level="series" id="cc030s3">
            <did>
                <unittitle label="Series III">50th Anniversary Paper</unittitle>
                <unitdate>1904</unitdate>
                <physdesc>1 folder</physdesc>
            </did>
            <scopecontent>
                <p>This series contains a paper read at the 50th anniversary of the first
                    50 years of the Dorchester Industrial School on June 7, 1904, which has a
                    summation of the first 50 years of the School.</p>
            </scopecontent>
            <c02>
                <did>
                    <container localtype="folder">5</container>
                    <unittitle>1904</unittitle>
                </did>
            </c02>
        </c01>
      </dsc>
    </archdesc>
</ead>
```

Appendix D

BIBFRAME Record

(Source Record: Library of Congress Online Catalog-Record Number 18660797.)
This is the BIBFRAME coding for the resource illustrated in Figure 5.4.

```
<rdf:RDF xmlns:bf = "http://id.loc.gov/ontologies/bibframe/" xmlns:bflc = "http://id.loc.gov/ontologies/
bflc/" xmlns:madsrdf = "http://www.loc.gov/mads/rdf/v1#" xmlns:rdf = "http://www.w3.org/1999/02/22-
rdf-syntax-ns#" xmlns:rdfs = "http://www.w3.org/2000/01/rdf-schema#">
    <bf:Work rdf:about="http://id.loc.gov/resources/works/18660797">
      <bflc:aap>Joudrey, Daniel N. Introduction to cataloging and classification</bflc:aap>
      <bflc:aap-normalized>joudreydanielnintroductiontocatalogingandclassification
      </bflc:aap-normalized>
      <rdf:type rdf:resource="http://id.loc.gov/ontologies/bibframe/Text"/>
      <rdf:type rdf:resource="http://id.loc.gov/ontologies/bibframe/Monograph"/>
      <bf:language>
        <bf:Language rdf:about="http://id.loc.gov/vocabulary/languages/eng">
          <rdfs:label xml:lang="en">English</rdfs:label>
          <bf:code rdf:datatype="http://www.w3.org/2001/XMLSchema#string">eng</bf:code>
        </bf:Language>
      </bf:language>
      <bf:supplementaryContent>
        <bf:SupplementaryContent rdf:about="http://id.loc.gov/vocabulary/msupplcont/bibliography">
          <rdfs:label>bibliography</rdfs:label>
          <bf:code>bibliography</bf:code>
        </bf:SupplementaryContent>
      </bf:supplementaryContent>
      <bf:supplementaryContent>
        <bf:SupplementaryContent rdf:about="http://id.loc.gov/vocabulary/msupplcont/index">
          <rdfs:label>index</rdfs:label>
          <bf:code>index</bf:code>
        </bf:SupplementaryContent>
      </bf:supplementaryContent>
      <bf:classification>
        <bf:ClassificationLcc>
          <bf:classificationPortion>Z693</bf:classificationPortion>
          <bf:itemPortion>.W94 2015</bf:itemPortion>
          <bf:assigner>
            <bf:Organization rdf:about="http://id.loc.gov/vocabulary/organizations/dlc">
              <rdfs:label>United States, Library of Congress</rdfs:label>
              <bf:code rdf:datatype="http://id.loc.gov/datatypes/orgs/code">DLC</bf:code>
              <bf:code rdf:datatype="http://id.loc.gov/datatypes/orgs/normalized">dlc</bf:code>
              <bf:code rdf:datatype="http://id.loc.gov/datatypes/orgs/iso15511">US-dlc</bf:code>
            </bf:Organization>
          </bf:assigner>
```

```xml
        <bf:status>
          <bf:Status rdf:about="http://id.loc.gov/vocabulary/mstatus/uba">
            <rdfs:label>used by assigner</rdfs:label>
            <bf:code>uba</bf:code>
          </bf:Status>
        </bf:status>
      </bf:ClassificationLcc>
    </bf:classification>
    <bf:classification>
      <bf:ClassificationDdc>
        <bf:classificationPortion>025.3</bf:classificationPortion>
        <bf:source>
          <bf:Source>
            <bf:code>23</bf:code>
          </bf:Source>
        </bf:source>
        <bf:edition>full</bf:edition>
        <bf:assigner>
          <bf:Organization rdf:about="http://id.loc.gov/vocabulary/organizations/dlc">
            <rdfs:label>United States, Library of Congress</rdfs:label>
            <bf:code rdf:datatype="http://id.loc.gov/datatypes/orgs/code">DLC</bf:code>
            <bf:code rdf:datatype="http://id.loc.gov/datatypes/orgs/normalized">dlc</bf:code>
            <bf:code rdf:datatype="http://id.loc.gov/datatypes/orgs/iso15511">US-dlc</bf:code>
          </bf:Organization>
        </bf:assigner>
      </bf:ClassificationDdc>
    </bf:classification>
    <bf:classification>
      <bf:Classification>
        <bf:classificationPortion>LAN025030</bf:classificationPortion>
        <bf:source>
          <bf:Source>
            <bf:code>bisacsh</bf:code>
          </bf:Source>
        </bf:source>
      </bf:Classification>
    </bf:classification>
    <bf:classification>
      <bf:Classification>
        <bf:classificationPortion>LAN020000</bf:classificationPortion>
        <bf:source>
          <bf:Source>
            <bf:code>bisacsh</bf:code>
          </bf:Source>
        </bf:source>
      </bf:Classification>
    </bf:classification>
    <bf:contribution>
      <bf:Contribution>
        <rdf:type rdf:resource="http://id.loc.gov/ontologies/bibframe/PrimaryContribution"/>
        <bf:agent>
          <bf:Agent rdf:about="http://id.loc.gov/rwo/agents/no2006073134">
            <rdf:type rdf:resource="http://id.loc.gov/ontologies/bibframe/Person"/>
            <rdfs:label>Joudrey, Daniel N.</rdfs:label>
```

```xml
          <bflc:marcKey>1001 $aJoudrey, Daniel N.</bflc:marcKey>
        </bf:Agent>
      </bf:agent>
      <bf:role>
        <bf:Role rdf:about="http://id.loc.gov/vocabulary/relators/aut">
          <rdfs:label>author</rdfs:label>
          <bf:code>aut</bf:code>
        </bf:Role>
      </bf:role>
    </bf:Contribution>
  </bf:contribution>
  <bf:title>
    <bf:Title>
      <bf:mainTitle>Introduction to cataloging and classification</bf:mainTitle>
    </bf:Title>
  </bf:title>
  <bf:content>
    <bf:Content rdf:about="http://id.loc.gov/vocabulary/contentTypes/txt">
      <rdfs:label>text</rdfs:label>
      <bf:code>txt</bf:code>
    </bf:Content>
  </bf:content>
  <bf:subject>
    <bf:Topic rdf:about="http://id.loc.gov/authorities/subjects/sh85037127">
      <rdfs:label xml:lang="en">Descriptive cataloging</rdfs:label>
      <bflc:marcKey>150 $aDescriptive cataloging</bflc:marcKey>
    </bf:Topic>
  </bf:subject>
  <bf:subject>
    <bf:Topic rdf:about="http://id.loc.gov/authorities/subjects/sh85129425">
      <rdfs:label xml:lang="en">Subject cataloging</rdfs:label>
      <bflc:marcKey>150 0$aSubject cataloging</bflc:marcKey>
    </bf:Topic>
  </bf:subject>
  <bf:subject>
    <bf:Topic rdf:about="http://id.loc.gov/authorities/subjects/sh85026721">
      <rdfs:label xml:lang="en">Classification--Books</rdfs:label>
      <bflc:marcKey>150 $aClassification$xBooks</bflc:marcKey>
      <madsrdf:componentList rdf:parseType="Collection">
        <madsrdf:Topic>
          <rdf:type rdf:resource="http://www.loc.gov/mads/rdf/v1#Authority"/>
          <madsrdf:authoritativeLabel xml:lang="en">Classification</madsrdf:authoritativeLabel>
          <madsrdf:elementList rdf:parseType="Collection">
            <madsrdf:TopicElement>
              <madsrdf:elementValue xml:lang="en">Classification</madsrdf:elementValue>
            </madsrdf:TopicElement>
          </madsrdf:elementList>
        </madsrdf:Topic>
        <madsrdf:Topic>
          <rdf:type rdf:resource="http://www.loc.gov/mads/rdf/v1#Authority"/>
          <madsrdf:authoritativeLabel xml:lang="en">Books</madsrdf:authoritativeLabel>
          <madsrdf:elementList rdf:parseType="Collection">
            <madsrdf:TopicElement>
              <madsrdf:elementValue xml:lang="en">Books</madsrdf:elementValue>
```

```xml
                </madsrdf:TopicElement>
              </madsrdf:elementList>
            </madsrdf:Topic>
          </madsrdf:componentList>
       </bf:Topic>
    </bf:subject>
    <bf:subject>
       <bf:Hub rdf:about="http://id.loc.gov/resources/hubs/d4b7d72a-1163-6c4d-caf8-5505ac16ed62">
          <rdfs:label>Resource description & access</rdfs:label>
          <bflc:marcKey>1300 $aResource description & access</bflc:marcKey>
          <bf:title>
             <bf:Title>
                <bf:mainTitle>Resource description & access</bf:mainTitle>
             </bf:Title>
          </bf:title>
          <bf:title>
             <bf:VariantTitle>
                <bf:mainTitle>RDA</bf:mainTitle>
             </bf:VariantTitle>
          </bf:title>
          <bf:title>
             <bf:VariantTitle>
                <bf:mainTitle>RDA: resource description & access</bf:mainTitle>
             </bf:VariantTitle>
          </bf:title>
          <bf:title>
             <bf:VariantTitle>
                <bf:mainTitle>RDA: resource description and access</bf:mainTitle>
             </bf:VariantTitle>
          </bf:title>
          <bf:title>
             <bf:VariantTitle>
                <bf:mainTitle>Resource description and access</bf:mainTitle>
             </bf:VariantTitle>
          </bf:title>
       </bf:Hub>
    </bf:subject>
    <bf:subject>
       <bf:Topic>
          <rdf:type rdf:resource="http://www.loc.gov/mads/rdf/v1#Topic"/>
          <rdfs:label>LANGUAGE ARTS & DISCIPLINES / Library & Information Science / Cataloging &
             Classification</rdfs:label>
          <madsrdf:authoritativeLabel>LANGUAGE ARTS & DISCIPLINES / Library & Information Science /
             Cataloging & Classification</madsrdf:authoritativeLabel>
          <bflc:aap-normalized>languagearts&disciplines/library&informationscience/cataloging&classi-
             fication
          </bflc:aap-normalized>
          <madsrdf:isMemberOfMADSScheme>
             <madsrdf:Authority rdf:about="http://id.loc.gov/vocabulary/subjectSchemes/bisacsh">
                <rdfs:label>BISAC subject headings</rdfs:label>
                <bf:code>bisacsh</bf:code>
             </madsrdf:Authority>
          </madsrdf:isMemberOfMADSScheme>
          <bf:source>
```

```xml
        <bf:Source rdf:about="http://id.loc.gov/vocabulary/subjectSchemes/bisacsh">
          <rdfs:label>BISAC subject headings</rdfs:label>
          <bf:code>bisacsh</bf:code>
        </bf:Source>
      </bf:source>
    </bf:Topic>
  </bf:subject>
  <bf:subject>
    <bf:Topic>
      <rdf:type rdf:resource="http://www.loc.gov/mads/rdf/v1#Topic"/>
      <rdfs:label>LANGUAGE ARTS & DISCIPLINES / Study & Teaching</rdfs:label>
      <madsrdf:authoritativeLabel>LANGUAGE ARTS & DISCIPLINES / Study &
          Teaching</madsrdf:authoritativeLabel>
      <bflc:aap-normalized>languagearts&disciplines/study&teaching</bflc:aap-normalized>
      <madsrdf:isMemberOfMADSScheme>
        <madsrdf:Authority rdf:about="http://id.loc.gov/vocabulary/subjectSchemes/bisacsh">
          <rdfs:label>BISAC subject headings</rdfs:label>
          <bf:code>bisacsh</bf:code>
        </madsrdf:Authority>
      </madsrdf:isMemberOfMADSScheme>
      <bf:source>
        <bf:Source rdf:about="http://id.loc.gov/vocabulary/subjectSchemes/bisacsh">
          <rdfs:label>BISAC subject headings</rdfs:label>
          <bf:code>bisacsh</bf:code>
        </bf:Source>
      </bf:source>
    </bf:Topic>
  </bf:subject>
  <bf:contribution>
    <bf:Contribution>
      <bf:agent>
        <bf:Agent rdf:about="http://id.loc.gov/rwo/agents/n80050006">
          <rdf:type rdf:resource="http://id.loc.gov/ontologies/bibframe/Person"/>
          <rdfs:label>Taylor, Arlene G., 1941-</rdfs:label>
          <bflc:marcKey>1001 $aTaylor, Arlene G.,$d1941-</bflc:marcKey>
        </bf:Agent>
      </bf:agent>
      <bf:role>
        <bf:Role rdf:about="http://id.loc.gov/vocabulary/relators/aut">
          <rdfs:label>author</rdfs:label>
          <bf:code>aut</bf:code>
        </bf:Role>
      </bf:role>
    </bf:Contribution>
  </bf:contribution>
  <bf:contribution>
    <bf:Contribution>
      <bf:agent>
        <bf:Agent rdf:about="http://id.loc.gov/rwo/agents/n00031008">
          <rdf:type rdf:resource="http://id.loc.gov/ontologies/bibframe/Person"/>
          <rdfs:label>Miller, David P. (David Peter), 1955-</rdfs:label>
          <bflc:marcKey>1001 $aMiller, David P.$q(David Peter),$d1955-</bflc:marcKey>
        </bf:Agent>
      </bf:agent>
```

```xml
            <bf:role>
              <bf:Role rdf:about="http://id.loc.gov/vocabulary/relators/aut">
                <rdfs:label>author</rdfs:label>
                <bf:code>aut</bf:code>
              </bf:Role>
            </bf:role>
          </bf:Contribution>
        </bf:contribution>
        <dcterms:isPartOf>
          <dcterms:isPartOf rdf:resource="http://id.loc.gov/resources/works"/>
        </dcterms:isPartOf>
        <bf:relation>
          <bf:Relation>
            <bf:relationship>
              <bf:Relationship rdf:about="http://id.loc.gov/vocabulary/relationship/series">
                <rdfs:label>series</rdfs:label>
                <bf:code>series</bf:code>
              </bf:Relationship>
            </bf:relationship>
            <bf:associatedResource>
              <bf:Series>
                <rdf:type rdf:resource="http://id.loc.gov/ontologies/bflc/Uncontrolled"/>
                <bf:status>
                  <bf:Status rdf:about="http://id.loc.gov/vocabulary/mstatus/t">
                    <rdfs:label>transcribed</rdfs:label>
                    <bf:code>t</bf:code>
                  </bf:Status>
                </bf:status>
                <bf:title>
                  <bf:Title>
                    <bf:mainTitle>Library and information science text series</bf:mainTitle>
                  </bf:Title>
                </bf:title>
              </bf:Series>
            </bf:associatedResource>
          </bf:Relation>
        </bf:relation>
        <bf:relation>
          <bf:Relation>
            <bf:relationship>
              <bf:Relationship rdf:about="http://id.loc.gov/vocabulary/relationship/relatedwork">
                <rdfs:label>related work</rdfs:label>
                <bf:code>relatedwork</bf:code>
              </bf:Relationship>
            </bf:relationship>
            <bf:relationship>
              <bf:Relationship rdf:about="http://id.loc.gov/entities/relationships/basedon">
                <rdfs:label>Based on</rdfs:label>
              </bf:Relationship>
            </bf:relationship>
            <bf:associatedResource>
              <bf:Hub rdf:about="http://id.loc.gov/resources/hubs/fc5bd467-56f3-1b0f-5db3-a5a07379160f">
```

```xml
              <rdfs:label>Taylor, Arlene G., 1941-. Introduction to cataloging and classification
              </rdfs:label>
              <bflc:marcKey>1001 $aTaylor, Arlene G.,$d1941-$tIntroduction to cataloging and
                    classification.</bflc:marcKey>
            <bf:contribution>
              <bf:Contribution>
                <rdf:type rdf:resource="http://id.loc.gov/ontologies/bibframe/PrimaryContribution"/>
                <bf:agent>
                  <bf:Agent rdf:about="http://id.loc.gov/rwo/agents/n80050006">
                    <rdf:type rdf:resource="http://id.loc.gov/ontologies/bibframe/Person"/>
                    <rdfs:label>Taylor, Arlene G., 1941-</rdfs:label>
                    <bflc:marcKey>1001 $aTaylor, Arlene G.,$d1941-</bflc:marcKey>
                  </bf:Agent>
                </bf:agent>
                <bf:role>
                  <bf:Role rdf:about="http://id.loc.gov/vocabulary/relators/ctb">
                    <rdfs:label>contributor</rdfs:label>
                    <bf:code>ctb</bf:code>
                  </bf:Role>
                </bf:role>
              </bf:Contribution>
            </bf:contribution>
            <bf:title>
              <bf:Title>
                <bf:mainTitle>Introduction to cataloging and classification</bf:mainTitle>
              </bf:Title>
            </bf:title>
          </bf:Hub>
        </bf:associatedResource>
      </bf:Relation>
    </bf:relation>
    <bf:hasInstance>
      <bf:Instance rdf:about="http://id.loc.gov/resources/instances/18660797">
        <bf:title>
          <bf:Title>
            <bf:mainTitle>Introduction to cataloging and classification</bf:mainTitle>
          </bf:Title>
        </bf:title>
        <bf:publicationStatement>Santa Barbara, California: Libraries Unlimited,
              [2015]</bf:publicationStatement>
      </bf:Instance>
    </bf:hasInstance>
    <bf:adminMetadata>
      <bf:AdminMetadata>
        <bf:status>
          <bf:Status rdf:about="http://id.loc.gov/vocabulary/mstatus/n">
            <rdfs:label>new</rdfs:label>
            <bf:code>n</bf:code>
          </bf:Status>
        </bf:status>
        <bf:date rdf:datatype="http://www.w3.org/2001/XMLSchema#date">2015-06-16</bf:date>
        <bf:agent>
          <bf:Agent rdf:about="http://id.loc.gov/vocabulary/organizations/dlc">
```

```xml
          <rdf:type rdf:resource="http://id.loc.gov/ontologies/bibframe/Organization"/>
          <rdfs:label>United States, Library of Congress</rdfs:label>
          <bf:code rdf:datatype="http://id.loc.gov/datatypes/orgs/code">DLC</bf:code>
          <bf:code rdf:datatype="http://id.loc.gov/datatypes/orgs/normalized">dlc</bf:code>
          <bf:code rdf:datatype="http://id.loc.gov/datatypes/orgs/iso15511">US-dlc</bf:code>
        </bf:Agent>
      </bf:agent>
    </bf:AdminMetadata>
</bf:adminMetadata>
<bf:adminMetadata>
    <bf:AdminMetadata>
      <bf:status>
        <bf:Status rdf:about="http://id.loc.gov/vocabulary/mstatus/c">
          <rdfs:label>changed</rdfs:label>
          <bf:code>c</bf:code>
        </bf:Status>
      </bf:status>
      <bf:date rdf:datatype="http://www.w3.org/2001/XMLSchema#dateTime">2017-06-
          07T11:12:20</bf:date>
      <bf:descriptionModifier>
        <bf:Organization rdf:about="http://id.loc.gov/vocabulary/organizations/dlc">
          <rdfs:label>United States, Library of Congress</rdfs:label>
          <bf:code rdf:datatype="http://id.loc.gov/datatypes/orgs/code">DLC</bf:code>
          <bf:code rdf:datatype="http://id.loc.gov/datatypes/orgs/normalized">dlc</bf:code>
          <bf:code rdf:datatype="http://id.loc.gov/datatypes/orgs/iso15511">US-dlc</bf:code>
        </bf:Organization>
      </bf:descriptionModifier>
    </bf:AdminMetadata>
</bf:adminMetadata>
<bf:adminMetadata>
    <bf:AdminMetadata>
      <bf:status>
        <bf:Status rdf:about="http://id.loc.gov/vocabulary/mstatus/c">
          <rdfs:label>changed</rdfs:label>
          <bf:code>c</bf:code>
        </bf:Status>
      </bf:status>
      <bf:agent>
        <bf:Agent rdf:about="http://id.loc.gov/vocabulary/organizations/dlcmrc">
          <rdf:type rdf:resource="http://id.loc.gov/ontologies/bibframe/Organization"/>
          <rdfs:label>United States, Library of Congress, Network Development and MARC Standards
              Office</rdfs:label>
          <bf:code rdf:datatype="http://id.loc.gov/datatypes/orgs/code">DLC-MRC</bf:code>
          <bf:code rdf:datatype="http://id.loc.gov/datatypes/orgs/normalized">dlcmrc</bf:code>
          <bf:code rdf:datatype="http://id.loc.gov/datatypes/orgs/iso15511">US-dlcmrc</bf:code>
        </bf:Agent>
      </bf:agent>
      <bf:generationProcess>
        <bf:generationProcess rdf:resource="https://github.com/lcnetdev/marc2bibframe2/
            releases/tag/v2.9.0-dev"/>
      </bf:generationProcess>
      <bf:date rdf:datatype="http://www.w3.org/2001/XMLSchema#dateTime">2025-03-
          17T14:36:45.548452-04:00</bf:date>
```

```xml
        </bf:AdminMetadata>
    </bf:adminMetadata>
    <bf:adminMetadata>
        <bf:AdminMetadata>
            <bf:descriptionLevel>
                <bf:descriptionLevel rdf:resource="http://id.loc.gov/ontologies/bibframe-2-4-0/"/>
            </bf:descriptionLevel>
            <bflc:encodingLevel>
                <bflc:EncodingLevel rdf:about="http://id.loc.gov/vocabulary/menclvl/f">
                    <rdfs:label>full</rdfs:label>
                    <bf:code>f</bf:code>
                </bflc:EncodingLevel>
            </bflc:encodingLevel>
            <bf:descriptionConventions>
                <bf:DescriptionConventions rdf:about="http://id.loc.gov/vocabulary/descriptionConventions/isbd">
                    <rdfs:label>ISBD: International standard bibliographic description</rdfs:label>
                    <bf:code>isbd</bf:code>
                </bf:DescriptionConventions>
            </bf:descriptionConventions>
            <bf:identifiedBy>
                <bf:Local>
                    <rdf:value>18660797</rdf:value>
                    <bf:assigner>
                        <bf:Organization rdf:about="http://id.loc.gov/vocabulary/organizations/dlc">
                            <rdfs:label>United States, Library of Congress</rdfs:label>
                            <bf:code rdf:datatype="http://id.loc.gov/datatypes/orgs/code">DLC</bf:code>
                            <bf:code rdf:datatype="http://id.loc.gov/datatypes/orgs/normalized">dlc</bf:code>
                            <bf:code rdf:datatype="http://id.loc.gov/datatypes/orgs/iso15511">US-dlc</bf:code>
                        </bf:Organization>
                    </bf:assigner>
                </bf:Local>
            </bf:identifiedBy>
            <bf:descriptionLanguage>
                <bf:Language rdf:about="http://id.loc.gov/vocabulary/languages/eng">
                    <rdfs:label xml:lang="en">English</rdfs:label>
                    <bf:code rdf:datatype="http://www.w3.org/2001/XMLSchema#string">eng</bf:code>
                </bf:Language>
            </bf:descriptionLanguage>
            <bf:descriptionConventions>
                <bf:DescriptionConventions rdf:about="http://id.loc.gov/vocabulary/descriptionConventions/rda">
                    <rdfs:label>Resource description and access</rdfs:label>
                    <bf:code>rda</bf:code>
                </bf:DescriptionConventions>
            </bf:descriptionConventions>
            <bf:note>
                <bf:Note>
                    <rdf:type rdf:resource="http://id.loc.gov/vocabulary/mnotetype/internal"/>
                    <rdfs:label>040 $aDLC$beng$cDLC$erda$dDLC</rdfs:label>
                </bf:Note>
            </bf:note>
            <bf:descriptionAuthentication>
```

```xml
            <bf:DescriptionAuthentication rdf:about="http://id.loc.gov/vocabulary/marcauthen/pcc">
              <rdfs:label>Program for Cooperative Cataloging</rdfs:label>
              <bf:code>pcc</bf:code>
            </bf:DescriptionAuthentication>
          </bf:descriptionAuthentication>
        </bf:AdminMetadata>
      </bf:adminMetadata>
</bf:Work>
<bf:Instance rdf:about="http://id.loc.gov/resources/instances/18660797">
    <bf:issuance>
      <bf:Issuance rdf:about="http://id.loc.gov/vocabulary/issuance/mono">
        <rdfs:label>single unit</rdfs:label>
        <bf:code>mono</bf:code>
      </bf:Issuance>
    </bf:issuance>
    <bf:provisionActivity>
      <bf:ProvisionActivity>
        <rdf:type rdf:resource="http://id.loc.gov/ontologies/bibframe/Publication"/>
        <bf:date rdf:datatype="http://id.loc.gov/datatypes/edtf">2015</bf:date>
        <bf:place>
          <bf:Place rdf:about="http://id.loc.gov/vocabulary/countries/cau">
            <rdfs:label xml:lang="en">California</rdfs:label>
            <bf:code rdf:datatype="http://www.w3.org/2001/XMLSchema#string">cau</bf:code>
          </bf:Place>
        </bf:place>
        <bflc:simplePlace>Santa Barbara, California</bflc:simplePlace>
        <bflc:simpleAgent>Libraries Unlimited</bflc:simpleAgent>
        <bflc:simpleDate>[2015]</bflc:simpleDate>
      </bf:ProvisionActivity>
    </bf:provisionActivity>
    <bf:publicationStatement>Santa Barbara, California: Libraries Unlimited, [2015]
    </bf:publicationStatement>
    <bf:identifiedBy>
      <bf:Lccn>
        <rdf:value>2015012911</rdf:value>
      </bf:Lccn>
    </bf:identifiedBy>
    <bf:identifiedBy>
      <bf:Isbn>
        <rdf:value>9781598848571</rdf:value>
        <bf:qualifier>hardback : acid-free paper</bf:qualifier>
      </bf:Isbn>
    </bf:identifiedBy>
    <bf:identifiedBy>
      <bf:Isbn>
        <rdf:value>9781598848564</rdf:value>
        <bf:qualifier>pbk : acid-free paper</bf:qualifier>
      </bf:Isbn>
    </bf:identifiedBy>
    <bf:identifiedBy>
      <bf:Isbn>
        <rdf:value>9781440837456</rdf:value>
        <bf:status>
```

```xml
      <bf:Status rdf:about="http://id.loc.gov/vocabulary/mstatus/cancinv">
        <rdfs:label>canceled or invalid</rdfs:label>
        <bf:code>cancinv</bf:code>
      </bf:Status>
    </bf:status>
    <bf:qualifier>ebook</bf:qualifier>
  </bf:Isbn>
</bf:identifiedBy>
<bf:responsibilityStatement>Daniel N. Joudrey, Arlene G. Taylor, and David P.
   Miller</bf:responsibilityStatement>
<bf:title>
  <bf:Title>
    <bf:mainTitle>Introduction to cataloging and classification</bf:mainTitle>
  </bf:Title>
</bf:title>
<bf:editionStatement>Eleventh edition</bf:editionStatement>
<bf:extent>
  <bf:Extent>
    <rdfs:label>xxv, 1048 pages</rdfs:label>
  </bf:Extent>
</bf:extent>
<bf:dimensions>27 cm</bf:dimensions>
<bf:media>
  <bf:Media rdf:about="http://id.loc.gov/vocabulary/mediaTypes/n">
    <rdfs:label>unmediated</rdfs:label>
    <bf:code>n</bf:code>
  </bf:Media>
</bf:media>
<bf:carrier>
  <bf:Carrier rdf:about="http://id.loc.gov/vocabulary/carriers/nc">
    <rdfs:label>volume</rdfs:label>
    <bf:code>nc</bf:code>
  </bf:Carrier>
</bf:carrier>
<bf:note>
  <bf:Note>
    <rdfs:label>Significant expansion of: Introduction to cataloging and classification. Tenth edition /
       Arlene G. Taylor ; with the assistance of David P. Miller.</rdfs:label>
  </bf:Note>
</bf:note>
<bf:note>
  <bf:Note>
    <rdf:type rdf:resource="http://id.loc.gov/vocabulary/mnotetype/biblio"/>
    <rdfs:label>Includes bibliographical references (pages 1001-1022) and index.</rdfs:label>
  </bf:Note>
</bf:note>
<dcterms:isPartOf>
  <dcterms:isPartOf rdf:resource="http://id.loc.gov/resources/instances"/>
</dcterms:isPartOf>
<bf:instanceOf>
  <bf:Work rdf:about="http://id.loc.gov/resources/works/18660797">
    <rdfs:label>Joudrey, Daniel N. Introduction to cataloging and classification</rdfs:label>
    <bf:contribution>
```

```xml
<bf:Contribution>
  <rdf:type rdf:resource="http://id.loc.gov/ontologies/bibframe/PrimaryContribution"/>
  <bf:agent>
    <bf:Agent rdf:about="http://id.loc.gov/rwo/agents/no2006073134">
      <rdf:type rdf:resource="http://id.loc.gov/ontologies/bibframe/Person"/>
      <rdfs:label>Joudrey, Daniel N.</rdfs:label>
      <bflc:marcKey>1001 $aJoudrey, Daniel N.</bflc:marcKey>
    </bf:Agent>
  </bf:agent>
  <bf:role>
    <bf:Role rdf:about="http://id.loc.gov/vocabulary/relators/aut">
      <rdfs:label>author</rdfs:label>
      <bf:code>aut</bf:code>
    </bf:Role>
  </bf:role>
</bf:Contribution>
</bf:contribution>
<bf:contribution>
  <bf:Contribution>
    <bf:agent>
      <bf:Agent rdf:about="http://id.loc.gov/rwo/agents/n80050006">
        <rdf:type rdf:resource="http://id.loc.gov/ontologies/bibframe/Person"/>
        <rdfs:label>Taylor, Arlene G., 1941-</rdfs:label>
        <bflc:marcKey>1001 $aTaylor, Arlene G.,$d1941-</bflc:marcKey>
      </bf:Agent>
    </bf:agent>
    <bf:role>
      <bf:Role rdf:about="http://id.loc.gov/vocabulary/relators/aut">
        <rdfs:label>author</rdfs:label>
        <bf:code>aut</bf:code>
      </bf:Role>
    </bf:role>
  </bf:Contribution>
</bf:contribution>
<bf:contribution>
  <bf:Contribution>
    <bf:agent>
      <bf:Agent rdf:about="http://id.loc.gov/rwo/agents/n00031008">
        <rdf:type rdf:resource="http://id.loc.gov/ontologies/bibframe/Person"/>
        <rdfs:label>Miller, David P. (David Peter), 1955-</rdfs:label>
        <bflc:marcKey>1001 $aMiller, David P.$q(David Peter),$d1955-</bflc:marcKey>
      </bf:Agent>
    </bf:agent>
    <bf:role>
      <bf:Role rdf:about="http://id.loc.gov/vocabulary/relators/aut">
        <rdfs:label>author</rdfs:label>
        <bf:code>aut</bf:code>
      </bf:Role>
    </bf:role>
  </bf:Contribution>
</bf:contribution>
<bf:title>
  <bf:Title>
```

```xml
          <bf:mainTitle>Introduction to cataloging and classification</bf:mainTitle>
        </bf:Title>
      </bf:title>
      <bf:language rdf:resource="http://id.loc.gov/vocabulary/languages/eng"/>
      <bf:hasInstance>
        <bf:Instance rdf:about="http://id.loc.gov/resources/instances/18660797">
          <bf:title>
            <bf:Title>
              <bf:mainTitle>Introduction to cataloging and classification</bf:mainTitle>
            </bf:Title>
          </bf:title>
          <bf:identifiedBy>
            <bf:Lccn>
              <rdf:value>2015012911</rdf:value>
            </bf:Lccn>
          </bf:identifiedBy>
          <bf:identifiedBy>
            <bf:Isbn>
              <rdf:value>9781598848571</rdf:value>
              <bf:qualifier>hardback : acid-free paper</bf:qualifier>
            </bf:Isbn>
          </bf:identifiedBy>
          <bf:identifiedBy>
            <bf:Isbn>
              <rdf:value>9781598848564</rdf:value>
              <bf:qualifier>pbk : acid-free paper</bf:qualifier>
            </bf:Isbn>
          </bf:identifiedBy>
          <bf:identifiedBy>
            <bf:Isbn>
              <rdf:value>9781440837456</rdf:value>
              <bf:status rdf:resource="http://id.loc.gov/vocabulary/mstatus/cancinv"/>
              <bf:qualifier>ebook</bf:qualifier>
            </bf:Isbn>
          </bf:identifiedBy>
          <bf:publicationStatement>Santa Barbara, California: Libraries Unlimited,
              [2015]</bf:publicationStatement>
          <bf:editionStatement>Eleventh edition</bf:editionStatement>
          <bf:extent>
            <bf:Extent>
              <rdfs:label>xxv, 1048 pages</rdfs:label>
            </bf:Extent>
          </bf:extent>
        </bf:Instance>
      </bf:hasInstance>
    </bf:Work>
  </bf:instanceOf>
  <bf:adminMetadata>
    <bf:AdminMetadata>
      <bf:status>
        <bf:Status rdf:about="http://id.loc.gov/vocabulary/mstatus/n">
          <rdfs:label>new</rdfs:label>
          <bf:code>n</bf:code>
```

```xml
          </bf:Status>
        </bf:status>
        <bf:date rdf:datatype="http://www.w3.org/2001/XMLSchema#date">2015-06-16</bf:date>
        <bf:agent>
          <bf:Agent rdf:about="http://id.loc.gov/vocabulary/organizations/dlc">
            <rdf:type rdf:resource="http://id.loc.gov/ontologies/bibframe/Organization"/>
            <rdfs:label>United States, Library of Congress</rdfs:label>
            <bf:code rdf:datatype="http://id.loc.gov/datatypes/orgs/code">DLC</bf:code>
            <bf:code rdf:datatype="http://id.loc.gov/datatypes/orgs/normalized">dlc</bf:code>
            <bf:code rdf:datatype="http://id.loc.gov/datatypes/orgs/iso15511">US-dlc</bf:code>
          </bf:Agent>
        </bf:agent>
      </bf:AdminMetadata>
    </bf:adminMetadata>
    <bf:adminMetadata>
      <bf:AdminMetadata>
        <bf:status>
          <bf:Status rdf:about="http://id.loc.gov/vocabulary/mstatus/c">
            <rdfs:label>changed</rdfs:label>
            <bf:code>c</bf:code>
          </bf:Status>
        </bf:status>
        <bf:date rdf:datatype="http://www.w3.org/2001/XMLSchema#dateTime">2017-06-07T11:12:20</bf:date>
        <bf:descriptionModifier>
          <bf:Organization rdf:about="http://id.loc.gov/vocabulary/organizations/dlc">
            <rdfs:label>United States, Library of Congress</rdfs:label>
            <bf:code rdf:datatype="http://id.loc.gov/datatypes/orgs/code">DLC</bf:code>
            <bf:code rdf:datatype="http://id.loc.gov/datatypes/orgs/normalized">dlc</bf:code>
            <bf:code rdf:datatype="http://id.loc.gov/datatypes/orgs/iso15511">US-dlc</bf:code>
          </bf:Organization>
        </bf:descriptionModifier>
      </bf:AdminMetadata>
    </bf:adminMetadata>
    <bf:adminMetadata>
      <bf:AdminMetadata>
        <bf:status>
          <bf:Status rdf:about="http://id.loc.gov/vocabulary/mstatus/c">
            <rdfs:label>changed</rdfs:label>
            <bf:code>c</bf:code>
          </bf:Status>
        </bf:status>
        <bf:agent>
          <bf:Agent rdf:about="http://id.loc.gov/vocabulary/organizations/dlcmrc">
            <rdf:type rdf:resource="http://id.loc.gov/ontologies/bibframe/Organization"/>
            <rdfs:label>United States, Library of Congress, Network Development and MARC Standards Office</rdfs:label>
            <bf:code rdf:datatype="http://id.loc.gov/datatypes/orgs/code">DLC-MRC</bf:code>
            <bf:code rdf:datatype="http://id.loc.gov/datatypes/orgs/normalized">dlcmrc</bf:code>
            <bf:code rdf:datatype="http://id.loc.gov/datatypes/orgs/iso15511">US-dlcmrc</bf:code>
          </bf:Agent>
        </bf:agent>
        <bf:generationProcess>
```

```xml
        <bf:generationProcess rdf:resource="https://github.com/lcnetdev/marc2bibframe2/releases/tag/v2.9.0-dev"/>
      </bf:generationProcess>
      <bf:date rdf:datatype="http://www.w3.org/2001/XMLSchema#dateTime">2025-03-17T14:36:45.548452-04:00</bf:date>
    </bf:AdminMetadata>
  </bf:adminMetadata>
  <bf:adminMetadata>
    <bf:AdminMetadata>
      <bf:descriptionLevel>
        <bf:descriptionLevel rdf:resource="http://id.loc.gov/ontologies/bibframe-2-4-0/"/>
      </bf:descriptionLevel>
      <bflc:encodingLevel>
        <bflc:EncodingLevel rdf:about="http://id.loc.gov/vocabulary/menclvl/f">
          <rdfs:label>full</rdfs:label>
          <bf:code>f</bf:code>
        </bflc:EncodingLevel>
      </bflc:encodingLevel>
      <bf:descriptionConventions>
        <bf:DescriptionConventions rdf:about="http://id.loc.gov/vocabulary/descriptionConventions/isbd">
          <rdfs:label>ISBD: International standard bibliographic description</rdfs:label>
          <bf:code>isbd</bf:code>
        </bf:DescriptionConventions>
      </bf:descriptionConventions>
      <bf:identifiedBy>
        <bf:Local>
          <rdf:value>18660797</rdf:value>
          <bf:assigner>
            <bf:Organization rdf:about="http://id.loc.gov/vocabulary/organizations/dlc">
              <rdfs:label>United States, Library of Congress</rdfs:label>
              <bf:code rdf:datatype="http://id.loc.gov/datatypes/orgs/code">DLC</bf:code>
              <bf:code rdf:datatype="http://id.loc.gov/datatypes/orgs/normalized">dlc</bf:code>
              <bf:code rdf:datatype="http://id.loc.gov/datatypes/orgs/iso15511">US-dlc</bf:code>
            </bf:Organization>
          </bf:assigner>
        </bf:Local>
      </bf:identifiedBy>
      <bf:descriptionLanguage>
        <bf:Language rdf:about="http://id.loc.gov/vocabulary/languages/eng">
          <rdfs:label xml:lang="en">English</rdfs:label>
          <bf:code rdf:datatype="http://www.w3.org/2001/XMLSchema#string">eng</bf:code>
        </bf:Language>
      </bf:descriptionLanguage>
      <bf:descriptionConventions>
        <bf:DescriptionConventions rdf:about="http://id.loc.gov/vocabulary/descriptionConventions/rda">
          <rdfs:label>Resource description and access</rdfs:label>
          <bf:code>rda</bf:code>
        </bf:DescriptionConventions>
      </bf:descriptionConventions>
      <bf:note>
        <bf:Note>
```

```
              <rdf:type rdf:resource="http://id.loc.gov/vocabulary/mnotetype/internal"/>
              <rdfs:label>040 $aDLC$beng$cDLC$erda$dDLC</rdfs:label>
           </bf:Note>
         </bf:note>
         <bf:descriptionAuthentication>
            <bf:DescriptionAuthentication rdf:about="http://id.loc.gov/vocabulary/marcauthen/pcc">
               <rdfs:label>Program for Cooperative Cataloging</rdfs:label>
               <bf:code>pcc</bf:code>
            </bf:DescriptionAuthentication>
         </bf:descriptionAuthentication>
      </bf:AdminMetadata>
    </bf:adminMetadata>
  </bf:Instance>
</rdf:RDF>
```

Appendix E

An Approach to Subject Analysis

The following outline offers a practical framework for applying the subject analysis concepts discussed in Chapter 11. It walks the analyst through the key features of a work, pinpoints essential questions for determining aboutness, and helps make the process more concrete. An example of subject analysis is provided after the outline.

E.1 Outline

I. **Analyze the information resource**

  A. Identify the overall discipline, branch of knowledge, or subject area in which the work fits. Consider the intended audience and the purpose of the information resource (e.g., why the resource was created, what it accomplishes, what questions it might answer, and for whom)

  B. Identify the important topics or concepts in the information resource. Look for frequently mentioned topics or ideas in the following:
  1. Title and subtitle
  2. Table of contents, chapter titles, section headings, or equivalents
  3. Preface and/or introduction, first chapter, etc.
  4. Illustrations and their captions
  5. Conclusion (e.g., last chapter, section, etc.)

  C. Identify names used as subject concepts

  D. Identify role(s) of any geographic name(s) present

  E. Identify chronological elements

  F. Identify form or genre of the resource being analyzed

II. **Construct an aboutness statement**

  A. Describe what the information resource is about

  B. Review the resource again. Look for support for your ideas. Refine the statement as needed

  C. Identify terms from the aboutness statement to be searched in the controlled vocabulary

  D. Sketch out a rudimentary hierarchy (discipline/sub-discipline/concept/topic, etc.) into which the aboutness concepts fall

III. **Translate the aboutness into controlled vocabulary**

　A. Search the chosen terms in the controlled vocabulary. Translate the terms into the specific headings or descriptors used in the controlled vocabulary list

　B. Using the hierarchy as a guide, search the classification for the most appropriate class(es) to describe the resource's aboutness. Convert the aboutness into specific classification notation(s)

IV. **Review your choices and compare to similar items**

E.2 Example

The summarization-level analysis below is for the website *Japanese Garden Reference Library*, created and maintained by the North American Japanese Garden Association (please see https://najga.org/japanese-gardening-reference/). Analysis of the website and construction of subject access mechanisms might proceed as follows:

I. **Analyze the information resource**

　A. **Identify the overall discipline, branch of knowledge, or subject area into which the work fits. Consider the intended audience and the purpose of the information resource**

　　This work falls into the arts, particularly in landscaping or garden design. It is for a general audience—anyone that may be interested in Japanese gardens. The organization's "About Us" page states, "NAJGA fosters knowledge sharing, research, and collaborations within the horticultural, human, and business communities of Japanese Gardens in North America to ensure their sustainability, enduring value, and social impact … Creating a more beautiful, healthy and peaceful world through Japanese gardens and championing the Art, Craft and Heart of Japanese Gardens in North America."

　B. **Identify concepts in:**

　　1. **Title and subtitle**

　　Japanese Garden Reference Library

　　Note that the title contains the terms *Japanese*, *garden*, and *reference library*. (Does this website fit the definition of a *reference library*?)

　　2. **Table of contents, chapter titles, section headings, or equivalents**

　　The section headings include design & theory; Japanese gardening tools; bamboo fences; stone lanterns & basins; pathways; Japanese garden plants; the tea garden; gardening terms; garden galleries; World Japanese Garden Database; Japanese gardening publications; and other resources.

Some sections contain articles and images about the topics related to the heading for the section. For example, in the section on Japanese garden plants, you find articles on Pruning Maples; Fall care for Japanese Black Pine; Plants for Dry Hot Climates, etc. Other sections contain a glossary, a database, image galleries, a bibliography, and links to outside resources.

Some of these are helpful for aboutness; some are not.

3. **Preface, introduction, and/or first chapter**

There is no introduction for this resource, but on the organization's homepage, this description is provided: "From design theory to the tools of the trade, our reference library is the go-to resource for Japanese garden enthusiasts and professionals alike."

4. **Illustrations and their captions**

Note that illustrations are of various gardens, some at varying times of year, and various feature of Japanese gardens.

5. **Conclusion (e.g., last chapter, section, etc.)**

None in this resource.

C. **Identify names used as subject concepts**

The personal names involved are names of authors and garden designers; there is also mention of the corporate body responsible for the website. The work is not about these entities, however.

D. **Identify role(s) of any geographic name(s) present**

The geographic area Japan provides the context for the topic of this work. The work is not *about* Japan, but the gardens discussed are of a type originally designed in Japan. Only some of the individual gardens discussed in this site are in Japan.

E. **Identify chronological elements**

The time periods addressed are too broad to be meaningful.

F. **Identify form of the resource being analyzed**

This resource consists of many kinds of information: text, pictures, links, and the like. Note that the word *database* is included, but the entire work is not a database. Much of the resource comprises internal web pages and links to outside resources. A sizable portion of this resource is dedicated to lists of articles about Japanese gardens (i.e., a bibliography).

II. **Construct an aboutness statement**

   A. **Describe what the resource is about**

   This resource is a bibliography related to Japanese-style gardens and gardening, including the history and design of Japanese-style gardens in Japan and around the world, elements needed in these gardens, plants to be included, and equipment. Much of the resource contains text and images of gardens and a database of important Japanese-style gardens.

   B. **Review the resource again. Look for support of your ideas. Refine the statement as needed**

   C. **Identify terms from the aboutness statement to be searched in the controlled vocabulary**

   Japan, Japanese, Japanese-style

   Gardens, Gardening

   Gardening equipment

   History, Historic

   Design

   Database

   Bibliography

   D. **Sketch out a rudimentary hierarchy (discipline/sub-discipline/concept/topic, etc.) into which the aboutness concepts fall**

   Arts / design / landscaping / gardens / Japanese

III. **Translate the aboutness into controlled vocabulary**

   A. **Search the chosen terms in the controlled vocabulary. Translate the terms into specific headings from the controlled vocabulary list**

   LCSH:

   Gardens, Japanese—History
   Gardens, Japanese—Design
   Historic gardens—Japan
   Gardens, Japanese—Bibliography
   Gardens, Japanese—Databases
   Gardening—Equipment and supplies

B. Using the hierarchy as a guide, search the classification for the most appropriate class(es) to describe the resource's aboutness. Convert the aboutness into specific classification notation(s)

LC Classification: SB458

Dewey Decimal Classification: 712.0952

IV. Review your choices and compare to similar items

How did you do?
Does this resource fit with others around it?
Would you search for it using these words?
If you searched using these words, would you be happy with this item?

Glossary

Defined in this glossary are basic terms for students of information organization, including terms used in descriptive cataloging, classification, controlled vocabulary, indexing, archival description, museum registration, and other topics treated in this text. Readers may wish to consult other sources for other terms used in the library and information professions. Some concepts are marked *obsolete* to indicate that the terms are no longer in common usage; these terms remain in the glossary, however, because they may be encountered in older LIS literature and in the workplace.

AACR *(Anglo-American Cataloguing Rules).* A set of cataloging rules, first published in 1967, for producing descriptive metadata and name and title access points in a surrogate record for a resource; later editions were published in 1978, 1988, 1998, and 2002; the editions published in 1978 and later were referred to as AACR2; the creation of these rules was the result of collaboration among representatives from Australia, Canada, Great Britain, and the United States. It was replaced in 2010 by *RDA: Resource Description & Access* (Original RDA).

AAP. *See* **Authorized access point.**

AAT. *See Art & Architecture Thesaurus.*

Abbreviation. A shortened form of a word. *See also* **Acronym; Initialism.**

Aboutness. The subject of a work contained in a resource, which is translated into controlled subject languages (e.g., classification schemes, subject heading lists); includes topical aspects but also genre and form. *See also* **Conceptual analysis; Is-ness; Of-ness; Subject analysis; Translation.**

Aboutness statement. A single sentence or a short paragraph describing and summarizing one's understanding of a resource's aboutness, the genre/form, and the relationships among the important subject concepts. The aboutness statement is used to identify the terms or concepts to be searched in the controlled vocabulary. The statement can also help the cataloger to construct a rudimentary hierarchy to get a better understanding of how the concepts fit together and how they might fit into a scheme of classification.

Abstract. A condensed narrative description (i.e., summary or synopsis) of a resource that may serve as a surrogate for the resource in a retrieval system; typically created for journal articles, conference papers, individual chapters, and the like; usually created by the author of the resource or by an indexer at the time of database indexing.

Abstracting. The process of creating an abstract. *See also* **Indexing.**

Access. That portion of cataloging in which access points are selected and formulated by a cataloger. *See also* **Description; Descriptive cataloging.**

Access point. Any word or phrase used to obtain information from a retrieval tool or other organized system; in cataloging and indexing, *access points* are specific names, titles, and subjects chosen by the cataloger or indexer, when creating metadata, to allow for the retrieval of the resource description. *See also* **Authorized access point; Controlled access point; Name/Title access point; Variant access point.**

Accession log. *See* **Museum accession record.**

Accession number. A notation assigned to an information resource that is unique to the resource; the notations may be based upon the order in which resources are acquired. In museum registration, accession numbers are used to track objects in the collection. They are used consistently throughout all documentation.

Accession record. In archives and museums, a record that contains basic information about the acquisition of a collection or object. It may include an identification number (i.e., an accession number), information about the donor, any associations, provenance, any information needed for insurance purposes, and so forth.

Accessioning. The accessioning process enters an object into the museum registration system, creating needed documentation for it. It comprises acquiring rights to the object, assigning an accession number, creating records for the object, and marking the object.

Accompanying materials. Dependent materials that accompany and are cataloged with the main component of the resource. Examples include, but are not limited to, answer books, teacher's manuals, atlases, slides, sound recordings, and software packages.

Acquisitions. The library technical services unit that, among other things, is responsible for managing orders and budgets for the collection.

Acronym. An abbreviation made up of initial letters of other words, but pronounced as its own word (e.g., *radar*). *See also* **Abbreviation; Initialism.**

Added entry. *Obsolete.* In AACR2, any access point in a resource description other than the main entry; replaced in RDA by *access point*, and access points are not considered to be primary or secondary unless a work identifier is being constructed. *See also* **Main entry (access point).**

Administrative metadata. Metadata created for the purposes of management, decision making, and recordkeeping; provides information about the technical, preservation, and storage requirements of digital resources; used for monitoring, accessing, reproducing, digitizing, and backing up digital resources.

Agent. A term generically referring to various roles associated with the creation and production of resources; an entity responsible for the existence, expansion, dissemination, etc., of resources (e.g., creators, contributors, and publishers of information resources). *See also* **Collective agent.**

Agent entities. A set of entities that have responsibility for the creation, manufacture, distribution, ownership, or modification of resources, among other possible actions. Includes persons and collective agents, such as corporate bodies and families. *See also* **Collective agent; Corporate body.**

Alphabetical catalog. A catalog with entries arranged or displayed in alphabetical order rather than according to the symbolic notation of a classification. *See also* **Classified catalog; Dictionary catalog; Divided catalog.**

Alphabetico-classed catalog. Catalog in which subject categories are used for the arrangement of resource descriptions; broad categories are subdivided by narrower categories that are placed alphabetically within each broad category.

Alternative. An Original RDA instruction that offers a different approach to what was specified in the preceding, main instruction.

Alternative title. A second title for a resource that is joined to the first title with the word *or* (e.g., *Frankenstein, or, The Modern Prometheus*). Both titles together constitute the *title proper* of the work. *See also* **Title proper.**

Analytical description. A description of a part or parts of a larger resource as opposed to a description of the whole resource; e.g., creating a description for one short story in a compilation. *See also* **Comprehensive description; Hierarchical description.**

Analytical entry. *Obsolete. See* **Analytical description**.

Analytico-synthetic classification. *See* **Faceted classification.**

Annotated bibliography. A bibliography where each entry contains annotations, i.e., brief notes providing additional information about the resource listed.

Annotation. A brief note indicating the subject matter or commenting on the usefulness of information in a particular resource.

ANSI (American National Standards Institute). A corporate body that takes responsibility for establishing voluntary industry standards; works closely with NISO.

Antonym. A term that has the opposite meaning of another term (e.g., *hot* and *cold* are antonyms). *See also* **Synonym.**

Appellation. A name, title, label, access point, or another form of nomen that is used within a given scheme or context to refer to an entity.

Appellation element. An element in Official RDA that provides some kind of label for the entity, such as a name, title, access point, or identifier.

Application profile. A document that describes a community's recommended best practices for metadata creation; a formal way to declare, using namespaces, which elements, qualifiers, vocabularies, etc., are used in a particular application or project or by a particular community.

APPM *(Archives, Personal Papers, and Manuscripts).* An older standard based on AACR2 for the description of archival materials. Replaced by DACS in the United States. See also ***Describing Archives: A Content Standard.***

Approval plan. A method in which a library contracts with one or more vendors to receive new resources according to pre-selected profiles outlining the collection's needs.

Archival description. The process of establishing intellectual control over the holdings of an archives through the creation of metadata (e.g., preparation of finding aids).

Archival series. *See* **Series (archives).**

Archives. (1) An organization that preserves records of enduring value that document activities of organizations or persons and are accumulated in the course of daily activities; (2) materials created by organizations or persons that document the course of daily activities.

Arrangement. The placing of entities in a certain order (e.g., alphabetical, by classification, by size). In card catalogs, this activity was called *filing*.

Art & Architecture Thesaurus **(AAT).** A thesaurus that covers the disciplines of art and architecture.

ASCII (American Standard Code for Information Interchange). A standard code that assigns specific bit patterns to letters, numbers, and symbols; used for exchange of textual data in instances where programs are incompatible, because ASCII can be read almost universally by any computer.

Associative relationship. A relationship between terms in a controlled vocabulary that might be of interest but that is not a hierarchical or an equivalence-based relationship; often expressed as a *related term* relationship. *See also* **Related term.**

Attribute. A characteristic or property of an entity that is useful in description, such as extent, edition, form, resource type, and so on.

Attribute element. An element in Official RDA that describes an entity by connecting it to a value, rather than to another entity; used to describe important characteristics of the entity not represented by a relationship. *See also* **Relationship element.**

Author. A specific type of creator primarily associated with writing books or other forms of text; a person who is responsible for all or some of the intellectual content of a text. *See also* **Creator.**

Author entry. *Obsolete.* The place in a retrieval tool where a surrogate record beginning with the name of the author (i.e., creator) of an information resource may be found.

Author/Title access point. *See* **Name/Title access point.**

Authority control. The result of the process of maintaining consistency in the verbal form used to represent an access point and the further process of showing the relationships among names, works, and subjects—all for the purpose of collocation; also, the result of the process of doing authority work with or without the necessity of choosing one form of name, title, or subject term to be the authorized selection. *See also* **Authority work.**

Authority data. The result of a cataloger gathering information about an entity. Authority data is explanatory information about agents (persons, families, corporate bodies), works (and their varying expressions), and subjects; this information is recorded in authority records during the process of authority work. *See also* **Authority record; Authority work.**

Authority file. A collection of authority records.

Authority record. Documentation of the decisions made during the course of authority work. An authority record contains a variety of authority data about the entity (e.g., person, family, corporate body, place, work, subject) being described, including all the forms used for a particular name, title, or subject and all the relationships among variants that have been identified in the process of authority work; typically the record designates one of the forms as the authorized or default one to use in catalog records.

Authority work. The process of determining and maintaining the form of a name, title, or subject concept to be used in creating access points. In the name and title areas, the process includes identifying all variant names or titles and relating the variants to the name or title forms chosen to be access points. In some cases, it may also include relating names or titles to each other. In the verbal subject area, the process includes identifying and maintaining relationships among terms—relationships such as synonyms, broader terms, narrower terms, and related terms. *See also* **Authority control.**

Authorized access point (AAP). The standardized character string established in an authority record that is used to represent an entity (e.g., person, family, corporate body, place, work, subject) consistently in bibliographic descriptions. *See also* **Controlled access point; Variant access point.**

Authorized term. *See* **Preferred term.**

Auto-Graphics. A bibliographic network offering its database and services to a variety of Canadian libraries and also to a few libraries in the northeastern United States; formerly Utlas International, which became ISM/LIS, and then A-G Canada.

Axiom. In ontologies, a statement or proposition that is accepted as true.

A–Z index. An alphabetical list of entries for the major concepts and entities in a web resource. Each entry has direct links to the web pages that contain information about the entries.

A–Z indexing. The process of creating an alphabetical list of entries for the major concepts and entities referred to in a website. Each entry is linked to the web pages that contain that information. This process is similar to that of *back-of-the-book indexing*.

Back-of-the-book index. An alphabetical list of entries for the major subjects, authors, and works referred to in an information resource. Each entry is accompanied by references or pointers (e.g., page numbers) to the locations in the resource that contain information about that entry.

Back-of-the-book indexing. The process of creating an alphabetical list of entries for the major subjects, authors, and works referred to in a resource. Each entry is accompanied by references or pointers (e.g., page numbers) to the locations in the resource that contain information about that entry.

Basic level categories. According to studies by Roger Brown, basic level categories are the first levels at which children learn categories, such as *flowers*, instead of *daisies* (more specific) or *plants* (more generic). Brown thought the children's level to be the "natural" or "universal" level.

BIBFRAME. Bibliographic Framework Initiative, a project started by the Library of Congress to provide a replacement for MARC as the primary encoding standard for library-generated metadata. Based on linked data principles, BIBFRAME replaces self-contained bibliographic and authority records with authoritative statements about resources—statements that are encoded for use in the Semantic Web.

BIBFRAME Model. A model of the structure of bibliographic resources and their potential relationships to other entities; it comprises three high-level core classes: *work, instance,* and *item.*

BIBFRAME Vocabulary. A defined set of classes (entities) and properties (relationships or attributes) used to describe bibliographic resources.

Bibliographic classification. *See* **Classification.**

Bibliographic control. *See* **Information organization.**

Bibliographic data. Information gathered in the process of creating resource descriptions; also refers to any discrete element in a bibliographic record. *See also* **Metadata.**

Bibliographic database. A collection of resource descriptions held in the format of a database. *See also* **Database.**

Bibliographic description. *See* **Resource description.**

Bibliographic family. A set of related resources that are derived from a common progenitor.

Bibliographic file. A grouping of bibliographic records. In a catalog or bibliographic database, a bibliographic file is distinct from, but might be linked to, one or more authority files and/or holdings files. *See also* **Authority file.**

Bibliographic Framework Initiative. *See* **BIBFRAME.**

Bibliographic identity. The concept that creators of works may use separate personae when creating different types of works. For example, Charles L. Dodgson and Lewis Carroll are two bibliographic identities used by a single person; one wrote about mathematics and the other wrote literature.

Bibliographic network. A corporate entity that has as its main resource a bibliographic database; access to the database is available for a price, and members of the network can contribute new records and download existing ones.

Bibliographic record. Catalog data in card, microform, machine-readable, or other form carrying full cataloging information for a resource. *See also* **Resource description; Surrogate record.**

Bibliographic tool. *See* **Bibliographic database; Bibliography; Catalog; Finding aid; Index; Register; Retrieval tool.**

Bibliographic universe. A concept that encompasses all instances of recorded information.

Bibliographic utility. *See* **Bibliographic network.**

Bibliography (discipline). The study of books as physical or cultural objects, often resulting in lists.

Bibliography (retrieval tool). A list of resources on a given subject, by a given author, from a particular period or place, and the like.

Book catalog. Catalog in which resource descriptions are printed on pages that are bound into book form.

Book number. *See* **Cutter number.**

Boolean operators. The terms AND, OR, and NOT as used to construct searches in a retrieval tool that uses post-coordinate indexing and/or keyword searching.

Boolean retrieval. A retrieval approach that uses exact-match queries, wherein the exact specifications of the query must be satisfied to create a match. This may include the use of Boolean operators. For this type of retrieval to work well, users must know what they are looking for and be able to construct a query that translates their interests into a logical search strategy.

Boolean searching. The process of searching with individual index terms or keywords that are linked with Boolean operators (either using actual operators or symbols for them, or using a system where operators are implied if not specified).

Broad classification. A method of applying a classification scheme that omits detailed subdivision of its main classes or that facilitates the use in smaller libraries of only its main classes and subdivisions. *See also* **Close classification.**

Broader term (BT). A term one level up from the term being examined in a listing where terms for subject concepts have been organized into hierarchical relationships. *See also* **Narrower term; Related term.**

Browsing. A process of looking, usually based on subject, at all the resources in a particular area of the stacks to find the items that best suit the needs of the person who is browsing. In online systems, browsing is the process of looking at all the metadata that is displayed under a certain subject, in a particular classification, or under a certain name or title.

Call number. A notation on a resource that matches the same notation in the metadata description and is used to identify and locate the item; it often consists of a classification notation and a cutter number, and it may also include a workmark and/or a date; it is the number used to "call" for an item in a closed stack library—thus the source of the name *call number*. *See also* **Cutter number; Work mark.**

Card catalog. Catalog in which every resource description is written, typed, or printed on cards that are placed in file drawers in a particular order (usually alphabetical or classified order).

Carrier. The physical or electronic format in which a resource's content is stored.

Carrier type. A category reflecting the physical format of a resource (e.g., *volume, audio disc, filmstrip cartridge*).

Catalog. A type of retrieval tool; an organized compilation of bibliographic metadata or an organized set of surrogate records that represent the holdings of a particular collection and/or resources to which access may be gained. It may be arranged alphabetically, by classification notation, by subject, or, in the case of an online catalog, the display may be arranged by date or any one of several other elements.

Catalog record. *See* **Bibliographic record.**

Cataloger. A librarian or a person in another information institution who creates metadata for the resources collected by the institution and works to maintain the system through which that metadata is made available to users; the person may also be an independent contractor.

Cataloging. The creation of metadata for information resources by describing a resource, choosing appropriate access points, conducting subject analysis, assigning subject headings and classification numbers, and maintaining the system through which cataloging data is made available. *See also* **Copy cataloging; Descriptive cataloging; Indexing; Original cataloging; Subject cataloging.**

Cataloging code. *Obsolete.* A set of rules (i.e., guidelines or instructions) for cataloging. *See also* **Content Standard.**

Cataloging Cultural Objects **(CCO).** A content standard for communities that describe works of art, architecture, cultural artifacts, and images.

Categories for the Description of Works of Art **(CDWA).** Guidelines and a metadata element set used for describing and accessing information about works of art, architecture, other material culture, and related images.

Categorization. The cognitive function that involves grouping together like entities, concepts, objects, resources, and so on.

Category. A cognitive label applied to a group of like entities.

Character-by-character filing. *See* **Letter-by-letter filing.**

Characteristic of division. In the context of classification or categorization, a chosen attribute or property that allows a larger group of entities to be divided into smaller, more specific groups.

Checksum. A value computed for a block of data, based on the contents of the block; used to detect corruption of the data.

Chief source of information. *Obsolete.* In AACR2, the location from which much of the information is to be taken that is used to create the descriptive part of a resource description (e.g., title page of a book, title screen of a motion picture, label on a sound recording tape or disc). *See also* **Preferred sources of information.**

CIP (Cataloging-in-Publication). A program in which cataloging is provided by an authorized agency to the publisher or producer of a resource so that preliminary cataloging data can be issued with the resource, usually on the verso of the title page; often the phrase is applied to cataloging provided by the Library of Congress to the publishers of books.

Citation. An entry in a bibliography containing a brief description of a resource; typically contains no more than creator, title, version information, publication information, volume, issue, and page numbers.

Citation order. A set sequence of the characteristics of division, which determines how multifaceted information resources are collocated within a classification scheme. *See also* **Characteristic of division.**

Class. In bibliographic classification, the first order of structure in a hierarchical classification, at which level major disciplines are represented. A class may incorporate one or more divisions, which in turn may incorporate one or more sections or subdivisions.

Class (ontology). In ontologies, a group or category of entities with something in common.

Classical theory of categorization. Theory based on Aristotle's hypothesis that categories contain entities or concepts based on what they have in common and that categories are like containers with things either in or out of the container.

Classification. The placing of subjects into categories; in information organization, classification is the process of determining where an information resource fits into a given hierarchy and often then assigning the notation associated with the appropriate level of hierarchy to the information resource and its metadata. *See also* **Enumerative classification; Faceted classification; Hierarchical classification.**

Classification notation. A set of numbers, letters, symbols, or a combination of these that is assigned to a certain concept in a classification scheme.

Classification schedule. The list of concepts found in a classification system in classified order, usually including a notation to be used for each concept.

Classification scheme. An organized framework for the systematic organization of knowledge, usually organized by subject. *See also* **Taxonomy.**

Classification table. Supplementary part of a classification scheme in which notations are assigned for concepts that can be applied in conjunction with many different topical subjects. Tables commonly exist for geographic locations, time periods, standard subdivisions (e.g., dictionaries, theory, serial publications, historical treatment), ethnic and national groups, languages, and so on.

Classified catalog. A catalog whose main part is arranged in the order of classification notations that represent the various subjects or aspects of subjects covered by the resources housed in the institution; supplementary part(s) usually exist for alphabetical indexes for creators, subject terms, and so on. *See also* **Alphabetical catalog; Dictionary catalog; Divided catalog.**

Close classification. The use of minute subdivisions to arrange materials by highly specific topics. *See also* **Broad classification.**

Closed stacks. Secure storage areas where the collection's materials are not directly accessible to or browsable by the general public, or are limited to only a small group of users; closed stacks are accessible only to the staff of the library, archives, or other institution. *See also* **Open stacks.**

Clustering. An algorithm-based sorting technique used by retrieval tools to group similar search results together based on content (and a variety of other factors), which can then be used to display the results.

Code (descriptive cataloging). A set of rules. *See also* **Cataloging code.**

Code (encoding). 1. (noun). A specific designation in an encoding standard that defines and limits the kinds of data that can be stored at that point (e.g., 245 for a title statement; <subject> for a subject). 2. (verb). The process of assigning the appropriate tags or numeric codes of an encoding standard to a document or portions of a document. *See also* **MARC tag; Tag (encoding).**

Codification. The process of creating sets of rules to govern such things as the making of resource descriptions. *See also* **Content Standard.**

Coextensive entry. A principle of subject analysis, by which a subject heading or a set of headings covers all, but no more than, the concepts or topics covered in the resource.

Coherent description. In Official RDA, a description of an information resource that conforms to the RDF data structure and is compatible with Official RDA's modeling of the WEMI entities. *See also* **Effective description; Minimum coherent description.**

Collation. *Obsolete.* In AACR2 and earlier, a statement of details about the physical description (e.g., pagination, illustrations, and size) of a book. The concept as applied to other types of resources is called *physical description* or *carrier description*.

Collection development. The process of building a library's collections to meet the needs of the population it serves.

Collection-level description. An approach to creating metadata in which two or more individual resources are described together as a unit; this approach is prevalent in archives where collections of documents are described; sometimes referred to as *collective description*.

Collective agent. Two or more persons, acting as a unit with a single name, that is responsible for the existence, expansion, dissemination, etc., of resources; families and corporate bodies are examples of collective agents. *See also* **Agent.**

Collective title. An inclusive title that represents a compilation that contains two or more individually titled parts.

Collocation. The bringing together of metadata descriptions or information resources that are related in some way (e.g., same author, same work, same subject).

Collocation device. A number or other designation on a resource used to place it next to (i.e., collocate with) other resources that are like it.

Colon Classification. Classification scheme devised by S. R. Ranganathan in the early 1930s; it was the first fully faceted classification scheme. Its name comes from Ranganathan's early use of the colon punctuation symbol to separate facets.

Colophon. A set of data at the end of a resource that gives varying kinds of bibliographic data. It might give information usually found on a title page, and, in items after the invention of printing with movable type, it gives such information as date of printing, printer, typeface used, and the like.

Command searching. The process of searching in which a code (e.g., "a" or "au" for *author*, "t" or "ti" for *title*) is followed by an exact string of characters that is matched against the system's internal indexes; common in first generation online catalogs.

Compilation. A collection of works (or parts of works) by one author published together, or a collection of two or more works or parts of works by more than one author published together. Each work in a compilation was originally written independently or as part of an independent publication.

Compound headings. In subject heading lists, multi-topic concepts combined in the form of a phrase (e.g., **Television programs for gay people**). *See also* **Subject heading string.**

Comprehensive description. A description of a whole resource (as opposed to describing only a part). *See also* **Analytical description; Hierarchical description.**

Computer output microform (COM) catalog. A catalog that is produced on either microfiche or microfilm and that requires a microform reader for its use.

Conceptual analysis. An examination of the intellectual or creative contents of an information resource to understand what the item is about and what the item is (i.e., its form or genre). *See also* **Subject analysis; Translation.**

Condition. In Official RDA, an indication of the circumstances under which a particular instruction should be applied.

Condition option. In Official RDA, an instruction that may be applied when a specific condition is met.

Container architecture. A model for pulling together distinct packages of metadata, which are related to the same information resource, into a single container. This conceptual model allows different communities to create, maintain, and share their metadata.

Container list. *See* **Finding aid.**

Content. The intellectual information transmitted in or by a resource or its metadata; content is distinguished from the encoding, packaging, or framework used for transmission.

Content standard. A set of rules or instructions to guide catalogers, indexers, and the like, in the creation and formatting of data for a bibliographic or index record, an authority record, a metadata statement, or some other form of resource description.

Content type. In RDA, a category representing how the content of a work is communicated or perceived (e.g., *text, performed music, still image*).

Contextualize. A user task in FRAD; to place in context or to clarify relationships. This task has been deprecated in LRM.

Continuing resource. *See* **Integrating resource; Serial.**

Contributor. An agent that has made significant contributions, other than principal creation, to a resource.

Control field. A field in the MARC format (00X) that includes numeric or other encoded data for retrieval.

Controlled access point. A name, term, or code found in an authority record; may be an authorized access point or a reference. *See also* **Access point; Authorized access point; Variant access point.**

Controlled title. A title that has been established as part of authority work; it is used for work and expression titles (including series titles). *See also* **Uncontrolled title.**

Controlled vocabulary. A list or database of terms in which all terms or phrases representing a concept are brought together. Often a preferred term or phrase is designated for use in resource descriptions in a retrieval tool; the non-preferred terms have references from them to the chosen term or phrase, and relationships (e.g., broader terms, narrower terms, related terms) among preferred terms are identified. There may also be scope notes to explain the terms.

Conventional collective title. In RDA, a collective title, referring to the form of the work, used for a compilation containing two or more works of that type (e.g., *Plays, Works, Speeches*), or it may be used for two or more parts of a work (e.g., *Selections*).

Cooperative cataloging. Collaboration between independent institutions to create cataloging that can be shared with others.

Coordinate terms. Terms that share the same parent terms (e.g., *green* and *blue* are coordinate terms; they are both child terms of *primary colors*).

Coordination. Joining two or more concepts together in the search process. *See also* **Post-coordinate indexing; Pre-coordinate indexing.**

Copy cataloging. Adapting original cataloging created by one library for use in another institution's catalog. *See also* **Original cataloging.**

Core element. An element in a metadata standard that is required in all descriptions (if the information is applicable and discernible).

Core-if element. An element in a metadata standard that is required only in certain circumstances or under specific conditions.

Corporate body. An organization or a group of persons that is identified by a collective name and that acts (or may act) as an entity.

Crawler. *See* **Spider.**

Creator. An agent that is responsible for the intellectual or artistic content of a work; includes authors, writers, enacting jurisdictions, composers, photographers, artists, and the like.

Critical cataloging. A movement in the metadata community focused on understanding and addressing oppressive knowledge organization structures (e.g., controlled vocabularies and classification schemes) to make metadata more inclusive and respectful.

CRM entity. The top-level generic entity in the CIDOC Conceptual Reference Model; a thing. Every other entity in CRM is a type of CRM entity. *See also* **Entity; RDA Entity; Res.**

Cross-reference. An instruction in a retrieval tool that directs a user to another place in the tool; also called a *reference*.

Crosswalk. A table, chart, or other device that indicates equivalence relationships among concepts, elements, or values in two or more controlled vocabularies, metadata schemas, encoding standards, and so on; for example, a crosswalk could be used to show which classification notation in DDC is equivalent to a notation in LCC.

Cultural heritage institution. A broad term that refers to organizations that acquire, preserve, and provide access to resources, bringing together libraries, archives, and museums. *See also* **Archives; Library; Museum.**

Cutter number. A designation that has the purpose of alphabetizing all works that have exactly the same classification notation; named for Charles Ammi Cutter, who devised such a scheme, but used with a lowercase *c* when referring to another such table that is not Cutter's own (e.g., the Library of Congress's general cutter table). *See also* **Call number.**

DACS. *See* ***Describing Archives: A Content Standard***.

Data. Unprocessed information, which may be in the form of numbers (binary data, numerical data sets), text (facts, information without context), images, etc. *See also* **Information; Knowledge; Wisdom.**

Data element identifier. A letter or number following a delimiter that specifies the type of content found in a MARC subfield (e.g., the letters in $a and $b). *See also* **Delimiter; Subfield code.**

Data value standard. A controlled list of terms or codes used to populate specific metadata elements. Examples include lists of resource types or subject headings. *See also* **Controlled vocabulary.**

Database. A set of records that are all constructed in the same way and are often connected by relationship links; the structure underlying most electronic retrieval tools.

Database index. A retrieval tool that provides access to the analyzed contents of information resources (e.g., articles in journals, short stories in collections, papers in conference proceedings, reviews, reports). A database index contains electronically accessible and searchable entries that provide descriptive and administrative metadata, as well as descriptor terms (and, in some instances, a classification notation) to represent aboutness. May be referred to as a *journal index* or a *periodical index*. *See also* **Index.**

Database indexing. A type of indexing where the goal is to provide access to the large body of periodical literature published for a specific subject area or discipline.

DC. *See* **Dublin Core.**

DDC. *See* ***Dewey Decimal Classification***.

Deep web. The invisible, hidden parts of the web that are not indexed in search engines.

Delimiter. A special character or symbol that indicates the beginning of a particular MARC subfield (e.g., $ or | or ‡). *See also* **Data element identifier; Subfield code.**

Demographic group. A subset of the general population; may refer to the group's age, occupation, nationality, ethnic background, medical condition, etc., as a distinguishing feature.

Depth indexing. Assignment of all the subject terms necessary to represent all the main concepts in a document, including many subtopics and underlying themes. *See also* **Exhaustivity; Summarization.**

Derived indexing. A form of indexing in which the terms used in the list (i.e., the index) come from the language used in the documents being indexed.

Derivative relationship. A connection between different works, where one resource is descended from another work. This may include translations, adaptations, revised editions, and so on.

Describing Archives: A Content Standard **(DACS).** A content standard for archival description used in the United States. It may be used with EAD-encoded finding aids and MARC records for archival collections. It has replaced APPM. *See also* **APPM; Archival description.**

Description (cataloging). The part of descriptive cataloging in which elements that identify a resource are recorded; also, the portion of the bibliographic record (i.e., descriptive data) that results from this process. *See also* **Access; Descriptive cataloging; Descriptive data; Metadata; Resource description.**

Description (Dublin Core). In the Dublin Core Metadata Initiative Abstract Model, a compilation of individual metadata statements that collectively describe a single resource.

Description set. In the Dublin Core Metadata Initiative Abstract Model, two or more metadata descriptions; describes more than one entity (e.g., a resource and the creator of the resource). *See also* **Metadata Description Set.**

Descriptive cataloging. The phase of the cataloging process that is concerned with the identification and description of a resource, the recording of this information in a bibliographic record, and the selection and formation of access points—except for subject access points. *See also* **Access; Description; Subject cataloging.**

Descriptive data. Data that describes a resource, such as its title, its edition, its date of publication, its extent, and notes identifying pertinent features.

Descriptive markup. In document encoding, code or tags that identify logical structures within a document rather than focusing on its appearance.

Descriptive metadata. Metadata that contains the important identifying characteristics of a resource and the analysis of its contents for the purposes of discovery, identification, selection, and acquisition.

Descriptor. A subject term, representing a single concept, usually found in thesauri and used in indexes. *See also* **Subject heading.**

Designation of edition. A word or number identifying the edition to which a resource belongs.

Devised title. A title provided for an untitled resource or collection by an archivist or by another information professional.

Dewey Decimal Classification **(DDC).** Classification devised by Melvil Dewey in 1876; it divides the world of knowledge hierarchically into 10 classes, which are in turn divided into 10 divisions, which are in turn divided into 10 sections, and so on with additional subdivisions, using the Arabic numeral system (i.e., 0–9).

Diachronic work. A work that is intended to be embodied over time.

Diacritic. Modifying mark over, under, or through a character to indicate that pronunciation is different from that of the character without the diacritic; also called *diacritical mark*.

Dictionary catalog. A catalog arranged or displayed in alphabetical order with records for names, titles, and subjects intermixed. *See also* **Alphabetical catalog; Classified catalog; Divided catalog.**

Digital collection. A collection of information resources in digital form that are selected, brought together, organized, preserved, and to which access is provided over digital networks for a particular community of users. May be referred to as a *digital library* or *digital archives. See also* **Institutional repository.**

Direct entry. A principle in the formulation of controlled vocabularies that stipulates the entry of a concept directly under the term that names it, rather than as a subdivision of a broader concept (e.g., **Child rearing**, not *Children—Development and guidance*).

Directory (MARC). A component of a MARC record containing a series of 12-character fixed-length segments that identify the field tag, length, and starting position of each data field in the record.

Directory (Web). *See* **Internet directory.**

Discovery layer. An application attached to a retrieval tool that provides additional ways to browse and organize search results; often allows for faceted browsing. *See also* **Faceted browsing; Retrieval tool.**

Divided catalog. A catalog in which different types of bibliographic records are arranged or presented in separate files or displays. In print catalogs, usually the subject entries are separated from other entries, and sometimes titles are also separated. Order is usually alphabetical in each section, but the subject section may be in classified order. Online catalogs are de facto divided catalogs when authors, titles, and subjects are searched and displayed separately. *See also* **Alphabetical catalog; Classified catalog; Dictionary catalog.**

Document. A resource; often associated in people's minds with text and illustrations having been produced on paper, but increasingly associated with other forms of information resources.

Document retrieval vs. Information retrieval. A dichotomy that is created by the level of exhaustivity used in subject indexing; summarization allows for retrieval of a document which can, itself, then be searched for relevant information, whereas information retrieval allows for retrieval of information at a much more specific level than the whole document. *See also* **Depth indexing; Exhaustivity; Summarization.**

Document structure. Refers to various components of a resource that are encoded to indicate their function within the document (e.g., title, section heading, paragraph).

Document type definition (DTD). An SGML or XML application; defines the structure of a particular type of document. *See also* **XML schema.**

Domain. A sphere of knowledge, influence, or activity.

Domain (metadata). The type of entity that an element, attribute, or relationship can be used to describe. *See also* **Range.**

Domain (networking). A group of computers whose host names share a common name (i.e., the domain name).

DTD. *See* **Document type definition.**

Dublin Core. An internationally agreed-upon set of metadata elements, with associated attributes and properties, developed and maintained by the Dublin Core Metadata Initiative as a simple standard for resource description; the 15 basic elements are broad and generic and therefore can be used to describe a wide range of resources.

EAC-CPF (Encoded Archival Context–Corporate Bodies, Persons, Families). An XML schema to encode metadata about agents involved in the creation of archival materials or agents that are the subjects of archival materials. Among other things, it puts agents into historical, geographical, and chronological context.

EAD (Encoded Archival Description). An XML schema created specifically to encode finding aids; it provides the structure for an archival finding aid and defines its data components.

Edition. A particular version of a resource; a specific expression of the intellectual content of the work found in a resource. *See also* **Designation of edition.**

Effective description. In Official RDA, a resource description that meets the minimum criteria for coherent description and includes additional elements or descriptions of related entities that are considered useful for identification or access. *See also* **Coherent description.**

Electronic resource. A resource that requires the use of a computer to access its intellectual contents.

Element. An individual category or field that holds an individual piece of description of a resource; typical metadata elements include title, dimensions, edition, and the like.

Element refinement. In Dublin Core, a qualifier that sharpens the focus of an element, that is, it makes the meaning of an element more specific. *See also* **Encoding scheme (Dublin Core).**

Encoded Archival Context–Corporate Bodies, Persons, Families. *See* **EAC-CPF.**

Encoded Archival Description. *See* **EAD.**

Encoding. The process of converting data into electronic form. Encoding ensures that metadata is structured logically and that it may be communicated, shared, and displayed easily. Encoding entails the setting off of each part of a record (or each metadata statement) so that (1) each of the parts can be identified clearly; (2) the parts or statements may be displayed in certain positions according to the wishes of those creating a display mechanism; and (3) certain parts of a record can be searchable.

Encoding scheme. A record syntax standard that is used to convert metadata to electronic form. Examples include the MARC bibliographic format, BIBFRAME, and any number of XML schemas.

Encoding scheme (Dublin Core). Additional metadata element refinement that indicates a controlled vocabulary or a data type that aids in the interpretation of an element value. *See also* **Element refinement; Vocabulary encoding scheme.**

Entity. A thing (a person, subject, work, resource, etc.); objects of interest that are described by listing their various attributes and relationships. *See also* **CRM entity; RDA entity; Res.**

Entity boundary. In Official RDA, a set of criteria to determine if a new entity is being described; this helps to determine if a new resource description is necessary.

Entity-relationship model. Data analysis method used to describe the requirements and assumptions in a system. These models comprise three components: *entities* are things about which information is sought, *attributes* are data collected about the things, and *relationships* provide structure for linking things within a system. FRBR, LRM, and RiC are based on this type of modeling.

Entry. *Obsolete.* The place in a print retrieval tool where a surrogate record is found.

Entry element. In authority control, the part of a name entered first, which should follow the conventions used with the person's native language or in the person's country of origin or residence. Depending on a person's language/place of origin, the entry element may be a surname, a forename, a title, etc.

Entry vocabulary. Cross-references in a controlled vocabulary list that point users to authorized subject terms; terms not chosen as the authorized terms in a controlled vocabulary.

Enumerative classification. A classification arrangement that attempts to assign a designation for every subject concept (simple or complex) required in the system. *See also* **Faceted classification; Hierarchical classification.**

Equivalence relationship. The relationship between synonymous or nearly synonymous terms; often represented by the thesaural labels *USE* or *UF.*

ERIC thesaurus. A commonly used name for the *Thesaurus of ERIC Descriptors,* a thesaurus for indexing and searching documents indexed by the Educational Resources Information Center.

Event. (1) An occurrence related to a work; something that takes place occurring at a specific location or over a specific period. (2) A class in the BIBFRAME model that addresses an occurrence related to a work.

Exception. An instruction in Original RDA that describes a situation where the cataloger is expected to deviate from standard practice based on special circumstances or based on particular resource types.

Exemplar. A typical or standard example; an excellent representation or model.

Exhaustivity. The number of concepts that will be considered in the process of providing subject analysis; the two basic degrees of exhaustivity are *depth indexing* and *summarization. See also* **Depth indexing; Summarization.**

Expansive Classification **(EC).** A late nineteenth-century classification scheme created by Charles Ammi Cutter in which a set of coordinated schedules gives successive development possibilities from very simple (broad) to very detailed (close) subdivision.

Explicit knowledge. Knowledge that is recorded, codified, or communicated in an overt form. *See also* **Tacit knowledge.**

Exploded search. A subject search in which the vocabulary term chosen is searched along with all its narrower terms.

Explore. A user task in LRM; to discover and to gain greater understanding of resources and entities.

Expression. An entity in LRM and RDA that reflects the way that a work is communicated through alphanumeric characters, signs, images, movement, sounds, or the like; an intangible, abstract entity that is made tangible in a *manifestation*.

Extensibility (metadata). The ability to use additional metadata elements or refinements to adapt a metadata schema to the specific needs of a community or project. *See also* **Element refinement; Encoding scheme (Dublin Core).**

Extension plan. In Official RDA, an indication of whether a work is intended to be extended or changed over time, as well as how and when it is planned to end. *See also* **Integrating determinate plan; Integrating indeterminate plan; Static plan; Successive determinate plan; Successive indeterminate plan.**

Extensional aboutness. The inherent subject properties of the work; relatively "objective," stable, recognizable subject matter. *See also* **Intensional aboutness.**

Extent. The number and type of units and/or subunits that make up the carrier of a resource.

Extrinsic relationship. A relationship to another resource that is informative but not essential to understanding the resource. *See also* **Intrinsic relationship.**

Facet. A component (piece, side, or aspect) of a subject.

Facet indicator. A symbol, punctuation mark, or reserved digit signifying that the digits or letters following that symbol represent another aspect of the topic. For example, in *Colon Classification,* a period (full stop) is used to indicate the upcoming space facet (i.e., geographic characteristic) in classification notations.

Faceted Application of Subject Terminology (FAST). FAST is a faceted version of *Library of Congress Subject Headings*. It has established nine facets including topical, geographic names, chronological, form/genre, personal names, named events, corporate names, meetings, and titles. *See also* **Faceted Vocabulary;** *Library of Congress Subject Headings.*

Faceted browsing. A type of system-based browsing; often featured in discovery layers that allows the searcher to browse retrieved search results by various categories established in the metadata, such as resource type, date, form, subject, place, etc. *See also* **Discovery layer; System-based browsing.**

Faceted classification. A classification arrangement that has small notations standing for subparts of the whole topic, which, when strung together, usually in a prescribed sequence, create a complete classification notation for a multipart concept. *See also* **Enumerative classification; Hierarchical classification.**

Faceted vocabulary. A controlled vocabulary where the terms are divided into defined categories representing specific aspects or angles of the subject matter.

Faceting. An approach to categorizing terms in a controlled vocabulary or an approach to organizing discrete concepts in a classification scheme so that terms/concepts with a similar function or a shared characteristic will be clustered together.

False drop. An irrelevant search result.

Family resemblances. Wittgenstein's notion that categories are not solely established based on a single, universal characteristic, but instead on a more complex network of similarities and relationships.

FAST. *See* **Faceted Application of Subject Terminology.**

Federated searching. The ability to search and retrieve results from multiple sources of information while using only a single, common interface. It features an all-inclusive search box for multiple systems, which may include catalogs, indexes, databases, and other electronic resources. Also known as *meta-searching*.

Field. A separately designated part of an encoded record; it may contain one or more subfields.

Filer. In personal information management, one who prefers to sort their documents and materials into folders and file them away. *See also* **Piler.**

Filing. The process of placing paper records (e.g., catalog cards, acquisition forms) in order, usually in drawers.

Find. A user task in LRM; to search for entities that match specific criteria.

Finding aid. An inventory-like description of an archival collection; it describes the whole collection as well as groupings within the collection.

Fixed field. A field in an encoded record that is always the same length from record to record. In MARC, the 008 field is often referred to as *the* fixed field, despite the existence of other fixed-length fields.

Fixed location. A set place where a physical information resource will always be found or to which it will be returned after having been removed for use. *See also* **Relative location.**

Flexibility (metadata). The ability to include as much or as little detail as needed in one's metadata.

Flyleaf. The blank pages at the end of a book.

Folksonomy. The aggregation of tags created by many individual users. The term is a blend of *folks* and *taxonomy*. *See also* **Tag (Web 2.0); Tagging.**

Form. A designation of what a resource is based on its physical characteristics, type of data, or arrangement of information. Examples include novels, maps, essays, videocassettes, questionnaires, and short stories.

Form heading. *See* **Genre/Form heading.**

Format. A designation of the physical medium, file format, or dimensions of a resource.

FRAD. See *Functional Requirements for Authority Data.*

FRBR. See *Functional Requirements for Bibliographic Records.*

FRSAD. See *Functional Requirements for Subject Authority Data.*

Full entry. *Obsolete.* A complete description of a resource containing all its details; a full catalog record, headed by the primary access point, which gives all the elements necessary for the complete identification of a manifestation of a work. This record also bears the tracings for all the other headings under which the work is entered.

Functional Requirements for Authority Data **(FRAD).** A conceptual entity-relationship model developed by IFLA that describes the need for and the uses of authority-controlled data by information professionals and information seekers; superseded by the *Library Reference Model.*

Functional Requirements for Bibliographic Records **(FRBR).** A conceptual entity-relationship model developed by IFLA that identifies various entities found in the bibliographic universe, attributes associated with those entities, relationships among the entities, uses of bibliographic data by information seekers, and the relationships between the attributes and the uses of bibliographic data; superseded by the *Library Reference Model.*

Functional Requirements for Subject Authority Data **(FRSAD).** A conceptual entity-relationship model developed by IFLA; designed as a companion to FRBR and FRAD, it focuses on subject authority data, particularly on *thema* and *nomen*; superseded by the *Library Reference Model. See also* **Nomen; Thema.**

Fundamental categories. *See* **PMEST.**

Fuzzy set theory. A theory that holds that some categories are not well defined and sometimes depend upon the observer, rather than upon a definition (e.g., people who are under five feet tall think the category *tall people* is larger than do people who are over six feet tall).

General International Standard Archival Description **(ISAD(G)).** An international content standard for archival description. It may be used as a national standard or as a basis for developing national standards. DACS, the standard for archival description in the United States, is ISAD(G) compliant. *See also* **Archival description.**

Genre. A designation of what a resource is based on its content, style, technique, themes, or a combination of these. Examples include science fiction, mystery, travel, romance, how-to, and fantasy.

Genre/Form heading. A controlled vocabulary term that refers to the literary genre, artistic form, or publication format of a work rather than to its topical content; sometimes said to reflect an item's *is-ness* when discussed in opposition to *aboutness. See also* **Is-ness.**

Genus–species relationship. In controlled vocabularies, a specific type of hierarchical relationship in which one term is a *type* or a *kind* (species) of the thing represented in the broader term (genus). For example, *pets* and *dogs* reflect a genus–species relationship because *dogs* are a type or kind of *pet*. Sometimes referred to as a *class–class member relationship*. See also **Broader term; Hierarchical relationship; Narrower term.**

Gifts and exchanges. Gifts are resources that are donated to an institution. Exchanges are when institutions swap duplicate or unwanted items according to a mutually beneficial trade agreement with other institutions.

GMD (General Material Designation). *Obsolete.* In an AACR2 record, an indication of the class of item being described (e.g., art original, electronic resource, motion picture); replaced in RDA with three metadata elements: *carrier type, content type,* and *media type.* See also **Carrier type; Content type; Media type.**

Granularity. In metadata description, the level and depth at which information resources are described; in database design, a measure of the size or number of segments into which memory is divided.

GUI (Graphical User Interface). A computer interface that uses icons and other such graphics to make a screen more intuitive for users.

Harvesting. A metadata collection process relying on automated agents that return metadata at a minimal level of complexity.

Heading. *Obsolete* (in descriptive cataloging). (1) An access point printed at the top (head) of a copy of a surrogate record, or column of records, in a printed tool, or appearing at the top of a listing of related works in an online retrieval tool. (2) The exact string of characters of the authorized form of an access point as it appears in the authority record. Replaced in RDA with *authorized access point.* Still used in subject cataloging in the term *subject heading.* See also **Access point; Authorized access point; Subject heading.**

Hierarchical classification. A classification that attempts to arrange subjects in a series of ordered groups, some of which are subordinate to others—proceeding from broad classes to more specific subdivisions. See also **Enumerative classification; Faceted classification.**

Hierarchical description. A description of two levels of a resource: a *comprehensive description* of the whole resource with *analytical descriptions* of one or more of its parts; also called *multilevel description;* generally, it is not used in cataloging, but is more common in describing archival collections. See also **Analytical description; Comprehensive description.**

Hierarchical relationship. In controlled vocabularies, a relationship in which one term is designated as being subordinate to (or narrower than) another term; identified by the relationship designators *BT* and *NT.* Hierarchical relationships may encompass a *genus–species, instance,* or *whole-part relationship.* See also **Broader term; Genus–species relationship; Instance relationship; Narrower term; Whole-part relationship.**

Hierarchy. An arrangement by which categories are grouped in such a way that a concept (e.g., class or discipline) is subdivided into sub-concepts that are equal in level of specificity to each other, each of those sub-concepts are further subdivided, and so on.

Holdings. The resources that an information institution owns or to which it can provide access (e.g., copies of print or digital books, issues of a journal, DVD sets).

Holonym. A term that represents the whole, which is made up of parts, for example, *face* is a holonym for the term *nose* (its part or *meronym).* See also **Meronym.**

Homograph. One of two or more words that look the same but have different meanings.

Homophone. One of two or more words that are spelled differently but are pronounced the same way.

Homosaurus. An international thesaurus of LGBTQ-related terms created to improve access to LGBTQ-themed resources in libraries and other information institutions.

HTML (Hypertext Markup Language). A scheme for encoding text, pictures, and the like for the web, so that they can be displayed using various browsers.

HTTP (Hypertext Transfer Protocol). The part of a URL that lets the system's browser know that a web page is being sought; the protocol itself defines how messages are formatted and is the protocol most often used to transfer information from web servers to system browsers.

Hyperlink. An electronic connection between two separate pieces of information on the web: it may be between two web pages, between two parts of an electronic resource, between text and an image, and so forth.

Hypernym. A term with a broad meaning under which more specific terms fall, following a genus–species relationship; it is a parent term or broader term (e.g., *fruit* is a hypernym and *strawberry* is one of its hyponyms). *See also* **Broader term; Hyponym.**

Hypertext. Documents in which words, pictures, references, and the like may be linked to other locations or documents so that clicking on one of the links takes a person to related information.

Hyponym. A term that is more specific in meaning, which is placed under terms with broader meanings; it is a child term or narrower term (e.g., *strawberry* is a hyponym and *fruit* is its hypernym). *See also* **Hypernym; Narrower term.**

ICP. *See* ***Statement of International Cataloguing Principles.***

Identifier. A unique character string (e.g., an ISBN, URI, a record number) associated with an entity (e.g., a person, a resource, a concept) that differentiates it from other entities.

Identify. A user task in LRM; to confirm that an entity corresponds to the one sought; to recognize a specific resource, agent, and so on.

IFLA (International Federation of Library Associations and Institutions). International organization for the promotion of library standards and the sharing of ideas and research.

IFLA LRM. *See* **Library Reference Model.**

ILL. *See* **Interlibrary loan.**

ILS. *See* **Integrated library system.**

Imprint. The information in a textual publication that tells where it was published, who published it, and when it was published.

Index. A retrieval tool that provides access to the analyzed contents of resources (e.g., articles in a journal, short stories in a collection, papers in a conference proceeding). A back-of-the-book index provides access to the analyzed contents of one work.

Index browsing. A type of system-based browsing using the retrieval tool's internal data organization to guide browsing activities. It relies on the system's indexes to provide browsable lists of names, subjects, titles, and so on. *See also* **System-based browsing.**

Indexer. A person who creates a brief description and determines access points that are needed to make metadata, often for smaller units of information (e.g., journal articles, conference papers), available to searchers. Indexers often are employed by for-profit organizations.

Indexing. The process of creating metadata, especially the access points, for information resources, often for smaller units of information (e.g., journal articles, conference papers). *See also* **Cataloging.**

Indicator. In MARC, indicators are two separate character positions following a MARC tag (e.g., 245). Indicators contain coded information that is needed for interpreting or supplementing data in the field. The functions of the indicators are established in the context of each MARC tag (e.g., the indicators for a 245 field are different than those for the 246 field).

Individual (ontologies). *See* **Entity.**

Infoglut. *See* **Information overload.**

Information. The communication or reception of knowledge; organized data. *See also* **Data; Knowledge; Wisdom.**

Information architecture. A methodology for planning, designing, building, organizing, and maintaining an information system (usually associated with systems on the web).

Information fragmentation. The situation that exists when information is scattered or spread across multiple devices or is found in different formats, such as when people have some documents or information kept on a smartphone, but other information is found on a desktop computer, a laptop, a tablet, and in other locations.

Information organization. The process of describing resources and then providing name, title, and subject access to the descriptions, resulting in resource descriptions that serve as surrogates for the actual items of recorded information and in resources that are logically arranged. Also referred to as *Bibliographic control* or *Organization of information*.

Information overload. When a person receives more information than can be processed or handled.

Information resource. *See* **Resource.**

Information retrieval. The process of gaining access to stored data for the purpose of becoming informed.

Information system. Technology used in information organization that addresses three basic functions: *storage, retrieval,* and *display*; may also be referred to as a *retrieval system* or an *information retrieval system*.

Inheritance relationships. The transfer of attributes and relationships from a superclass to its subclasses.

Initialism. An abbreviation made up of initial letters of words in a phrase, but each letter is pronounced separately (e.g., ABC is an initialism for the American Broadcasting Company). *See also* **Abbreviation; Acronym.**

Instance. In BIBFRAME, one or more material embodiments of a work. It is like the manifestation entity in LRM and RDA. *See also* **Manifestation.**

Instance relationship. In controlled vocabularies, a specific type of hierarchical relationship in which one term is an example of another term. For example, *oceans* and *Indian Ocean* represent an instance relationship because *Indian Ocean* is an example of an *ocean*. *See also* **Broader term; Hierarchical relationship; Narrower term.**

Institutional repository. An online system that collects and preserves digital resources (e.g., articles, manuscripts) related to the intellectual activity of an academic community, such as a university, college, or department. *See also* **Digital collection.**

Instruction sheet. In the *Subject Headings Manual* (SHM), a memo explaining policies of the Library of Congress for the correct application of and the establishment of terms for *Library of Congress Subject Headings* (LCSH).

Integrated library system. Computer system that includes various modules to perform distinct functions while sharing access to the same database. *See also* **Library services platform.**

Integrating determinate plan. In Official RDA, an extension plan that includes resources in which content is replaced, updated, or integrated over time with a definite intended endpoint. *See also* **Extension plan; Integrating resource.**

Integrating indeterminate plan. In Official RDA, an extension plan that includes resources in which content is replaced, updated, or integrated on an ongoing basis with no intended endpoint. *See also* **Extension plan; Integrating resource.**

Integrating resource. A bibliographic resource that is added to or changed by means of updates that are integrated into the whole resource (includes updating loose-leaf publications and updating websites).

Intensional aboutness. Subject properties of a resource that are associated with users, their requests, or the reasons for which the document has been acquired. It is a meaning-based, changing, interpretive aboutness. *See also* **Extensional aboutness.**

Interlibrary loan (ILL). The process of acquiring a physical resource or a copy of it from a library that owns it by a library that does not own it, usually for the purpose of re-lending it to a patron.

International Standard Archival Authority Record for Corporate Bodies, Persons, and Families
(**ISAAR(CPF)**). A content standard that provides guidance on creating archival authority records for corporate bodies, persons, and families who have created and maintained the records, documents, and other resources that comprise archives.

International Standard Bibliographic Description. See **ISBD**.

International Standard Book Number. See **ISBN**.

International Standard Serial Number. See **ISSN**.

Internationalized Resource Identifier. See **IRI**.

Internet directory. A collection of links to websites organized by topics.

Interoperability. The compatibility of two or more systems such that they can exchange information and data and can use the exchanged information and data without any special manipulation.

Intrinsic relationship. A relationship that is essential for the identification of a work being cataloged. *See also* **Extrinsic relationship**.

Inventory. A tool whose purpose is to provide a record of what is owned.

IRI (Internationalized Resource Identifier). On the web, a means to uniquely identify entities such as people, corporations, books, abstract concepts, or network-accessible things via a character string, an address, a name, a number, or another such device; not limited to things that have network locations; uses Unicode as its character set. *See also* **URI**.

ISAAR(CPF). See *International Standard Archival Authority Record for Corporate Bodies, Persons, and Families.*

ISAD(G). See *General International Standard Archival Description.*

ISBD *(International Standard Bibliographic Description).* A standard that was designed in the early 1970s to facilitate the international exchange of cataloging records by standardizing the elements to be used in the description, assigning an order to those elements, and specifying a system of symbols to be used in punctuating the elements.

ISBN (International Standard Book Number). An internationally distinctive and unique number assigned to a monographic item.

Is-ness. The form or genre of a work; what the work is, rather than what it is about. *See also* **Aboutness; Genre/Form headings; Of-ness**.

ISO (International Organization for Standardization). A corporate body that oversees the creation and approval of standards.

ISSN (International Standard Serial Number). An internationally distinctive and unique number assigned to a serial.

Item. An entity in LRM and RDA; a copy of a manifestation of a work, such as a book, a map, an electronic file, or a sound recording, as distinct from its intellectual content (i.e., the work or expression of the work that it contains).

Journal index. *See* **Database index**.

Justify. A user task in FRAD; to document the choice of name of, or inclusion of other attributes about, an entity (person, family, subject, etc.) and the reasons for the choices made. This task has been deprecated in LRM.

Keyword. A term that is representative of the content of a resource; it can be considered *key* to finding information. It may be a term that is extracted from a document or chosen by the searcher.

Keyword indexing. Use of significant words from a title or a text as index entries.

Keyword matching. A type of querying in retrieval systems where the computer matches discrete words, rather than exact phrases, to the data stored in the system's indexes. If more than one word is searched at the same time, the words do not necessarily need to be stored in the same index or table. *See also* **Phrase matching.**

Keyword searching. The use of one or more keywords as the intellectual content of a search command.

Knowledge. What exists in the mind (rather than in any stored form) of an individual who has studied a subject, understands it, and perhaps has added to it through research or other means; a combination of information, context, and experience. *See also* **Data; Information; Wisdom.**

Knowledge management. The attempt to capture, evaluate, store, and reuse what the employees of an organization know.

Knowledge organization. The work done to create and manage classification schemes and controlled vocabularies.

Knowledge organization system (KOS). A generic term for all types of schemes for organizing information, including classification schemes, categories, authority files, subject heading lists, thesauri, and ontologies.

Knowledgebase. A set of products, traditionally housed in separate databases but functionally integrated for the purposes of library resource management and discovery. Knowledgebases underlying *library services platforms* (LSPs) go beyond the functions typically included in *integrated library systems* to include the offerings of library materials vendors (e.g., descriptions of accessibility of e-journals and e-books, URL link resolvers, discovery tools), dynamically updated within the LSP. *See also* **Library services platform.**

Known-item searching. Searching for a specific name or title within a retrieval tool to retrieve a particular information resource.

LC/NACO Authority File (LCNAF). A file housed at the Library of Congress containing not only the authority records created by LC and PCC contributors but also records contributed from Australia, Canada, Great Britain, and others; also called the *Library of Congress Name Authority File.*

LC-PCC PSs. See **Library of Congress–Program for Cooperative Cataloging Policy Statements.**

LCC. *See* **Library of Congress Classification.**

LCRIs. See **Library of Congress Rule Interpretations.**

LCSH. *See Library of Congress Subject Headings.*

Leader. A component of a MARC record that identifies the beginning of a new record and provides coded information for record processing. The leader is fixed in length and contains 24 characters.

Left-anchored searching. A search in a retrieval tool in which the exact phrase is matched against data from the index starting with the first letter of the first word (or text string) moving from left to right letter-by-letter. Each letter in the query must exactly match the indexed data for it to be retrieved. *See also* **Phrase matching.**

Letter-by-letter filing. An arrangement of entries in a retrieval tool in which spaces and some punctuation marks are ignored so that an entry files as if it is all run together into one word (e.g., "New York" is treated as "Newyork" and follows "Newark"). *See also* **Word-by-word filing.**

Librarian. A person who works in a library. (This is not the venue for a discussion of who is and who is not a librarian, what qualifications are or are not required, the status of professionals and paraprofessionals in libraries, the need for a master's degree, and so on.)

Library. An institution in which collections of resources (such as books, periodicals, DVDs, etc.) are kept for people to use or borrow, rather than purchase.

Library guide. *See* **Research guide.**

Library hand. A method of writing taught to librarians in which the letters were carefully formed to be completely readable on catalog cards.

Library management system. *See* **Integrated library system; Library services platform.**

Library of Alexandria. The largest and most famous library of antiquity that was founded in Alexandria, Egypt around 300 BCE; it was a prestigious research hub in that era.

Library of Congress Classification **(LCC).** Classification scheme created by the Library of Congress beginning in the late 1890s; it divides the world of knowledge hierarchically into categories using letters of the English alphabet and then using Arabic numerals for further subdivisions. LCC is an enumerative scheme, allowing only a limited amount of faceting.

Library of Congress–Program for Cooperative Cataloging Policy Statements (LC-PCC PSs). Interpretations or decisions—that have been made by the Library of Congress, the Program for Cooperative Cataloging, or both—as to how catalogers will interpret, apply, or supplement specific RDA instructions.

Library of Congress Rule Interpretations **(LCRIs).** *Obsolete.* A collection of the decisions made by the Library of Congress as to how its catalogers would interpret and apply AACR2; replaced by the Library of Congress–Program for Cooperative Cataloging Policy Statements.

Library of Congress Subject Headings **(LCSH).** A list of terms established and managed by the Library of Congress used to express the subject matter of resources.

Library Reference Model **(LRM).** A conceptual model of the bibliographic universe; an entity-relationship model designed to harmonize and replace FRBR, FRAD, and FRSAD.

Library services platform (LSP). An extension of traditional integrated library systems, using current technology to address barriers to efficient use of divergent material types, particularly electronic resources. Typical characteristics include unified management of physical and electronic materials; use of global knowledgebases in addition to, or rather than, local databases; cloud computing as the basis for system architecture; and development of application programming interfaces to facilitate interaction of LSP system software with that of external vendors. *See also* **Integrated library system.**

Linked data. A method of encoding and publishing data on the web, so that a wide range of different resources can be understood by computers as being related to the same entity or concept (e.g., if two documents are about Abraham Lincoln, they both can be identified as being about Lincoln, and they can be linked through automated means with the metadata used to identify the subject matter). Linked data makes possible the discovery of knowledge about entities that would otherwise have been separated by disassociated means of encoding or by different data silos. Linked data is referred to as *open* if it is made freely available with minimal or no restrictions on access or re-use. *See also* **Semantic Web.**

Literal. In metadata, a string of alphanumeric characters (e.g., "French" or "1985") providing the value for an attribute (as opposed to a URI).

Literary warrant. The principle that new notations are created for a classification scheme and new terms are added to a controlled vocabulary only when information resources actually exist about the new concepts.

Location device. A number or other designation on an item to tell where it is physically located.

MADS (Metadata Authority Description Schema). An XML schema for an authority data element set that has been developed for library applications; designed as a companion to MODS. *See also* **MODS.**

Main entry (access point). *Obsolete.* An access point that is chosen as the main or primary one; may also be referred to as *primary access point* in libraries and archives.

Main entry (record). *Obsolete. See* **Full entry.**

Manifestation. An entity in LRM and RDA that identifies the physical form in which an expression of a work can be found.

Manuscripts. Papers created by an individual (not papers of a corporate body); original handwritten, typed, or word-processed documents that usually exist in single copies (unless they have been carbon-copied, photocopied, or printed multiple times).

MARC (Machine-Readable Cataloging). A standard that prescribes codes that precede and identify specific elements of a bibliographic, authority, or holdings record, allowing the record to be read by a machine, which then displays the data in a fashion designed to make the record intelligible to users.

MARC 21. A MARC standard agreed upon by Canadian and U.S. representatives ("21" stands for the twenty-first century). MARC 21, which represents a consolidation of USMARC and CAN/MARC, two previous national MARC schemes, has also been adopted by Great Britain, Germany, and other countries.

MARC record. An electronic bibliographic record that has its content designated according to MARC conventions.

MARC tag. A three-digit number that designates the kind of content to be added to a field in a MARC record. *See also* **Code (encoding); Tag (encoding).**

Markup language. A scheme that allows the tagging and describing of individual structural elements of text for the purpose of digital storage, appropriate layout display, and retrieval of individual components; examples of markup languages include HTML and XML.

Media type. A category indicating the type of intermediation device (e.g., a computer, a projector) needed to interact with a resource.

***Medical Subject Headings* (MeSH).** A list of terms created by the National Library of Medicine to be used as controlled vocabulary for subject concepts in the field of medicine.

Menu searching. A process of searching that allows one to navigate by making choices from menus, rather than by giving commands.

Meronym. A term that represents one part of a whole (e.g., *nose* is a meronym of *face* [the holonym]). *See also* **Holonym.**

Meta tag. A tag in the header of an HTML document that contains metadata.

Metadata. Structured information that describes the attributes of resources for the purposes of identification, discovery, selection, use, access, and management; an encoded description of a resource (e.g., an RDA record encoded with MARC, a Dublin Core record); the purpose of metadata is to provide a level of data at which choices can be made as to which resources one wishes to view without having to search through massive amounts of irrelevant full text. *See also* **Bibliographic data; Description; Resource description; Surrogate record.**

Metadata Authority Description Schema. *See* **MADS.**

Metadata description set. In Official RDA, a collection of one or more metadata statements. *See also* **Metadata statement; Metadata work.**

Metadata Encoding and Transmission Standard. *See* **METS.**

Metadata Object Description Schema. *See* **MODS.**

Metadata registry. A database used to organize, store, manage, and share metadata schemas and their components.

Metadata statement. An assertion about a single attribute or property of a resource (e.g., an RDF triple indicating the title of a resource); multiple metadata statements comprise a metadata description set; metadata statements are the foundation of bibliographic or metadata records. *See also* **Metadata description set; Metadata work.**

Metadata work. In Official RDA, a metadata statement or a metadata description set comprises a metadata work. If the metadata is considered a work, then RDA elements can be used to describe the metadata (i.e., meta-metadata). *See also* **Metadata description set; Metadata statement; Meta-metadata.**

Meta-language. A set of rules for designing markup languages.

Meta-metadata. Data describing metadata (e.g., administrative data used to track metadata).

Meta-searching. *See* **Federated searching.**

METS (Metadata Encoding and Transmission Standard). A standard for encoding descriptive, administrative, and structural metadata for objects in digital collections.

Microdata. An HTML specification used to nest metadata annotations within the content of web resources; used by search engines and web crawlers to provide more relevant results for users.

Minimum Coherent Description. In Official RDA, a description of a resource that meets the criteria for a coherent description and includes a description of at least one of its WEMI entities. That entity must be described by at least one element that provides some kind of label for the entity, such as a name, title, access point, or identifier. *See also* **Coherent description.**

Mixed notation. In a classification scheme, notation that uses more than one type of symbol.

Mode of issuance. A category reflecting how a resource is produced in terms of the number of parts, distribution, updating, and termination. *See also* **Integrating resource; Monograph; Multipart monograph; Multiple unit; Serial; Single unit.**

Model. An abbreviated description of a complex situation, paradigm, or process used to explain or demonstrate the situation, paradigm, or process.

MODS (Metadata Object Description Schema). A schema for a bibliographic element set that has been particularly developed for library applications; a subset of MARC expressed in XML; MADS, a set of authority data elements, has been established as a companion schema. *See also* **MADS.**

Monograph. In AACR2 and Original RDA, a complete bibliographic unit or information resource. It is often a single work but may also be one work or more than one work issued in successive parts; unlike serials, it is not intended to continue indefinitely. In Official RDA, monograph has been replaced by *single unit*. *See also* **Single unit.**

Monographic series. *See* **Series (bibliographic).**

Multilevel description. *See* **Hierarchical description.**

Multipart monograph. A monograph issued in a finite number of parts; it may be issued in successive parts at regular or irregular intervals, but it is not intended to continue indefinitely. In Official RDA this term has been replaced by *multiple unit*. *See also* **Multiple unit.**

Multiple unit. A resource issued in multiple parts. *See also* **Mode of issuance; Single unit.**

Museum. An institution that collects objects, artifacts, and other specimens of material culture to exhibit to the public in order to better understand humanity and the world. It may contain collections of art, natural history specimens, artifacts related to human culture, history, and society among other things.

Museum accession record. A record used as a surrogate for an object acquired by a museum; it contains many kinds of information about the object, such as its accession number, financial history, location in the museum, and other forms of initial documentation. The aggregate of museum accession records is the accession log or accession file.

Museum registration. *See* **Registration.**

Namespace. The authoritative space created to hold a collection of metadata elements or attributes, each identified by a unique URI; the namespace itself is also identified by a unique URI.

Name/Title access point. An authorized access point that includes the authorized name of an agent and the preferred title for a work. It serves to identify a work. *See also* **Standard citation.**

Narrower term (NT). A term one level down from the term being considered in a listing where terms for subject concepts have been organized into hierarchical relationships. *See also* **Broader term; Related term.**

Natural language. The language used by a person when expressing a concept about which information is desired.

Natural language processing (NLP). Computer analysis of written or spoken language to interpret meaning in a way that can allow the computer to understand and respond; a foundation of artificial intelligence.

Navigate. In the ICP, a function of the catalog in addition to the ones articulated in FRBR and LRM. To navigate is to use the internal data structures of the information system to find sought information.

NISO (National Information Standards Organization). A corporate body that oversees the creation and approval of standards to be used in information processing; an American counterpart to ISO.

NLP (Natural language processing). *See* **Natural language processing.**

Nomen. In LRM and Official RDA, the association between a name (label, appellation) and another entity. Each entity in LRM can have a relationship with a nomen.

Nomen string. An attribute of the *nomen* entity; it represents a single text string (i.e., the actual characters that make up a name, label, or appellation) that identifies a nomen that is associated with another entity. For example, a nomen string could be an alternate spelling of the name associated with an author.

Non-book materials. Terminology used for resources that are not textual monographs (e.g., audiovisual materials, maps, microforms, kits).

Non-literal. In metadata, an actual physical, digital, or conceptual entity, as opposed to a *literal* (i.e., an alphanumeric string representing an entity).

Non-linear browsing. Browsing that is more unstructured, serendipitous, and multidirectional; may involve using hyperlinks to navigate between assorted items; it is more exploratory and random.

Normalization. Removing punctuation and excess characters from a string of text to provide better potential for matches.

Notation. A representation in a system, such as a classification scheme, with a set of marks, usually consisting of letters, numbers, and/or symbols.

Number building. In DDC, the process of developing a complex classification number for a resource by appending digits from tables or other parts of the schedules to a base number.

Obtain. A user task in LRM; to gain access to the resource described.

OCLC Online Computer Library Center. The largest and most comprehensive bibliographic network in the world; OCLC, based in Dublin, Ohio, was instrumental in the development of Dublin Core and FAST; they are owners and custodians of the *Dewey Decimal Classification*.

Official RDA. *See* **RDA: Resource Description & Access (Official RDA).**

Of-ness. Of-ness represents what a visual resource is depicting; the object(s) that the image is *of*, as opposed to what the work is (genre/form) or what the work is about (subject matter). *See also* **Aboutness; Is-ness.**

One-to-one principle. In Dublin Core, the principle that descriptions should refer to only one resource at a time.

ONIX (Online Information Exchange). The publishing industry standard for representing and communicating product information in an electronic format.

ONIX message. Electronic information about a book, serial, or another resource transmitted by publishers and other participants in the publishing industry.

Online catalog. A catalog, available for use by the general public, in which resource descriptions are encoded for computer display; typically, part of an ILS or LSP; also referred to as an *online public access catalog* or *OPAC*.

Ontology. A formal representation to machines of what, to a human, is common sense or reality; a formal naming of the entities that exist for a particular domain, with an attempt to define the types, properties, and relationships among them, which then define the essence of a situation, domain, or conceptual framework.

OPAC (Online public access catalog). *See* **Online catalog.**

Open stacks. Storage areas where patrons of a facility are allowed to access the information resources themselves to browse and to retrieve items of interest. *See also* **Closed stacks.**

Option. In Official RDA, a suggested way to record metadata, which the cataloger can choose to apply or not.

Optional addition. An instruction in Original RDA that allows catalogers to supplement the information required by the preceding instruction.

Optional element. Metadata elements included at the discretion of the agency or the individual creating the metadata content.

Optional omission. An instruction in Original RDA that allows catalogers to omit some information called for in the preceding instruction.

Organization of information. *See* **Information organization.**

Organization of knowledge. *See* **Information organization.**

Organize. To perform the process of forming unity and arranging separate parts into a whole that functions as an integrated unit.

Original cataloging. The process of creating a bibliographic description "from scratch," especially without reference to other records for the same resource; also, the cataloging data created by this process. *See also* **Copy cataloging.**

Original order. In archival collections, the organization or sequence of records as established by the creator of those records; the archival order reproduces the order employed when the records were in active use. *See also* **Provenance;** *Respect des Fonds.*

Original RDA. See *RDA: Resource Description & Access* (Original RDA).

Other title information. Words or phrases (e.g., a subtitle) that appear in conjunction with and are subordinate to the title proper of a resource; an additional title, phrase, or statement that helps to qualify or amplify the title proper (e.g., *A Moon for the Misbegotten: A Play in Four Acts*).

Parallel title. A title proper that is repeated in another language or script.

Paris Principles. The conventional name of the Statement of Principles agreed upon by attendees at the International Conference on Cataloguing Principles in Paris, October 9–18, 1961; replaced by IFLA's *Statement of International Cataloguing Principles.* See also **Statement of International Cataloguing Principles** (ICP).

Party. *See* **Agent.**

Pathfinder. *See* **Research guide.**

Patron-driven acquisitions. A process in which a library obtains certain resources only after the need for them has been definitively expressed by patrons; also known as *demand-driven acquisitions.*

PCC (Program for Cooperative Cataloging). An international cooperative program coordinated jointly by the Library of Congress and participants around the world; effort is aimed at expanding access to collections through useful, timely, cost-effective cataloging that meets internationally accepted standards.

Periodical. A publication with a distinctive title, which appears in successive numbers or parts at stated or regular intervals and which is intended to continue indefinitely. Usually each issue contains articles by several contributors. *See also* **Serial.**

Periodical index. *See* **Database index.**

Periodical indexing. A process similar to database indexing but focused on a single publication. *See also* **Database indexing.**

Person. According to LRM and Official RDA, an individual human being who lives or is assumed to have lived.

Personal information management. The activities that individuals perform to organize, store, and retrieve information for their own purposes.

Phrase matching. A type of querying in retrieval systems where the computer matches exact phrases, rather than discrete words, to the data stored in the system's indexes. The exact phrase must be found with all the words together in the same index. *See also* **Keyword matching; Left-anchored searching.**

Pick list. *See* **Simple term list.**

Piler. In personal information management, one who relies on piles of material, sometimes spread across a room beyond one's desk. *See also* **Filer.**

Pinakes. *Pinakes* is the plural of *pinax*, a word that means tray or dish. It is thought that wax could be poured in the middle of such trays, and when hardened the wax could be written in with a stylus. Thought to have been used by Callimachus at the Library of Alexandria for their catalog or bibliography.

Place. (1) A given extent of space; a bounded, named geographic area or region. (2) An entity in LRM and Official RDA.

PMEST. A mnemonic device for identifying Ranganathan's five fundamental categories: *personality, matter/material, energy, space*, and *time*. The fundamental categories delineate five general facets that might be represented in any topic. *See also* **Faceted classification.**

Policy statement. Supplemental information used in coordination with RDA that provides an interpretation of or additional guidance for an instruction. *See also* **Library of Congress–Program for Cooperative Cataloging Policy Statements.**

Post-coordination. Indexing that enters subject concepts as discrete, single concepts so that searchers are required to coordinate them using Boolean operators to locate resources about the compound and/or complex subjects in which the searchers are interested.

Precision. The measurement of how many of the documents retrieved by a search are relevant. *See also* **Recall.**

Pre-coordination. The assigning of subject terms to surrogate records in such a way that some concepts, sub-concepts, place names, time periods, and form concepts are put together in subject strings, and searchers of the system do not have to coordinate these particular terms themselves.

Preferred name. The name or form of name chosen to represent an agent; it is used as the basis for the AAP representing that agent.

Preferred sources of information. In Original RDA, the source or sources in an information resource considered to be the major location(s) for the bibliographic data to be used in preparing a description (e.g., title page of a book, title screen of a motion picture, label on a sound recording tape or disc); unlike the concept it replaced (i.e., *chief source of information* in AACR2), more than one location within the resource may be considered primary; it varies according to the type of resource. *See also* **Chief source of information.**

Preferred term. A term or phrase chosen in a controlled vocabulary to be used consistently to represent a concept. Also referred to as an *authorized term*. *See also* **Descriptor; Subject heading.**

Preferred title for work. A standardized title chosen to identify a work that has been known by various titles over time or across multiple languages; formerly known as *uniform title*.

Preservation metadata. Metadata that supports and documents the preservation process used in libraries, archives, etc., to ensure usability into the future or to salvage damaged materials.

Primary access point. *See* **Main entry (access point).**

Printed catalog. A catalog in which the resource descriptions appear in static printed form—cards in a card catalog, columns in a book, or on microform.

Probabilistic retrieval. A retrieval model based on term weighting and frequency, which attempts to estimate the probable relevance of information to a query; it returns results that match the query to some degree and are displayed in the order of decreasing similarity.

Property. (1) In metadata, an element or attribute of a resource, such as the title, the description, or the creator of the resource. (2) In legal terms, it designates ownership or proprietorship, as in *intellectual property*.

Property-value pair. An underlying model for metadata statements in Dublin Core; for metadata to be useful, each resource is described using attributes (e.g., publication date) and their value (e.g., 2025). Paired together they communicate a statement about a resource. If either the value or the property is missing, the statement is incomplete. This structure can be seen as two-thirds of an RDF triple (the predicate and the object). Also referred to as *Attribute-value pair*. *See also* **RDF Triple.**

Protocol. A standard set of rules that determines how computers communicate with each other across networks (e.g., HTTP and Z39.50 are protocols); it describes the format that a message must take and the way in which computers must exchange a message.

Prototype theory. The theory that categories have prototypes (i.e., best examples); for example, most people think a robin is a better example of a bird than is an ostrich.

Provenance (archives). *Provenance* refers to the individual, family, organization, or institution that is responsible for the creation, maintenance, or use of the materials. It is a primary organizing principle in archives. *See also* **Original order;** *Respect des fonds.*

Provenance (museums). The origins and ownership trail of a museum object (i.e., information about its origins, custody, or ownership).

Proximity (searching). The concept of *nearness* of search terms to one another in a text.

Proximity operators. A tool in information retrieval that allows searchers to specify the maximum distance between two or more words in a query.

Public services. A library's front-of-house operations, which focus on serving patrons through reference services, library instruction, reserves, circulation, and so on. *See also* **Technical services.**

Publisher. The agent (e.g., corporate body or person) responsible for disseminating information resources to make them available for public use.

Pure notation. In a classification scheme, notation that uses only one type of symbol.

Qualifier (controlled vocabulary). An addition or annotation that is affixed to a subject term to clarify its meaning. In LCSH, qualifiers are often placed in parentheses (e.g., **Tablets (Medicine)**) or after a comma if the concept is entered in inverted form (e.g., **Authors, Basque**).

Qualifier (Dublin Core). In Dublin Core, a qualifier is either an element refinement or an encoding scheme. *See* **Element refinement; Encoding scheme (Dublin Core).**

Querying. The act of requesting information from a retrieval tool; conducting a search. *See also* **Browsing.**

Range. The value of an element, attribute, or relationship that is used to describe an entity. *See also* **Domain (metadata).**

***RDA: Resource Description & Access* (Official RDA).** A cataloging content standard built on an extensive set of elements, conditions, and options, based on LRM, and published in 2020. Used to produce the description and access points representing a resource. Intended to replace Original RDA.

***RDA: Resource Description & Access* (Original RDA).** A set of cataloging instructions, originally based on FRBR and FRAD, published in 2010 and implemented in 2013, for producing the description and access points representing a resource; the descriptive cataloging standard that replaced AACR2.

RDA entity. The top-level generic entity in Official RDA. Equivalent to the entity *res* in LRM and CRM entity in CIDOC CRM. Every other entity in Official RDA is a type of RDA entity. *See also* **CRM entity; Entity; Res.**

RDA Toolkit. A subscription-based electronic tool that contains the text of both versions of RDA, AACR2, related policy statements, and other resources useful in descriptive cataloging.

RDF (Resource Description Framework). An infrastructure that enables the encoding, exchange, and reuse of structured metadata, using a serialization format such as XML, Turtle, or JSON as the means for exchanging and processing the metadata. RDF is based on the premise that resources have attributes and relationships, and they have values. Some values can be other resources with their own properties and values, and all these relationships can be linked within the framework. The basic structure of RDF is the RDF triple. RDF is the foundation for linked data and the Semantic Web. *See also* **RDF Triple.**

RDF dataset. A group of RDF graphs.

RDF graph. A set of RDF triples.

RDF triple. The model used to structure metadata statements. A triple consists of a subject (a resource), a predicate (a property), and an object (a value). This is the underlying structure of linked data and the Semantic Web.

Recall. The measurement of how many of the relevant documents in a system are *actually* retrieved. *See also* **Precision.**

Record. *See* **Bibliographic record; Metadata; Surrogate record.**

Records management. The process of maintaining records for an organization; it includes such functions as making decisions about what records should be created, saving necessary records, establishing effective systems for retrieval of records, and archiving important records for posterity.

Reference. *See* **Cross-reference.**

Reference database. A database that contains links or pointers to the actual information held outside the database. *See also* **Source database.**

Refinement. *See* **Element refinement; Encoding scheme (Dublin Core).**

Register. One of the control tools for a museum; it functions like a catalog with additional kinds of data and access points (e.g., donors, style, provenance).

Registration. The process of creating documentation that uniquely identifies an object belonging to a museum; the object descriptions form the register (or catalog) for the museum.

Related term (RT). A term at the same level of specificity or bearing a non-hierarchical relationship to another term in a listing where terms for subject concepts have been organized into relationships that are hierarchical; this relationship suggests that if the concept already located is more or less relevant, there are other associated concepts that might also yield relevant material. *See also* **Associative relationship.**

Relationship. In E-R models, the reciprocal connection between entities.

Relational database. A form of database architecture in which records are structured in such a way that information is not all stored in the same file; files for different kinds of information are created (e.g., a bibliographic file, a personal name file, a corporate name file, a subject file, a classification file); records in the bibliographic file contain pointers to records in the other files and vice versa. A relational database structure conserves storage space, allows for faster searching, and allows for easier modification of records. Pointers establish relationships among records.

Relationship. A reciprocal association, link, or connection between two entities.

Relationship designator. A device (i.e., a label, phrase, or term) that clearly identifies the specific nature of the relationship that exists between entities.

Relationship element. In Official RDA, an element that connects two RDA entities.

Relative location. The situation in which an information resource will be or might be in a different place each time it is reshelved because it is shelved in relation (usually classificatory) to entities already shelved. *See also* **Fixed location.**

Relevance. A measure of how pertinent retrieval results are to particular queries or user needs. This concept is defined and calculated quite differently among various information retrieval systems.

Relevancy ranking. An algorithmic method used by search engines and other retrieval tools to order the search results so that the records most likely to be of interest to users will be listed first.

Representative expression. In Official RDA, a canonical realization of a work that contains attributes considered to be essential in characterizing the work. *See also* **Expression; Work.**

Reprint. A new printing of an item either by photographic methods or by resetting unchanged text.

Res. The Latin word for *thing* or *entity*; used in LRM as the top-level generic entity. Every other entity in LRM is a type of res. *See also* **CRM entity; Entity; RDA entity.**

Research guide. A subject bibliography that leads users to the resources a library has on a specific topic; may be in print or online; also known as a *library guide, subject guide,* or *pathfinder.*

Resource. An instance of recorded information (e.g., book, article, video, web page, sound recording, electronic journal); *resource* is used to avoid using *book, DVD,* or other such specific designations; also called *document, information resource, library materials, object,* and so on.

Resource description. Full descriptive and access information for a resource; a set of metadata statements referring to the same resource; other terms used for descriptions of resources are *bibliographic description* and *metadata*. A resource description is contained in a *surrogate record*. *See also* **Bibliographic record; Metadata; Surrogate record.**

Resource Description and Access. See *RDA: Resource Description & Access.*

Resource Description Framework. *See* **RDF.**

Resource discovery. The process of locating, accessing, retrieving, and bringing together relevant information from widely distributed networks.

Resource entities. Entities that are components of an information resource (i.e., work, expression, manifestation, and item). *See also* **Expression; Item; Manifestation; Work.**

Resource management system. A generic term that refers to various kinds of technology applications used to manage work processes in libraries and other information institutions. *See also* **Integrated library system; Library services platform.**

Resource type. A category that reflects the nature or overall form of the resource (i.e., a book, a map, a serial).

Respect des fonds. The principle that states that archival materials created or collected together should be kept together without mixing in records or materials from other creators or collections. *See also* **Original order; Provenance.**

Retrieval tool. A device such as a catalog, an index, a search engine, and the like, created for use as an information retrieval system.

Retrospective conversion. The process of changing information in eye-readable surrogate records into machine-readable form.

Rights and access metadata. Metadata addressing access, use of information resources, or intellectual property rights.

Robot (Internet). *See* **Spider.**

Romanization. The representation of the characters or script of a non-Roman alphabet by Roman characters.

Rule of three. *Obsolete.* In AACR2, a restriction placed on the number of access points for creators of and contributors to the resource—if more than three were involved, only the first of each kind was recorded; also, there was a restriction on the numbers of persons or corporate bodies listed in statements of responsibility—if more than three were found on the chief source of information, only the first was recorded and the others were replaced by the Latin abbreviation *et al.* (meaning *and others*). In RDA, no such restrictions apply.

Schedule. *See* **Classification schedule.**

Schema. (1) A set of metadata elements created by a particular community or for a particular type of resource. (2) A document or piece of code that controls a set of terms in another document or piece of code; similar in function to a master checklist.

Schema-neutral. The idea that a content standard, controlled vocabulary, or some other standard may be used with more than one metadata schema, display format, or encoding format.

Scope note. A statement delimiting the meaning and application of a subject heading, index term, or classification notation.

Search engine. A computerized retrieval tool that, in general, matches keywords input by a user to words found in documents of the site(s) being searched; the more sophisticated search engines may allow other than keyword searching.

Search engine indexing. An automated process, performed by spiders (or crawlers or bots), that records key information from websites and their locations for inclusion in a search engine.

Search engine optimization (SEO). An activity aimed at raising the visibility of websites by getting sites to be ranked higher in search engine results.

Sears List of Subject Headings (Sears). A controlled vocabulary of terms and phrases that is used mostly in small libraries to provide subject access to resources available from those libraries.

See also note (SA). A reference in LCSH instructing the cataloger to consider other ways to express the concept found in the main heading (e.g., as a subdivision, or in a phrase heading).

Select. A user task in LRM; to choose a resource that is appropriate to the user's needs.

Selection (Collection development). The process in which collection development librarians learn about the existence of works through vendors' product catalogs, reviews, publishers' announcements, and the like, and then choose the most appropriate materials for the collection.

Semantic Web. An extension of the World Wide Web. The traditional web provides linkages between online resources, generally at the level of the whole resource or a discrete part of it. The Semantic Web provides linkages among statements about resources, in a format semantically meaningful to, and actionable by, computers. Linked data, structured according to RDF, is generally considered to be the foundation for the Semantic Web. *See also* **Linked data; RDF.**

Semantics. The meaning of a string of characters, words, elements, etc.

Serial. A publication (physical or electronic) issued in successive parts (regularly or irregularly), and usually consecutively numbered, that is intended to continue indefinitely. Included are periodicals, newspapers, proceedings, reports, memoirs, annuals, numbered monographic series, and online journals. *See also* **Integrating resource.**

Series (archives). A logical group of materials in an archival collection; a logically grouped set of files, correspondence, documents, etc.

Series (bibliographic). A number of separate works, commonly related in subject or form, which are issued successively and with some regularity. They are usually issued by the same publisher, distributor, etc., and are in uniform style, with a collective title. Each monograph in the series frequently is given a number, usually in chronological order. Works in a series *may* be cataloged together as a serial, especially if numbered, but more frequently they are cataloged separately.

SGML (Standard Generalized Markup Language). An international standard for document markup for machine readability.

Shelf browsing. The activity of inspecting an area of the stacks where an item of interest is located to see if other relevant items are in proximity.

Shelf reading. The process of scanning call numbers of shelved items to determine whether they are in correct order.

Shelflist. *Obsolete.* A list of physical information resources owned by an institution in the order in which they appeared on the shelves of the institution where they were housed.

Shelving. The process of placing physical information resources on shelves in the order of their call numbers or other notations that indicate their appropriate locations.

Simple term list. A straightforward list of values that may be used for a particular metadata element, usually in alphabetical order (or some other logical arrangement); often accessed through pull-down menus.

Single unit. A resource issued as a single physical or logical unit; this term has replaced *monograph* in Official RDA. *See also* **Mode of issuance; Monograph; Multiple unit.**

SkyRiver. A computer-based bibliographic network offering its database and services to a variety of libraries.

Social tagging. *See* **Tagging.**

Source database. A database that contains the actual information sought, rather than one that points to outside data sources. *See also* **Reference database.**

Specific entry. A principle observed in the application of controlled vocabularies, by which a cataloger or an indexer assigns to an information resource the most precise term available in the controlled vocabulary (or allowed to be created by the rules of the vocabulary), rather than assigning a broader heading. *See also* **Specificity.**

Specificity. The level of semantic depth that is addressed by a particular controlled vocabulary (e.g., LCSH has greater specificity in its established headings than does *Sears*). *See also* **Specific entry.**

Spider. An automated internet program that gathers content from web pages (storing URLs and indexing keywords, links, and text) for inclusion in a search engine; may also be referred to as *crawler, web crawler, agent,* or *robot.*

SRU (Search/Retrieval via URL). A standard XML search protocol for internet search queries that uses the Contextual Query Language (CQL), a standard syntax for representing queries.

Standard. Something established by authority or custom as a model or example; in the information field, standards are approved by national and/or international bodies after discussion and voting by representatives.

Standard citation. A consistent way to refer to the resource; a name/title access point is sometimes used to provide a standard citation. *See also* **Name/Title access point.**

***Statement of International Cataloguing Principles* (ICP).** An IFLA document, first published in 2009, that outlines principles and values associated with cataloging; designed as a replacement for the 1961 Paris Principles. *See also* **Paris Principles.**

Statement of responsibility. A transcription of a statement, from the preferred sources of information, naming the agents responsible for the intellectual or artistic content of a work, contributions, performances, revisions, subsequent editions, and so on.

Static plan. In Official RDA, an extension plan that includes resources in which all the content is embodied simultaneously, such as a novel or a photograph. Single-unit monographs and multipart monographs in which all the parts are issued at once are included in this category. *See also* **Extension plan; Monograph; Multipart monograph; Single unit.**

Static work. A work intended to be embodied in a single act of production or publication. This category includes most monographs, including multiple-unit monographs in which all the parts are issued simultaneously.

Stereotyping. A method of printing using a metal copy of a typeset image.

Stopwords. A list of words that are so common that they are of no use when searching, such as *the, it, an, to,* and so on; these are words *not* included in, or they are filtered out of, the indexes of underlying retrieval tools.

String encoding scheme. A set of rules or instructions used to convert two or more metadata values into a structured string.

Structural metadata. Metadata addressing the "makeup" or structural composition of an electronic resource.

Structure. (1) Arrangement in a definite pattern of the parts of a whole. (2) The data model used to shape the way that metadata statements are expressed.

Structured description. A formal string of organized or controlled data constructed using a string encoding scheme or a vocabulary encoding scheme.

Subdivision (classification). A level of structure in a hierarchical classification at which subordinate concepts are represented; the level below classes, divisions, and sections.

Subdivision (controlled vocabulary). A term or phrase appended onto a subject heading to provide additional specificity, to show special treatment of a subject, or to bring out additional facets of the topic (e.g., geographic, chronological, form).

Subfield. A separately designated segment of a field in an encoded record.

Subfield code. A code, comprising a delimiter and an alphanumeric character, identifying the meaning of a particular segment of a field in an encoded record. *See also* **Data element identifier; Delimiter.**

Subject. What a resource is about; the topic(s) of a resource. *See also* **Aboutness.**

Subject (RDF). The topic of an RDF statement; it is the resource being described in the RDF triple. *See also* **RDF Triple.**

Subject access. The provision to users of the means of locating information using subject terminology and/or classification notations.

Subject analysis. The part of indexing or cataloging that deals with the conceptual analysis of an information resource; the translation of that conceptual analysis into a framework for a particular classification, subject heading, or indexing system; and then using the framework to assign specific notations or terminology to the information resource and its surrogate record. *See also* **Conceptual analysis; Translation (Subject cataloging).**

Subject authority file. A record of choices made in the development of terms for a controlled vocabulary. The authority records within the file contain such things as justification for the choice of one synonym over another; references from unused synonyms or near-synonyms; references for broader terms, narrower terms, and related terms; scope notes; citations for references used; and the like. *See also* **Subject heading list.**

Subject cataloging. The process of providing subject analysis, including subject headings and classification notations, when creating resource descriptions for archives, libraries, museums, and the like. *See also* **Descriptive cataloging.**

Subject entry. *Obsolete.* The place in a retrieval tool where a surrogate record containing a particular controlled vocabulary term is found.

Subject gateway. *See* **Directory (Web).**

Subject guide. *See* **Research guide.**

Subject heading. A subject term or phrase found in a subject heading list and used in resource descriptions; sometimes used in indexes. *See also* **Descriptor.**

Subject heading list. A list of authorized controlled vocabulary terms or phrases together with any references, scope notes, and subdivisions associated with each term or phrase. *See also* **Subject authority file; Thesaurus.**

Subject heading string. A subject heading with one or more subdivisions appended onto it to create additional context for the concept; subdivision may reflect additional topical, geographic, chronological, or form aspects of the resource. *See also* **Subdivision (controlled vocabulary).**

Subject language. A generic term for classification schemes and subject-focused controlled vocabularies.

Subject subdivision. *See* **Subdivision (controlled vocabulary).**

Subtitle. An additional title, subordinate to the title proper, that augments, expands, or limits the title proper; considered to be one kind of *other title information*.

Successive determinate plan. In Official RDA, an extension plan that includes resources with content that is accumulated over time and has a definite planned end or termination point. *See also* **Extension plan; Multipart monograph.**

Successive indeterminate plan. In Official RDA, an extension plan that includes resources with content that is accumulated over time and does not have a definite planned end or termination point. *See also* **Extension plan; Serial.**

Summarization. Indexing that identifies only a dominant, overall subject of an information resource, recognizing only concepts embodied in the main theme. *See also* **Depth indexing; Exhaustivity.**

Surrogate record. A presentation of the attributes and relationships of a resource in one complete package (i.e., a *record*). *See also* **Bibliographic record; Metadata; Resource description.**

Switching language. A mediation language used to establish equivalencies between or among different subject indexing languages or classification schemes.

Syndetic structure. An organizational framework in which related names, topics, and other controlled terms are linked to each other via connective terms such as *See* and *See also*, or the thesaural indicators BT, NT, RT, USE, and UF.

Synonym. A term with the same meaning as another term; often, in controlled vocabularies, used for a term that has nearly the same meaning as well as for a term that has the same meaning. *See also* **Antonym.**

Synonym ring. A feature of a search system used to enhance keyword searching by expanding a search with equivalent terms; data tables, synonym lists, or lexical databases used to help expand recall in keyword searching.

Syntax. The arrangement of parts or elements so that they become constituents of a connected or orderly system; metadata's syntax is described by its encoding schema (e.g., MARC, XML), just as a language's syntax is described by its grammar.

System. *See* **Information system.**

System design. The process of creating an architecture for the different components, interfaces, and modules of an information system; the specification of the working relations among all parts of a system.

System-based browsing. A type of browsing available in retrieval tools. One sub-type is pre-sequenced, linear, index browsing. This entails users scanning lists of topics, creators, or titles to find items of interest. The other is faceted browsing that allows the searcher to browse through search results divided into categories based on facets found in the metadata. *See also* **Faceted browsing; Index browsing.**

Table. *See* **Classification table.**

Tacit knowledge. Knowledge that is not recorded formally or is difficult to codify or share; it is knowledge still stored in the human mind. *See also* **Explicit knowledge.**

Tag (encoding). A number, set of letters, certain set of punctuation marks, and so forth, that designates the kind of field in an encoding standard. *See also* **Code (encoding); MARC tag.**

Tag (Web 2.0). In social media, the terms (keywords, subjects, etc.) assigned to a resource by a user; sometimes referred to as a *hashtag*.

Tag cloud. A visual representation of tags that have been assigned to a resource by users.

Tagging. A populist approach to description. It is a process by which a distributed mass of users applies keywords to various types of web-based resources for the purposes of collaborative information organization and retrieval. Tagging allows individual users to group similar resources together by using their own terms or labels, with few or no restrictions. Also referred to as *user tagging, social tagging,* and *social indexing.*

Taxonomist. A person responsible for designing a controlled vocabulary or a classification scheme.

Taxonomy. A classification or controlled vocabulary, usually in a restricted subject field, arranged to show presumed natural relationships. *See also* **Classification scheme; Controlled vocabulary.**

Technical metadata. Metadata that describes the physical characteristics, origins, and lifecycles of digital resources; it is key to the preservation of the resource for future use. It gives the basic technical information that is needed to understand the nature of the information resource, the software and hardware environments in which it was created, and what is needed to make the resource accessible to users.

Technical services. The activities in an institution that involve acquiring, organizing, housing, maintaining, and conserving collections and automating these activities. In some places circulating collections is also considered to be a technical service. *See also* **Public services.**

TEI Header. A set of encoded metadata at the beginning of a TEI document that describes the document, its contents, and its origins.

Text Encoding Initiative (TEI). Refers to both the corporate organization with that name and to the encoding standard created by that group. The encoding standard was originally intended for the encoding of literary texts, although it has expanded to be used for other types of texts as well.

Thema. In FRSAD, it refers to the subject matter of a work; replaced in LRM by the entity *res*. *See also* **Res.**

Thesaurus. A specialized authority list of controlled vocabulary terms (usually restricted to a particular subject area) used with information retrieval systems; terms represent single concepts, together with any references, scope notes, and subdivisions associated with each term, and are organized so that the relationships between concepts are made explicit; similar to a list of subject headings, except for the emphasis on single terms rather than phrases and subject strings. *See also* **Subject heading list.**

Time-span. In LRM, an entity reflecting a chronological period having a beginning, an end, and a duration.

Timespan. In Official RDA, an entity reflecting a chronological period having a beginning, an end, and a duration; when LRM was implemented in RDA, the time-span entity lost its hyphen.

Title. A name given to a resource. There are many types of titles. *See also* **Alternative title; Collective title; Conventional collective title; Devised title; Other title information; Parallel title; Subtitle; Title proper.**

Title entry. *Obsolete.* The place in a retrieval tool where a surrogate record containing the name of an information resource may be found.

Title proper. The main or primary title by which a resource is known; excludes parallel titles and other title information; includes alternative titles and part titles.

Tracing. *Obsolete.* On printed surrogate records (e.g., catalog cards, records in book catalogs), the set of name, title, and subject access points, other than the primary access point, appearing at the bottom of the record and used to find (i.e., trace) the additional copies of the surrogate record.

Translation. The conveyance of the content of a work in another language. In RDA, a translation is considered a different expression of a work, not a new work.

Translation (Subject cataloging). The second stage of the subject analysis process, in which the aboutness is converted into terminology or symbols from one or more subject languages—controlled vocabularies, classification schemes. *See also* **Aboutness; Conceptual analysis; Subject analysis.**

Tree structure. A strict hierarchical arrangement with successive subdivisions; a diagram of which is said to resemble the branches of a tree.

Triple. *See* **RDF triple.**

Triplestore. A database specifically designed to house RDF structured data for the Semantic Web.

Turnkey system. A computer system customized to include all the hardware and software necessary for a particular function or application (e.g., a circulation system).

UBC. *See* **Universal Bibliographic Control.**

UCS (Universal Character Set). ISO standard for encoded representation of characters in computers; has the purpose of including all characters in all written languages of the world.

UDC. See *Universal Decimal Classification.*

Uncontrolled access point. A name, title, or term that does not appear in an authority record; for example, a title proper is an access point but one that is transcribed and not standardized. *See also* **Authorized access point (AAP).**

Uncontrolled title. A title that is transcribed from a manifestation; it is not an authority-controlled title recorded in an authority record.

Unicode. An American industry counterpart to UCS, which permits computers to be able to handle the large number of character sets used in various languages. Both UCS and Unicode provide a unique number for every character to be used regardless of platform or format.

Uniform Resource Identifier. See **URI.**

Uniform Resource Locator. See **URL.**

Uniform title. *Obsolete.* A title chosen for a work so that all manifestations will be displayed together under the same primary access point and will be displayed together among all the entries for that access point. Uniform titles also are used to distinguish between and among different works that have the same title. The concept is replaced in RDA by *preferred title of work.*

UNIMARC (Universal MARC). Originally conceived as a conversion format, in which capacity it requires that each national agency create a translator to change records from UNIMARC to the particular national format and vice versa; some countries have adopted it as their national format.

Union catalog. A catalog that represents the holdings of more than one institution or collection.

Universal Bibliographic Control (UBC). The concept that it will someday be possible to have access to metadata for all the world's information resources.

Universal Decimal Classification **(UDC).** A classification devised by Paul Otlet and Henri La Fontaine in the late 1890s. It was originally based on the fifth edition of DDC but has evolved into a much more faceted scheme than DDC.

Universal design. A strategy that extends system design to be as inclusive as possible (e.g., including ways for persons with hearing impairment or visual impairment or other disabilities to have the same access to digital information as do non-impaired persons).

Unstructured description. An informal string of narrative data, such as a free-text note or a transcription of data directly from a source.

Upward reference. A type of equivalence relationship used when a term that might be added to a controlled vocabulary is considered too specific for the vocabulary; the term is listed in the vocabulary with a USE reference pointing to its broader term.

URI (Uniform Resource Identifier). On the web, a means to uniquely identify entities such as people, corporations, books, abstract concepts, or network-accessible things via a character string, an address, a name, a number, or another such device; not limited to things that have network locations; unlike IRIs, URIs are limited to a subset of the ASCII character set, which limits their ability to display non-Roman scripts. *See also* **IRI.**

URL (Uniform Resource Locator). One form of URI: the address of an information resource on the internet; it indicates what protocol to use (e.g., *http*) and then gives the IP address or the domain name where the resource is located: most often server address, directory path, and file name.

User tagging. *See* **Tagging.**

User tasks. In several IFLA reports (i.e., FRAD, FRBR, FRSAD, ICP, and LRM), a set of activities that users hope to accomplish when interacting with information retrieval tools and bibliographic data. *See also* **Contextualize; Explore; Find; Identify; Justify; Navigate; Obtain; Select.**

USMARC. The version of MARC used in the United States until it was superseded by MARC 21.

Value. A specific name of an attribute (or property) of a resource; for example, the value of a *language* attribute might be "French," or the value of a *duration* attribute might be "approximately 90 min."

VAP. *See* **Variant access point.**

Variable data field. A field of an encoded record that can be as long or as short as the data to be placed into that field.

Variant access point (VAP). A string of alphanumeric characters, which represents an entity but is not authorized for use in resource descriptions; a variant access point is a cross-reference that points users to an authorized access point. *See also* **Access point; Authorized access point; Controlled access point; Cross-reference.**

Variant name. A name or form of name *not* chosen as the preferred name to represent an agent; it is used as the basis for a cross-reference (i.e., a variant access point). *See also* **Preferred name.**

Vocabulary control. The process of creating and using a controlled vocabulary.

Vocabulary encoding scheme. A controlled vocabulary or data value standard. *See also* **Controlled vocabulary; Data value standard; Encoding scheme (Dublin Core).**

VRA Core. A set of guidelines created by the Visual Resources Association that contains a metadata element set for describing visual resources depicting works of art, architecture, and artifacts or structures from material, popular, and folk culture.

Web. Short for World Wide Web (WWW); a nonlinear, multimedia, flexible system to provide information resources on the internet and to gain access to such resources; based on hypertext and HTTP.

Web 2.0. The trend in web technology that emphasizes collaboration among users and interactivity between users and content. Examples of Web 2.0 features include rating resources, reviews, and tagging.

Web crawler. *See* **Spider.**

Web indexing. The process of creating indexes in the internet environment. There are usually two types: search engine indexing (an automated process) and A–Z indexing, a human endeavor similar to the process of creating a back-of-the-book index but for websites and containing hyperlinks rather than page references. *See also* **A–Z indexing; Search engine indexing.**

Whole-part relationship. In controlled vocabularies, a specific type of hierarchical relationship in which one term is a component of its broader term (i.e., the whole). For example, *nose* and *face* reflect a whole-part relationship because a *nose* is part of a *face*. *See also* **Broader term; Hierarchical relationship; Holonym; Meronym; Narrower term.**

Wisdom. The quality of having extensive experience, knowledge, and good judgment; the accumulation and application of collected knowledge to generate an understanding of others and society. *See also* **Data; Information; Knowledge.**

Word-by-word filing. An arrangement of terms in a retrieval tool in such a way that spaces between words take precedence over any letter that may follow (e.g., "New York" appears before "Newark"). *See also* **Letter-by-letter filing.**

Work. An entity in LRM and RDA that identifies a distinct intellectual or artistic creation; an abstract instance of content or ideas, regardless of the packaging in which the content or ideas may be expressed.

Work mark. In a call number, a work mark is a designation added to a cutter number that usually stands for the first non-article word of the title, but depending upon the circumstances, may stand for other entities such as the name of a biographee.

WWW (World Wide Web). *See* **Web.**

XML (Extensible Markup Language). A subset of SGML, designed specifically for web documents, which omits some features of SGML and includes a few additional features (e.g., a method for reading non-ASCII text); it allows designers to create their own customized tags, thus overcoming many of the limitations of HTML.

XML schema. An XML schema provides definition and structure to XML documents. It outlines the constraints of XML documents and provides a mechanism for their validation by identifying approved elements and attributes, the number and order of elements, data types, and some values. An XML schema is expressed in XML syntax, supports namespaces and inheritance, can define data types, and follows XML rules, unlike the document type definitions that preceded XML schemas. *See also* **Document type definition.**

Z39. The standards section of ANSI/NISO that is devoted to libraries, information science, and publishing.

Z39.50. A national standard that provides for the exchange of information, such as surrogate records or full text, between otherwise incompatible computer systems.

Z39.50 protocol. A standard applications-level tool that allows one computer to query another computer and transfer search results without the user having to know the search commands of the remote computer.

Selected Bibliography

Allemang, Dean, Jim Hendler, and Fabien Gandon. *Semantic Web for the Working Ontologist*. 3rd ed. New York: Association for Computing Machinery, 2020.

ALA Filing Rules. Chicago: American Library Association, 1980.

American National Standards Institute and National Information Standards Organization. *Criteria for Indexes*, ANSI/NISO Z39.4-2021. Baltimore, MD: National Information Standards Organization, 2021.

American Society for Indexing. *Best Practices for Indexing Guide*. Tempe, AZ: ASI, 2015.

Anglo-American Cataloguing Rules, Second Edition, 2002 Revision, prepared under the direction of the Joint Steering Committee for Revision of AACR. Ottawa: Canadian Library Association; Chicago: American Library Association, 2002.

Antoniou, Grigoris, Paul Groth, Frank van Harmelen, and Rinke Hoekstra. *A Semantic Web Primer*. 3rd ed. Cambridge, MA: MIT Press, 2012.

Avram, Henriette. "Machine Readable Cataloging (MARC): 1961–1974." In *Encyclopedia of Library and Information Sciences*. 4th ed., edited by John D. McDonald and Michael Levine-Clark. Boca Raton, FL: Taylor & Francis, 2017.

Baca, Murtha, ed. *Introduction to Metadata*. 3rd ed. Los Angeles: Getty Research Institute, 2016. http://www.getty.edu/publications/intrometadata/.

Baca, Murtha. "A Picture Is Worth a Thousand Words: Metadata for Art Objects and Their Visual Surrogates." In *Cataloging the Web: Metadata, AACR, and MARC 21*, edited by Wayne Jones et al., 131–8. Lanham, MD: Scarecrow, 2002.

Baca, Murtha, and Patricia Harpring, eds. *Categories for the Description of Works of Art*. Revised 2024 by Emily Benoff. Los Angeles: The Getty, 2024. http://www.getty.edu/research/publications/electronic_publications/cdwa/.

Baca, Murtha, Patricia Harpring, Elisa Lanzi, Linda McRae, and Ann Whiteside. *Cataloging Cultural Objects: A Guide to Describing Cultural Works and Their Images*. Chicago: American Library Association, 2006. https://www.vraweb.org/cco.

Badgett, Nan. *The Accidental Indexer*. Medford, NJ: Information Today, 2015.

Badke, William. *Research Strategies: Finding Your Way Through the Information Fog*. 7th ed. Bloomington, IN: iUniverse, 2021.

Baker, Nicholson. "Discards." *New Yorker* 70, no. 7 (April 4, 1994): 64–86.

Baldoni, Emily, and Daniel N. Joudrey. "Cataloging." In *Encyclopedia of Libraries, Librarianship, and Information Science*, edited by David Baker and Lucy Ellis. Cambridge, MA: Elsevier, 2024.

Banerjee, Kyle. *Building Digital Libraries: A How-to-Do-It Manual for Librarians*. 2nd ed. Chicago: ALA Neal-Schuman, 2019.

Banerjee, Kyle. "The Linked Data Myth." *Library Journal* [website]. August 13, 2020. https://www.libraryjournal.com/story/the-linked-data-myth.

Banerjee, Sujata, and Vibhu O. Mittal. "On the Use of Linguistic Ontologies for Accessing and Indexing Distributed Digital Libraries." In *Digital Libraries '94: Proceedings of the First Annual Conference on the Theory and Practice of Digital Libraries, June 19-21, 1994, College Station, Texas*, edited by John L. Schnase. College Station: Texas A&M, 1994. https://www.jcdl.info/archived-conf-sites/dl94/paper/banerjee.html.

Bastian, Jeannette, Megan Sniffin-Marinoff, and Donna Webber. *Archives in Libraries: What Librarians and Archivists Need to Know to Work Together*. Chicago: Society of American Archivists, 2015.

Bates, Marcia J. "The Design of Browsing and Berrypicking Techniques for the Online Search Interface." *Online Review* 13, no. 5 (October 1989): 407–24.

Bauer, Florian, and Martin Kaltenböck. *Linked Open Data: The Essentials*. 2nd ed. Vienna: DGS, 2016. https://reeep.org/wp-content/uploads/2023/10/LOD-TheEssentials2016.pdf.

Berman, Sanford. *Joy of Cataloging*. Phoenix, AZ: Oryx, 1981.

Berman, Sanford. *Prejudices and Antipathies: A Tract on the LC Subject Heads Concerning People*. Metuchen, NJ: Scarecrow, 1971. http://www.sanfordberman.org/prejant.htm.

Berner, Richard C. "Historical Development of Archival Theory and Practices in the United States." *Midwestern Archivist* 7, no. 2 (1982): 103–17.

Berners-Lee, Tim. "Linked Data." W3C Design Issues, July 2006. https://www.w3.org/DesignIssues/LinkedData.

Berners-Lee, Tim, with Mark Fischetti. *Weaving the Web: The Original Design and Ultimate Destiny of the World Wide Web by Its Inventor*. New York: HarperCollins, 1999.

Berners-Lee, Tim, James Hendler, and Ora Lassila. "The Semantic Web." *Scientific American* 284, no. 5 (May 2001): 34–8, 40–3.

Berners-Lee, Tim, Roy Fielding, and Larry Masinter. "Uniform Resource Identifier (URI): Generic Syntax." IETF [Internet Engineering Task Force] Documents. January 2005. http://tools.ietf.org/html/rfc3986.

Besson, Alain. *Medieval Classification and Cataloguing: Classification Practices and Cataloging Methods in France from the 12th to 15th Centuries*. Biggleswade, UK: Clover, 1980.

Bettington, Jackie, ed. *Keeping Archives*. 3rd ed. Canberra: Australia Society of Archivists, 2008.

Bierbaum, Esther Green. "Records and Access: Museum Registration and Library Cataloging." *Cataloging & Classification Quarterly* 9, no. 1 (1988): 97–111.

Bilal, Dania. Library *Automation: Core Concepts and Practical Systems Analysis*. 3rd ed. Santa Barbara, CA: Libraries Unlimited, 2014.

Billey, Amber. "Just Because We Can, Doesn't Mean We Should: An Argument for Simplicity and Data Privacy with Name Authority Work in the Linked Data Environment." *Journal of Library Metadata* 19, no. 1/2 (2019): 1–17.

Billey, Amber, Elizabeth Nelson, and Rebecca Uhl, in collaboration with Core, eds. *Inclusive Cataloging: Histories, Context, and Reparative Approaches*. Chicago: ALA Editions, 2024.

Billey, Amber, Emily Drabinski, and K. R. Roberto. "What's Gender Got to Do with It? A Critique of RDA 9.7." *Cataloging & Classification Quarterly* 52, no. 4 (2014): 412–21.

Block, Carson. *Managing Library Technology: A LITA Guide*. Lanham, MD: Rowman & Littlefield, 2017.

Bourcier, Paul, Heather Dunn, and Nomenclature Task Force, ed. *Nomenclature 4.0 for Museum Cataloging*. 4th ed. Lanham, MD: Rowman & Littlefield, 2015.

Borgman, Christine L. *From Gutenberg to the Global Information Infrastructure: Access to Information in the Networked World*. Cambridge, MA: MIT Press, 2000.

Borgman, Christine L. "Why Are Online Catalogs Hard to Use? Lessons Learned from Information Retrieval Studies." *Journal of the American Society for Information Science* 37, no. 6 (June 1986): 387–400.

Borgman, Christine L. "Why Are Online Catalogs *Still* Hard to Use?" *Journal of the American Society for Information Science* 47, no. 7 (July 1996): 493–503.

Bowker, Geoffrey C., and Susan Leigh Star. *Sorting Things Out: Classification and Its Consequences*. Cambridge, MA: MIT Press, 1999.

Breeding, Marshall. "Library Services Platforms: A Maturing Genre of Products." *Library Technology Reports* 51, no. 4 (2015): 1–40.

Breeding, Marshall. "Library Systems Report." *American Libraries*. May 1st issue each year.

Breeding, Marshall. *Library Technology Buying Strategies*. Chicago: ALA Editions, 2016.

Breeding, Marshall. *Library Technology Guides*. http://www.librarytechnology.org/.

Breeding, Marshall. *Next-Gen Library Catalogs*. New York: Neal-Schuman, 2010.

Broughton, Vanda. *Essential Classification*. Chicago: ALA Neal-Schuman, 2015.

Brown, A. G., in collaboration with D. W. Langridge and J. Mills. *An Introduction to Subject Indexing*. 2nd ed. London: Bingley, 1982.

Brown, Christopher C. *Librarian's Guide to Online Searching: Cultivating Database Skills for Research and Instruction*. 6th ed. Santa Barbara, CA: Libraries Unlimited, 2021.

Buckland, Michael K. "What Is a 'Document'?" *Journal of the American Society for Information Science* 48, no. 9 (September 1997): 804–9. https://people.ischool.berkeley.edu/~buckland/whatdoc.html.

Burke, Frank G. "Archives: Organization and Description." In *World Encyclopedia of Library and Information Services*. 3rd ed., edited by Robert Wedgeworth, 63–8. Chicago: American Library Association, 1993.

Bush, Vannevar. "As We May Think." *Atlantic Monthly* 176 (July 1945): 101–8. https://www.theatlantic.com/magazine/archive/1945/07/as-we-may-think/303881/.

Caplan, Priscilla. *Metadata Fundamentals for All Librarians*. Chicago: American Library Association, 2003.

Carlson, Scott, Cory Lampert, Darnelle Melvin, and Anne Washington. *Linked Data for the Perplexed Librarian*. Chicago: ALA Editions, 2020.

Carmicheal, David W. *Organizing Archival Records*. 4th ed. Lanham, MD: Rowman & Littlefield, 2019.

Carpenter, Michael. "The Original 73 Rules of the British Museum: A Preliminary Analysis." *Cataloging & Classification Quarterly* 35, no. 1/2 (2002): 23–36.

Casson, Lionel. *Libraries in the Ancient World*. New Haven, CT: Yale University Press, 2001.

Cataloging Ethics Steering Committee. "Cataloguing Code of Ethics." 2021 version. https://alair.ala.org/handle/11213/16716.

Chambers, Sally, ed. *Catalogue 2.0: The Future of the Library Catalogue*. Chicago: Neal-Schuman, 2013.

Chan, Lois Mai. *Library of Congress Subject Headings: Principles and Applications*. 4th ed. Westport, CT: Libraries Unlimited, 2006.

Chan, Lois Mai, and Athena Salaba. *Cataloging and Classification: An Introduction*. 5th ed. Lanham, MD: Rowman & Littlefield, 2023.

Chan, Lois Mai, Phyllis A. Richmond, and Elaine Svenonius, eds. *Theory of Subject Analysis: A Sourcebook*. Littleton, CO: Libraries Unlimited, 1985.

Chan, Lois Mai, Sheila S. Intner, and Jean Weihs. *A Guide to the Library of Congress Classification*. 6th ed. Santa Barbara, CA: Libraries Unlimited, 2016.

Change the Subject. A film by Sawyer Broadley, Jill Baron, Óscar Rubén Cornejo Cásares, and Melissa Padilla. 2019. Dartmouth Digital Library Program. https://n2t.net/ark:/83024/d4hq3s42r.

Chen, Peter Pin-Shan. "The Entity-Relationship Model: Toward a Unified View of Data." *ACM Transactions on Database Systems* 1, no. 1 (1976): 9–36.

Clack, Doris Hargrett, ed. *The Making of a Code: The Issues Underlying AACR2* Chicago: American Library Association, 1980.

Clark, Alexander, Chris Fox, and Shalom Lappin, eds. *The Handbook of Computational Linguistics and Natural Language Processing*. Malden, MA: Wiley-Blackwell, 2010.

Classification Research Group. "The Need for a Faceted Classification as the Basis of All Methods of Information Retrieval." In *Theory of Subject Analysis: A Sourcebook*, edited by Lois Mai Chan, Phyllis A. Richmond, and Elaine Svenonius, 154–67. Littleton, CO: Libraries Unlimited, 1985.

Cleveland, Donald B., and Ana D. Cleveland. *Introduction to Indexing and Abstracting*. 4th ed. Santa Barbara, CA: Libraries Unlimited, 2013.

Collantes, Lourdes Y. "Agreement in Naming Objects and Concepts for Information Retrieval." PhD diss., Rutgers University, 1992.

Collison, Chris J., Paul J. Corney, and Patricia Lee Eng. *The KM Cookbook: Stories and Strategies for Organisations Exploring Knowledge Management Standard ISO30401*. London: Facet, 2019.

Cooey, Nancy, and Amy Phillips. "Library of Congress Subject Headings: A Post-Coordinated Future." *Cataloging & Classification Quarterly* 61, no. 5/6 (2023): 491–505.

Coronel, Carlos, and Steven Morris. *Database Systems: Design, Implementation, & Management*. 14th ed. Boston, MA: Cengage, 2023.

Covert, Abby. *How to Make Sense of Any Mess: Information Architecture for Everybody*. North Charleston, SC: CreateSpace, 2014.

Cutter, Charles A. *Rules for a Dictionary Catalog*. 4th ed. Washington, DC: Government Printing Office, 1904; Reprint, London: The Library Association, 1962.

Dalkir, Kimiz. *Knowledge Management in Theory and Practice*. 4th ed. Cambridge, MA: MIT Press, 2023.

Danskin, Alan, et al. "FAST the Inside Track: Where We Are, Where Do We Want to Be, and How Do We Get There?" *Cataloging & Classification Quarterly* 61, no. 5/6 (2023): 506–24.

Denton, William. "FRBR and the History of Cataloging." In *Understanding FRBR: What It Is and How It Will Affect Our Retrieval Tools*, edited by Arlene G. Taylor, 35–57. Westport, CT: Libraries Unlimited, 2007.

Describing Archives: A Content Standard. Version 2022.0.1.1. Chicago: Society of American Archivists, 2022. http://www2.archivists.org/groups/technical-subcommittee-on-describing-archives-a-content-standard-dacs/dacs.

Desouza, Kevin C., and Scott Paquette. *Knowledge Management: An Introduction*. New York: Neal-Schuman, 2011.

DeWeese, Keith P., and Dan Segal. *Libraries and the Semantic Web*. San Rafael, CA: Morgan & Claypool, 2015.

Digital Libraries and Institutional Repositories: Breakthroughs in Research and Practice. Hershey, PA: IGI Global, 2020.

Dillon, Andrew. "Information Architecture in JASIST: Just Where Did We Come From?" *Journal of the American Society for Information Science and Technology* 53, no. 10 (2002): 821–76.

Dillon, Andrew, and Don Turnbull. "Information Architecture." In *Encyclopedia of Library and Information Sciences*. 3rd ed., edited by Marcia J. Bates and Mary Niles Maack, 2361–8. New York: Taylor & Francis, 2009.

Dublin Core Metadata Initiative. http://dublincore.org/.

Dunkin, Paul S. *Cataloging U.S.A.* Chicago: American Library Association, 1969.

"EAD: Encoded Archival Description." Library of Congress. http://www.loc.gov/ead/.

EDItEUR. "ONIX: Overview." http://www.editeur.org/83/Overview/.

Eisenstein, Jacob. *Introduction to Natural Language Processing*. Cambridge, MA: The MIT Press, 2019.

Enis, Matt. "Open for Growth." *Library Journal* 147, no. 10 (2022): 41–4.

"Encoded Archival Context: Corporate Bodies, Persons, and Families (EAC-CPF)." Society of American Archivists. http://eac.staatsbibliothek-berlin.de/.

Evans, G. Edward, Sheila S. Intner, and Jean Weihs. *Introduction to Technical Services*. 8th ed. Santa Barbara, CA: Libraries Unlimited, 2011.

Fairthorne, Robert A. "Content Analysis, Specification, and Control." In *Annual Review of Information Science and Technology*. Vol. 4, edited by Carlos A. Cuadra and Ann W. Luke. Chicago: Encyclopedia Britannica, 1969.

Fishbein, Meyer H. "Archives: Records Management and Records Appraisal." In *World Encyclopedia of Library and Information Services*. 3rd ed., edited by Robert Wedgeworth, 60–3. Chicago: American Library Association, 1993.

Foster, Elvis, with Shripad V. Godbole. *Database Systems: A Pragmatic Approach*. 3rd ed. Boca Raton, FL: CRC Press, 2023.

Fox, Richard. *Information Technology: An Introduction for Today's Digital World.* 2nd ed. Boca Raton, FL: CRC Press, 2021.

Fox, Violet, ed. *Sears List of Subject Headings.* 23rd ed. Armenia, NY: H. W. Wilson/Grey House Publishing, 2022.

Franks, Patricia C. *Records and Information Management.* Chicago: ALA Neal-Schuman, 2018.

Furrie, Betty. *Understanding MARC Bibliographic: Machine-Readable Cataloging.* 8th ed. Washington, DC: Library of Congress, Cataloging Distribution Service, 2009. http://www.loc.gov/marc/umb.

Gartner, Richard. *Metadata in the Digital Library: Building an Integrated Strategy with XML.* London: Facet, 2021.

Gates, Lynn E., and Joel D. Tonyan. *Making the Most of Your ILS: A User's Guide to Evaluating and Optimizing Library Systems.* Santa Barbara, CA: Libraries Unlimited, 2023.

Gerolimos, Michalis. "Tagging for Libraries: A Review of the Effectiveness of Tagging Systems for Library Catalogs." *Journal of Library Metadata* 13, no. 1 (2013): 36–58.

Getty Research Institute. "Art & Architecture Thesaurus Online: About the AAT." http://www.getty.edu/research/tools/vocabularies/aat/about.html.

Getty Research Institute. "Getty Vocabularies." http://www.getty.edu/research/tools/vocabularies/index.html.

Gilliland, Anne J. *Conceptualizing 21st-century Archives.* Chicago: Society of American Archivists, 2014.

Gilliland, Anne J. "Setting the Stage." In *Introduction to Metadata.* 3rd ed., edited by Murtha Baca. Los Angeles: Getty Research Institute, 2016. http://www.getty.edu/publications/intrometadata/setting-the-stage.

Glushko, Robert J., ed. *The Discipline of Organizing.* 4th Professional ed. Berkeley, CA: University of California, 2020.

Godby, Carol Jean. *Mapping ONIX to MARC.* Dublin, OH: OCLC Research, 2010.

Gorman, Michael. "AACR2: Main Themes." In *The Making of a Code: The Issues Underlying AACR2*, edited by Doris Hargrett Clack. Chicago: American Library Association, 1980.

Gorman, Michael. "From Card Catalogues to WebPACs: Celebrating Cataloguing in the 20th Century." In *Proceedings of the Bicentennial Conference on Bibliographic Control for the New Millennium: Confronting the Challenges of Networked Resources and the Web, Washington, D.C., November 15–17, 2000,* sponsored by the Library of Congress Cataloging Directorate; edited by Ann M. Sandberg-Fox. Washington, DC: Library of Congress, Cataloging Distribution Service, 2001. https://www.loc.gov/catdir/bibcontrol/gorman_paper.html.

Gorman, Michael. "The Longer the Number, the Smaller the Spine; or, Up and Down with Melvil and Elsie." *American Libraries* 12, no. 8 (September 1981): 498–9.

Gross, Tina, and Arlene G. Taylor. "What Have We Got to Lose? The Effect of Controlled Vocabulary on Keyword Searching Results." *College & Research Libraries* 66, no. 3 (May 2005): 212–30.

Gross, Tina, Arlene G. Taylor, and Daniel N. Joudrey. "Still a Lot to Lose: The Role of Controlled Vocabulary in Keyword Searching." *Cataloging & Classification Quarterly* 53, no. 1 (2015): 1–39.

Guenther, Rebecca S. "MODS: The Metadata Object Description Schema." *Portal: Libraries and the Academy* 3, no. 1 (2003): 137–50.

Guerrini, Mauro, and Tiziana Possemato. "Linked Data: A New Alphabet for the Semantic Web." *Italian Journal of Library, Archives, and Information Science* 4, no. 1 (2013). https://www.jlis.it/index.php/jlis/article/view/256.

Hagler, Ronald. *The Bibliographic Record and Information Technology.* 3rd ed. Chicago: American Library Association, 1997.

Hamill, Lois. *Archival Arrangement and Description: Analog to Digital.* Lanham, MD: Rowman & Littlefield, 2017.

Harris, Michael H. *History of Libraries in the Western World.* 4th ed. Lanham, MD: Scarecrow, 1999.

Haynes, David. *Metadata for Information Management and Retrieval.* 2nd ed. Chicago: ALA, 2018.

Heath, Tom, and Christian Bizer. *Linked Data: Evolving the Web into a Global Data Space.* San Rafael, CA: Morgan & Claypool, 2011.

Hedden, Heather. *The Accidental Taxonomist.* 3rd ed. Medford, NJ: Information Today, 2022.

Hernandez, Michael J. *Database Design for Mere Mortals, 25th Anniversary edition: A Hands-on Guide to Relational Database Design.* 4th ed. Hoboken, NJ: Pearson Education, 2020.

Hider, Philip. *Information Resource Description: Creating and Managing Metadata.* 2nd ed. Chicago: ALA Editions, 2018.

Hider, Philip, and Gemma Steele, "LibraryThing and Literary Works Revisited," *Library Resources & Technical Services* 65, no. 3 (2021): 113–26.

Hildreth, Charles R. "The Use and Understanding of Keyword Searching in a University Online Catalog." *Information Technology and Libraries* 16, no. 2 (June 1997): 52–62.

Hoffman, Gretchen. *Organizing Library Collections: Theory and Practice.* Lanham, MD: Rowman & Littlefield, 2019.

Hoffman, Gretchen, and Karen Snow, eds. *Cataloging and Classification: Back to Basics.* New York: Routledge, 2022.

Holley, Ralph M., and Daniel N. Joudrey. "Aboutness and Conceptual Analysis: A Review." *Cataloging & Classification Quarterly* 59, no. 2/3 (2021): 159–85.

"Homosaurus: An International LGBTQ+ Linked Data Vocabulary." https://homosaurus.org/.

Hopkins, Judith. "The 1791 French Cataloging Code and the Origins of the Card Catalog." *Libraries & Culture* 27, no. 4 (Fall 1992): 378–404.

Humbert, de Romans. *Regulations for the Operation of a Medieval Library.* St. Paul: Associates of the James Ford Bell Library, University of Minnesota, 1980.

Hunter, Eric J. *Classification Made Simple: An Introduction to Knowledge Organisation and Information Retrieval.* 3rd ed. Farnham, UK: Ashgate, 2009.

Husain, Shabahat. *Knowledge Management Systems: Concepts, Technologies and Practices.* Bingley, UK: Emerald Publishing, 2021.

International Conference on Cataloguing Principles, Paris, 9th–18th October, 1961. *Report.* London: International Federation of Library Associations, 1963.

International Council on Archives. *International Standard Archival Authority Record for Corporate Bodies, Persons, and Families* (ISAAR(CPF)). 2nd ed. Paris: International Council on Archives, 2004.

International Council on Archives. *ISAD(G): General International Standard Archival Description*, 2nd ed. Ottawa: International Council on Archives, 2000. https://www.ica.org/app/uploads/2024/01/CBPS_2000_Guidelines_ISADG_Second-edition_EN.pdf.

International Council on Archives. *Records in Contexts: Conceptual Model.* Version 1.0. November 2023. https://github.com/ICA-EGAD/RiC-CM/

International Council of Museums, International Committee for Documentation. "CIDOC CRM: Conceptual Reference Model." https://cidoc-crm.org/.

International Federation of Library Associations and Institutions, IFLA Study Group. *Functional Requirements for Bibliographic Records: Final Report.* Munich: Saur, 1998. http://www.ifla.org/publications/functional-requirements-for-bibliographic-records.

International Federation of Library Associations and Institutions, Meetings of Experts on an International Cataloguing Code. *Statement of International Cataloguing Principles (ICP).* 2016 edition. The Hague: IFLA, 2016. https://www.ifla.org/g/cataloguing/international-cataloguing-principles-icp/.

International Federation of Library Associations and Institutions, Working Group on Functional Requirements and Numbering of Authority Records. *Functional Requirements for Authority Data: A Conceptual Model.* The Hague: IFLA, 2009. https://www.ifla.org/publications/functional-requirements-for-authority-data.

International Federation of Library Associations and Institutions, Working Group on the Functional Requirements for Subject Authority Records (FRSAR). *Functional Requirements for Subject Authority Data: A Conceptual Model.* The Hague: IFLA, 2010. https://www.ifla.org/functional-requirements-for-subject-authority-data/.

International Federation of Library Associations and Institutions, Working Group on GARE Revision. *Guidelines for Authority Records and References.* 2nd ed. Munich: K. G. Saur, 2001. https://www.ifla.org/resources/?oPubId=8079.

International Organization for Standardization. *Information and Documentation—Format for Information Exchange*, ISO 2709:2008. 4th ed. Geneva: ISO, 2008.

International Organization for Standardization. *Information and Documentation—Guidelines for Bibliographic References and Citations to Information Resources*, ISO 690:2021. Geneva: ISO, 2021.

International Organization for Standardization. *Information and Documentation: Guidelines for the Content, Organization and Presentation of Indexes*, ISO 999:1996. Geneva: ISO, 1996.

International Organization for Standardization. *Information and Documentation: Records Management*, ISO 15489-1. Pt. 1. Concepts and Principles. Geneva: ISO, 2016.

International Standard Bibliographic Description (ISBD). Consolidated ed. Berlin: De Gruyter Saur, 2011. https://repository.ifla.org/handle/20.500.14598/1939.

Jackson, Sidney L. *Libraries and Librarianship in the West: A Brief History.* New York: McGraw-Hill, 1974.

Jacob, Elin K. "Classification and Categorization: A Difference That Makes a Difference." *Library Trends* 52, no. 3 (Winter 2004): 515–40.

Jacob, Elin K. "Ontologies and the Semantic Web." *Bulletin of the American Society for Information Science and Technology* 29, no. 4 (April/May 2003): 19–22. https://asistdl.onlinelibrary.wiley.com/doi/10.1002/bult.283.

Jewett, Charles Coffin. *On the Construction of Catalogues of Libraries, and Their Publication by Means of Separate, Stereotyped Titles.* 2nd ed. Washington, DC: Smithsonian Institution, 1853.

Jones, William. *Keeping Found Things Found: The Study and Practice of Personal Information Management.* San Francisco, CA: Morgan Kaufmann, 2008.

Jones, William. "Personal Information Management." In *Annual Review of Information Science and Technology*, Volume 41, edited by Blaise Cronin, 453–504. Medford, NJ: Information Today, 2007.

Jones, William, and Jaime Teevan, eds. *Personal Information Management.* Seattle: University of Washington Press, 2007.

Joudrey, Daniel N. "Building Puzzles and Growing Pearls: A Qualitative Exploration of Determining Aboutness." PhD diss., University of Pittsburgh, 2005. http://d-scholarship.pitt.edu/id/eprint/10357.

Joudrey, Daniel N. "Cataloging." In *Encyclopedia of Library and Information Sciences.* 4th ed., edited by John D. McDonald and Michael Levine-Clark. Boca Raton, FL: Taylor & Francis, 2017.

Joudrey, Daniel N., Arlene G. Taylor, and David P. Miller. *Introduction to Cataloging and Classification.* 11th ed. Santa Barbara, CA: Libraries Unlimited, 2015.

Kao, Anne, and Stephen R. Poteet, eds. *Natural Language Processing and Text Mining.* London: Springer, 2007.

Kendall, Kenneth E., and Julie E. Kendall. *Systems Analysis and Design.* 11th ed. New York: Pearson, 2023.

Keyser, Pierre de. *Indexing: From Thesauri to the Semantic Web.* Oxford: Chandos, 2012.

Knowlton, Steven A. "Three Decades since Prejudices and Antipathies: A Study of Changes in the Library of Congress Subject Headings." *Cataloging & Classification Quarterly* 40, no. 2 (2005): 123–45.

Kumar, Shiv. "From Clay Tablets to Web: Journey of Library Catalogue." *DESIDOC Journal of Library & Information Technology* 33, no. 1 (January 2013): 45–54.

Kwasnik, Barbara. "The Influence of Context on Classificatory Behavior." PhD diss., Rutgers University, 1989.

Lakoff, George. *Women, Fire, and Dangerous Things: What Categories Reveal about the Mind.* Chicago: University of Chicago Press, 1987.

Lancaster, F. W. *Indexing and Abstracting in Theory and Practice.* 3rd ed. Champaign: University of Illinois, Graduate School of Library and Information Science, 2003.

Lancaster, F. W. *Vocabulary Control for Information Retrieval.* 2nd ed. Arlington, VA: Information Resources, 1986.

Lancaster, F. W. "Whither Libraries? or Wither Libraries." *College & Research Libraries* 39, no. 5 (September 1978): 345–57.

Landis, William E., and Robin L. Chandler, eds. *Archives and the Digital Library*. Binghamton, NY: Haworth Information, 2006.

Langridge, D. W. *Classification: Its Kinds, Elements, Systems, and Applications*. London: Bowker-Saur, 1992.

Langridge, D. W. *Subject Analysis: Principles and Procedures*. London: Bowker-Saur, 1989.

Library of Congress. "BIBFRAME: Bibliographic Framework Initiative." http://www.loc.gov/bibframe/.

Library of Congress. *Bibliographic Framework as a Web of Data: Linked Data Model and Supporting Services*. Washington, DC: Library of Congress, 2012. http://www.loc.gov/bibframe/pdf/marcld-report-11-21-2012.pdf.

Library of Congress. "Library of Congress Classification." https://www.loc.gov/catdir/cpso/lcc.html.

Library of Congress. "Library of Congress Demographic Group Terms PDF Files." https://www.loc.gov/aba/publications/FreeLCDGT/freelcdgt.html.

Library of Congress. "Library of Congress Genre/Form Terms PDF Files." https://www.loc.gov/aba/publications/FreeLCGFT/freelcgft.html.

Library of Congress. "Library of Congress Subject Headings PDF Files." https://www.loc.gov/aba/publications/FreeLCSH/freelcsh.html.

Library of Congress. "MADS: Metadata Authority Description Schema." http://www.loc.gov/standards/mads/.

Library of Congress. "MARC Standards." http://www.loc.gov/marc/.

Library of Congress. "MARCXML: MARC 21 XML Schema." http://www.loc.gov/standards/marcxml/.

Library of Congress. "METS: Metadata Encoding and Transmission Scheme." https://www.loc.gov/standards/mets/.

Library of Congress. "MODS: Metadata Object Description Schema." http://www.loc.gov/standards/mods/.

Library of Congress, Working Group on the Future of Bibliographic Control. *On the Record: Report of the Library of Congress Working Group on the Future of Bibliographic Control*. Washington, DC: Library of Congress, 2008. http://www.loc.gov/bibliographic-future/news/lcwg-ontherecord-jan08-final.pdf.

Liu, Jia. *Metadata and Its Applications in the Digital Library: Approaches and Practices*. Westport, CT: Libraries Unlimited, 2007.

Lubetzky, Seymour. *Cataloging Rules and Principles: A Critique of the A.L.A. Rules for Entry and a Proposed Design for their Revision*. Washington, DC: Library of Congress, 1953.

Malone, Thomas W. "How Do People Organize Their Desks? Implications for the Design of Office Information Systems." *ACM Trans Office Info Systems* 1, no. 1 (1983): 99–112.

Mann, Thomas. "'Cataloging Must Change!' and Indexer Consistency Studies: Misreading the Evidence at Our Peril." *Cataloging & Classification Quarterly* 23, no. 3/4 (1997): 3–45.

Mann, Thomas. *The Oxford Guide to Library Research*. 4th ed. New York: Oxford University Press, 2015.

Markey, Karen. "The Online Library Catalog: Paradise Lost and Paradise Regained?" *D-Lib Magazine* 13, no. 1/2 (2007). http://www.dlib.org/dlib/january07/markey/01markey.html.

Marshall, Brianna H., ed. *The Complete Guide to Personal Digital Archiving*. Chicago: ALA Editions, 2018.

Marshall, Joan K. *On Equal Terms: A Thesaurus for Nonsexist Indexing and Cataloging*. Santa Barbara, CA: ABC-CLIO, 1977.

Martin, Lisa Marie. *Everyday Information Architecture*. New York: A Book Apart, 2019.

Maxwell, Robert L. *FRBR: A Guide for the Perplexed*. Chicago: American Library Association, 2008.

Maxwell, Robert L. *Maxwell's Handbook for RDA, Resource Description & Access: Explaining and Illustrating RDA: Resource Description and Access Using MARC21*. Chicago: American Library Association, 2013.

McIlwaine, I. C. *The Universal Decimal Classification: A Guide to Its Use*. Rev. ed. The Hague: UDC Consortium, 2007.

Meissner, Dennis. *Arranging and Describing Archives and Manuscripts*. Chicago: Society of American Archivists, 2019.

Millar, Laura A. *Archives: Principles and Practices*. 2nd ed. Chicago: Neal-Schuman, 2017.

Miller, Steven J. *Metadata for Digital Collections: A How-to-Do-It Manual*. 2nd ed. Chicago: Neal-Schuman, 2022.

Milsap, Larry. "A History of the Online Catalog in North America." In *Technical Services Management, 1965–1990: A Quarter Century of Change, A Look to the Future: A Festschrift for Kathryn Luther Henderson*, edited by Linda C. Smith and Ruth C. Carter, 79–91. Binghamton, NY: Haworth, 1996.

Mitchell, Erik T. *Library Linked Data: Early Activity and Development*. Chicago: ALA TechSource, 2016.

Mitchell, Erik T. *Metadata Standards and Web Services in Libraries, Archives, and Museums*. Santa Barbara, CA: Libraries Unlimited, 2015.

Moulaison, Heather Lea, and Raegan Wiechert. *Crash Course in Basic Cataloging with RDA*. Santa Barbara, CA: Libraries Unlimited, 2015.

Muller, Samuel, Johan A. Feith, and Robert Fruin. *Handleiding voor het Ordenen en Beschrijven van Archieven*. Groningen: Erven B. van der Kamp, 1898.

Muller, Samuel, Johan A. Feith, and Robert Fruin. *Manual for the Arrangement and Description of Archives*. Translation of the second edition by Arthur H. Leavitt; with new introductions by Peter Horsman [and others]. Chicago: Society of American Archivists, 2003.

Mulvaney, Nancy C. *Indexing Books*. 2nd ed. Chicago: University of Chicago Press, 2005.

National Library of Medicine. "Medical Subject Headings." https://www.nlm.nih.gov/mesh/meshhome.html.

Neal, Diane Rasmussen, ed. *Indexing and Retrieval of Non-text Information*. Berlin: De Gruyter Saur, 2012.

Neilson, Dixie. "Museum Registration and Documentation." In *Encyclopedia of Library and Information Sciences*. 4th ed., edited by John D. McDonald and Michael Levine-Clark, 3199–213. Boca Raton, FL: CRC Press, 2017.

Norris, Dorothy May. *A History of Cataloging and Cataloging Methods*. London: Grafton, 1939.

Noy, Natalya F., and Deborah L. McGuinness. *Ontology Development 101: A Guide to Creating Your First Ontology*. Stanford, CA: Knowledge Systems Laboratory, Stanford University, 2000. https://protege.stanford.edu/publications/ontology_development/ontology101.pdf.

OCLC. *Bibliographic Formats and Standards*. http://www.oclc.org/bibformats/.

OCLC. "Dewey Services." http://www.oclc.org/en/dewey.html.

OCLC. *Online Catalogs: What Users and Librarians Want: An OCLC Report*. Dublin, OH: OCLC, 2009.

O'Connor, Brian C., Jodi Kearns, and Richard L. Anderson. *Doing Things with Information: Beyond Indexing and Abstracting*. Westport, CT: Libraries Unlimited, 2008.

Oh, Kyong Eun. "The Process of Organizing Personal Information." PhD diss., Rutgers University, 2013.

Oh, Kyong Eun. "Personal Information Organization in Everyday Life: Modeling the Process." *Journal of Documentation* 75, no. 3 (2019): 667–91.

Oh, Kyong Eun. "Types of Personal Information Categorization." *Journal of the Association for Information Science & Technology* 68, no. 6 (2017): 1491–504.

Oliver, Chris. *Introducing RDA: A Guide to the Basics After 3R*. Chicago: ALA Editions, 2021.

Olson, Hope A. *The Power to Name: Locating the Limits of Subject Representation in Libraries*. Dordrecht, The Netherlands: Kluwer Academic, 2002.

Olson, Hope A., and John J. Boll. *Subject Analysis in Online Catalogs*. 2nd ed. Englewood, CO: Libraries Unlimited, 2001.

Osborn, Andrew D. "The Crisis in Cataloging." *Library Quarterly* 11, no. 4 (October 1941): 393–411.

Pace, Andrew. "21st Century Library Systems." *Journal of Library Administration* 49, no. 6 (2009): 641–50.

Petroski, Henry. *The Book on the Bookshelf*. New York: Knopf, 1999.

Pettee, Julia. "The Subject Approach to Books and the Development of the Dictionary Catalog." In *Theory of Subject Analysis: A Sourcebook*, edited by Lois Mai Chan, Phyllis A. Richmond, and Elaine Svenonius, 94–98. Littleton, CO: Libraries Unlimited, 1985.

Pitti, Daniel V. "Creator Description: Encoded Archival Context." *Cataloging & Classification Quarterly* 39, no. 1/2 (2004): 201–26.

Pustejovsky, James, and Amber Stubbs. *Natural Language Annotation for Machine Learning*. Sebastopol, CA: O'Reilly Media, 2013.

Quintarelli, Emanuele. "Folksonomies: Power to the People." Paper presented at the ISKO Italy-UniMIB Meeting, 2005. http://www.iskoi.org/doc/folksonomies.htm.

Ranganathan, S. R. *Prolegomena to Library Classification*. 3rd ed. London: Asia Publishing House, 1967.

RDA: Resource Description & Access. Chicago: American Library Association, 2010– . http://www.rdatoolkit.org/.

Records and Information Management Core Competencies. 2nd ed. Overland Park, KS: ARMA International, Education Development Committee, 2017.

Reibel, Daniel B., and Deborah Rose Van Horn. *Registration Methods for the Small Museum*. 5th ed. Lanham, MD: Rowman & Littlefield, 2018.

Reyes, Vanessa. *Saving Your Digital Past, Present, and Future: A Step-By-Step Guide*. Lanham, MD: Rowman & Littlefield, 2020.

Reynolds, Dennis. *Library Automation: Issues and Applications*. New York: Bowker, 1985.

Riley, Jenn. *Understanding Metadata*. Bethesda, MD: National Information Standards Organization, 2017. http://groups.niso.org/higherlogic/ws/public/download/17446/Understanding%20Metadata.pdf.

Riva, Pat, Patrick Le Boeuf, and Maja Žumer. *IFLA Library Reference Model: A Conceptual Model for Bibliographic Information*. The Hague, Netherlands: IFLA, 2017. https://www.ifla.org/resources/?oPubId=11412.

Roe, Kathleen D. *Arranging & Describing Archives & Manuscripts*. Chicago: Society of American Archivists, 2005.

Rosenfeld, Louis, Peter Morville, and Jorge Arango. *Information Architecture: For the Web and Beyond*. 4th ed. Sebastopol, CA: O'Reilly, 2015.

Rowley, Jennifer, and Richard Hartley. *Organizing Knowledge: An Introduction to Managing Access to Information*. 4th ed. Burlington, VT: Ashgate, 2008.

Rules for Archival Description. Revised version. Ottawa: Bureau of Canadian Archivist, 2008.

Russell, Beth M. "Hidden Wisdom and Unseen Treasure: Revisiting Cataloging in Medieval Libraries." *Cataloging & Classification Quarterly* 26, no. 3 (1998): 21–30.

Saffady, William. *Records and Information Management: Fundamentals of Professional Practice*. 4th ed. Lanham, MD: Rowman & Littlefield, 2009.

Sandberg, Jane, ed. *Ethical Questions in Name Authority Control*. Sacramento, CA: Library Juice Press, 2018.

Satija, M. P., and Alex Kyrios. *A Handbook of History, Theory and Practice of the Dewey Decimal Classification System*. London: Facet Publishing, 2023.

Schopflin, Katharine, and Matt Walsh. *Practical Knowledge and Information Management*. London: Facet, 2019.

Shatford, Sarah. "Analyzing the Subject of a Picture: A Theoretical Approach." *Cataloging & Classification Quarterly* 6, no. 3 (1986): 39–62.

Simmons, John E., and Toni M. Kiser, eds. *MRM6: Museum Registration Methods*. 6th ed. Lanham, MD: Rowman & Littlefield, 2020.

Smalley, Joseph. "The French Cataloging Code of 1791: A Translation." *Library Quarterly* 61, no. 1 (January 1991): 1–14.

Smiraglia, Richard P. "Authority Control and the Extent of Derivative Bibliographic Relationships." PhD diss., University of Chicago, 1992.

Smiraglia, Richard P. *The Nature of "A Work": Implications for the Organization of Knowledge*. Lanham, MD: Scarecrow, 2001.

Snow, Karen. *A Practical Guide to Dewey Decimal Classification*. Lanham, MD: Rowman & Littlefield, 2024.

Snow, Karen. *A Practical Guide to Library of Congress Classification*. Lanham, MD: Rowman & Littlefield, 2017.

Sowmya, V. B. *Practical Natural Language Processing: A Comprehensive Guide to Building Real-World NLP Systems*. Sebastopol, CA: O'Reilly, 2020.

Stauffer, Suzanne M., ed. *Libraries, Archives, and Museums: An Introduction to Cultural Heritage Institutions Through the Ages*. Lanham, MD: Rowman & Littlefield, 2021.

Stoll, Clifford. *Silicon Snake Oil: Second Thoughts on the Information Highway*. New York: Doubleday, 1995.

Strout, Ruth French. "The Development of the Catalog and Cataloging Codes." *Library Quarterly* 26, no. 4 (October 1956): 254–75.

Svenonius, Elaine. *The Intellectual Foundation of Information Organization*. Cambridge, MA: MIT Press, 2000.

Taylor, Arlene G. "Cataloguing." In *World Encyclopedia of Library and Information Services*. 3rd ed., edited by Robert Wedgeworth, 177–81. Chicago: American Library Association, 1993.

Taylor, Arlene G. "The Information Universe: Will We Have Chaos or Control?" *American Libraries* 25, no. 7 (July/August 1994): 629–32.

Taylor, Arlene G. *Introduction to Cataloging and Classification*. 10th ed., with the assistance of David P. Miller. Westport, CT: Libraries Unlimited, 2006.

Taylor, Arlene G. "On the Subject of Subjects." *Journal of Academic Librarianship* 21, no. 6 (November 1995): 484–91.

Taylor, Arlene G., ed. *Understanding FRBR: What It Is and How It Will Affect Our Retrieval Tools*. Westport, CT: Libraries Unlimited, 2007.

Taylor, Arlene G., and Barbara Tillett, eds. *Authority Control in Organizing and Accessing Information: Definition and International Experience*. New York: Haworth Information, 2004.

Text Encoding Initiative. "TEI: P5 Guidelines." Version 3.1.0. http://www.tei-c.org/release/doc/tei-p5-doc/en/html/index.html.

Thompson, Kelly J. "More Than a Name: A Content Analysis of Name Authority Records for Authors Who Identify as Trans." *Library Resources & Technical Services* 60, no. 3 (2016): 140–55.

Tillett, Barbara B. "Bibliographic Relationships." In *Relationships in the Organization of Knowledge*, edited by Carole A. Bean and Rebecca Green, 9–35. Dordrecht, The Netherlands: Kluwer Academic, 2001.

Tillett, Barbara B. "A Taxonomy of Bibliographic Relationships." *Library Resources & Technical Services* 35, no. 2 (April 1991): 150–8.

UDC Consortium. "About Universal Decimal Classification and the UDC Consortium." http://www.udcc.org/about.htm.

Van Hooland, Seth, and Ruben Verborgh. *Linked Data for Libraries, Archives and Museums: How to Clean, Link and Publish Your Metadata*. Chicago: American Library Association, 2014.

Vanderwarf, Sandra, and Bethany Romanwoski. *Inventorying Cultural Heritage Collections: A Guide for Museums and Historical Societies*. Lanham, MD: Rowman & Littlefield, 2022.

"VRA Core: A Data Standard for the Description of Images and Works of Art and Culture." Library of Congress. https://www.loc.gov/standards/vracore/.

W3C. "Extensible Markup Language." http://www.w3.org/XML/.

W3C. "RDF 1.1 Primer." https://www.w3.org/TR/rdf11-primer/.

Web Hypertext Application Technology Working Group (WHATWG). "HTML Living Standard." https://html.spec.whatwg.org/.

Webber, Desiree, and Andrew Peters. *Integrated Library Systems: Planning, Selecting, and Implementing*. Santa Barbara, CA: Libraries Unlimited, 2010.

Weihs, Jean, and Sheila Intner. *Beginning Cataloging*. 2nd ed. Santa Barbara, CA: Libraries Unlimited, 2017.

Weinberger, David. *Everything Is Miscellaneous: The Power of the New Digital Disorder*. New York: Times Books, 2007.

Weiss, Andrew. *Using Massive Digital Libraries: A LITA Guide*. Chicago: American Library Association, 2014.

Wellisch, Hans H. "Aboutness and Selection of Topics." *Key Words* 4, no. 2 (March/April 1996): 7–9.

Whittaker, Steve. "Personal Information Management: From Information Consumption to Curation." *Annual Review of Information Science and Technology*, Volume 41. Medford, NJ: Information Today, 2007.

Wilson, Patrick. "The Catalog as Access Mechanism: Background and Concepts." In *Foundations of Cataloging: A Sourcebook*, edited by Michael Carpenter and Elaine Svenonius, 253–68. Littleton, CO: Libraries Unlimited, 1985.

Wilson, Patrick. *Two Kinds of Power: An Essay on Bibliographical Control*. Berkeley: University of California Press, 1968.

Witty, Francis J. "The Beginnings of Indexing and Abstracting: Some Notes Towards a History of Indexing and Abstracting in Antiquity and the Middle Ages." *The Indexer* 8 (1973): 193–8.

Wythe, Deborah, ed. *Museum Archives: An Introduction*. Chicago: Society of American Archivists, 2004.

Yee, Martha M. "Guidelines for OPAC Displays: 1999." In *From Catalog to Gateway: Charting a Course for Future Access: Briefings from the ALCTS Catalog Form and Function Committee*, edited by Bill Sleeman and Pamela Bluh, 83–90. Chicago: Association for Collections & Technical Services, American Library Association, 2005.

Yee, Martha M., and Sara Shatford Layne. *Improving Online Public Access Catalogs*. Chicago: American Library Association, 1998.

Yeo, Geoffrey. *Record-making and Record-keeping in Early Societies*. New York: Routledge, 2021.

Zeng, Marcia Lei, and Jian Qin. *Metadata*. 3rd ed. Chicago: ALA Neal-Schuman, 2022.

Index

Italic page numbers indicate tables and figures.

A-Z indexes/indexing 33–4, 125
AACR see *Anglo-American Cataloguing Rules* (AACR/AACR2)
AACR2 see *Anglo-American Cataloguing Rules* (AACR/AACR2)
AAPs *see* authorized access points
AAT see *Art & Architecture Thesaurus* (AAT)
abbreviations 472, 542
   in AACR2 *vs.* RDA 77, *334–6*
   in access points 395
   in CCO 276
   in controlled vocabularies 463, 472
   in display of records 146–7
   in filing rules 540, 542
   in ISBD 331
   in resource descriptions 270, 294–5
aboutness 14, 425
   aboutness statements 427, 449–50, 477
   analysis by humans *vs.* machines 450–1
   artificial intelligence and 450–1
   Cohesion Method 440
   conceptual analysis process 441–2
   consistency in determining 433–4
   extensional 426
   Figure-Ground Method 440, 448
   indexing 31
   intensional 426
   Langridge's approach to 439
   methods to determine 438–41
   non-textual materials 434–5
   Objective Method 440, 448
   objectivity 437–8
   outline of determination process 571–5
   perceptions of 433
   purpose, confusing with 433–4
   Purposive Method 440, 448
   stages in aboutness determination 427–8, 449
   subject analysis and 425–6
   translation into controlled vocabularies 14, 427, 433, 477, 513
   use-based approaches 440–1
   Wilson's approach to 440
   see also subject analysis
abstracts/abstracting 31, 34–5
   critical 34
   indicative 34
   informative 34
   modular 34
   structured 34
AC-Administrative Components 215
access metadata *see* rights and access metadata
access points
   AACR2 75–6, 333–4, *335–6*
   for agents 13, 288, 395–8
   alphabetical display *vs.* relevancy ranking 115
   in archives 115, 116, 292, 299, 408–11
   in the art and museum community 299, 411–12
   authority control 9, 102–3, 152, 287, 299, 365–6, *408*
   authorized access points (AAPs) 13, 152, 235, 287, 299, 366–7, 369–70, 371, *372*, 383, 407
   bibliographic records 292, 402
   in bibliographies 100
   in catalogs 102–3, 114–15, *175*, 292
   choosing 13, 28, 273, 292, 322
   as collocation device 3, 152, 229, 287–8, 298, 334, 365, 367, 369–70, 397
   controlled/uncontrolled titles 272–3, 287–8
   for creators 235, 287, 298–9, 384–7
   defined 9, 99, 270, 286, 312n
   descriptive cataloging 13, 269
   displays in online tools 114–15, 144–5, 543–4
   for finding aids 115, 116
   in FRAD 235, 379–80, 381
   International Cataloguing Principles (ICP) (IFLA) 272–3, 382–3
   in LRM 278, 380–2
   main entry/primary access point 75–6, 177n, 333–4, 545
   name/title 76, 289, 370, 381, 399
   need for 287
   not used in ISBD 329

Index 625

in objects of the catalog (Cutter) 103
persons 384–8, *389*, 395–8, 406
in RDA 75, 77, 319, 322, *335–6*, 384–7, *389*, 390–1, 395–8, 399–405
relationships among 287, 369, 402–5, 407
relationships, representation of 270, 285, 286–7, 288–90, 292, 390
in resource description 269–70, 298–9, 311–12
sample list of *372*
vs. statements of responsibility 298–9
title-only 290, 399
title proper 287
types of 287–8
uncontrolled 272–3
variant access points (VAPs) 366–7, 407
works and expressions 278, *310*, 369, 370, 381, 390–1, 399–405, *400*
see also subject headings
accession log *see* registers
accession numbers 20, 116, 120, 299, 533
accession records 17, 20, 119
accessioning process, museums 19, *20*, 20–1, 159
Ackoff, R. L. 5
acquisitions
in libraries 13, 279
in museums 19–20, *20*
acronyms xxiv–xxvii, 1, 270, 286, 395, 459, 472, 543–4
added entries 74, *174*, *177*, 334, *335*
administrative metadata
defined *207*, 211
in METS 217–18
need for 211, 213
in ONIX messages 354
types of 205–6, *207*, 211–15
see also meta-metadata; preservation metadata; rights and access metadata; technical metadata
agents 381
access points 395–8
BIBFRAME Model 195–6
collective 231, 232, 233–4, 308, 381
entities 214, 230, 231, 232, 233–4, 238–40, *238*, *242*, 243–4, 245, 247–8, 308, 381, 386–91
relationships 288, 290–3, 297–9
ALA *see* American Library Association (ALA)
A.L.A. Cataloging Rules for Author and Title Entries 69
ALA, *List of Subject Headings for Use in Dictionary Catalogs* 78
Alphabetical catalogs 111, 113–14
alphabetical order
arranging resources 14
Bodleian library 59
in catalogs/indexes 31, 56, 57, 59, 105, *107*, 110, 111, 113–14, *114*
in classification indexes 111, 521

in controlled vocabularies 465, 491
cutter numbers 529n, 546, 547
filing rules 540, 544
Gessner 59
Harvard University 63
KWIC/KWAC/KWOC indexing 85
Library of Alexandria 52–3
limited use 53
Rostgaard 59
of search results 115, 145, 146
St. Martin's Priory 56
Trithemius 57
Zenodotus 52
alphabetico-classed catalogs 111, 113
alphabets, non-Roman *see* transliteration
Alta Vista 124
alternative titles 294
alternatives (RDA) 311, *318*, 326, 401
Amazon.com 127, 251, 367–8, 533, 534
American Documentation Institute 84, 86
American Libraries 159n
American Library Association (ALA) 66, 67, 68, 69, 78, 447, 540
American Society for Indexing (ASI) 34, 127, 356, 357
American Society for Information Science & Technology (ASIS&T) *see* Association for Information Science and Technology (ASIS&T)
analytical description 282
analytical entries 56, 59, 60
analytical metadata 206, *207*
analytico-synthetic classification *see* faceted classification
analyzable units 8, 206, 437 *see also* exhaustivity
Anderson, J. 356
Andresen, L. 215
Anglo-American Cataloguing Rules (AACR/AACR2) 75, 76–7, 82, 278–9, 306, 321–2, 329, 333–4, *334–6*, 345, 354, 378, 395, 405–7
annotations
in abstracting 34
in bibliographies 100
in HTML coding 184, 208
RDA guideline for AAPs 400
ANSI/NISO Standards
Z39.2 170
Z39.4 127, 356–7
Z39.19 458, 460–1
Z39.50 154
Z39.85 336
antonyms 463, 467
appellations
authority control 385–94
element (RDA) 315, 319, 385, 387–8, *389*
identifier as 237

nomen as 234, 318, 381
persons 382, 387–8, 390
relationships 226, 239, 244, 319
title as 236, 237
works and expressions 391–2
application profiles
   in DC 261, 336, 339
   defined 218–19, 315–16
   DPLA Metadata Application Profile 28
   as metadata management tools 218–19
   in Official RDA 311, 314, 315–16, 384, 392
APPM see *Archives, Personal Papers, and Manuscripts* (APPM)
approval plans 12
Arango, J. 24, 29, 30, 38
archival description 82, 273–5, 278, 285, 342, 345–7, 410
archival theory 81, 345
archives
   accession records 17
   authority control 408–11
   authorized access points 286, 292, 408–11
   collection-level description 208, 283
   conceptual model 241–8, *242*, *245–6*, 342, 409
   controlled vocabularies 83
   Describing Archives: A Content Standard (DACS) 82, 115, 206, 273–5, 278, 285, 292–3, 342, 345–7, 409, 410
   descriptive practices 16, 17, 82, 273–5, 285, 294, 342, 345–7
   digital 27 *see also* digital collections
   dissemination information 296
   "Dutch Manual" 81–2
   EAD (Encoded Archival Description) 18, 116, 191–2, 345, 549–54
   Encoded Archival Context for Corporate Bodies, Persons, and Families (EAC-CPF) 409, 410–11
   finding aids 8, 17, 115–16, *117–19*, 128
   General International Standard Archival Description (ISAD(G)) 115, 273 342, 345, 409
   hierarchical description 282–3
   history 81–2
   information systems 159–60
   International Standard Archival Authority Record for Corporate Bodies, Persons, and Families (ISAAR(CPF)) 409, 410, 411
   Machine-Readable Cataloging 18, 82, 170
   metadata schemas 342, 345–7, 408–11
   in museums 22
   online access 17
   organization of information in 16–18
   original order 16, 17, 81, 82, 242
   principles for 81–2, 274–5
   processing collections *17*
   provenance 16, 19, 81, 82, 242
   Records in Contexts (RiC) 241–8, *242*, *245–6*, 342, 409
   and records management 35
   respect des fonds 16–17, 81, 242, 275
   Rules for Archival Description (RAD) 115
   series 17, 345
   standardizations and cooperation 17
   standards for description and access 342, 345–7
   subject access 438, 479, 488, 493
   theory 81–2, 345
   types and formats 16
Archives, Personal Papers, and Manuscripts (APPM) 82, 345
Archives Portal Europe 411
ArchivesGrid 116, 159–60
ArchivesSpace 159
Aristotle 78, 515, 516
arrangement
   alphabetical arrangements of catalogs 111, 113–14
   catalogs 109–15, *110*, *112*, *114*
   letter-by-letter 540–2
   metadata 539–44
   online public access catalogs (OPACs) 114–15
   physical information 545–8, *546–7*
   word-by-word 540–2
Art & Architecture Thesaurus (AAT) 83, 293, 349–50, 414, 430, 464, 465–6, 471, 488–9, *490*
art collections
   authority control 411–17, *413*
   Cataloging Cultural Objects (CCO) 275–6, *277*, 278, 285, 293, 294, 347–8, 350n, 412–15, *413*
   Categories for the Description of Works of Art (CDWA) 350–1
   non-textual information, subject analysis of 434–5
   VRA Core 217, 275, 347, 348–50, 416–17, 448
Art of Medieval Technology: Images of Noah the Shipbuilder (Unger) 434
articles, initial 149, 177, 180, 543–4
artificial intelligence (AI) xxii, 23, 206
   hallucinations 23
   internet search results 25, 122, 123
   large language models and 455, 501
   natural language processing 499, 501, 505
   ontologies and 496–7
   resource management systems 157, 159
   Semantic Web and 26, 260
   subject analysis and 437, 450–1
Artstor 22
Ashurbanipal 51
Association for Information Science and Technology (ASIS&T)
   Dublin Core 336
   prior names of 86

associative relationships in controlled vocabularies 461, 465
attribute elements 311
    persons *389*, 390
    works and expressions 393–4
attribute-value pair 136, 184, 210, 255, 261, 270, 309–11
attributes 7, 182, 269
    common attributes across resource types 293–9, *298*
    dissemination information 295–7
    edition 294–5
    entity-relationship models (E-R models) 226
    Library Reference Model (LRM) (IFLA) 236, *236–7, 238*
    physical description 297
    Records in Contexts (RiC) 244–5, *245–6*
    titles 293–4
    variation across communities 293
audience, subject analysis and 446–7
Augustus, C. 53
Austin, J. L. 517
author, primacy of 53 *see also* main entry
authority control
    access points 287, 377–407, *408*
    access points for agents 395–8
    agent 386–90
    Anglo-American Cataloguing Rules (AACR/AACR2) 405–7
    appellation elements 385–94, *389*
    archives 408–11
    art collections 411–17
    authority data 370
    authority files 373, 376
    authority records 367, *374*
    authority work 370–1, *371, 372,* 373
    authorized access points (AAPs) 367, 369–70
    bibliographic standards for 377–407, *408*
    Cataloging Cultural Objects (CCO) 412–15, *413*
    in catalogs 102–15
    Categories for the Description of Works of Art (CDWA) 415–16
    collocation 365, 367
    in controlled vocabularies 457–8, 460–1
    cultural heritage collections 411–17
    DCMI Agents Working Group 417–18
    defined 9, 103
    Describing Archives: A Content Standard (DACS) 410
    descriptive cataloging 13
    effect on federated searching if missing 141
    Encoded Archival Context for Corporate Bodies, Persons, and Families (EAC-CPF) 409, 410–11
    encoding 171
    in finding aids 17
    in FRAD/FRSAD/LRM 227–8, 379, 380–2
    Functional Requirements for Authority Data (FRAD) 379–80
    Functional Requirements for Bibliographic Records (FRBR) 378–80
    Functional Requirements for Subject Authority Data (FRSAD) 227–8
    goals of 365–6
    headings 371
    integration, standardization of 151–4, *153*
    International Cataloguing Principles (ICP) 382–3
    international efforts 377
    International Standard Archival Authority Record for Corporate Bodies, Persons, and Families (ISAAR(CPF)) 409, 410, 411
    International Standard Name Identifier (ISNI) 388, 418
    InterParty 417
    lacking, for names in indexes 125
    Library Reference Model (LRM) (IFLA) 227–8, 379, 380–2
    Metadata Authority Description Schema (MADS) 407, *408*
    modules in library systems 156
    museums 411–17
    names 366–9, 395–6, 406–7
    nomens 384–5
    online settings 417–18
    ORCID (Open Researcher and Contributor ID) 388, 418
    persons 387–90
    preferred names 366–7
    processes of 365
    RDA (2010) 394–405
    RDA (2020) 383–94
    timespans 384
    variant access points (VAPs) 367
    variant names 367
    VRA Core 416–17
    works and expressions 369–70
    see also controlled vocabularies
authority data 370
authority files 373, 376
    access provided by bibliographic networks 155
    art world files 480
    in CCO 275, 412, 414
    in CDWA 416
    future uses 417
    integration (of bibliographic and authority files) 151–4
    Virtual International Authority File (VIAF) 377
    in VRA Core 351

authority records 367, *374*
    in bibliographic network files 155
    CCO recommended elements 412–14
    in FRAD 379
    guidelines for archival 345, 409–10
    in ICP 382
    linkages between authority records and bibliographic records 151–4, *153*
    listing of variants in 366, 373, 377
    in LRM 381
    MARC encoding of 171, *375*, *482*, *483*
    in RDA 398
authority work 370–1, *371–2*, 373
authorized access points (AAPs) 13, 367, 369–70, 383, 396–8
authorized/preferred terms 456–7
automatic indexing 34, 127, 206
automation *see* systems and system design; technology
Avram, H. 86–7, 170, 196n
axioms 495

Baca, M. 241
back-of-the-book indexes/indexing 31–2, 125, 357, 436, 443
Bacon, F. 78, 79, 519
Banerjee, S. 499
Barritt, M. R. 81–2
basic level categories 517–18
Benardino, P. 173
Berlin, B. 432, 517–518
Berman, S. 469
Berners-Lee, T. 250, 252
biases 276, 433, 451, 468–9, 476, 501
BIBFRAME (Bibliographic Framework Initiative) 260
    BIBFRAME Model 195–6, *196*
    BIBFRAME Vocabulary 195
    coding 555–70
    current state regarding 181, 260
    development of 194–6, *196*
Bible, heading for 59, 67
bibliographic classification 518–29, *522, 524, 525, 526*
Bibliographic Classification (BC2) 81, 519
bibliographic control *see* information organization
bibliographic control, five functions of 7–10
bibliographic databases 7, 15, 136–7
bibliographic features in subject analysis 427, 438, 439, 441–3
Bibliographic Framework Initiative *see* BIBFRAME (Bibliographic Framework Initiative)
bibliographic identities 396, 402–3, 406
bibliographic networks 10, 14, 15, 78, 87, 105, 155, 271
Bibliographic Record and Information Technology, The (Hagler) 7–10

bibliographic relationships *see* relationships
bibliographical significance 288
bibliographies
    annotated 100
    antiquity 49, *50*, 51–53
    citations 100–1
    focus/arrangement 101–2
    on the Internet 23, 27, 135, 138
    ISO standard for 357
    lacking location information 10
    Middle Ages and Renaissance 55–7, 519
    research guides 102
    as retrieval tools 3, 7–9, 99–102
    sixteenth century 57–8
    style manuals for 100–1
bibliography
    discipline 57, 59, 69
    mechanization of 83–6
Bizer, C. 259
Bliss, H. 519
Bliss Bibliographic Classification 81, 519
Bliss Bibliographic Classification Association 519
Bodleian Library 59
Bodley, T. 59
Boll, J. 520
book catalogs 105–6, *107*, 109
    example *107, 112*
    history 105–6, 539
book indexing *see* Indexes/Indexing
Boolean operators 89, 138, 140, 150, 151, 474
Boolean retrieval 138
Borgman, C. 28, 160–1, 161n
Boston Athenaeum 66, 78
Boston Public Library 65
Bowman, J. H. 151
Breeding, M. 156–7, 158, 159n
British Library 171, 316, 493
British Museum 63, 65
broad classification 529–30
broader term (BT) relationships 464
Brown, A. G. 435
Brown, J. D. 68
Brown, R. 517–18
Brown University Library 65
browsing 1, 4, 111, 115
    faceted 16, 141, *142*, 146, 158
    indexes 140–1
    non-linear 141
    shelf 111, 140, 531, 532
    subjects 473, 491, 502
    of systems 89, 111, 115, 138, *139*, 140–1, *142*, 145, 147, 148, 157–8
Bush, V. 85

Caesar, J. 53
call numbers 14, 59, 81, *112*, 114, 115, 229, 299, 529, 530, 533, 545–8
Callimachus 52–3, 78
card catalogs
    arrangement in 109–11, 113–14, *114*, 539, 544
    description of 106–8, *108*
    first 61–2, *61*, 61n
    history 61–2, 88, 105–6, 133, 135
    replaced book catalogs 105–6
    replaced by online catalogs 106, 108, 133
    size of cards 106
    standardization issues 143
Cassiodorus 55
Catalog Rules: Author and Title Entries (1908) 68
Catalog Rules: Author and Title Entries (1941) 68–9
catalogers
    and AACR2 333, 334–6
    CCO 285, 347
    choices in RDA 307, 311, 312, 313, 314, 316, 324–6, 334–6, 387, 391, 392, 398
    choosing access points 99, 286, 292, 333
    defined 7
    doing authority work 369, 370, 373, 384, 387, 396–9
    and FAST 492
    first cataloger 52
    after French Revolution 60–2
    handwriting cards 83
    judgment 69, 271, 300, 321, 326, 347, 398
    knowledge of MARC and other encoding 195, 197
    major activities of 7–10, 13–14
    metadata creation 211, 271, 277–8
    original vs. copy cataloging by 14, 155
    providing subject access 433, 435, 437, 473–5, 477–8, 479, 527
    supplying titles 294
    and TEI Headers 189
cataloging codes
    contention in developing 75–6
    filing rules 539
    first instance of 60–2, 306
    first international 68
    and ISBD 329
    metadata standards 270–1
    Panizzi's 63, 305–6
    principles for 104, 271
    Smithsonian Institution's 65–6
    see also content standards
Cataloging Cultural Objects (CCO) 275–6, 277, 278, 285, 293, 294, 347–8, 350n, 412–15, *413*
catalogs/cataloging
    access points 102–3
    alphabetical 111–14

alphabetical arrangements 111, 113–14
Anglo-American Cataloguing Rules (AACR/AACR2) 75, 76–7
antiquity 49, *50*, 51–53
archives 82
arrangement and display 109–15, *110, 112, 114*
authority control 103
book catalogs 105–6, *107*, 109
British Museum 63
call numbers 14
card catalogs 61–2, *61*, 61n, 88, 105, 106–8, *108*, 109–11, 113–14, *114*, 133, 135, 143, 539, 544
classified 110–11
code, international 68
codes 60–2, 270
cooperative 14, 15, 22, 24, 155, 170, 373
conceptual analysis 13–14
controlled vocabularies 78–9
cooperative cataloging 14, 15, 22, 24, 155, 170, 373
copy cataloging 14
cutter numbers 14
Cutter's objects of 67, 103, *104*, 128, 229, 287, 431
definition 13, 49n, 102
descriptive cataloging 13
dictionary *107*, 113–14, 540
discovery layers 15–16
divided 113–14, *114*
early OPACs 88–9
ethics code 276–7
European Renaissance 56
filing rules 539–44
as finding lists 59
forms of 105–9
functions of 103–5, *104*
history of information organization 49, *50*, 51–3
intellectual works/physical items 76, 278
interlibrary loans 15, 126, 155
International Cataloguing Principles (ICP) (IFLA) 271–3
International Standard Bibliographic Description (ISBD) 75, 329–33
knowledge management 39
known-item searching 103
main entries 69, 74–6
major outcomes of 15
MARC 14, 345
microform 108, 109
Middle Ages 55–7
museums 21–2
nineteenth century 62–3, 64–7
On the Construction of Catalogues of Libraries, and Their Publication by Means of Separate, Stereotyped Titles (Jewett) 65–6
online 15, 87, 108–9, *109*

original cataloging 14, 87, 155, 170, 278, 450
other arrangements 114–15
outcomes of cataloging 15
Paris Principles 69, 74–5, 76, 104, 229, 272, 278, 333, 382
principle theories of cataloging (Osborn) 69
printed 110
purposes of 103
Registrum Librorum Angliae 55
relevance ranking 115, 123, 138, 146, 158
Rostgaard, F. and 59, *60*
Rules for a Dictionary Catalog (Cutter) 66–8
seventeenth century 59
shelflists 56, 105
special materials 81–2
standardization issues 143
subject cataloging 13–14
translation 14
twentieth century 68–9, *70–3*, 74–8
union catalogs 15, 22, 66, 87, 105, 126, 478
United States, nineteenth century 63, 65–8, *65–7*
Vatican Code 68
Web-PACS (web-accessible) 88
see also standards for description and access
Catalogue of English Printed Books 59
Catalogue of Printed Books in the British Museum, The 63
Cataloguing Code of Ethics 276–7
Categories for the Description of Works of Art (CDWA) 350–1, 415–16
  core categories 350–1, 415–16
  elements 416
  groupings for authority data 415–16
  in XML 351
Categories/categorization
  basic level categories 517–18
  classical theory of categories 516–18
  classification and 513–15
  cognition as 2
  collaborative in folksonomies 504
  color categories 432, 517
  daily life 1–3, 516
  defined 513–15
  early subject categories 55, 78, 79, 447
  fuzzy set theory 517, 518
  history 52, 55, 79, 513
  in information architecture 29–30
  in knowledge management 39
  of metadata 210–18
  museums 21
  online uses of 24, 127, 367, 533–5
  prototype theory 518
  systems for 513–35, *522, 524–6*
  see also classification

CC see *Colon Classification* (CC)
CCO see *Cataloging Cultural Objects* (CCO)
CDWA see *Categories for the Description of Works of Art* (CDWA)
characteristics of division 522–3
Chenhall, R. G. 83
chief source of information
  see preferred sources of information
China, early printing techniques in 57
chronological elements in subject analysis 445
CIDOC Conceptual Reference Model (CRM) 248–50
citation order 523, 527
citations, bibliographic 100–1
Clarke, S. 241
classical theory of categorization 516–18
classification
  bibliographic 518–29, *522, 524–6*
  broad *vs.* close 529–30
  categorization and 513–15
  collocation device 533
  components of schemes for 520–2
  concepts 529–33
  defined 514–15
  enumerative 79, 522–3, *525–6*, 529
  facet indicators 81, 528
  faceted 80–1, 450, *466*, 522, 523, 527–9
  fixed location 533
  fixed *vs.* relative location 533
  fourteenth century 55
  hierarchical 514, 515, 521, 522–3, *522, 524, 526*, 527, 529, 531
  history 79–81
  indexes 521
  integrity of numbers 530–2
  keeping pace with knowledge 530–2
  literary warrant 530
  location/collocation devices 533
  MARC 21 classification data format 171
  modern era 78–81, *80*
  notation 14, 520–1
  PMEST 527–8
  relative location 533
  schedules 520, 521, 523, 529
  schemes 520
  special materials 83
  tables 520
  theory 513, 516–18
  translating aboutness into 427, 450
  see also Categories/categorization
Classification Research Group (CRG) 81, 519
A Classification System for Libraries of Judaica 520
classified catalogs 110–11, *112*
  collocation function in 533
  description of 110–11

example *112*
history 59, 62
influence on filing 113, 539
close classification 529–30
closed stacks 18, 22, 532, 545
coextensive entry 478
coherent description 315
Cohesion Method of subject analysis 440
Collantes, L. 433, 440
collations 62
collection development process 12–13
    approval plans 12
    gifts and exchanges 12
    patron-driven acquisitions 12
    selection of resources 12
collection-level description 208, 283
collections 8–9, 12–15
    acquisitions 13, 279
    in archives 16–18, 81–82, 115–16, 128, 408–11
    classification of 530
    digital 27–9
    in libraries 12, 56, 88
    lists and 9
    in museums 18–22, 82, 116–21, 411–17
    personal 2
    for profit 4
collective agents
    in LRM 231, 233–4, 235, *239–40*
    in RDA 308, 382, 386
collective titles 294, 336
collocation 3, 15, 21, 74, 365, 367
    and authority control 152, 229, 287–8, 298, 334, 365, 367, 369–70, 397
    and classification 431, 518, 522–3, 529–30, 533
    and controlled vocabulary 14, 431, 456–7, 470
    and Cutter 67, 135
    and Maunsell 59, 67
    in print tools 135–6
Colon Classification (CC) (Ranganathan) 81, 519, 527–9
colophons 51
color categories 432, 517
COM catalogs 108
compound headings 470
comprehensive description 282
computer output microform catalogs (COM catalogs) 108
computers
    see information systems; technology
CONA see *Cultural Objects Name Authority* (CONA)
conceptual analysis
    aboutness determination methods 438–41
    defined 13–14, 427
    identifying concepts in 444–5
    independent of classification schemes 439

levels of meaning in art 434–5
objectivity in 437–8
process 427–31, 441–9
resource examination 441–4
conceptual models
    archives 241–8, *242, 245–6*
    background to development of 225
    Conceptual Reference Model (CRM) (CIDOC) 248–50
    DCMI Abstract Model (DCAM) 261–2
    entity-relationship models (E-R models) 226, *226*
    Library Reference Model (LRM) (IFLA) 3–4, 4n, 76, 77, 227–41, *230–1, 235, 237–40*, 278
    linked data 250–7
    models defined 225
    museums 248–50
    Records in Contexts (RiC) 241–8, *242, 245–6*, 342, 409
    Resource Description Framework (RDF) 250–7
    Semantic Web 250–60
    user tasks (LRM) 228–30
Conceptual Reference Model (CRM) (CIDOC) 248–50
conditions, options and condition options (RDA) 307, 311, 313–15, *313, 314*, 316, 318, 384, 387, 391
consistency in subject analysis 433–4
container lists 18
containers, subject analysis and 442
content examination 444–9, 571–3
    chronological elements 445
    content characteristics 445–8
    corporate bodies 444
    genre and form 447–8
    geographic names 445
    identification of concepts 444–5
    language, tone, audience, and intellectual level 446–7
    named entities 445
    persons 444
    point of view 446
    research methods 446
    strategies 448–9
    table of contents *429*
    titles 445
content standards 9, 168, 209, 270–1
    history 62–78
    for publishers *see* ONIX (Online Information Exchange)
    use for semantics in metadata 206, 209
    vary by community 270, 293
Contextual Query Language (CQL) 154
continuing resources 279
contributors 288
    access points in cataloging 13, 269, 298, 370, 383
    Dublin Core element 336, *340*
    entities/agents in metadata *207*, 298, 417, 488–9, *489*

control fields (MARC) 171, *179*
controlled access points 9, 18, 235, 287–8, 299, 365, 366, 379-80, 381
controlled titles 287
    of works 269, 289–90, 369–70, 378, 381, 383, 391, 395, 399–401
controlled vocabularies
    abbreviations 472
    aboutness and 427, 433–4, 445–6, 449–50, 572, 574–5
    acronyms 472
    application of terms, principles for 477–9
    Art & Architecture Thesaurus (AAT) 83, 293, 349–50, 414, 430, 464, 465–6, 471, 488–9, *490*
    assignment of, by machines 450
    associative relationships 461, 465
    authority files and 373
    authorized/preferred terms 456–7
    challenges 467–75
    coextensive entry 478
    compound headings 470
    concepts not in the 479
    creating, principles for 475–7
    defined 456–7
    direct entry 477
    displaying relationships 465–6
    equivalence relationships 458, 462–3
    Faceted Application of Subject Terminology (FAST) 474, 492–3
    folksonomies 504
    hierarchical relationships 125, 459, 460–1, 464, 466, 475–6, 483, *490*, 491, 493, *494*, 495
    homographs 10, 25, 122, 154, 457, 471, 498, 503
    homophones 471
    Homosaurus 493, *494*
    inclusive terms 468–9
    inconsistencies 470
    information environments, different 455–6
    initialisms 472
    lexical relationships 466–7
    Library of Congress Demographic Group Terms (LCDGT) 447, 487–8
    Library of Congress Genre/Form Terms for Library and Archival Materials (LCGFT) 484, 486–7
    Library of Congress Subject Headings (LCSH) 78, 83, 444, 461, 469, 470, 473–5, 479–80, *481–2*, 482–3, 492–3, 542–3
    literary warrant 68, 476
    Medical Subject Headings (MeSH) 483–4, *484–5*
    metadata *204*, 209, 219
    modern era 78–9
    multi-word terms and phrases 470
    natural language approaches to subjects 498–505, *503*
    new concepts 479
    numbers of terms assigned 478–9
    ontologies 248, 494–7, 515
    popular *vs.* technical terms 472
    pre-coordination/post-coordination 473–5, 493
    principles for applying 477–9
    principles for creating 475–7
    qualification of terms 471–2
    relationships in 456–7, 461–7
    Sears List of Subject Headings (*Sears*) 78–9, 461, 475–6, 482–3, *483*
    sequence and form for multiword terms and phrases 470
    simple term lists 458
    specific entry 478
    specific *vs.* general terms 467–8
    specificity 475–6
    standards 479–94, *481–5*, *490*, *494*
    standards for art and museums 411–17, *413*
    subdivision of terms 177, 178, 460–1, 473–5, 477, 479, 482, 483, 487, 493
    synonym rings 458–9, *459*
    synonymous concepts 468
    tagging 501–5, *503*
    taxonomies 459–60
    thesauri 460–1
    thesauri *vs.* subject heading lists 460–1
    Thesaurus of ERIC Descriptors 460, 476, 491
    types of 458–61
    use of qualifiers 471–2
    used in database indexing 32, 125, 147
    word form for one-word terms 469
    see also authority control; subject headings; thesauri
conventional collective titles 294, 401n
cooperative cataloging 14, 15, 22, 24, 155, 170, 373
coordinate terms 466
coordination of subject terms 473–5, 493
copy cataloging 14, 155
core elements 324, 398
core-if elements 324
corporate bodies 308
    access points in RDA 394, 396, 401
    as creators 63, 65, 401
    in DACS 410
    entities in FRBR 278
    filing order 113, 539–40, 543
    history (Panizzi and Jewett) 67
    in ICP principles 382
    names in subject analysis 444
    RDA chapters on 322
    relationships in FRBR/FRAD 380
    in statements of responsibility 298
    used as subject concepts 444–5

Index 633

covers/jackets/containers, subject analysis and 442
creators 7, 288, *298*, 298–9
    as access points 13, 15, 297–9, *298*
    in archives 16, 115, 273, 409–10
    in authority control 365, 369, 376, 379, 383
    as basic attribute 7, 16, 297–9
    as basis for Cutter number 14, 545
    in bibliographic relationships 286–7
    in bibliographies 100–2
    as catalogers/metadata generators 225, 229–30, 299
    in catalogs/cataloging 103, 104, 113–15, 114, *114*, 155
    element in Dublin Core 336, 339, 340
    encoding of 168, 173, 177, 181
    of FRBR entities 241
    identifying 298
    intellectual property rights of 214
    meaning 210
    in metadata 24, 217–18
    in museums 414–16
    in RDA 287, 334–6, 308, 383, 399, 401
    in RDF 254, 255, 257
    in records management 35
    in resource description 270
    in searching/display 144, 146–8, 150
    in statements of responsibility 298
CRG *see* Classification Research Group (CRG)
critical cataloging 276
cross-references 31, 56, 60, 125, 152, 289, *336*, 366, 367, 370, 376, 381, 396, 455, 457, 462–3, 468, 477, 520
crosswalks 220–1
cultural heritage collections
    authority control 411–17
    Cataloging Cultural Objects (CCO) 275–6, 277, 278, 285, 293, 294, 347–8, 350n, 412–15, *413*
    VRA Core 217, 275, 347, 348–50, 416–17, 448
Cultural Objects Name Authority (CONA) 414, 480
Cutter, C. A. 66–8, *67*, 78, 79, 103, *104*, 111, 113, 128, 135, 382, 431, 519, 539, 545, 546
cutter numbers 14, 67, 529, 529n, 545–6, *546*
Cutter's objects of the catalog 67, 103, *104*, 128, 229, 287, 431

DACS see *Describing Archives: A Content Standard* (DACS)
D'Alembert, J. 79
data administration *see* records management
data in DIKW pyramid 5, *5*
Data Documentation Initiative (DDI) 217
data element identifiers 178
data normalization 151
data recording methods, *RDA* and 311–12, *312*
data value standards *see* controlled vocabularies

database indexes/indexing 32, 125, 126
databases
    arrangement of retrievals in 539
    checkbook example 136, *137*
    classification and 519
    defined 136–8
    entity-relationship model 226
    federated searching of 22, 141, 143, 151, 158, 411
    lexical databases 498–9
    non-relational (NoSQL) 137
    normalization of data 151
    order of records in 110
    reference 137
    relational 137
    source 137
    Structured Query Language (SQL) 137
    in system design 136–8
    triplestores 257
    underlying retrieval tools 87, 88, 100, 102, 116, 119–20, 122, 138, 155, 156, 373
    see also bibliographic networks
DC *see* Dublin Core
DCAM *see* DCMI Abstract Model
DCMI *see* Dublin Core Metadata Initiative
DCMI Abstract Model (DCAM) 261–2
DCMI Description Set Model 261
DCMI Resource Model 261
DCMI Vocabulary Model 261
deep web 122
delimiters (encoding) 178, *179*, 183
demand-driven acquisitions 12
demographic groups 245, 447, 456, 487–8
Dent, C. 514–15
depth indexing 435–7
derivative relationships 76, 288–9
derived indexing 31
Describing Archives: A Content Standard (DACS)
    access points 292–3
    authority control 410
    creating finding aids using 115, 206, 278, 345–7
    principles 273–5
    purpose 82
    relation to other standards 273, 342, 345, 409
    rules 346–7
    sources of information 285
    structure 345–6
description
    see resource descriptions; standards for description and access
description, collection-level 208, 283
description set 262
descriptive cataloging 13

descriptive markup 181
descriptive metadata 211
    in METS 217–18
    need for access points with 286
    as part of larger digital object 208
    from preferred sources of information 283, *284*, 285
    types of 206, *207*
    see also standards for description and access
descriptors in thesauri 460
devised titles 294
Dewey, M. 23, 66, 67, 79–80, *80*, 81, 106, 143, 519, 530, 531
Dewey Decimal Classification (DDC) 79–80, 111, 433, 519, 520, 521, 523, *524–5*, 529, 530, 531, 547
diachronic work 281
dictionary catalogs *107*, 113–14, 540
digital collections 27–9
digital libraries 27–9, 208, 283, 437
Digital Object Identifier (DOI) 32, 100
digital objects 158
    describing with METS 217
    need for administrative metadata 211, 213
    use of FAST for 492
digital preservation 211, 213, 214
Digital Public Library of America (DPLA) 27–8
DIKW pyramid *5*, 5–6
Dillon, A. 29
direct entry 477
directories 23–4, 27, 124, 535
directory (MARC) 171, *172*
discourse analysis 501
discovery interface (or discovery layer, or discovery service) in catalogs 15–16, 161
    and faceted browsing 16, 141, *142*, 146, 158
    and tagging 501–5
display 30, 103, 108–9, *110*, 114, 123, 126, 134, 144–7
    of authorized names and references 370, 373, 377, 383, 414–15
    based on MARC records *172*, 173, 333
    of characters 168
    of digital objects 217–18
    encoding for 174, *175*, 183, 186, 287
    of retrieved results 144–6, 539–44
    standard for, in ISBD 326, 329
    structural metadata and 216–17
    use of labels for 333
    variable information in display of records 146–7
dissemination information 295–7
divided catalogs 113–14, *114*
document type definition (DTD) 168, 183, 186–7
Documentation Movement 83–6

documents 84 *see also* information resources
domain and range 309
DTD *see* document type definition (DTD)
Dublin Core 24
    application profiles 218–19
    Metadata Element Set (DCMES) 336–9, *338*, *340*
    one-to-one principle 262, 339
Dublin Core Libraries Working Group (DC-Lib) 219
Dublin Core Metadata Element Set (DCMES) 336–9, *338*, *340*
Dublin Core Metadata Initiative (DCMI) 262, 336, 339
    Administrative Working Group 215
    Agents Working Group 417–18
    element refinements 219, 339, *340*
"Dutch Manual" 81–2

EAC-CPF *see* Encoded Archival Context for Corporate Bodies, Persons, and Families (EAC-CPF)
EAD *see* Encoded Archival Description (EAD)
Eastman Kodak 84
EBSCO 146, 157, 158
Educational Resources Information Center (ERIC) 491
effective description (RDA) 309, 315
EGAD *see* International Council on Archives, Expert Group on Archival Description (EGAD)
Electronic Binding DTD (Ebind) 217
element mapping 189, 220, 311, 321, 349, 355 *see also* crosswalks
element refinement 210, 219, 339, *340*
elements 182, 208, 270
    appellation 315, 385–6
    attribute 311
    Cataloging Cultural Objects (CCO) 347–50
    core 324
    Describing Archives: A Content Standard (DACS) 345–7
    domain and range 309
    Dublin Core 336–7, 339
    General International Standard Archival Description (ISAD(G)) 342–5
    Metadata Object Description Schema (MODS) 339–42
    optional 186, 210, 270, 336, 337
    range and domain 309–10
    RDA: Resource Description & Access 309, *310*, 311
    relationship 309, 311
    VRA Core 348–50
elisions 543–4
Empedocles 516
Encoded Archival Context for Corporate Bodies, Persons, and Families (EAC-CPF) 409, 410–11

Encoded Archival Description (EAD)
    and EAC-CPF 410–11
    EAD3 191–2, *549–54*
    EAD4 192
    purpose 18, 116, 345
    Version 2002 191
encoding and encoding standards
    BIBFRAME 194–6, *196*
    contexts for 167–9
    creation of resource descriptions 271
    different languages and 169–70
    Encoded Archival Description (EAD) 18, 116, 191–2, *549–54*
    encoding standards 167–201
    HTML (Hypertext Markup Language) 25, 125, 168, 183–4, *185*, 206, 251, 336
    ISO/IEC 10646 Universal Coded Character Set (UCS) 168–9
    Machine-Readable Cataloging (MARC) format 167, 170–81, *172–4*, *175–6*, *180*
    MARCXML 192, *193*
    ONIX 351, *352–3*, 354–5
    records 169–93
    SGML (Standard Generalized Markup Language) 167–8, 181–3, 184–6
    surrogate records 169–70
    TEI (Text Encoding Initiative) 169, 188–91, *190*
    Unicode 88, 167, 168–9, 171
    XML DTDs and schemas 168, 169, 181, 183, 186–7, 192
    XML (Extensible Markup Language) 167–8, 169, 181, 186–92 *see also* markup languages
entities 182, 226
    agents 233–4
    boundaries 309
    collective agents 233–5
    Conceptual Reference Model (CRM) (CIDOC) 248–50
    Library Reference Model (LRM) (IFLA) 230–1, 230–5, *236–7*, 238
    nomens 234–5, *235*
    non-human 233, 307, 319, 381, 386–7
    place 234
    RDA: Resource Description & Access 308–9
    Records in Context (RiC) *242*, 243–4
    resource entities (WEMI) 195, 232–3, *239–40*, 278, 288, 290, *310*, 378, 381, 390–1
    time-span 234
entity boundaries (RDA) 309
entity-relationship models (E-R models) 226, 226n, 232, 241
entries 53
entry elements (access points) 397
entry vocabulary 462 *see also* cross-references

enumerative classification 79, 522–3, *526*, 529
equivalence relationships
    in controlled vocabularies 458, 462–3
    in crosswalks 220
    among resources 288
ERIC *see* Educational Resources Information Center (ERIC)
ERIC thesaurus *see Thesaurus of ERIC Descriptors*
ethics
    cataloging code of 276–7
    personal data in authority records 373
    in subject analysis 437–8
Europeana Data Model (EDM) 28
events in BIBFRAME 196
Evergreen (ILS) 158
Exchangeable Image File Format (Exif) *212*, 213
exchanges (collection development) 12
exhaustivity in subject analysis 435–7, *437 see also* depth indexing; summarization
existence of information, making known 8
expanded searching 158
Expansive Classification (EC) (Cutter) 67, 79, 519
explicit/tacit knowledge 38–9
exploded searches 154
explore (user task) 4, 105, 229, 230, 382
expressions 232, 308, 310
    access points 399–405
    authority control and 369–70, 391–4, *392–3*
    in BIBFRAME 195
    in FRBR/LRM 231, 236–8, 278
    in ICP 273
    identification of an entity 285, 298
    in international authority control 377
    representative expression 394
    in RDA 285, 308–9, 324, 334–6, 373, 395, 399–401
extensibility of metadata 210
Extensible Markup Language (XML) 186–92
    DTDs and schemas 168, 169, 181, 183, 186–7, 192
extension plans 281, *282*, 319
extensional aboutness 426
extrinsic relationships 414–15

facet formulas 527–8
facet indicators 81, 528
Faceted Application of Subject Terminology (FAST) 474, 492–3
faceted browsing 16, 141, *142*, 146, 158
faceted classification 80–1, 450, *466*, 522, 523, 527–9
faceted vocabulary 293, 473, 488, *489*, *490*, 492
faceting 39, 80, 519
facets 16, 80, 474, 519, 527
Fagan, L. 63

Fairthorne, R. 425–6
false drops 25, 25n, 153
families 77, 196, 228, 243, 273, 274, 286, 288, 298, 308, *318*, *319*, 335, 383
family resemblances (in categories) 517
federated searching 22, 141, 143, 151, 158, 411
Feith, J. 81
fictitious persons 233, 307, *319*, 381, 386–7, 444
Figure-Ground Method of subject analysis 440
filing
    arrangement 540–2
    difficulties in 542–4
    history of 539–40
    rules 113, 114, 135, 521, 539–44
find (user task) 4, 105, 229
finding aids 17–18, 82, 115–16, *117–19*, 128, 159–60, 549–54
    and hierarchical description 282–3
    standards for 191–2, 217, 273, 345–6
    see also inventories
finding lists 57–62, 88
finite resources 279
fixed fields (MARC) 171, *173*, 174, 179, 180, *375*
fixed location (classification) 53, 56, 519, 533, 547
flexibility of metadata 210
flyleaf 55
FOLIO LSP 157–8
folksonomies 504
form, subject analysis and 447–8
FRAD see *Functional Requirements for Authority Data* (FRAD)
FRBR see *Functional Requirements for Bibliographic Records* (FRBR)
Freitag, R. 87
French Revolution 60–2, 306
Frost, W. 141, 143
FRSAD see *Functional Requirements for Subject Authority Data* (FRSAD)
Fruin, R. 81
full entries 74–5
Functional Requirements for Authority Data (FRAD) 76, 77, 227–8, 229–30, 236–7, 272, *318*, 321, 378
    attributes of person 371
    authority control 379
    entities 379–80
    relationships between entities 380, 382
Functional Requirements for Bibliographic Records (FRBR) 4n, 76, 77, 227–8, 229–30, 236, 237–8, 241, 272, 278
    authority control 378–9
    entities and attributes 237–8
    Group 1 entities 378, 380
    Group 2 entities 378, 379, 381
    Group 3 entities 378, 380
    relationships 238
    user tasks 4, 104–5, 228–30, *230*
Functional Requirements for Subject Authority Data (FRSAD) 76, 228, 230, 377, 378, 379, 380, 381
fuzzy set theory 517, 518

gender attribute 373, 379, 390, 398, 412, 416
General International Standard Archival Description (ISAD(G)) 273, 342–5
    elements 342, 345
    encoding 345
    international exchange of descriptive information 345
general material designations (GMD) 77, *334*
general *vs.* specific terms 467–8
generative AI, subject analysis and 437, 450–1
genre, subject analysis and 447–8
genre/form headings 484, 486–7
genus-species relationships 464, 535
geographic names in subject analysis 445
Gerolimos, M. 502
Gessner, C. 57, 59
Getty Research Institute 411, 480
Getty vocabularies 275, 376, 414, 480
    Art and Architecture Thesaurus (AAT) 83, 293, 349–50, 414, 430, 464, 465–6, 471, 488–9, *490*
    Cultural Objects Name Authority (CONA) 414, 480
    Thesaurus of Geographic Names (TGN) *340*, 414, 480
    Union List of Artists Names (ULAN) 412, 414, 480
gifts and exchanges (collection development) 12
Glastonbury Abbey 55
GMD *see* general material designation
Goldfarb, C. 181
Goodfellow, J. 505
Google 25, 122–4, 127–8, 455
    influence of 147, 157, 183
    synonyms and 123
Gorman, M. 75, 76, 278, 530, 533
granularity
    defined 8
    levels in metadata 116, 206, 208, 220, 237, 251
    in MARC 173, 177
    in subject analysis 436 *see also* exhaustivity
graphical user interface (GUI) 88
Greek civilization 51–3
Gross, T. 153
Gruber, T. 495, 504
Guidelines for Indexes and Related Information Retrieval Devices (Anderson) 356
"Guidelines for OPAC Displays" (Yee) 143
Guiles, K. 87
Gutenberg, J. 57

Hagler, R. 7–10
Han, M.-J. 505
Hansen, H. 215
Hanson, J. 68
Harnad, S. 2
harvesting technologies 221
headings 56, 56n *see also* access points; subject headings
Heath, T. 259
Hensen, S. 82
Hildreth, C. 88, 138
Hider, P. 505
hierarchical classification 514, 515, 521, 522–3, *522, 524, 526,* 527, 529, 531
hierarchical databases 137
hierarchical description in archives 242, 282–3
hierarchical relationships
 between corporate bodies 380
 in CIDOC CRM 249
 in controlled vocabularies 125, 459, 460–1, 464, 465, 475, 483, *490,* 491, 493, *494,* 495
 in DIKW pyramid 5
 in directories 24, 124
 and inheritance relationships 227, 231, 233, 236, 240, 245, 249
 in LRM and RDA 227, 231, 232, 233, 236, 240, 386
 in MARC 180
 online taxonomies 533–5
 in OWL 497
 in RiC *242,* 243, 245
 in structural metadata and METS 216, 218
 in subject analysis 427, 450, 571–2, 574, 575
 in XML *182,* 183
Historia Animalium 515
history of information organization
 antiquity 49, *50,* 51–3
 bibliographic classification 518–19
 catalogs 49, *50,* 51–3
 Greek civilization 51–3
 Middle Ages to the Renaissance 54
 modern era 62–89, *64–7, 70–3, 80,* 83
 nineteenth century 62–3, *64–7,* 65–8
 Renaissance to nineteenth century 57, *58,* 59–62, *60, 61*
 Roman libraries 53
 twentieth century 68–9, *70–3,* 74–89, *80,* 83
 Western world focus 49
Hittites 51
holonyms 466
homographs 10, 25, 122, 154, 457, 471, 498, 503
homophones 471
Homosaurus 493, *494*
HTML *see* Hypertext Markup Language (HTML)

H. W. Wilson 106, 127, 356
hypernyms 466
Hypertext Markup Language (HTML) 25, 125, 168, 183–4, *185,* 206, 251, 336
 Extensible (XHTML) 183
 HTML4 183
 HTML5 183
 HTML Living Standard 183
 metadata embedded in 208
 microdata 25, 184, *185,* 208
hyponyms 466

Iconclass 83, 520
ICP *see International Cataloguing Principles* (ICP)
identifiers 9, 125, 312, *312*
 accession number as 20, 117, 119–20
 in authority control 370, 379, 381, 384, 385–6, 387–8, 391, 398, 399, 409, 410
 in controlled vocabularies 457, 483
 in description/metadata 205, 208, 211, 215, 235, 237, 244, 299, 312, *312,* 323, 324, 329, 331, 337, 341
 in linked data/RDF 251–4, 287
 as nomen/appellation element 235, 308, 315, *319,* 386, 387–8, 391
 work 289–90 *see also* name/title access points
identify (user task) 4, 104, 229
IFLA *see* International Federation of Library Associations and Institutions (IFLA)
IFLA LRM *see Library Reference Model* (LRM)
IFLA OPAC display guidelines 143
IFLA Principles *see* Paris Principles
ILL *see* interlibrary loan (ILL)
illustrations/visual features, subject analysis and 443
ILS *see* integrated library system (ILS)
impartiality in subject analysis 437–8
inclusive terms in controlled vocabularies 468–9
index browsing 140–1
indexers
 choice of access points 99, 286
 choice of subject terms 125, 468, 473, 475, 477, 479, 535
 variations among 433, 455
indexes/indexing
 A-Z 33–4, 125
 ANSI/NISO Standard Z39.85-2012 336
 automatic 127, 206, 450
 back-of-the-book 31–2, 125, 357, 436, 443
 in bibliographic relationships 289
 in classification schemes 521
 commercial 147
 creator 139

database/journal/periodical 32, 35, 125, *126*, 282
  defined 31
  depth 435, 437, *437*
  derived 31
  history 57–9, *58*, 62, 78, 81, 85
  information system 134, 137–8
  internet/web 23, 24, 33–4, 121–2, 124
  KWAC (Key Word And Context) 86
  KWAC (Key Word Augmented in Context) 86
  KWIC (Key Word in Context) 85–6
  KWOC (Key Word Out of Context) 85
  online, standardization issues 143
  organization of information in 31
  periodical 32–3, 125
  pre-coordinated 473–5, 493
  records 356–7
  as retrieval tools 125–7, *126*
  search engine 33
  software tools for 34
  spider 25, 122
  standardization, lack of 143, 148, 151
  standards for description and access 356–7
  subject 110–11
  web 33–4, 125
indicators (MARC) 177, *179*
individuals (OWL) 497
infoglut *see* information overload
INFOMINE 124
information
  arrangement of physical resources 81, 513, 545–8, *546–7*
  definition of 5–7
  in DIKW pyramid *5*, 6
  fragmentation 37
  history of the organization of 49–97
  international exchange of descriptive 345
  nature of 5–7
  nature of organization of 7–10
  non-textual/non-book 75, 277, 434–5, 442–3
  organization of, in different contexts 11–39
  overload 37
  preferred sources of 283–5, *284*, 287–8, 542
  preservation of 188, 203, 213–14
  reasons for organizing 3
  resources, major activities involved in organizing 7–10
  retrieval tools 99–100
  vs. knowledge 5–7
information architecture 29–30, 39
information fragmentation 37
information hierarchy/DIKW pyramid *5*, 5–6
information organization 1–575
  abstracting 34–5

access to resources, provision of 9–10, 285–93
activities involved in 7–11
archives 16–18, *17*
arrangement 545–8
authority control 365–418
call numbers 545–8
cataloging 13–15
categories 513–35
classification 513–35
conceptual models 225–63
controlled vocabularies in 455–505
cutter numbers 545–8
defined 7
description and access 269–300
descriptive standards 305–57
in different contexts 11–39
encoding and encoding standards 167–97
filing 539–44
functions of 7–10
history 49–89
indexes/indexing 31–4
knowledge management 37–9
libraries 11–16, *12*
lists, creation of 8–9
location of resources, providing 10
metadata 203–21
museums 18–22, 20
nature of 7–10
the need for 2–4
online settings and contexts 22–30
personal information management 2, 37
reasons for 3
records management 35–6
resource description for 269–300
retrieval tools 99–128
standards for 305–57
subject analysis and aboutness 425–51, 571–5
system design 134–6
systems, retrieval, and technology 133–61
vocabulary control 455–505
Western civilization and 49–89
information overload 37
information resources 269
  use of term 7
  see also resource descriptions
information retrieval 25, 85, 108, 209, 366, 436, 458, 474, 499, 535
information systems
  archives 159–60
  bibliographic networks 155
  browsing 89, 111, 115, 138, *139*, 140–1, 142, 145, 147, 148, 157–8
  databases 136–8

Index

design of 134–6, *135*
discovery layers 141
displays 144–7
functions of 134
as hard to use 160–1
museums 160
querying 139–40
resource management systems 155–9
retrieval models 138
searching 138–43, *139*, *142*, 229
standardization issues 143–54, *153*
storage 134
system defined 134
inheritance relationships 227, 231, 233, 236, 240, 245, 249
initial articles 149, 177, 180, 543–4
initialisms xxiv–xxvii, 472
initials, filing of 543
instance in BIBFRAME 196
instance relationships 464
institutional repositories 27–8
integrated library systems (ILSs) 14, 87–9, 155–9 *see also* library services platforms
integrating determinate plans 281
integrating indeterminate plans 281
integrating resources (mode of issuance) 280, *280*
integrity of numbers (classification) 530–2
intellectual level, subject analysis and 446–7
intensional aboutness 426
inter-indexer consistency studies 455
interlibrary loans (ILL) 15, 126, 155
International Cataloguing Principles (ICP) (IFLA) 271–3, 321, 382–3
International Conference on Cataloguing Principles 69, 104, 272
International Council on Archives 241, 409
International Council on Archives, Expert Group on Archival Description 241, 409
International Federation for Documentation 84
International Federation of Library Associations and Institutions (IFLA)
    conceptual models 76, 77, 104–5, 227–41, 278, 306, 321, 378–82
    display guidelines 144, 147
    Guidelines for Authority Records and References (GARR) 377
    International Cataloguing Principles (ICP) 271–3, 321, 382–3
    ISBD 75
    ISBD Review Group 329
    Library Reference Model (LRM) 3–4, 4n, 4, 76, 227–41, 278, 306, 378–82
    Meeting of Experts on an International Cataloguing Code 382
    Paris Principles 69
    UNIMARC 180
    Universal Bibliographic Control 99
International Standard Archival Authority Record for Corporate Bodies, Persons, and Families (ISAAR(CPF)) 409, 410, 411
International Standard Bibliographic Description (ISBD)
    and AACR2 333
    aims of 75, 329
    areas of description 329–32, *332*
    cataloging codes and 329
    consolidated edition 329
    history of 75
    IFLA ISBD Review Group 329
    and MARC records 329, 333
    punctuation 75, 322, 326, 329–33
    and RDA 311, 322, 329
International Standard Book Number (ISBN) 299, 312, 331
International Standard Name Identifier (ISNI) 388, 418
International Standard Serial Number (ISSN) 125, 331
Internationalized Resource Identifiers (IRIs) 251, 253n, 299, 312, *312*, 376 *see also* Uniform Resource Identifiers (URIs)
internet
    deep web 122
    directories 23–4, 27, 124, 535
    information organization and 23, 25–6
    microdata 25, 124, 184, *185*, 208
    organization of information in 23–6
    search engine optimization (SEO) 25
    search engines 24–5, 121–4
    Semantic Web 26
    web crawlers 24, 25, 122, 251
interoperability of metadata 209–10
InterParty 417
intrinsic relationships 414
introductions, subject analysis and 442
inventories 18, 55, 56, 57, 82
IRI *see* Internationalized Resource Identifiers (IRIs)
ISAAR (CPF) *see International Standard Archival Authority Record for Corporate Bodies, Persons, and Families*
ISAD(G) *see General International Standard Archival Description* (ISAD(G))
ISBD *see International Standard Bibliographic Description* (ISBD)
ISBN *see* International Standard Book Number (ISBN)
ISSN *see* International Standard Serial Number (ISSN)
is-ness 427 *see also* genre/form headings
ISO/IEC 10646 Universal Coded Character Set (UCS) 168–9

item
    in BIBFRAME 195, *196*
    in LRM *231*, 233, 239, 278
    in RDA 290, 308, 310, 322

jackets, subject analysis and 442
Jacob, E. 495, 514
Jefferson, T. 79, 519
Jewett, C. C. 63-7, *66*
Joudrey, D. N. 153, 271-2, 277, 329, 438, 446, 448-9
journal indexing 32-3

Kay, P. 432, 517
keyword 124
    access 9-10
    early uses 62-3
    faceted browsing 16, 141, *142*, 146, 158
    false drops 25, 25n, 153
    HTML meta tags 183-4
    indexes 126-7
    matching 140
    problems of 25, 286, 431, 455, 468
    search engines 184, 455
    searching 10, 103, 114-15, 120, 122, 127-8, 139-40, 148, 150-1, 153, 208, 252, 285-6, 368, 455, 498-9, 535
    subjects 153, 498
    tagging 501-5, *503*, 507
Kilgour, F. 85, 87
knowledge
    categories 513, 515, 518, 530-2
    classification of 530
    defined 6-7, 38
    in DIKW pyramid *5*, 6
    forms of 439
    tacit/explicit 38-9
knowledge management 6-7, 37-9
knowledge organization systems (KOS) 7
knowledge pyramid/hierarchy *5*, 5-6
Knowlton, S. 469
known-item searching 103
Koch, T. 519
Koha (ILS) 158
Korea, early printing techniques in 57
KWAC (*Key Word and Context*) 86
KWAC (*Key Word Augmented in Context*) 86
KWIC (*Key Word in Context*) 85
KWOC (*Key Word Out of Contex*) 85-6

La Fontaine, H. 80, 84, 99, 519
labeled displays 147
Lai, L.-L. 39
Lakoff, G. 432, 516

Lambe, P. 39
Lancaster, F. W. 426, 441, 515
Langridge, D. W. 433, 439, 445, 446-7
language(s)
    authority control, forms of 377
    bibliographies and 101-2
    classification and 517, 519
    encoding standards and 169-70
    names in different 367-8
    subject analysis and 446-7
    and UCS 168
LaPlante, W. 220
large language models 455, 501
Layne, S. S. 435
LC *see* Library of Congress
LCC *see Library of Congress Classification* (LCC)
LCDGT *see Library of Congress Demographic Group Terms* (LCDGT)
LCGFT *see Library of Congress Genre/Form Terms* (LCGFT)
LC-PCC PS *see* Library of Congress-Program for Cooperative Cataloging Policy Statements (LC-PCC PSs)
LCRI *see Library of Congress Rule Interpretations* (LCRI)
LCSH *see Library of Congress Subject Headings* (LCSH)
leader (MARC) 171
learning, organization and 2
left-anchored searching 139-40
letter-by-letter arrangement 540-2
levels of description 282-3, 315
lexical databases, keyword searching with 499
lexical relationships in controlled vocabularies 466-7
lexical variants 463
lexicons *see* thesauri
librarians 11, 133
Librarian's Convention (1853) 66-7
libraries
    antiquity 49, *50*, 51-3
    automation of 86-9
    cataloging 13-15
    catalogs 15-16
    church/monastery 55, 519
    collections of resources 12-13
    college 56
    computers, use of in 1960s and 1970s 87-8
    digital 27-9
    educational institutions in fourteenth century 56
    integrated library systems 87-9
    monastic 55-7, 519
    in museums 22
    overview of organization of information in 11-16
    physical information, arrangement of 545-8, *546, 547*

Index 641

physical processing 15
research guides 102
technical services 11, *12*, 155, 279
library automation 14, 83–9, 133
library hand 83, *83*
Library of Alexandria 51–3, 519
Library of Congress (LC) 63, 77–8, 79–80, 86–8, 143n, 154, 157, 170, 181, 192, 194, 259, 306, 321, 322, 326, 345, 377, 448, 469, 480, 483n, 546
    catalog cards 63, 78, 106
    destruction in the war of 1812 79
    homepage as an example 259
    Linked Data Service 376
    Network Development and MARC Standards Office 339
Library of Congress Classification (LCC) 79, 519, 521, 523, *525*, *526*, 529, 529n, 530, 531, 533, 546
Library of Congress Demographic Group Terms (LCDGT) 447, 487–8
Library of Congress Genre/Form Terms for Library and Archival Materials (LCGFT) 484, 486–7
Library of Congress Metadata Guidance Documentation (MGDs) 283, 290, *291*, 316–17, *318*, 384, 390, 391, 393
Library of Congress/NACO Authority File (LCNAF) 312, 373, 376, 385, 388, 398, 480
Library of Congress-Program for Cooperative Cataloging Policy Statements (LC-PCC PSs) 77, 283n, 285, 316, 326, 384, 387, 391, 392
Library of Congress Rule Interpretations (LCRI) 76–7
Library of Congress Subject Headings (LCSH) 78, 83, 444, 461, 469, 470, 473–5, 479–80, *481–2*, 482–3, 492–3, 542–3
Library of Pergamum 51
Library portals 15
Library Reference Model (LRM) (IFLA) 3–4, 4n, 76, 77, 227–41, 278
    agent entities 233–4, 381
    aims 227
    attributes 236, *236–7*, *238*
    authority control 379, 380–2
    basis for RDA (2020) 306, 308
    entities *230–1*, 230–5, *237–8*
    entities similarity to BIBFRAME entities 195–6
    as high-level conceptual model 228
    history 227–8
    nomens 234–5, *235*, 379, 381–2, 384
    places 234
    relationships 236, 238–41, *239–40*, 381
    res 232
    resource entities (WEMI) 232–3, 278, 381
    time-spans 234
    user tasks 4, 105, 228–30

library services platforms (LSPs) 14, 155–9 *see also* integrated library systems (ILSs)
Lilley, O. 433
linked data 26, 159, 252, 260
    BIBFRAME as a form of 194, 322
    support for 124
Linnaeus 459, 515
List of Subject Headings for Use in Dictionary Catalogs (ALA) 78
lists, creation and use of 8–9
literals 234, 253, 255–6, 261
literary warrant 68, 476, 530
location devices 533
Lorie R. 181
Lounsbury, F. 517
LRM see *Library Reference Model* (LRM)
LSP *see* Library services platform (LSP)
Lubetzky, S. 69, 75, 76, 104, 278
Luhn, H. P. 85

Machine-Readable Cataloging (MARC) 14, 18, 170–81
    archives and 82
    bibliographic format *172-6*, 195, 217
    control fields 171, *179*
    data element identifiers 178
    delimiters 178
    development of 86–7, 170
    directory 171–2, *172*
    displays 174, *175–6*
    as encoding standard 167
    fields, components of 173, *173–6*, 176–8, *180*
    fixed fields 171, *173*, 174, *180*, 375
    future of 179
    indicators 177, *180*
    leader 171
    MARC 21, 170–1, *180*
    metadata 203, 205
    records, components of *172*, 173
    subfield codes 177, *180*
    subfields 173
    tags 173, *173–4*, *180*, 375
    UNIMARC 180
    variable data fields 173, *180*
MADS *see* Metadata Authority Description Schema
main entry 69, 74–6, 333–4
    justification 333–4
Making of America II (MOA2), 217
manifestation 230, 232, 233, 237, 238, 278, 308, *310*
Mann, T. 455
MARC *see* Machine-Readable Cataloging (MARC)
MARCXML 192, *193*
markup languages
    descriptive markup 181

Encoded Archival Description (EAD) 18, 116, 191-2, *549-54*
HTML (Hypertext Markup Language) 183-4, *185*
MARCXML 192, *193*
SGML (Standard Generalized Markup Language) 167-8, 181-3, 184-6
TEI (Text Encoding Initiative) 169, 188-91, *190*
XML (Extensible Markup Language) 186-92
Maslow, A. 128
Maunsell, A. 59, 67
McDaniel, C. 517
Medical Subject Headings (MeSH) 483-4, *484-5*
medieval libraries 55
memex concept 85
meronyms 466
Merriam-Webster 225, 514
MeSH see *Medical Subject Headings* (MeSH)
meta-languages 181
meta-metadata *207*, 215
meta-searching 141, 143
metadata
    administrative 211, *212*, 213-15
    analytical 206, *207*
    application profiles 218-19
    arrangement of 539-44
    authorized access points 13
    basics of 205-7, *207*, 269
    categories and types of 205-6, *207*, 210-18
    characteristics 209-10
    complexity level 206
    components *204*
    content standards 9, 209
    contextual 206, *207*
    controlled vocabularies 209
    crosswalks 220-1
    defined 77, 203, 205
    description sets 307-8
    descriptive 211
    digital collections 27-9
    display, encoding standards and 169
    Dublin Core 24
    element refinement 210, 219, 339, *340*
    elements 208
    encoded in HTML 183-4
    encoding standards 168, 168n, 210
    extensibility 210
    flexibility 210
    granularity levels 116, 206, 208, 220, 237, 251
    harvesting technologies 221
    interoperability 209-10
    labeling of 147
    levels of complexity 206, 208
    location and form of 208
    location of resources, providing 10-11
    Machine-Readable Cataloging (MARC) 14, 203, 205
    management tools 218-21
    meta-metadata *207*, 215
    Metadata Encoding & Transmission Standard (METS) 217-18
    models *204*, 225-64
    museum objects 22
    namespaces 187, 219, 255, 256
    optional elements 186, 210, 270, 336, 337
    preservation 214
    qualifiers 210
    registries 219-20
    relational databases 137
    retrieval tools 7
    rights and access 214-15
    schemas *204*, 205, 208-9
    search engine optimization (SEO) 25
    search engines and 123-4
    semantics 209
    standardization and control 208-9
    statements 269, 307
    structural 216-17
    structure 209
    surrogate records 99, 99n
    syntax 209
    technical *212*, 213, 216, 347
    templates 221
    use of term 2n
    work 308
    see also access points; conceptual models; resource descriptions; standards for description and access
metadata application profiles *see* Application profiles
Metadata Authority Description Schema (MADS) 407, *408*
Metadata Encoding & Transmission Standard (METS) 217-18
Metadata Guidance Documentation (MGDs) 283, 290, *291*, 316-17, *318*, 384, 390, 391, 393
metadata models *204*, 225-64
Metadata Object Description Schema (MODS) 271, 341-2, *343-4*
    excerpt *343-4*
metadata registries 219-20
Metis: Library Classification for Children 520
METS *see* Metadata Encoding & Transmission Standard
Michael, B. 505
microdata 25, 124, 184, *185*, 208
microfilm/microphotography 84, 85, 108
microform catalogs 108
Miller, D. P. 271-2, 277
Milsap, L. 133

Index

Milton, N. 39
minimum coherent description 315
Mittal, V. 499
mixed notation (classification) 520–1
mode of issuance 279–81, *280*, *282*, *319*
    integrating resource 280
    multipart monograph 279–80
    multiple unit 281
    serial 280
    single unit 279
models *see* metadata models
MODS *see* Metadata Object Description Schema
Moen, W. 173
monastery libraries 55, 519
monographs
    mode of issuance 279–80
    multipart monograph 279–80, *280*, 331
    single unit 279–82, *280*
Mooers, C. 85
morphology 500
Morville, P. 24, 29–30, 38
Mosher, E. 181
movable type printing, invention of 57
Muller, S. 81
multi-word terms and phrases 470
multipart monographs (mode of issuance) 279–80, *280*
multiple units (mode of issuance) 281
museums
    access and storage 22
    accessioning process *20*, 20
    acquisition process 19–20
    authority control 411–17
    categorization 21
    changes in 19
    conceptual models 248–50
    Conceptual Reference Model (CRM) (CIDOC) 248–50
    definitions 18–19
    information systems 160
    libraries in 22
    metadata about objects 22
    modern era 81–2
    museum registers and databases *see* registers and registration
    online databases 119–20
    provenance 20
    registration *see* registers and registration
    retrieval tools 120, *121*
    visual material, description of 21–2

Name Authority Cooperative Program (NACO) 373
name/title access point 74, 76, 290, 292, *335*, 369–70, 381, 383, 399–401

names
    access points for 102, 272–3, 395–6
    authority control 366–9, 395–6, 406–7
    corporate 383, 412–13, 444
    describing persons 395–6
    geographic 445
    in subject analysis 444–5
    as subject concepts 444–5
    using multiple 402
    variant forms 370, 373, 383, 401, 410
namespaces 187, 219, 255, 256
narrower term (NT) relationships 103, 125, 154, 457, 464, 465, 466, 480n
NASA Thesaurus 460, 495
National Agricultural Library 77, 321
National Gallery of Art (NGA), 120
National Information Standards Organization (NISO) 127, 154, 355, 356, 357
National Library of Australia 75, 158, 326, 411
National Library of Medicine 77, 86, 321, 472, 483–4
Native American kinship systems 517
natural language approaches to subjects
    discourse analysis 501
    keywords 498–9
    morphology 500
    natural language processing 499–501
    phonetics 500
    phonology 500
    pragmatics 501
    semantics 501
    syntax 501
    tagging and folksonomies 501–505
91 Rules (Panizzi) 63, 65, 135
Nineveh, library 51
Nisbett, R. E. 432
NISO *see* National Information Standards Organization (NISO)
NLP *see* natural language approaches to subjects
nomen
    attributes of 238, 385
    authority control 384–5
    in LRM 231, 234–5, 379, 380, 381–2
    nomen string *vs.* 234–5
    in RDA 308–9, *318*, *319*, 384–5
    relationships *239–40*
nomen string 234–5
Nomenclature (Chenhall) 21, 83
non-human entities 233, 307, *319*, 381, 386–7
non-linear browsing 141
non-relational databases 137
non-textual information, subject analysis and 434–5, 443–4
Nonaka, I. 38

normalization 151
Norris, D. M. 63
notation (classification) 520–1
notes
  contents notes (libraries), 148, 299
  scope and contents (archives) 116, 299
  scope notes (thesauri) 457, 479–80, 489
  use of 21, 331, 347
number building (classification) 79, 81, 523
numbers integrity in classification 530–2

OAI *see* Open Archives Initiative (OAI)
OAI-PMH *see* Open Archives Initiative, Protocol for Metadata Harvesting
Objective Method of subject analysis 440
objectivity/subjectivity in subject analysis 437–8
objects of the catalog (Cutter) 67, 103, *104*, 128, 229, 287, 431
obtain (user task) 4, 105, 229
OCLC (Online Computer Library Center) 10, 14, 24, 78, 85, 87, 89n, 105, 155, 173, 174, 336, 377, 492
  ArchiveGrid 159–60
  WorldCat 15, 22, 24, 493
ODRL *see* Open Digital Rights Language (ODRL)
Office of Information Systems Specialists 87
Office of Strategic Service (OSS) 84–5
Official RDA see *RDA: Resource Description & Access*
of-ness 435
Ohio College Association 87
Ohio College Library Center *see* OCLC (Online Computer Library Center)
Olafsen, T. 426
Olson, H. 469, 520
On the Construction of Catalogues of Libraries, and Their Publication by Means of Separate, Stereotyped Titles (Jewett) 65–6
one-to-one principle 262, 339, 347
ONIX messages 351, *352–3*
ONIX (Online Information Exchange) 351, *352–3*, 354–5
Online Public Access Catalogs (OPACs) 88–9, 108–10, *109*
  bibliographic record from *110*
  display 144–7, 371, 539–42
  generations of 89
  searching 138–9, 147–8
  standardization issues 143
online records
  content 271
  elements 270
  retrieval tools for 270
  syntax 271
online settings and contexts
  authority control projects in 417–18

information organization in 22–3
  see also digital collections; information architecture; internet; linked data; Semantic Web
ontologies 248, 494–7, 515
OPACs *see* Online Public Access Catalogs (OPACs)
Open Archives Initiative (OAI) 28
  Protocol for Metadata Harvesting (OAI-PMH) 221
Open Digital Rights Language (ODRL) 215
Open Metadata Registry 220
Open Researcher and Contributor ID *see* ORCID (Open Researcher and Contributor ID)
open source software 102, 158
open source systems 157, 158, 159
open stacks 18, 22, 532
Opesade, A. 505
optional additions 313, *318*, 326
optional element 186, 210, 270, 336, 337
optional omissions 313, *318*, 326
optional punctuation 322, 329
options, conditions, and condition options 307, 311, 313–15, *313*, *314*, 316, 318, 384, 387, 391
ORCID (Open Researcher and Contributor ID) 388, 418
organization of information *see* information organization
original cataloging 14, 87, 155, 170, 278, 450
original order 16, 17, 81, 82, 242
Original RDA see *RDA: Resource Description & Access*
Osborn, A. 69
other title information 178, 294, 326
Otlet, P. 80, 84, 85, 99, 519
OWL Web Ontology Language 241, 497

page-turner model *207*, 216
Palatine Library 53
Pandectarum (Gessner) 59
Panizzi, A. 63, 65, *65*, 67, 135, 305, 469n
Panofsky, E. 434–5
parallel titles 294
Paris Principles 69, 74–5, 76, 104, 229, 272, 278, 333, 382
Parker, R. 87
PastPerfect 160
patron-driven acquisitions 12
Pergamum, library 51
periodical indexing 32–3, 125
person (entity) 308, 381
personal information management 2, 37
personal names in subject analysis 444
phonetics 500
phonology 500
phrase matching 139–40, 148, 151
physical information, arrangement of in libraries 545–8, *546–7*
pilers 2

Index

pinakes (Library of Alexandria) 52–3, 52n, 519
Pitt Rivers Museum 119
Pitti, D. 411
place (entity) 234, 308
Plato 78
PMEST 527–8
point of view, subject analysis and 446
policy statements 316, 326 *see also* Library of Congress-Program for Cooperative Cataloging Policy Statements (LC-PCC PS)
Pollio, A. 53
popular *vs.* technical terms 472
post-coordination/pre-coordination 473–5, 493
pragmatics (NLP) 501
pre-coordination/post-coordination 473–5, 493
PRECIS *(Preserved-Context Indexing System)* 81
precision 151–3, 436–7, 499
prefaces, subject analysis and 442
preferred names 366–7, 395–6
preferred sources of information 283, *284*, 285
preferred titles 76, 290, 370, 391–2, 399–400
PREMIS Data Dictionary for Preservation Metadata *207*, 213, 214, 218
preservation metadata *207*, 213, 214, 218
Preserved-Context Indexing System (PRECIS) 81
principles for information organization 4
printed catalogs *see* book catalogs; card catalogs; COM catalogs
printing 57
probabilistic retrieval 138
Program for Cooperative Cataloging (PCC) 260, 316–17, 322, 326, 329, 373, 384, 387
Project Gutenberg 27
properties 7, 26, 183
   in BIBFRAME 195
   in CRM 249–50
   in DCAM 261–2
   in ontologies 495, 497
   in RDF 253, 255
   in Schema.org 184
   see also attributes; relationships
property-value pair 136, 184, 210, 255, 261, 270, 309–11
prototype theory 518
provenance
   archives 16, 17, 81, 82, 116, 242, 247
   in Dublin Core 340
   museums 19–20, 21, 116, 120, 285
   preservation metadata 214
   in RDA 307
proximity operators 150
punctuation
   in classification 528
   filing 540–42
   in ISBD 75, 322, 326, 329–33

marks 542
standardization 150–1
pure notation (classification) 521
purpose of information organization 3–4, *4*
Purposive Method of subject analysis 440
Pythagoras 516

Qin, J. 219, 495
qualification of terms 471–2
qualifiers
   in access points 290, 383
   in Dublin Core 339
   in metadata extensibility 210, 219, 339
   in subject headings 445, 470, 471–2, 483, *484–5*
query languages 137
querying 139–40 *see also* searching
Quintarelli, E. 504

Ranganathan, S. R. 81, 519, 527–8
range and domain 309
RDA Registry 306, 311
RDA: Resource Description & Access 75, 77–8
   AACR2 and 333, *334–6*
   agents 386–90, *392–3*
   access points for agents 395–8
   access points for works and expressions 399–401
   access points in bibliographic records 402–5
   alternatives 326
   appellation element 385–6
   application profiles 315–16
   attributes of manifestation & item 323–4
   authority control 383–4
   core elements 324, 326
   data recording methods 311–12, *312*
   elements 309, *310*, 311
   entities 306, 308–9
   establishing an AAP 399–401
   example of RDA data *327–8*
   exceptions 325, *325*
   International Cataloguing Principles (ICP) 271–3
   ISBD and 311, 322, 329
   levels of description 315
   Library of Congress-Program for Cooperative Cataloging Policy Statements (LC-PCC PS) 77, 283n, 285, 316, 326, 384, 387, 391, 392
   Metadata Guidance Documentation (MGDs) 283, 290, *291*, 316–17, *318*, 384, 390, 391, 393
   mode of issuance and 279–81, *280*, *282*, 319
   name/title access point 290
   nomens 308–9, 384–5
   Official RDA 306–17, *310, 312, 314, 317–320*, 383–94
   options, conditions, and condition options 307, 311, 313–15, *313, 314*, 316, 318, 384, 387, 391

Original RDA 306, *318–19*, 321–7, *325, 327–8*, 394–405
   place of publication element 316, *317*
   policy statements 316
   relationship designators *291*
   relationship elements 287, 290, *291*, 292, *318, 335*, 388, 403–4
   resource types and 277–8
   sources of information 283, *284*, 285
   as standard for description and access 306–27, *310, 312*, *313–14, 317, 318–20, 327–8*
   work identifiers 289–90
   works and expressions 390–4, *392–3*
   works and expressions, access points for 399–405
RDA Toolkit Restructure and Redesign Project (RDA 3R) 306
RDF and related concepts *see* Resource Description Framework (RDF)
reasons for information organization 3–4, *4*
recall 151–3, 436–7, 499
re-classification of resources 530–2
Records
   in databases 136–8
   display of 146–7, 539–44
   encoding of 169–70
   syntax of 14
Records in Contexts (RiC) 241–8, *242, 245–6*, 342, 409
records management
   information organization and 35–6
   in museums 22
reference databases 137
registers and registration (museums) 19–21, *20*, 82, 116, 119
registrars 21, 116, 211
registries, metadata 219–20
Registrum Librorum Angliae 55
Reibel, D. B. 21
related term (RT) relationships 125, 456–7, 465
relational databases 88, 137, 308 *see also* entity-relationship models
relationship designators 287, 290, *291*, *292, 318*, 335, 388, 403–4
relationship elements 290, 309, 311
   persons 388–90, *388–9*
   works and expressions 392–3, *392–3*
relationships 226, *239–40*
   agents, relationships with resources 288
   associative relationships in controlled vocabularies 461, 465
   in controlled vocabularies 457, 461–7
   displaying 465–6
   equivalence relationships in controlled vocabularies 458, 462–3
   extrinsic relationships 414–15
   hierarchical relationships in controlled vocabularies 125, 459, 460–1, 464, 466, 475–6, 483, *490*, 491, 493, *494*, 495
   intrinsic relationships 414
   Library Reference Model (LRM) (IFLA) 236, 238–41, *239–40*, 381
   Records in Contexts (RiC) 246–8, *246*
   representation of 286–7
   resource descriptions 285, 290, *291,* 292–3
   between resources 288–90, 380
   taxonomy of bibliographic 288–90
relative location (classification) 533
relevance/relevance ranking 115, 123, 138, 146, 158
representative expression 394
res 230, 232, 234–5, 238–40, 308, 381–2
research guides 102
Research Libraries Information Network 87
research methods, subject analysis and 446
Resource Description and Access (RDA) *see RDA: Resource Description & Access*
Resource Description Framework (RDF) 209, 252, 253–60, *258*, 376
   and BIBFRAME 197
   dataset 255, 257, *257, 258*
   DCAM compared to 261–2
   encoding 255
   graph 225, 255, 256–7, *258*
   for Semantic Web 257
   tabular form *255–6*
   triples 253–5, *254, 257*
Resource Description Framework in Attributes (RDFa) 124, 184
resource descriptions
   analytical 282
   archives 273–5
   Cataloging Cultural Objects (CCO) 275–6, 277, 278, 285, 293, 294, 347–8, 350n, 412–15, *413*
   collection level 283
   common attributes across resource types 293–9, *298*
   comprehensive 282
   continuing 279
   creation of 270–1
   creators 297–9, *298*
   defined 253
   definitions and terminology 269–70
   Describing Archives: A Content Standards (DACS) 82, 115, 206, 273–5, 278, 285, 292–3, 342, 345–7
   developing collection of 8–9, 11–13
   dissemination information 295–7
   edition 294–5
   electronic 141, 158, 277, 306
   ethical principles for 276–7
   examination for subject analysis 427, 441–4
   finite 279

General International Standard Archival Description (ISAD(G)) 273
hierarchical 242, 282–3
identification of works within 8
identifying 8
initial questions 277
integrating 280
International Cataloguing Principles (ICP) (IFLA) 271–3, 321, 382–3
level of description 282–3
mode of issuance 279–81, *280, 282, 319*
physical description 297
preliminary considerations 277–99
principles of 271–7
producing lists of 8
providing the means of locating 10
relationship and contextual information 299
relationships 285, 290, 291, 292–3
sources of information for 283, *284*, 285
titles 293–4
types of resources 277–8
use of term 7
visual 148, 348–51, 411–17, 434–5
see also standards for description and access
resource discovery 24, 134, 158, 203, 308
resource entities (WEMI) 195, 232–3, *239–40*, 278, 288, 290, *310*, 378, 381, 390–1
resource examination for subject analysis 427, 441–4
resource management systems 155–9
resource types 277–8
respect des fonds 16–17, 81, 81n, 274–5, 532
responsibility, statements of *see* statements of responsibility
retrieval and retrieval tools 134
    access to recorded information 99
    bibliographies 100–2
    catalogs 102–15, *104, 107–10, 112, 114*
    display of results 144–7, 539–44
    finding aids 115–16, *117–19*
    hard to use 160–1
    indexes 125–7, *126*
    internet directories 23–4, 27, 124, 535
    metadata 7
    models 138
    museums 116, 119–20, *121*
    need for 99–100, 127–8
    organization and 3
    over-reliance on one 128
    registers 116, 119–20
    research guides 102
    search engines 121–4
retrieval in information systems 134
retrieval models 138

rights and access metadata 214–15
Romanization, of scripts *see* transliteration
Roman libraries 53
Rosch, E. 518
Rosenfeld, L. 24, 29, 30, 38
Rostgaard, F. 59, *60*
Rowley, J. 4–5
rule of three *335*
Rules for a Dictionary Catalog (Cutter) 66–8, 78
Rules for Descriptive Cataloging 69

schedules (classification) 520, 521, 523, 529
schema-neutral 308, 322, 347
Schwartz, C. 27
SciCentral 24
scope notes 309, 457, *460*, 479, 483, *483, 484*, 489, *491, 494*
scripts, and multiple languages 88, 169–70, 383
search engine optimization (SEO) 25
search engines
    automatic indexing 34, 127, 206
    metadata's role in 184, 208, 259
    need for other tools 127–8
    and online catalogs 109
    proximity formulations 150
    reliance on keywords 455, 498–9
    as retrieval tools 7, 24–6, 121–4
    spiders 24, 25, 122
searching
    authority control integration 151–4, *153*
    Boolean operators 89, 138, 140, 150, 151, 474
    browsing 1, 4, 89, 111, 115, 138, *139*, 140–1, *142*, 145, 147, 148, 157–8
    derived key 88–9, 89n
    expanded 158
    exploded 154
    faceted 16, 141, *142*, 146, 158
    federated 22, 141, 143, 151, 158, 411
    genre/form 148
    keyword 10, 103, 114–15, 120, 122, 127–8, 139–40, 148, 150–1, 153, 208, 252, 285–6, 368, 455, 498–9, 535
    left-anchored 88–9, 139–40, 141, 148
    phrase 139–40, 148, 151
    standardization 147–8
    stopwords 148
Sears, M. E. 78, 229
Sears List of Subject Headings (Sears) 78–9, 461, 475–6, 482–3, *483*
see also reference 31, 373, *375*, 402–5, 465
see/USE reference 31, *375*, 403, 462–3
select (user task) 4, 105, 229
selection of resources for collections 12

Semantic Web 26, 250–2
   BIBFRAME and 194–6
   future for 260
   goal of 26
   linked data 251–2, 260
   microdata 124, 184, 259
   ontologies 248, 494–7, 515
   RDF (Resource Description Framework) 209, 252, 253–60, *258*, 376
semantics 209, 501
   in controlled vocabularies 455, 458, 460, 467, 475
   interoperability 209, 219–20
   in metadata schemes 209–10
   in microdata 124, 184, 259
   and NLP 501
   and ontologies 248, 494–7, 515
   and RDF 124, 256
serials
   mode of issuance 279–81, *280*
   ONIX for 351
   organizing 330, 435
series
   access points 148, 287, 292, 292n
   in archival description 17, 345
   authority control 375, 399
   in ISBD 329, 331
   in library description 13, 74, 152, 323, 324, *325*
   in MARC *174*, 292
   in museum description 414
   as relationship 289
   searching 148
SGML *see* Standard Generalized Markup Language (SGML)
Shaw, R. 85
shelf browsing 111, 140, 531, 532
shelf reading 105
shelflists 56, 105
SHM see *Subject Headings Manual* (SHM)
Silicon Snake Oil (Stoll) 5–6
Simple Knowledge Organization Scheme (SKOS), 256, 376
simple term lists 458
single unit (mode of issuance) 279, *280*, 281
SKOS *see* Simple Knowledge Organization Scheme (SKOS)
SkyRiver 87, 155
Smiraglia, R. 76, 289
Smithsonian Institution, cataloging code for 65–6
Snowden, D. 38–9
Social Networks and Archival Context (SNAC) 411
software
   in archives 159
   digital collections 28

filing 543
for indexing 34
in information systems 134, 157, 158, 159, 169
for integrated library systems 87–8, 156, 158
interoperability 209
for knowledge management 39
in museums 160
open source 102, 158
preservation 214
for research guides 102
technical metadata 211, 213
Sorbonne 1338 catalog 55
source databases 137
sources of information for resource descriptions 283, *284*, 285
specific entry 478
specificity in controlled vocabularies 467–8, 475–6
spiders 24, 25, 122
SRU (Search/Retrieval via URL) 154
St. Augustine's Abbey 56
St. Martin's Priory 56
St. Pierre, M. 220
stacks 15, 18, 111
   browsing 18, 103, 111, 140
   open *vs.* closed 18, 22, 532, 545
Stacy, R. D. 38
standard citation 74 *see also* name/title access point
Standard Generalized Markup Language (SGML) 167–8, 181–3, 184, 186
standardization in information systems
   authority control integration 151–4, *153*
   basic search queries 147–8
   Boolean operators 140, 150, 151
   card catalogs 143
   display 144–7
   initial articles, handling of 149
   proximity operators 150
   punctuation 150–1
   search queries 147–8
   system displays 144–7
   systems and 143–51
   truncation 149–50
   Z39.50 154
standards for controlled vocabularies
   Art & Architecture Thesaurus (AAT) 83, 293, 349–50, 414, 430, 464, 465–6, 471, 488–9, *490*
   Faceted Application of Subject Terminology (FAST) 474, 492–3
   Homosaurus 493, *494*
   Library of Congress Demographic Group Terms (LCDGT) 447, 487–8
   Library of Congress Genre/Form Terms for Library and Archival Materials (LCGFT) 484, 486–7

Index

Library of Congress Subject Headings (LCSH) 78, 83, 444, 461, 469, 470, 473–5, 479–80, *481–2*, 482–3, 492–3, 542–3
Medical Subject Headings (MeSH) 483–4, *484–5*
Sears List of Subject Headings (Sears) 78–9, 461, 475–6, 482–3, *483*
Thesaurus of ERIC Descriptors 460, 476, 491
standards for description and access
    Anglo-American Cataloguing Rules, Second Edition (AACR2) 333–4, *334–6*
    archives 342, *343–4*, 345–7
    bibliographic references 357
    Cataloging Cultural Objects (CCO) 275–6, 277, 278, 285, 293, 294, 347–8, 350n, 412–15, *413*
    Categories for the Description of Works of Art (CDWA) 350–1
    Describing Archives: A Content Standard (DACS) 82, 115, 206, 273–5, 278, 285, 292–3, 342, 345–7, 409, 410
    Dublin Core (DC) 336–9, *338, 340*
    General International Standard Archival Description (ISAD(G)) 342–5, *343–4*
    history 305–6
    indexes 356–7
    International Standard Bibliographic Description (ISBD) 306, 329–33, *332*
    Metadata Object Description Schema (MODS) 339, 341–2, *343–4*
    ONIX (Online Information Exchange) 351, *352–3*, 354–5
    RDA: Resource Description & Access 306–27, *310*, 312–14, 317–20, 325, 327–8
    VRA Core 217, 275, 347, 348–50, 416–17, 448
    see also authority control
Statement of International Cataloguing Principles (ICP) (IFLA) see *International Cataloguing Principles* (ICP)
statements of responsibility 13, 178, 237, 298, 330, 333, 335, 387
static plans 281
static works 281
Steele, G. 505
stereotyping 66
Stoll, C. 5–6
stopwords 148
string encoding scheme 311–12, 319, 384
Strout, R. F. 49n, 53, 57, 59, 63
structural metadata 28, 205, *207*, 209n, 211, 216–18, 221
structure standards *see* metadata schemas
structured description (RDA) 311–12, *312*
Structured Query Language (SQL) 137
style guides for citations 100–1

subdivision of terms 177, 178, 460–1, 473–5, 477, 479, 482, 483, 487, 493
subdivisions (classification) 79, 80, *525*, 529
subfields (MARC) 173
    codes 177–8
subject access
    in archives 115, 342, 345, 410
    and authority control 151–4, 365–6, 376
    in BIBFRAME 195
    in CCO 348, 412, 414
    in CDWA 350, 415
    and Cutter 67, *104*, 113
    in directories 23–4, 27, 124, 535
    in Dublin Core 336–7, *338*
    history of 49, 52, 61, *70*, 72, 83, 85
    in indexes 125–7
    keyword 148, 153
    in LRM 238, *239*, 380–2
    through MARC 173, *176*, 177, 179
    modern era 78–81, *80*
    natural language approaches 498–505
    in OPACs 88–9
    in RDA 322, 326
    special materials 83
    in VRA Core 350
    see also classification; controlled vocabularies
subject analysis
    aboutness and 425–6
    aboutness statements 427, 449–50
    analyzable units 437
    artificial intelligence and 437, 450–1
    challenges of 425, 431–8
    chronological elements 445
    Cohesion Method 440
    concept identification 444–5
    conceptual analysis 427, 441–9
    consistency 433–4
    content characteristics 445–8
    content examination 444–9, 571–5
    controlled vocabularies and 450
    cover/jacket/container 442
    cultural differences 432–3
    definition of 427–31
    determining aboutness 438–41
    exhaustivity 435–7, *437*
    Figure-Ground Method 440
    future for 450–1
    genre/form 447–8
    illustrations/visual features 443
    introductions/prefaces 442
    knowledge, forms of 439
    Langridge's approach 439
    language, tone, audience and intellectual level 446–7

    names 444–5
    non-textual information 434–5, 443–4
    Objective Method 440
    objectivity 437–8
    outline of process 571–5
    point of view 446
    purpose of documents 439
    Purposive Method 440
    research methods 446
    resource examination 441–4
    stages in aboutness determination 449
    steps in process of 427, *428–30*, 430–1
    tables of contents 442
    technological advances and 450–1
    text, examination of 443
    titles/subtitles 442
    topics 439, 444
    use-based approaches 440–1
    visual material 21–2
    Wilson's approach 440
subject arrangement in Vivarium library 55
subject authority files 373, 376
subject headings
    as access points 9–10, 15, 32–3, 99, 102, 111–14,
        125, 269, 270, 286, 287–8, 292, 312, 455
    in archives 18, 83, 115–16, 292, 342
    authority control 103, 152–4, 365, 366, 373, 376
    chronological elements as 445
    co-extensive entry 477
    compound 470
    consistency 433
    direct entry 477
    exhaustivity 435–7
    genre/form *vs.* 447–8
    geographic names 445
    history of 52–3, 55, 56, 59, 62–3, 68, 78–9
    lists 312, 376, 425, 426, 430, 458, 460–1, 479–87, 505
    literary warrant of 476
    in MARC 171, *174*, 177–8
    in museums 21, 83, 120, 412, 415
    names as 444–5
    as nomen 234
    number assigned 478–9
    post-coordination 473–5, 493
    pre-coordination 473–5, 493
    relationships among 456, 461–7, 470
    searching 103–4, 140, 141, 145, 146, 147, 148, 455
    specific entry 478
    specificity 475–6
    strings 460–1, 473–5, 492
    thesauri *vs.* subject heading lists 460–1
    titles as 445
    see also controlled vocabularies; subjects/subject
        matter; thesauri

Subject Headings Manual (SHM) 435, 477, 479, 480
subject in RDF 253–4, 261, 307, 315
subject languages *see* classifications; controlled
        vocabularies; subject headings; thesauri
subjectivity/objectivity 437–8
subjects/subject matter
    and aboutness 425–6
    attributes of resources 3, 6, 7, 211, 234, 299, *310*,
        337, 341, 347, 350, 410, 412, 415, 425, 431
    in BIBFRAME 196
    in categories and classifications 513–35
    and cultural differences 432–3
    in Cutter's objects 103, *104*
    early approaches to 52–3, 55, 79, 425
    gateways 23–4, 27, 124
    modeling of 76, 228, 230, 236, 240, 247, *318*, 378,
        380–2
    natural language approaches to 498–505
    and objectivity 438–9
    used to organize resources 13–14, 28, 51–3, 100,
        101, 102, 110–11, 208
    in user tasks 104
    of visual materials 21–2, 434–5, 443
    see also classifications; controlled vocabularies;
        subject analysis; subject headings; thesauri
subtitles 14, 210, 294, 442
successive indeterminate plans 281
Sumerians 49, 51
summarization
    in RDA 326
    in subject access
surrogate records 269–70
    and access points 9, 287, 382, 387, 404, 484
    for art and artifacts 82
    and authority control 151–4, *153*, 376
    displaying 146–7
    encoding of 167–70, 171, *175*, *176*, 182
    in retrieval tools/systems 7, 99, 99n, *110*, 128,
        137–8, 155, 158, 208, 269–70
    and system design 135–6
    in UBC 84
syndetic structure 366, 457, 504
synonym rings 458–9, *459*, 498
synonyms and synonymous concepts 122–3, 466
    control 10, 31, 103, 123, 209, 365, 456–7, 459,
        462–3, 468–70 *see also* authority control
    in Google 122–3
    lack of control 25, 153–4, 160–1, 251, 459
    in natural language 466, 498–9
synsets 458–9, *459*, 498
syntax 168–9, *204*, 209, 255, 261, 271, 319
syntax (natural language processing) 501
syntax encoding schemes (Dublin Core) 261–2, 339, *340*
Systema Naturae (Linnaeus) 459, 515

system-based browsing 89, 111, 115, 138, *139*, 140–1, *142*, 145, 147, 148, 157–8
systems and system design 133–6, *135*
    authority control integration 151–4
    bibliographic networks 155
    databases 136–8
    defined 134, *135*
    federated searching 22, 141, 143, 151, 158, 411
    functions 134, *135*
    integrated library systems (ILSs) 14, 87–9
    library history of 87–9
    library services platforms (LSPs) 88–9
    organization of information and 134–6
    other aids for users 151–4
    querying languages 137
    retrieval models 138
    searching methods 138–43, *139*
    standardization and systems 143–54
    use in the LIS professions 155–60

tables (classification) 79, 520, 523, 529
tables (databases) 134, 137
tables of contents 15, 211, 299
    subject analysis and 442, 498
Tables of Persons Eminent in Every Branch of Learning Together with a List of Their Writings (Library of Alexandria) 52–3, 52n, 519
tacit/explicit knowledge 38–9
tag clouds 502, *503*
tags and tagging 134, 154, 158, 169, 450, 498, 501–5, *503*
    MARC 171, 173, *173–4*, 177–8, 179, 287, 375
    MARCXML and MODS *193*, 341
    HTML/XML 181, *182*, 183–4, 186–7, 188–9, 191–2, 206
Takeuchi, H. 38
Taube, M. 85
taxonomies 459–60, 495, 513–5, 533–5
taxonomists 463, 470, 473, 475, 476
Taylor, A. G. v, xx, 6, 39, 153, 271–2, 277, 329
technical metadata *212*, 213, 216, 347
technical services in libraries 11, *12*, 155, 279
technical *vs.* popular terms 472
technology
    resource management systems 157–9
    standardization issues 143–54
    subject analysis and 450–1
    used in LIS professions 155–60
    see also information systems
TEI (Text Encoding Initiative) 169, 188–91, *190*
    header *182*, 189, *190*, 191, 217
    schema 188–91
    TEI Lite 188–9
texts, examination of for subject analysis 443
TGN *see Thesaurus of Geographic Names* (Getty) (TGN)

thema (FRSAD) 235, 380, 381
thesauri 83, 125, 460–1
    associative relationships 461, 465
    challenges 467–70
    equivalence relationships 458, 462–3
    hierarchical relationships (BT/NT relationships) 464
    see also controlled vocabularies; subject headings
Thesaurus of ERIC Descriptors 460, 476, 491
Thesaurus of Geographic Names (Getty) (TGN) *340*, 414, 480
Thomas, D. 143, 147
Thompson, K. J. 373
Tillett, B. 288–9, 377
time periods in subject analysis 337, 445, 473, 477, *489*, 492, 520, 522–3, 527–8, 542, 571, 573
time-span (LRM) *231*, 234, *236–7*, 238, 239, 308
timespan (RDA) 308–9, *318*, 384, *388*, *393*
titles 7, 293–4, 442, 445
    abbreviated 326
    access points 7, 9–10, 13–14, 56, 63, 69, 74, 99–100, 102, 104, 111, 113–14, 270, 272–3, 286–7, 292, *319*, 333, 382–3, 542, 543
    alternative 294
    authority controlled 10, 13, 67, 74, 103, 151–3, 287, 333, 365–6, 369–70, 373, 381, 383, 391, 399–401
    collective 294, *336*
    conventional collective 294
    corrected 294
    cover 294
    in DACS 346
    devised 273, 278, 294
    earlier/later 210, 326
    in finding aids 115
    in the FR models 241
    indexing and abstracting 31, 32, 35, 125, 126
    initial articles 149, 177, 180, 543–4
    key 326
    keywords 124, 128, 140, 148, 154, 286
    in KWIC/KWAC indexes 85–6
    in MARC 14, 147, 160, 171–3, *173–4*, 176–7, 178, 179
    name/title access point 74, 76, 290, 292, *335*, 369–70, 381, 383, 399–401
    other title information 178, 294, 326
    parallel 178, 294, 326
    recording 294
    searching/browsing 88–9, 99–100, 103, 104, 110, 111, 114, 115, 145, 147, 148
    series 148, 152, 287, 292, 331
    spine 294
    in subject analysis 21, 161, 427, 431–2, 435, 441–5
    subtitle 14, 210, 294, 442
    on title page 59–60, 62, 67, *298*

title proper 13, 14 147, 177, *178*, 272–3, 287, 294, *314*, *320*, 324, 325, *327*, 382
   uncontrolled 287
   variant 10, 103, 210
   for visual materials 21–2, 348, 350–1, 435
   work title 269, 289–90, 369–70, 378, 381, 383, 391, 395, 399–401
titles of persons 396, 397, 398, 406
tone, subject analysis and 446–7
translation in subject analysis 13–14, 432 *see also* classification, controlled vocabulary
transliteration 169, 322, 370, 383, 396, 406, 541
tree structure 137, 483, 484, *485*, 488, 522
triplestores 257, 269, 308
Trithemius, J. 57
truncation 89, 140, 148, 149–50
Turnbull, D. 29–30
turnkey systems 88
twentieth century, history of information organization and 68–9, 70–3, 74–78, 89–84
typewriters 35, 83, 106

uncontrolled access points 272–3, 287, 382
uncontrolled titles 287 *see also* title proper
Unicode 88, 167, 168–9, 171
Uniform Resource Identifiers (URIs) 184, 251–2, 253, 253n, 299 *see also* Internationalized Resource Identifiers (IRIs)
Uniform Resource Locators (URLs) 10, 15, 100, 251, 299
uniform titles 395, 404, 543
UNIMARC 180
union catalogs 15, 22, 66, 87, 105, 126, 478
Union List of Artists Names (ULAN) 412, 414, 480
Universal Bibliographic Control (UBC) 84, 99, 377
Universal Coded Character Set (UCS) 168–9
Universal Decimal Classification (UDC) 80, 84, 519, 521, 523
University of Oxford library 59
unstructured description 311, *312*, *313*
upward references 463
URI *see* Uniform Resource Identifiers (URIs)
use-based approaches to subject analysis 440–1
users
   needs of 18, 30, 136, 161
   system designs for 10
   user tasks 4, 76, 104–5, 136, 138, 147, 227, 228–30, 269, 379, 382

value 136, 184, 210, 255, 261, 270, 309–11
Vander Wal, T. 503
variable data fields (MARC) 171, 173, *180*
variant access points (VAPs) 235, 367, 381, 385–6, 387, *389*, 401, 402
variant names 10, 31, 59, 74, 273, 290, 366, 367, 373, 383, 387, 395–6
Vatican Code 68
Vellucci, S. 209
Verona, E. 69, 74
Virtual International Authority File (VIAF) 377, 417
visual material
   description of, museums and 21–2
   subject analysis of 21–2, 434–5, 443
   see also *Cataloging Cultural Objects* (CCO); *Categories for the Description of Works of Art* (CDWA); VRA Core
Visual Resource Association Core *see* VRA Core
Vivarium library 55
vocabulary control
   see controlled vocabularies
vocabulary encoding schemes 262, 307, 312, 339
Vokac, L. 426
VRA Core 217, 275, 347, 348–50, 416–17, 448

Warner, A. 515
Wason, T. 515
web crawlers 24, 25, 122, 251
web indexing 31, 33–4, 125
Web Ontology Language *see* OWL Web Ontology Language
Web Ontology Working Group 497
Weibel, S. 209
Wellisch, H. 468
WEMI 195, 232–3, *239–40*, 278, 288, 290, *310*, 378, 381, 390–1
White, H. 146
whole-part relationships *239*, 289, 414, 464
Whytefield, J. 56
Wilson, P. 431, 440, 442, 443, 448
wisdom 5, 6
Wittgenstein, L. 517
Women, Fire, and Dangerous Things (Lakoff) 517
word-by-word arrangement 540–2
word form for one-word terms 469
WordNet 466–7, 499
work
   access points 288–90, 399–401, 403–5
   authority control and 369–70, *392–3*
   in BIBFRAME 195–6
   in CCO 278, 347–8, 414–15
   in FRBR 230, *231*, 232, 234, 236, *238–40*, 278–9
   identifiers 289–90
   in LRM 230–2, 236, 278–9, 294, 378, 381
   in RDA 322–4, 390–1, 399–401
   in VRA Core 349–50, 417

work marks 81, 546
World Wide Web Consortium (W3C), 183, 253, 257
WorldCat 22, 24, 87, 126, 155, 493
Wu, S. 504

XHTML 183–4
XML (Extensible Markup Language) 167–8, 169, 181, 186–92
XML DTDs and schemas 168, 169, 181, 183, 186–7, 192

Yahoo! 24, 25, 124, 535
Yang, S. 505
Yee, M. 143

Z39.2 170
Z39.4 127, 356–7, *357*
Z39.19 458, 460, 461
Z39.50 154
Z39.85 336
Zadeh, L. 517
Zeng, M. 219, 495
Zenodotus 52

About the Author

Daniel N. Joudrey, MLIS, PhD, is Professor, School of Library and Information Science, Simmons University, Boston, Massachusetts, where he teaches information organization, subject cataloging and classification, and descriptive cataloging. His published works include *Introduction to Cataloging and Classification*, 11th ed. (with Dr. Arlene G. Taylor and David P. Miller, Libraries Unlimited, 2015); the third and fourth editions of *The Organization of Information*; "Cataloging" in *The Encyclopedia of Library and Information Sciences*; "Cataloging" in *The Encyclopedia of Libraries, Librarianship, and Information Science*, and various articles. With Janis Young, he is co-instructor of the Library of Congress's LCSH and LCC Online Training videos. He is currently a member of the *Dewey Decimal Classification* Editorial Policy Committee. His research interests include aboutness determination, subject access to information, and cataloging education. He holds an MLIS and a PhD from the School of Computing and Information (formerly the School of Information Sciences) at the University of Pittsburgh, where his studies, guided by Dr. Taylor, focused on subject cataloging, particularly that of determining aboutness.